T0189560

Lecture Notes in Computer Science 12780

More information about this subseries at http://www.springer.com/series/7409

Marcelo M. Soares · Elizabeth Rosenzweig ·
Aaron Marcus (Eds.)

Design, User Experience, and Usability

Design for Diversity, Well-being, and Social Development

10th International Conference, DUXU 2021
Held as Part of the 23rd HCI International Conference, HCII 2021
Virtual Event, July 24–29, 2021
Proceedings, Part II

 Springer

Editors
Marcelo M. Soares
Hunan University, School of Design
Changsha, China

Department of Design
Federal University of Pernambuco
Recife, Brazil

Aaron Marcus
Aaron Marcus and Associates
Berkeley, CA, USA

Elizabeth Rosenzweig
World Usability Day and Rabb School
of Continuing Studies, Division of
Graduate Professional Studies
Brandeis University
Newton Center, MA, USA

ISSN 0302-9743 ISSN 1611-3349 (electronic)
Lecture Notes in Computer Science
ISBN 978-3-030-78223-8 ISBN 978-3-030-78224-5 (eBook)
https://doi.org/10.1007/978-3-030-78224-5

LNCS Sublibrary: SL3 – Information Systems and Applications, incl. Internet/Web, and HCI

This Springer imprint is published by the registered company Springer Nature Switzerland AG
The registered company address is: Gewerbestrasse 11, 6330 Cham, Switzerland

Foreword

Human-Computer Interaction (HCI) is acquiring an ever-increasing scientific and industrial importance, and having more impact on people's everyday life, as an ever-growing number of human activities are progressively moving from the physical to the digital world. This process, which has been ongoing for some time now, has been dramatically accelerated by the COVID-19 pandemic. The HCI International (HCII) conference series, held yearly, aims to respond to the compelling need to advance the exchange of knowledge and research and development efforts on the human aspects of design and use of computing systems.

The 23rd International Conference on Human-Computer Interaction, HCI International 2021 (HCII 2021), was planned to be held at the Washington Hilton Hotel, Washington DC, USA, during July 24–29, 2021. Due to the COVID-19 pandemic and with everyone's health and safety in mind, HCII 2021 was organized and run as a virtual conference. It incorporated the 21 thematic areas and affiliated conferences listed on the following page.

A total of 5222 individuals from academia, research institutes, industry, and governmental agencies from 81 countries submitted contributions, and 1276 papers and 241 posters were included in the proceedings to appear just before the start of the conference. The contributions thoroughly cover the entire field of HCI, addressing major advances in knowledge and effective use of computers in a variety of application areas. These papers provide academics, researchers, engineers, scientists, practitioners, and students with state-of-the-art information on the most recent advances in HCI. The volumes constituting the set of proceedings to appear before the start of the conference are listed in the following pages.

The HCI International (HCII) conference also offers the option of 'Late Breaking Work' which applies both for papers and posters, and the corresponding volume(s) of the proceedings will appear after the conference. Full papers will be included in the 'HCII 2021 - Late Breaking Papers' volumes of the proceedings to be published in the Springer LNCS series, while 'Poster Extended Abstracts' will be included as short research papers in the 'HCII 2021 - Late Breaking Posters' volumes to be published in the Springer CCIS series.

The present volume contains papers submitted and presented in the context of the 10th International Conference on Design, User Experience, and Usability (DUXU 2021), an affiliated conference to HCII 2021. I would like to thank the Co-chairs, Marcelo M. Soares, Elizabeth Rosenzweig, and Aaron Marcus, for their invaluable contribution to its organization and the preparation of the proceedings, as well as the members of the Program Board for their contributions and support. This year, the DUXU affiliated conference has focused on topics related to UX design and research methods and techniques, design education and practice, mobile UX, visual languages and information visualization, extended reality UX, and experience design across cultures, as well as UX design for inclusion and social development, health and well-being, and the creative industries.

I would also like to thank the Program Board Chairs and the members of the Program Boards of all thematic areas and affiliated conferences for their contribution towards the highest scientific quality and overall success of the HCI International 2021 conference.

This conference would not have been possible without the continuous and unwavering support and advice of Gavriel Salvendy, founder, General Chair Emeritus, and Scientific Advisor. For his outstanding efforts, I would like to express my appreciation to Abbas Moallem, Communications Chair and Editor of HCI International News.

July 2021   Constantine Stephanidis

HCI International 2021 Thematic Areas and Affiliated Conferences

Thematic Areas

- HCI: Human-Computer Interaction
- HIMI: Human Interface and the Management of Information

Affiliated Conferences

- EPCE: 18th International Conference on Engineering Psychology and Cognitive Ergonomics
- UAHCI: 15th International Conference on Universal Access in Human-Computer Interaction
- VAMR: 13th International Conference on Virtual, Augmented and Mixed Reality
- CCD: 13th International Conference on Cross-Cultural Design
- SCSM: 13th International Conference on Social Computing and Social Media
- AC: 15th International Conference on Augmented Cognition
- DHM: 12th International Conference on Digital Human Modeling and Applications in Health, Safety, Ergonomics and Risk Management
- DUXU: 10th International Conference on Design, User Experience, and Usability
- DAPI: 9th International Conference on Distributed, Ambient and Pervasive Interactions
- HCIBGO: 8th International Conference on HCI in Business, Government and Organizations
- LCT: 8th International Conference on Learning and Collaboration Technologies
- ITAP: 7th International Conference on Human Aspects of IT for the Aged Population
- HCI-CPT: 3rd International Conference on HCI for Cybersecurity, Privacy and Trust
- HCI-Games: 3rd International Conference on HCI in Games
- MobiTAS: 3rd International Conference on HCI in Mobility, Transport and Automotive Systems
- AIS: 3rd International Conference on Adaptive Instructional Systems
- C&C: 9th International Conference on Culture and Computing
- MOBILE: 2nd International Conference on Design, Operation and Evaluation of Mobile Communications
- AI-HCI: 2nd International Conference on Artificial Intelligence in HCI

List of Conference Proceedings Volumes Appearing Before the Conference

1. LNCS 12762, Human-Computer Interaction: Theory, Methods and Tools (Part I), edited by Masaaki Kurosu
2. LNCS 12763, Human-Computer Interaction: Interaction Techniques and Novel Applications (Part II), edited by Masaaki Kurosu
3. LNCS 12764, Human-Computer Interaction: Design and User Experience Case Studies (Part III), edited by Masaaki Kurosu
4. LNCS 12765, Human Interface and the Management of Information: Information Presentation and Visualization (Part I), edited by Sakae Yamamoto and Hirohiko Mori
5. LNCS 12766, Human Interface and the Management of Information: Information-rich and Intelligent Environments (Part II), edited by Sakae Yamamoto and Hirohiko Mori
6. LNAI 12767, Engineering Psychology and Cognitive Ergonomics, edited by Don Harris and Wen-Chin Li
7. LNCS 12768, Universal Access in Human-Computer Interaction: Design Methods and User Experience (Part I), edited by Margherita Antona and Constantine Stephanidis
8. LNCS 12769, Universal Access in Human-Computer Interaction: Access to Media, Learning and Assistive Environments (Part II), edited by Margherita Antona and Constantine Stephanidis
9. LNCS 12770, Virtual, Augmented and Mixed Reality, edited by Jessie Y. C. Chen and Gino Fragomeni
10. LNCS 12771, Cross-Cultural Design: Experience and Product Design Across Cultures (Part I), edited by P. L. Patrick Rau
11. LNCS 12772, Cross-Cultural Design: Applications in Arts, Learning, Well-being, and Social Development (Part II), edited by P. L. Patrick Rau
12. LNCS 12773, Cross-Cultural Design: Applications in Cultural Heritage, Tourism, Autonomous Vehicles, and Intelligent Agents (Part III), edited by P. L. Patrick Rau
13. LNCS 12774, Social Computing and Social Media: Experience Design and Social Network Analysis (Part I), edited by Gabriele Meiselwitz
14. LNCS 12775, Social Computing and Social Media: Applications in Marketing, Learning, and Health (Part II), edited by Gabriele Meiselwitz
15. LNAI 12776, Augmented Cognition, edited by Dylan D. Schmorrow and Cali M. Fidopiastis
16. LNCS 12777, Digital Human Modeling and Applications in Health, Safety, Ergonomics and Risk Management: Human Body, Motion and Behavior (Part I), edited by Vincent G. Duffy
17. LNCS 12778, Digital Human Modeling and Applications in Health, Safety, Ergonomics and Risk Management: AI, Product and Service (Part II), edited by Vincent G. Duffy

18. LNCS 12779, Design, User Experience, and Usability: UX Research and Design (Part I), edited by Marcelo Soares, Elizabeth Rosenzweig, and Aaron Marcus

19. LNCS 12780, Design, User Experience, and Usability: Design for Diversity, Well-being, and Social Development (Part II), edited by Marcelo M. Soares, Elizabeth Rosenzweig, and Aaron Marcus

20. LNCS 12781, Design, User Experience, and Usability: Design for Contemporary Technological Environments (Part III), edited by Marcelo M. Soares, Elizabeth Rosenzweig, and Aaron Marcus

21. LNCS 12782, Distributed, Ambient and Pervasive Interactions, edited by Norbert Streitz and Shin'ichi Konomi

22. LNCS 12783, HCI in Business, Government and Organizations, edited by Fiona Fui-Hoon Nah and Keng Siau

23. LNCS 12784, Learning and Collaboration Technologies: New Challenges and Learning Experiences (Part I), edited by Panayiotis Zaphiris and Andri Ioannou

24. LNCS 12785, Learning and Collaboration Technologies: Games and Virtual Environments for Learning (Part II), edited by Panayiotis Zaphiris and Andri Ioannou

25. LNCS 12786, Human Aspects of IT for the Aged Population: Technology Design and Acceptance (Part I), edited by Qin Gao and Jia Zhou

26. LNCS 12787, Human Aspects of IT for the Aged Population: Supporting Everyday Life Activities (Part II), edited by Qin Gao and Jia Zhou

27. LNCS 12788, HCI for Cybersecurity, Privacy and Trust, edited by Abbas Moallem

28. LNCS 12789, HCI in Games: Experience Design and Game Mechanics (Part I), edited by Xiaowen Fang

29. LNCS 12790, HCI in Games: Serious and Immersive Games (Part II), edited by Xiaowen Fang

30. LNCS 12791, HCI in Mobility, Transport and Automotive Systems, edited by Heidi Krömker

31. LNCS 12792, Adaptive Instructional Systems: Design and Evaluation (Part I), edited by Robert A. Sottilare and Jessica Schwarz

32. LNCS 12793, Adaptive Instructional Systems: Adaptation Strategies and Methods (Part II), edited by Robert A. Sottilare and Jessica Schwarz

33. LNCS 12794, Culture and Computing: Interactive Cultural Heritage and Arts (Part I), edited by Matthias Rauterberg

34. LNCS 12795, Culture and Computing: Design Thinking and Cultural Computing (Part II), edited by Matthias Rauterberg

35. LNCS 12796, Design, Operation and Evaluation of Mobile Communications, edited by Gavriel Salvendy and June Wei

36. LNAI 12797, Artificial Intelligence in HCI, edited by Helmut Degen and Stavroula Ntoa

37. CCIS 1419, HCI International 2021 Posters - Part I, edited by Constantine Stephanidis, Margherita Antona, and Stavroula Ntoa

38. CCIS 1420, HCI International 2021 Posters - Part II, edited by Constantine Stephanidis, Margherita Antona, and Stavroula Ntoa
39. CCIS 1421, HCI International 2021 Posters - Part III, edited by Constantine Stephanidis, Margherita Antona, and Stavroula Ntoa

http://2021.hci.international/proceedings

List of Contents Proceedings Volumes appearing before the Conference   x

38. CCIS 1420, HCI International 2021 Posters – Part II, edited by Constantine Stephanidis, Margherita Antona, and Stavroula Ntoa

39. CCIS 1421, HCI International 2021 Posters – Part III, edited by Constantine Stephanidis, Margherita Antona, and Stavroula Ntoa

http://2021.hci.international/proceedings

10th International Conference on Design, User Experience, and Usability (DUXU 2021)

Program Board Chairs: **Marcelo M. Soares,** *Hunan University, China, and Federal University of Pernambuco, Brazil* **and Elizabeth Rosenzweig,** *World Usability Day and Brandeis University, USA* **and Aaron Marcus,** *Aaron Marcus and Associates, USA*

- Sisira Adikari, Australia
- Claire Ancient, UK
- Roger Ball, USA
- Eric Brangier, France
- Silvia de los Rios, Spain
- Marc Fabri, UK
- Ernesto Filgueiras, Portugal
- Josh A. Halstead, USA
- Chris Hass, USA
- Zhen Liu, China
- Wei Liu, China
- Martin Maguire, UK
- Judith Moldenhauer, USA
- Gunther Paul, Australia
- Francisco Rebelo, Portugal
- Christine Riedmann-Streitz, Germany
- Patricia Search, USA
- Dorothy Shamonsky, USA

The full list with the Program Board Chairs and the members of the Program Boards of all thematic areas and affiliated conferences is available online at:

http://www.hci.international/board-members-2021.php

HCI International 2022

The 24th International Conference on Human-Computer Interaction, HCI International 2022, will be held jointly with the affiliated conferences at the Gothia Towers Hotel and Swedish Exhibition & Congress Centre, Gothenburg, Sweden, June 26 – July 1, 2022. It will cover a broad spectrum of themes related to Human-Computer Interaction, including theoretical issues, methods, tools, processes, and case studies in HCI design, as well as novel interaction techniques, interfaces, and applications. The proceedings will be published by Springer. More information will be available on the conference website: http://2022.hci.international/:

General Chair
Prof. Constantine Stephanidis
University of Crete and ICS-FORTH
Heraklion, Crete, Greece
Email: general_chair@hcii2022.org

http://2022.hci.international/

Contents – Part II

Experience Design across Cultures

Cultural Usability of E-Government Portals: A Comparative Analysis
of Job Seeking Web Portals Between Saudi Arabia and the United States ... 3
  Asma Aldrees and Denis Gračanin

Spatial Analysis and Comfort Optimal Experience Design of Rural
Landscape in Water Network Area of Southern China.............. 18
  Yali Chen, Zhenxi Gong, and Shuo Wang

Relations on Cultural Behavior and Technology Adoption:
A Chilean Perspective...................................... 34
  Jaime Díaz, Danay Ahumada, Jorge Hochstetter, and Freddy Paz

User Experience Centered Application Design of Multivariate Landscape
in Kulangsu, Xiamen....................................... 43
  Fengze Lin, Fengming Chen, and Mingjian Zhu

A Study on the Application of Innovative Strategies on Intelligent
Mutual-Aid Delivery Services on College Campuses.............. 60
  Hong Liu, Zhong Siyang, Wan Yixin, Junya Yu, and Wei Cao

Product Interventions and User Performance: Implications for Public
Design to Achieve Sustainable Practice 78
  Ming Jun Luo, Jia Xin Xiao, and Wenhua Li

Participatory Design to Create Digital Technologies for Batik Intangible
Cultural Heritage: The Case of iWareBatik..................... 88
  Puspita Ayu Permatasari and Lorenzo Cantoni

Methods for Multiple Roles to Build Brands of Service System–A Case
Study of Guangzhou Baiyun International Airport................. 107
  Qixuan Su and Yi Liu

Analysis and Design of Household Intelligent Planting Products Based
on Hall Three-Dimensional Structure.......................... 121
  Wei Xiong, Zhengli Zhang, Yi Liu, and Zhen Liu

Lacquer Jewelry Design of Shanghai Style Based on User
Perception Preference 132
  Yalan Yu and RongRong Fu

Innovation in Teaching Model Based on University Museum Resources:
Taking the Course of Study on Chinese Ethnic Costume Decoration
as an Example   148
    Chi Zhang, Xiaomei Hu, and Minghong Shi

Research on Intelligent Classified Trash Can and Smart Application
Design—Achieving Green Smart Home Living in China   160
    Nan Zhang, Yanlin Wu, Yingao Kong, and Jinsong Lv

Research on Design Collaboration Strategy for the Transformation
of Historical and Cultural Blocks in Beijing   178
    Fumei Zhang, Tian Cao, and Ran Huo

Design for Inclusion and Social Development

GA-Based Research on Suitability of Recreational Space in Gardens
to the Elderly—With Yangzhou Geyuan Garden as an Example   195
    Tian Cao and Fumei Zhang

Accessibility Evaluation of E-Government Web Applications:
A Systematic Review   210
    Daniela Cisneros, Fernando Huamán Monzón, and Freddy Paz

Emergence of Polarization and Marginalization in Online Education System
of Bangladesh Due to COVID-19: Challenges and Policies to Ensure
Inclusive Education   224
    Md Montaser Hamid, Tanvir Alam, Md Forhad Rabbi, Khalad Hasan,
    Anastasia Kuzminykh, and Mohammad Ruhul Amin

Performing a Disembodied Mind: Neurotechnology Between
Empowerment and Normalization   239
    Johannes Kögel

Studying the Phenomenon of Verbal Bullying in High School Students
for Video Experience Design: A Case of an International School
in Guangzhou, China.   252
    Zhen Liu and Yue Cai

A Study of Teaching Aids Design for Autistic Children with Focus
on Hand-Eye Coordination   270
    Zaixing Liu, Lijun Jiang, Xiu Wang, and Zhelin Li

A Video Experience Design for Emotional Bullying in Public High School
in Guangzhou, China.   284
    Zhen Liu and Zihao Zhuang

Adapting Participatory Design Activities for Autistic Adults: A Review   300
    Rachael Maun, Marc Fabri, and Pip Trevorrow

A Case Study of Augmented Physical Interface by Foot Access with 3D
Printed Attachment   315
   Tatsuya Minagawa and Yoichi Ochiai

Towards a Conceptual Model for Consideration of Adverse Effects
of Immersive Virtual Reality for Individuals with Autism.   333
   Matthew Schmidt and Nigel Newbutt

Usability of a Digital Elder Mistreatment Screening Tool for Older Adults
with Visual and Hearing Disabilities   343
   Sarah J. Swierenga, Jennifer Ismirle, Chelsea Edwards,
   and Fuad Abujarad

Ergonomic and Usability Analysis of Platform for Communication
of People with Limited Talk.   361
   Caroline Torres and Marcelo M. Soares

Design Your Life: User-Initiated Design of Technology to Support
Independent Living of Young Autistic Adults.   373
   Thijs Waardenburg, Niels van Huizen, Jelle van Dijk, Maurice Magnée,
   Wouter Staal, Jan-Pieter Teunisse, and Mascha van der Voort

Design for Health and Well-Being

Building a Digital Health Risk Calculator for Older Women
with Early-Stage Breast Cancer.   389
   Fuad Abujarad, Shi-Yi Wang, Davis Ulrich, Sarah S. Mougalian,
   Brigid K. Killelea, Liana Fraenkel, Cary P. Gross,
   and Suzanne B. Evans

Design of Form and Motion of a Robot Aimed to Provide Emotional
Support for Pediatric Walking Rehabilitation   403
   Jaime Alvarez, Eriko Hara, Toshihiko Koyama, Koji Adachi,
   and Yoshihito Kagawa

Exploring the Factors Aiding Speech-to-Text Emotional Restoration   420
   Xin Chen and Qingxin Deng

Reprojecting a Fitness App Regarding Retention and Usability Using
Nielsen's Heuristics.   434
   Renata Faria Gomes and Maria de Fátima Costa de Souza

Lessons Learned in Developing a Patient-Centered Website to Support
Stroke Patients and Caregivers During Transitions of Care.   450
   Michele C. Fritz, Sarah J. Swierenga, Paul P. Freddolino,
   Constantinos K. Coursaris, Amanda T. Woodward,
   and Matthew J. Reeves

Usability Evaluation of Music Applications for Stress Reduction. 467
  Moushume Hai, Ariana Lacue, Yuwei Zhou, Yogesh Patel,
  Asturias Roncal, and Patricia Morreale

The Art Therapy Experience Based on Online Education System for Higher
Education During the COVID-19 Pandemic: A Case Study of
Communication Method. 477
  Zhen Liu, Lingfeng Ren, and Ke Zhang

Spatial Interaction Design for Children's Magnetic Resonance Imaging
Examination Based on Embodied Cognition 490
  Bao Quan Luo

Persuasive Design of a Mobile Application for Reducing Overcrowding
in Saudi Hospital Emergency Departments 506
  Khalid Majrashi, Hashem Almakramih, and Mohammed Gharawi

Eco-activism, Human-Computer Interaction and Fast Fashion 519
  Antonio Nucci and Matthew Hibberd

SeatPlus: A Smart Health Chair Supporting Active Sitting
Posture Correction. 531
  Zuyu Shen, Xi Wan, Yucheng Jin, Ge Gao, Qianying Wang, and Wei Liu

Potential Usability Design Strategies Based on Mental Models, Behavioral
Model and Art Therapy for User Experience in Post-COVID-19 Era 548
  Zulan Yang, Zhen Liu, Ke Zhang, and Chang Xiao

DUXU Case Studies

Improving the Withdrawal Functionality on ATM Using a UCD
Framework. A Case Study 565
  Joel Aguirre, Fiorella Falconi, Rodrigo Serrano, Arturo Moquillaza,
  and Freddy Paz

Check-!n Toolkit for Capturing Guests' Momentary Experiences Without
Disturbing Their Traveling 581
  Jingrui An, Yaliang Chuang, and Pengcheng An

Content and Mechanism of Car Experience: A Case Study Based
on Interpretive Phenomenological Analysis. 599
  Jingpeng Jia and Xueyan Dong

Design of Traditional Brand H5 Game Advertisement Based on EEG
and Eye Movement Analysis: Example of MAXAM 613
  JunXuan Li and RongRong Fu

Modular Approach to Designing 3D Printed Products: Custom HCI Design
and Fabrication of Functional Products   627
    Robert Phillips, James Tooze, Paul Smith, and Sharon Baurley

The Effect of User Interface on Experiential Value for E-Book
Platforms Users   647
    Yen-Shan Tsai, Elena Carolina Li, and Chih-Liang Yeh

A Designer Embedded Book Space Experiment   661
    Tao-Tao Yu and Teng Wen Chang

Author Index   671

Experience Design across Cultures

Cultural Usability of E-Government Portals: A Comparative Analysis of Job Seeking Web Portals Between Saudi Arabia and the United States

Asma Aldrees[✉] and Denis Gračanin[iD]

Virginia Tech, Blacksburg, VA 24060, USA
{aaldrees,gracanin}@vt.edu

Abstract. Saudi Arabia has obtained a very high e-government index value for the first time in 2020. However, there is a need to address the multicultural requirements in the design of the e-government services. In this paper, we investigated the multicultural usability of the Saudi job seeking web portal, "Taqat", compared to the United States (US) job seeking web portal, "USAJOBS", from the perspective of Saudi and US citizens. We assessed the compatibility of both portals with the US web design guidelines (USWDS). The Saudi web portal lacks only three out of nineteen US design guidelines. Then, we conducted a user study with 200 participants, 100 Saudi citizens, and 100 US citizens using a web-based survey instrument with twenty close-ended questions measured on five-point Likert scale and Nielsen's ten heuristic usability principles. The results of the Mann-Whitney U test revealed a significant multicultural gap in the usability of the Saudi web portal design compared to the US web portal. Future efforts and investigations are highly needed to reduce the multicultural differences in the usability and adoption of the Saudi job seeking web portal.

Keywords: Cultural usability · Cross-cultural testing · Heuristic evaluation · E-government · Web portal · Comparative analysis · Saudi Arabia · The United States

1 Introduction

Electronic government is a fundamental basis of any government revolution that adopts new digital transformations and aims to improve the accountability and transparency of the government towards its citizens [7]. It is defined as a medium for offering government services to targeted users through electronic channels [37]. The web portal is one of the electronic channels the government utilizes to disseminate its services. The usability of government web portals is an essential component of their success. Developers of government web portals should regularly monitor and improve the portals' quality to ensure the satisfactory levels of the offered e-government services to the public. The quality of such web portals is affected by the expected contents and their usability [36].

© Springer Nature Switzerland AG 2021
M. M. Soares et al. (Eds.): HCII 2021, LNCS 12780, pp. 3–17, 2021.
https://doi.org/10.1007/978-3-030-78224-5_1

Lack of usability leaves many users unable or unwilling to adopt the offered electronic services [13]. Nations worldwide have embraced e-government initiatives and adopted the usability aspects that suit their social and cultural backgrounds. However, there are a lot of multicultural perspectives in each society, which spawned many research interests to address and evaluate the usability requirements for multicultural societies to ensure its benefit for all users.

In this paper, we have conducted a comparative analysis of the job seeking web portals' usability between the Saudi and US governments due to two reasons. First, one of the researchers is a Saudi citizen, and this research furthers the mission to help in the development of the Saudi government services. Second, the effective way to improve the e-government systems is by comparing its system with one of the leading countries with a prominent e-government foundation. Hence, we have adopted the US web portal design to improve the design of the Saudi web portal. We mainly aim to investigate the multicultural usability of both web portals to improve the Saudi web portal and gauge to what extent it is ready to serve multicultural societies.

Motivation—The Saudi government seeks to bring its society into the global digital age by implementing efficient e-government services that serve multicultural users locally and globally. Therefore, the Saudi government needs to improve the current systems and follow a comprehensive design that encompasses the multicultural preferences of target users. However, due to the global pandemic of COVID'19, the unemployment rates in Saudi Arabia reached its highest rate in the second quarter of 2020 to 15.4%, which indicates the highest unemployment rate for the past five years. According to the Saudi General Authority for Statistics [19], the Labor Force Survey results have been highly impacted by the effects of the COVID'19 pandemic on the Saudi economy. Therefore, Saudi government should boost the Saudi labor market by offering useful and usable services for training and employment, which upskill Saudi citizens and provide equal opportunities.

"Taqat" is the Saudi job seeking web portal that delivers job offers and helps Saudi job seekers find the right jobs with care and concern [28]. For further improvements, "Taqat" was compared to the US job seeking web portal, "USAJOBS", which connects job seekers with federal employment opportunities [39]. The findings of this study could help Saudi government practitioners and decision makers support the labor market by improving the design of the "Taqat" web portal on a multicultural basis.

The remainder of this paper is organized as follows: Sect. 2 elaborates on the overall background of cultural usability in e-government systems and Sect. 3 reviews the related literature. A preliminary analysis of the adopted web portals is articulated in Sect. 4 while Sect. 5 describes the research methodology. The results of the study are provided in Sect. 6. Finally, Sect. 7 discusses the empirical results and identifies areas for future research.

2 Background

2.1 E-Government

E-government initiatives have emerged in the late 1990s [26]. It is simply defined as the use of technology through seamless online interaction between government entities and citizens for the fast delivery of government services [17]. It is also defined as the implementation and delivery of cost-effective e-services for all stakeholders [11]. In [22], the author considered e-government as the sum of all electronic connections among government employees, citizens, businesses, and industries where subordinating relationships exist. Undoubtedly, the e-government initiatives make life better and more comfortable for all parties. They offer the public the opportunity to break down any temporal and geographical barriers and efficiently fill in the gap between governments and their citizens [41].

Government Models: According to [10,43], there are different models of e-government based on the type of their stakeholders. The stakeholder can be defined as any organization, group or individual that is involved and affected by the government's achievements [14]. These models can be categorized as follows:

- Government-to-Citizen (G2C): refers to the electronic communications and service delivery between governments and their citizens.
- Government-to-Business (G2B): refers to the electronic transaction initiatives between governments and businesses. It provides the electronic purchases for government marketplace.
- Government-to-Government (G2G): refers to services delivery program across government entities, agencies, and employees. It offers a large database for efficient communication and effective information sharing among different levels of government.
- Government-to-Employees (G2E): refers to the interaction between a government and its employees. It provides employees with the required training, data access, and resources to support their tasks.

In this study, the G2C model will be adopted to investigate the multicultural usability of the Saudi job seeking web portal.

E-Government Implementation in Saudi Arabia: Saudi government has invested heavily in the e-government initiatives and radically improved its e-government services [16]. The first Saudi e-government project, called "Yesser", was initiated in 2005 [42]. This project aimed to allow everyone to have online access to e-government services by the end of 2010 [3]. Since then, many research efforts have been placed to improve the e-government initiatives in Saudi Arabia. Some are focused on citizens' acceptance and satisfaction of e-government services [23]. Others investigated the importance of incorporating the usability in e-government projects [1], the development of security transactions of e-government services [4], evaluation of government web portals [16], as well as exploring the factors that negatively affected the e-government implementations in Saudi Arabia [7].

Saudi government has currently shifted from a high to very high E-Government Development Index (EGDI) group for the first time in 2020. According to the United Nations' annual report, its EGDI rank has dramatically increased to 43th compared to the 52nd in 2018 [38]. However, it has not accomplished significant progress in e-government projects with The Online Services Index (OSI) of 0.6882. Although it has a very high EGDI value, it's OSI value is considered low. Therefore, continuous and extensive investigations of Saudi government e-services would significantly accelerate its overall e-government development.

On the other hand, the US government has a very high EGDI value with a global rank of 9 and a considerable high OSI value of 0.9471. It is considered one of the leading countries in e-government implementations [38]. Therefore, it is highly beneficial to follow the successful practices of e-government services by pioneering countries in this field, such as the US government.

2.2 Usability

Usability is the significant contributor for enhancing digital systems. According to the International Organization for Standardization (ISO), usability is defined as "the extent to which a system, product or service can be used by specified users to achieve specified goals with effectiveness, efficiency, and satisfaction in a specified context of use" [30]. In the e-government practices, it has been proven that usability is the main key factor for the success of their implementation [29]. It allows e-governments to provide a better performance, increase citizen's satisfaction, and boost citizens' experiences with their systems [6]. Therefore, many studies have been carried out to assess the usability regarding the e-government quality [40], e-government functionality [32], and citizens perceptions of e-government initiatives [33].

Cultural Usability: In the global context, usability of e-government initiatives should be evaluated across multicultural perspectives. Its importance is growing with the large number of culturally different users. Culture is defined initially by Hofstede as "the collective programming of the mind that distinguishes the members of one group or category of people from another" [27]. However, the relationship between usability and culture is known as cultural usability or "culturability" [9]. Culture usability can be defined as "the extent to which a computer system, especially in intercultural contexts of use, matches the cultural background of its users, such that it supports their activities efficiently and pleasurably" [24]. Therefore, it is worth considering the usability aspects of e-government systems for boosting multicultural perspectives while offering e-services.

Usability Evaluation Methods: There are various usability evaluation methods (UEMs) that can be adopted to assess the usability of e-government web portals. The heuristic evaluation model by Jacob Nielsen is one of the most effective usability heuristic methods where we can evaluate the web portal against a set of ten usability principles as illustrated in Table 1 [34].

We adopted Nielsen's model to explore the multicultural usability of job seeking web portals in Saudi Arabia and the US from the perspective of Saudi and US citizens.

Table 1. Nielsen's ten heuristic usability principles [34].

No.	Principles	Explanation
1	Visibility of system status	The design keeps users informed about what is going on by providing appropriate feedback in a reasonable time
2	Match between system and the real world	The design speaks the users' language. It uses words and phrases familiar to the user
3	User control and freedom	An "emergency exit" is clearly designed when users make mistakes and want to leave without going through an extended process
4	Consistency and standards	Users should not have to wonder whether different words, situations, or actions mean the same thing
5	Error prevention	The interface is carefully designed that prevents errors or problems from occurring in the first place
6	Recognition rather than recall	The design is straightforward and visible. It minimizes the user's memory load
7	Flexibility and efficiency of use	Users can use shortcuts and customized frequent actions
8	Aesthetic and minimalist design	The interface contains relevant and needed information
9	Help users recognize, diagnose, and recover from errors	Error messages are expressed in plain language, precisely indicate the problem, and suggest a solution
10	Help and documentation	The interface provides documentation to help users understand how to complete their tasks

3   Related Work

Many research studies have provided interesting findings to support the e-government initiatives for multicultural societies. Cross-cultural differences in users' perceptions of e-government quality attributes between Kuwaiti and British citizens were discussed in [5]. No significant cultural differences between the two groups were found in terms of important quality features. However, the study revealed a significant variation between Kuwaiti and British citizens regarding the perceived performance of quality attributes in e-government web portals, indicating the need to thoroughly understand cross-cultural quality variations in e-government systems.

Another study compared e-government adoption in the UK and the US [12]. The study aimed to specify if the same factors are prominent in both countries and proposed an e-government adoption model in the UK based on the salient factors in the USA. A survey was conducted and 260 UK citizens were recruited in London to evaluate the proposed model. The results indicated significant cultural differences in e-government adoption between the UK and the US government systems.

The user interface design of Saudi government websites compared to their counterparts in the Philippine and India was investigated in [2]. The study incorporated the web design attributes used commonly in these three countries. The results showed no such cultural differences in the government websites design attributes among the three cultures. This study's findings can be used as guidelines to help Saudi web developers and designers develop government websites that are culturally appropriate for users with diverse cultural backgrounds, such as expatriates.

Another study investigated the e-government initiatives in Saudi Arabia in comparison with the US and UK e-government systems [31]. The study revealed that Saudi e-government web portals need more attention. The comparison of Saudi web portals with the US and UK portals would suggest various improvements to the Saudi portals. However, they argued that the Saudi e-government had not yet achieved the required maturity level as the US and UK e-government systems. They also asserted that the state of the Saudi e-government was still infancy and needed more investigation to improve the Saudi e-government initiatives.

In light of the previous studies, we focused on addressing the challenges facing the Saudi e-government initiatives. The goal is to investigate the multicultural usability of the Saudi job seeking web portal, "Taqat", compared to the US job seeking web portal, "USAJOBS", to suggest potential improvements to the Saudi web portal based on the US web portal specifications.

4   Preliminary Analysis

The United States Web Design System (USWDS) is the federal government design system created by the US government in 2015 [21]. It is a library of guidelines, codes, and tools that helps government digital teams to share the design solutions of e-government portals and provide effective user-centered design practices. This library supports the design of dozens of US agencies and nearly 200 portals; the US job seeking web portal is one of them. Therefore, it is worth conducting a preliminary analysis that evaluates the Saudi job seeking web portal using the USWDS guidelines. We have considered the USWDS guidelines as the reference design components to boost the Saudi e-government initiatives in improving the portal's design and empowering users. Hence, we verified the compatibility of the Saudi job seeking web portal with each design guideline, out of the nineteen design guidelines in the USWDS toolkit.

The compatibility evaluation results of the Saudi web portal with the USWDS guidelines are illustrated in Table 2. The Saudi web portal lacks three USWDS design guidelines: banner, breadcrumb, and side navigation to become completely aligned to these guidelines. Usually, there are huge design libraries and large lists of standards for improving the design of e-government portals. However, the USWDS guidelines have been adopted due to their superb and optimal design specifications.

Table 2. The compatibility of the Saudi web portal with the USWDS guidelines.

No.	USWDS components	Functionality	Taqat compatibility
1	Accordion headings	Enable users to reveal or hide the associated sections	Provided
2	Alerts	Display important messages that attract user's attention	Provided
3	Banner	Appears at the top of all webpages and shows the website is official and secur	Missing
4	Buttons	Slightly change in style to draw attention to specific action	Provided
5	Button Groups	Display important messages that attracts user's attention	Provided
6	Breadcrumb	Facilitates orientation to specify users' position	Missing
7	Cards	Contain contents about a single subject	Provided
8	Form controls	Allow users to enter information	Provided
9	Form template	Provide patterns of common forms	Provided
10	Header	Provides a quick and organized way to reach main sections of the website	Provided
11	Footer	Provides links for users who are lost	Provided
12	Identifier	Identifies the agency responsible for the website	Provided
13	Search	Allows users to search for specific content	Provided
14	Side navigation	The hierarchical-vertical navigation that is placed at the side of a page	Missing
15	Step indicator	Updates users of their progress with multiple-steps process	Provided
16	Tables	Show tabular data in columns and row	Provided
17	Tag	Draws user's attention to new content	Provided
18	Tooltip	Brief message appears when a user hovers on an element	Provided
19	Typography	Provides clear and consistent typefaces	Provided

5 Research Methodology

5.1 Research Design

Both the Saudi and US job seeking web portals are official government web portals that require users to register using their real information to be allowed to use them. Therefore, in this study, we built and designed two prototypes that match and mirror both web portals. The web prototypes allow participants to explore them as if they were using the original web portals. They can also apply for a job by searching for their preferred one, and then proceed to the job application process to complete the job application and submit the request. The web prototypes are only user interfaces that we designed using front-end techniques. They do not have any back-end structure, database, or servers. Hence, participants do not have to enter any credential information to use them, and also their job applications are not saved, which would increase the likely of participation.

Additionally, we paid attention to a significant cultural difference between Saudi and US citizens regarding the language, which would affect their evaluation and hinder us from getting precise results. Therefore, we designed the web prototypes of the Saudi and US original job seeking web portals in English and Arabic. The English version of both web prototypes was distributed among the US participants, while the Saudi participants explored the Arabic version of both web portals. Also, the survey instrument itself was written in English and Arabic to ensure reliable and credible participation from all participants. Moreover, we anonymously designed both prototypes by removing the portals' titles, logos, and recognizable keywords. So, the web prototypes are just abstract designs of both web portals with no identity to prevent any biased incline by participants due to their loyalty towards their country's web portal.

This study followed the quantitative approach using a web-based questionnaire instrument that encourages participants to browse the web prototypes and provide their evaluations regarding the usability of both prototypes. Web-based surveys are mostly used due to their quick, inexpensive, and accurate means of assessing information [44]. As mentioned in Table 1, the questionnaire was designed based on the ten usability heuristic principles with twenty close-ended questions measured on a five-point Likert scale, ranging from strongly disagree (1) to strongly agree (5).

5.2   Research Setting and Sampling

The target sampling for this research study are the citizens or legal residents in Saudi Arabia and the US whose age range is 18–37 years old. Participants must confirm their nationality and age to be allowed to participate in the study. We limited the age range because it represents the majority users of job seeking web portals in both countries.

Participants will be selected through random sampling strategies. In [18], the authors suggested having at least 100 subjects in each major subgroup. That suggestion will be considered to recruit the sample size of this study, with 100 subjects selected from each subgroup (Saudi and US citizens). The total sample size was about 200 participants (100 Saudi citizens and 100 US citizens or legal residents). The Saudi citizens were recruited by sharing the survey link widely on the web and social media channels. Also, Google ads campaigns were used to promote the link among Saudi citizens and encourage them to participate [20]. US citizens were recruited using Amazon Mechanical Turk (MTurk) services. It is an effective crowdsourcing website helping researchers hire the workers who meet the study conditions [8]. An incentive of USD 2 was paid to each US participant.

5.3   Data Collection

The data collection was done using Qualtrics online survey software [35]. To maintain confidentiality, the data collection process was free of any participant names or identifiers. Participants spent approximately 20–40 min to explore and evaluate the usability of both web portals. Participation in the study was voluntary. Respondents were allowed to choose to quit the survey any time they want without saving their responses. The social desirability effect can lead to inaccuracies in findings when participants feel uncomfortable providing sincere answers that might make them unfavorable. Therefore, we included a confidentiality clause in the survey confirms that all answers will remain completely confidential.

As a result, a total of 200 valid surveys comprised the final sample for this study. We received 100 valid and complete responses from the Saudi participants out of 130 responses, while 100 valid and complete responses were received from the US participants out of 110 responses.

6   Results and Findings

6.1   Demographic Data

The demographic distributions of the survey participants are presented in Table 3. In terms of gender, the Saudi participants showed larger participation of women (69%) than men (31%). In contrast, the US participants presented larger participation of men (76%) than women (24%). The age range was encoded into four age groups. The age groups did not show any variation among Saudi participants. On the other hand, there was a significant difference in the US participants' age groups. Only 4 US participants were in 18–22 years old range while the other three age ranges were approximately equal in size. The most common educational category of the Saudi participants was undergraduate degree (49%) followed by graduate degree (20%). Almost half of the US participants pursued a graduate degree (46%), followed by undergraduate degree (42%). These two degrees represent the majority of the US participants (88%).

6.2   Reliability Analysis

We measured the reliability of the survey responses using the Cronbach's alpha indicator, considering a minimum value of $\alpha = 0.7$ [15]. Reliability is the internal consistency of a scale that gauges the degree to which the survey items are reliable. The survey items refer to the ten usability heuristic principles used to evaluate the usability of the Saudi and US web portal from the perspectives of Saudi and US citizens. Overall, Cronbach's alpha value in both web portals is above 0.7, indicating that the survey's items for both web portals are reliable and consistent, as shown in Table 4.

6.3   The Saudi Job Seeking Web Portal

Descriptive Analysis: The usability of the Saudi web portal from the perspectives of Saudi and US citizens is illustrated in Fig. 1. The inspection of the

Table 3. Demographic data.

Demographics	Category	Saudi sample	US sample
Sample size		100	100
Gender	Male	31	76
	Female	69	24
Age	18–22 years old	25	4
	23–27 years old	35	30
	28–32 years old	22	39
	33–37 years old	18	27
Education level	High school degree	13	9
	Associate degree	18	3
	Undergraduate degree	49	42
	Graduate degree	20	46

Table 4. Cronbach alpha values of the web portals.

Web portals	Cronbach alpha	No. of items
The first web portal: the Saudi job seeking web portal "Taqat"	**0.898**	10
The second web portal: the US job seeking web portal "USAJOBS"	**0.906**	10

usability results indicated that majority of the US participants considered the Saudi web portal usable more than the Saudi participants with (17%) strongly agree and (70%) agree. While approximately half of the Saudi participants agreed to its usability (8%) strongly agree and (49%) agree. In terms of usability issues, only (5%) of the US citizens disagreed with the usability of the web portal with (4%) disagree, and (1%) strongly disagree while (13%) of Saudi participants were not satisfied and disagreed to its usability.

Inferential Analysis: As stated earlier, we want to investigate whether the Saudi web portal is usable and accepted by all multicultural users. In this vein, we adopted the inferential analysis of the data by applying a non-parametric test of ordinal data. Mann-Whitney U test was used to measure the cultural difference between two independent samples (the Saudi and US participants) in the usability of the Saudi web portal. The test illustrated a null hypothesis before conducting the analysis, which states that the distribution of the usability of the Saudi web portal is the same across categories of participants (Saudi and US citizens), with the significance level at 95%, ($p < 0.05$) [25]. Based on the obtained results in Table 5, there is a significant cultural gap in the usability of the Saudi web portal based on p value ($p = .000$). Hence ($p < 0.05$), the null hypothesis has been rejected.

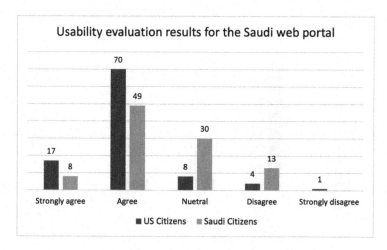

Fig. 1. Usability evaluation results for the Saudi web portal.

Table 5. Mann-Whitney U test results of the Saudi web portal's usability.

Null hypothesis	Significance	Decision
The distribution of the usability of the Saudi web portal is the same across categories of participants	**.000**	**Reject** the null hypothesis

6.4   The US Job Seeking Web Portal

Descriptive Analysis: Figure 2 represents the usability of the US web portal from the perspectives of Saudi and US citizens. The US participants were satisfied with the US web portal and agreed to its usability more than the Saudi participants with (14%) strongly agree and (68%) agree. While the majority of Saudi participants rated its usability with (13%) strongly agree and (55%) agree. However, a small percentage of the US and Saudi participants disagreed with the portal's usability with (7%) and (11%) respectively.

Inferential Analysis: We adopted the Mann-Whitney U test again to examine the cultural usability of the US web portal between the independent groups of participants. The null hypothesis assumed that the distribution of the usability of the US web portal is the same across categories of participants (Saudi and US citizens) with ($p < 0.05$). Table 6 showed no cultural difference in the usability of the US portal based on p value ($p = .077$). Since ($p > 0.05$), the null hypothesis has been retained.

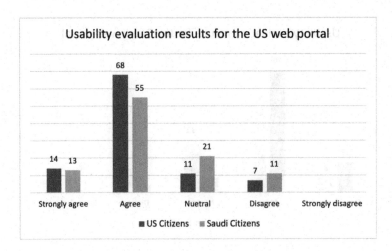

Fig. 2. Usability evaluation results for the US web portal.

Table 6. Mann-Whitney U test results of the US web portal's usability.

Null hypothesis	Significance	Decision
The distribution of the usability of the US web portal is the same across categories of participants	**.077**	**Retain** the null hypothesis

7   Discussion and Conclusion

The main goal of our research was to find out where the Saudi e-government system stands, especially the job seeking web portal, "Taqat". It highlighted the importance of the cultural factor in the improvement of e-government services.

We conducted a user study that assessed the multicultural usability of the job seeking web portal in Saudi Arabia, "Taqat", in light of comparison with the modern e-government paradigms used in a leading country, "USAJOBS"; the US job seeking web portal. The study focused on investigating the cultural gap in the usability of both web portals from the perspective of the Saudi and US citizens. A preliminary analysis was carried out to evaluate the compatibility of the Saudi web portal with the global design guidelines such as the United States Web Design Systems (USWDS) to provide potential design recommendations for improving and enhancing the Saudi web portal's interface design.

The comparative analysis of the findings between "Taqat" and "USAJOBS" web portals showed that the "USAJOBS" web portal gained overall acceptance from both the Saudi and US participants. They claimed that it was usable, efficient, and has a clear structure more than the Saudi web portal. Some comments were received from participants regarding the web portals, one participant assured that the functionality of the US web portal was better and easy going. Another participant commented that the Saudi web portal provides a good filter style. Four participants mentioned that the Saudi web portal needs more design improvements in the job search functionality and the application process while five participants argued that both web portals are very similar.

Regarding the multicultural usability, the Mann-Whitney U test was used to inspect the cultural differences in the usability of both web portals. The US web portal showed no cultural difference in its usability from the perspectives of the Saudi and US participants with ($p = .077$) which asserted the multicultural usability of the US web portal. On the other hand, a significant cultural gap emerged in the usability of the Saudi web portal with ($p = 0.000$). It showed that the Saudi web portal has not achieved the required multicultural usability in its design. These findings aligned with the results of the study conducted in [31].

Finally, the results of this paper help support the Saudi government's plan for boosting the e-government initiatives by shedding light on the design gaps of its web portal such as the cultural gap and recommending prompt attention to narrow them down. Practitioners and designers in the Saudi government teams should increase their efforts and improve the design of the Saudi web portal to accelerate its development and acceptance by all target multicultural users, which holds great promise if ministered as it should be. Based on these findings, the culture factor will be included in our future investigation to explore the adoption factors that significantly affect the Saudi citizen's intention to use e-government employment services in Saudi Arabia.

References

1. Al-Fakhri, M.O., Cropf, R.A., Higos, G., Kelly, P.: E-government in Saudi Arabia: between promise and reality. Int. J. Electron. Gov. Res. 4(2), 59–82 (2008). https://doi.org/10.4018/978-1-60566-918-2.ch011
2. Al-Khalifa, H.S., Garcia, R.A.: Website design based on cultures: an investigation of Saudis, Filipinos, and Indians government websites' attributes. In: Marcus, A. (ed.) DUXU 2014. LNCS, vol. 8518, pp. 15–27. Springer, Cham (2014). https://doi.org/10.1007/978-3-319-07626-3_2
3. Al-Nuaim, H.: An evaluation framework for Saudi e-government. J. E-Gov. Stud. Best Pract. 1–12 (2011). https://doi.org/10.5171/2011.820912
4. Al-Zahrani, M.: Integrating IS success model with cybersecurity factors for e-government implementation in the Kingdom of Saudi Arabia. Int. J. Electr. Comput. Eng. (IJECE) 10(5), 4937 (2020). https://doi.org/10.11591/ijece.v10i5.pp4937-4955
5. Aladwani, A.M.: A cross-cultural comparison of Kuwaiti and British citizens' views of e-government interface quality. Gov. Inf. Q. 30(1), 74–86 (2013). https://doi.org/10.1016/j.giq.2012.08.003
6. Albert, W., Tullis, T.: Measuring the User Experience: Collecting, Analyzing, and Presenting Usability Metrics (Interactive Technologies), 2nd edn. Elsevier Inc., Oxford (2013)
7. Alghamdi, S., Beloff, N.: Towards a comprehensive model for e-government adoption and utilisation analysis: the case of Saudi Arabia. In: Proceedings of the 9th Federated Conference on Computer Science and Information Systems - FedCSIS 2014, vol. 2, pp. 1217–1225. IEEE, Warsaw, September 2014. https://doi.org/10.15439/2014F146

8. Amazon: Amazon Mechanical Turk. https://www.mturk.com/. Accessed 12 Feb 2021
9. Barber, W., Badre, A.: Culturability: the merging of culture and usability. In: Proceedings of the Conference on Human Factors and the Web, Basking Ridge, p. 10. AT&T Labs, New Jersey (1998)
10. Belanger, F., Hiller, J.S.: A framework for e-government: privacy implications. Bus. Process. Manag. J. **12**(1), 48–60 (2006). https://doi.org/10.1108/14637150610643751
11. Buckley, J.: E-service quality and the public sector. Manag. Serv. Qual. **13**(6), 453–462 (2003). https://doi.org/10.1108/09604520310506513
12. Carter, L., Weerakkody, V., Phillips, B., Dwivedi, Y.K.: Citizen adoption of e-government services: exploring citizen perceptions of online services in the United States and United Kingdom. Inf. Syst. Manag. **33**(2), 124–140 (2016). https://doi.org/10.1080/10580530.2016.1155948
13. Casal, L., Flavin, C., Guinalu, M.: The role of perceived usability, reputation, satisfaction and consumer familiarity on the website loyalty formation process. Comput. Hum. Behav. **24**(2), 325–345 (2008). https://doi.org/10.1016/j.chb.2007.01.017
14. Chourabi, H., Mellouli, S.: E-government: integrated services framework. In: Proceedings of the 12th Annual International Digital Government Research Conference on Digital Government Innovation in Challenging Times - DG.O 2011, p. 36. ACM Press, College Park (2011). https://doi.org/10.1145/2037556.2037563
15. Cronbach, L.J.: Essentials of Psychological Testing. Harper & Row, New York (1984)
16. Eidaroos, A.M., Probets, S.G., Dearnley, J.A.: Heuristic evaluation for e-Government websites in Saudi Arabia. In: Aloqbi, A., Alsini, I., Alzimani, K. (eds.) Proceedings of the 3rd Saudi International Conference - SIC 2009, p. 5. Saudi Students Clubs and Schools in the UK and the Republic of Ireland, Guildford, June 2009. https://hdl.handle.net/2134/5779
17. Fagan, M.H.: Exploring city, county and state e-government initiatives: an East Texas perspective. Bus. Process. Manag. J. **12**(1), 101–112 (2006). https://doi.org/10.1108/14637150610643797
18. Gall, M.D., Gall, J.P., Borg, W.R.: Educational Research: An Introduction, 8th edn. Pearson (2006)
19. GASTAT: Saudi labor market statistics Q2 2020. Gov, Saudi Arabia, June 2020. https://www.stats.gov.sa/en/814. Accessed 12 Feb 2021
20. Google: Google Ads. https://ads.google.com/. Accessed 12 Feb 2021
21. U.S. Government: U.S. Web Design System (USWDS). https://designsystem.digital.gov/. Accessed 12 Feb 2021
22. Greunz, M., Schopp, B., Haes, J.: Integrating e-government infrastructures through secure XML document containers. In: Proceedings of the 34th Annual Hawaii International Conference on System Sciences, p. 10. IEEE Computer Society, Maui (2001). https://doi.org/10.1109/HICSS.2001.926518
23. Hamner, M., Al-Qahtani, F.: Enhancing the case for Electronic Government in developing nations: a people-centric study focused in Saudi Arabia. Gov. Inf. Q. **26**(1), 137–143 (2009). https://doi.org/10.1016/j.giq.2007.08.008
24. Hertzum, M.: Usability Testing: A Practitioner's Guide to Evaluating the User Experience, vol. 1. Morgan and Claypool Publisher (2020). https://doi.org/10.2200/S00987ED1V01Y202001HCI045
25. Hettmansperger, T., McKean, J.: Robust Nonparametric Statistical Methods. Kendall's Library of Statistics: An Arnold Publication No. 5, Arnold (1998)

26. Ho, A.T.: Reinventing local governments and the e-government initiative. Public Adm. Rev. **62**(4), 434–444 (2002). https://doi.org/10.1111/0033-3352.00197
27. Hofstede, G.: Dimensionalizing cultures: the hofstede model in context. Online Read. Psychol. Cult. **2**(1), 26 (2011). https://doi.org/10.9707/2307-0919.1014
28. HRDF: TAQAT The National Labor Gateway. https://www.taqat.sa/. Accessed 12 Feb 2021
29. Huang, Z., Benyoucef, M.: Usability and credibility of e-government websites. Gov. Inf. Q. **31**(4), 584–595 (2014). https://doi.org/10.1016/j.giq.2014.07.002
30. ISO: Ergonomics of human-system interaction part 210: human-centred design for interactive systems (2019). https://www.iso.org/obp/ui/#iso:std:iso:9241:-210:ed-2:v1:en. Accessed 12 Feb 2021
31. Khan, H.U., Alsahli, A., Alsabri, H.: E-government in Saudi Arabia: analysis on present and future. J. Electron. Commun. Eng. Res. **3**, 1–13 (2013)
32. Kossak, F., Essmayr, W., Winiwarter, W.: Applicability of HCI research to e-government applications [case study]. In: Proceedings of the 9th European Conference on Information Systems - ECIS 2001, pp. 957–968. European Conference on Information Systems, Association for Information Systems, Bled, June 2001
33. Magoutas, B., Schmidt, K.U., Mentzas, G., Stojanovic, L.: An adaptive e-questionnaire for measuring user perceived portal quality. Int. J. Hum Comput Stud. **68**(10), 729–745 (2010). https://doi.org/10.1016/j.ijhcs.2010.06.003
34. Nielsen, J.: 10 usability heuristics for user interface design, November 2020. https://www.nngroup.com/articles/ten-usability-heuristics/. Accessed 12 Feb 2021
35. Qualtrics: Qualtrics Online Survey Software. https://www.qualtrics.com/. Accessed 12 Feb 2021
36. Scott, J.K.: Assessing the quality of municipal government web sites. State Local Gov. Rev. **37**(2), 151–165 (2005). https://doi.org/10.1177/0160323X0503700206
37. Sharifi, H., Zarei, B.: An adaptive approach for implementing e-government in I.R. Iran. J. Gov. Inf. **30**(5–6), 600–619 (2004). https://doi.org/10.1016/j.jgi.2004.10.005
38. UN: E-Government Survey 2020 Digital Government in the Decade of Action for Sustainable Development. Gov 11, The United Nations, New York (2020)
39. US-Office: USAJOBS. https://www.usajobs.gov/. Accessed 12 Feb 2021
40. Wang, Y.D., Emurian, H.H.: An overview of online trust: concepts, elements, and implications. Comput. Hum. Behav. **21**(1), 105–125 (2005). https://doi.org/10.1016/j.chb.2003.11.008
41. West, D.M.: E-government and the transformation of service delivery and citizen attitudes. Public Adm. Rev. **64**(1), 15–27 (2004). https://doi.org/10.1111/j.1540-6210.2004.00343.x
42. Yesser: Saudi e-Government Program. https://www.yesser.gov.sa/en. Accessed 12 Feb 2021
43. Yildiz, M.: E-government research: reviewing the literature, limitations, and ways forward. Gov. Inf. Q. **24**(3), 646–665 (2007). https://doi.org/10.1016/j.giq.2007.01.002
44. Zikmund, W.G., Babin, B.J., Carr, J.C., Griffin, M.: Business Research Methods, 9th edn. South-Western, Cenage Publishing Co. (2013)

Spatial Analysis and Comfort Optimal Experience Design of Rural Landscape in Water Network Area of Southern China

Yali Chen[1(✉)], Zhenxi Gong[2], and Shuo Wang[3]

[1] School of Design, South China University of Technology, Guangzhou 510641, China
[2] School of Architecture, Hunan University, Changsha 410082, China
[3] School of Architecture, South China University of Technology, Guangzhou 510641, China

Abstract. Under the background of the coordinated development of urban and rural areas, rural rejuvenation is a hot topic. The research focuses is on the spatial form of characteristic landscape. From the perspective of rural experience, it uses the analysis methods of settlement space and landscape space to construct an updated experiential characteristic rural style. Rural landscape is the basic spatial carrier of developing characteristic rural pattern. It is of operational significance to discuss the spatial form of rural "experiential" landscape under the target framework of "characteristic rural landscape". With the help of the practice of "experience" in traditional rural design, based on the principles and objectives of improving the quality of public space, this paper puts forward some strategies such as shape shaping and functional reorganization, focusing on solving the spatial quality problems such as point, line, area and landscape, among which the shape shaping strategy is mainly aimed at improving the environmental quality of traditional rural space, and functional reorganization promotes the functional demand quality of "comfort" in traditional rural areas, with a view to injecting new vitality into diversified villages.

Keywords: Rural experience landscape space · Analysis and optimization strategies · Comfort optimal experience · Environmental improvement

1 Introduction

Rural landscape reflects the result of adaptation and transformation of natural environment and social needs in a specific region for thousands of years, especially the rural landscape after adaptation and transformation of human and natural environment. Since the reform and opening up, China's urbanization process has triggered dramatic changes in the traditional rural landscape. As a result of the new rural construction, the rural landscape has become fragmented and disorderly [1]. With the in-depth development of people's ecological awareness and traditional cultural protection concept, the unique historical rural landscape has attracted great attention of scholars in recent years, and has become an important research topic showing the characteristic value in the current rural social development [2].

© Springer Nature Switzerland AG 2021
M. M. Soares et al. (Eds.): HCII 2021, LNCS 12780, pp. 18–33, 2021.
https://doi.org/10.1007/978-3-030-78224-5_2

Traditional rural public space, as the main place for villagers' activities and communication, is the material carrier of daily life and production, and maintains the relationship between geography and blood. In the process of development and construction of traditional villages, the public space is squeezed and occupied by residential buildings, which leads to the change of rural spatial functions. In the village planning and construction, there are some problems in public space, such as monotonous form, single function, homogeneous landscape, lack of vitality in space and fault of local culture. As a result, it is difficult to meet the needs of modern rural life and adapt to the landscape features of local areas.

2 Literature Review

Experience is one of the important ways to measure spatial texture and atmosphere, participation is the core of experience, and the feeling of subject in the process of spatial experience is an important factor to evaluate the recognition and pleasure of landscape space [3]. With the progress of society, the improvement of human living standards and the diversified development of material elements, human expectations for the outside world are no longer satisfied with the coverage of basic needs, but tend to yearn for a series of comprehensive psychological demands and emotional experiences such as curiosity, exploration, immersion, reflection and recollection [4]. The acquisition of these experiences comes from the perception of the external spatial order.

Among the elements of traditional rural landscape, productive farming space, living space and spiritual living space constitute three important plates. Farmland, streets, squares, rivers, dwellings and other spaces bear the role of rural experience places. Through the optimization design of "experiential" intensity and "comfort", residents or tourists can be promoted to understand the traditional rural feelings, folk customs, and the tourism experience way of staying and participating in rural life, and stimulate rich rural activities according to the behavioral intensity of the behavioral subjects, thus optimizing the quality of village landscape [5]. The excavation of the essence of experience can enable us to have a brand-new thinking about the usual experience cognition and behavior needs through the thinking of experience design, and conduct more in-depth and research on the needs and feelings of users, and guide and optimize the continuous development of traditional rural landscape according to the concept of experience design.

In the theoretical study of rural landscape by foreign scholars, Hugh Clout, a rural geographer, thinks that rural areas have less population density and obvious local characteristics [6]. Gareth Lewis, a rural social geographer, pointed out that "the countryside is a rural form represented by scattered farmhouses to market towns that can provide production and living services" [7]. International research on rural landscape focuses on the study of the comprehensive form of landscape view type, regional landscape nature and regional landscape connotation in the regional space of human settlement and related behaviors. Compared with the urban landscape, the regional settlement landscape is less disturbed by human beings, so its natural attributes are stronger [8]. Compared with the pure natural landscape, the settlement landscape discussed in western landscape architecture has a certain artificial flavor, which is the production landscape and the unique cultural and living landscape of the settlement under the influence of human activities, and embodies the dual meanings of "experience subject" and "multiple values". Whether it is a natural landscape or a cultural landscape, what it contains is the diversity of rural landscape. However, different people or groups may have completely different perceptions and descriptions of the same landscape. Therefore, the universal research of western scholars holds that the rural landscape was "invented" by the cognitive person after the experience, and the landscape was endowed with rich diversity and significance in the process of being recognized, described and displayed. Since the 1960s, Germany has stimulated the enthusiasm of rural residents to participate in the construction of their homes spontaneously through the landscape and design competition of their hometown and the villagers' sense of experience and acquisition, which laid a good foundation for the renovation of German villages in the future. In the 1970s, Germany enacted laws and regulations in various States to implement the "rural renewal" plan, which combined with the experience of sightseeing and ecological civilization, and laid a solid foundation for rural renovation and transformation through years of planning renovation and action measures. Rural Environmental Planning promoted by the United States aims to build a sustainable "comfortable" rural community with balanced economic and environmental development through land, and promote the sustainable development of rural communities. In 1950, Japan's rural environment was weakened due to the population gathering in cities. By improving the rural public environment and inheriting traditional culture and handicrafts, Japan enhanced the villagers' regional presence and stimulated the rural vitality [9].

3 Research Method

The sample selected in this paper is located in the villages in the water network area of South China, that is, the core water network villages in the Pearl River Delta. Traditional village space in south China's water network area is also a daily public space in the life of water residents, and its form and layout are closely related to the daily life of water residents [13]. In the historical period, the rich water network plain of the Pearl River Delta attracted a large number of immigrants, forming a traditional settlement of commodity circulation network, all of which can not be separated from the influence of the unique region interwoven by water and land. In the process of adapting to the unique climate type and natural environment, the traditional water villages in South China have grown organically [14]. The social living environment has created a multi-layered and harmonious village landscape. The interaction between man and water has established the relationship between man and natural environment, shaped the ecological network with regional characteristics and realized the recognizable local landscape pattern [15]. Nowadays, people's experience in the water environment is based on the paddy field landscape, bridge port landscape, street landscape and other rural landscape elements in the traditional water settlements in the Pearl River Delta [16]. Traditional water towns and villages in southern China are a complex regional space interwoven by land and water environment. The landscape of traditional water towns and villages is a comprehensive system based on the integration of local natural environment, agricultural production, rural space and social life, which produces natural landscape, agricultural landscape, rural landscape and cultural landscape correspondingly. The hierarchical structure of rural landscape as shown in Fig. 1.

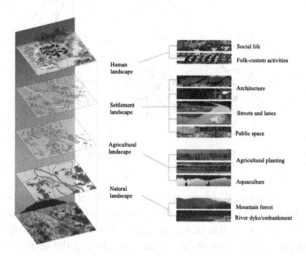

Fig. 1. Hierarchical structure of rural landscape

4 Data Collection and Analysis

The development characteristics of traditional rural landscape space can be interpreted with the help of the theory of "location characteristics" in human geography. "Location characteristics" is a method of spatial arrangement of various geographical phenomena in human geography. [17] "Location" refers not only to an absolute position, such as longitude or latitude, but also to the relative position expressed by place or position. Among them, the location is generally related to natural factors such as topography, soil, vegetation and water system, while the location is usually related to the social region of human activities, such as the settlement center, settlement area and settlement boundary [18]. In 1950s, hagt, an American geographer, imitated the work of ancient Greek cartographers and developed the theory of location characteristics by using geometric methods. Hagt formulated and put forward six geometrical features with regional characteristics: first, the movement characteristics of inter-regional factor flow and interaction; The second is the path of element movement or the path of movement network; The third is the spatial layout characteristics of network nodes; Fourth, the hierarchical structure characteristics of nodes; Fifth, the characteristics of ground space organization formed by nodes and networks, such as different forms and degrees of land use; The sixth is the spatial diffusion process that reflects the spatio-temporal changes of the pattern of human occupation of the surface [19]. The study of location characteristics has promoted human geography to positivist science, and made geography begin to pay attention to the general law of accurately and quantitatively expressing spatial organization mode [20], as shown in Fig. 2, hagt spatial system diagram.

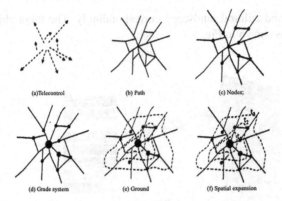

(a)Telecontrol   (b) Path   (c) Nodes;

(d) Grade system   (e) Ground   (f) Spatial expansion

Fig. 2. Hagt spatial system diagram

"Location characteristics" interprets the development characteristics and order of traditional rural landscape space, and the formation of rural landscape takes human activities as the trigger point, that is, various types of rural public activity areas. Through the diffusion degree of the activity, the path of expanding the activity area is formed, and new gathering points are further derived. Because of the experience of "main" and "secondary", people's activity areas have different degrees of density [21]. With the continuous replication and diffusion of the subject of "experience", the degree of spatial diffusion is further increased, and the mode of "adaptability" exists in rich forms in rural areas of China [22]. For example, the entrance space in traditional rural public space, the point space such as big trees and old bridges at the entrance of the village, the linear public space such as village roadways and roads, and the square space for organizing collective activities in the village can all become public spaces for villagers to gather and exchange. These places not only bear the daily production, life, leisure and entertainment functions of villagers, but also inherit rural culture and stimulate villagers' common memory, sense of belonging and identity [23].

In this paper, the traditional rural public communication space in southern China is taken as the analysis object. The form of the rural public communication space is free and flexible. Geographically, it is influenced by the environment resources with dense water network and few people and land, and forms various functional public communication spaces with water as the pulse. In spiritual space, it is influenced by the communication mode of rural society, and develops the social and cultural space with water system as the guide. With the help of the water system-oriented street-river interaction structure level, the spatial analysis focuses on the integration and promotion of rural landscape space in the local environment, and explores the relationship between people-oriented "experiential" landscape space form and subject behavior participation. Taking Xiaozhou Village in the Pearl River Delta as a typical example, this paper analyzes the hierarchy and dynamic sequence structure of its landscape space, and further puts forward new ideas and methods for the renewal design and optimization of rural landscape space.

The main purpose of experiential design is people-oriented, creating humanized design from people, which is the core content advocated in environmental design, and is reflected in all aspects. Experiencing is people-oriented and revolves around people's participation, so the principle of interactive participation is particularly important, which is the most fundamental characteristic of experiential design. For the design of communication space, we should pay more attention to experience and people's participation, such as the experience of function, space, culture and service. The spirit of place is not only limited to the concept of place, but also a sense of spiritual belonging that people consciously acquire in the process of active participation, which is a more meaningful expression of space sense. In the campus activity center, the communication space is not only a place for villagers to gather, but also an environment for life communication, and a meeting point with place spirit for people to communicate with each other. Therefore, from the perspective of experience, the communication space design of activity center should pay more attention to the participation and expression of people's spirit and feelings, so that the traditional rural communication space will have deeper spiritual feelings and experiences, thus having the spirit of place.

In view of the topographical features of water network villages in South China, under the specific historical and geographical conditions that there is more water and less land, and it is necessary to save land as much as possible, most of the water towns and villages in South China adopt the layout of lane system to build villages, and finally the typical comb layout village style is presented, which is a typical and common village construction mode. Generally speaking, in the traditional villages with comb layout, the houses are arranged neatly and regularly along the main street of the village in the north-south direction or generally in the north-south direction. However, some villages are built according to the village orientation, such as the river in front of the village.

The main skeleton of rural road network system in southern China is called "main street", which realizes the leading connection between internal traffic and internal and external traffic. The main street is the whole structure connecting villages, which mainly undertakes the functions of traffic, social activities, trade and commerce, etc. The width of traditional main roads ranges from 5 to 5–10 m. "Lane", as a living lane for residents in water towns and villages in southern China, has the main function of connecting the main street with the space of Lane, and has the functions of material transportation and pedestrian. Generally speaking, the square is perpendicular to the main streets in the countryside or to the pond in front of the countryside, which is conducive to the wind passing through the pond entering the streets and houses by wind pressure, with a general width of 2–4.5 m. "Lane Lane" is a branch network structure which is carried out from "Lane Lane Lane" down, and plays a role in connecting rural households. Usually, it is set in the front and back of residential buildings, and has strong privacy. The width of "alley" is generally 0.5–2 m, which is suitable for walking alone and facilitating direct communication between people. Its strong privacy is conducive to the safety of villages, because outsiders are easy to find and get lost when walking through the roadway, as shown in Table 1, Street and Lane Scale Levels in Traditional Water Towns and Villages in South China. As shown in Table 1, the street level in traditional water towns and villages in southern China.

Table 1. Street scale hierarchy in traditional water towns and villages in southern China

Class	Structure	Scale	Characteristics
The first class	Main street	More than 3 m	Public space and traffic street, with formal pavement
The second class	Secondary street	0.8–2 m	Semi-private communication space, connecting with large-scale residential buildings in rural areas
The third class	Inner lane	About 1 m	Private and very quiet, which is used for passing functions

Xiaozhou Village belongs to the grid street structure in the water towns of South China, and the street space, architectural space and landscape environment together constitute the entity part of the grid village. Roadways with grid comb structure form the relationship between lines and interweave into a structural space. Generally, a village with a complete spatial scale system forms a closed grid, while a single village forms a discrete grid space guided by one or two main streets. Grid street structure can be divided into aggregation, traffic, communication and other types according to its level of function, and its privacy gradually increases according to the scale of hierarchical structure, while the frequency of traffic function gradually decreases with the scale. Figure 3 shows the structure and function of rural streets in traditional water towns in southern China.

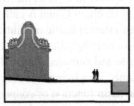
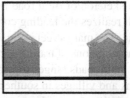

Leisure gathering place in front of ancestral hall with wide vision

0.8<D/H<1.2,Form a relatively open red sandstone main roadway

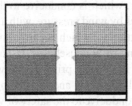
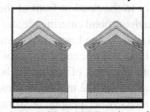

0.3<D/H<0.45 Roadways mainly used by residents

0.25<D/H<0.375 Roadway for residents to pass quickly

Fig. 3. Structure and function of rural streets in traditional water towns in southern China

We can classify the streets and lanes in the countryside according to the scale. The street and lane structure divides the rural space into non-dry spaces, at the same time, it also divides the street and lane structure into various grades. Streets with different grades and height-width ratios assume different functional roles in the rural space, and meet the traffic and communication functions of water towns and villages respectively. Streets with aspect ratio of $0.8 < D/H < 1.2$ form wide red rock roadway, which is often a meeting place in waterfront space; Roadways with height-width ratio of $0.3 < D/H < 0.45$ become vertical roadways for residents, while roadways with height-width ratio of $0.25 < D/H < 0.375$ become cross roadways for residents to travel rapidly. As shown in the figure, Fig. 4 is the width-height ratio represented by the D/H value of rural streets and lanes in traditional water towns in southern China.

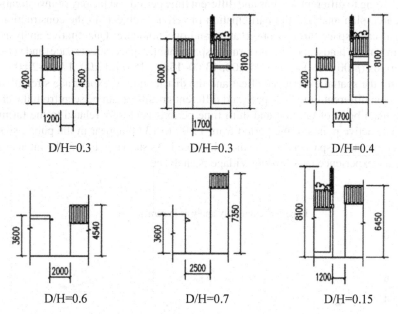

Fig. 4. Width-height ratio represented by spatial D/H value of rural streets and lanes in traditional water towns in southern China

In the 1950s, the Greek sociologist Dausadias (1913–1975) thought that inhabitation was composed of nature, man, society, architecture and supporting network, and the concrete physical space of human inhabitation could be divided into four parts: noumenon, landmark center, circulation system and communication area [24]. In the solid landscape form of rural settlement, ontology includes the overall pattern, style and features, groups and clusters of villages in a broad sense; Landmark center refers to buildings and structures or specific place nodes with obvious single functionality and aggregation in the settlement system, which has typical representative or guiding attributes for the development of village residence form; Circulation system refers to the traffic space in the streets where the villages live in compact communities, and the communication area refers to the special functional space such as village assembly square which is obviously different from the surrounding functions [25]. Therefore, through the investigation of the villagers, this paper analyzes the relationship between the stay time and activity types of the subjects in different spaces and the spatial form and function of rural landscape. In order to improve the accuracy of the information provided by the interviewees, the questionnaire survey was conducted in the countryside, and the interviewees were all villagers familiar with the local public space. Researchers ask and complete respondents according to the questions in the questionnaire; the form of direct questionnaire is mainly aimed at young respondents with higher education level, and researchers are responsible for explaining the questionable parts. These two forms of questionnaires can effectively avoid errors in the process of filling out questionnaires.

According to different seasons and different time periods on the day of investigation, the research plan analyzes the participation of activity subjects in the construction of rural landscape space through observation and questionnaire; Quantitative analysis of people in various landscape spaces (farming space, public space, street space) and various time periods (8:00–11; 00, 11:00–13:00, 13:00–15:00, 15:00–17:00, 17:00–20:00), so as to infer the spatial experience effect and the distribution of experience strength and weakness in different time and space and different groups. It can be seen from the chart that the main body of the first and third time periods is closely related to the farming space; The active points in the period from 11:00 to 13:00 appear in the public space; However, the street space activity is more balanced. As shown in Fig. 5, the intensity of rural space experience in Xiaozhou Village is analyzed.

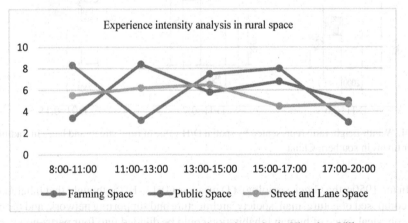

Fig. 5. Analysis of rural space experience intensity in Xiaozhou Village

According to the observation and records of main street space, secondary street space, roadway space and waterway space during the field investigation, it can be found that most of residents' daily activities are concentrated in the main street space, accounting for 80%, secondary street as traffic space accounts for 70%, and waterway space communication behavior accounts for 60%, which is still in a relatively active state, and the difference of people's communication degree is small, while the inner lane space accounts for 30%. Through the detailed analysis of the crowd distribution characteristics of various types of street space nodes, it can be found that the main activities in the countryside are still in the traditional public space, while the secondary streets bear the communicative ties between the rural people, and the waterway space in the water network village still plays the role of water transportation in the traditional villages, which also shows that the traditional life experience and comfort in the water town can continue in the modern rural landscape to a certain extent. As shown in Fig. 6.

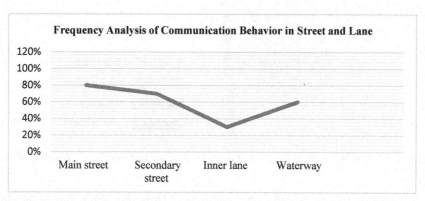

Fig. 6. Frequency analysis of communication behavior in street and lane main street main street lane

The traditional rural public communication space in southern China reflects the integration of geographical conditions and settlement environment. Its rural regional characteristics and overall spatial form can be seen from the level of street-river communication structure under the guidance of water system, and the practical choice of villagers in rural life, as well as the experience formed by historical period, which continues to the choice of comfort in contemporary rural life. According to Fig. 5 and Fig. 6, the relationship between behavior patterns, experience intensity and spatial types can be used as one of the important bases for landscape planning mode, function setting and industrial layout.

5   Discussion

In the optimization measures of rural structure in Xiaozhou Village, it is considered that the street lane structure is composed of several main streets, and the branch lanes extend to both sides with the main street as the guide. The branch lanes keep a vertical relationship with the main street, and at the same time, the two sides of the branch lanes extend out the alley lanes perpendicular to it, while the rural buildings keep a neat layout along the main street, the branch lanes and the alley lanes, forming a similar grid shape as a whole. The road width of the outermost river in Xiaozhou Village connecting the ancestral hall is generally 3–5 m, which is combined with the square and the pond. It is the widest public place of all roads in the village and meets the meeting and communication in the waterfront space; The roadway whose width is between 1.2 and 3 m is the main vertical roadway for residents, while the roadway whose width is less than 1.2 m becomes the cross roadway for residents to travel quickly and quickly. Figure 7 shows the optimized hierarchical structure of roadway structure and function in Xiaozhou Village.

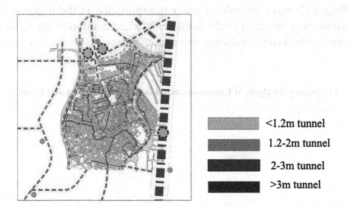

<1.2m tunnel

1.2-2m tunnel

2-3m tunnel

>3m tunnel

Fig. 7. Optimized hierarchical structure of roadway structure and function in Xiaozhou Village

Xiaozhou Village is located in the southwest of Drowning Valley Bay in the plain of South China, on the north bank of the back channel of Pearl River. It is a typical network-shaped water town with criss-crossing large and small rivers, time and time, and twists and turns. Its village water system runs through the whole rural space like meridians. In the protection and continuation measures of Xiaozhou Village, according to the width, location, runoff size of the water system and the structural relationship between the water system and the village, it can be roughly divided into three levels: the first level is Xijiangyong Dayong River, which is the largest river stream connecting the peripheral water system of the village, and several types can be seen: Jiehelin (section 1-1), Jiehewu (section 2-2), and House and House (section 3-3) The second stage is a small river channel, which accepts three small rivers in the village and merges into a big one. The structure of the small river system shows the house and house (section 4-4), house and tree (section 5-5), street river house (section 6-6) and street river street (section 7-7). The waterway in the second stage structure is suitable for the daily communication space between villages. On the third level, Shigang Jiaoyong River belongs to the inland river system, which constitutes the network waterway in the village. The third level river system houses and houses (section 8-8), Jiehe Street (section 9-9) and Jiehe House (section 10-10) maximize the communication among the villagers, which is the system with the highest communication frequency among all river systems. In addition to retaining its original functions, the third-class river system also optimizes the land and water space, promotes the communication among villagers, and the landscape characteristics of the connection between the village and the Pearl River water network structure.

Optimization strategy of street space in Xiaozhou Village, beautiful and continuous spatial interface for the optimization of street space in Xiaozhou Village, it is necessary to beautify the spatial interface. The beautiful and continuous spatial interface can not only enhance the visual experience and satisfaction of residents in street space activities, but also organically integrate into the surrounding beautiful water environment. The road width-height ratio of comfortable scale lane space reflects the relationship among people, streets and buildings, and the ratio of street width to the height of buildings on both sides. Street space, as the main place for rural residents' daily activities, should take the ratio of road width to height as the standard, create a comfortable and pleasant spatial scale, reasonably demolish some buildings in areas where space is depressed due to serious occupation of street space, and make the space become compact by adding structures to areas where space affinity is decreased due to over-opening, thus becoming a street space suitable for walking. The main street space bears many functions of traffic passing through, so its street space scale should tend to be comfortable and open, and the roadway space, as a place for daily walking activities in rural residential areas, should be more compact and have affinity, which can promote the communication between neighbors, while the secondary street space is between the main street space and the roadway space, and the spatial scale transits from open to comfortable and intimate. Table 2: Optimization measures of water network structure in Xiaozhou Village.

Villagers in traditional water towns and villages in southern China have their own big quays in the middle lanes to meet people's needs of borrowing water, while each lane has a small quay as a transfer station or a connection point. This layout and spatial distribution of villages in water towns is the result of the positive role played by waterways. Historically, due to the different functions of transportation, trade, water pumping, washing and entertainment, quays of different sizes and shapes have been formed in water towns. Nowadays, although the importance of waterways has been reduced, there are still many quays in the villages, which are scattered in the villages and around large and small rivers. The land-water spatial connection of traditional water towns in southern China also needs to meet the needs of modern rural life and meet the functions of rural landscape. Therefore, the optimized design of brick, stone, boron, soil slope and other revetments on both sides of the rural flood road can realize the life experience of the residents in the water town and meet the comfort requirements of modern life. Optimizing the design of revetment has a strong practical effect on water towns and villages. One is to stabilize the bank wall to protect the flooded bank from being washed, collapsed or flooded, and the other is to derive from the experience of villagers living in water in southern China. Residential houses are built beside the flood to facilitate residents to take water and drive boats. Most important buildings, such as ancestral halls, are built near the flood, and the solid and moisture-resistant masonry materials provide a solid foundation for ancestral halls. The revetment on both sides of Chongdao is a unique landscape of water towns and villages in southern China. As shown in Table 3, the optimized setting of water quay in Xiaozhmou Village.

Table 2. Optimization measures of water network structure in Xiaozhou village

First-class waterway		Street River Forest Section
		Street River House Section
		Roof and roof sections
Second-class waterway		Roof and roof sections
		Roof and tree profiles
		Street River House Section
		Street River street Section
Third-class waterway		Roof and roof sections
		Street River street Section
		Street River House Section

Table 3. Optimal setting of water port in Xiaozhou village

Form 1	Concave vertical water port		
Form 2	External concave vertical water port		
Form 3	Concave horizontal water port		
Form 4	External concave horizontal water port		

6 Conclusion

This paper discusses the life and production mode of rural users in traditional space in South China's water network area, studies the behavior and activities of people living in it by introducing the concept of "experience", puts forward that the root of vital signs in rural space lies in the people who are active in it, and clarifies the correlation between the elements of rural space and people's experience of space. Through the comparative analysis of integration degree and selection degree of rural space in South China's water network area, this paper explores the spatial structure of rural space itself, and analyzes the comfort choice caused by people's experience in rural space, so as to put forward targeted optimization strategies for rural space.

With the rapid development of urbanization in China, the promotion of rural landscape space has become an important link in rural transformation and development. How to lead the countryside to a scientific and rational construction road undoubtedly needs more practical exploration, especially for villages with obvious local characteristics. Nowadays, researches on rural texture, architectural pattern and landscape optimization are emerging one after another. However, it is worth discussing how to put forward more adaptive lifting methods in the face of rural environment. In a sense, from the people-oriented perspective, it is particularly important to put the participation, relevance and compound of spatial subjects into practice, form a long-term mechanism of "experience + optimization + practice", and use the advantages of rural areas to construct rural landscape in this process. If the current rural space scale can't meet the current demand of public space, when another site is needed for expansion, the overall rural space texture should be considered, and the overall rural space should not be destroyed. At the same time, the new space should incorporate traditional cultural elements on the basis of meeting public activities to meet the protection, comfort and pleasure of space. Rural construction from the perspective of experience is intended to enhance the "combination" between people's subjective feelings and objective reality conditions, that is, to explore the landscape mode, spatial sequence and experience depth under the guidance of experience. This combination is an important manifestation of the success of rural construction, and it is also the key to discuss the trend of rural construction in the future.

Acknowledgements. We thank the Guangzhou philosophy and social science development "13th Five-Year Plan" project number: 2020GZGJ19, and the Central University Project Number: BSQD201910.

References

1. Yuncai, W., Binyi, L.: China rural landscape planning and rural landscape planning Chinese gardens (01), 56–59 (2002)
2. Zhongyu, Y.: A study on the promotion of rural tourism landscape based on the coupling analysis of landscape perception experience and ecological environment. Hefei University of Technology (2018)
3. Fuping, D.: History and logic of experience design decoration (12), 92–94 (2018)
4. Yuhan, S, Binyi, L.: Analysis of visual perception of rural landscape; and Chinese gardens **32**(09), 5–10 (2016)
5. Liangzhi, W.: Introduction to the Science of Human Settlements. China Construction Industry Press (2001)
6. Yinan, C.: An interactive study on spatial form and behavior in ancient countryside; and beauty and times (city edition) (09), 50–51 (2015)
7. Fen, X.: A study on the development of rural tourism based on experience. Hubei University (2011)
8. Cong, S., Jialin, L.: A study on the renewal of village street and lane space from the perspective of. Habitat Environment Urban Architecture (06), 99–103 (2019)
9. Xing, L., Xiaodan, W.: Hierarchy and change of public space—analysis of the form of village public space; and Central China Architecture (02), 41 (2008)
10. Yu, Z., Baihua, W., Wei, G., Xuchu, G.: A review on the method of quantitative measurement of street interface morphology southern architecture (1), 88–93 (2017)
11. Fang, Z., Danyin, Z., Chengxia, X.: A study on the function continuity index of street interface based on near-human space perspective; and new buildings (5), 116–121 (2017)

12. Yuan, L., Xin, Y.: Aesthetics of the Street Yin Peitong, Translated. Baihua Literature and Art Press, Tianjin (2006)
13. Tolman, E.C.: Cognitive maps in rats and men. Psychol. Rev. **55**(4), 189–208 (1948)
14. Bafna, S., Syntax, S.: A brief introduction to its logic and analytical technique. Environ. Behav. **01**, 17–19 (2003)
15. Nadai, L.: Discourses of urban public space, USA 1960–1995 a historical critique, Ph.D. thesis. Columbia University (2000)
16. Bachi, L., Ribeiro, C., Hermes, J., Saadi, A.: Cultural Ecosystem Services (CES) in landscapes with a tourist vocation: Mapping and modeling the physical landscape components that bring benefits to people in mountain tourist destination in southeastern Brazil. Tour. Manag. **77**, 104017 (2020)
17. Wen, Z.: A study on the cooperative development of "production-life-ecology" in rural areas; and Qufu normal University (2018)
18. Guimin, L.: A pilot project of pastoral complex: ideas, models and advancing ideas. Local Finance Res. (07), 8–13 (2017)
19. Kun, W.: A study on the spatial delimitation of production-life-ecology (Sansheng) based on suitability evaluation. Zhejiang University (2018)
20. Ying, H., Lin, Z.: A continuation of the spatial image of traditional streets and alleys planner (06), 36–39 (2003)
21. Ying, H., Lin, Z.: Continuation of traditional street spatial image planner (06), 36–39 (2003)
22. Cannel, M.D.: Staged authenticity: arrangements of social space in tourist settings. Am. J. Sociol. **79**(3), 589–603 (1973)
23. Manfredo, M.J., et al.: A test of concepts inherent in experience based setting management for outdoor recreation areas. J. Leisure Res. **15**(3), 263–283 (1983)
24. Bohua, L., Peilin, L., Yindi, D.: Characteristics of rural habitat environment evolution and micro-mechanism in the less developed areas of transition human geography **27**(06), 56–61 (2012)
25. Rundong, Z., Qin, T., Xulin, Z.: Exploration and Practice on Renovation of Existing Residential Facade in Villages and Towns Based on Regional Cultural Inheritance and Innovation. Central China Arch **35**(03), 27–32 (2001)

Relations on Cultural Behavior and Technology Adoption: A Chilean Perspective

Jaime Díaz[1]([✉]) [iD], Danay Ahumada[2] [iD], Jorge Hochstetter[1] [iD], and Freddy Paz[3] [iD]

[1] Depto. Cs. de la Computación e Informática, Universidad de La Frontera, Temuco, Chile
{jaimeignacio.diaz,jorge.hochstetter}@ufrontera.cl
[2] Depto. Procesos Diagnósticos y Evaluación, Universidad Católica de Temuco, Temuco, Chile
dahumada@educa.uct.cl
[3] Department of Engineering, Pontificia Universidad Católica del Perú, Lima, Peru
fpaz@pucp.pe

Abstract. Digital transformation is the change associated with applying digital technologies in all aspects of human society. This need for digital transformation is beginning to be transversal for all industries, but especially in those small and medium-sized. Some initiatives seek to promote these transformation processes through technology adoption models. However, on a few occasions, it has been studied under a particular socio-cultural context. In this document, we begin our research by analyzing Tornatzky's proposal for technology adoption, but under a socio-cultural vision specific to the Chilean market.

Keywords: Technology adoption · Digital transformation · Human behavior · Cultural dimensions · Micro and small enterprises

1 Introduction

The need for digital transformation is evident in all industries. However, the path to achieving this is unclear. For many companies, this challenge lies in choosing to adapt and expand their technology infrastructure and internal business processes for the challenges ahead [1, 2].

To survive in this new economy, companies, including Micro and Small Enterprises (MSEs), are forced to adopt this digital trend. Companies that do not implement this practice and philosophy will be left behind by those that do [3, 4].

According to the Chilean Association of IT Companies: *"The MSEs that do not jump on the bandwagon of innovation, digitization, and digital transformation, will be left out of this world, and that it will be difficult for them to achieve high-impact or massive businesses"* [5].

The problem arises when studying technology adoption by small and medium-sized companies, which still lags behind large companies. In developing countries such as Chile, such digital approaches will be the primary conditions to survive in this new economic era. Additionally, this segment's studies related to digital transformations are rarely found in a Latin American sociocultural context [6–11].

© Springer Nature Switzerland AG 2021
M. M. Soares et al. (Eds.): HCII 2021, LNCS 12780, pp. 34–42, 2021.
https://doi.org/10.1007/978-3-030-78224-5_3

Given this need for study, we will begin our research proposal with a preliminary exercise. We will analyze the cultural characteristics of Hofstede, associated with the approach of Tornatzky's technological adoption model [12]. We seek to identify some preliminary adaptation considerations when applied in particular socio-cultural contexts.

1.1 Theoretical Foundation in Technology Adoption Research - The TOE Framework

The TOE framework was developed initially by Tornatzky, Fleischer and Chakrabarti [12] to describe the influence of contextual factors in the adoption of an innovation. In this framework, there are three aspects of a firm's context that influence adoption of technology innovation: *technological context, organizational context and environmental context.*

Technological context refers to internal and external technologies important to the company. The *organizational context* concerns nature and the resources of the company, which depends on firm size and the decentralization, formalization and complexity of its managerial structure. Then, the *environmental context* refers to other parties surrounding the firm such as competitors, suppliers and government [13, 14].

From the theories above, the TOE framework was chosen as the theoretical basis for the development of our research model. The TOE framework has been widely recognized by previous studies as a well-established framework to study e-commerce adoption [13, 15–19].

1.2 Cultural Behavior and Evaluation

Culture is considered as a *"collective mental programming that distinguishes the members of a group or category of people from others."* It is a collective phenomenon shared by people who live or have lived in the same social environment [20–22].

There have been various discussions on constructing an *"enterprise culture"*. The organizational culture builds the visible face of the brand. It is juxtaposed with the business's values to identify the credibility and nature of the organization's services. Understanding these sociocultural behaviors is positive as they provide new characteristics of functioning and well-being in the company.

Geert Hofstede conducted what can be considered the most comprehensive study on the cultural influence of people on their activities [21, 22]. He proposes the creation of indexes to generate *"cultural dimensions"*. The generation of these indices results from surveys, evaluations, and interviews carried out with various industry players globally.

Hofstede developed a model that identifies the six main dimensions to differentiate cultures: (1) Power Distance (PDI), (2) individualism vs. collectivism (IND), (3) masculinity vs. femininity (MAS), (4) uncertainty avoidance (UAI), (5) long-term orientation (based on Confucian dynamism; LTO) and (6) Indulgence and restraint (IVR) [21]. Any initiative that positively impacts adopting methods, technologies, or behavior should consider such approaches [9, 23–28].

2 Methods and Materials

The following proposal seeks to associate Hofstede's cultural characteristics with Tornatzky's pillars of technological adoption. First, we identify the particular cultural properties of Chile [29].

The analysis of the cultural characteristics of Chile (see Table 1) yields some interesting guidelines. Especially those that refer to Long-Term Orientation dimensions. This type is not necessarily favorable when implementing transformation processes that can take some time to implement.

Table 1. Chile's culture through the lens of the 6-D model from Hofstede [29].

Cultural dimension	Index	Description
Power Distance (PDI)	63/100	This dimension deals with the fact that all individuals in societies are not equal. Organizational arrangements show taller pyramids and low degrees of delegation. A hierarchical social structure and relatively rigid social classes are present
Individualism (IND)	23/100	*"Degree of interdependence a society maintains among its members"*. Blue and white-collar workers alike tend to look for more autonomy and variety in their positions, are far more assertive than in the past, and do not hesitate to change employers. These changes can be expected given the remarkable increase in Chile's GDP
Masculinity (MAS)	28/100	In Feminine countries, the focus is on "working in order to live." People need to feel a sense of "belonging" within a social group; they place value on warm interpersonal links and tacitly search for their group's approval. Consequently, they tend to be supportive team members, and managers strive for consensus. People value equality, solidarity, and quality in their working lives. Conflicts are resolved by compromise and negotiation
Uncertainty Avoidance (UAI)	86/100	The dimension of Uncertainty Avoidance has to do with how a society deals with the fact that the future can never be known. Chile shows a strong need for rules and elaborate legal systems to structure life, significant dependence on experts, and the authorities, particularly among non-managerial employees
Long-Term Orientation (LTO)	31/100	"This dimension describes how every society has to maintain some links with its past while dealing with the challenges of the present and future". Chile is said to have a normative culture. People in such societies have a vital concern with establishing the absolute Truth; they are normative in their thinking. They exhibit great respect for traditions, a relatively small propensity to save for the future, and a focus on achieving quick results

(continued)

Table 1. (*continued*)

Cultural dimension	Index	Description
Indulgence (IVR)	68/100	"The extent to which people try to control their desires and impulses based on how they were raised". Chile has a relatively Indulgent orientation. People generally exhibit a willingness to realize their impulses and desires with regard to enjoying life and having fun. They possess a positive attitude and have a tendency towards optimism. In addition, they place a higher degree of importance on leisure time, act as they please and spend money as they wish

Continuing with Tornatzky's proposal [12], he notes that three types of contexts can affect technology acceptance, creativity, and implementation. We summarize the three TOE framework contexts in Table 2.

In summary, we can identify that the technology adoption model's properties are inconsistent with Chile's specific cultural characteristics. This inconsistency of statements makes us present our central research problem (P1): *"The theories of technology adoption are not contextualized in socio-cultural environments for Chile, which causes particular technological gaps that prevent a digital transformation".*

Figure 1 provides a general description of the topics described: (P1) MIPEs in Chile are conditioned by their sociocultural factors, which implies that the theoretical proposals for adopting technology (such as the TOE framework) must have specific, explicit specifications for every situation. Furthermore, it is not enough to identify and acknowledge the technology gap; there is also the job of achieving the right adoption for the much-desired *"digital transformation."* The final proposal should allow the generation of a digital transformation model for MSEs in Chile.

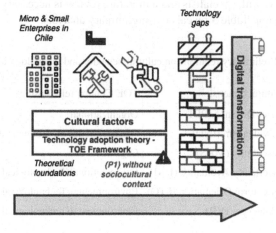

Fig. 1. Towards a digital transformation model for MSEs in Chile: general overview

Table 2. Tornatzky's TOE framework contexts [30].

Context	Description
Technological	*"The studies establish that system integration, complication, perceived intended benefits, perceived unintended benefits, and standardization are important variables while observation is found irrelevant"*
Organizational	*"Specifically refers to concise measures relating to organizations, for example, size, scope, and executives' principles. Adoption inclination is affected by formal and casual intra hierarchical systems for correspondence and control; alongside assets and creativity of the company". - "The huge variables in business scenery incorporate money related assets, top administration support, company's structure, business's slack, development limit, information ability, operational ability, vital utilization of innovation, trust, mechanical assets, support for advancement, nature of human capital, hierarchical information collection, aptitude and framework and authoritative preparation"*
Environmental	*"It emphasizes on areas in which a company leads its business tasks, with the need given to outside elements affecting the business, for example, government motivating incentive and guidelines". – "It incorporates factors identified with industry qualities, for example, competition, relations with purchasers and providers, just as the phases of the business life cycle"*

3   A Preliminary Approach

There is a scenario where each of the TOE context's recommendations is justified appropriately for each cultural dimension. The relationship between both approaches and the justification of actions is relevant for this proposal. For clarification, the respective associations are based on the descriptions above and the studies that support them. A subsequent analysis with specialists and a literature review is necessary to reach a more consistent conclusion. Table 3 reveals our preliminary analysis.

Table 3. Preliminary relations on cultural behavior and technology adoption.

Cultural dimension	TOE Context relationship
Power Distance (PDI)	Organizational
Individualism (IND)	Organizational/Environmental
Masculinity (MAS)	Organizational
Uncertainty Avoidance (UAI)	Organizational/Technological
Long-Term Orientation (LTO)	Environmental/Technological
Indulgence (IVR)	Environmental/Technological

The first dimension of Power Distance (PDI) emphasizes the difference between the different members within society. We can then associate these characteristics with the organizational aspects of how the company works. Some key points for the eventual process of technology adoption: *"The members depend on a high command"; "An institutional change management is necessary, led by a member of the management"; "The decision-making to implement or not a system supported by technology, depends only on a single person."*

The Individualism dimension (IND) refers to the relationship between social individuals and how meaningful their relationship is. In a small organization such as MSEs, there is more significant engagement behavior. These characteristics can be associated with what is related to the organizational context, but also to environmental incentives: *"Small organizations act as a family group"; "Initiatives within its members should be rewarded and encouraged."*

Regarding the Masculinity dimension (MAS), Chile has a more equitable society (FEM index). It aims to seek a *"sense of belonging"; and "support team members."* All characteristics of the organizational context.

In the dimension of the Long-Term Orientation (LTO), one essential feature appears. Chile is a "short-term," normative society that expects quick results. This characteristic supposes an eventual conflict to the basis of what a digital transformation implies. Since by definition, it is a process of change. Implementing software (which could be considered a short-term initiative) is not the answer to a digital transformation. Software is a tool, not a panacea for these kinds of initiatives. A solution to this scenario is to create a roadmap for early implementations (win-win) with immediate visible results, without stopping thinking about long-term initiatives.

Finally, the Indulgence dimension (IVR) speaks of society's impulsiveness and freedom of expression. The impetus can conclude the relationship with the technology context for acquiring software or similar perceived benefits and decision making. The mix with environmental topics is related to the external incentives that may arise.

4   Discussion

Digital transformation is the change associated with applying digital technologies in all aspects of human society. This need for digital transformation is beginning to be transversal for all types of industries. For many companies, this challenge lies in adapting and expanding their technology infrastructure and internal business processes for the challenges ahead.

While it is true that there are studies on technology adoption for the industry [31–33], most of these initiatives focus on large companies and developed countries. Studies that focus on SMEs in developing countries are less common [31, 32, 34–37]. The problem is that the validation and use of these initiatives have been carried out in large companies, or other cultures or realities. This first approach manages to give a research initiative to carry out more exhaustive studies.

Regarding the proposal, we can highlight a couple of conclusions: (i) Considering that Tornatzky's "Organizational" context appears in four of the six pillars, it will make more sense to emphasize this type of recommendation? Are they more important when we work on a cultural-based technology adoption proposal?

If the previous question is positive, then the transformation efforts are motivational: Emphasizing change management, rewards for participating teams, assurance of future work, and a plan for short, medium, and long-term implementations.

Regarding the Technology context, being a culture of an established hierarchy (ii) Would it be enough for a technology specialist to suggest an alternative for improvement for the company? Perhaps the government could offer a general basic solution? This scenario leads to an escalation problem. There are not so many specialists to analyze each company and suggest something particular. Could the escalated solution be to deliver basic systems to start a technology adoption with things like payment platforms or simple ERP systems?

Finally, (iii) the Environmental context plays a fundamental role: Considering that the target organizations are small companies, the government or some public entity should encourage this initiative. All of the above entail's implementation and training expenses. Given the nature of our objective, it is not possible to pay individually.

Although the exercise has been mainly theoretical and positional, we seek, as future work, systematically analyze studies that talk about related topics and support the results through surveys and interviews with experts. We finally seek to propose a digital transformation model that serves as a theoretical basis for making decisions at the governmental level.

Acknowledgment. The authors would like to thank all the participants involved in the preliminary experiments. Also, all the members of the *"Centro de Estudios de Ingeniería de Software, CEIS"*, *"User Experience & Game Design - Research Group, UXGD"* and *"HCI, Design, User Experience, Accessibility & Innovation Technologies Group, HCI-DUXAIT"*. UXGD is a member of the HCI-COLLAB network. Funded by Universidad de La Frontera, Proyecto DI21–0016.

References

1. MacGregor, R., Vrazalic, L.: Role of small-business strategic alliances in the perception of benefits and disadvantages of E-commerce adoption in SMEs. In: Advanced Topics in Electronic Commerce, vol. 1, pp. 1–27. IGI Global (2005)
2. Achrol, R.S., Kotler, P.: Marketing in the network economy. J. Mark. **63**, 146–163 (1999)
3. Digitaliza tu Pyme. https://www.digitalizatupyme.cl/. Accessed 13 Apr 2020
4. TODO X LAS PYMES. https://www.todosxlaspymes.cl/. Accessed 14 Apr 2020
5. La urgencia de la pyme por subirse al nuevo carro tecnológico - La Tercera (2019). https://www.latercera.com/pulso/noticia/la-urgencia-la-pyme-subirse-al-nuevo-carro-tecnologico/717575/
6. Bianchi, C., Mingo, S., Fernandez, V.: Strategic management in Latin America: challenges in a changing world. J. Bus. Res. **105**, 306–309 (2019). https://doi.org/10.1016/j.jbusres.2018.10.022
7. Katz, R., Callorda, F.: Accelerating the development of Latin American digital ecosystem and implications for broadband policy. Telecommun. Policy **42**, 661–681 (2018)
8. Kabanda, S., Brown, I.: A structuration analysis of Small and Medium Enterprise (SME) adoption of E-commerce: the case of Tanzania. Telematics Inform. **34**, 118–132 (2017)
9. Lu, Q.(Steven), Pattnaik, C., Xiao, J., Voola, R.: Cross-national variation in consumers' retail channel selection in a multichannel environment: evidence from Asia-Pacific countries. J. Bus. Res. **86**, 321–332 (2018)

10. Hadi Putra, P.O., Santoso, H.B.: Contextual factors and performance impact of e-business use in Indonesian small and medium enterprises (SMEs). Heliyon. **6**, e03568 (2020)
11. Abed, S.S.: Social commerce adoption using TOE framework: an empirical investigation of Saudi Arabian SMEs. Int. J. Inf. Manag. **53**, 102118 (2020)
12. Tornatzky, L.G., Fleischer, M., Chakrabarti, A.K.: The Processes of Technological Innovation. Lexington Books (1990)
13. Zhu, K.: The complementarity of information technology infrastructure and e-commerce capability: a resource-based assessment of their business value. J. Manag. Inf. Syst. **21**, 167–202 (2004)
14. Rahayu, R., Day, J.: Determinant factors of e-commerce adoption by SMEs in developing country: evidence from indonesia. Procedia Soc. Behav. Sci. **195**, 142–150 (2015)
15. Ghobakhloo, M., Arias-Aranda, D., Benitez-Amado, J.: Adoption of e-commerce applications in SMEs. Ind. Manag. Data Syst. **111**, 1238–1269 (2011)
16. Ramdani, B., Chevers, D., Williams, D.A.: SMEs' adoption of enterprise applications: a technology-organisation-environment model. J. Small Bus. Enterp. Dev. **20**, 735–753 (2013)
17. Cruz-Jesus, F., Pinheiro, A., Oliveira, T.: Understanding CRM adoption stages: empirical analysis building on the TOE framework. Comput. Ind. **109**, 1–13 (2019)
18. Oliveira, T., Martins, R., Sarker, S., Thomas, M., Popovič, A.: Understanding SaaS adoption: the moderating impact of the environment context. Int. J. Inf. Manag. **49**, 1–12 (2019)
19. Jia, Q., Guo, Y., Barnes, S.J.: Enterprise 2.0 post-adoption: extending the information system continuance model based on the technology-organization-environment framework. Comput. Hum. Behav. **67**, 95–105 (2017)
20. Hameed, M.A., Counsell, S., Swift, S.: A conceptual model for the process of IT innovation adoption in organizations. J. Eng. Tech. Manag. **29**, 358–390 (2012)
21. Hofstede, G.J., Hofstede, G: Cultures and Organizations - Software of the Mind, pp. 1–29 (2001)
22. Hofstede, G.: Culture's Consequences, 2nd edn. Sage Publications, Thousand Oaks (2001)
23. Huang, S.(Sam), Crotts, J.: Relationships between Hofstede's cultural dimensions and tourist satisfaction: a cross-country cross-sample examination. Tour. Manag. **72**, 232–241 (2019)
24. Ameen, N., Tarhini, A., Hussain Shah, M., Madichie, N.O.: Employees' behavioural intention to smartphone security: a gender-based, cross-national study. Comput. Hum. Behav. **104**, 106184 (2020)
25. Gilboa, S., Mitchell, V.: The role of culture and purchasing power parity in shaping mall-shoppers' profiles. J. Retail. Consum. Serv. **52**, 101951 (2020)
26. Radojevic, T., Stanisic, N., Stanic, N.: The culture of hospitality: from anecdote to evidence. Ann. Tour. Res. **79**, 102789 (2019)
27. Song, C., Park, K.M., Kim, Y.: Socio-cultural factors explaining technology-based entrepreneurial activity: direct and indirect role of social security. Technol. Soc. **61**, 101246 (2020)
28. Díaz, J., Rusu, C., Collazos, C.A.: Experimental validation of a set of cultural-oriented usability heuristics: e-Commerce websites evaluation. Comput. Stand. Interfaces. **50**, 160–178 (2017). https://doi.org/10.1016/j.csi.2016.09.013
29. Country Comparison - Hofstede Insights. https://www.hofstede-insights.com/country-comparison/chile/. Accessed 26 Jan 2021
30. Dube, T., Van Eck, R., Zuva, T.: Review of technology adoption models and theories to measure readiness and acceptable use of technology in a business organization. J. Inf. Technol. Digit. World **02**, 207–212 (2020)
31. Fischer, M., Imgrund, F., Janiesch, C., Winkelmann, A.: Strategy archetypes for digital transformation: defining meta objectives using business process management. Inf. Manag. **57**(5), 103262 (2020)

32. Guinan, P.J., Parise, S., Langowitz, N.: Creating an innovative digital project team: levers to enable digital transformation. Bus. Horiz. **62**, 717–727 (2019)
33. Zapata, M.L., Berrah, L., Tabourot, L.: Is a digital transformation framework enough for manufacturing smart products? The case of Small and Medium Enterprises (2020). https://doi.org/10.1016/j.promfg.2020.02.024
34. Williams, M.D., Dwivedi, Y.K., Lal, B., Schwarz, A.: Contemporary trends and Issues in IT adoption and diffusion research. J. Inf. Technol. **24**, 1–10 (2009)
35. Roth, S., Dahms, H.F., Welz, F., Cattacin, S.: Print theories of computer societies. Introduction to the digital transformation of social theory. Technol. Forecast. Soc. Change **149**, 119778 (2019)
36. Tekic, Z., Koroteev, D.: From disruptively digital to proudly analog: a holistic typology of digital transformation strategies. Bus. Horiz. **62**, 683–693 (2019)
37. Mergel, I., Edelmann, N., Haug, N.: Defining digital transformation: results from expert interviews. Gov. Inf. Q. **36**, 101385 (2019)

User Experience Centered Application Design of Multivariate Landscape in Kulangsu, Xiamen

Fengze Lin, Fengming Chen, and Mingjian Zhu[✉]

School of Design, South China University of Technology, Guangzhou 510006,
People's Republic of China
zhumj@scut.edu.cn

Abstract. As nominated as World Heritage Site in 2017 by UNESCO, Kulangsu Island in Xiamen, China, is a unique historic international settlement from 19th century. One important feature of Kulangsu is its dual identities of community for local residents and tourist attractions for visitors. Thanks to abundant cultural and natural resources, its famous visual landscape of Amoy Art deco architecture and various foreign-style architecture, together with Kulangsu's historic-contemporary soundscape, like piano melody sound, wave sound and lost church music once satisfied both local inhabitants and visitors all over the world. Unfortunately, many unique sounds and views in the history has disappeared gradually because of local population decline and rush tourism development. Smart application provides us another perspective and tool for landscape design on a multivariate space like Kulangsu. Although the development of smart phone application is successful in China nowadays, its technology is seldom combined with landscape design methods. There is lack of technical implementation and testing for application in Landscape design field. The aim of this study and application design is to promote user experiences for visitors. The research firstly investigates users' preferences for Kulangsu's landscapes and travel behaviors by the means of investigation. Concluded from user interview results, there are three key objectives predefined before the design and development process. Eventually, the application design is proposed to demonstrate how user experience centered design and augmented reality technology can be utilized for virtual revival and digital restoration of Kulangsu's multivariate landscape in different historic periods.

Keywords: User experience · Augmented reality · Multivariate landscape · Kulangsu

1 Introduction

As nominated as World Heritage Site in 2017 by UNESCO, Kulangsu island in Xiamen, China, is a unique historic international settlement since 19th century. But as the most famous tourist spot in Fujian, over development by tourist industries and following consequences resulted by this phenomenon, like improper exploitation of multivariate heritage, social and natural environmental deterioration and deceasing population of

© Springer Nature Switzerland AG 2021
M. M. Soares et al. (Eds.): HCII 2021, LNCS 12780, pp. 43–59, 2021.
https://doi.org/10.1007/978-3-030-78224-5_4

local inhabitants, bring the essence of this beautiful island under the danger of destroying and vanishing. Due to the decline of indigenous culture and chaos of landscape development, original renovation and manage methods can no longer satisfy the needs of the future tourism development of Kulangsu. Thus, it is significant to apply emerging technologies to design and develop a guide tour application for tourists, which should be capable of reducing the impact of outside visitors on local community and reviving historic multivariate landscapes.

2 Background

2.1 Multivariate Landscape in Kulangsu

Multivariate landscape refers to visual landscape and soundscape, which means the notion of visual landscape and that of soundscape are covered by the term "Multivariate Landscape" in this paper. Actually, the term of soundscape is a neologism coined by a Canadian composer Raymond Murray Schafer in the 1970s. The notion of "Soundscape" refers to those audio elements that compose a landscape from the acoustic perspective [3]. It is worth mentioning that this concept is not merely about aesthetic, but also in the sense of historic, cultural and geographic, same as that of landscape. As a result, as for tourists, both visual landscape perception and auditory landscape perception determine their understanding, attitude and behavior towards Kulangsu [4].

Originally before 19th century, Kulangsu only had few settlements formed by residents of southern Fujian. As Xiamen was opened a port to the outside world, more and more foreign missionaries, diplomatic officers and businessmen began to live in this small island. Afterwards, Kulangsu became an international Settlement in 1903, attracting huge number of overseas Chinese returning from Southeast Asia to settle down and make contribution to Kulangsu's development. Ever since, Kulangsu island completely evolved into a modern interactional multicultural settlement.

Thanks to abundant natural resources and developed history, Kulangsu has unique multivariate landscape features in different periods of time. As for visual landscape, the island is famous its Historical-Cultural heritages and rich natural environments. The combination of diverse architectures distinguishes Kulangsu from other regions of Xiamen, which absorbs and preserves traditional Southern-Fujian architectural style, veranda colony style, diverse foreign architectural styles brough by architects from different countries, and the most magnificent Amoy Deco style developed by returned overseas Chinese [1]. Natural landscapes also vary on Kulangsu, because of the fact that there are several granite mountains, countless ravines and springs scattered on the island, as well as disjointed distribution of rocks and beautiful beaches around the islands. In addition to southern China mild but changeable climate, the island is full of different of kinds of animals and plants, from ocean to land and air. No matter for historic architecture or natural scenery, the visual landscapes of Kulangsu are picturesque and exceptional. Certainly, all above visual landscapes are accompanied by Kulangsu's unique soundscape, composited of wave sound, piano melody, organ melody, anthem from churches, conversation or quarrel in multi-languages. Besides, the origin of island's name is related to the strange wave sound like beating drum, generated from huge reef at the southwest sea of island.

Unfortunately, all these unique sounds and sceneries in the history are at the risk of disappearing with the passage of time. Because of local population decline and rush tourism development, Kulangsu's unique multivariate landscapes gradually loses the original Social-Cultural medium, and is also suffered from excessive interference and damage from some outside visitors (Tables 1 and 2).

Table 1. Soundscapes of Kulangsu.

Soundscapes
Wave Sound Like Drum Beats (from Drum Wave Stone)
Family Party Music (Historically from Elite Families)
The Noise of the Market of Historic International Residents (Historically from Market)
Piano Music (from Churches and Music Halls, Iconic Acoustic Elements)
Organ Music (from Churches and Music Halls)
Ambient Sound of Soccer Court (from Foreigner's Soccer Court)
Wave Sound (from Sea)
Dialogue in Southern Fujian Dialect (from Local Community and Overseas Chinese Community)

Table 2. Landscapes of Kulangsu.

Landscapes	
Historic-cultural landscapes	Catholic Church (Religion Place)
	Sanhe Taoist Temple (Religion Place)
	Former Southern Hokkien Christian Bookstore (Historical Infrastructure)
	Former Kulangsu Water Supply Company (Historical Infrastructure)
	Former Office of Kulangsu Telegraph Company (Historical Infrastructure)
	Huang's Ancestral Hall (Traditional Residential Buildings)
	Former Office of British Asiatic Petroleum Company (Historical Institute)
	Former Foreigner's Soccer Court (Historical Sport Facilities)
	Cliff Inscription (Cultural Relics)
Natural landscapes	Drum Wave Stone (Iconic Landscape Element)
	Sunlight Rock (Iconic Landscape Element)
	Flag-Raising Hill

2.2 User Experience

Even though have been introduced and explained in design field for decades, the concept and connotation of User Experience are still vaguely and widely defined. Because rapid development of technology service and product, the concept of User Experience can be applied to evaluate and measure artifacts in more fields, including game, education, and tourism. People now commonly can be aware of the importance of User Experience, but designer and researchers are still unable to reach an agreement or consensus about User Experience [8]. For now, the meaning of User Experience is open and controversial.

Actually, the definition varies and differs from the form of technology and medium. In other words, User Experience is constrained by the capability of technology strength and the characteristics of certain medium. In terms of mobile application, what's significant for users using experiences are customization, usability and user engagement [9].

User engagement is a sub-category of User Experience, which is used to describe the user mental state and should be determined by user's instant intuition and pleasure they obtain from using it. Generally speaking, user engagement can be attributed to some experience characteristic, including aesthetic, variety, interactivity and challenge [6].

2.3 Augment Reality Technology

Augment Reality Overview. Technically, augmented reality is a field of computer research which focuses on the integration of the computer-generated virtual world and the physical world. But on the other hand, to be more practical, augmented reality is about providing users with real-time interactive experience of the real-world environment, with the augment of digital virtual contents. It is a mixed reality combining real surroundings and digital information into a multi-dimensional composite environment. With the development of technology, AR can support media in various forms, like text, audio, images, video, and geo-positioning data. Thus, the technology gradually involves more sensory modalities, including visual module, auditory module, haptic module as well as olfactory module.

Augmented Reality Concepts and Mechanism. There are three significant concepts within an AR system, tracking, registration and calibration, as shown in Fig. 1. Tracking is to dynamically determine the spatial properties in physical environment in real-time. Registration refers to the alignment systems between virtual contents and real environment. And calibration relates to checking and adjusting of sensors' measurement and accuracy [2].

Feedback loop is another sample scenario concisely describes how AR system actually works (Fig. 2). The system firstly would pose-track the user's viewport, register the pose in the physical world with corresponding digital contents, and eventually presents situated visualizations on AR display devices.

Augmented Reality Application in Tourism. Many different sectors have been using augmented reality technologies to upgrade service or product, including AR therapy in medial field, AR MOOC in education field, and AR games in entertainment industry. Furthermore, augmented reality is potential to utilized in tourist industry, especially

Fig. 1. Three important concepts of AR (created by the authors based on references).

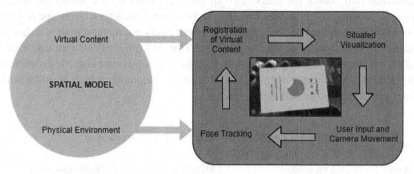

Fig. 2. Feedback loop of AR system (created by the authors based on references).

for heritage attractions like Kulangsu. With similar conditions and requirements, many heritage sites have already employed AR technologies to bring out improved user experiences, like Greece's Crete's Chania old town and Olympia archaeological site. These examples use AR guide applications on handheld devices to virtually reconstruct and revive lost ancient architectures and monuments, return to the faded world, enriching their historical-cultural connotation and attracting more potential tourists. Many other studies have researched into this field, and implemented sophisticated augmented reality application framework, which contains geolocation tracking system, AR reconstruction, AR animation, AR virtual avatar guide, and AR life simulation [5]. All above examples and studies reveal the advantages of utilizing AR technologies in tourism, especially for scenic spots known for historic heritages.

2.4 Comparison of Current Kulangsu Guide Tour Application

For the tourism of Kulangsu, the most popular travel style is the traditional group tour with a professional guide in charge of introducing and explaining the implication of attractions [10]. As the result, there are no much guide tour applications for Kulangsu in the market. So as to research and analyze the strength and weakness of different Kulangsu guide tour applications, products on different platforms, with different functions and features are within the scope of this study.

As shown in the Table 3 below, characteristic and function of guide tour applications differs from product to product. Firstly, aesthetic user interface design is necessary and vital for user experience centered application. Illustration map in Lvji Guide and 3D virtual display in Meet Kulangsu are two methods worth learning from. Even though applications' accurate functions and user scenarios are quite different, contents of guide tour are consistent, but with different preferences. With the aim of designing a guide tour application with knowledge about multivariate landscape, professional landscape knowledge should be included. Another issue of current applications is monotonous travel route, with no other alternatives to choose. Since the definition of User Experience in this study includes the aspect of customization, it is crucial to provide more and personalized tour routes for users. Two of three applications use audio narratives to improve the complexity of guide, which is ought to augment with soundscape resources in the application prototype. Only Meet Kulangsu apply augmented reality technology and achieve satisfactory results through testing. Thus, it's obvious that application of AR greatly contributes to user engagement. Before the user interviews later, this comparison briefly determines and emphasize the key elements and methods, which are enlightening for later prototype design and development.

Table 3. Comparison of current guide tour application.

Category	Lvji guide	Meet Kulangsu	Kulangsu guide
Platform	IOS/Android	IOS	WeChat Applet
Application contents	Most contents are about travel instructions, only few related to landscape knowledge	Primary game contents, lack of detailed guide and explanation	Professional and faultless professional contents about Kulangsu, including landscape knowledge
User interface	Professional UI design; Rigid and monotonous	Attractive and aesthetic; Imperfect UI adaption; Interactive and playful	Outdated user interface design; Rigid and monotonous
Navigation function	Fixed tour route and display on map; Explanation of attractions in text form; Location information for toilet, entrance and exit and souvenir shop	Location information for toilet, entrance, exit and souvenir shop	Fixed tour routes; Detailed explanation of attractions in text form with images
Augment reality function	None	By scanning the AR markers scattered on Kulangsu to collect virtual assets	None

(continued)

Table 3. (*continued*)

Category	Lvji guide	Meet Kulangsu	Kulangsu guide
Graphical element	Illustration map	3D models of attractions and Kulangsu landscape; Illustration map; Explanation images	Images for guide tour and explanation of attractions
Audio element	Voice navigation and guide	AI narrative guide	None
Notification content	Promotion notification	Promotion notification	None

3   Evaluation

3.1   Respondents Interview

Tourists of Kulangsu is the target participant group of the user interviews, covering various demographic background and different travel behaviors. All 21 respondents are provided with seven questions from seven prospective, which are usability, customization, user engagement, emotional experience, interactive experience and visual experience (Table 4).

Table 4. Interview questions.

Serial number	Questions
1	Have you ever paid attention to the historical landscape pattern of Kulangsu?
2	Have you encountered any obstacles in the process of inquiring about the historical landscape of Kulangsu?
3	How do you know the historical landscape of Kulangsu? (e.g. books, web queries, TV shows, etc.)
4	What do you think of the effect of querying Historical landscapes from different ways?
5	Do you think it is necessary to design and develop a special software or app to restore historical landscape?
6	Dis you use any software or app with similar functions?
7	What do you think is the future development trend of this kind of software?

3.2 Results and Discussions

After the interview stage, results are collected and analyzed as follows.

(1) Only a few people have paid attention to the historical landscape pattern and landscape evolution of Kulangsu. Most tourists are more interested in the current landscape and put more energy on sightseeing.
(2) The biggest problem tourists encounter in the process of understanding the historical landscape is the lack of official information sources, so tourists cannot guarantee that the information they find is accurate. In addition, the lack of historical landscape image information also makes the search results unable to accurately identify.
(3) Most people search online on the computer, while some tourists search through the mobile social platform or Knowledge-Sharing app, or ask the surrounding residents to learn about the local landscape history.
(4) Tourists reflect that the quantity and quality of historical landscape information obtained varies among different sources. The information obtained through TV is authoritative, but it lacks the right of independent choice. The audience can only follow the program arrangement to obtain information, which is lack of initiative. However, the Internet is full of we media without authority, and the information is too complex and difficult to distinguish the true from the false. The information provided by books is relatively authoritative and perfect, but the content form is relatively boring and the speed of access is slow. The oral history of local residents has a strong subjective color, and cannot directly understand the historical landscape.

3.3 User Personas

Tourists of Kulangsu is the target participant group of the user interviews, covering various demographic background and different travel behaviors. All 21 respondents are provided with seven questions from seven prospective, which are usability, customization, user engagement, emotional experience, interactive experience and visual experience. Then, User Personas of this study can be summarized and generated as below (Figs. 3 and 4).

Fig. 3. User Persona 1.

Habits:
- To travel by oneself;
- To search for the history of the landscape on internet in advance before setting off;
- To take books about historic landscape on tour

Problems in tour:
- Information on the internet is mostly lack of authority;
- Books are too heavy to take with, and there are few images of historic landscape. It is not convenient to understand the changes of the historic landscape.

Name: Mr. Sun
Gender: Male
Age: 21

Fig. 4. User Persona 2.

4 Problem Statement

4.1 User Personas

See Table 5.

Table 5. User requirements.

Type	Needs
User engagement	Users can continuously maintain in a mental state that encourage users to conduct interactions or be immersed in
	Application should sensorily appeal to users by user interface design, and induce they to make interactions using predefined mechanisms
Usability	All of the users' requirements are met, and there are no missing critical features
	The application should be easy for all ages to use
	The application should response to users' action quickly
Customization	The layout and color of the application can be customized by users
	Users can freely choose the order in which they browse the landscape
Emotional experience needs	Users are able to ensure the authority of the information
	App focus on landscape restoration and provide introduction
Interaction experience needs	Users can quickly switch between different function modules
	Voice information has high recognition
	App can automatically identify the location and provide the historical landscape change information of the location
Visual experience needs	The interface layout should be as simple as possible
	The information and buttons are bright and easy to identify
Functional requirement	App can reproduce disappeared landscape Through the vision and voice
	GPS Positioning function
	Through the message prompt, environmental education and important aboriginal activities are carried out to remind tourists
	Independent tour guide function
	Push tips for important activities

4.2 Objectives

The user centered application prototype design of multivariate landscape in Kulangsu is entitled "Historic Landscape Kulangsu". Based on user requirements and current application's problem explained above, *Historic Landscape Kulangsu* should be designed to achieve three objectives as shown below.

(1) To develop a guide tour mobile application to promote multivariate landscape knowledge, including natural and cultural landscape contents.
(2) To design appropriate aesthetic user interface to improve user experience.
(3) To apply augmented reality technology to generate visual landscape and soundscape in virtual environment.

5 Prototype Design

5.1 Use Case Diagram

As shown in Fig. 5 below, the Use Case Diagram concisely outline the interaction scenario user involved in *Historic Landscape Kulangsu*, as well as the communication process between user and application system.

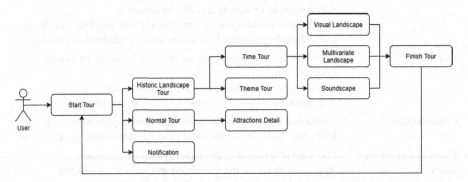

Fig. 5. Use case diagram of *Historic Landscape Kulangsu*.

5.2 User Flow

User flow explain how the users implement the application by conducting different tasks in a certain pre-defined sequence. In the diagram below, it presents various and complex systematic pathways that user can choose from when using application.

After registering in the Historic Landscape Kulangsu, users have 2 main ways to experience the journey of landscape restoration: Normal Tour and Historic Landscape Guided Tour referring to Fig. 6.

Normal Tour. Users can choose from Attraction List and Other Facilities. App would provide detailed information according to users' action.

Historic Landscape Guided Tour. Historic landscape guided tour can provide information in the order of time or by various theme. Specific tour modes are classified in 3 categories: Visual Landscape mode, Multivariate Landscape mode and Soundscape mode, where Visual Landscape mode focuses on visual landscape augmented reality restoration, Soundscape mode merely concentrate on reviving lost historic sounds on Kulangsu island, and Multivariate Landscape mode can provide both acoustic and scenery guide tour information.

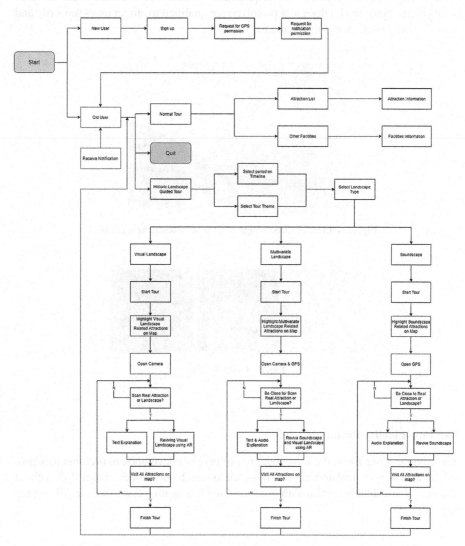

Fig. 6. User flow.

5.3 User Interface Design Style

Because of the unique theme of historic multivariate landscape and Kulangsu's culture identity, the vibe of literary and vintage of old book suits the prototype UI design. Nostalgic texture, colors of old book are selected as the design style to coordinate with application's contents. Accordingly, in the specific color design, light yellow, bright orange and dark brown are applied to complete all the UI color matching. As mentioned in Sect. 4.1 User Requirement, the requirement of aesthetic is fundamental for user engagement. Thus, the UI design of prototype are qualified to attract users sensorily and promote user experience (Figs. 7 and 8).

Fig. 7. Old Book (free image asset from www.pexels.com).

Fig. 8. Color board.

5.4 Low-Fidelity Prototype

According to User Flow, the Low-Fidelity prototype is developed to preliminarily provide an overview of final appearance. It is used to sketch out the idea of user flow without coloring. Some details remain ambiguous and unclear in this stage, like the AR display page (Fig. 9).

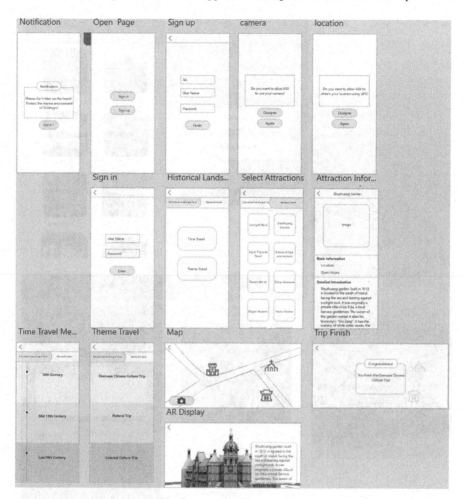

Fig. 9. Low-fidelity prototype.

5.5 High-Fidelity Prototype

Integrating the Low-Fidelity Protype and design style discussed in Sect. 5.2, the High-Fidelity Prototype is more detailed and easier for tester to find specific components to make further amendments. In addition, it is presentable enough to show how the application looks and works for stakeholder involved (Figs. 10 and 11).

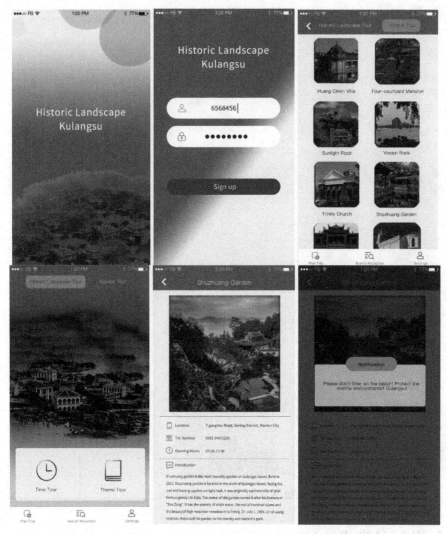

Fig. 10. High-fidelity prototype.

5.6 Wire Flow

Wire Flow is constructed according to the High-Fidelity Prototype. Instead of viewing page individually, Wire Flow is appropriate for showing the page-to-page communication of dynamic application prototype. Making all pages linked and clickable, the purpose of wire flow is to show the relationship between all user interfaces and convey whole prototype context to the users. Besides, the layout and design elements on each page are also clear in Wire Flow (Fig. 12).

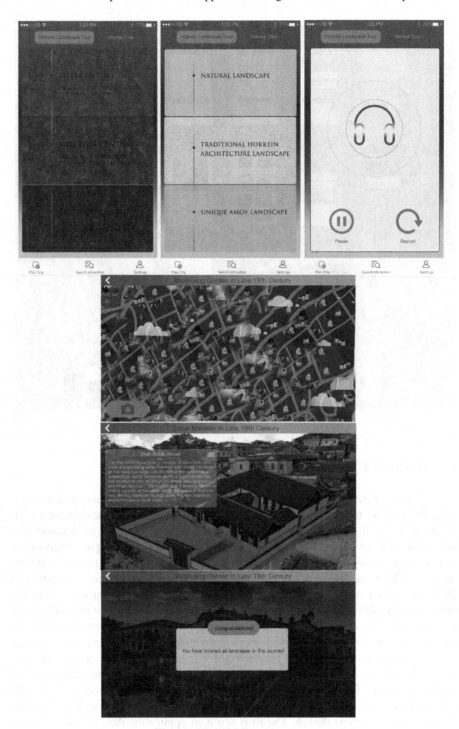

Fig. 11. High-fidelity prototype.

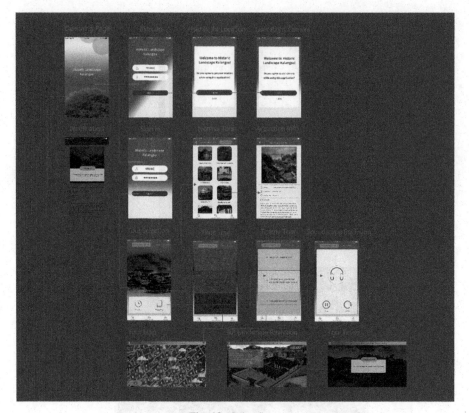

Fig. 12. Wire flow.

6 Conclusion

To conclude, this study provides a vision for how user experience centered design and augmented reality technology can be utilized to design a mobile application for virtual revival and digital restoration of Kulangsu's multivariate landscape in different historic periods. Been through the vicissitudes of over a century, Kulangsu's exceptional and stunning multi-dimensional landscapes are suffering from rush tourism industry currently. Therefore, by introducing an AR-featured mobile guide tour application, it allows the tourists to self-exploration and appreciate sceneries and learning landscape environment of different eras in Kulangsu. As for research phrase, the method of user interview has been conducted accordingly to find out authentic user requirements. To solve these current issues and achieve user requirements, three objectives are proposed to guide and direct further design processes. Moreover, the prototype of application is designed following the three aspects of User Experience, usability, customization and user engagement. To meet these user requirements, aesthetic user interfaces and 3D augmented reality design correlating with landscape restoration are employed in final High-Fidelity prototype design. The final result of application design offers a guide tour alternative for tourists of Kulangsu to provide improved user experience, as well as a modern-technologies-involved solution for protecting and promoting multivariate landscapes of Kulangsu.

References

1. UNESCO. https://whc.unesco.org/en/list/1541/documents/. Accessed 11 Nov 2020
2. Dieter, S., Tobias, H.: Augmented Reality: Principles and Practice. Addison-Wesley, Boston (2016)
3. Élise, G.: Soundscape revisited. Metropolitics (2014)
4. Mengyuan, Q., Jie, Z., Chunhui, Z.: Exploring tourists' soundscape emotion and its impact on sustainable tourism development. Asia Pacific J. Tour. Res. **23**(9), 826–879 (2018)
5. Jihad, A., Hend, H.: Employing augmented reality for reviving heritage site: an AR vision for Qsar Al-Abd in Jordan. Am. J. Tour. Res. **8**(1), 1–10 (2019)
6. Heather, O., Elaine T.: What is user engagement? A conceptual framework for defining user engagement with technology. J. Am. Soc. Inf. Sci. Technol. **59**, 939–955 (2008)
7. Sun, Y.: HUL and conservation of the historic city of Kulangsu: a scoping case. Historic Environ. Policy Pract. **9**(3–4), 376–388 (2018)
8. Bin, Y., Long, W., Zihan, P.: Measuring and improving user experience through artificial intelligence-aided design. Front. Psychol. **11**, 3000 (2020)
9. Amir, D., Teemu, L.: User experience in mobile augmented reality: emotions, challenges Opportunities and Best Practices. Computers **7**, 33 (2018)
10. Lin, Z.: The renovation trouble, strategy, and experience of Gulangyu Island in Xiamen. Planners, 64–70 (2016)

A Study on the Application of Innovative Strategies on Intelligent Mutual-Aid Delivery Services on College Campuses

Hong Liu[1]([⊠]), Zhong Siyang[1], Wan Yixin[2], Junya Yu[2], and Wei Cao[2]

[1] Beijing City University, No. 269 Bei si Huan Zhong Lu, Hai Dian District, Beijing, China
[2] GuoLin Financial Information Services Co., Ltd., Beijing, China

Abstract. As China's e-commerce has entered an "Internet+" era in recent years, the number of express parcels on college campuses has been soaring exponentially. However, delivery service is not allowed on many campuses, leading to a missing "last mile". Taking Beijing City University as an example, this study studies and analyses the degree of satisfaction of users about picking up and shipping parcels on the campus by means of field survey, questionnaire survey and in-depth interview. The demands on the missing "last-mile" delivery service on the campus are also studied by using the empathy map as one of the service design methods and are then categorized using the Kano model. The contact points of the on-campus delivery service are analysed and a user journey graph is produced on this basis. Then, a campus mutual-aid delivery service is optimally designed, leading to a final service blueprint. A campus intelligent mutual-aid service platform is also planned, featuring the delivery service as its main function so as to address the missing "last-mile" delivery service issue. Students are considered as the basic users of this service. Background data analysis offers suggestions on how to accurately mate students who would like to ship or pick up a parcel, which effectively integrates the resources and needs and sends them to mobile clients, thus integrating users, Internet of Things and the Internet and virtually landing the service design concept.

Compared to traditional delivery processes, this intelligent mutual-aid service is more stable, efficient and convenient. It also features high availability and extensibility. The data searching algorithm accurately matches users while making full use of their overlapping time. This service enhances the efficiency of on-campus delivery services and promotes the transition from a traditional digital campus to a mutual-aid intelligent one.

The landing of this mutual-aid platform significantly improves the efficiency of delivery services on the campus and makes it standardized, alleviating the chaotic situation to a large extent. In addition, the platform also streamlines the on-campus delivery procedure. In the meantime, it can help develop an initiative in students and enhance their practical ability, therefore promoting the innovative development of this service and formulating a harmonious campus featuring mutual aid.

Keywords: Mutual aid · Intelligent · On-campus delivery · Service design

© Springer Nature Switzerland AG 2021
M. M. Soares et al. (Eds.): HCII 2021, LNCS 12780, pp. 60–77, 2021.
https://doi.org/10.1007/978-3-030-78224-5_5

1 Background and Industry Analysis of Intelligent Mutual-Aid Delivery Services on College Campuses

1.1 Background

Online shopping has become increasingly important for college students thanks to the development of Internet. According to the Industry Development Report on Campus Parcel (2019) issued by China Education Logistics Association and Ali Research, the number of campus parcels in China is expected to grow from 2.5 billion in 2018 to 3 billion in 2019. Assume that China has a total number of 38 million college students and that the average annual expenses on educational, recreational and social activities per person is 4000 yuan, then the average number of parcels each college student receives in a year totals 78, 1.8 times that of the national average. It should be noted that the college market is worth over 200 billion yuan although college students earn no income. Such a unique market is especially worthy of attention for logistics and e-commerce businesses considering the much higher average number of parcels that college students receive compared to the national average.

1.2 Industry Analysis

The rapid development of Internet economy has made online shopping n integral part of people's daily lives. Online shopping has brought about substantial convenience for students, but the "last-mile" delivery services on campuses are impeded.

80% of students reportedly have encountered delays or difficulties while picking up their parcels during "Double 11" and "Double 12" shopping festivals. There are primarily two views about picking up parcels on campuses from college students: it is too far away; it takes too long due to too many people and slow processes. Students have to pick up their parcels at designated on-campus parcel centres in person because delivery persons are now allowed onto campus. It costs time for both students and delivery persons as both of them need to wait. There are also other problems. For example, there are much fewer students picking up parcels at lunchtime but it can be quite crowded after class; students may forget bringing their ID cards while picking up parcels and that costs them much more time to handle the issue. Considering these problems, it is of vital practical significance to investigate the application of efficient and large-scale "last-mile" delivery services on college campuses.

College students are not only the largest consumer group but also the largest Internet population, who assimilate new ideas and spread knowledge fast and are favoured by enterprises. Despite some existing problems, campus e-commerce and delivery services are bound to grow rapidly in the near future thanks to improvement in digital campus construction. The intelligent mutual-aid delivery services on college campuses enjoy substantial market potential as long as science-based management approaches are adopted which take into consideration students' consumption features.

1.3 Intelligent Campus

China issued the Overall Framework for Intelligent Campus in 2018, which systematically elaborated on the overall planning of intelligent campus and made clear provisions for intelligent teaching environment, teaching resources, campus management, campus service and information security system, setting national standards for intelligent campus construction. "Intelligent campus" uses highly-developed computer network as its core technology, uses information and knowledge sharing as its means, centres teachers and students, and serves teaching, research and management activities. "Intelligence" is shown in four aspects, namely, in-depth sharing of resources, high-speed flow of information, intelligent delivery service, mating and sharing of information.

Intelligent campus is a complex formed with Internet of Things (IoT) and cloud computing. It can also be seen as an upgrade of digital campus. One of the features of intelligent campus is that its information platforms are constructed thanks to the rapid development in network and communication technologies, which enables sharing of resources to a certain extent. Maximal transmission efficiency can be obtained and businesses are streamlined. It also enables intelligent management of the campus through these platforms. Unified treatment is also available for campus delivery through intelligent individualized services. Since the intelligent services have to be available throughout the campus, a fully operating network is necessary for the construction of information platforms. Schools need to pay due attention to Internet infrastructure development and keep abreast of new software and hardware systems. A stable and high-speed network connection is pivotal for accessing the information platforms at any time at any place. Moreover, intelligent campus also enables communication with other schools in terms of logistics information, which integrates the school's achievements in mutual-aid delivery services into the international academic circle and promotes the school's reform and innovation.

2 Status Quo of Last-Mile Delivery Service on Campus

2.1 Status Quo of Campus Parcels at Home and Abroad

The parcel industry is growing rapidly with campus beings its huge potential market, but the last-mile delivery service still needs huge improvement in most domestic colleges, which impose similar restrictions: off-campus personnel are now allowed onto campus, including delivery persons for parcels and takeaways. In the meantime, many schools have been exploring new ways of parcel management. At the present, many Chinese colleges have implemented pilot experiments in campus parcel centres. There are mainly three modes: under the direct management of the school, jointly managed by enterprises, intelligent parcel lockers. The first is guided by the school authorities and implemented by the school logistics department. The school offers a venue for parcel companies and manages these companies. The second mode allows parcel companies to establish agents on campus. The "Remin University Parcel 100" mode that was put into use in 2013 has been widely used in many other schools. Many colleges established self-service parcel lockers since then. Parcel receivers would pick up their parcels with passcodes sent to them by delivery persons.

Outside China, campus parcel delivery services usually belong to Third-Party Logistics (TPL). It appeared in as early as the 1980s in Europe, where it was generally believed that logistics services not offered by manufacturers and retailers belong to TPL. In the United States, 57% of logistics services are offered by TPL. The figure in Japan reaches as high as 80%. So far, TPL services account for one third of the global total and are growing at an annual rate of 15%. A number of parcel institutions outside China have established their own campus terminals, avoiding the issue of chaos with too many parcel companies to some extent. A mature campus parcel service scheme known as Campus Express has been formulated over many years of development in western campuses. These campuses would normally have their own logistics websites that integrate campus parcel services and campus online shopping. Take Harvard University: Chinese consumers may purchase Harvard souvenirs through the University's shopping website, and shipping of the souvenirs would be processed by Harvard logistics including designating a parcel company and finally shipping the goods. In most examples, campus parcel centres are responsible for managing different parcel companies in an integrated platform and for delivering the parcels on campus. Their services are continuously improved to form a complete parcel ecological environment featuring all of shopping, shipping and transporting.

2.2 Campus Service Environment Analysis

The campus service environment is a key component of the overall service process. Incorporating its service design into the study of campus service environment construction is thus of crucial significance to improving the intelligent campus services. This can be done by considering four aspects of work, namely: people, things, process, environment. This requires analysing, planning, optimizing and innovating components of the environment system from a holistic view. The essence of campus services is service. The prerequisite of intelligent campus service is the holistic study of campus services and implementation of a system. Service design is a key engine propelling the service sector in foreign countries. It is therefore of paramount importance to introduce it into the design of campus services, spanning from top-level design to service management, from organization to personnel, from environmental optimization to information construction, so as to establish a college campus service system throughout all dimensions. The present investigation uses the tool of service design and bases the study on the service feature of college campus service environment. It summarizes the main components of college campus service environment, with a focus on the construction of a service environment on the organizational and individual levels. The study aims to address the construction issue of system, platform and holistic layout of campus services. The ultimate output is a service application scenario of intelligent mutual-aid campus services.

3 Analysis of the Intelligent Mutual-Aid Delivery Service Design at Beijing City University

3.1 Existing Problems

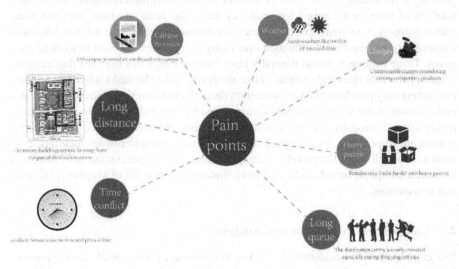

Fig. 1. Users' concerns

All the parcels of Beijing City University are collected at one distribution centre, which takes up an area of around 300 m^2. Campus parcel delivery services arise as a result of restricting parcel delivery persons from entering campuses. After investigating student users who receive and ship parcels, this study summarizes six existing problems, namely: time conflict, long distance, long-time queuing, carrying, sanitation concerns, extreme weather (Fig. 1). For problem 1, time conflict, students may not have the time to pick up parcels either when they are off campus due to weekends, holidays, field studies and researches, or when they need to attend certain classes and have no spare time. Problem 2 is long distance. This campus has nine dormitory buildings, six of which are over 1000 m away from the parcel distribution centre. Students would not like to travel that far to pick up only a few parcels (Fig. 2). Problem 3 is the time spent on queuing. Delivery persons would normally send the passcodes at around the same time for too many parcels, leading to too many students coming to pick up parcels at approximately the same time and the distributing centre being overly crowded (Figs. 3 and 4). Problem 4 is the difficulty in carrying heavy parcels, more often in the cases of female users. Whey the parcels are too big or too heavy, the user may find it difficult to carry the parcels back. During shopping festivals, it can also be difficult to carry too many parcels without convenient tools. Problem 5 is poor sanitation conditions at the parcel distribution centre, which needs to be improved. Problem 6 happens in extreme weathers. On extremely hot or cold days, for example, students are not willing to go out. The above six problems are especially prominent, although there still exist many other minor problems, all of which affect the delivery service experience that users receive to some extent.

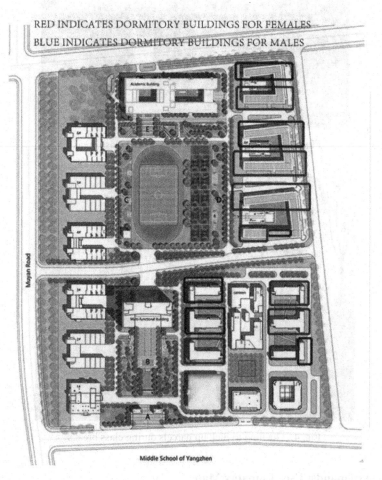

Fig. 2. Dormitory buildings for males (blue) and females (red) (Color figure online)

Fig. 3. Queuing to pick up parcels during class breaks

Fig. 4. Queuing to pick up parcels during class breaks

3.2 Real Demands: User Empathy Map

User empathy map may better help discover users' concerns so as to find better solutions. The present study targets the problems found in the last-mile delivery services and proposes attempted solutions. Numerous trials are made to verify its effects, feedbacks and influences. The following seven questions are used to better analyse users' real demands.

- Who discovers the problems?
- How do users think about last-mile delivery?

- What do users see?
- What comments do users hear from others?
- What do users talk about the most as a result?
- What are users' biggest concerns?
- What rewards make users feel happier?

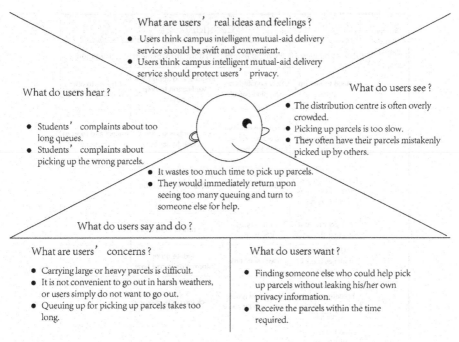

Fig. 5. Empathy map

The empathy map shows that more improvements are still needed in picking up and shipping parcels. It also shows the contradictions between what users want and what is in need. The comparison reveals the real demands of users when they pick up parcels.

Figure 5 shows that students discover the problems in last-mile delivery services. They might find that the distribution centre is too often overly crowded; their parcels are mistakenly picked up by others; they have to wait a long time in the queue; it is difficult for them to carry the parcels that are too big or too heavy, etc. The research has revealed what students are thinking about and what difficulties they are having while picking up parcels. It is also found that they also would like a platform where they could find someone who would help them pick up their parcels without leaking their own privacy, so that they have more time spent on what they enjoy doing.

3.3 User Demand Classification and User Satisfaction Analysis

Kano model is a customer satisfaction model that classifies and sorts quality factors. It is based on analysing the influence of customer demand on customer satisfaction and reflects the nonlinear relationship between quality factors and customer satisfaction. According to the different influences that different quality factors have on customer satisfaction, quality factors are classified into five types in Kano model: one-dimensional quality (O), attractive quality (A), mandatory quality (M), indifferent quality (I), reverse quality (R). One-dimensional quality means that customer satisfaction would increase should the service is offered, otherwise customer satisfaction would fall.

Concerns and demands	Category			
	Picking up parcels	Shipping parcels	Platform management	Sanitation
1	Need to pick up parcels	Post demands on shipping parcels	Register and apply for a verification to help others	Choose to offer cleaning services
2	Place orders on various items of goods	Compare different parcel companies to find the best one	On-campus students post demands	Collect and redeem coupons
3	The parcel arrives at the centre but is too heavy	Match the most appropriate one	Offer services via the platform	
4	In urgent need of receiving the parcel	Fill in basic information	Take orders from users	
5	The platform matches users in need	Save users' time	Update order information in real time	
6	Users need to predetermine the time to pick up parcels	The parcel is light but is too far away	Check the order progress	
7	Drop the parcel in the doorway, instead of			
8	For convenience of filling in picking-up information next			
9	Frequently-visited on-campus places			

Fig. 6. Classification of users' concerns

In this study, questionnaires were distributed online. A total number of 354 responses were collected, with 280 effective ones. In-depth analysis on the responses based on Kano model is carried out, leading to 23 indexes. As shown in Fig. 6, the concerns are classified as: picking up parcels, shipping parcels, sanitation, platform experience. Respondents chose among "very satisfied", "satisfied", "neutral", "unsatisfied", "very unsatisfied" (Fig. 7).

Figure 8 shows that there are a total number of 23 service quality indexes, including 10 mandatory properties, 7 one-dimensional properties, 3 attractive properties, 3 indifferent properties. This implies that basic needs of shipping and picking up parcels should be prioritized in the service design ahead of improving other services. In the

Quality classification table in Kano model					
Campus parcel service demands	Not offered services				
	Very satisfied	Satisfied	Neutral	Unsatisfied	Very unsatisfied
Already offered services	Very satisfied	Q	A	A	A	O
	Satisfied	R	I	I	M	A
	Neutral	R	I	I	I	M
	Unsatisfied	R	I	R	I	M
	Very unsatisfied	R	R	R	R	Q

Fig. 7. Quality classification table in Kano model

No.	Property type						Classification
	A	O	M	I	R	Q	
A1	25	78	138	30	5	4	M
A2	116	66	68	25	0	5	A
A3	35	109	72	42	4	5	O
A4	45	98	60	22	4	6	O
A5	14	102	154	5	2	3	M
A6	12	171	62	15	6	3	O
A7	32	120	98	18	4	8	M
A8	54	53	152	12	1	8	M
A9	98	105	65	10	0	2	A
A10	21	126	122	8	2	1	M
A11	15	147	105	8	3	2	M
A12	8	125	89	9	0	6	O
A13	16	110	134	12	4	4	M
A14	9	109	55	105	0	2	I
A15	9	136	117	15	2	1	M
A16	105	63	63	45	2	2	A
A17	16	128	72	23	1	1	O
A18	17	109	70	37	6	2	O
A19	26	38	166	45	2	3	M
A20	23	67	56	123	4	7	I
A21	27	67	124	56	1	5	M
A22	13	72	78	114	1	2	I
A23	15	134	45	82	2	2	O

Fig. 8. Corresponding property type in Kano model

meantime, customers' expected demands should be emphasized. That means, to enlarge the service scope to include more apartment buildings and people of different ages. Enhanced customer experience requires cutting-edge technology and intelligence that should be applied on parcel equipment. The attractive demand should also be satisfied which requires that the parcels are not damaged.

3.4 Feasibility Analysis

The above research data reveals that intelligent campus mutual-aid delivery service is more stable, efficient and convenient. It also features high availability and extensibility.

Therefore, the implementation of such a service plan is analysed from three aspects of user experience, technology and platform management.

The experience of users, the first beneficiary in service design, is the most important part in the whole design process. After conducting researches through field study, questionnaire and in-depth interview, the present design analyses numerous issues including the real demands, user concerns and solutions in terms of the "last-mile" delivery service at Beijing City University and obtains various kinds of analysis data. The application of last-mile delivery is carefully reviewed under various scenarios. The influence scope, user expectation and rigid demand on the service are compared. The results indicate that the present design is suitable for Beijing City University. Meanwhile, the technology level and platform management in the service sector remain immature in its development. Data screening and search algorithms may well be combined with 5G technology to offer better services for users. Platform management is mainly used to cultivate the mutual-aid consciousness in students and to enhance its service performance management. A series of stimulus and reward mechanisms are devised for some key elements in the service, so as to enhance the integrated quality of service personnel. This might also help cultivate the mutual-aid consciousness among students and their own managerial ability. Personnel management is key to enhancing the integrated quality of service personnel, the quality of campus last-mile delivery services, and the overall satisfaction of users. In addition, an effective management system helps stimulate sustained passion among its service personnel and generate more businesses to the company. Judging from the platform management, the present service design is feasible.

4 Intelligent Mutual-Aid Delivery Service Design at Beijing City University

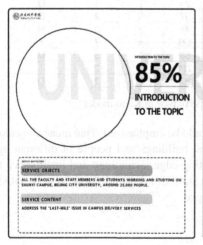

Fig. 9. Scheme of the plan

Mutual-aid is a natural law that describes how mutual benefits can be guaranteed through cooperation. Intelligent mutual-aid delivery service is an intelligent campus delivery mechanism in the form of mutual help. Official accounts on WeChat may have a number of premium functions where developers are able to define autoreplies to certain texts sent from users. They may also respond to users' messages and requests through information matching. The following functions are therefore made possible: Users enter the official WeChat account and place an order according to his/he demand. The keywords for shipping parcels include: intended shipping time, place, reward for urgent tasks, fee check, etc. Students need to register before using the service. They offer services after taking orders posted from others. The features include: (1) Online communication, offline pick-up. Demands from both parties are efficiently communicated and chosen on WeChat. Parcels are distributed to different time periods throughout a day, enhancing the convenience of the service. (2) A service is formed where students help students and on-campus demands are addressed on campus. It further integrates parcel services into students' daily lives and extends the depth of the system (Fig. 9). (3) The shipping service is optimized. On-campus students have various types of demands on shipping, such as shipping common parcels, parcels during winter and summer holidays, parcels on graduation, etc. The latter two types are usually larger and heavier and are costlier. The parcel distribution centre may offer some discounts to benefit students and improve the college campus parcel market. (4) It extends the service contents. In addition to shipping common parcels, the distribution centre may also offer personalized services on campus, such as sending flowers and gifts, personalizing wrappers, etc. The documents to be communicated between different school departments may also be delivered by students as well after they take the order.

4.1 Design Process

The service studies user demands and behaviours in different service stages through various types of technology. It also portraits users through correlation study and cluster analysis, so as to offer clearer demands. The service design starts from designing a blueprint and analyses user concerns by combining offline service processes. The user experience is continuously enhanced by address user concerns and optimizing the service process. Meanwhile, the service design is based on online platforms considering user preference. The small app prevalent on WeChat is also used in the service design. Linear, layered and network structures are combined with user behaviour processes. User habits, features of their grade and major are interactively integrated in the design. Diversified service design is used to satisfy users' different needs.

The service design has users' demands and campus delivery as its core. Based on the frameworks of WeChat official account and online shopping platform, it is an intelligent, convenient and open platform that incorporates shipping parcels and picking up parcels.

User Registration and Verification. Users need to fill in their identity information on the first login after entering the WeChat official account. They need to choose their school, grade, major, etc. They are only allowed to post orders within their school. Users will be directed to the verification page after successful registration. The verification status can be of one of the three types: not under review, under review, verified. Only verified users can post or take orders.

Developers have to strictly handle identify verification requests and approve verification only after careful review.

Users Post Orders. Verified users may post detailed information about the parcels, including its size, type, intended receiving time, comments (if the parcel if a fragile one, etc.), the complete message, receiving address. Users may track the order status at the personal centre. They can also cancel orders that have yet to be taken. Orders not taken by 8 pm will be deleted.

Users Take Orders. The order list shows all the orders of the school that the user belongs to. Users may choose appropriate orders to take and then drop the parcels at designated places. Users may confirm the order upon dropping and obtain corresponding scores. Parcels not dropped within the designated time range will be withdrawn and scores will be deleted.

Users Confirm Each Other. The server needs to confirm the order on the platform after dropping the parcel, otherwise the order would be withdrawn. The receiver has to confirm the receipt on the platform then. If the receiver does not confirm it beyond the set time, the order would be automatically confirmed.

Credit Rating. The receiver may rate the server according to his/her attitude, speed and parcel quality. The sender may also rate the receiver according to his/her attitude and whether the information provide is accurate. The rating is linked to scores.

Feedback. Users may provide feedbacks on any problems and complaints. Users may also contact customer service staff who will help check the parcel location, delivery time and server information.

Management by the Manager. The platform manager may manage various kinds of information, including: users, identity verification, order list, parcel type, address, parcel standard, feedback, etc.

4.2 Framework of the Service Functions

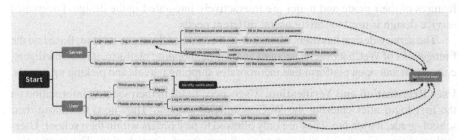

Fig. 10. Framework of the login page

The login page demonstrates the essence of communication between people and things, which is a natural process in app. Users may access the app's various functions only after successful login. The above figure classifies users into two types: "servers" who help deliver parcels and "users" who posts demands on the app. Different usage properties are used to determine the different functions of app users. Different login methods are assigned on the login page. For "servers", he/she has to log in with a mobile phone number in order to better collect servers' information, which is also the first step in identify verification. For "users", he/she may log in with the method he/she finds the most appropriate. After logging in with different roles, he/she may have operations specific to that role (Fig. 10).

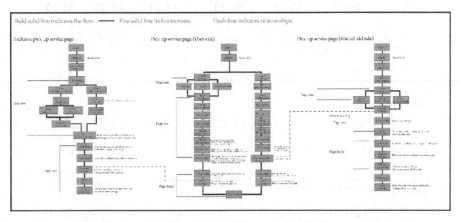

Fig. 11. Functional framework of the mutual-aid delivery service

The framework design focuses on the navigation bar and page layout, so that users may find the required information in the shortest time possible. The interface design is demonstrated in the form of a functional framework. It helps organize and optimize the design process as well as compare and convert different functions. This functional framework (Fig. 11) is centred on users and servers. It is formulated after numerous updates and satisfies the habits of both servers and users while minimizing the contradiction between the two. The pick-up, sharing and mutual-aid procedures are streamlined and standardized on different pages. In the framework, the functions that link one interface to another are also matched and verified, making the app management more reasonable. It also enables users in different roles to better understand the order status.

4.3 Service Blueprint

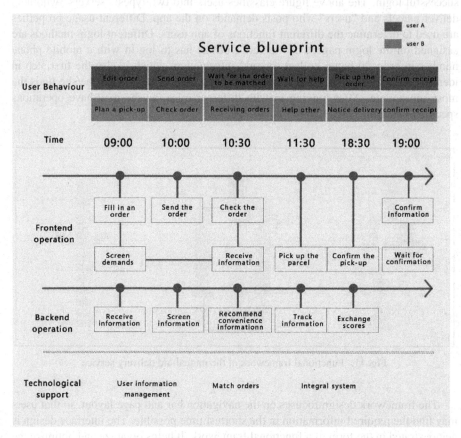

Fig. 12. Service blueprint

The service blueprint offers an easy-to-perceive design process for service design. In the design of the campus intelligent mutual-aid delivery service, the service blueprint may be used to categorize users' behaviours. The design may integrate elements like users' time spent on these processes, frontend operation, backend operation, technology support, etc. The service blueprint (Fig. 12) starts from user behaviour. While users edit the order, the frontend operation and backend operation work simultaneously to share users' demand information in real time. This ensures that all the steps are closely linked and accurately matched, so that the overall service is normally running. Each operation made by the user on the app would be matched to a backend operation, which records the user's operations in real time. For example, while users enter information in the frontend page, the backend is receiving the information and sharing the formation in real time. The information is tracked throughout the process and is therefore made fully transparent.

4.4   Conceptual Graph

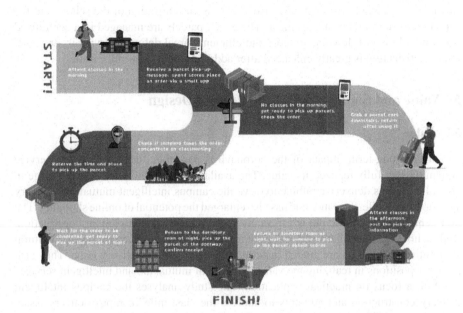

Fig. 13. Flowchart of the designed service

The intelligent mutual-aid delivery service perfectly matches the online small app and offline delivery service in a real-time, comprehensive and accurate manner. The online small app is easy to use and has a concise layout and clear steps. The information is tracked throughout all steps to ensure accuracy. In the offline delivery process, users may confirm each step on their own. Steps are interlinked and cannot be missed. The parcel information is automatically tracked by the system. Each parcel has a unique code that ensures accuracy. User privacy is also protected to the greatest extent by offering only necessary information like name, telephone and address. User photos and parcel contents are hidden. Big data technology is adopted to analyse the different demands of students in different majors, grades and study levels on the service. The delivery service is available throughout the campus. It incorporates different parcel companies and enables a multi-layered and multidimensional "last-mile" delivery service engaging many users. This service fully implements the idea of "students helping each other".

The present design vividly shows the procedure of campus intelligent mutual-aid delivery service. A big data-enabled analysis presents the most representative procedure. For example, Wei Zhang goes to the teaching building to attend classes and receives text messages about picking up a parcel. Since he is in class, he opts to spend his scores and place an order on the WeChat small app. If anyone takes his order, he would be notified. In this way, Wei could concentrate on his class. He may reserve the time and place to pick up the parcel and confirm receipt on the small app. The service system (Fig. 13) shows that the service is intelligent, convenient and humane since it incorporates the idea of "users serving users" throughout the overall service procedure and addresses users' concerns about time, distance, weather, conflict, queuing and charges. For overly large and heavy parcels, carts are available to help users better handle them. This also enhances the overall efficiency and also serves as an innovation of the school and the parcel company in their management. Therefore, parcels are managed in a centralized way, and a low-cost, low-energy-cost and efficient parcel delivery service is available. Users' satisfaction is greatly enhanced after addressing the "last-mile" issue.

5   Value and Significance of the Present Design

5.1   Value

Due to the long-term impact of the coronavirus pandemic, campus delivery service system ha snot fully realized its value. The availability, reliability and value change in last-mile campus delivery combine to drive the campus intelligent mutual-aid delivery system. Meanwhile, the pandemic has also enlarged the potential of online shopping. The user-centred design principle is especially used in campus environment construction. Both school-led intelligent service system construction and campus service cultural environment expansion are crucial in addressing the last-mile delivery issue. They also hold key positions in realizing the value and goal of mutual aid and intelligent service.

With a focus on practical application, this study analyses the campus intelligent delivery construction and attempts to address the "last-mile" campus delivery issue. Big data screening and search algorithms offer more practical user experiences and form the ultimate last-mile delivery service design scheme. The design may cultivate students' innovation and entrepreneurship consciousnesses and in the long term, could formulate effective joint mechanisms with off-campus enterprises and training centres. This may help on-campus students better manage their time in study and work, and develop their self-study and practical capabilities. Students are also able to develop their own networks and accumulate social experience. The design also helps the school handle cooperation with parcel companies in a more standardized way and improve campus sanitation situations in a short time. The school may also benefit from upgrading from information to intelligence. The long-term cooperation between the school and parcel companies also engages the latter into the campus environment and makes them an integral part of the school's employment opportunities and campus culture.

5.2   Significance

The campus intelligent mutual-aid delivery design is an open platform that could enhance cooperation between various parcel companies and promotes their service quality and available traffic. This is not only an innovation of service design in terms of last-mile campus delivery, but also an innovation of school and parcel companies in management and cooperation. The centralized management is low-cost, efficient and consumers less energy, significantly enhancing users' experience. The service could be part of campus intelligence construction. If the geology, culture, history and environment factors of the campus are all taken into account, then quality innovation services and products are expected to be generated in the future. This study offers an integrated intelligent mutual-aid online platform, which implements the idea of intelligent service, mutual-aid delivery, college-wide participation and develops a culture of teachers and students helping each other.

6 Conclusions

The campus intelligent mutual-aid delivery design effectively addresses the campus last-mile delivery issue and offers reasonable user experience throughout the whole design process. The study focuses on Beijing City University and intelligent service and mutual-aid delivery. By collecting and analysing users' demands and determining demand factors, the study converts concerns into pleasures so that users are more willing to use and enjoy the service. Similar designs could be applied to other universities in the future, but their different situations should be considered in the design process. Only in this way can the campus intelligent mutual-aid delivery design be applied more widely.

References

1. Huang, Y., Lin, L., Liu, H., Zhu, C., Zhang, M.: Siting of intelligent parcel locker on college campuses in the "Internet+" era: take Nanjing Forestry University for example. Log. Sci-Tech **43**(12), 46–50 (2020)
2. Wang, S., Zhu, H., Yang, Y., Huang, X., Ye, Z.: A study on the development mutual-aid service platform in college students. Invest. Coop. **11**, 157–159 (2020)
3. Halley, S.: Campus officials express dissatisfaction with COVID-19 safety precautions on campus. Dean Provost **22**(4) (2020)
4. Qiu, Z., Xu, Z., Su, H., Liang, Z.: A study on the parcel package recycling based on "green logistics": take higher education institutions in Guangzhou for example. China Circ. Econ. (32), 9–11 (2020)
5. Wang, X., Li, N.: An optimization study on parcel package recycling logistics in higher education institutions: take Xi'an University of Finance and Economics for example **42**(11), 67–69+55 (2020)
6. Zhou, X.: Design of new parcel scenarios in higher education institutions campuses considering coronavirus pandemic containment measures. Log. Mater. Handl. **25**(11), 148–149 (2020)
7. Yan, B.: Research on the new mode of campus express based on WeChat platform. J. Simul. **7**(2) (2019)
8. Liang, W., Yin, X.Z.: The feasibility analysis of the convenience store express service in colleges. In: Proceedings of 2014 4th International Conference on Education and Education Management (EEM 2014 V67). Information Engineering Research Institute, USA: Consortium on Application of Intelligent Information Technology, p. 4 (2014)

Product Interventions and User Performance: Implications for Public Design to Achieve Sustainable Practice

Ming Jun Luo[1], Jia Xin Xiao[2(✉)], and Wenhua Li[3]

[1] Guangdong Industry Polytechnic, Guangzhou 510000, China
[2] School of Art and Design, Guangdong University of Technology, 729 Dongfengdong Road, Guangzhou 510000, China
[3] Guangzhou Academy of Fine Arts, Guangzhou 510000, China

Abstract. This paper explains the practice-oriented approach to design and examines the relationship between people and products. A theoretical framework is proposed after reviewing the literature on product intervention and usability. Taking public facilities as a case study, this paper illustrates the ways in which people use them to make communities more sustainable for their inhabitants. The final conclusion is that public facilities should be designed by applying appropriate product interventions based on the social context and user acceptance.

Keywords: Design Strategies · Product Intervention · Practice-oriented

1 Introduction

The relationship between people and products has long been regarded as that of 'master and slave' (Bhamra et al. 2008). In recent years, some researchers and designers have suggested that a product should not only serve the user but also influence human behaviour and reduce the potential for error. The balance between products and users should be carefully configured within the social context.

Public facilities play an important role in daily life, from indoor areas such as shopping malls and metro stations to outdoor areas such as parks and roads. Indeed, these facilities offer not only convenience but also serve to control our behaviour to ensure social sustainability. Hence, to design high-quality public facilities, the interrelationships between products and users should be examined by studying user behaviour, needs and acceptance, and the social impact of the facilities (Siu 2005). To some extent, interventions can influence user behaviour. However, designers should carefully configure the balance between product interventions and user performance, because inappropriate or problematic interventions may be counterproductive and are often short-lived (Dan et al. 2010; Lille 2009). Moreover, in-depth studies on user practice are necessary to examine user responses and feedback on interventions.

Products provided with 'scripts' can steer user behaviour (regarding the definitions of 'scripts' 'affordances' and 'constraints', see Norman 1998; Crilly et al. 2004). However,

© Springer Nature Switzerland AG 2021
M. M. Soares et al. (Eds.): HCII 2021, LNCS 12780, pp. 78–87, 2021.
https://doi.org/10.1007/978-3-030-78224-5_6

some researchers emphasise that changing human behaviour can be challenging, as users tend to be slow to accommodate sustainable practices (DeVries 2006; Scott 2004). In other words, trying to alter human behaviour in an inappropriate way may be deemed unacceptable and lead to annoyance and frustration.

Using railings in Hong Kong as a public facility case study, this paper illustrates how railings are used to maintain order in society, explores the relationship between product interventions and user performance, and finally discusses the design of public facilities by applying appropriate product interventions based on the social context and user acceptance.

2   Method

2.1   Public Space Facilities in Hong Kong

Hong Kong is a small but fast-paced modern city with a high population density. Compared with other developed cities, Hong Kong citizens are more reliant on public facilities such as buses and the mass transit railway (MTR) due to the convenience of public transportation and the high cost of private cars. Meanwhile, people from mainland China and countries worldwide visit Hong Kong for holidays. Every day, people interact with various public facilities and share them with others (both locals and non-locals). Therefore, public facilities are of great importance in providing convenience while also ensuring safety in society.

2.2   Research Method

This paper aims to investigate the potential for guiding human behaviour via product interventions and explores the role of the 'practice-oriented' method in the design process. To obtain various product design strategies and find the most effective way to design public facilities, we reviewed the literature on user perspective (experience, behaviour) and product design methods (usability, ergonomic engineering and sustainability).

Non-participant observation is a qualitative methodology that aims to gain in-depth insights into human behaviour without interacting with users (Marshall and Rossman 1998). Observation is a direct way to learn how people interact with (user or misuse) an existing product and then to establish appropriate (acceptable) forms of intervention. In this study, we conducted non-participant observations in streets, roads, metro stations, shopping malls, parks and other open spaces to examine the behaviour of users as they interacted with different forms of 'railings'. Through observation, we were able to uncover unexpected ideas that may have been overlooked and provide some guidance for the design of public facilities.

3   Results and Discussions

Instead of following the traditional way of 'separating space' by erecting railings, we could consider the use of signs, notices, chairs, pillars, trees, blocks, people, etc. for this purpose. Many kinds of interventions can be introduced to steer human behaviour. For example, they may be informative or compulsory, and tangible or intangible.

3.1 Tangible Interventions

In public spaces, tangible interventions can be seen everywhere. For instance, workers erect temporary railings during road repairs to prevent pedestrians from endangering themselves. Railings are sometimes set up in streets to guide people to behave appropriately. Bollards are often installed at the entrances to open spaces to prevent the entry of bicycles, even though this overlooks the accessibility and satisfaction of certain city users, such as people with disabilities, and especially those with visual impairment, for whom they are inconvenient or even dangerous (see Fig. 1).

Fig. 1. Tangible interventions set up to prevent the entry of pedestrians (left) and bicycles (right)

3.2 Intangible Interventions

In Hong Kong in most cases, an 'intangible railing' divides escalator space into two parts: the right side for people who are willing to wait in line patiently, and the left side for those in a hurry who want to move faster (Fig. 2). Hong Kong is known for its rapid pace of life and dense population. Hence, policies and measures are required to ensure social order in the city. Although interventions in the form of notices and information were enacted to encourage people to conform to this escalator etiquette, it took years for people to adopt it. However, once the rule became established, it has not been easy to change.

These types of intangible intervention have already become ingrained social norms among many local citizens, who apply them spontaneously through self-discipline (Fig. 3). People who obstruct the walking lane on escalators may be regarded as impolite and boorish. Nonetheless, people from mainland China and other countries may be unaware of these invisible 'railings' and unwittingly obstruct the walking lane, leading to misunderstandings and conflict with locals.

Fig. 2. An 'intangible railing' divides escalator space into two parts

3.3   Product interventions and user performance

Recently, for safety reasons, walking on escalators has been discouraged, yet citizens accustomed to the previous norm still provide a walking lane on the left while using escalators. User performance may change gradually from reluctant to spontaneous during the intervention period, because users are often slow to accommodate sustainable practices. Once a habit has formed, it may then be difficult to change. However, if we really want to alter user behaviour, persuasive product interventions and policies should be implemented. Users may then once again undergo the process of attitude change (reluctant-accepted-spontaneous).

In public spaces, we noticed that people waiting for a bus conscientiously stand in line at the kerbside, one by one, even if they are in a hurry. It was obvious that people have formed a sustainable practice of waiting in line, whether railings were set up or not

Fig. 3. The pillars are considered to represent 'railings' that separate the pedestrian bridge into two parts and avoid crowds becoming chaotic.

(Fig. 4 and Fig. 5). Indeed, as all individuals are involved in social relations, they quickly learn from each other via social norms and individual practice. In general, the bus stop sign is deemed the starting point of the 'railing'. No one would risk stepping over it, because those who jump the queue would be ejected for their unethical behaviour and severely criticized by others. Moreover, in Hong Kong, only a few buses share the same bus stop, enabling people to queue without crowding. In this case, product intervention is less necessary because people have achieved spontaneous sustainable behaviour (i.e., positive practices) without the need to impose restrictions. However, in some cases, such as a bus stop located in the middle of road, interventions are necessary to prevent people (e.g., children or the elderly) from accidentally entering the vehicle stream.

On some streets and footbridges in Hong Kong, the researchers noticed a phenomenon in which people would gather around a rubbish bin, smoking and relaxing (Fig. 6). Over the past three decades, the Hong Kong government has put considerable effort into preventing people from smoking in both indoor and outdoor public spaces such as public transport interchanges (Smoking Public Health Ordinance). With no designated smoking areas in the streets, smokers are willing to stand close to bins because it is convenient for disposing of their cigarette ash (smoking or carrying a lit tobacco product in a statutory no smoking area in Hong Kong is an offence carrying a $1,500 fine).

In this case, the rubbish bin and the small area nearby could be regarded as a 'railing' separating a smoking area from public space. Thus, a bin with a cigarette butt container,

Fig. 4. People standing in line to board a bus with the intervention of railings.

similar to a designated area with a sign stating 'smoking area', gives the impression that smoking is allowed in this area. Hence, to reduce the smoking rate in a specific area, we could deliberately remove the rubbish bin to increase the difficulty of accessing one. However, we would need to balance the relationship between intervention and user acceptance. Inappropriate controls (interventions) may lead to overwhelming annoyance or irritation. In these circumstances, decreasing the distribution density of rubbish bins may be considered a gentler form of persuasive intervention.

Although people have their own individual conscience and attitudes, they still behave similarly to others because they quickly learn practices from each other, such as waiting in line to board a bus. However, changes may not occur if people do not recognise the underlying issue. In that case, appropriate rules are needed to get everyone to follow the instructions and ensure social security.

3.4 Implications for in Public Design to Achieve Sustainable Practice

'Railings' are facilities designed to govern social order in public areas such as streets, roads, stations and parks. However, if we shift the focus from 'railings' to 'space separators', they can be viewed as ways of separating spaces to ensure social security. By focusing on 'separating', designers can identify a range of products that may be more suitable for a given situation.

Fig. 5. People standing in line waiting for buses, even in the absence of railings. They have clearly formed a sustainable practice of waiting in line with or without railings.

As both social contexts and human behaviour are complex and dynamic, designers should shift their focus onto practices rather than products. Nowadays, some researchers propose 'practice orientation', which focuses on investigating user behaviour in social practice as an effective approach to designing appropriate strategies to suit the dynamic social context. Although people learn from each other, the actions (i.e., practices) of individuals differ due to personal perspectives and attitudes. The variety of human behaviour demonstrates that it is impossible to insist on a static way to deal with a constantly changing situation. As user practices and social norms are not constant across space and time, flexibility should be considered as a form of sustainability in the design process. In other words, a product that was suitable and met people's requirements in the past may not serve the public interest in the present. Similarly, practices people previously rejected may be deemed totally accepted in the current situation, and vice versa.

'Practice orientation' may be regarded as an alternative approach to product design that adapts to social change and encourages users to participate in the design process and co-create the product along with the designers. Indeed, user participation is imperative, because those who are directly affected by a decision should have the greatest say in making the decision. Designers can identify appropriate interventions to alter inappropriate behaviour through user (practitioner) activities. Through the practice-oriented

Fig. 6. A rubbish bin, together with a small area nearby separating a smoking area from public space. Smokers are willing to stand close to rubbish bins because of the convenience of disposing of their cigarette ash.

approach, designers should aim to understand the complex and dynamic social interactions between users, objects and society, rather than focusing on individual products (Fig. 7). Simply speaking, 'product' is a 'noun' and practice is a 'verb'. For example, if we consider a product such as a cup, merely focusing on the shape of a cup, even when considering usability and user experience, will produce a design outcome that is no more than a utensil. If we focus on drinking, however, a variety of options arise, such as by hand, paper, a straw. As a result, an innovative straw with a filter, namely 'Lifestraw', was designed for some areas in Africa to drink water directly from a freshwater lake. This solution was by no means without foundation, but rather more reliant on the findings from everyday user practices. In other words, designers should shift their focus from 'product' to 'practice' to explore how people interact with public facilities in different situations (spatiotemporally), and then design appropriate interventions to influence user behaviour.

People are influenced not only by the social context (norms, culture) but also by the behaviour of others (actions). These elements (users, other people, products, society) influence each other in a systemic and integrated society.

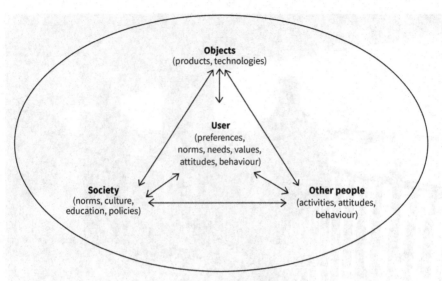

Fig. 7. Practice-oriented model

4 Conclusions

Public facilities play an important role in society. On the one hand, they provide us with convenience; on the other hand, they help to govern social order and security. In other words, a high-quality public facility is designed not only for user satisfaction but also to encourage sustainable practices. As some studies have shown, products have the potential to influence user behaviour. To ensure change and meet user needs, a sustainable approach to design is required that takes into account both product interventions and user performance. Furthermore, in terms of practice orientation, designers should shift the focus from products to practices to explore how people interact with public facilities in different situations (spatiotemporally), and then identify appropriate interventions that will influence user behaviour.

Taking public facilities in Hong Kong in the form of 'railings' as a case study, we examined how facilities influence user behaviour in daily life. We found that interventions may not be required to encourage sustainable user practices in every situation. Social norms, culture and policies can be combined to influence user performance. Thus, users generally experience a change in attitude towards different interventions from passive to active. The kind of intervention that is most suitable for a specific facility should be open to discussion.

This paper does not propose a solution for how to deal with every problem in public design, but instead offers a potential approach to the design of public facilities to influence sustainable user practices through effective and appropriate interventions. It aims to explore the potential of facilities to guide user behaviour, and proposes a direction and strategies for public design. Due to the complexity and dynamic nature of social contexts and user behaviour, the design of every public facility requires in-depth exploration.

Comprehensive and long-term studies should therefore be carried out in the design of public facilities to respond to the dynamic situation.

Acknowledgments. The authors would like to acknowledge the National Natural Science Foundation Youth Fund (52008114) and the Young Scholars in Yangcheng of the 13th Five Year Plan for the Development of Philosophy and Social Sciences in Guangzhou (2019GZQN41) for the data collection and the preparation of the paper. The authors also acknowledge Prof. Siu, the Chair professor of Public Design Lab of The Hong Kong Polytechnic University, during the final analysis and preparation of this paper.

References

Bhamra, T.A., Lilley, D., Tang, T.: Sustainable use: changing consumer behaviour through product design. In: Design Visions, proposals and tools, Italy (2008)

Crilly, N., Moultrie, J., Clarkson, P.J.: Seeing things: consumer response to the visual domain in product design. Des. Stud. **25**(6), 547–577 (2004)

Lockton, D., Harrison, D., Stanton, N.A.: The design with intent method: a design tool for influencing user behaviour. Appl. Ergon. **41**(3), 382–392 (2010). https://doi.org/10.1016/j.apergo.2009.09.001

de Vries, M.J.: Ethics and the complexity of technology: a design approach. Philos. Reformata **71**(2), 118–131 (2006). https://doi.org/10.1163/22116117-90000383

Lilley, D.: Design for sustainable behaviour: strategies and perceptions. Des. Stud. **30**(6), 704–720 (2009)

Marshall, C., Rossman, G.B.: Designing Qualitative Research. Thousand Oaks, CA: Sage (1998)

Norman, D.A.: The Design of Everyday Things. The MIT Press, Cambridge, MA (1998)

Scott, F.: Behaviour Change: Believing You Can Make a Difference! BTCV. Global Action Plan and the Environment Council Workshop, London (2004)

Siu, K.W.M.: Pleasurable products: public space furniture with userfitness. J. Eng. Des. **16**, 545–555 (2005)

Participatory Design to Create Digital Technologies for Batik Intangible Cultural Heritage
The Case of iWareBatik

Puspita Ayu Permatasari(✉) and Lorenzo Cantoni

USI – Università della Svizzera italiana, via Buffi 13, 6900 Lugano, Switzerland
puspita.ayu.permatasari@usi.ch

Abstract. Heritage communication is more and more integrating digital media, which help to offer a wider and deeper understanding of heritage and its values. In particular, intangible cultural heritage (ICH) can find in information and communication technologies a powerful ally to share its facets and different dimensions, through multimedia technologies (especially videos), storytelling, and several other applications like mixed realities and artificial intelligence.

Such media can help not only to provide access to information and knowledge, but also to enrich the experience of people exposed to such heritage, and to promote a deep connection between the heritage itself and interested persons.

This paper presents the process through which goals and needs to communicate and promote Indonesian Batik textile heritage, which has been inscribed by UNESCO among the Intangible Cultural Heritage list in 2009, have been collected and transformed into the design of digital communication outlets, namely a website and a mobile app. Such process has encompassed an extensive analysis of the presence itself of Batik in digital media through benchmarking, as well as the elicitation of needs and requirements of relevant stakeholders and target audiences, through in-depth interviews and surveys. The design has been done ensuring at every step that it was considering and integrating, as much as possible, the results of the previous analyses. While presenting the iWareBatik case, which has been successfully implemented and launched, with the support of the highest Indonesian cultural-related institutions, the paper describes in detail the used methodology, hence providing an itinerary, which can be adopted by other similar projects.

Keywords: Participatory design · Intangible cultural heritage · AWARE model · Website development · Mobile application · Online communication model

1 Introduction

The integration of Information and communication technology (ICT) plays a central role in bringing improvements and innovations in the field of cultural heritage (CH) conservation and communication, both for tangible and intangible cultural heritage (ICH) [6, 22]. Tangible heritage refers to the physical artefacts possessing socio-cultural importance

© Springer Nature Switzerland AG 2021
M. M. Soares et al. (Eds.): HCII 2021, LNCS 12780, pp. 88–106, 2021.
https://doi.org/10.1007/978-3-030-78224-5_7

such as monuments, temples, palaces, and other natural/cultural heritage sites [17], while the ICH is defined as the knowledge behind the living traditions and cultural expressions preserved by local communities and transmitted from generation to generation through cultural practices [18]. According to Cantoni [6], ICT in heritage tourism contributes to five areas namely (i) Access, ICT provides access to heritage-related information; (ii) Better experience as ICT improves the experience of the travelers in acquiring information about the heritage; (iii) Connect, ICT connects locals, tourists and the concerned heritage; (iv) Dis-intermediate, to facilitate and streamline (some) relationships, so to ensure that local players can benefit from the heritage valorization activities; (v) Educate, ICTs facilitate learning and upskilling of the concerned professionals. Digital technologies also facilitate researchers in terms of documentation, scientific process, interpretation and its dissemination [1, 2, 5]. In particular, the integration of ICTs also helps to support culture, education, and societal development of heritage related to fashion [8, 9]. Given the wide range of roles and functions, ICT has been strongly integrated within the implementation of UNESCO's "Five Cs" strategic objectives: Credibility, Conservation, Capacity building, Communication, and Communities [7]. A number of studies further elaborate the effectiveness of mixed reality [43], artificial intelligence [40], gamification [12], videos, storytelling [4, 10] and mobile applications [44], in order to provide different experiences for users in cultural heritage sites, as well as improve their engagement towards ICH [2, 3, 42].

Answering the challenge of building human computer interaction (HCI) for ICH, this study presents iWareBatik digital technologies [13] as a case study of promoting a wise use of digital technology for ICH preservation.

Despite a growing interest on Indonesian Batik as UNESCO ICH since 2009, there is still a considerable gap to balance the online narratives that focus on usage values and the ones stressing the importance of tradition and its conservation [14–16]: the multifacet dimensions of Batik ICH are not well-communicated within the digital publication outlets. This phenomenon might lead to a lack of people's awareness of the importance of Batik as intangible cultural heritage, which may degrade the value of this intergenerational legacy. Facing the challenges in communicating Batik as textile heritage, the paper outlines the process of developing iWareBatik, a digital initiative in forms of a website (www.iwarebatik.org) and a mobile app.

iWareBatik stands for "I am aware of Batik", it is designed to communicate all dimensions of Batik ICH to domestic and international tourists, by providing users insightful contents about 124 Batik motifs, its meanings, and wearing rules, as well as about 129 tourism sites and UNESCO sites. It presents one-minute visual journey videos of 34 regions and interactive features such as an interactive map and a Batik Recognition Tool, an AI-driven tool built within the app to recognize 8 motifs [13].

2 Literature Review

Hereafter, Batik as ICH, the Online Communication Model as well as the AWARe Model are presented, with their background literature. A few lines are also devoted to outlining the final iWareBatik products.

2.1 Batik as an Intangible Cultural Heritage

Batik is a wax resist dyeing tradition, existed since 5000 BC-2600BC [19]. In 2009, it was inscribed among the list of UNESCO ICH of humanity because of the following exceptional cultural values: namely historical production technique, socio-cultural meanings contained in its patterns and symbols, special wearing rules (characterizing life events and the social class of the wearer), and social empowerment within its valorization activities [20]. Batik visual art represents the traces of cultural adherence, intercultural exchanges as well as many cultural dimensions associated with Indonesia since 6th Century until today [21]. Since 2016, the presence of Batik tradition is not only focused in Java island, yet this tradition has been spread and valorized across all 34 Indonesian regions [23, 24]. The nationwide Batik safeguarding practice provides employment to more than 200,000 people working on this cultural industry, and has thus become one of the major economic pillars of the nation [24].

2.2 Online Communication Model (OCM)

One of the seven grand challenges in human computer interaction domain is related to ubiquitous learning and foster creativity [11]. Building experiential design of ICT is an essential aspect to help leverage on tourism branding [49, 50], and facilitate learning experience of local traditions and heritage of the destination [47, 48]. The challenge lies on designing hypermedia intensive communication outlets [32] that address the needs and expectations of all stakeholders.

To this end, iWareBatik adopts the Online Communication Model (OCM, Fig. 1) [37, 38]. The OCM is singled out in 4 main pillars and a fifth element, namely: (i) contents and services; (ii) technical instruments (software and hardware) that make accessible the contents and online activities; (iii) providers i.e. people who run the website or the application; (iv) users, intended audiences; and (v) the relevant information/communication context or market [38].

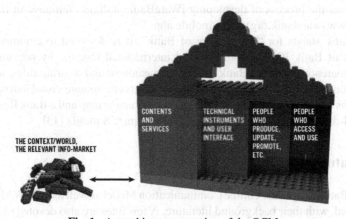

Fig. 1. A graphic representation of the OCM.

The design process moves along the five elements, addressing them as follows (Fig. 2): it takes into account the relevant information context (v) analyzed through benchmark activities; elicits needs and wants of intended users (iv) and of main stakeholders (iii) through interviews, surveys and other strategies, in order to define (and prioritize) all technical dimensions (ii) as well as contents and functionalities (i).

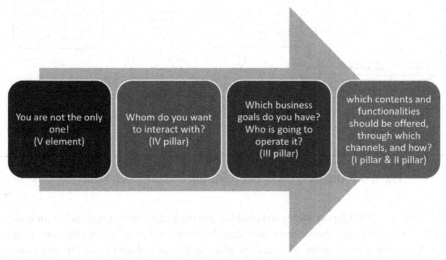

You are not the only one!
(V element)

Whom do you want to interact with?
(IV pillar)

Which business goals do you have? Who is going to operate it?
(III pillar)

which contents and functionalities should be offered, through which channels, and how?
(I pillar & II pillar)

Fig. 2. Design process according to the OCM.

2.3 Participatory Design and AWARe – Analysis of Web Applications Requirement

The design of iWareBatik has implemented, once the benchmark has been conducted, a participatory service design approach [4, 45, 46]; in order to elicit and properly organize requirements, the AWARe (Analysis of Web Applications Requirement) model has been adopted [32, 35].

AWARe design leverages on five different areas: hypermedia design, communication theory, software engineering, information systems, and human computer interaction design [32]. It provides toolsets to analyze goal-oriented and stakeholder-oriented requirements through iterative refinements of user requirement elicitation (URE) [35]. The user requirement elicitation (URE) analysis [27–29] provides documentation, identification of requirements related to hypermedia structure and taxonomy, conflicts and influence analysis on personas, roles, goals, and user scenarios. AWARe further refines the priority goals, and thus strengthen the validation and consensus between designers and stakeholders [31, 35].

The AWARe model emphasizes on the iterative refinement of requirements and of the needs elicited from stakeholders, as well as the analysis of user scenarios [32, 35, 36], in order to build a final conceptual design (see Fig. 3). Hereafter its main elements.

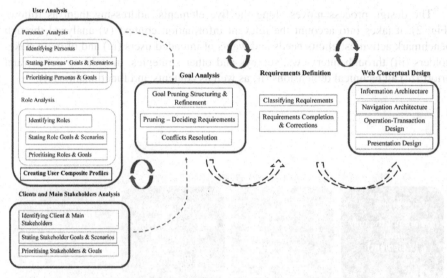

Fig. 3. AWARE (Analysis of Web Applications Requirement) Model [32].

Stakeholders. AWARe organizes stakeholders into two categories, *users* and *main stake-holders*. Site *users* are the persons who may be interested in accessing the web or the app. A classification of users' personas, profiles, and roles is done in order to map potential users and audiences. *Main stakeholders* are project owners and main influencers: clients of the design process, decision- and opinion-makers, and the development team. *Clients* are defined as the persons/institutions who own and assign the digital project to the development team.

Goal Refinement Process. AWARe classifies goals into *communication goals* and *ill-defined goals* or *soft goals*. Each stakeholder might have also tacit and implicit goals with regards to the design of a digital technology. Soft goals are more general, visionary, and describe general expectations of the stakeholders towards the digital application. The different goals and priorities, including their constraints, shall be clearly documented.

Scenarios and Priorities. AWARe takes into account different scenarios and goal priorities of users and main stakeholders, which are fundamental to guide the design process.

Transition to Goal Graph and Hypermedia Taxonomy. Once goals, soft goals, scenarios, priorities and constraints are set, a requirement analysis is conducted by mapping all gathered requirements into a goal graph and converting them into a requirement taxonomy. AWARe classifies requirements into six types namely, Access (A); Content (C); Presentation (P); Structure of Content (SC); Navigation (N); User Operation (U); Interaction (I); System Operation (O) [36].

Systematic Evaluation (Usability). Results of the requirement analysis can be traced back and reused for a systematic evaluation, in order to check if, how and how well they have been taken into account in the actual implementation of the project.

In light of obtaining high quality data, two methods of user requirement elicitation are adopted, namely a data driven method [27, 33] and a model inquiry method [27, 34]. Those two methods are used to explore both tacit and explicit needs/requirements.

2.4 The iWareBatik Case

The successful integration of complex HCI design and the involvement of several stakeholders has helped to boost the online visibility of the iWareBatik digital initiative, encompassing a website and a dedicated app, available on both iOS and Android platforms.

Since the launching day on August 17th, 2020 until February 11th, 2021, iWareBatik has attracted 22′426 visitors on the website and a total of 1′476 mobile app downloads. Such results have been reached through extensive communication and promotion activities, which have been supported by USI UNESCO Chair (Switzerland), Indonesian Presidential Cabinet, Indonesian Embassy in Bern, Indonesian Ministry of Foreign Affairs, LPDP – Indonesian Ministry of Finance, Sobat Budaya Cultural Association, Caventer Indonesia, and Overseas Indonesian Student Association Alliances (OISAA).

3 Methodology

Adopting OCM and AWARe, the iWareBatik design has been conducted along the following activities.

Benchmark. The research has adopted a model-driven approach, which was done by analyzing previous works/models designed and built for similar goals. Such benchmarking activities have allowed to define major types of contents and functionalities, to be used in order to inform subsequent analyses, especially to define a survey and to guide interviews.

Focus Group Discussion (FGD) and Prototyping Activities. Prior to the interview and survey, several FGD and some prototyping activities had been conducted from September until December 2018 with 12 Master students in Media Management and International Tourism of USI. Those activities were intended to obtain some ideas about main features of the digital technology from the potential users' perspective [27, 30]. The first design elements as a result of the prototyping activities were also used and integrated within the interview and survey.

Interviews. A series of interviews was conducted from February until March 2019. In order to gain international and Indonesian (domestic) perspectives, the selection of 15 respondents was based on convenience sampling, consisting of 11 Indonesian representatives, and four international respondents from Croatia, Italy, Japan and USA. Some of them have several profiles, occupations and characteristics, making it easier to obtain several perspectives. Each participant was interviewed on average for 45 min, in a semi-structured fashion.

Survey. The survey was conducted from 8–15 April 2019 using Qualtrics Survey Software. It obtained a total of 191 responses, from 123 Indonesian and 68 international respondents. The link of the survey was disseminated through social media networks, emails, and during workshops of two master courses at USI. The survey recorded international respondents from 16 different countries (Albania, China, Croatia, Estonia, France, Germany, Italy, India, Iran, Japan, Lithuania, Malaysia, Maldive, Nigeria, Poland, Switzerland, Thailand, Turkey, Uganda, and Ukraine).

Based on the previous activities, the iWareBatik tools – website and mobile app – have been designed and eventually developed and launched.

4 Results

The design elements of iWareBatik digital technologies were iteratively built mainly upon the result of benchmarking, interview, and survey, presented as follows.

4.1 Benchmarking

The benchmarking study has been conducted through an analysis of the online presence of Batik, mapping websites and mobile apps on Batik, as well as other apps related to UNESCO properties in Indonesia.

The content analysis of websites [14] has contributed to identify the relevant themes/topics covered while communicating Batik online.

164 mobile apps on Batik have been classified into different categories. 70% of the apps cover Batik fashion and apparels for different publics (men, women, family, and kids), while the rest are classified as apps for Batik textile catalogues and encyclopedia. Only 2 mobile apps provide (limited) information about Batik and tourism in Indonesia. Also some elements learned from previous digital technology projects for Batik [39–41] have been taken into account in the design process.

Further benchmarking studies were conducted by analyzing 322 mobile apps dedicated to 18 tangible/intangible UNESCO heritage in Indonesia [16].

The overall result of benchmarking studies (the fifth element in the OCM) provides an overview on the online communication world of Batik ICH. First of all, it has highlighted essential elements to communicate it, which have been later used to inform interviews and especially the survey: the found communication "ingredients" have been presented in order to get a feedback and to define priorities for the iWareBatik design. Moreover, the benchmark has also unveiled gaps and areas of improvement in order to build a better HCI design for Batik ICH communication: in particular, the authenticity and the identity behind ICH practices shall be better captured and showcased in more detail, so to provide an effective information design [5, 25, 26].

4.2 Interviews

The result of interview shows a huge interest of different stakeholders towards iWareBatik digital technologies. Table 1 provides an overview on the interviewed sample.

Table 1. Interviewed persons.

Occupation	Nationality	#	Type of Stakeholders		Roles			
			Site User	Main Stakeholder	Client	Domain Expert in Tourism	Domain Expert in Batik	Opinion Maker
Indonesian diplomat in Switzerland	Indonesian	1	V	V	V	V		V
USI Master student	USA	1	V					
Fashion journalist	Japanese	1	V					
USI PhD student/fashion follower	Italian	1	V					
Head of tourism promotion in Indonesian Ministry of Tourism	Indonesian	1	V	V	V	V		V
Journalist	Croatian	1	V					
Indonesian textile collector/travel blogger/public official	Indonesian	1	V					
Batik practitioners	Indonesians	3	V	V			V	
Lecturers in institute of tourism	Indonesians	2	V	V		V		V
Head of Batik association (Batik expert and gallery owner)	Indonesian	1	V	V			V	
Batik researcher/cultural tourism consultant	Indonesian	1	V	V		V	V	V
Head of Sobat Budaya Association/cultural digital library	Indonesian	1	V	V			V	V
	Total	**15**						

All stakeholders expect contents related to (a) Batik motifs, meanings and history, production process, wearing rules; (b) Local motifs, Batik galleries, things to do, tourism attractions, how to get there.

In relation to interactive features, all respondents are also interested in having (c) a feature like a "Spinning wheel", which could be played by the users to randomly access a motif or a region, so to inject some serendipity within the app, to accompany a more structured navigation; 14 respondents favor map features such as (d) "Batik Around You", a map connected to the GPS that would indicate the nearest Batik event; and (e) an Interactive Map of Indonesia.

In terms of visual presentation, 13 respondents specifically require (f) Images of Batik fashion, products, and accessories.

With regards to gamification, respondents were allowed to choose maximum two most preferred gamification features and give priority to the chosen ones. 9 respondents preferred (g) a Selfie function with the possibility of using a Batik motif as the frame; 5 people preferred (h) Drawing Batik motif with knowledge quiz (natural dye, specific plants, motif names); while 4 people opted for having (i) an Artificial Intelligence tool within the app to scan and recognize motifs; and (j) a Batik fashion mix match to redress male/female avatars with Batik dress/shirt. Only 2 people choose (k) a Batik puzzle game with Batik meanings. One person proposed to add (l) a Storytelling video with cartoon animation that explains the meaning of Batik motifs.

4.3 Survey

The survey is an important process to capture the needs and expectations of a larger population of potential users with regards to the iWareBatik design. The age range of respondents is 18 to 65, 145 respondents (76%) are young adults (18–30 years old), 46 respondents (15%) are 30–40, and the rests (9%) are 40–65. 103 respondents (53%) are students, 47 (26%) employees and professionals, while 41 (21%) are lecturers/PhD candidates. 180 respondents (94%) are aware of Indonesian Batik, but only 68% (126) are aware of its exceptional cultural values as inscribed by UNESCO in 2009. 124 respondents (64%) show the willingness to download an educative mobile application on Batik.

While asked about the visual contents, 128 people (67%) responded 'strongly agree' to see (i) images or videos depicting Batik products (such as garments and textiles) and its production process; 117 (61%) wanted to discover (ii) a map of Batik regions in Indonesia, each showing its typical Batik motifs; and 97 respondents (51%) to play (iii) a Spinning Wheel, which allows users to play and discover each motif or region; 38% expected to see (iv) a lady and/or a man wearing Batik at Indonesian touristic destinations or heritage sites (palaces, temples, beaches, etc.) as the main screen of the app.

When it comes to contents, two third of the respondents recommended to include contents related to (i) philosophical meanings and history of Batik motifs; as well as (ii) a map of Batik regions showcasing typical Batik motifs and production process. 103 respondents (53%) expected contents related to (iii) Batik production centers, local tourism attractions, and how to get there. The survey recorded 126 respondents (65%) interested in having a (iv) Batik recognition tool, to scan batik patterns and find information on them, making it as the most preferred augmented reality (AR) feature by the survey respondents. The remaining AR options, such as photo montage tool, Batik puzzle game, and fashion mix and match tool were chosen by less than 50% respondents. About two third of the respondents expected that the iWareBatik web and mobile application would offer (v) the possibility to discover tourism regions to see their Batik motifs and their tourism attractions; while 119 respondents (60%) would use the app (vi) to gain information related to Batik Exceptional Cultural Values (production process, motifs, meanings, wearing rules).

5 Design Process

5.1 Refinement of User Goals

The first stage of goal refinement, moving from the interviews with main stakeholders and the survey was conducted by using NVivo software. As the survey received 114 textual answers from the respondents, the most frequent words of those texts were computed. Similarly, some parts of the interview transcripts containing the needs and requirements of the participants were added, so to find the most important keywords.

The result of the computing process using NVivo show that some words were frequently mentioned such as learn, production process, history, meanings, types of Batik, interactive, contemporary, tourism, regions, pictures, games, fashion, video, copyright, educate, young people, map, story, workshop, price, local producers, and souvenirs. Those main keywords were used in order to inform the design of iWareBatik contents.

The second step of the analysis was done by analyzing, annotating, and translating each textual input into a table of indicators based on the AWARe requirement categories, detailed in Table 2. Some inputs imply ill-defined goals of the stakeholders. For instance, a respondent wrote, "Really put appreciation and hope for this app, because (it can be used) to attract awareness especially of Indonesian young generations". This textual inquiry data is classified as soft goals of the respondent, anchoring other design elements and outputs to support this idea. The analyst and development team further worked on textual inputs, in order to understand which features, functionalities, contents were desired by respondents.

Table 2. List of user requirements annotated from the 114 survey textual inputs. Numbers beside requirements indicate how many respondents mentioned them.

Contents				Content Structure		Content Access		Navigation		Interface		User Operations	
Exceptional Cultural Values of Batik (motifs, history, meanings, etc)	81	Across Indonesia (Whole Regions)	9	Batik motifs and its meanings, history	71	Batik and Locals	62	Region > motif and meanings	67	Easy to use (uncomplicated menu)/user friendly/prompt response	7	Able to read/see contents	82
Identity (place of origin / region)	39	Promotion	8	Batik villages/workshops/local producers	25	Thematic Batik	23	Batik motif/meanings/ production technique > locals villages	30	Simple and Elegant	2	Able to choose options or categories	45
Production technique	25	Fashion / Special wearing rules	6	Regions pages	20	Batik and tourism regions/sites	13	See certain themes of Batik	15	Engaging storytelling with short/synthetic text	7	Able to discover interactive map, pages	19
Types of Batik	21	Batik making classes	4	Tourism sites	7	Buy Batik	7	Buy batik	11	Engaging design for young people	6	Able to purchase from the platform	13
Producers	15	Specific philosophy, Meanings for personal life	3	local culture	3	People wearing Batik	5	Region > tourism sites	11	**Visual Presentation**		Able to watch video material	5
Batik products	14	Design evolution	2	Traditional Batik (royals, local motifs, etc)	2	Thematic Sites	5	Price	8	Video	9	Able to play (games, AR, AI, etc)	2
Raise Awareness	13	UNESCO	1	**Types of App**				Highlight the classification of Batik wearing rules	5	Short Film	4		
Where to buy	12	Batik events	1	Informative			80	Promote Batik (for seller)	4	Images	6		
Destinations	12			Interactive			13						

Another example of textual input is the following one: "Hope that this application can give the essence of Batik and its related history and development, the position of Batik in the world, and explanations about batik producers across Indonesia". The text implies more practical needs to discover the complexity of contents related to Batik, its history and the development of its motifs across centuries. Such input is easier to be defined and fit in the set of requirements.

The keywords inferred from the computed analysis of textual data and the requirements table are combined and translated into an holistic paragraph, capturing the overview of stakeholders' goals towards iWareBatik: "The iWareBatik digital innovation helps to better communicate Batik to international and domestic (Indonesian) tourists, it is helpful to educate and raise the awareness of young people. It is designed in a way that engages users to discover, learn, and comprehend the ancestor traditions through short stories about the beautiful motifs, different meanings, emotions, history, and philosophical contemplation behind the Batik making. iWareBatik offers interactive features both in its website and mobile app, such as games or maps, in order to highlight the images and videos of local Batik textiles, tourism regions, as well as the cultural experience of Batik workshops across Indonesia. As Batik symbolizes friendship, iWareBatik may be used to recommend consumers to buy meaningful batik souvenirs. The platform also provides information about the price and even a possibility to buy Batik within the app, or where to go to get one. It displays how to wear Batik as formal attire, dress in contemporary fashion for individuals or couples. All Batik patterns reflect cultural identity, which shall be protected with the proper legal instruments."

5.2 User Composite Profiles, Scenarios, and Priorities

The design of the website and of the application should meet the needs and expectations of users and main stakeholders. AWARe model defines users as the audience whom the site aims to attract and serve. On other hand, main stakeholders are those who have the interest in building the digital platform, aiming at communicating certain topics in a way that is in line with their organizational strategy and objectives [32], at the same time meeting users' needs and interests. For example, USI UNESCO Chair and Indonesian government, as the clients-main stakeholder of this digital project, ensure that the system design is in line with the safeguarding objectives of Batik ICH. In addition, the designer or the project analyst must be able to identify the objectives of all stakeholders, both from the users' perspective and from the main stakeholder's one [31]. The next step of the design process is to define the personas and roles, in order to create composite profiles and scenarios/story of both users and main stakeholders.

Personas refer to personal characteristic of people who might be potential users in accessing the services provided by the platform. They encompass several dimensions such as age, profession, mindset, and roles characterizing a profile. Roles refer to the behavioral attitude of the user when using and accessing the site. Role goals refer to the objectives of specific online activities performed by the user. The combination of goals of a persona and a role generates a user composite profile, which informs the overall needs, tasks, and requirements inferred by the identity of the overall profile. Several personas are identified during the elicitation stage, namely: Tourist (International/Indonesian), Journalist, Art Student, Batik SME/Designer. The user roles applicable for the design of iWareBatik project are Casual Surfer, Material Gatherer, Facts Finder, and Ideas Seeker. All elements of user personas and user roles are combined in a holistic description.

Defining user composite profiles helps analyst to assign the degree of importance of the addressed users during the goal refinement process. Once the user composite profile is generated, the user scenarios can be outlined in order to describe the situations or story on where, when, and how the user would access the digital communication outlet. Five different user scenarios were defined such as Tourist, Journalist, Fashion Designer, Art Student, and Indonesian Diplomat. Among them, two examples illustrating the site user and client user scenario were presented as follows.

Site User Scenario. A high school student living in a village in East Java heard about iWareBatik website and application from her friend. She had an assignment to present the art of Indonesian Batik and explain its meanings in the class. She looks into the website and finds a large collection of Batik motifs existing in 34 provinces in Indonesia. She discovers the interactive map of iWareBatik and clicks into East Java region. She finds it interesting to see the short story of the region and its Batik motifs, presented in one-minute visual journey video. As she lives in a village with limited access to internet, she is able to use the offline mode of iWareBatik app to learn and share stories about Batik with her peers, as well as to help Batik producers in her village.

Client User Scenario. A diplomat working at Indonesian Embassy in London, England has a mission to conduct a Batik exhibition in his city. He is informed about iWareBatik website and application from his colleague in Bern, Switzerland. He needs to prepare a material for the exhibition. He browses the iWareBatik website and finds all the information of Batik motifs, including its thematic meanings and places of origin across Indonesia, which are available in English and Indonesian language. He finds out that iWareBatik app has an artificial intelligence feature that can be used to recognize Batik motifs. It inspires him to integrate iWareBatik app in the event, so the visitors can learn Batik textile heritage in a better and different way.

Based on the previous analysis, all the goals/soft goals associated to each stakeholder are converted into a table of user composite profiles (see Table 3). It appears that some stakeholders share similar objectives. The priority of a goal is weighed upon the number of stakeholders who have similar goals/soft goals.

Table 3. The list of user composite profiles of all stakeholders (site users and main stakeholders).

Site User Profile	Roles	Goals	Soft Goals
Tourist	Casual Surfer	- Discover cultural/natural destinations and UNESCO sites in Indonesia - Get to know Indonesian Batik - To know the reason why Batik was inscribed by UNESCO - Batik picture and read short story about its meaning - Discover Indonesian Batik regions - Search for Batik villages and workshops	Attractivity Interactivity Simpleness
Journalist	Material Gatherer	- To know the reason why Batik was inscribed by UNESCO - Discover Batik in each region and its difference - Learn history of Batik - See Batik picture and find its meanings	Richness Accuracy
Art Student	Facts Finder	- Get to know Batik in each region and its differences - To know the reason why Batik was inscribed by UNESCO - Learn history of Batik - Learn how to make Batik textile - Discover the evolution of Batik across centuries	Richness Attractivity Accuracy
Batik Small Medium Enterprise (SME)/Designer	Ideas Seeker	- Get to know Batik in each region and its differences - Learn how to make Batik - Learn how to wear Batik according to its purposes - Do something with the platform (to contribute article, to promote, to buy)	Attractivity Richness
Main Stakeholder Profile	Roles	Goals	Soft Goals
USI UNESCO Chair	Client, Decision Maker, Representative, Opinion Maker	- Raise people's awareness in preserving tangible and intangible cultural heritage (ICH) - Preserve UNESCO Sites in Indonesia - Safeguard Indonesian Batik	Accuracy Accessibility Attractivity
Indonesian Government (LPDP scholarship)	Client, Representative, Opinion Maker	- Safeguard Indonesian Batik - Preserve UNESCO sites in Indonesia - Promote Indonesian tourism - Promote Indonesian creative products	Attractivity Richness Accuracy
Sobat Budaya Cultural Association	Representative, Domain Expert, Opinion Maker	- Safeguard Indonesian Batik - Protect Indonesian cultural properties	Accuracy Security
Batik Artisans/SMEs	Representative, Domain Expert,	- Promote Batik motifs and products - Safeguard Indonesian Batik	Attractivity Accessibility
Communication Manager	Decision Maker, Domain Expert, Opinion Maker, Development Team	- Effective Communication - Reduce costs and maintenance - Attract visitors and users	Effectiveness Attractivity

5.3 Transition to Design Model

The goals of users and main stakeholders gathered during the elicitation process (interview and survey) are combined within the joint requirement analysis. Joint requirement analysis illustrates all goals/soft goals of users and main stakeholder, as well as the associated requirements that are systematically arranged into a goal graph. The requirements are classified into 7 set of requirements namely Access (A); Content (C); Presentation (P); Structure of Content (SC); Navigation (N); User Operation (U); Interaction (I), System Operation (O) [36]. The goal graph illustrates goal refinement along with the identification of conflicts and influences, hypermedia taxonomy and set of requirements (see Fig. 4). The elements of the goal graph are presented in Table 4.

Table 4. Elements of goal graph based on AWARe model.

The goal graph is divided into two parts, namely the main stakeholders (from the center to the right side) who aim to supply information and the site user profiles (from the center to the left side), whose goals are to obtain information. Eventually the main goal(s) of a user composite profile and main stakeholders need to be detailed in more specific goals. For example, a tourist wants 'to know Indonesian Batik culture'. This goal is specified into several goals such 'to know the reason why Batik was inscribed by UNESCO', 'see Batik picture and find its meaning', discover Indonesian Batik regions', 'search for Batik villages and Batik workshop'. Subsequently, each goal is linked to specific requirements that satisfy the goals outlined. For example, USI UNESCO Chair and Indonesian government, as the clients-main stakeholders, share similar priorities with regards to raise people's awareness to preserve UNESCO Sites in Indonesia and safeguard Batik as UNESCO ICH. Those main goals are linked to several Requirements of Content (C) such as 'Highlight UNESCO sites in Indonesia' and 'Highlight Exceptional Cultural Values of Indonesian Batik UNESCO ICH in 2009'. The contents with regards to the exceptional cultural values of Batik are organized into requirements of structure of contents (SC) that outline 'the history of Batik, Batik production process, meanings, sociocultural aspects, wearing rules, and evolution across centuries'. Those contents are systemized in a way that satisfies the goals of the site user profiles (Tourist, Journalist, Art Student in the left part), who wants to know the reason why Batik was inscribed by UNESCO.

Apart from that, another shared priority is to 'discover Batik in each region and learn its differences'. This goal is interpreted into more specific goals such as 'learn how to wear Batik according to its purposes' and 'learn how to make Batik', which are different from one region to another. Those priorities implicate several requirements of visual presentation (P) such as 'display typical Batik production video in each region' and 'display images of persons (male/female) wearing Batik and videos of Batik fashion shows', requirements of structure of content (SC) 'provide info how to wear Batik in Casual events, Formal Functions, and for Ritual Ceremonies', as well as a requirement of access path (A) that provide 'feature to explore Batik motifs according to classifications and thematic meanings'.

When it comes to fulfil the soft goals, several requirements were set in order to satisfy the expectations of associated stakeholders. For instance, 'Attractivity' is a soft goal shared by USI UNESCO Chair, Indonesian Government, Tourist, Journalist, and Art Student. In order to create attractive content, two sub goals are defined such as to provide 'engaging multimedia' and 'storytelling'. The requirements of visual presentation (P) for those objectives are to provide 'clear, beautiful, high resolution pictures', to create 'one-minute visual video of the region and its Batik' for each region, and to manage 'short text (4 sentences max), engaging description, semi-formal language'. Some requirements of interaction (I) also serve two soft goals: 'Attractivity' and 'Interactivity', such as to provide 'Interactive Map covering 34 Indonesian regions', 'Spinning Wheel feature', and 'Artificial Intelligence tool to detect Batik motif within the app'. In terms of 'Accuracy' and 'Richness', requirements of system of operation (O) and navigation (N) are put in place, such as 'system provides structured content database of Batik motifs, meanings, history and the regions, which is built according to the valid resources such as scientific papers, books, governmental sites, etc.' and provide 'the evolution of Batik motifs across century through timeline feature'. These two requirements are in line with the goal of the Communication Manager, which is to effectively communicate Batik and its all dimensions.

In terms of 'Accessibility', it is fulfilled by the provision of '2 languages: English and Indonesian' and 'spinning wheel feature' and 'off line mode for mobile app for non internet connection usage in rural areas'. Several conflicts were mapped such as the needs of Batik SME/Designer to sell Batik from the app are in contrast with goal of Communication Manager that aims at reducing costs and maintenance. It is decided that iWareBatik digital technology serves as an educative online platform to help people

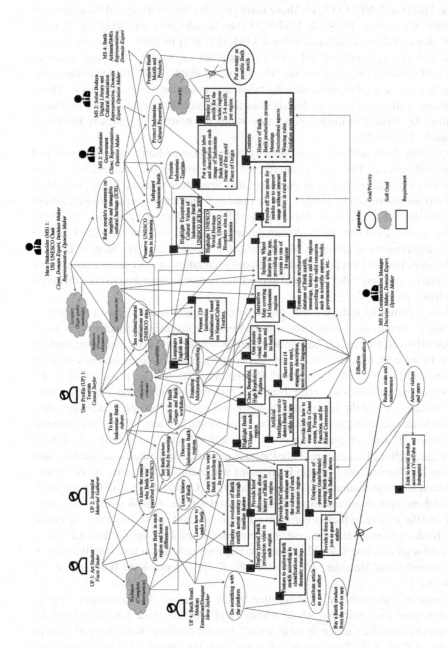

Fig. 4. The goal graph as the result of Joint Requirement Analysis in AWARe model

understand the Batik ICH. Another conflict is also identified in relation to the provision of Batik motifs information. Sobat Budaya Association cares for the security to protect the information of Batik motifs as cultural property. Two requirements and limitation are hence justified, namely 'put a copyright label and description on each image of Indonesian Batik motif and 'display 124 motifs for the whole regions or 3–4 motifs per region'.

6 Discussion and Conclusion

The development of iWareBatik digital technology is an example of digital innovation that is built upon the triangulation of participatory service design research, online communication model framework, and AWARe method that extensively captures all requirements and the needs of the stakeholders involved within the field of Batik ICH.

Designing ICT for ICH requires a holistic approach that integrates not only the safeguarding goals of UNESCO Convention in 2003 and scientific elements of Batik as a thousand years-old visual art, but also the main stakeholders in connection with this heritage, especially the Batik artisans. The project has been designed and implemented not only to meet the explicit goals stated by its main stakeholders, but it also covers the underlying expectations of end users, which contribute to the satisfaction of user experience when accessing and exploring the digital platform. The AWARe model is a communication-oriented design methodology that effectively outlines the goals, both from the stakeholders' point of view and from the one of the design team. The goal oriented and participatory nature of AWARe model makes it suitable methodology for designing hypermedia intensive online platforms, especially those that address complex issues, are multidisciplinary, and involve large audiences.

The documentation of iWareBatik design process could serve as an exemplary model for building other similar projects related to cultural heritage and ICH. This research contributes to provide conceptual design thinking through iterative refinement of user requirement elicitation, involving various categories of stakeholders. The case offered in the paper may contribute to improve the measurement and the standard of online communication design for intangible cultural heritage related to textile.

This study also provides an example of AWARe model that is implemented with huge data samples taken from the interviews and survey. Different methods were used during the process of data analysis, in order to extract them into user composite profiles and convert them into the goal graph. The implementation of conceptual frameworks outlined in this study may serve as a guide and an illustration for the design practitioners, in order to perform benchmarking analysis, identify the needs of the stakeholders through iterative refinement, manage the design transition, treat all the requirements and conflicts into applicable solutions, and accordingly build an effective user experience of digital technology.

Since the scope of this study is limited to the documentation process of the design, the study can be further developed into the evaluation and the usability studies based on the set of requirements outlined above. The research topics can also be expanded to address other cultural heritage projects. It is deemed important that the online communication design of intangible cultural heritage truly corresponds to the safeguarding mission of the UNESCO, while taking into account various dimensions and effectively attract more stakeholders for supporting the preservation of the ICH.

Acknowledgement. LPDP (Lembaga Pengelola Dana Pendidikan) Endowment Funds Scholarships, Ministry of Finance, Republic of Indonesia; UNESCO Chair in ICT to develop and promote sustainable tourism in World Heritage Sites USI - Università della Svizzera Italiana, Switzerland.

References

1. Arnold, D., Geser, G.: EPOCH research agenda for the applications of ICT to cultural heritage, pp. 27–39. Archaeolingua, Budapest (2008)
2. Garbelli, M.: World heritage sites, tourism, and ICT. In: Workshop Material Presented in UNESCO Summer School in ICT for Gastronomic Tourism (2015)
3. Robbins, C.: Beyond preservation: new directions for technological innovation through intangible cultural heritage. Int. J. Educ. Dev. ICT **6**(2), 115–118 (2010)
4. Noor, N.L.M., Nordin, A.: Requirements elicitation for the technology conception of a community information system for the indigenous microenterprise: a contextual multi-analysis approach on business and community requirements of Batik making. Electron. J. Inf. Syst. Eval. **15**, 102–115 (2012)
5. Owen, R., Buhalis, D., Pletinckx, D.: Identifying technologies used in cultural heritage. In: Chrysanthou, Y., Cain, K. (eds.) VAST 2004 5th International Symposium on Virtual Reality, Archaeology Intelligence and Cultural Heritage 2nd proceedings, pp. 155–163. Eurographics, Belgium (2004)
6. Cantoni, L.: Heritage and sustainable tourism. The role and challenge of information and communication technologies. In: De Ascaniis, S., Gravari-Barbas, M., Cantoni, L. (eds.) Tourism Management at UNESCO World Heritage Sites, pp. 68–74. Università della Svizzera italiana, Lugano (2018)
7. Albert, M.T.: Perspectives of world heritage: towards future-oriented strategies with the five 'Cs.' In: Albert, M.T., Richon, M., Viñals, M.J., Witcomb, A. (eds.) Community Development Through World Heritage, pp. 16–26. United Nations Educational, Scientific and Cultural Organization (UNESCO), Paris (2012)
8. Kalbaska, N., Sádaba, T., Cantoni, L.: Editorial: fashion communication: between tradition and digital transformation. Stud. Commun. Sci. **18**(2), 269–285 (2019). https://doi.org/10.24434/j.scoms.2018.02.005
9. Noris, A., Nobile, T.H., Kalbaska, N., Cantoni, L.: Digital fashion: a systematic literature review. A perspective on marketing and communication. J. Global Fashion Market. **12**(1), 32–46 (2021). https://doi.org/10.1080/20932685.2020.1835522
10. Tussyadiah, I.P., Fesenmaier, D.R.: Access to places via shared videos. Ann. Tour. Res. **36**, 24–40 (2009). https://doi.org/10.1016/j.annals.2008.10.001
11. Stephanidis, C., et al.: Seven HCI grand challenges. Int. J. Hum. Comput. Interact. **35**(14), 1229–1269 (2019). https://doi.org/10.1080/10447318.2019.1619259
12. Adukaite, A., Cantoni, L.: Raising awareness and promoting informal learning on World Heritage in Southern Africa: The case of WHACY, a gamified ICT-enhanced tool. Int. J. Educ. Dev. Inf. Commun. Technol. **12**, 50–67 (2016)
13. iWareBatik. https://www.iwarebatik.org/. Accessed 12 Feb 2021
14. Permatasari, P.A., Cantoni, L.: Mapping mobile apps on Batik: a journey across heritage and fashion. In: Kalbaska, N., Sádaba, T., Cominelli, F., Cantoni, L. (eds.) FACTUM 2019, pp. 166–178. Springer, Cham (2019). https://doi.org/10.1007/978-3-030-15436-3_15

15. Permatasari, P.A., Cantoni, L.: Indonesian tourism and Batik: an online map. e-Review Tour. Res. **16**(2/3), 184–194 (2019)
16. Permatasari, P.A., Qohar, A.A., Rachman, A.F.: From web 1.0 to web 4.0: the digital heritage platforms for UNESCO's heritage properties in Indonesia. Virtual Archaeol. Rev. **11**, (2020). https://doi.org/10.4995/var.2020.13121
17. UNESCO: Convention concerning the protection of the world cultural and natural heritage in 1972. http://whc.unesco.org/uploads/activities/documents/activity-562-4.pdf. Accessed 04 Jan 2021
18. UNESCO: Convention for the safeguarding of the intangible cultural heritage (2003). http://portal.unesco.org/en/ev.php-URL_ID=17716&URL_DO=DO_TOPIC&URL_SECTION=201.html. Accessed 04 Jan 2021
19. Druding, S.C.: Dye history from 2600BC to the 20th century. Bi-annual gathering of weavers, dyers, and spinners (1982)
20. UNESCO ICH: Indonesian Batik inscription in 2009. https://ich.unesco.org/en/RL/indonesian-batik-00170. Accessed 14 Jan 2021
21. Hann, M.: Symbol, Pattern and Symmetry: The Cultural Significance of Structure. Bloomsbury, London (2013)
22. De Ascaniis, S., Cantoni, L.: Pilgrims in the digital age: a research manifesto. Int. J. Relig. Tour. Pilgrim. **4**(3), 1–5 (2016)
23. Indonesian Ministry of Industry, KINA: Karya Indonesia [The Made in Indonesia). https://kemenperin.go.id/download/4554. Accessed 04 Jan 2021
24. Indonesian Ministry of Industry, [Batik as an oriented export creative industry]. https://kemenperin.go.id/artikel/21115/Selain-Padat-Karya,-Industri-Batik-Punya-Orientasi-Ekspor. Accessed 14 Jan 2021
25. Crofts, N.: Grasping the intangible: how should museums document intangible heritage? In: CIDOC 2010: ICOM General Conference, pp. 1–15 (2010)
26. Purba, E.J., Putra, A.K., Ardianto, B.: Perlindungan hukum warisan budaya takbenda dan penerapannya di Indonesia [Protection on intangible cultural heritage and its application in Indonesia]. Uti Possidetis J. Int. Law **1**(1), 87–109 (2020)
27. Hartson, R., Pyla., P.S.: The UX Book: Process and Guidelines for Ensuring a Quality User Experience. Elsevier, USA (2012)
28. De Ascaniis, S., Cantoni, L., Sutinen, E., Talling, R.: A LifeLike experience to train user requirements elicitation skills. In: Marcus, A., Wang, W. (eds.) DUXU 2017. LNCS, vol. 10290, pp. 219–237. Springer, Cham (2017). https://doi.org/10.1007/978-3-319-58640-3_16
29. Coughlan, J., Macredie, R.D.: Effective communication in requirements elicitation: a comparison of methodologies. Requirements Eng. **7**(2), 47–60 (2002). https://doi.org/10.1007/s007660200004
30. Suchman, L.: Making work visible. Commun. ACM. (1995). https://doi.org/10.1145/223248.223263
31. Bolchini, D., Paolini, P.: Capturing web application requirements through goal-oriented analysis. In: 2nd Proceedings of the Workshop on Requirements Engineering, pp. 16–28 (2002)
32. Bolchini, D., Paolini, P.P.: Mastering the requirements analysis for communication-intensive websites. A dissertation presented by Università della Svizzera italiana (2003)
33. Beyer, H., Holtzblatt, K.: Contextual Design: Defining Customer-Centered Systems. San Francisco (1998)
34. Constantine, L.L., Lockwood, L.A.D.: Software for Use: A Practical Guide to the Models and Methods of Usage-Centered Design. Addison-Wesley Professional, Reading (1999)
35. Perrone, V., Bolchini, D.: Designing communication-intensive web applications: a case study. In: 4th Proceedings of the Workshop on Requirements Engineering, pp. 239–250 (2004)

36. Bolchini, D., Mylopoulos, J.: From task-oriented to goal-oriented web requirements analysis. In: 4th Proceedings of International Conference on Web Information Systems Engineering, WISE 2003 (2003)
37. Cantoni, L., Tardini, S.: Internet. Routledge, London (2006)
38. Bolchini, D., Arasa, D., Cantoni, L.: Teaching websites as communication: a "Coffee shop approach.". In: Proceedings of the ED-MEDIA, pp. 4119–4124 (2004)
39. Tresnadi, C., Sachari, A.: Identification of values of ornaments in Indonesian Batik in visual content of NITIKI game. J. Arts Humanit. UE (2015). https://doi.org/10.18533/journal.v4i 8.797
40. Hermawan, H.D., Arifin, F.: The development and analysis of quality of Batik Detector as a learning media for Indonesia Batik motifs Android based in Indonesian School of Singapore. In: Proceedings 2015 International Conference on Science and Technology (2015). https://doi.org/10.1109/TICST.2015.7369371
41. Widiaty, I., Riza, L.S., Abdullah, A.G., Mubaroq, S.R.: Application of desktop-based Batik information system. In: IOP Conference Series: Materials Science and Engineering (2018). https://doi.org/10.1088/1757-899X/288/1/012086
42. Cozzani, G., Pozzi, F., Dagnino, F.M., Katos, A.V., Katsouli, E.F.: Innovative technologies for intangible cultural heritage education and preservation. The case of i-Treasures. Pers. Ubiquit. Comput. **21**(2), 253–265 (2017)
43. Alivizatou-Barakou, M., et al. (eds.): Intangible Cultural Heritage and New Technologies: Challenges and Opportunities for Cultural Preservation and Development. Springer, Cham (2017). https://doi.org/10.1007/978-3-319-49607-8_5
44. Schieder, T., Adukaite, A., Cantoni, L.: Mobile apps devoted to UNESCO world heritage sites: a Map. In: Xiang, Z., Tussyadiah, I. (eds.) Information and Communication Technologies in Tourism 2014, pp. 17–29. Springer, Cham (2013). https://doi.org/10.1007/978-3-319-039 73-2_2
45. Qinghua, Y., Nagai, Y., Yinghuang, L.: Co-creation with ceramic practitioner for improving the marketing and enhancing the customer purchase experiences. Asian Bus. Res. J. (2019). https://doi.org/10.20448/journal.518.2019.41.44.53
46. David, S., Cantoni, L.: Co-design of eTourism application. The case of Ilha de Mozambique. e-Rev Tourism Res. (eRTR) **1**(6), 1–5 (2015). https://doi.org/10.13140/RG.2.1.1785.6488
47. Pucciarelli, M., Cantoni, L.: Mobile access to knowledge. Mob. Sci. Learn., 71–77 (2012)
48. Miralbell, O., Cantoni, L., Kalbaska, N.: The role of e-learning applications within the tourism sector. eLearn Center Res. Paper Ser., 04–05 (2014)
49. Marcus, A., Schieder, T., Cantoni, L.: The travel machine: mobile UX design that combines information design with persuasion design. In: Marcus, Aaron (ed.) DUXU 2013. LNCS, vol. 8015, pp. 696–705. Springer, Heidelberg (2013). https://doi.org/10.1007/978-3-642-39253-5_78
50. Buditomo, B.P.: The design and development of a mobile app: Branding Indonesia as an experience tourism destination. A Master thesis presented by Auckland University of Technology Library (2018)

Methods for Multiple Roles to Build Brands of Service System–A Case Study of Guangzhou Baiyun International Airport

Qixuan Su[1] and Yi Liu[1,2(✉)]

[1] Guangzhou Academy of Fine Arts, No. 257 Changgang Road, Guangzhou, People's Republic of China
[2] Province Key Lab of Innovation and Applied Research On Industry Design, No. 257 Changgang Road, Guangzhou, People's Republic of China

Abstract. With service economy booming, service brand has drawn attention of scholars and practitioners worldwide. Service brand building involves multiple roles of enterprises, employees and customers, which complicates the service system. Therefore, this paper puts forward methods for different stakeholders to realize the brand value unity and reconcile the contradiction between brand integrity and personalization in the aim for cognitive unity of the brand system within the enterprise. With Guangzhou Baiyun Airport as the case of building service brand, this paper exploits methods of building complex service brand system with multiple stakeholders. Firstly, in regard to the service suppliers, it is necessary to define the brand, build a framework, position the role so as to present the services as a brand. The process of building the airport service system is hereby divided into two phases. We shall first establish a consistent service brand, which refers to a total brand with extracted values and connotations out of prominent brand features. The second is to build a service system, based on the core concepts of the total brand, with clear-cut levels and explicit roles within, and set up sub-brands. The innovation of this paper lies in exploring with systematic thinking the methods for building complex service brand system in which the total brand value serves as the core. Meanwhile, the sub-brands showcase both personality and diversity while maintaining integrity. The three roles of leaders, employees and customers mainly constitute the analytical model. When the former two participants build service brand together, the value and cognition of the brand can achieve integrity within the companies.

Keywords: Multiple roles · Service brand · Service system

1 On Topic Selection

1.1 Connotation and Significance of Service Brand Building

Traditional brand theories are mainly centering on the physical products of manufacturing industry. Products are easy to copy, but services are not, which means building a brand out of service is more complex. Services feature intangibility and heterogeneity

© Springer Nature Switzerland AG 2021
M. M. Soares et al. (Eds.): HCII 2021, LNCS 12780, pp. 107–120, 2021.
https://doi.org/10.1007/978-3-030-78224-5_8

[1], so customers can not evaluate the quality of the service prior to purchase, and also brands enjoying high popularity and reputation can increase customers' trust. Values of the service brand tend to transmit to customers through their experience of the brand [2]. What the service brand conveys is communicated to the customers via their interactions with the service providers [3]. Therefore, brand is one of the tangible forms for customers to perceive the intangible services. With the development of economy, consumers pay more attention to spiritual needs. In the homogeneous society, good service can impress consumers with one or more points. Service brand meets consumers psychological needs with its unique values, which may strengthen their evoked feelings and impressions attached to the brand values. Good services also improve consumers' understanding of the service function with greater satisfaction. As the consumption level of consumers upgrades, it can be seen that service enterprises are inevitable to enhance the value of services by building brands [4].

Building service brand is part of the corporate culture, finally affecting customers in an "invisible" way. Different enterprises can communicate service information through brands to show their uniqueness. Thus, building a successful service brand is one of the ways for higher recognition and competitive advantages of enterprises [5], which is of great strategic significance for the business development.

1.2 "Multiple Roles" in Service System

Due to the to the inherent particularity of services, a service system involves many stakeholders, elements and segments. On the service provider side, a large service system contains multiple subsystems each as a "role" with interactions in between. It is needed not only to meet the overall requirements of the large ones, but also operate separately to provide personalized services and transmit service value. In the case of Guangzhou Baiyun Airport, the subsystems coordinate and operate for a large system, and they meanwhile own particular systems. One the service receiver side, different types of users call for differentiated requests for the large service system, and each type is consisted of multiple "roles". The large service system provides specific services according to the characteristics and requirements of the roles. For instance, Baiyun Airport will classify passengers and confirm the role portrait so as to build sub-brands for providing services.

1.3 Methods and Innovations

Since the 1990s, some scholars have begun to discuss about building service brand, among which there are several representative service brand models. Berry, a well-known American service marketing scientist, put forward a service brand building model [1] by studying 14 mature and high-performance service enterprises. The model emphasizes that customer service experience plays a prominent role in brand building (see Fig. 1), but it just estimates and predicts customer perception of service brand from the perspective of service marketers. British scholars de Chernatony and Segal-Horn [6] conducted in-depth interviews with 28 leading-edge consultants on issues related to service brands, and put forward a closed loop model (see Fig. 2). It integrates the external customer communication, internal staff management and the interaction between staff and customers of service brands. Brodie [7] ran a sampling survey of 552 airline customers and proposed a triangle model of service brand-customer relationship-customer value (see Fig. 3). This model illustrates that service brands are used to create value for customers and other stakeholders. On this basis, Skaalsvik et al. [8]. put forward an interactive model for service brand building from a holistic and systemic perspective, with leaders, employees and customers as three main roles (see Fig. 4).

The above models possessing their own focus gradually transit from the perspective of just one single role to a systematic perspective in regard to service brand building. However, it is difficult to ensure the consistency of the brand value during its transmission among multiple levels and elements. Meanwhile, the interaction between roles also affects the integrity of service brand. Therefore, based on the multiple roles, this paper puts forward a method of building service brand system so as to achieve the unity of service brand value and maintain the diversity.

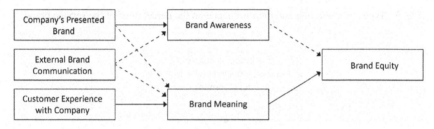

Fig. 1. A service-branding model

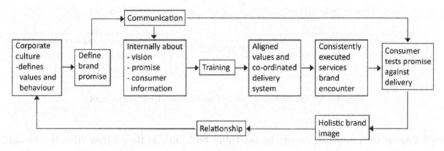

Fig. 2. The criteria influencing the success of services brands

2 On Service Brand

2.1 Service Brand

It is a relatively new trend in recent years to research on service brand [9]. Berry [1] points out that branding is the cornerstone of services marketing for the 21st century which defines service brand. He holds that a strong service brand is essentially a promise to satisfy customers in the future. Customer experience influences their association and attitude towards the service brand [10]. De Chernatony et al. [11, 12]. believe that

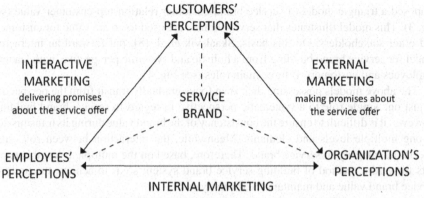

Fig. 3. Types of marketing and their influence on the perceptions of the service brand.

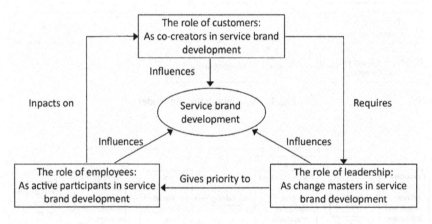

Fig. 4. An interactive model of service brand development

employees play a key role in the brand value building, as they often "live the brand" within the organization and in their interactions with the consumers. Brands represent the vision and culture of the enterprise, and the employees, as participants, would definitely reflect and represent the enterprise values.

However, the above researches just focus on the relationship between a single role and service brand. Hence some scholars broaden the discussions from the perspective of stakeholders, taking brand as a continuous social process [13]. Brand value is achieved through the negotiation among stakeholders [7, 14]. Therefore, Skaalsvik and others [8] believe that the development of enterprise service brand is "the efforts initiated and implemented by service providers in order to increase customer service brand assets."

It is evident that the concept and definition of service brand is becoming profound and extensive. Under this circumstance, building service brand becomes complicated which shifts from a static condition to a dynamic process involving a network featuring more elements and participants rather than individuals in linear manners.

2.2 Roles in Service System

The service system involves multiple elements and sufficient subjects, including not only static and tangible parts, such as name, logo, employee image, but also dynamic and intangible ones, for example service environment, employee behaviors, customer emotions. A more dynamic service system presents abundance and complexity.

The participants in the service system are also stakeholders. Through the connection via funds, information and materials, all stakeholders cooperate to create differentiated services and achieve shared benefits [15]. A role is an established identity underpinning any relationship [16]. From an external view, customers are the role involved, who interact with the service system and whose emotions and experiences will affect the communication of the value with the service system. From an internal perspective, the main participants are enterprise leaders and employees. Leaders are the front-runners to build the service system and maintain the consistency among numerous elements. The employees interact with customers directly or indirectly, playing a key role in the communication of the service system value. Customer experience can also be affected by the attitude and behaviors of the employees.

In a holistic view, the service system is built by multiple roles, the relationship among who is connected by space, personnel, process, facilities, information and other elements inside the network; the value of the service system is communicated through the interaction between roles and elements.

2.3 Complexity of Service Brand Building

The service industry started its late entry to building the service brand due to the complexity [6]. First and the foremost, there are diverse roles in different dimensions within the service system represented by service providers, stakeholders and environment. Ranging from the service providers to the users of a service system, each role faces different service steps and touchpoints, with certain elements interrelated. When the relationship between roles is not well handled, the service process will lack of integrity and stability.

Secondly, the promotion of different functions of the brands complicates the task of building service brands which have a variety of functions conveying differential brand information and brand images, thus affecting customers' association of the brands. Brands should not only present and meet the personalized needs of customers via differentiated functions, but also transmit the unified brand values, which, in the sense of brand communication, is complex and difficult.

Finally, diversity gives rise to the difficulty of brand management. Service brand should first manage multiple factors, mainly including physical factors and human-centered ones. Physical factors bring on the customer's first impression, and the other ones affect customers' emotions and expectations. Secondly, it is more important to maintain customer experiences, which accumulate in the process of interactions with the service brands. Multiple elements make the experience lively and diversified. Also, customer experience features complex mental activities on a number of levels [17]. It is by no means easy to improve the customers' brand experience in terms of brand management.

3   Research on Role Relationship in Service Brand System

3.1   Roles of Services

From the perspective of brand evolution, brand is a relationship formed with stakeholders [18]. The relationships involved in service brands are linked by the roles of the service system: mainly service maker, service personnel and customers. As shown in Fig. 5 (see Fig. 5), the service maker is the enterprise leader who, with the basic understanding of the service objectives and expectations, require the service personnel or the employees to provide specific service measures, and at the same time, formulate the rules, processes, roles, standards, assessment and evaluation of the services. Whereas, service brands cannot directly act on end users, and service personnel, as the "interface" between them, can facilitate communication and influence customers. When recognizing the brand values and having been encouraged, customer-facing employees will unconsciously improve the service quality to satisfy the customers by understanding the service process, environment and challenges, meanwhile communicating the value of service brands. Elements such as service channels, scenarios, touchpoints, and functions are involved at the same time. Customers purchase and participate in the service out of their own experience and needs, and the service personnel complete the service objectives.

Fig. 5. Relationship between roles and interests of service system

3.2   Role Diversity and Brand Consistency in Service System

Service system stresses on multiple stakeholders with each role having its own personality and unique points as well as interactions in between. The service brand highlights the customer's experience of services, which is essentially a commitment. Multiple roles imply more service touchpoints, which makes it difficult to ensure the consistency of customer brand experience if with inconsistent information conveyed. Besides, the process of the service system is also diversified, with different hierarchical relationships and service steps aiming for different needs. Brand consistency refers to the identity and stability of brand image, value and experience perceived by brand stakeholders [3]. The ultimate goal of brand building is to provide a consistent and unique customer experience [20]. Customer's perception of service brand mainly comes from the results and process of the services, so brand consistency affects perceived value [21]. Baiyun Airport has many service departments inside and various types of users outside. To brand these elements by coordinating them in the framework of brand strategy requires controls of touchpoints, internal and external communication of value and consistent customer experience.

In the process of brand building, value communication is mainly realized through the interaction between employees and customers in service encounters [2], which signifies that internal and external communication should be consistent. In the eyes of consumers, employees represent the brands [19]. With internalized understanding and consistent belief of the brand values, employees connect brand identification with brand image and put it into services. Baiyun Airport actively mobilizes employees to participate in the establishment of brand values when building service brand and puts forward practical measures so as to realize the internal communication of brand value through co-creation. Furthermore, the hub airport broadcasts information to customers after achieving close contacts between employees and service brand, which refers to the external communication. The aim is to maintain the consistency of internal and external communication of the brand values.

3.3 Levels and Branding of Service System

Branding is essentially a process of interactions between service enterprises, Service employees and customers [22]. From the cognitive level, the branding of service system demands leaders to pinpoint the direction of brand development and formulate relevant strategies. Employees identify with and participate in brand building, and effectively communicate brand value to customers. The presentation of service brands is of variety and diversity, relating more environmental factors apart from brand design and identification along with brand communication. Customers' perception of service brand not only comes from five senses, but also owns advanced cognition, that is, emotional cognition. To improve the customer experience, branding the customer experience is a must. Baiyun Airport has a variety of customer types. According to differentiated characteristics and needs, they need to be branded separately, so that different customers can perceive the brand value of Baiyun Airport from their own perspective.

From a systematic view, the branding of service system should first establish service brand orientation, the key of which is brand identification (mission, vision, values), which advocates meeting customer needs within the scope of brand identification, and underlines the brand as a resource and strategy center [23]. The second is to conduct the organizational design of the brand with all personnel in the service value chain participating in brand building. The elements, roles, hierarchical relationships and others in the system can finally be clearly presented through branding. On these grounds, the stakeholders of Baiyun Airport all join in building the brand, who first carry out the general branding, and then subdivide the brand by building the industry brand through the internal efforts and setting up the user brand with the external ones, so as for a top-down branding.

4   On Service Brand Innovation of Baiyun Airport

Guangzhou Baiyun International Airport, as one of the three major aviation hubs in China, undertakes a large number of passenger throughput over the year, with multiple and varied passenger groups. The functional and emotional needs of users of the airport services have been paid more attention. Therefore, this paper selects Baiyun Airport service brand building as the case study to explore the methods of complex service brand system with multiple roles.

4.1   Method

The first task is to establish the core value of service brand [24], which is generally created by enterprise founders or senior managers [25]. Baiyun Airport builds its total brand presented by "Cordial service", namely spring breeze, standing for cordial service (hereafter referred to as Cordial Service) in accordance with its own positioning and vision (see Fig. 6).

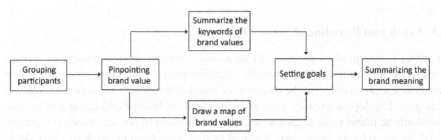

Fig. 6. Methods of Building Total Brand

1. Grouping participants: The enterprise leaders set up workshops with grouped employees and let participants play the roles of different user groups so as to discuss and analyze the user needs in the pursuit of building the total brand.
2. Pinpointing brand value: A clear-cut understanding of the current situation of the airport, the brand vision and goal is a prerequisite for putting forward representative key values. The next if to classify and summarize the keywords in line with the brand vision in order that participants can vote for the best options.
3. Working on delivering the brand values: An important thing is to dissect the business processes and detail the touchpoints, in combination of the value keywords into the service scenes closely related to the users, to ultimately draw a map of brand values.

4. Setting goals: Marks of the most important brand value innovation point and the link that can best reflect the service brand value should be highlighted on the map. The decision-maker does the final confirmation of the innovation point.
5. Summarizing the brand meaning: The aviation hub is famous for its cordial, warm and natural services. It is still needed for extended meaning in terms of person, space and process. The final step is to confirm the brand logo and let the total brand fall to the ground.

The service system of Baiyun airport is huge and diverse. In the pursuit of the total brand, it is conducive to maintaining the consistency of service brands with established brand value, which answers the code of conduct and cultural concept of building sub-brands. In the process of building the total brand, the enterprise leaders, as the decision-makers, play a leading and decisive role.

Then we continue to work on building brand under the guidance of brand values, and build the service brand framework with clear levels of service roles and service system as well as define the key words of each role. Service roles should find a balance between user needs and their own capabilities in order to undertake competent and differential roles [16], as each role has its own uniqueness in the service system. In view of this, it can be done to brand their personality as the sub-brands.

There are two phases in building the sub-brands of Cordial Service of Baiyun Airport. According to the core concept of the total brand, two types of sub-brands are respectively built in regard to the staff and user groups of each department. (see Fig. 7).

• Cordial service industry brand

While leaders established and maintained the core value of the service brand of the hub airport, it is the employees, especially the customer-facing ones, that communicate the values to the users. In addition, there are many service departments of the airport, each of which presents different working patterns, thus bringing on varied touchpoints during the whole service process. Therefore, employees need to understand brand values and act on their role accordingly to build the sub-brand of Cordial Service.

First, take brand value as a gene integrated into the whole process. By drawing service flow chart and role plays, the intangible brand is personified, urging the employees to explore the personality of their own department, including the service content, characteristics and advantages. Also, to show the image and concept of the sub-brand in a comprehensive way calls for the established personality of the service role, the pursuit of its value and branding and confirmation of the name, slogan and vision as well as the developing strategies of the sub-brand.

Employees' participation in the building the sub-brands means establishment of a close relationship between employees and service brands. Multiple departments form into a sub-brand in concert, leading employees shape their values in accordance with the value of the total brand and behave as expected.

• Cordial service user brand

The service brand is not only built by the leaders and employees of the enterprise, but also by the users, an important role in the service system. Baiyun Airport has huge passenger throughput and diversified user types with different needs. After exploiting the advantages and disadvantages of service departments in the interaction with users, it is a must to focus on seven types of key players that need service, establish a target user model with advanced needs recognized and analyze the demand model from multiple dimensions of physical situation, interactive relationship, emotional goal and rational goal. Furthermore, a detailed scheme of specific service optimization should come out with the help of the model, encompassing suggestions on space, facilities, communicative wordings, process and other aspects. It is also needed to outline the departments considered most closely linked in the entire product (service) upgrade process and system in seek of expected support. If the above service content can be branding with defined values and mission of the sub-brand as well as clarified goal and vision, it will do good to the total brand and further name sub-brands and design brand image in the future.

Building user brand is connecting service with users, who obtain experience via sub-brands, and forms overall perception of the functional and emotional quality of service and brand.

4.2 Summary and Analysis

In consideration of the above ways, a model of building service brand (see Fig. 8) is as follows with three stages:

1. Enterprise leaders, as the front-runner of brand building, position the core value of the total brand. The value of service can be represented by care, response, use and experience, and according to these elements, the total brand is built. Guangzhou Baiyun Airport has established the general brand of "Cordial Service" with "cordial, warm and natural" service as the core value, deepening the total brand from BI and VI, including the five dimensions of personnel, space, process, equipment and information.
2. The internal construction and external construction of sub-brands are carried out respectively according to the brand value transmitted by the total brand. Employees are participants with their professional and psychological elements to build and perform industry brands. Baiyun Airport's main service departments are namely, Airport Terminal 1, Terminal 2, passenger bridge, security inspection, customer service and transfer departments, along with a total of 6 sub-brands, namely the brand image, slogan, vision and development strategy. Customers are the co-creators of brand building, who can enjoy a good experience when user brand manages to consider the function and psychological elements. Baiyun Airport has targeted 7 types of user sub-brands for 7 groups of specific passengers, namely, children, passengers insensitive to technology, transfer passengers, tourists, time-sensitive passengers, the elderly and passengers on their first flight. The hub has provided personalized names, slogans, brand images, business lines and service lines, vision and development strategies for the above sub-brands.
3. In terms of brand building, enterprise leaders, employees and customers, as the main roles, share corresponding relations. Leaders establish brand value and empower employees to participate in brand building. Employees, as brand communicators, influence customers. Out of their own needs and brand experience, customers will have feedback to the whole service system, based on which leaders and employees

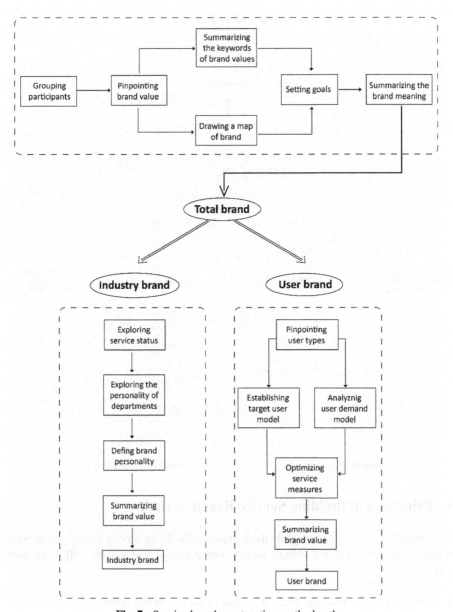

Fig. 7. Service brand construction method path

improve the brand further. All levels of brands maintain the same value and diversity at the same time, and have corresponding sub-brands for different roles and different scenes.

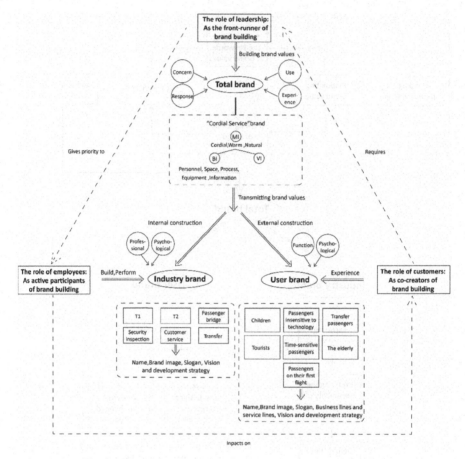

Fig. 8. Brand building model of service system under multi-role.

5   Principles of Building Service Brand System

Through this research, we integrate the methods of building service brand system with multiple roles to form the overall service brand design and get the following four principles:

1. Value-centered principle. The core value of service brand reflects the essence and positioning of brand, which is a competitive advantage uneasy to be imitate. Brand value can mirror the uniqueness and culture of the enterprise and enhance customers' cognition and loyalty. The core value of service brand requires stability. If it changes frequently, it will confuse employees and customers. The concept of cordial, warm and natural service underpins the process of building all the brands of Baiyun Airport, serving as a stable cornerstone for specific practice.
2. Consistency. Brand, essentially as a commitment, must be consistent in communications. To that end, the brand value should be taken as a gene in the process of

building the service brand. In addition, we should also establish a complete service system with a brand management organization encompassing unified instructions, coordinated department and efficiency. In this way, the consistency of the service brand can be guaranteed.

3. Diversity and unity. Due to the large number of roles and stakeholders involved, it calls for consistency of internal and external communication. The difficulty of service branding lies in controlling and managing the impact of human. Baiyun Airport allows stakeholders to participate in building service brand, especially to lead employees to identify with brand value and present motivations in practices. Meanwhile, enterprises should control the information transmitted by multiple touchpoints. Unified brand management can improve the customer experience.

4. Extendibility. The process of building service brand is not static with the change of environment and the needs of stakeholders, thus leading to further requirements that enterprises should have a holistic view to regularly evaluate the brand and adjust the service quality, experience and relationship [26]. Holding the principle of extending the brand constantly to keep the whole service brand alive, so that customers can recognize the brand and gradually form loyalty.

6   Summary

To sum up, this paper takes Guangzhou Baiyun Airport service brand building as a case to explore the model of complex service brand system building with multiple roles. The model includes the establishment of a general brand, from which sub-brands are extended. Under this circumstance, it not only maintains the consistency of brand value, but also preserves diversity out of different situations and with multiple roles. In the process of building service brand, enterprise leaders, employees and customers are involved as the main participants, and according to their characteristics achieve appropriate positioning.

As an exploratory study, the model proposed verifies the effectiveness with actual cases, which can enhance the depth and abundance of the research. However, there are many categories of service industry with a large gap in between. More cases can be combined as planned to verify the general applicability of the model in the future.

References

1. Berry, L.L.: Cultivating service brand equity. J. Acad. Market. Sci. 28(1), 128–138 (2000)
2. de Chernatony, L., Cottam, S., Segal-Horn, S.: Communicating services brands' values internally and externally. Serv. Ind. J. 26(8), 819–836 (2006)
3. de Chernatony, L., Segal-Horn, S.: Building on services characteristics to develop successful services brands. J. Mark. Manag. 17(7–8), 645–669 (2001)
4. Geng, P.M.: Research on brand cultivation of service enterprises. Market Mod. J. 02, 136–137 (2009)
5. Cheng, M., Wu, Z.M.: A review of western service brand research. Foreign Econ. Manage. 28(05), 53–60 (2006)
6. de Chernatony L., Segal-Horn S.: The criteria for successful services brands. Eur. J. Market. 37(7–8) (2003)

7. Brodie, R.J., Whittome, J.R.M., Brush, G.J.: Investigating the service brand: a customer value perspective. J. Bus. Res. **62**(3), 345–355 (2009)
8. Skaalsvik, H., Olsen, B.: Service branding: suggesting an interactive model of service brand development. Kybernetes **43**(8), 1209–1223 (2014)
9. Grnroos, C.: Service Management and Marketing: A Customer Relationships Management Approach. Wiley, London (2000)
10. O'Cass, A., Grace, D.: Exploring consumer experiences with a service brand. J. Product Brand Manage. **13**(4), 257–268 (2004)
11. de Chernatony, L.: Brand management through narrowing the gap between brand identity and brand reputation. J. Mark. Manag. **15**, 157–179 (1999)
12. de Chernatony, L.: A model for strategically building brands. J. Brand Manag. **9**(1), 32–44 (2001)
13. Muniz, A.M., O'Guinn, T.: Brand community. J. Consum. Res. **27**(4), 412–432 (2001)
14. Brodie, R.J.: From goods to service branding: an integrative perspective. Mark. Theory **9**(1), 103–107 (2009)
15. Manzini E.: Design, When Everybody Designs: An Introduction to Design for Social Innovation. The MIT Press, Cambridge (2015)
16. Shu, H.M., Gong, M.S., Liu, S.Q.: Role-playing strategy of service system in the perspective of role interaction. Packag. Eng. **38**(24), 166–170 (2017)
17. Fan, X.C.: Customer experience-driven service brand building. Nankai Bus. Rev. **4**(6), 16–20 (2001)
18. Merz, M.A., He, Y., Vargo, S.L.: The evolving brand logic: a service-dominant logic perspective. J. Acad. Mark. Sci. **37**(3), 328–344 (2009)
19. McDonald, H.B., de Chernatony, L., Harris, F.: Corporate marketing and service brands– moving beyond the fast- moving consumer goods model. Eur. J. Mark. **35**(3–4), 335–353 (2001)
20. Mosley, R.W.: Customer experience, organisational culture and the employer brand. J. Brand Manag. **15**(2), 123–134 (2007)
21. Sarker, M., Mohd-Any, A.A., Kamarulzaman, Y.: Validating a consumer–based service brand equity (CBSBE) model in the airline industry. J. Retail. Consum. Serv. **59** (2020)
22. Dall'Olmo, R.F., de Chernatony, L.: The service brand as a relationship builder. J. Brand Manage. (11), 137–150 (2000)
23. Urde, M., Baumgarth, C., Merrilees, B.: Brand orientation and market orientation—from alternatives to synergy. J. Bus. Res. **66**(1), 13–20 (2013)
24. Zhang, H., Bai, C.H., Lu, H.L.: Major participants and their roles in internal services branding: the hotel industry as an example. Tour. Tribune **29**(05), 58–67 (2014)
25. de Chernatony, L., Drury, S., Segal-Horn, S.: Building a services brand: stages, people and orientations. Serv. Ind. J. **23**(3), 1–21 (2003)
26. Shang, Y.Q., Zhu, H.L.: The building path of strong service brand. China Bus. Market **29**(03), 94–100 (2015)

Analysis and Design of Household Intelligent Planting Products Based on Hall Three-Dimensional Structure

Wei Xiong[1](✉), Zhengli Zhang[1], Yi Liu[2], and Zhen Liu[1]

[1] School of Design, South China University of Technology, Guangzhou 510006, People's Republic of China
[2] Guangdong Provincial Key Laboratory of Innovation and Applied Research on Industry Design, Guangzhou Academy of Fine Arts, Guangzhou 510220, People's Republic of China

Abstract. In this paper, Hall three-dimensional structure model has been applied in the design of household intelligent planting products. There are some short-comings in the current household intelligent planting products, which can not well meet the needs of users, and the user experience needs to be improved. Therefore, in order to establish a complete design process of household intelligent planting products, optimize the design steps and improve the design efficiency, Hall three-dimensional structure theory is used as a guide in this study, and a design model of household intelligent planting products is proposed, which is composed of three dimensions: knowledge, time and logic. In general, this study is based on the guidance of Hall three-dimensional structure theory, and takes improving user interaction experience as the core, and Kano model and AHP as tools to carry out the design practice of household intelligent planting products. Finally, an intelligent planting product and matching software were proposed, which can help improve user experience and satisfaction in the planting process.

Keywords: Product design · Hall three-dimensional structure theory · Home environment · Intelligent planting · User evaluation

1 Introduction

With the development of urbanization and the increase of population density, the per capita green area decreases year by year. Urban residents' aesthetic and emotional needs for natural scenery have led to the rapid development of home gardening. The development of various cultivation techniques makes it possible to grow plants intelligently, which provides more convenient conditions for the construction of urban ecological civilization. Putting ornamental plants in the home environment has become the hobby of many people, and various ornamental plants have gradually are regarded as an important decorative element in the home environment. However, the existing household intelligent planting products in the market have been found to have some problems such as single shape and thin function, which bring certain difficulties for users to successfully complete the planting of plants. This paper aims to propose a standardized intelligent planting

© Springer Nature Switzerland AG 2021
M. M. Soares et al. (Eds.): HCII 2021, LNCS 12780, pp. 121–131, 2021.
https://doi.org/10.1007/978-3-030-78224-5_9

product design process based on hall three-dimensional structure theory and home environment. Through this process the designer can adjust the design work according to the orderly steps in time and complete the design task at a higher level.

2 System Engineering Methodology

Hall three-dimensional structure was proposed by A.D. Hall, an American systems engineering scholar, in 1969 to optimize systems engineering practice. It consists of three dimensions, namely time dimension, logic dimension and knowledge dimension, and its goal is to define work objectives to achieve optimal results [1].

Hall 3D structure model has been applied to the design of related products by many researchers, and some research results have been achieved. Zhang R et al. [2], by building a Hall three-dimensional structure model of the main furniture for growing children, transformed various design tasks into multiple nodes to achieve the design objectives in an orderly manner. Zheng Y et al. [3] used Hall three-dimensional structure for reference to conduct logical analysis and construction of the wearable intelligent products, making the design process proceed in an orderly manner and improving the design efficiency.

On the whole, Hall three-dimensional structure is a method to manage design logically and sequentially and solve problems integrally by summarizing all kinds of knowledge [4]. Therefore, this paper attempts to introduce the Hall three-dimensional structure into the design and development process of household intelligent planting products, so that the design process can be systematically promoted, the design level can be effectively improved.

3 Hall Three-Dimensional Structural Model of Household Intelligent Planting Products

3.1 Time Dimension

Firstly, the time dimension of the design project, which reflects the sequence of each design step in the design process, is established. The traditional Hall three-dimensional structure can be divided into seven stages from planning to updating in time dimension [1]. In this design project, considering that the design task involves the professional knowledge of plant planting and cultivation, and the final product is realized in the form of combination of software and hardware in the preliminary design conception, additional technical preparation and matching APP design stage are added to ensure the smooth development of the subsequent design. As a result, This design project is implemented in seven stages, including market and user survey, technical preparation, scheme design, scheme selection, matching APP design, product production and product update iteration.

3.2 Logical Dimension

Logical dimension refers to the system analysis thinking and design steps followed in each stage of the design process [5]. It is a dimension oriented by solving problems and guided by logical analysis. When constructing the logical dimension of this design project, it is divided into seven stages, which are design background investigation, clear design requirements, collection of design data, proposal of design scheme, evaluation of design scheme, implementation and update. Moreover, the logical dimension and the time dimension are consistent in development. For example, the time dimension develops from the stage of market and user research to the stage of technical preparation, and the logical dimension correspondingly presents the stage from clear design requirements to design data collection. However, in logic dimension, the design of the supporting APP is also included in the stage of design proposal, while the subsequent evaluation stage is to judge both the physical design and the design of the APP. The design of physical products and APP is sequential in time dimension, but parallel in logical dimension. Both dimensions end up with production and renewal.

3.3 Knowledge Dimension

The knowledge dimension is not linear as the logic dimension and the time dimension. It is called at any time according to the requirements of the work steps. It has the flexibility and comprehensiveness of technology application. Reasonable use of knowledge can ensure the rationality of design and production.

In this system, the knowledge dimension can be divided into two aspects: on the one hand, it is related to plant cultivation technology and knowledge, which has a strong professional nature, covering soilless cultivation technology, medium water and fertilizer monitoring technology, etc. This part of knowledge reserve needs to be realized through the technical preparation stage in the time dimension. On the other hand, it is related to the knowledge needed for the design work, such as engineering technology, social science and design theory. In these two parts, there is no direct connection between the knowledge points. All kinds of knowledge can be reasonably applied to each step under the guidance of Hall three-dimensional structure, and the whole design process can be ensured to complete in an orderly and efficient way.

4   Specific Design Process

4.1 Market and User Research

In the time dimension, the market and user research is the first stage of the design project. Market and user information is collected at this stage, which is then further analyzed and refined to obtain the overall design purpose. In the logical dimension, this step is divided into the investigation of design background and the definition of design requirements. Its significance is to point out the direction for the subsequent steps such as design proposal and design evaluation. In addition, this stage needs to be supported by user research and user psychological knowledge in the knowledge dimension, and at the same time, certain data processing ability is required to sort out and summarize the collected information.

First of all, several existing household intelligent planting products which are popular in the market are selected as comparison objects. The products' functions, loss of functions, other shortcomings, and technical rationale were compared.

The comparison details are shown in Table 1. It can be found that these products can provide basic functions to ensure plant growth to a certain extent, but at the same time, there are some functional deficiencies. The missing functions of each product are different. In order to clarify which functions are necessary, user evaluation will be carried out in the next step to summarize and rank the functions of household intelligent planting products.

Table 1. Comparison of existing products

Name	Function	Loss of function	Other shortcomings	Technology
Haier intelligent planting box	Simulate sunlight, provide soilless cultivation function	Monitor the growing environment	Not suitable for home environment modeling	Sunlight simulation, soilless cultivation
Xiaomi smart flower pot	Monitor soil moisture and fertilizer and alert on your mobile phone	Simulate sunlight	/	EC and pH sensing, Internet of Things
HuiU planter	Simulate sunlight and monitor illumination	Monitor soil moisture and fertilizer	Must be connected to the wired power supply, assembly trouble	Sunlight simulation, Internet of Things
iGrow intelligent brightening flowerpots	Simulate sunlight	Monitor soil moisture,fertilizer and illumination	/	Sunlight simulation

The user requirements are sorted through the Kano model. First, preliminary questionnaire survey, in-depth interview and other research methods are used to collect preliminary user survey data. The functional requirements of users are sorted out and summarized, as shown in Table 2.

Then, the requirements are classified and integrated through questionnaires combined with Kano model, and the better-worse coefficient is calculated according to the questionnaire results, indicating which functions can increase user satisfaction and which functions can reduce user satisfaction [6]. Accordingly, the classification results of user requirements are obtained, as shown in Fig. 1.

As can be seen from Fig. 1, the focus needs of users are mainly in the aspects of convenient planting of plants and embellishment of home environment. Since the cultivation of ornamental plants is a behavior with a more aesthetic nature, most users emphasize that the overall device can ensure the good growth of plants and at the same time have ornamental and aesthetic value. In a word, the follow-up design should firstly monitor the plant growth environment, provide light and moisture and other functions

Table 2. Scoring result

Number	Function	Number	Function
1	Easy to operate	11	Time-saving
2	Provide illumination	12	Noiseless
3	Provide water	13	Powerfrugal
4	Monitoring the growth environment	14	Small size
5	Monitor growth	15	Safe
6	Record growth	16	Allow replacement of plants
7	Appreciate the plant	17	Clean
8	Allow replacement of plants	18	Portable
9	Decorative interior space	19	Easy to maintenance
10	Remote control	20	Free switch

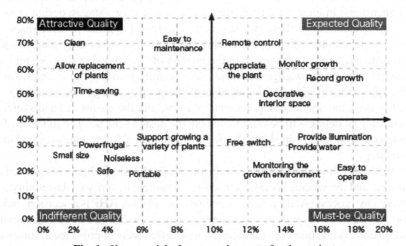

Fig. 1. Kano model of user requirements for the project

to conveniently complete plant planting and maintenance. Its adornment property and ornamental property is also considered to be a very important requirement.

Through the above analysis, the positioning and direction of the design can be clarified, and the design can be carried out in a targeted way, so that the user's acceptance and liking of the final design scheme will be improved.

4.2 Technical Analysis

Technical analysis is the second stage of the time dimension. Correspondingly, it is embodied in the third stage in the logical dimension, namely the collection of design data. In this stage, the information and data related to intelligent culture technology are collected and summarized, so as to ensure that the gaps in botanical knowledge in the knowledge dimension are filled. Without the data obtained from the technical analysis, the subsequent stages of the time dimension would not proceed smoothly. On the basis of these data, the technical feasibility of subsequent scheme design will be guaranteed in the logical dimension.

As can be seen from the literature and other materials, in recent years, with the development of new agriculture, intelligent cultivation technology has been widely studied. It mainly includes soilless cultivation technology, plant block seedling cultivation technology, water solution monitoring technology, red and blue light regulation plant growth technology, etc. Potted plants can grow healthily with these techniques when left unattended. Therefore, the comprehensive application of these technologies in the scheme design will be helpful to the realization of related functions and design.

4.3 Scheme Design and User Evaluation Centered Scheme Selection

The design of the scheme and the selection of the scheme are the third and fourth stages in the time dimension. These two stages are almost equivalent in terms of time and logic dimensions; In logic dimension, they are regarded as two stages: design proposal and design evaluation. In these two stages, the design of specific product shape and function is carried out at first, and then the best scheme is selected by the evaluation method centered on user evaluation. In the process of design and evaluation, all kinds of knowledge in the knowledge dimension will be fully invoked. For example, in the specific appearance design, the knowledge of design psychology and modeling will be used to meet the aesthetic requirements of users, and the means of hand-sketching and computer modeling will be used to display the design scheme; The function of the product needs to be determined by referring to the botanical knowledge acquired in the previous step.

On the basis of the obtained design scheme, the final design scheme is screened and determined, and the scheme is evaluated before refinement to verify its desirability. analytic hierarchy process (AHP) is used to evaluate the scheme. AHP is a decision-making method for quantitative analysis of qualitative indicators. By introducing quantitative evaluation criteria into qualitative indicators, it can effectively improve the accuracy and scientificity of decision making [7]. The detailed analysis process is as follows.

First, the factors considered in the design process are divided into four aspects according to the difference in nature: functionality, technical feasibility, integrity and aesthetics, as shown in Table 3.

In addition, 10 horticultural industry workers and 10 designers were invited to compare, discuss and score the above four factors according to the requirements of Table 3, and then the obtained data were sorted out.

The numbers entered in the table are determined by the difference in importance of the two factors. When the importance of the column factor is the same as that of the row factor, fill in 1, and in the same way, the intensity of importance can be divided into five levels: equally important, slightly important, generally important, relatively important and very important. The corresponding Numbers are 1, 3, 5, 7 and 9 respectively. Fill in 2, 4, 6, 8 if there is a situation between the two levels. If the opposite happens, that is, when the row factor is more important than the column factor, fill in the reciprocal of the

Table 3. Design evaluation system property index

	Indicator	Particulars
Evaluation system	Functionality	Easy to operate
		Load the plant
		Provide illumination
		Provide water&fertilizer
		Monitor growth
		Provide water&fertilizer
		Record
		Cultivation of a variety of plants is allowed
	Technical feasibility	The material process conforms to the production standard
		The structure conforms to the existing production technology
		The technology is ready
	Aesthetics	Do not cover up the form of plants, easy to ornamental plants
		Blend in and decorate the home environment to a certain extent
	Integrity	Help with plant selection and purchase
		Covers the entire life cycle of the plant

corresponding figure, such as 1/3, 1/5, etc. Finally, according to the weight calculation formula, the general scoring situation of each table is obtained as shown in Table 4.

Table 4. Scoring result

Importance evaluation	Functionality	Technical feasibility	Aesthetics	Integrity
Functionality	1	4	5	3
Technical feasibility	0.25	1	2	0.25
Aesthetics	0.2	0.5	1	0.2
Integrity	0.33	4	5	1

This table is taken as a reference and calculated according to the weight calculation formula

$$W_i = \frac{1}{n} \sum_{j=1}^{n} \frac{a_{ij}}{\sum_{k=1}^{n} a_{kj}} \tag{1}$$

Then we can get the weight value of each index, as shown in Table 5.

Table 5. Weight of 4 indicators

Importance evaluation	Functionality W1	Technical feasibility W2	Aesthetics W3	Integrity W4
Weighted value	0.5101	0.1139	0.3043	0.0717

In order to verify the rationality of the weight table, consistency test is carried out.

First, the maximum eigenvalue of the matrix is calculated. According to the calculation formula of maximum eigenvalue

$$\lambda_{max} = \frac{1}{n} \sum_{i=1}^{n} \frac{\sum_{j=1}^{n} a_{ij}\omega_j}{\omega_i} \qquad (2)$$

The maximum eigenvalue of the matrix is obtained: $\lambda_{max} = 4.1930$.

Next, its consistency index is calculated

$$C.I. = \frac{\lambda_{max} - n}{n - 1} = 0.061 \qquad (3)$$

The reference table shows that the average random consistency index $R.I. = 0.90$.

Therefore, the test coefficient can be calculated

$$C.R. = \frac{C.I.}{R.I.} \approx 0.068 < 0.1 \qquad (4)$$

After calculation, it can be concluded that the test coefficient of this table is about 0.068, which passes the consistency test.

Next, the participants were asked to rate each indicator again. Five evaluation indicators were established, which were very good, good, general, poor and very poor, respectively, represented by 2, 1, 0, -1 and -2. The obtained data are normalized to obtain the fuzzy evaluation matrix of the design:

$$R = \begin{Bmatrix} 0.50 \ 0.30 \ 0.00 \ 0.10 \ 0.00 \\ 0.10 \ 0.40 \ 0.10 \ 0.20 \ 0.10 \\ 0.20 \ 0.40 \ 0.20 \ 0.20 \ 0.00 \\ 0.30 \ 0.30 \ 0.10 \ 0.20 \ 0.10 \end{Bmatrix} \qquad (5)$$

The matrix is calculated using the weighted average type of fuzzy operator, the final draw five evaluation set weights are: 0.378, 0.364, 0.081, 0.157, 0.020. It can be seen from the above table that the best weight value in the five comments is the highest (0.378), followed by the best weight value (0.363). Combined with the maximum membership rule, it can be known that the final comprehensive evaluation result is "very good" and the overall scheme is highly satisfactory. Therefore, this design will be regarded as the final design for further improvement. In addition, it can be seen that the evaluation degree of completeness in the scheme is relatively general, because the design of the supporting APP has not been completed yet, and the design of this part will be strengthened in the next step.

4.4 Design of Supporting APP

As the fifth stage of the time dimension, the design of supporting APP can complete the design scheme, which is complementary to the design of the physical product obtained in the fourth stage, and can also prepare for the next stage. In the logical dimension, this stage is completed by repeating the design proposal and design evaluation. The design knowledge of interaction design and interface design in the knowledge dimension is invoked, and the page prototype is made based on the function classification and ordering obtained in the early stage, so as to ensure that the supporting APP can provide users with planting functions in all aspects in combination with the physical design. Some of the resulting high-fidelity prototypes are shown in Fig. 2.

Fig. 2. APP design

4.5 Final Design Project Introduction

To sum up, the final overall design scheme is shown in Fig. 3.

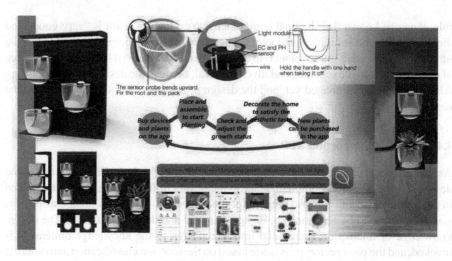

Fig. 3. Final design

The final design project is composed of hardware and APP. The hardware part is mainly composed of vertical bracket and modular planting cup. The whole bracket is connected to the power supply, and the implant cup can be connected to the power supply for operation. A single implant cup is composed of light module, EC (aqueous solution electrical conduction) sensor and pH sensor, etc. Such combination simulates light and can monitor all indexes of aqueous solution. After transplanting, the plant can be fixed in the planting cup and cultivated soilless with nutrient solution. Users can easily take the planting cup for observation or other operations such as adding water, changing water, etc. The software is operated mainly through the mobile APP. Users can check the water, nutrition and light of plants at any time.

The main difference between this design and existing products lies in the vertical design of the scheme and the design of the planting cup module. The vertical design can not only cover the form of the plant itself, but also save interior space; Combined with the planting cup module, the user's operating costs can also be reduced. Convenience and freedom of operation are provided by the planting cup. Multiple planting cups can be randomly matched and combined to create personalized planting combinations, and the fun of using the product will be enhanced.

The overall scheme is easy to operate, and the overall shape is mainly made of matte plastic and translucent acrylic materials, with black, white and gray tones to create a refined visual sense, which can be well integrated into the daily home environment.

4.6 Product Production and Update

As the final stages, the production and update of the product are basically consistent in terms of logical dimension and time dimension. In the production process of products, technology, cost, time and other factors need to be considered comprehensively; the support APP also needs to be developed synchronously. After the product launches, user feedback will be collected for subsequent optimization and improvement.

5   Conclusion

In order to improve the use experience of household intelligent planting products, Hall three-dimensional structure theory is used in the planning and design process, and a series of user evaluation methods including Kano model and AHP are used in the analysis of the design process. The final design results show that Hall three-dimensional structure theory can guide the design process well, and the design based on user evaluation can also improve the use experience of the product.

References

1. Lu, C., Guan, S.: User participatory design model research based on hall three dimensional structure. In: Chung, WonJoon, Shin, C.S. (eds.) AHFE 2018. AISC, vol. 790, pp. 92–101. Springer, Cham (2019). https://doi.org/10.1007/978-3-319-94601-6_11
2. Zhang, R., Sun, W., Zhang, R., Deng, T.: Research on the growth model of children's furniture design based on hall three-dimensional structure. Packag. Eng. **39**, 200–202 (2018)
3. Zheng, Y., Peng, H.: Analysis of the design system of wearable intelligent products based on hall three-dimensional structure industrial design **04**, 134–135 (2019)
4. Xie, J., Xiong, Z.: Analysis and research of electric bicycle design based on hall three-dimensional structure. In: Journal of Physics. Conference Series 1, vol. 1631 (2020)
5. Wang, H., Yu, Y., Li, M., Wang, R., Zhu, B.: Research on industrial design model based on hall three-dimensional structure. Chin. J. Med. Libr. Inf. Sci. **33**, 76–79 (2012)
6. McGoldrick, P.J., Nieroda, M.E.: Prioritizing retail CSR strategies: developing and applying the Kano approach. In: Obal, M.W., Krey, N., Bushardt, C. (eds.) Let's Get Engaged! Crossing the Threshold of Marketing's Engagement Era. DMSPAMS, pp. 821–822. Springer, Cham (2016). https://doi.org/10.1007/978-3-319-11815-4_240
7. Imran, M., Agha, M.H., Ahmed, W., Sarkar, B., Ramzan, M.B.: Simultaneous customers and supplier's prioritization: an AHP-based fuzzy inference decision support system (AHP-FIDSS). Int. J. Fuzzy Syst. **22**(8), 2625–2651 (2020). https://doi.org/10.1007/s40815-020-00977-9

Lacquer Jewelry Design of Shanghai Style Based on User Perception Preference

Yalan Yu and RongRong Fu[✉]

College of Art Design and Media, East China University of Science and Technology,
Shanghai, China

Abstract. Shanghai style lacquer art (A kind of Chinese traditional lacquer art integrated with the regional cultural characteristics of Shanghai) is used to make daily furniture and commodity, but as a living art, it can also be extended to the fashion jewelry design field. At present, Shanghai style Lacquer ware is facing the dilemma of the disconnection between product design and contemporary aesthetics, and It is difficult to integrate into modern life. For the Shanghai style lacquer jewelry design should match contemporary aesthetic and emotional needs, the paper uses EEG Muse technology and eye movement technology to obtain the signal data of user preference evaluation, combined with questionnaire survey, the user's perception preference for lacquer jewelry modeling is objectively obtained from both physiological and psychological perspectives, position the jewelry design form that meets the user's preference, and then assist the subsequent jewelry design practice. The final design evaluation verifies that this method can effectively improve user satisfaction in shanghai lacquer jewelry design, providing methods for the application of Shanghai style lacquer art in modern product design.

Keywords: Shanghai style lacquer art · Jewelry design · User perception preference · Orthogonal experiment · Muse experiment · Eye movement experiment

1 Introduction

As a kind of Chinese traditional lacquer art, the lacquer industry in Shanghai integrated Shanghai culture constantly in its development and has formed its unique style and pattern [1]. The profound cultural deposits of Shanghai style lacquer art of "color reflects all things, color implies all things" are worthy of our in-depth excavation and inheritance. In the research process, I found that product categories and decorative patterns of Shanghai style lacquer ware was pretty traditional, and lacked novelty. Both aesthetics and patterns are out of line with contemporary aesthetics and are difficult to integrate into modern people's living conditions. The key to the development of traditional lacquer art is to enter the life of modern people. When it is far away from people's life, lacquer art will lose the soil of survival [2]. In another perspective, lacquer art has been used in jewelry design for a long time. The combination of lacquer art and jewelry design has great advantages. While giving jewelry design more development space, it also provides some good ideas for traditional lacquer art to integrate into modern design [3]. To design Shanghai lacquer jewelry in accord with the aesthetics and emotional needs of modern people, this paper starts with the study of user's perception preference for lacquer jewelry, uses EEG technology and eye movement technology to explore user's preference and the tendency for lacquer jewelry modeling from a more physiologically objective perspective, and locates the appearance design form of lacquer jewelry in accord with user'spreference, to assist Shanghai lacquer jewelry design practice.

2   User Perception Preference of Lacquer Jewelry

2.1   Modeling Perception and Emotional Elements in Jewelry Design

As a product that people wear everyday, modern jewelry reflects the user's unique personality and fashion concept. For the user, the jewelry not only is an ornament but also bears the user's affection. As a bridge between users and products, emotions accomplish the uniqueness of each work [4]. It has become a more significant direction in modern jewelry design to be people-oriented and pays more attention to people's physiological and psychological needs. Modeling, material, and color are three important parts in the visual expression of jewelry, which have a direct impact on the generation of user emotion, and are important contents in jewelry emotional design [5]. User perceived preference means the degree of user perception of product modeling, which is influenced by the modeling and functional factors of the product itself, the emotional and aesthetic needs of users, and other factors [6]. For jewelry design, the user's perception preference is reflected in the preference of the product's shape, color, surface texture, and other different perception factors. The more obvious the user's perceived preference is, the more compatible the product's modeling design is with the user's emotional needs, which means the user's satisfaction is higher, and it is easier to cause purchase or choice behavior.

2.2   Evaluation of User-Perceived Preference of Lacquer Jewelry

According to the basic characteristics of modern jewelry design, this paper defines six groups of user preference evaluation words of lacquer jewelry as aesthetics, practicability, commerciality, uniqueness, artistry, and culture, respectively evaluating the aesthetic degree of lacquer jewelry, applicability in life, commercialization potential, uniqueness of products, the artistic appeal of products, and the perception of lacquer art culture in jewelry [7]. Based on the six evaluation degrees as the standard to measure the user's perception preference, starting from the jewelry modeling, material, color, decorative design elements, this paper investigates the target consumer groups' perception preference for lacquer jewelry appearance design, and locates the jewelry design form that meets the user's preference, to assist the subsequent jewelry design practice.

3 User Preference Acquisition Experiment of Lacquer Jewelry Based on EEG Technology

3.1 Identify the Target User Groups for Lacquer Jewelry

This paper chooses women aged 20−35 as the target group. Above all, this group accounts for about 23.61% of the national population, which is a large consumer group. As one generation growing up in a rather rich environment, the consumer behavior of consumer groups between 20 and 35 has distinct features: refuse to follow the crowd and pursue individuality; have a strong consumption desire and seek for high quality [8]. And relevant researches show that this group has more consumption desire about jewelry products which manifest their personality. And lacquer art can just give jewelry design a unique temperament and cultural connotation, which is in line with the demand of the millennials for jewelry. Because women's demand for jewelry is far higher than men's, this paper sets the target group of lacquer art jewelry as women aged 20−35.

3.2 Summarize the Design Elements and Forms of Lacquer Jewelry

Through the network, magazines, and books, we collected 100 kinds of lacquer ware jewelry. The works come from college teachers and students, independent jewelry designers, jewelry studios, fashion and luxury brands, etc. It can be summarized into four design elements, shape, material, color, and decorative pattern. According to the morphological analysis method [9], the design forms included in the shape can be divided into three types: circular, polygonal geometry, and natural bionics. The design forms of surface materials can be divided into four types: paint, paint and metal, paint and diamond/pearl, paint and mica/shell. The colors can be divided into three types: cold color, warm color, and no color. Decorative patterns can be divided into three forms: realistic, freehand, and geometric. To eliminate the interference of color, gray-scale photos are used in EEG experiments, so the color is not considered in the selection of experimental samples. At the end of the EEG experiment, an eye movement experiment was used to explore the subjects' preference for the color of lacquer jewelry. Each group of jewelry samples showed three forms of gray, warm, and cold color, and the selection of the subjects was counted to determine their color tendency for jewelry (Table 1).

3.3 Obtaining Experimental Samples by Orthogonal Test

To simplify the experiment times and improve the experiment efficiency, the orthogonal experiment method of SPSSAU is used to reconstruct the inductive design elements, and the orthogonal design table L12 (3 × 4 × 3) is obtained. According to the orthogonal design table, the representative product samples meeting the conditions are selected, as shown in Table 2.

Table 1. Design elements and forms of lacquer jewelry.

Design elements	Shape A			Material B				Decorative pattern C		
Design form	Circular	Polygonal-geometry	Natural-bionics	Paint	Paint and metal	Paint and diamond/p-earl	Paint and mica/shell	Realistic	Freehand	Geometric
Number	A_1	A_2	A_3	B_1	B_2	B_3	B_4	C_1	C_2	C_3

Table 2. Lacquer jewelry samples.

Number	1	2	3	4	5	6
Sample image						
Design form	$A_1B_1C_1$	$A_2B_2C_1$	$A_3B_3C_1$	$A_3B_4C_2$	$A_2B_4C_3$	$A_1B_3C_3$
Number	7	8	9	10	11	12
Sample image						
Design form	$A_1B_2C_2$	$A_2B_1C_2$	$A_3B_1C_3$	$A_3B_2C_3$	$A_2B_3C_2$	$A_1B_4C_1$

3.4 Experimental Design

To objectively obtain the target user's perception of lacquer jewelry, the experiment is divided into two parts: EEG Muse experiment and eye movement experiment. Guided by the principle of EEG and eye movement technology, record the eye movement behavior data and EEG data of target users for lacquer jewelry samples, and calculate the mean value of experimental indicators of each design form (the calculation formula is as follows: formula 1–10) [10]. Through the numerical value of the experimental index, the user's preference for the four design features of lacquer jewelry samples in color, shape, material, and decoration is obtained.

$$A_1 = \frac{\text{Experimaent index(sample1 + sample6 + sample7 + sample12)}}{4} \tag{1}$$

$$A_2 = \frac{\text{Experimaent index(sample2 + sample5 + sample8 + sample11)}}{4} \tag{2}$$

$$A_3 = \frac{\text{Experimaent index(sample3 + sample4 + sample8 + sample10)}}{4} \tag{3}$$

$$B_1 = \frac{\text{Experimaent index(sample1 + sample8 + sample9)}}{3} \tag{4}$$

$$B_2 = \frac{\text{Experimaent vindex(sample2 + sample7 + sample10)}}{3} \tag{5}$$

$$B_3 = \frac{\text{Experimaent index(sample2 + sample7 + sample10)}}{3} \tag{6}$$

$$B_4 = \frac{\text{Experimaent index}(\text{sample4} + \text{sample5} + \text{sample12})}{3} \tag{7}$$

$$C_1 = \frac{\text{Experimaent index}(\text{sample1} + \text{sample2} + \text{sample3} + \text{sample12})}{4} \tag{8}$$

$$C_2 = \frac{\text{Experimaent index}(\text{sample4} + \text{sample7} + \text{sample8} + \text{sample11})}{4} \tag{9}$$

$$C_3 = \frac{\text{Experimaent index}(\text{sample5} + \text{sample6} + \text{sample9} + \text{sample10})}{4} \tag{10}$$

In the Muse experiment, 12 lacquer jewelry samples were divided into 12 groups as 12 test materials, and the EEG data of the subjects were recorded respectively; the eye movement experiment was divided into two stages. In the first stage, 12 lacquer jewelry samples were divided into three groups, with four in each group. After Latin square sorting [11], 12 test materials were made, and the eye movement data of the subjects were recorded; In the second stage, the color preference of lacquer jewelry was tested. The jewelry samples of each group are presented in three forms: gray, warm and cold. The selection of the subjects is counted to determine their color preference for jewelry.

Experimental Equipment: The EEG equipment is muse2, iPhone and Muse: Mediation & sleep app analysis software; the eye movement equipment is SMI eye tracker (eye movement tracking frequency is 60Hz) produced by SMI company of Germany, Lenovo notebook computer, begaze, iView ETG data analysis software, etc.

Participants: In this study, 30 women aged 20–35 who wear jewelry every day were selected as subjects. All the subjects voluntarily participated in the experiment. They had a good rest before the experiment, were in good mental and physical health, and had normal vision or corrected vision. To eliminate the interference, the subjects were asked to clean their hair before the experiment and keep their face without makeup.

Experimental Environment: The experiment was carried out in the laboratory with sound insulation, light insulation, and other functions. In the process of the experiment, there was no interference from other people and noise except the main test and the subjects. It was better to keep the room at a suitable temperature and humidity to feel comfortable.

The Experimental Indexes Were as Follows

① EEG Muse index: In this experiment, the three data active, neutral and calm in the Muse app was used as the experimental indexes of this Muse experiment. Among them, active, neutral, and calm refer to the activity of the human brain. The higher the active value is, the higher the arousal degree of the sample for the subject is, and the stronger the stimulation is, the more interesting the subject is; on the contrary, the higher the neutral and calm value is, the lower the arousal degree of the sample for the subject is, and the lower the interest degree of the subject for the sample is.

② Eye movement indicators: In this experiment, the total fixation duration/fixation points/first fixation duration/hot-spot graph in eye movement data are used as indicators to evaluate users' perceptual preferences [12].

Total fixation duration: In the study of product preference, it reflects the degree of preference for different regions. The longer the total fixation time is, the higher the degree of preference or interest is; Fixation points: In the study of product preference, it reflects the degree of preference for different samples. The more the total fixation times, the higher the degree of preference or interest for the sample; First fixation duration: the longer the duration of the first fixation, the stronger the salience of the target; Hot-spot map: Refers to the degree to which the subjects pay attention to a certain area in the sample. In this experiment, it is mainly used to test the user's perception preference for jewelry color.

3.5   Experimental Materials

3.5.1   Muse Experimental Materials

Twelve jewelry samples were obtained by orthogonal test.

3.5.2   Eye Movement Test Materials

Experimental materials of stage one: To avoid the cognitive overload of users, the 12 experimental samples obtained in the previous paper are divided into three groups, with 4 samples in each group. The images of each group adopt the same size, accuracy, and white background effect. The experimental materials are as follows: to eliminate the possible interference error caused by the reading order of the subjects, the Latin square method is used to arrange the position of each sample on the display screen, and all the arranged pictures are made into 12 stimulus materials (Fig. 1).

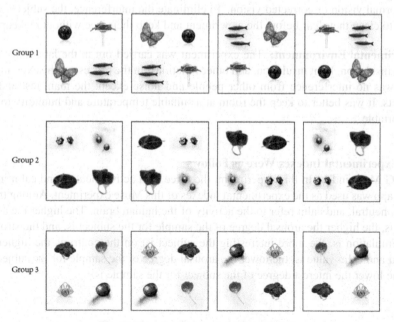

Fig. 1. Experimental materials for stage 1

The second stage of experimental materials: 12 jewelry samples are presented in three forms: gray, warm and cold. One of the stimulating materials is as follows in Table 3, and the user's choice of color in the stimulating materials is counted.

Table 3. Experimental materials for stage 1.

Color mode	D₁ Warm	D₂ Gray	D₃ Cold
Stimulus material			
User selection		D₁	

3.6 Experimental Process

3.6.1 Procedure of EEG Muse Experiment

The experiment instruction tells the subjects to perceive the lacquer jewelry picture as a whole. The computer screen first presents a white screen of 1000 ms, then presents the first stimulus material for 1 min, then presents a white screen of 1000 ms, and then presents the second stimulus material for 1 min, until the twelve stimulus materials are presented. The experimental process is shown in Fig. 2.

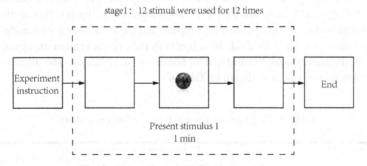

Fig. 2. Flow chart of EEG Muse experiment

3.6.2 Eye movement Experiment Process

In the first stage, the experimental instruction tells the subjects to perceive the lacquer jewelry picture as a whole, and then the cross 1000 ms will be displayed in the center of

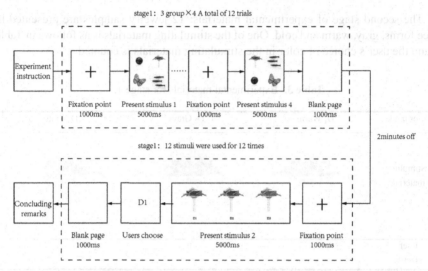

Fig. 3. Flow chart of eye movement experiment

the computer screen to guide the subjects' attention, and then the first stimulus 5000 ms, then the 1000 ms white screen, and then the second stimulus 5000 ms, until the twelve stimulus materials are presented. After resting for 10 min, the subjects entered the second stage of the experiment and then presented the first stimulus material for 5000 ms, followed by 1000 ms white screen, and then presented the second stimulus material for 5000 ms, until the twelve stimulus materials were presented (Fig. 3).

3.7 Questionnaire Investigation

To obtain the user's preference more comprehensively, this paper adds a questionnaire based on EEG and eye movement to test them subjectively. Six preference evaluation indexes were combined with 12 jewelry samples, and a questionnaire was made according to the Likert five scale method. 30 subjects in the eye movement experiment were selected for the survey, and 30 valid questionnaires were collected. The intention of the user preference component is shown in Table 4:

Table 4. Design elements and forms of lacquer jewelry.

Sample	User preference evaluation index				
	aesthetics	1	2	3	4	5
	practicability,	1	2	3	4	5
	commerciality	1	2	3	4	5
	uniqueness	1	2	3	4	5
	artistry	1	2	3	4	5
	culture	1	2	3	4	5

4   Data Analysis

4.1   Analysis of EEG Muse Data

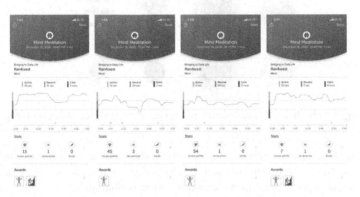

Fig. 4. Data diagram of mind mediation app

Statistics 12 jewelry samples of Muse index data and calculate the mean value, as shown in Table 3, on this basis, calculate the mean value of each design element under the three indicators, as shown in Table 4. From Table 4, we can see that the combination of design elements with the highest active index is $A_2B_2C_1$, the combination of design elements with the lowest neutral index is $A_2B_3C_2$, and the combination of design elements with the lowest calm index is $A_2B_2C_1$. Therefore, based on the results of EEG data analysis, $A_2B_2C_1$ is the best combination of design forms (Fig. 4).

Table 5. Mean value of user Muse experiment index of design elements.

Muse index	Design		
	Shape A	Material B	Decorative C
Active (sec)	17. 25	22. 33	31. 5
	23. 25	26. 67	22. 5
	20	23	16. 75
	–	18. 67	–
Neutral (sec)	33. 25	32. 33	31. 5
	31. 25	35. 67	30
	32. 75	29. 67	35. 75
	–	32	–
Calm (sec)	9. 5	9. 67	4. 75
	5. 5	5. 33	7. 5
	7. 25	7. 67	7. 5
	–	9. 33	–

4.2   Eye movement Data Analysis

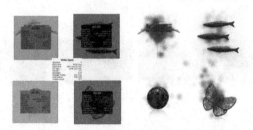

Fig. 5. The division of sample interest region and the sketch of hot spot map

Be gaze data analysis software is used to process and analyze the eye movement behavior, and the average value of each jewelry sample in three aspects of total fixation duration, fixation points, and first fixation duration is obtained. The results are shown in Table 5. On this basis, the average value of each design element under three eye movement indicators is calculated, as shown in Table 6. From Table 6, we can see that the design form combined with the highest total fixation duration index is $A_2B_4C_1$, the design form combined with the highest fixation point index is $A_2B_3C_1$, and the design form combined with the highest first fixation duration index is $A_2B_4C_1$. Therefore, based on the results of eye movement data analysis, $A_2B_4C_1$ is the best combination of design forms (Fig. 5).

Table 6. Mean value of eye movement index of design elements users.

Eye movement index	Design		
	Shape A	Material B	Decorative C
The total fixation duration/ms	2401. 60	1504. 49	2784. 89
	3223. 9	2663. 38	2564. 35
	1860. 79	2759. 59	2137. 05
	–	3054. 25	–
fixation points	5. 94	4. 76	6. 975
	8. 46	6. 91	6. 69
	5. 23	7. 36	5. 99
	–	7. 15	–
First fixation duration/ms	335. 28	307. 45	362. 56
	358. 94	357. 37	341. 42
	338. 82	354. 82	328. 74
	–	357. 68	–

The user's color preferences for lacquer jewelry samples are as follows:

From the hot-spot map, we can see that users' regions of interest are mainly concentrated in warm color jewelry samples. The statistical table of users' color preference data

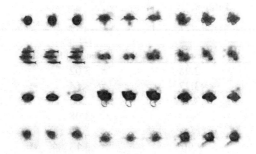

Fig. 6. Color preference hot spot map of 12 jewelry samples

shows that the mean value of D_1 warm color is 0.45, D_3 cold color is 0.37, and D_2 gray level is 0.19. Among the 12 jewelry samples, 7 samples have the highest selection ratio of D_1 warm color, especially in the jewelry samples with metal materials. Therefore, we can find that lacquer jewelry with D_1 warm color design features has higher user attention (Table 7).

Table 7. User color preference data sheet

Sample number	1	2	3	4	5	6	7	8	9	10	11	12	Mean value
D_1 Warm	0.42	0.65	0.54	0.42	0.39	0.45	0.52	0.61	0.58	0.16	0.16	0.42	0.45
D_2 Gray	0.13	0.16	0.23	0.06	0.19	0.26	0.29	0.16	0.29	0.16	0.13	0.23	0.19
D_3 Cold	0.45	0.19	0.23	0.52	0.42	0.29	0.19	0.23	0.13	0.68	0.71	0.35	0.37

4.2.1 Questionnaire Data Analysis

By processing the questionnaire data of six user preference evaluation indexes, the average value of each jewelry sample in each preference evaluation degree is calculated. The results are shown in Table 8.

From the results of the questionnaire data, it can be seen that the design form combined with the highest aesthetic value of user preference is $A_2B_2C_2$, the design form combined with the highest practicability is $A_1B_2C_2$, the design form combined with the highest commercial value is $A_2B_2C_2$, the design form combined with the highest uniqueness is $A_3B_2C_2$, the design form combined with the highest artistic value is $A_2B_2C_2$, and the design form combined with the highest cultural value is $A_2B_2C_2$. It can be seen that the user preference of lacquer jewelry with design form $A_2B_2C_2$ is relatively high, and that of jewelry with design form C_1 and C_2 is equivalent. This paper hopes that the lacquer jewelry design can carry more cultural connotation of Shanghai style lacquer art, that is, it has higher cultural perception, C_1 has higher cultural perception than C_2.

Based on the data of EEG muse, eye movement experiment, and questionnaire survey, we can find that the combination of design forms that meet the user preferences

Table 8. User color preference data sheet

User preference	Design		
	Shape A	Material B	Decorative C
aesthetics	2.98	3.02	3.03
	3.27	3.54	3.42
	3.12	2.85	2.91
	-	3.08	-
practicability,	3.98	2.67	3.09
	2.90	3.13	2.94
	2.95	2.77	2.71
	-	2.75	-
commerciality	2.72	2.64	3.07
	3.16	3.42	3.02
	3.01	2.95	2.79
	-	2.83	-
uniqueness	2.78	2.7	2.78
	2.94	3.13	3.00
	2.95	2.85	2.89
	-	2.88	-
artistry	2.87	2.82	2.96
	3.12	3.31	3.12
	2.98	3.02	2.89
	-	2.81	-
culture	2.83	2.76	3.03
	2.99	3.36	2.94
	2.79	2.63	2.64
	-	2.73	-

of the target user group is $A_2B_2C_1D_1$ or $A_2B_4C_1D_1$, that is, polygon shape, material combination of paint and metal or paint and mica shell, warm color, and the decorative pattern is concrete.

5 Lacquer Jewelry Design Practice Based on User Perception Preference

5.1 Design Scheme

The design form with the highest user preference obtained by the orthogonal experiment is integrated into the overall design of Shanghai lacquer jewelry. The whole design process is as follows (Fig. 7).

Source of inspiration: The name of the product "dark fragrance" comes from the ancient poem "remote knowledge is not snow, only dark fragrance". The design inspiration comes from "MEI LAI Zhu Ju", a masterpiece of Shanghai style high relief inlaid lacquer art. The plum blossoms inlaid with mica and Cassia obtusifolia stand out from

Fig. 7. Zhang Jun's MEI LAI Zhu Ju and its partial pictures

behind the rockery. Some of them are in full bloom, some of them are in bud, and they are as bright as moonlight. They are vivid and natural (Fig. 8).

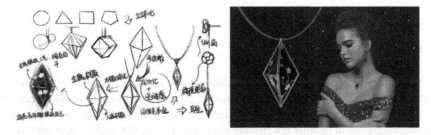

Fig. 8. Design sketch and effect picture of wearing necklace and earrings

Design Description: The whole work is based on black, supplemented by gold, white as embellishment, simple geometric modeling with the traditional plum blossom pattern, The material is painted with metal and white mica, integrated into the unique cultural connotation of Shanghai-style lacquer art, to bring users a sense of delicacy and modernity, and meet the spiritual and material needs of users.

6   Design Evaluation

Fig. 9. Design verification hot-spot map

Table 9. Mean value of user preference evaluation for design scheme

Sample	Design form	Aesthetics	Practicability	Commercial	Uniqueness	Artistry	Culture	Mean value
Design	A2B2C1D1	3.86	3.22	3.72	3.67	3.75	3.44	3.61

To verify whether the design scheme is in line with the preferences of the target users, the final design scheme is compared with three kinds of jewelry with high evaluation from the previous users. The eye movement experiment is carried out again. The hot figure is shown in Fig. 6. It can be seen from the figure that the attention of the design scheme is higher than that of the other three jewelry samples. At the same time, a 5-level satisfaction questionnaire was designed, and 15 users in the experiment were selected for investigation. The average value of user preference is shown in Table 6. According to the results of the questionnaire data, the average evaluation degree of user preference of the design scheme is higher than that of 12 lacquer jewelry samples (Fig. 9 and Table 9).

7   Conclusion

Based on the user's perceptual preference, Shanghai style lacquer jewelry is designed to meet the modern aesthetic and emotional needs. By analyzing the modeling perception and emotional information in jewelry design, the representation elements of user perception preference of lacquer jewelry are obtained. The design form of user preference evaluation is summarized by using morphological analysis method, and the experimental samples are selected by combining with orthogonal experiment method. Using EEG and eye movement technology to obtain the signal data of user preference evaluation degree, combined with questionnaire survey, the user's perception preference for lacquer jewelry modeling is objectively obtained from both physiological and psychological perspectives, so as to locate the jewelry design form. On this basis, the Shanghai lacquer jewelry design is completed. The final design evaluation verifies that this method can effectively improve the user satisfaction of Shanghai lacquer jewelry design, and provides ideas for Shanghai lacquer into modern product design.

References

1. Li, H.: Research and exploration on the development of modern lacquer industry in Shanghai. Shanghai Cult. (06), 73–82+126 (2018). [李洪忠.上海近现代漆艺产业发展考述与探究[J].上海文化,2018(06):73-82+126.]
2. Qiao, S.: Ongoing to the present age and abiding by tradition. Chinese Academy of Art (2008). [乔十光. 再论走向当代与恪守传统[C]// 中国艺术研究院, 2008.]
3. Yu, Q.: Application of traditional lacquer art in modern jewelry. Drama House (2017) (10). [余青莲. 传统漆艺在现代首饰中的应用研究[J]. 戏剧之家, 2017(10).]
4. Wu, J., Jin, H.J.: Research on the emotional expression of jewelry design. Design (2016) (019), 62–63.[吴金金, 金慧建. 首饰设计情感化表达的研究[J]. 设计, 2016, 000(019):62-63.]

5. Fu, X.: Emotion in art – emotional expression factors in modern jewelry design. Works Art (05), 32–33 (2020). [傅曦.艺术中的情感——现代珠宝首饰设计中的情感表达因素[J].艺术品鉴,2020(05):32-33.]
6. Tan, Z.Y.: Research on product conceptual design technology for user perception information. Zhejiang University (2007). [谭征宇.面向用户感知信息的产品概念设计技术研究[D]. 浙江大学, 2007.]
7. Duan, S.: Symbolic application of Han Dynasty culture in modern jewelry design. [段思萌. 汉代文化在现代首饰设计中的符号化应用研究[D].]
8. Cao, Z.: Research on the fashion consumption characteristics of the Millennials. Mod. Commer. (028), 21–22 (2019). [曹子益. 千禧一代时尚消费特征研究[J]. 现代商业, 2019, 000(028):21-22.]
9. Li, D.: Introduction of shape analysis in product design. Tianjin Textile Technol. (02), 26–28+62 (2003). [李德义.形态分析法在产品设计中的引入[J].天津纺织科技, 2003(02):26-28+62.]
10. Su, J., Tang, Z., Jing, N., et al.: Research on product design method for user cluster. Mech. Design 36(4), 119–123 (2019). [苏建宁, 唐钊山, 景楠, 等. 面向用户集群的产品设计方法研究[J]. 机械设计, 2019, 36(4): 119-123.]
11. Li, Y., Guo, G.: Product modeling scheme selection model based on multiple eye movement data. Comput. Integr. Manuf. Syst. (6), 658–665 (2015). [李运, 郭钢. 基于多项眼动数据的产品造型方案评选模型［J］. 计算机集成制造系统, 2015（6）：658－665.]
12. Tian, S., Shen, P., Guo, Y.: Research on color emotion based on eye tracking technology. Mod. Commun. J. Commun. Univ. China (6), 70–76 (2015). [田少煦, 申品品, 郭昱竹. 基于眼动跟踪技术的色彩情感研究［J］. 现代传播：中国传媒大学学报, 2015（6）：70－76.]

Innovation in Teaching Model Based on University Museum Resources

Taking the Course of Study on Chinese Ethnic Costume Decoration as an Example

Chi Zhang[1](✉), Xiaomei Hu[1], and Minghong Shi[2]

[1] Beijing Institute of Fashion Technology, East Yinghua Street 1,
Chaoyang, Beijing 100029, China
[2] Shenzhen Technology University, Lantian Road 3002, Pingshan, Shenzhen,
Guangdong 518118, China

Abstract. In recent years, many domestic schools of fashion design have enhanced their efforts in teaching study of ethnic costume culture as more and more novel ideas and scientific teaching methods are applied. Digging, sorting out, transforming, and applying the national costume culture in the school teaching of fashion design is a main way to inherit and develop the national costume culture. As a knowledge transfer space in universities, museums pass knowledge to students via exhibitions and teaching activities, seek for answers across the space and time by exploratory learning as a practice since ancient times. Ethnic costume museums are important premises to study and inherit national costume culture and natural teaching resources. Taking the Study on Chinese National Costume Decoration opened by the Museum of Ethnic Costumes, Beijing Institute of Fashion Technology as an example, this paper analyzes the teaching resources, content, methods, and results, etc. of courses to reflect on the university museums related to ethnic costume culture and its course teaching. It also discusses the potential advantages of university museums in teaching to combine with national costume culture innovation and inheritance courses for innovation in teaching model as a reference.

Keywords: Ethnic costume culture · Ethnic costume design · University museum · Innovation in teaching model

1 Introduction

As a knowledge transfer space, museums pass knowledge to students via exhibitions and teaching activities, and seek for answers across the space and time by exploratory learning as a practice since ancient times. The museum hall is a spatial foundation of teaching; the collection of materials constitutes the material basis of teaching; the textual criticism, research, knowledge production and transmission are the motivation foundation of teaching [1]. In recent years, more and more university museums start to further participate in teaching activities for greater values via teaching and to back feed

M. M. Soares et al. (Eds.): HCII 2021, LNCS 12780, pp. 148–159, 2021.
https://doi.org/10.1007/978-3-030-78224-5_11

the research of collections in museums. Ethnic costume culture relies on the history, life, habits, emotion, aesthetics, and faith of ethnics, and is the cultural carrier of all ethnics throughout the long-term historical development, which reflects their wisdom in a concentrated manner. The Chinese ethnic costume civilization has a long history, a unique design system and aesthetic ideas. However, since 1980s, the modernization and economic globalization have been stripping the ethnic costume culture gradually from its original land. The academic research and education on ethnic costume culture are relatively backward. In recent years, along with the national strength enhancement and promotion of national policies, the populace's acceptance of national culture is also significantly increased as some domestic universities' fashion design disciplines and schools are enhancing efforts in the teaching and study of ethnic costume culture. More and more novel ideas and scientific teaching methods are applied in teaching. The early development of Chinese professional education on costume is based on the western design education system and refers to the western model from design mode to process and workmanship. A relatively sound and mature teaching model has formed. In such a context, how to utilize all resources for active exploration of innovation in teaching model becomes a main link in inheriting and developing national costume culture.

As the first professional clothing museum in China, the Museum of Ethnic Costumes, Beijing Institute of Fashion Technology has a collection of more than 10,000 pieces of Chinese national costumes, accessories, fabrics, batik, and embroidery. Since its opening, the museum has been actively studying and transmitting ethnic costume culture, and engaged in teaching and study related to innovation design of national costume, in order to find a new train of thinking and a new way to combine museum research with teaching and design practice from aspects like costume culture study, fashion design study costume design research and costume skill practice, etc. In 2010, the museum planned and opened a course of Study on Chinese Ethnic Costume Decoration for master students. In the framework of regional and ethnic classifications, the course teaches students the decoration and application of classical ethnic costumes, social customs, and aesthetic psychology from point to area like costume characteristics, materials, workmanship, color, pattern, and decoration, etc. Since its opening, the course has continuously integrated multiple teaching resources, adjusted teaching content and made innovation in teaching methods, so that students can learn and master the colorful traditional costume art from the perspectives of study, inheritance, development, and application of outstanding cultural heritage. In this process, students complete the final innovative work through the cognitive transformation of ethnicity, design, and fashion.

With Study on Chinese Ethnic Costume Decoration opened by the Museum of Ethnic Costumes of Beijing Institute of Fashion Technology as an example and in combination with the Constructivism learning theories, this paper analyzes the teaching resources, content, methods, and results of this courses to reflect on the university museums related to ethnic costume culture and its course teaching. It also discusses how to combine the resources of university museums in teaching with ethnic costume culture innovation and inheritance courses for innovation in teaching model. In details, this paper introduces the 4 implementation stages of the Study on Chinese Ethnic Costume Decoration, the content and focus of each stage, and discusses how museum resources leverage their advantages in teaching.

2 Research Background

At present, the emphasis and efforts on ethnic costume culture teaching vary from university to university in domestic professional education of fashion design. Universities which stress this course are mainly ethnic university with fashion design major, universities in minority areas and some universities upholding the tradition of ethnic costume culture research. They generally enjoy advantages of ethnic culture resources and research systems. Except for the above three types of universities, most universities that have courses related to fashion design pay little attention to ethnic costume culture. The content of the courses is superficial and the curriculum is not profound enough or strongly related to the overall teaching system, resulting in low innovation conversion rate.

Teaching model refers to a structural form to develop education activities in a context, and is a dynamic system consisting of specific teaching methods and means [2]. Teaching model shall be based on teaching. Therefore, the author believes that teaching model is the key to solve the problems mentioned above. Teaching resources and means shall be re-sorted, and new teaching ways shall be introduced to structure new learning processes and evaluation methods of learning results.

Ethnic costumes usually have distinctive folk customs and artistic aesthetic appeal, and the exquisite traditional national skills contained in them are precious intangible cultural heritage and rare teaching and research resources. Since 1980s, ethnic costume culture has been facing the elimination of age. Except for some elderly living in remote areas, fashion cloth becomes the first choice of men and women in most of the minority areas while the traditional costume carrying the ethnic wisdom disappear with the elderly or are boxed forever. How to inherit and make innovation in traditional ethnic costumes, enhance the new generation's pride of ethnic culture, and form an open systematic ethnic culture inheritance gene in the context of modernization and globalization by diversified teaching means are questions to be carefully considered and explored by higher education courses focusing on inheritance and innovation of ethnic costume culture.

Ethnic costume courses are generally carried out by collection in minority areas. In such a process, students visit local museums and dwellings under the teacher's leadership to investigate and experience the overall dressing posture, style, fabrics, pattern, and color of ethnic costume, and to learn about their making process. The investigation focuses on ethnic costumes and data collection to form an investigation report. This allows students to understand ethnic costume to a certain degree but is less closely related to the design course and fails to guide students to sufficiently unearth and extract traditional elements. It also fails to combine ethnic costume with modern costume language and design methods, let alone any reference or innovation in ethnic elements. On the other hand, referring to ethnic culture is a frequently used design mode in modern costume design field. Ethnic costumes carry the unique personality symbols of culture and inspire designers. In view of this, the course of Study on Ethnic Costume decoration is opened to help students understand the aesthetic taste and humanistic connotation of traditional costume culture of minorities and to further express the spiritual connotation of ethnic costume, so that students can apply the essence of ethnic costume arts in future research and practice. They also have a chance to master and understand the general decoration rules, cultural connotations, origin, and development of ethnic costumes, and can learn more colorful ethnic costume arts from research, inheritance, development, and application of the outstanding cultural heritage.

3   Theoretical Framework

Constructivism Learning Theory believes that learning is to guide students to develop (construct) new theories from their original experience. Piaget's Individual Constructivism organically combines the structural concepts with action concepts to reveal that essentially wisdom is a kind of structural action (operation) [3]. He holds the ground that learners understand nature, society, others, and self in the process of interacting with the surrounding society, develop knowledge about the external world and gradually improve their recognition structures. This process emphasizes the active role of individual in recognition growth, namely, student centralization Lev Vygotsky believes that the cognition of our human beings is affected by society, culture, and historical factors. Knowledge is constructed based on social development. Learners form their understanding and derive their recognition from outer to inner by interacting with the society. Therefore, he stresses the sociality and interaction of learning, and supports the application of cooperative learning methods to obtain new knowledge and structure new recognition structure [4]. In combination with the views of Piaget and Lev Vygostsky, the acquisition of knowledge is the result of co-construction by individual and society. To be specific for talent training of design discipline, according to the Constructivism learning theory, students shall be put at the center and a project-driven mechanism shall be adopted to structure a new recognition process by creasing a learning situation for students and to measure their learning results via diversified ways.

4   Schema and Procedure

Based on the Constructivism Learning Theory and the museum's unique teaching resources, the Museum of Ethnic Costumes, Beijing Institute of Fashion Technology has carried out a hybrid curriculum model innovation in the course of Study on Chinese Ethnic Costume Decoration for master students. The specific implementation methods are as follows:

Stage 1: Study on ethnic culture and history based on collections

The course begins with concepts and theories related to ethnic costume. Teachers outline the content and give necessary tips for main and difficult points. Then, they take out appropriate costume collections from the museum as the case for detailed elaboration to help students understand the framework and research method of ethnic costume culture and related design knowledge, so that some space is left for them to learn independently. In 2015, the Museum launched an online ethnic costume database platform (www.biftmuseum.com) to provide abundant digital resources of visualized museum collections for students' fundamental learning. They can obtain basic information of costume texture and workmanship from the ethnic collections in a straightforward manner.

After theoretical study, students are grouped to select and research a suit of ethnic costume they are interested in from the museum. Relevant literature research is carried out under the teachers' instructions. The main content is to make breakthrough from a suit of ethnic costume and further research its ethnics and costume cultural characteristics of the specific branches from history, geographical characteristics, and cultural connotation, to deepen students' knowledge and understanding on the costume culture of the ethnics owning the costume, and to summarize its design features. This stage aims to help students build up the knowledge framework and research method of Chinese ethnic costume culture, guide the thinking on the reasons and influence of cultural formation, and motivate their interests and willingness in exploring ethnic costume culture.

Stage 2: design practice based on ethnography and anthropological research methods

At this stage, students start analyzing the design elements, process characteristics and methods of ethnic costume and decoration to lay a foundation for the innovative design of costumes in the next stage. The material study of ethnic costume samples allows students to intuitively understand the morphological characteristics of ethnic costume culture for data collection, picture and text recording and analysis from many aspects like texture, patter, structure, decoration, and workmanship. The next step is 1:1 grey cloth sample to deepen the understanding on the shape, structure, and workmanship of research objects, including their patterns, color, cultural connotation, and fabrication process.

Example: Master students Liu Sitong and Gao Xing studied the splendid upper outer garment for Siyin Miao Branch Females found at Niuchangba, Xinyao Village, Liuzhi, Guizhou with the collection No. of MFB008394 (Figs. 1, 2, 3 and 4).

Fig. 1. Splendid upper outer garment for Siyin Miao Branch Females found at Niuchangba, Xinyao Village, Liuzhi, Guizhou (MFB008394)

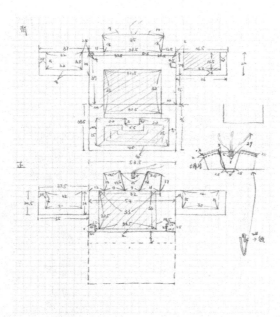

Fig. 2. Manuscript of measured material data (by Liu Sitong)

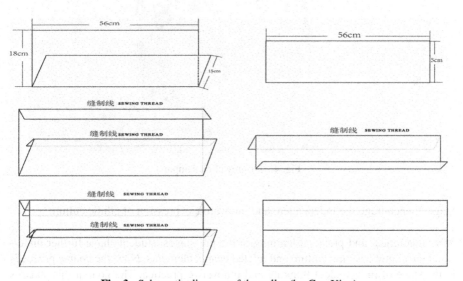

Fig. 3. Schematic diagram of the collar (by Gao Xing)

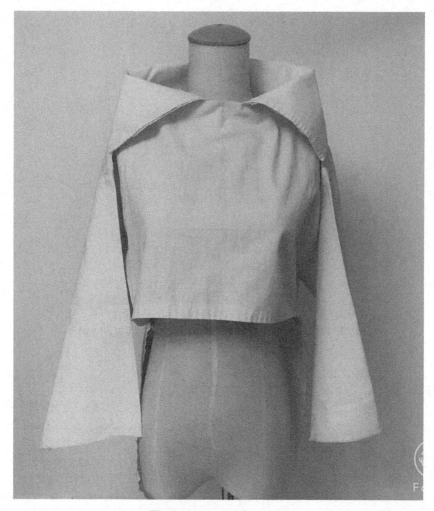

Fig. 4. 1:1 grey cloth sample

Stage 3: encourage the independent and innovative expression of ethnic culture

After theoretical and practical learning in the pre-stages, students have further understood the ethnic costume culture and related design elements. Now, the course proceeds to the stage of independent thinking and innovative practice. The goal at this stage is to enlighten students in expression and innovation of ethnic costume culture in such a diversified age based on pre-stages teaching. Through learning the structure and pattern of the research objects, students shall combine with concepts of creation in ethnic costume culture of the minorities with self-recognition and design experience for innovative design to produce new costume works.

Example: the two students designed two innovative works by taking the structure and patter of the splendid upper outer gourmet for Siyin Miao Branch Females as the creation origin and combining with the modern aesthetical standards (Fig. 5).

Fig. 5. Innovation design works by Gao Xing (left) and Liu Sitong (right)

Stage 4: multiple identities for interdisciplinary innovation

The innovative works do not mark the end of this course. After design, students take photos of their works as the model after makeup with assistance from the teachers to present their works by photography and scene layout. Online exhibitions for their innovative design works are planned under the leadership of the teachers. Outstanding works have a chance to participate in the offline innovative design exhibition organized by the museum.

Such a way of course setting breaks the barrier between disciplines. Students are not only required to learn design costume but also teamwork to explain their works from multiple dimensions and in multiple identities. This teaching model helps students to absorb and digest knowledge and innovatively transform learning results in diversified teaching practice. It is beneficial to expand their thinking broadness across disciplines and culture, cultivate the spirits of intellectual enquiries and the capacity of cultural research and integration (Fig. 6).

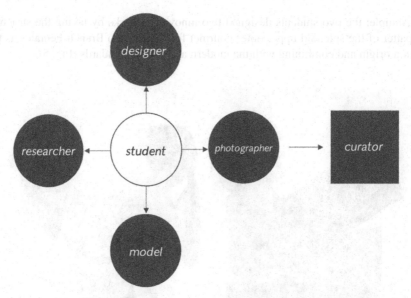

Fig. 6. Multiple identities and role transformation in this course

The four progressing course stages realize the detailing of theories of the knowledge system at the same longitudinal direction by theoretical study, design measurement and analysis, innovative design practice and interdisciplinary innovation practice while horizontally expanding the knowledge accumulation in other related disciplines to achieve the innovation of teaching models (Fig. 7).

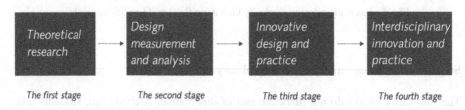

Fig. 7. Four stages of course implementation

5 Reflection and Findings

5.1 Museum Resources as Course Resources

The advantages of course teaching in museum include: 1. The Museum of Ethnic Costumes has massive ethnic costumes that it can provide abundant, optional, and concentrated study resources for students. To students from the design discipline, these study objects are observable, touchable, and measurable, creating valuable conditions for further study. 2. The curator of the Museum has abundant experience in ethnic costume culture collection and study to provide professional guidance on study experience and knowledge. 3. Collection is a main function of the Museum. After the course, some valuable fruits of students by knowledge production can be saved to support future relevant studies of the Museum.

5.2 The Inspiring and Question-Guided Teaching Mode is Adopted to Offer a Stage for Students to Transform from "Research to Designer, Model/Photographer and Curator". From Point to Surface, Knowledge Production is Boosted and the Inheritance and Innovation of Ethnic Costume Culture Are Realized

It is a wonderful learning experience to be involved in the process of knowledge creation in person. "Interaction" is the keyword in the main concept of the centralism of constructivism. Largely the teaching activities are to review knowledge and information. Learners go through and experience significant or valuable structuring process. Attention shall be paid to their self-values in this process while practical and interactive experience establishes a direct relationship between teaching content and learners to enhance their consciousness of subject. After theoretical learning and case analysis, the teacher transforms from a lecturer to a collaborative researcher by transferring the learning initiative to students so that they become a major participant and practitioner in teaching activities. Students choose a piece of works they are interested in from the museum to learn the costume culture and history of its ethnics from the text information. They understand the design and fabrication modes as well as the wisdom of life behind them by measuring and analyzing relevant data, to evaluate these modes and expression forms for innovation conforming to the aesthetic characters of the age in combination with what they have learned in course. Finally, the process of transforming from existing knowledge to producing new knowledge is done. Compared to traditional lecturing, this method can motivate students' activity and initiative.

5.3 The Combination of Exhibition and Teaching is also Adopted. Online Exhibitions Are Planned and Resources Platforms Are Structured to Beneficially Supplement the Teaching from Teachers and Provide Students a Source of Independent Learning. It also Archives, Accumulates, and Displays Teaching Results and Further Enriches the Research and Collections of the Museum

The teaching activities of the most museums are related to exhibitions to a certain degree while exhibitions are optimal education product and typical education activity. Exhibition is the most straightforward and intuitive way to show collections and the study results of scientific researchers to the public [5]. As a process-based teaching mode, exhibition pays attention to the dual experiences of knowledge transfer (teaching) and reproduction (study) to constantly refresh teaching activities. The planning and completion of exhibition is a creative process from nothing to something, which is a good chance for students to learn. Modern education stands for "student centered", which means paying attention to the learning imitative and process, emphasizing what learners know (knowledge) and how they think about (recognition process) the knowledge. The exhibition of costumes from design to conception exactly allows teachers and outsiders of teaching activities to understand how students think about (recognition process) the knowledge [6]. Exhibition is present online and as a part of the teaching activities, they can be used archive, accumulate and display teaching fruits, form a foundation for future teaching and provide data sources of learning and study for these who want to learn or understand relevant study fields.

6 Conclusion

At present, there are many defects in the courses related to ethnic costume culture and design, including outdated teaching mode, superficial and fragmented courses which can't realize effective innovation transformation. Confronted with such a dilemma, educators shall keep on learning advanced teaching ideas, seeking for new teaching resources, and enhancing exploration and study of course teaching mode. Guided by the Constructivism Learning Theory, this paper combines the resource advantages of university museums to think about and explore the specific design and development of teaching modes for courses from teaching goals and process, and to reflect on the advantages of museum resources in teaching. The abundant and diversified first-hand materials in museums, the professional halls with education and study properties and the experienced curators as the faculty are the advantages of museums to develop courses related to ethnic fashion design. The participation of university museums in courses of ethnic fashion design can make sure that the courses are student centered and function are a broader stage to break the barrier of disciplines and achieve the longitudinal in-depth professional study and horizontal development of comprehensive accomplishments. From point to surface, knowledge production is boosted and the inheritance and innovation of ethnic costume culture are realized. Courses are finally presented by online exhibition. The combination of exhibition and teaching is also adopted. Resources platforms are structured to beneficially supplement the teaching from teachers and provide students with a source of independent learning. It also archives, accumulates, and displays teaching results and further enriches the study and collections of the museum.

Acknowledgements. This research was financial supported by the Initiation Program for New Young Teachers, Beijing Institute of Fashion Technology (No. BIFTXJ201914).

References

1. Jingye, C.: Combination of exhibition and teaching: the origin and development of university museums. Chinese Museums (03), 105 (2020)
2. Haibing, L.: Preliminary exploration of the research type teaching mode of national costume culture of China. Teach. Res. Hubei Inst. Fine Art (01), 064 (2019)
3. Zhiyuan, W., Xiaoxi, C.: From structuralism to constructivism – introduction to piaget's genetic epistemology I. Philosophical Trends **02**, 17 (1983)
4. Huang, S.: Research on the hybrid teaching mode of design discipline based on constructivism. Yangtze River Series **06**, 13–14 (2020)

5. Office of Policy and Analysis: Lessons for Tomorrow: A Study of Education at the Smithsonian. Summary Report **1**, 19 (2009)
6. Anderson, W.L.: A taxonomy for learning, teaching and accessing – a revision of bloom's taxonomy of educational objectives. 30, Foreign Language Teachng and Research Press, Beijing (2009)

Research on Intelligent Classified Trash Can and Smart Application Design—Achieving Green Smart Home Living in China

Nan Zhang[✉], Yanlin Wu, Yingao Kong, and Jinsong Lv

School of Design Art and Media, Nanjing University of Science and Technology, Nanjing 210094, China

Abstract. Garbage classification has been implemented abroad for a long time, but for China, it is still in the initial stage of consciousness germination. This paper is aiming to build an intelligent garbage classified system to solve the problem of garbage sorting for Chinese users and improve the user experience. According to user research and market research, we found that due to the lack of correct classification knowledge guidance, the process of garbage sorting made users feel troubled. The trash cans in current market generally do not have the intelligent function of garbage classification. In order to simplify the process of garbage disposal and popularize the classification knowledge, we put forward the concept of intelligent classified trash can with deep learning-based image recognition and speech recognition classification system and a supporting smart application to help users achieve green smart home life. Finally, we invited 16 users to carries out the usability test and optimized the prototype of intelligent trash can hoping to bring users a better experience of garbage classification.

Keywords: Intelligent garbage classification · Smart home · Usability · User experience

1 Introduction

With the development of the green city, garbage classification has become an inevitable trend for China in the future. However, how to carry out the correct classification is becoming a tricky business for the population of China. In the context of smart home, this paper mainly focuses on how to design a household intelligent classified trash can (ICTC) with smart interactive system to solve the problem of garbage sorting for Chinese users and help them to achieve a green smart home life.

This study firstly looks for the field research and user research to found that the pain point of garbage classification in China is caused by the lack of correct knowledge popularization and guidance. In the next part, we focus on the existing household trash cans in the Chinese market. We found some "smart cans" mainly focus on the "contactless opening /closing" technology, which only achieves the purpose of freeing hands up by using sensing and foot stepping measures. Then carries out the relevant research about deep learning, image recognition technology, smart classification technology.

© Springer Nature Switzerland AG 2021
M. M. Soares et al. (Eds.): HCII 2021, LNCS 12780, pp. 160–177, 2021.
https://doi.org/10.1007/978-3-030-78224-5_12

Based on these studies, we proposed the concept of a household intelligent classified trash can (ICTC) with a deep learning-based image recognition and speech recognition system. The concept of deep learning originates from the research of artificial neural networks, which is a type of machine learning, and it is the necessary path to realize artificial intelligence. Deep learning is the internal rule of learning sample data and the level of presentation. Its goal is to make machines as analytical as humans, capable of recognizing data such as words, images, and sounds.

In terms of its external interactive hardware of ICTC, it has an intelligent scanning instrument, LCD screen, rechargeable interface, four different types of cans with controllable opening/closing form. The embedded interactive software of garbage classification system is deployed on the Raspberry Pie system, including image recognition and speech recognition. Also, a supporting smart application assists garbage classification, displays operating parameters of the ICTC, popularizes knowledge and social sharing also proposed to improve user experience.

2 Related Work

2.1 Field Research and User Research

Field Research. We conducted the field research in residential garbage collection sites and found that despite garbage classification policy has been gradually implemented and announcement has been published on the bulletin board, garbage is still mixed or misplaced. The chaotic situation is mainly caused by the residents who have not handled the garbage sorting problem well at home (Fig. 1).

Fig. 1. Current status of garbage sorting in residential areas.

User Research. We interviewed some residents, mainly housewives who spend lots of time to deal with housework. They belong to the user group with strong demand for garbage classification. The results showed that most of the interviewees began to pay attention to garbage classification under the existing policies, but due to the lack of correct classification knowledge, the process of garbage classification became tedious, complex, and boring, which made them feel troubled. Besides, it is very inconvenient for them to sort garbage at home, requiring multiple trash bins to dispose of different types of garbage. Mobile news and social media are the main channels for them to acquire garbage classification knowledge, but the information is difficult to distinguish between true and false. In terms of trash can, interviewees expressed expectations for the intelligent classification function, and hope that the use flow could be as simple as possible so that all family members can operate by themselves.

According to the research data, the pain points and opportunities are analyzed and organized as follows Table 1.

Table 1. Pain points and opportunities.

No.	Pain points	Opportunities
1	The flow of garbage classification is tedious and complex, users do not want to spend too much time to deal with it	Simplify the garbage classification flow through an intelligent interactive system
2	Users hold a negative attitude towards garbage classification	Popularize garbage classification knowledge through intuitive forms such as images or sounds to attract users
3	It is necessary to have more than one trash can for garbage sorting at home	Need a trash can containing different types of trash partitions
4	The knowledge acquisition channels of garbage classification are not centralized, and the information is difficult to distinguish between true and false	A professional garbage classification knowledge popularization and query system to ensure the accuracy of information

2.2 Market Research

Material. At present, the main materials of household trash cans in the Chinese market include Acrylonitrile Butadiene Styrene (ABS), Polypropylene (PP), Resin, Stainless steel, Carbon steel with spray paint, Hardwood, etc. Among those, Polypropylene, stainless steel and ABS are the most used. We made a comparative analysis of these three materials on multiple attributes, the results are shown in Table 2.

Table 2. Material performance comparison.

Category	PP	Stainless steel	ABS
Density	Low	High	Medium
Hardness	Medium	High	Low
Impact resistance	Low	High	Medium
Coloration	Good	Poor	Excellent
Surface gloss	Poor	Excellent	Good
Environmental performance	Good	Excellent	Good
Cost	Low	High	Medium

Volume. In the home space, different areas have different requirements for the volume of garbage cans. Therefore, we made statistics on the volume requirements for the trash cans in different areas of the home, and the results are shown in Fig. 2. The height of most household trash cans in the market is 30~40 cm (Fig. 3), the bottom area is more than 400 cm^2, and the volume range from 4 L to 20 L, mostly 10–12 L.

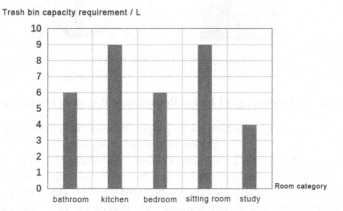

Fig. 2. Volume requirements.

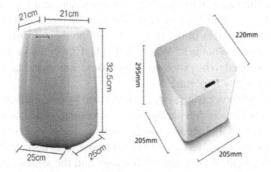

Fig. 3. Routine size of trash can.

Functions. Currently, there are some intelligence trash cans on the market, and the so-called "intelligence" is mainly focused on the contactless "opening/closing" technology, which only achieves freeing hands up. Through the infrared heat sensor and touch sensor, the corresponding signal is sent to the sensor in the trash can by palm scanning the designated area and kicking the can, to achieve the non-contact way. However, they do not have the function of garbage identification and classification, and lack a more in-depth interaction system between user and product (Fig. 4).

Fig. 4. Existing intelligent trash can.

2.3 Research on Technology of Image Recognition Based on Deep Learning

Deep learning is a complex machine learning algorithm especially in the fields of natural language processing, speech recognition and image processing. Typical deep learning models include convolutional neural network, DBN, and stacked auto-encoder network models. There are three main types of learning in the field of deep learning: supervised learning, unsupervised learning, and semi-supervised learning. This project mainly uses the target detection network in deep learning for supervised learning training.

Target detection, also called target extraction, is a kind of image segmentation based on the geometric and statistical characteristics of the target. It combines the segmentation and recognition of the target into one. The accuracy and real-time performance are important capabilities of the whole system. The task of target detection is to find all the targets (objects) of interest in the image, determine their positions and sizes, and solve the question about "What is it? Where is it" [1]. Especially in the complex scene, when multiple targets need to be processed in real time, automatic target extraction and recognition are particularly important.

At present, the image processing system constructed by convolutional neural network (CNN) can effectively reduce over-fitting, and can recognize the content of large-pixel images well. After fusing GPU acceleration technology, the neural network can better fit the training data in practice, and recognize most of the pictures faster and more accurately [2]. With the development of computer technology and the widespread application of computer vision principles, the use of computer image processing technology to track targets in real time is becoming more and more popular. Considering that the construction of speech recognition system has been very mature, this paper mainly focused on the deep learning-based image recognition technology and try to apply it to the construction of the smart home system.

3 Design Concept

We try to apply the deep learning-based image recognition and speech recognition technology to the construction of smart home system, and proposed an intelligent classified trash can (ICTC). It aims to attract users through this kind of intelligent form and makes all the family members (including the elderly and children) can easily master the garbage classification knowledge. In addition, the trash can comprise a controllable opening/closing system to simplify the waste disposal process, and we also proposed a supporting smart application to provide a reliable classification knowledge query and sharing platform for Chinese users.

3.1 Intelligent Classified Trash Can (ICTC)

We will elaborate the design concept of the ICTC in four aspects including the product's modeling and structural, task flow, hardware control system, software classification and identification system.

Product Modeling and Structural. The trash can mainly compose of four parts: lid, body, camera, and display screen.

- The camera and display screen are located on the front of the can, which is convenient for the system to capture images and display information.
- In order to solve the problem that families always use multiple bins for sorting garbage, we divide the internal structure of the ICTC into four independent sub-buckets, corresponding to four categories of garbage: Recyclable, Harmful waste, Kitchen waste, and other waste.
- The lid divided into four independent opening and closing pieces, corresponding to the four sub-buckets, which manage the four categories of garbage.
- Due to this structure, the volume of the ICTC should be larger than the ordinary household bin, which is estimated to be 40 L. The bottom size should be set as 40 cm * 40 cm. Considering that the user needs to bend down to dispose the garbage, the height of the ICTC needs to be increased to 60 cm, and the size of the four sub-buckets should be 9 cm * 9 cm * 54 cm.
- Considering the strong hardness, impact resistance and easy transfer, the material of body and lids should be Acrylonitrile Butadiene Styrene (ABS). The four independent sub-buckets should be Polypropylene (PP) to reduce the cost (Fig. 5 and 6).

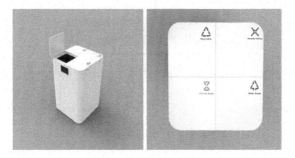

Fig. 5. ICTC modeling.

Harmful Waste   Kitchen Waste   Recyclable   Other Waste

Fig. 6. The four types of garbage classification.

Task Flow. The recognition system takes in two forms: image recognition and speech recognition, users can choose according to their preferences. No matter which form is chosen, once the garbage is identified, the lid of the corresponding sub-buckets will open and close automatically by the control system. At the same time, the classification knowledge related to the garbage will be displayed on the screen and feeds back to users via voice broadcast. The specific task flow is shown in Fig. 7.

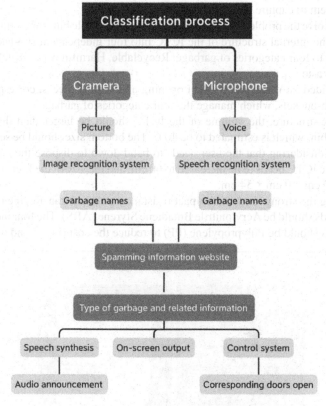

Fig. 7. Task flow.

Hardware Control System. This project uses Raspberry Pi 4B as the embedded system, which is a miniature ARM-based computer motherboard (the same size as a credit card) and complete related tasks by connecting it with hardware such as camera, display, sensor, steering gear. the hardware control system mainly consists of two input modules and three output modules (Figs. 8, 9 and Table 3).

If user selects the image input button and put the garbage in front of the camera, it will send the captured garbage picture to the recognition system and then outputs the name of the garbage. If the voice input button is selected, users can directly speak the garbage name, then microphone will receive the audio and convert it to text information through the API interface. No matter which input module is selected, once the garbage name is detected by the identification system, its category and other information will be obtained from the garbage sorting website through the crawler module and then displayed on the screen, followed by voice broadcast.

The opening/closing door control module converts the detected garbage category into a control signal to control the steering gear to implement operations such as opening the corresponding door. ICTC has four independent sub-buckets and four lids, each lid is connected to the wall of corresponding sub-buckets through a steering gear. The control system corresponds different steering gear through control codes. Once the identification system determines the garbage category, it will send a pulse signal to the corresponding steering gear and rotates the corresponding lid to complete the 90° opening and closing action.

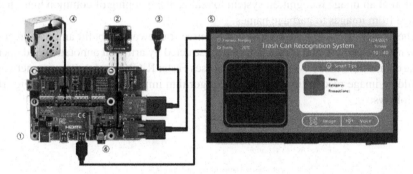

Fig. 8. Hardware equipment.

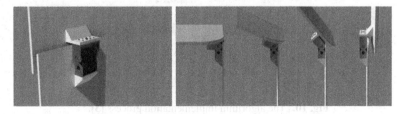

Fig. 9. Door control module.

Table 3. Hardware details.

Category	Module name	Sensor	Function
Control module	①System control module	Raspberry Pi 4B	Program operation and signal control
Input modules	②Image input module	Camera	Capture garbage pictures for image recognition
Input modules	③Sound input module	Microphone	Capture the user's voice for speech recognition
Output modules	④Door control module	Steering gear	Control the opening/closing of doors
Output modules	⑤Display module	LCD display	Displays information such as garbage name and category
Output modules	⑥Audio output module	3.5 mm interface	Voice output detection results

Software Classification and Recognition System. Considering that the construction of speech recognition system has been very mature, this part mainly focuses on the construction of an image recognition system to realize the mapping of common household garbage from images to garbage names.

The system uses the TensorFlow open-source framework to build an image recognition neural network, and uses a data set constructed by artificial annotation and open-source data to train the network. This project uses Faster R-CNN target detection network to build an image recognition system. The algorithm implementation process (Fig. 10) is as follows:

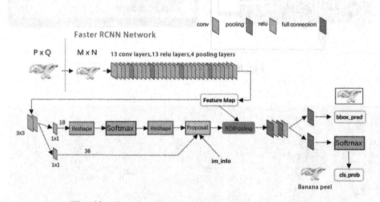

Fig. 10. The algorithm implementation process [3].

Feature Extraction
Take the entire picture of garbage as Input, and extract features through basic networks such as convolutional layer CNN to obtain Feature Map.VGG16 is used as the feature

extraction module in this network. In the step of inputting the image, the original image is reshaped into an M × N size image.

Region Proposal Networks (RPN)

The Fig. 11 shows the specific structure of the RPN network. We can see that the feature map is divided into two lines after a 3 × 3 convolution kernel convolution. The upper one uses SoftMax to classify the anchors (the smallest unit on a feature map) to obtain foreground and background (the detection target is foreground), the following line is used to calculate the offset of the bounding box regression of the anchors in order to obtain an accurate proposal. After synthesizing the two results and removing proposals that are too small and beyond the boundary, the final proposal layer is obtained. Finally, according to the score of the region proposal, the first 300 region proposals are selected as the input of Fast R-CNN for target detection [3].

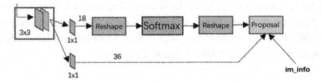

Fig. 11. RPN network [3].

RoI Pooling

The RoI Pooling layer (Fig. 12) is responsible for collecting proposals calculating proposal feature maps, and sending them to the subsequent network. From the algorithm flow chart, you can see that the RoI pooling layer has 2 inputs: one is Original feature map, another one is Proposal boxes output by RPN (different sizes). After processing, even for proposals of different sizes, the output results are all 7 * 7 in size, achieving fixed-length output (fixed-length output) [3, 4].

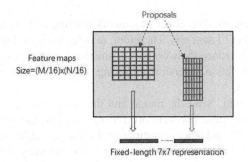

Fig. 12. RoI Pooling layer [3, 4].

Classification and bbox Regression

The classification part uses the obtained proposal feature map, calculates which category each proposal belongs to (such as banana, apple, etc.) through the full connect layer and SoftMax, outputs the cls_prob probability vector and uses Bounding box regression again to obtain the position deviation of each proposal. The displacement bbox_pred is used to return to a more accurate target detection frame [3].

The target detection network implements the mapping between the image and the name and location of the garbage, and then uploads the identified garbage name to the garbage classification query platform to obtain the final category. Compared with the judging method of directly corresponding garbage images to the four categories of garbage, the judgment method of "image-name-category" uses the name as an intermediate quantity, and other methods (such as voice input, text input, etc.) can be used to obtain the name and then carrying out the type judgment, through the input judgment of other auxiliary methods, has improved the garbage classification ability of the whole system. The specific training process of the recognition network is as follows:

(1) Create data set: use the "labelimg" open source tool to label the image, frame the location of the object to be detected, and finally form an xml label file containing category information and location information (Fig. 13).

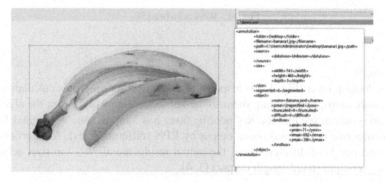

Fig. 13. Label picture.

(2) Data enhancement: The effect of network training and fitting is generally proportional to the number of data sets. Therefore, in order to expand the data set, improve the training effect and reduce the workload of manual annotation, data enhancement is adopted. Random translation, inversion, mirroring, and other operations were performed on the image (Fig. 14).

(3) Network training: Send the image and the label information obtained by the annotation to the target detection network for training, and the network will perform features extraction, RPN and other operations on the image. Fitting with the category and location information in the label, through continuous loop training, adjusting parameters, and finally obtaining a network weight with a good fitting effect.

(4) Prediction: The weight file obtained by the above training can form a detection network with good fitting effect. Input the image to be detected into the network,

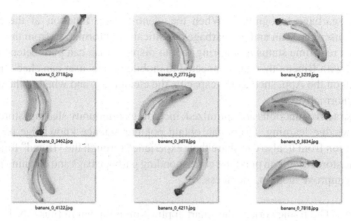

Fig. 14. Data enhancement.

and the result will be output, including category, location information, and confidence information (Fig. 15).

Fig. 15. Spam identification interface information.

3.2 Supporting Smart Application

In order to improve user experience, a supporting smart application which is compatible with the ICTC was proposed.

Functions. The smart application as an auxiliary tool to make the garbage sorting more accurate and enhance people's awareness of environmental protection. The APP mainly consists three main functions, which can improve user experience while completing garbage classification. The specific function modules are as follows:

- Auxiliary garbage recognition. When the identification function of the ICTC is impaired, user can scan and get garbage classification information from the App.
- Serve as a real-time status monitoring tool to display trash can parameters. ICTC is equipped with Bluetooth, once connected to mobile phone, user can check the status of the can on the App, such as the capacity, the cleanliness and whether the device is working normally.
- More interactive functions are optimized, including community sharing, store supply, and knowledge learning. Users can obtain popular science knowledge of garbage classification from it, also can share their experience through the "friend" function. In the online store, users can purchase corresponding garbage bags and cleaning products online to improve the user stickiness.

Framework. The framework of the smart application is shown in Figs. 16, 17.

Interactive System. The interactive interface design of each module as shown in the figure below.

4   Usability Test

User Testing. For usability test, we built the prototype of the ICTC by Acrylonitrile Butadiene Styrene (ABS). And invited 16 users including two elderly people, two children, and fourteen adults to identify six garbage objects in four categories: Kitchen waste, Recyclable, Harmful garbage, and other garbage, respectively for 16 times. The test content mainly included the accuracy rate of recognition and classification, the time spent on the whole process of garbage disposal and the user experience of using it (Fig. 18, Tables 4, 5).

Result. The test feedback was positive, the identification accuracy rate was 87.5% and the average recognition speed was 3 s, but the average garbage disposal speed was 7.2 s (Finding the location of the camera takes up lots of time), average user experience score was 3.75 (Full marks is 5) which all within the acceptable range. Most testers said that the process is simple, the information display and the voice broadcast are clear, and the interaction mode can attract users well. However, we found some problems that need to be improved, such as the position of the display screen causes some users to bend down when watching the screen. Finally, we sorted out these problems and summarized the key points of optimization:

- The speed of garbage identification needs to be accelerated.
- The accuracy of garbage identification needs to be improved.
- The size and position of the camera need to be adjusted to be more eye-catching.
- The position of the display screen needs to be adjusted to facilitate interaction.

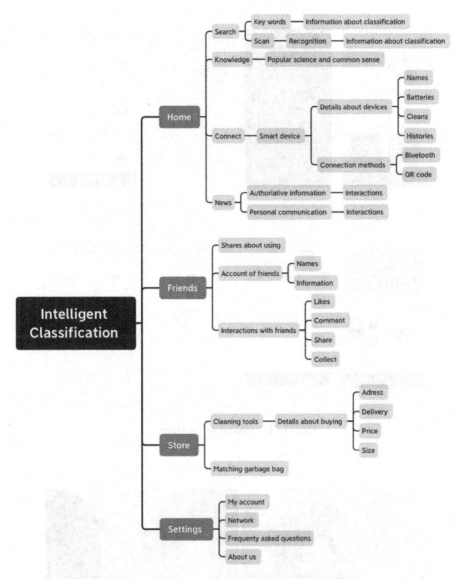

Fig. 16. The framework of the smart application.

Based on these, we optimized the initial concept, especially adjusted the position of the display screen to the top of the trash can to facilitate interaction; expanded the size of the camera to make it more visible. The further iterative product as shown in Fig. 19.

Fig. 17. The interactive interface.

Fig. 18. The use process of the first-generation trash can.

Table 4. Usability test.

	User1				User2				User3				User4			
Garbage No.	1	2	3	4	1	2	3	4	1	2	3	4	1	2	3	4
Identify the results	√	√	√	√	√	×	√	√	√	√	√	√	√	√	×	√
Time (s)	8	6	5	5	8	8	7	5	7	8	6	7	10	5	7	7
Experience（1-5）	5				5				4				3			

	User5				User6				User7				User8			
Garbage No.	1	2	3	4	1	2	3	4	1	2	3	4	1	2	3	4
Identify the results	√	√	√	√	√	√	√	√	×	√	√	√	√	√	√	√
Time (s)	8	5	5	7	11	8	5	6	10	8	6	6	8	6	5	5
Experience（1-5）	4				3				3				5			

	User9				User10				User11				User12			
Garbage No.	1	2	3	4	1	2	3	4	1	2	3	4	1	2	3	4
Identify the results	√	√	×	√	√	√	√	×	×	√	√	√	√	√	√	√
Time (s)	8	7	11	10	8	6	6	10	8	8	7	7	8	5	5	6
Experience（1-5）	2				4				3				5			

	User13				User14				User15				User16			
Garbage No.	1	2	3	4	1	2	3	4	1	2	3	4	1	2	3	4
Identify the results	×	√	√	×	√	√	√	√	√	√	√	×	√	√	√	√
Time (s)	11	9	7	9	10	8	5	6	8	8	6	10	7	7	6	6
Experience（1-5）	2				4				4				4			

Table 5. User evaluation

No.	
1	The accuracy of garbage identification is so high! Let me feel that garbage classification is no longer difficult in daily life
2	The accuracy rate of garbage identification is not very good. I tried 4 but 2 of them were wrong
3	I must bend or even squat to watch the display screen
4	It would be better if the recognition and opening speed could be faster
5	The camera is so small that it took me a few seconds to find out where it was
6	The voice broadcast function is very convenient for the elderly and children

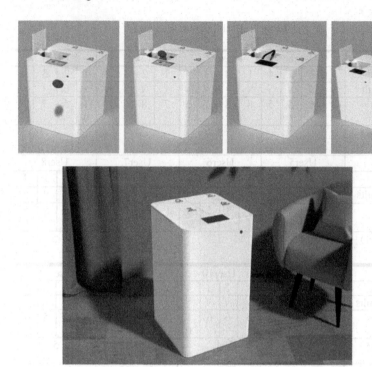

Fig. 19. Iterative product.

5   Conclusion

To solve the problem of difficult garbage classification for Chinese users while helping them achieve a green smart home life, this paper mainly focuses on how to build an intelligent garbage classification system with deep learning-based image recognition and speech recognition technology to improve the user experience of garbage classification. We proposed an intelligent classified trash can (ICTC) as the carrier of this classification system. The user test results show that this study greatly improves the efficiency of garbage classification, simplifies the garbage disposal process, and is helpful for users to master the classification knowledge.

For future studies, we will do more research on how to establish the connection system between the ICTC and the supporting smart application to improve the usability and user experience of the smart home.

References

1. A review of target detection algorithms based on deep learning. http://www.360doc.com/content/18/0424/23/41501311_748500691.shtml. Accessed 24 Apr 2018
2. TensorFlow Series III: An Introduction to Deep Learning. http://www.rendingren.com.cn/news/15817606045645.shtml. Accessed 15 Feb 2020

3. Detailed procedure of Faster R-CNN algorithm. https://blog.csdn.net/qq_37392244/article/det ails/88837784. Accessed 27 Mar 2019
4. Introduction to the principle of Fasters-RCNN. https://blog.csdn.net/Lin_xiaoyi/article/details/ 78214874. Accessed 26 Feb 2019

Research on Design Collaboration Strategy for the Transformation of Historical and Cultural Blocks in Beijing

Fumei Zhang[1]([envelope]) [iD], Tian Cao[2] [iD], and Ran Huo[1] [iD]

[1] Beijing Institute of Graphic Communication, Xinghua Street 1, Beijing 102600, China
[2] Nanjing University of Science and Technology, Xiaolingwei 200, Nanjing 210094, Jiangsu, China

Abstract. Transformation of historical and cultural block has become an important research topic nowadays. This paper taking the research perspective of human geography, investigates the transformation of historical and cultural blocks in Beijing, looking into their real situations and social cooperative environment through the reconstruction. In the specific course of study, examining Dashilar, The White Pagoda, Shichahai and other typical blocks' reconstruction cases, to explore the synergy and cooperation strategies between the government and the forces of all sectors of society. In the analysis of specific cases, this paper discusses the methods and paths of urban block renovation and reconstruction from two aspects of cultural space and cultural ecology. Cultural memory is an important cultural basis in the construction of Beijing's historical and cultural blocks, which hides the city's cultural genes and is also the historical background of the reconstruction of city's cultural space. Cultural ecology, which performs as the environment and soil for the existence and development of culture, is the state of cultural development that adapts to the social form. The presence and participation of people, as well as the positive interaction between people and the environment, are the important basis for investigating the cultural ecology of urban blocks. In the case study, we survey the role of cross-boundary integration of architectural culture, art, commercial design and other fields is considered and analyzed, mainly with participants of different identities.

Keywords: Design collaboration · Cross-boundary integration · Transformation of historical and cultural block · Cultural space · Cultural ecology

1 Introduction

Beijing is a famous cultural city with a long history. Like many cities in China, Beijing has experienced a complex process of demolition, transformation and construction in the course of urban modernization construction. Under current environment that the times pays close attention to cultural heritage protection and cultural inheritance, the protection and activation of historical and cultural blocks in Beijing has become a hot topic. In 2012, Beijing was successfully selected as the world's "Design Capital" and officially joined the creative city network of UNESCO (the United Nations Educational

Scientific and Cultural Organization). Modern design participates in the development of Beijing's modern city in many levels. The core content explored in this topic is the collaboration effect of modern design in the process of the transformation of historical and cultural blocks, as well as the methods and strategies that may be adopted.

2 Investigation of the Current Situation of Historical and Cultural Blocks in Beijing

2.1 Historical Origin and Current Situation of Historical and Cultural Blocks in Beijing

As the medium level of cultural heritage protection system in Beijing, the historical and cultural blocks in the old city of Beijing are the kernel of the famous historical and cultural city of Beijing, and the important carrier of the ancient capital style and historical culture. As a well-known proverb in Beijing says, "Beijing is one city, half of which is alleyway". Beijing takes alleyway (Hutong) and quadrangle courtyard (Siheyuan) as basic elements to form the basic framework of the old city.

In 1999, Beijing Municipal Government officially approved the *Plan for Protection and Control Scope of Historic and Cultural Conservation Districts in the Old City of Beijing*, which designated 25 historical and cultural conservation districts with an increase of 15 in 2002 and an increase of 3 in 2012. Currently, Beijing Municipality has designated and published 43 historical and cultural protection blocks, among which 33 historical and cultural blocks are located in the old city of Beijing, where are important places to accommodate cultural relics and historical and cultural buildings and have a relatively intact block style (Fig. 1).

List of Three Batches of Historical and Cultural Conservation Districts Published by Beijing Municipality	
The first batch	Xisibei First Alley to Eighth Alley
Nanchang Street	Dongsibei Third Alley to Eighth Alley
Beichang Street	Dongjiao Minxiang
Xihuamen Street	Dashilar
Nanchizi	East Liulichang
Beichizi	West Liulichang
Donghuamen Street	Xianyukou
Wenjin Street	
Jingshan Front Street	**The second batch**
Jingshan East Street	Imperial City
Jingshan West Street	North Luogu Lane
Zhibumen Street	North Zhang Zizhong Road
Jingshan Back Street	South Zhang Zizhong Road
Di' anmen Inner Street	Fayuan Temple
Wusi Street	
Shichahai District	**The Third Batch**
South Luogu Lane District	New Taicang
Guozijian District	Dongsi South
Fuchengmen Inner Street	South Naoshikou

Fig. 1. List of three batches of historical and cultural conservation districts published by Beijing municipality.

2.2 Alleyway and Quadrangle Courtyard: Basic Constitution of Historical and Cultural Blocks in Beijing

Alleyway and quadrangle courtyard are the basic elements of the space composition in the old city of Beijing, and bear the cultural characteristics of Beijing. Since the Yuan Dynasty, Beijing began to build quadrangle courtyards on a large scale, which developed into mature courtyard residence in the Ming and Qing Dynasties, becoming the main architectural form with regional characteristics in Beijing. In the Ming and Qing Dynasties, Beijing began to emerge more abundant and complex street structures and block forms.

Since the 20th century, the change in the number of alleyway and quadrangle courtyard is a vivid epitome of the city construction course of Beijing. According to the research data, the number of alleyway and quadrangle courtyard in Beijing decreases with the acceleration of urban modern transformation (Figs. 2 and 3).

Statistical table of the number change of alleyway (Hutong) in the old city of Beijing		
Years of data	The number of alleyway(Hu tong)	The number of alleyway(Hu tong) changed compared with the previous period (+/-)
1931	2623	546
1944	3200	577
1949	3073	-127
1965	2382	-169
1980	2290	-92
1990	2242	-48
2003	1559	-683
2005	1353	-206
2017	a little more than 1000	The specific data of reduction is unknown

Fig. 2. Statistical table of the number change of alleyway in the old city of Beijing [1].

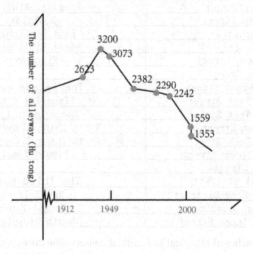

Fig. 3. Statistical table of the number change of alleyway in the old city of Beijing [1].

After the renovation of dangerous houses in Beijing advanced to the center of the city, alleyway and quadrangle courtyard within the Second Ring Road of Beijing vanished at an extraordinary speed. In the nearly 20 years from 11980 to 2000, Beijing has experienced the high-speed and modernized urban construction of "big demolition and big construction" [2], while alleyway and quadrangle courtyard contain and express Beijing history and culture, they also gradually die out in the city construction of the new era. In modern social life, the historical and cultural conservation districts are faced with many problems, such as weak awareness of cultural heritage protection, ruin and disrepair of houses, disorder and occupation of public space, unclear property ownership, aging of residents, hollowing out of the core area of the old city and so on.

In the meanwhile, due to the attachment to "Old Beijing" and the nostalgia of "Alleyway Tour", alleyway and quadrangle courtyard become the tourism culture resources that need to be protected urgently, and the comprehensive improvement of historical and cultural blocks has become an important proposition of Beijing city construction (Fig. 4).

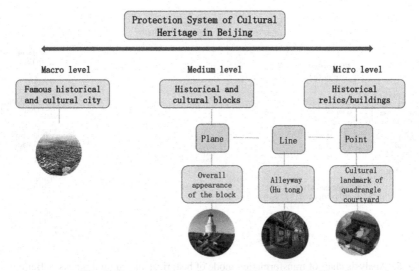

Fig. 4. Protection system of cultural heritage in Beijing

After entering the 21st century, along with the promotion of the awareness of cultural heritage protection, the strength of the protection of the old city in Beijing is gradually increasing. *The Beijing Urban Master Planning (2004–2020)* formulated in 2004 clearly put forward the "protection of chessboard road network framework and the patterns of streets, alleys and alleyway" in the old city of Beijing. In 2008, Beijing Municipal Government issued important government documents, such as *The Protection Plan of Famous Historical and Cultural City of Beijing* and *The Protection Plan of 25 Historical and Cultural Protection Districts in the Old City of Beijing*. The holding of 2008 Beijing Olympic Games and the founding of 2009 Beijing International Design Week provided an important opportunity for modern design to participate in urban construction. In 2017,

The Beijing Urban Master Planning (2016–2035) was formulated, clearly proposing the overall urban planning in the block level to create a city cultural image with both international and regional characteristics.

3 Transformation Mode of Historical and Cultural Blocks in Beijing

The transformation and renewal of historical and cultural blocks adopt different paths and methods in different historical periods, resulting to different effects. Based on the diversity of the implementation subjects, the transformation mode of historical and cultural blocks in Beijing can be divided into two types: government-oriented and comprehensive collaborated. In the early stage, the government-oriented type was the primary. In recent years, with the conversion of government functions and the diversification of project implementation subjects, the comprehensive collaborated block transformation mode has further made prominent effect (Fig. 5).

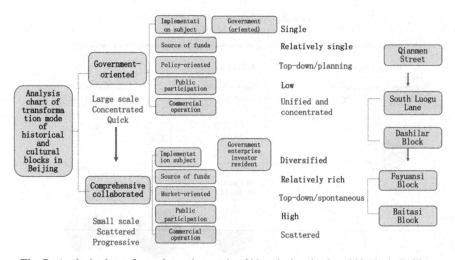

Fig. 5. Analysis chart of transformation mode of historical and cultural blocks in Beijing.

3.1 Government Oriented-Transformation and Renewal of Qianmen Street

In the transformation of historical and cultural blocks in Beijing, the government-oriented transformation projects take the early transformation of Dashilan Historical Block, Qianmen Street, South Luogu Lane and other blocks as the typical cases. The implementation subject type of this kind of project is relatively single, which is led by government to show a top-down policy orientation. The time limit of the project is clear, public participation is weak, and the commercial operation form is relatively unified.

Qianmen Street is a famous commercial street with a long history in Beijing, where was once the commercial center of the city in history. In the city construction after the reform and opening up, Qianen Street was tore down and built time and again, and most of the original wooden houses were demolished and built as commercial buildings. The block transformation project started at the end of 2006 and was led by Beijing Municipal Government, and its finishing was completed in May 2008 before the opening the Beijing Olympic Games. The implementation subject of the project is Beijing Municipal Government and SOHO China. Beijing tourism culture landmark is remodeled through the transformation and renewal of the blocks, and SOHO China is responsible for the actual investment management. The high-end brands and Beijing time-honored brands have been entered. For the transformation project of Qianmen, there are different comments in the industry. The transformation project of Qianmen Street is an overall demolition and renovation in large scale, with the street surface widened and only a small part of the original buildings preserved and repaired. The pseudo-classic architecture business street, which is called "fake antique" that is the transformation project completed based on the idea of "historical image restoration", is controversial in evaluation.

3.2 From Government-Oriented to Comprehensive Collaborated-South Luogu Lane and Dashilan Blocks

Renovation and Revitalization Project of South Luogu Lane Block. South Luogu Lane is one of the oldest cultural blocks in Beijing, which has been renovated and repaired many times since the founding of new China. The block renovation from 2006 to 2008 improved the overall quality of road facilities, formed a fish-bone distribution of east-west alleyway with South Luogu Lane as the central axis, and retained the alley-way texture and "neighborhood" style in the Great Capital of the Yuan Dynasty [3]. In 2015, aiming at the specific problems of the blocks, Dongcheng District Government launched the protection and revitalization plan of South Luogu Lane district with the purpose of "protecting the style, improving the people's livelihood, promoting the environment and revitalizing the culture", to carry out comprehensive renovation and repair of the blocks. In 2016, *The Regulatory Guidelines on Style Protection of Historical and Cultural Blocks of South Luogu Lane* was issued and implemented, which was the first regulatory guidelines on style protection in Beijing. In the course, the implementation subject of renovation and renewal of historical and cultural blocks has changed. Jinyu Dongcheng Real Estate Co., Ltd., as the implementation subject of the project of "protection, renovation and revitalization" in South Luogu Lane district, promoted the block transformation and formed a benign working mechanism of "department leading, street managing and society participating" [4]. Through the cases of South Luogu Lane and Dashilan Blocks, we can see the changes of the guiding ideology, strategic direction and actual implementation of the Beijing Municipal Government in the transformation project of historical and cultural blocks. The transformation of historical blocks in the early stage involves the transformation and renewal of municipal infrastructure, and the unified management and concentrated demolition, transformation and renovation at the government level, which have the problem that the thought of demolition and transformation is relatively single. In the later period, the professional company is the implementation subject of the block renewal, which effectively enhances the subjective initiative, makes up the shortage of government funds and introduces various social forces to participate in the block transformation.

Transformation/Renewal Plan of Dashilar Historical Block. The historical and cultural background of Dashilan block can be traced back to the period of Yong Le in the Ming Dynasty, and the framework and pattern of the block reflect the urban changes of Beijing from the Jin Dynasty to the Ming and Qing Dynasties. The transformation project of Dashilan block started in 2004, and Beijing Municipal Government was the implementation subject to lead the overall transformation with Architectural Design and Research Institute of Tsinghua University as the design subject. The design for the plan of protection, renovation and revitalization of Beijing Dashilan West Street won the outstanding scheme award of public buildings in the 17th capital urban planning and architectural design scheme report exhibition [5]. In 2011, Dashilan Investment LLC., as the implementation subject, launched the "Dashilan Renewal Plan", which formed a positive interaction with the annual Beijing International Design Week and became a typical case of exploring the organic renewal of historical and cultural blocks in a comprehensive collaborative mode.

Through the cases of South Luogu Lane and Dashilan Blocks, we can see the changes of the guiding ideology, strategic direction and actual implementation of the Beijing Municipal Government in the transformation project of historcal and cultural blocks. The transformation of historical blocks in the early stage involves the transformation and renewal of municipal infrastructure, and the unified management and concentrated demolition, transformation and renovation at the government level, which have the problem that the thought of demolition and transformation is relatively single. In the later period, the professional company is the implementation subject of the block renewal, which effectively enhances the subjective initiative, makes up the shortage of government funds and introduces various social forces to participate in the block transformation.

3.3   Construction of the Comprehensive Collaborated Cultural and Creative Blocks-Regeneration Plan of Baita Temple Block and Fayuan Temple Block

In the comprehensive collaborated transformation project, the dominance of government is transferred to the enterprises, investors and residents to collaborate and develop the blocks, and the implementation subject shows a more diversified feature. The starting time and completion time of the project are relatively vague, and the duration is long. The project is guided by the market demand from bottom to top, the commercial operation form presents a more diversified feature, and the public participation is high. The blocks of Baita Temple and Fayuan Temple are typical for the construction of "cultural and creative blocks".

Regeneration Plan of Baita Temple Block. Baitasi block is a historical and cultural block in the old city with complex texture and without large-scale demolition and transformation, where relies on Miaoying Baita Temple, the ancient temple in the Yuan Dynasty, and there are Beijing cultural landmarks, such as Beijing Lu Xun Museum and Lu Xun former residence. In 2013, Beijing Huarong Financial Investment and Development Co., Ltd launched the "regeneration plan of Baita Temple", which negotiated to vacate part of the courtyard space of the block, improved the overall environment while retaining the alleyway culture, and introduced the renewable resources of the block against the disorder of the "additional building" of the original quadrangle courtyard and the "narrowing" of alleyway in Baitasi block. Since 2015, the regeneration plan of Baita Temple has been deeply involved in the annual Beijing International Design Week, introduced multiple dimensional resources such as art, design, culture and commerce, and explored and realized the gradual block transformation of "micro circulation" and "organic renewal" [6].

Regeneration Plan of Fayuan Temple Block. Fayuansi block, relying on one of the most famous temples in Beijing which has a long history, is the core area of Xuannan culture since the Ming and Qing Dynasties. After the changes of the times, it faces the transformation problems similar with other blocks. In 2014, the transformation of Fayuansi block was conducted under the leading of government, and the implementation subject were the School of Architecture of Tsinghua University and Beijing Institute of Ancient Architectural Design Co., Ltd., to carry out "protection and renovation of courtyard and single structure". In 2018, *Detailed Planning for the Construction of Historical and Cultural Protection District of Fayuan Temple* was prepared. Subsequently, in order to further activate the vitality of the old city, Xiceng District launched the renewal plan of Fayuansi block, and took Beijing Xuanfang Dade Real Estate Co., Ltd. as the implementation subject to connect with Beijing International Design Week to carry out activities and explore a new mode of "participatory construction and sustainable renewal".

4 Design Collaboration Strategy Creating Based on Cultural and Creative Blocks

The regeneration plans of Baita Temple Block and Fayuan Temple Block mentioned above are closely linked with the activities of Beijing International Design Week in recent years. The transformation and activation projects of historical and cultural blocks with the construction goal of cultural and creative blocks reflect the role of modern design in the transformation of historical and cultural block in Beijing. The intervention of design can be discusses from two progressive levels: cultural space shaping and cultural ecological cycle. For the collaborative design strategy based on cultural heritage, on the one hand, it can play the advantages of modern design in the management and coordination to optimize the overall human environment of the block, on the other hand, it can promote block transformation and cultural renewal through creative design and collaborative research and development (Fig. 6).

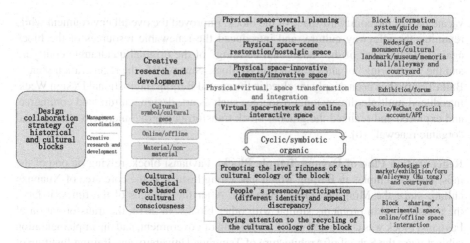

Fig. 6. Design collaboration strategy of historical and cultural blocks.

4.1 Cultural Space Shaping Based on Cultural Memory

Cultural space not only refers to the physical place or regional space that blends human factors, but also refers to the human information platform and virtual space built by digital information era through network channels. The historical and cultural blocks in the old city of Beijing bears a long period of historical context and cultural memory with rich levels, which are both the impression of the block cultural space and the core content of tourism culture.

In the cultural memory theory of Jan Assmann, a German scholar, "cultural memory is a long-term memory of more than several generations in collective memory" [7], which is extended through the exchange of various cultural forms, and the cultural space is an important place to bear cultural memory. The cultural memory of historical and cultural block in Beijing is sorted out and excavated again though design collaboration, based on which the block cultural space is constructed.

Shaping and Renewing the Physical Cultural Space

Planning the Overall Cultural Landscape of the Block, Constructing the Information System of Cultural Space. The overall planning of Beijing historical and cultural blocks at the level of cultural landscape is an important premise that the cultural space with multiple dimensions and multiple levels in historical blocks can be effectively distributed and built. We should play the role of design management and coordination, reasonably distribute the cultural landscape on the basis of meeting the residential, commercial, traffic and tourism and other functions, connect the cultural landmarks in the historical blocks, timely update the information system of cultural space, and realize the visual visualization of the overall cultural landscape of the blocks through modern design.

For example, Dashilan renewal plan formulated an overall strategy of "system consideration of the region and organic renewal of micro circulation", and publicized its idea through the theme website; since 2015, Baitasi renewal plan has held many activities during Beijing International Design Week every year, and the guide map in the block activity manual is the actual effect presentation of the state of the block every year. The mini program of "Play Qianmen" consumption map launched in the Qianmen Historical and Cultural Festival in 2019 is a program development that integrates tourism guide, commercial payment, game interaction and other functions, and also shows the overall planning of the block to the tourists and consumers.

Establishment and Protection of Core Cultural Landmarks: Historical Nostalgia and Narrative Display. The core cultural landmark in Beijing historical and cultural blocks is the cultural soul of the blocks. It is beneficial to the formation of the finishing touch of cultural space and the memory point of cultural transmission to protect the core cultural buildings and site landscape in historical and cultural blocks and complete the remodeling and reappearance of cultural space. The cultural landmarks that are remolded from former residences of celebrities in modern China, such as Mei Lanfang Museum and Lu Xun Memorial Hall in the historical block of the old city of Beijing, are not only the concentrated presentation of the historical and cultural features of the block, but also the model of the traditional quadrangle courtyard residential pattern. The construction of alleyway museum is also a typical case of shaping cultural space on the basis of combing cultural memory.

Innovative Cultural Space: Space Reconstruction with Innovative Elements. Innovative cultural space in Beijing historical and cultural blocks refers to the space reconstruction experiment that integrates the art, architecture, commerce, daily life and other fields of resources through design so as to extract innovative concept or core cultural element. For historical and cultural blocks, the addition of new elements is experimental and exploratory in cultural space, which is often controversial. We should carefully consider the "degree" of the implementation. The minimum residential renovation in South Luogu Lane by Zhoushan Qingping, a Japanese architect, is a case that provides living experience through residential innovative design; in addition, the project of guesthouse transformed from old house and the implantation of well-known brand concept stores in historical and cultural blocks are also an attempt to introduce innovative cultural space into the blocks, for example, One Page bookstore in Qianmen Beijing Fun and Starbucks flagship store are the effective exploration of the integration of the new and old space.

Docking and Interaction of Online/Offline Cultural Space. In addition to the above-mentioned cultural space with material substance in urban space as the carrier, along with the exploitation of digital media and information channels, online cultural space with non-material information media as the carrier has also become an important component of the digital survival of Beijing historical and cultural blocks. Through investigation and survey, the historical and cultural blocks such as Dashilan and Bama Temple have been established special websites in recent years, while the WeChat official accounts of the "Fun Nanluo" in South Nanluo Lane and the "Xuanfang Dade" in Fayuansi block are all the network interactive cultural space participated with blocks as the subject. The linkage of "online-virtual cultural space" and "offline-physical cultural space" is conductive to presenting cultural memory more systematically and realizing the interaction and integration of information.

According to statistics, it can be seen that the official account of the "Fun Nanluo" has relatively stable activity publicity and promotion per month since it was established in 2016. As to the utilization efficiency of online cultural space, different historical blocks also show great differences. In contrast, the WeChat official account of "Xuanfang Dade" has more intensive articles promotion during the Beijing International Design Week every year, while it shall be in a relatively quiet state in other times, and doesn't play the complete publicity role of the cultural space. In addition, there are cases presented the single project, such as the release of long-scroll digital illustration with the theme of Yu'er alleyway on the internet, which is a case of the combination of historical humanities and digital art (Figs. 7 and 8).

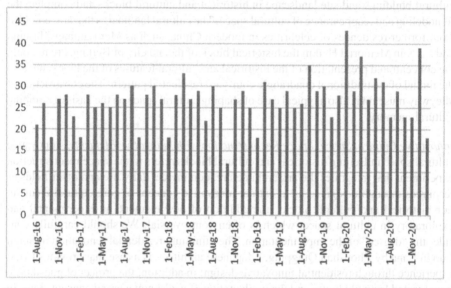

Fig. 7. Bar graph of articles number issued by WeChat official account of the Fun Nanluo since founding.

4.2 Cultural Ecological Cycle Based on Cultural Consciousness

In Fei Xiaotong's theory of "cultural consciousness", the people in specific regions and cultural environment should have "self-knowledge" to the culture in which they live, and should form the self-consciousness of protecting and inheriting the history and culture. Cultural ecology is the state of cultural development that adopts to the social formation, and is the environment and soil for the emergence, existence and development of culture. In the renewal and activation of historical and cultural blocks in the old city of Beijing, it is an important goal to construct a recyclable cultural ecology and is also the manifestation of cultural self-consciousness in the level of social practice.

Promoting the Level Richness of the Cultural Ecology of the Blocks. The development goal of historical and cultural blocks is comprehensive. The richer the cultural and

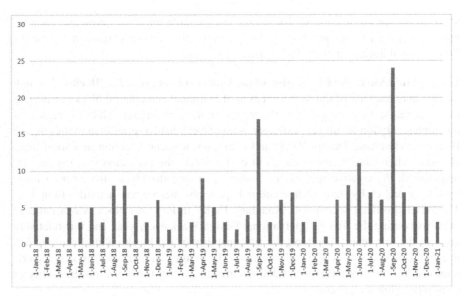

Fig. 8. Bar graph of articles number issued by WeChat official account of Xuanfang Dade

ecological level of the blocks, the more people can be attracted to visit and stop. The WeChat official account of "Xuanfang Dade" claimed that the renewal goal of Fayuansi block is to create a "historical and cultural essence district with highlighted culture, livable environment, green ecology, efficient wisdom and inter-generational transition" [8]. In recent years, in the process of linkage between Beijing International Design Week and historical blocks, various activities such as forum, exhibition, workshop, market and lecture are carried out, and the daily life, historical exhibition, space art, commercial operation and other contents present more subdivided business forms in the block environment. The richness of cultural ecology means the diversity of cultural factors of self-restraint blocks and the diversity of crowd who participate in the shaping of block cultural ecology.

People's Presence and Participation is the Key to the Construction of Cultural Ecology. In the theory of new urbanism, street and alley space is an important public space to provide social communication. The construction of a benign and sustainable cultural ecology requires the presence and participation of people to consciously carry out cultural renewal in the process of developing the tourism and cultural industry and publicizing the historical culture of the block.

Corresponding to different levels of the cultural ecology of the block, the related groups pf historical and cultural blocks include aborigines, tourists, researchers and tourism operators. The people with different identities have differences in the participation and demand of the block activities. The cultural ecology is ultimately implemented in the effective operation and quality improvement of block functions such as tourism, commerce, residence and transportation. In the process of transformation of Dashilan, Baitasi and Fayuansi blocks, the concept of "sharing" and the implementation of "micro courtyard", "symbiotic courtyard" and "alleyway parasitism" and other experimental space forms are all mentioned. The design can promote the cooperation and communication among different groups of people, which is the thinking expansion against the finiteness and limitation of the block space resources.

Paying Attention to the Circulation of the Cultural Ecology of the Blocks. Through the dynamic tracking of the transformation of historical and cultural blocks in Beijing in recent years, it can be seen that the overall strategy of different blocks is close, but the implementation is still very different. Some blocks held a series of activities during Beijing International Design Week, and won a lot of social attention in a short time. However, after more than one month of design week, the exhibition space is directly demolished, the creative space is no longer open, and the block also enters a long-term plain and chilly state. Online cultural space also has no new activities to update. The WeChat official account of "Xuanfang Dade" in Fayuansi block is concentrated to release during the Beijing International Design Week every year, and it is relatively quiet in the rest time. Therefore, the sustainability of the block cultural ecology lies in the effectiveness of design collaboration. The goal of cultural ecology is not short-term results, but long-term sustainable circulation, so that the block has the ability of conscious cultural regeneration.

5 Conclusion

To sum up, with the progress of the times and the accumulation of experience, the transformation of the old city of Beijing shows a more positive feature, and the collaborative strategy of modern design provides an important reference scheme for the sustainable and recyclable development of historical and cultural blocks in Beijing. The cases of the transformation and activation of the historical blocks in the old city of Beijing discussed in this paper also have certain reference significance for the discussion of the two-way mutual construction of modern design in improving the human and cultural environment.

Acknowledgements. This research is financial supported by Art Discipline Project of The National Social Science Fund of China (No. 17CG203) and the Youth Project of Philosophy and Social Science Foundation of Beijing (No. 19YTC035).

References

1. Haojie, S.: Study on the revolution of space scale of alleyway in the old city of Beijing (Master Dissertation). Beijing University of Civil Engineering and Architecture (2020)
2. Zuqun, Z.: Study on Beijing. Collaborative Research on Heritage Tourism and Cultural Creative Industry of Beijing. Capital University of Economics and Business Press, Beijing, p. 70, 1st edn. (2014)
3. Zuqun, Z.: Study on Beijing. Collaborative Research on Heritage Tourism and Cultural Creative Industry of Beijing. Capital University of Economics and Business Press, Beijing, pp. 275–276, 1st edn. (2014)

4. Report of Dongcheng District People's Government on Implementation of Protection and Revitalization Plan of Historical and Cultural Block-South Luogu Lane District. http://www.bjdch.gov.cn/n3201130/n3203907/n3203909/n6275910/c6276315/content.html. Accessed 4 Feb 2021
5. Beijing Survey, Design and Mapping Administration Office: Beijing Design, Development Report on Survey and Design Industries of Beijing, 2010–2011. China City Press, Beijing, p. 122 (2011)
6. Regeneration plan of Baita Temple. https://www.btsremade.com/. Accessed 16 Jan 2021
7. Xin, C., Gang, P.: Cultural Memory and Historism. Zhejiang University Press. Hangzhou, vol. 1, p. 36 (2014)
8. Brief introduction to the WeChat official account of Xuanfang Dade. Accessed 20 Jan 2021

Design for Inclusion and Social Development

GA-Based Research on Suitability of Recreational Space in Gardens to the Elderly—With Yangzhou Geyuan Garden as an Example

Tian Cao[1][⊠] and Fumei Zhang[2]

[1] Nanjing University of Science and Technology, Xiaolingwei 200, Nanjing 210094, Jiangsu, China
[2] Beijing Institute of Graphic Communication, Xinghua Street 1, Beijing 102600, China

Abstract. This study focuses on the relationship between the outdoor recreational space for the elderly and the landscaping design of gardens, and centers around gardens of the Southern Yangtze Delta where the elderly gathers spontaneously. With the Four-season Artificial Hills in Geyuan Garden, Yangzhou City, Jiangsu Province as an example, genetic algorithm (GA) is used to locate the optimal recreational point for the elderly, which situates close to "Yiyu Pavilion" according to the results. Analysis shows that this point is characterized by a large angle of perception, multiple layers of scenery and diversified attractions, which inspires the suitability design of today's urban public spaces for the elderly and puts forward related suggestions on modification.

Keywords: GA · Gardens · Recreational space · Suitability for the elderly

1 Introduction

As the global aging continues in recent years, activities of the elderly are drawing concerns, including urban outdoor recreation, a type which can't be ignored. The elderly usually chooses outdoor creational spaces according to their needs. Observing and analyzing these premises would be a source of inspiration and reference for the suitability design of urban public space for the elderly.

The classical gardens of the Southern Yangtze Delta in China are typical cases because of their long history and representation of the highest ancient landscaping arts level of China. Till now, there are many such gardens over this country, amongst which, many become attraction or urban parks after protection and development, offering a place where people can play and rest. Through observation, it is found that the gardens of the Southern Yangtze Delta are more attractive to the elderly, evidenced by the fact that not only these living around but also those who live far away may gather in such parks by riding or public transport. Unlike common tourists who just skim the surface, the elderly often goes directly to some specific areas in the gardens for concentrated recreational

© Springer Nature Switzerland AG 2021
M. M. Soares et al. (Eds.): HCII 2021, LNCS 12780, pp. 195–209, 2021.
https://doi.org/10.1007/978-3-030-78224-5_14

activities. This paper studied the design problems behind such a phenomenon based on Geyuan Garden in Yangzhou City, Jiangsu Province, China.

In Yangzhou City, Jiangsu Province, a historical renowned city of the Southern Yangtze Delta, there are some gardens built in Ming or Qing Dynasty, including Geyuan Garden. Originally it was privately owned by Huang Zhijun, a local salt dealer of the Qing Dynasty. After several times of expansion upon the foundation of China, it is opened to the public as an urban park. The Garden consists of the residential area, the Four-season Artificial Hills and the expansion area, of which, the Four-season Artificial Hills are the core, the most intact part in this Garden and a fixed recreational and exercise premises for most of the elderly. With the Four-season Artificial Hills as the study object, this paper analyzed the correlation between the outdoor recreation of the elderly and the landscaping design of the Garden.

2   Research Methodology

As the major research method used in this paper, GA, also known as a parameterized algorithm, relies on computer-based algorithm simulation for data analysis and computation by simulating the basic logics of biological evolution in the nature. Its main principle is to find data results that are close to the target through intergenerational data transmission, feedback and correction (namely data evolution); after repeated times of transmission and correction, GA can find the optimal data result infinitely close to the target. This algorithm is preferred to seek for the optimal solution of a set target in a certain data structure. In recent years, as AI is increasingly followed in architecture, geography and meteorology, GA also receives attention gradually as one of the computer intelligence technologies. Some scholars applied this algorithm to find the optimal solution in academic issues such as floor-area ratio of buildings, mountain path exploration, and weather forecast, which produced good research effect [3].

The outdoor recreational activities of the elderly are subject to subjective and objective factors. Consequently, the research is complicated and impossible through only some calculation. However, scientific tools like GA are helpful to find the optimal solution with certain spatial conditions, and provide a solving idea and practical reference for the design of outdoor recreational space for the elderly. Meanwhile, the research on this topical based on GA also expands its application in humanities and social sciences.

3   GA-Based Research Process

3.1   Identify the Breakthrough Point of "Perception"

From May 2020 to December 2020, the author visited the Four-season Artificial Hills of Geyuan Garden more than 10 times and randomly investigated 20 elderly who came for recreational purpose. Most of them believed that the "beautiful scenery" here made them "pleasant physically and mentally". Generally speaking, humans communicate with external things via perceptive activities. The experiment by D.O.Hebb and W.H.Bexton,

2 Canadian psychologists from the 1950s proved that moderate sensory stimulation is vital in our daily life and our physical and mental health would be seriously affected without sensation [2]. Through eyes, ears and nose, the elderly perceives scenery and produces abundant sensory stimulation, ultimately achieving the recreational purpose of "physical and mental pleasure".

The landscaper Mr. Chen Congzhou once pointed out that "scenery in a garden can be static or dynamic. Static scenery refers to these points where tourists stop to enjoy" [1]. The garden builder would predefine the optimal perception point for people to enjoy and rest. Occupying an area of about 5,000 square meters, the Four-season Artificial Hills consist of majestic artificial hills, vibrant plants, elegant buildings and diversified spaces. Amongst many of the locations for the elderly to rest, which one is the best? It can be located by GA from the breakthrough point of "perception".

3.2 Establish Parameter Cells

Analyze the Forms of Perception Range Model. Generally, our perception activities are directed. For example, when a building attracts us, we look into its direction. In a garden, people are usually immersed in the superimposed effect of multiple layers of perception [4]. The perceptive information may come from different sources, for instance, birds singing and flower fragrance from nowhere when we see an artificial hill. Based on such analysis, the perception range model is set as a sphere with human as the core, and the space occupied by the sphere is our perception range.

The local elderly who frequently visit the garden seldom climb up to the artificial hills or buildings. Instead, they rest on the ground. Therefore, with the elderly as P, their perception range model is a hemispheroid (S) with themselves as the geometric, and the volume occupied by S represents the perception range of the elderly.

Define the Size of the Perception Range Model. The size of the perception range model depends on our perception. As a result of physical degeneration, the elderly's perception is weaker than these of the middle or young age, and varies from people to people [5]. Through field tests, with visual perception as an example, when the elderly stands at the highest point-the peak of "Hill Autumn" at the east-in the garden, those who have better eyes can see clearly the "Hill Summer" at the west across the whole garden (about 80 m); these who are visually impaired can enjoy the "Wind and Moon Pavilion" in the middle (about 50 m) and the "Zhuqiu Pavilion" close to the "Hill Autumn" (about 25 m). Few older people have perceptual capacity below 25 m. Hence, 80 m, 50 m and 25 m are taken as the radius R of the elderly's perception range model, so as to cover the elderly with different perception.

Build the Perception Range Model. The spatial model is built in Rhinoceros, a kind of software usually used in parameterized design, and the Grasshopper is adopted for GA programming to form the elderly's perception range model (Figs. 1 and 2).

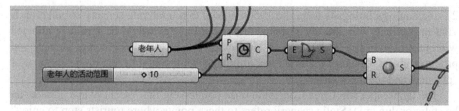

Fig. 1. Programming of the elderly's perception model

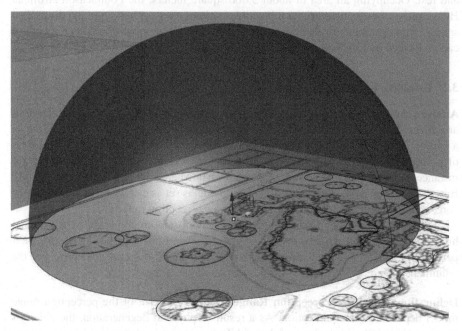

Fig. 2. The elderly's perception range model S

3.3 Write GA

Scenario Modeling. The elderly P stands in the Four-season Artificial Hills, and its perception range model S overlaps with the surrounding scene. He or she can be considered as having perceived the scene.

The Four-season Artificial Hills are modeled. According to the elements of traditional gardens, including "superimposed mountains, flowing water, buildings and plants", the Four-season Artificial Hills contain 8 artificial hills, 3 water bodies, 5 buildings and 32 places of plants (arbors and shrubs), which are modeled in order to form the scene model collection Y. instead of detailed structuring of scenes, the simplified geometric structuring mode is adopted to improve the computation efficiency of computer (Fig. 3). In order to reproduce the scenes of the Four-season Artificial Hills factually, the geometry matches with the overall appearance of the scenes, for example, buildings and green fences represented by cuboids, high arbors by round columns, pavilions by hexagonal columns and artificial hills by polygonal columns in consistent sizes.

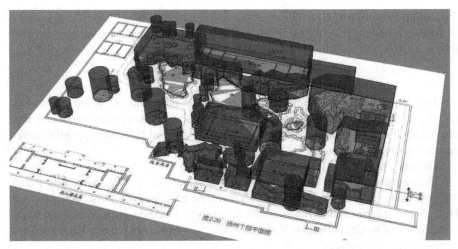

Fig. 3. Scene model collection Y for the four-season artificial hills in Geyuan garden

By placing the perception range model S of the elderly P into the scenario, when the elderly P is at a certain position, his/er perception range model S intersects with the scenario model Y, represented as the collection U:

$$U = P \cap Y \tag{1}$$

As long as the collection U is established, the elderly P can perceive the scenes in the scenario (Fig. 4).

Fig. 4. Intersection between the elderly P and the four-season artificial hills scene model Y

Operation Principle of GA. To calculate the optimal recreational point for the elderly in the Four-season Artificial Hills by GA, the location coordinates are the key and also the final results to be obtained by GA. Set the location coordinates of the elderly P as:

$$P(X_p, Y_p) \tag{2}$$

Take 50 m as the test parameter of the perception range model. As the coordinates (X_p, Y_p) change, the perception range model S moves on the basic plane, indicating that the elderly P is walking around in the Four-season Artificial Hills and upgrading his/er perception range.

The basic principles of GA are as follows:

The computer tries to change X_p and Y_p continuously so that the elderly P and the perception range model S moves on a real-time basis in the Four-season Artificial Hills. When the perception range model S moves to a certain position and intersects with the scene model collection Y, the computer automatically records the number of intersections (N) produced.

Generally speaking, people tend to perceive the most scenes in a limited range. The richer the scenes, the more ideal the residing point. According to this principle, when the elderly P stays at the most ideal point, the scenes he perceives shall reach the maximum. Therefore, the maximal intersection value N is taken as the GA's objective and its basis to automatically correct (X_p, Y_p).

In accordance with the above rules, the computer calculates based on (X_p, Y_p), outputs and examines N0 and feeds back the corrected (X_p, Y_p), followed by new N_1, N_2, N_3…Via such a circulation, multiple N_s are obtained to structure the genetic iteration of data.

After repeated intergenerational computing, GA will output a set of (X_p, Y_p) close to the set objective. The P point represented by the value is accepted as the optimal perception point of the elderly.

3.4 Computer Operation Results

The algorithmic routine for the intersection between the perception range model S and scene model Y of the elderly P is edited in Grasshopper. The input terminal and the output terminal of the GA ALU are correlated to the (X_p, Y_p) of the elderly P and the intersection value N recorded in the computer for operation according to the basic principles of GA.

As the GA ALU is operating, the computer can perform computation infinitely to obtain a result infinitely close to the optimal solution. When the computer operates for a period of time, the result is almost stable. In this operation, when the computer operates for 30 min and the GA iterations reach 99, the result tends to stabilize. 5 points obtain the N of 29, the highest value with the given parameters (Figs. 5 and 6), and are considered as 1 point (P_1) as they are less than 1 m distanced. This is the ideal perception point for the elderly with the perception range radius of 50 m in the Four-season Artificial Hills. Similarly, GA is performed by changing the perception range radius of the elderly P to 25 m and 80 m. When the computer operates for 30 min and the GA iterations reach 99, the result tends to stabilize and the optimal perception points P_2 and P_3 are obtained and indicated in the figures below (Figs. 7, 8, 9, 10):

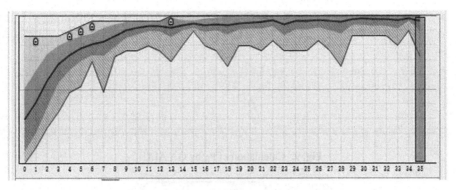

Fig. 5. Calculation of P_1 by GA ALU

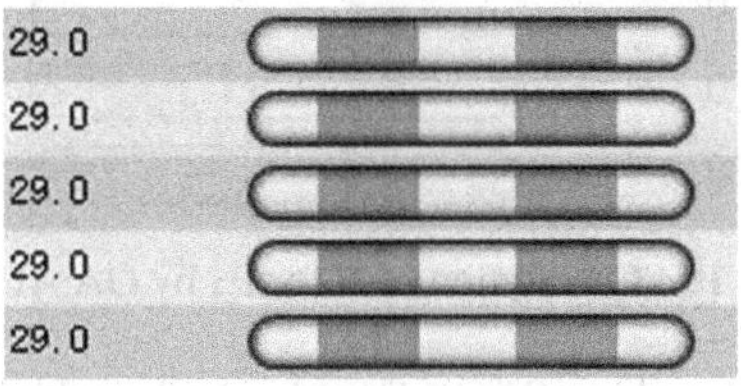

29.0

29.0

29.0

29.0

29.0

Fig. 6. Calculation of N for P_1 by GA ALU

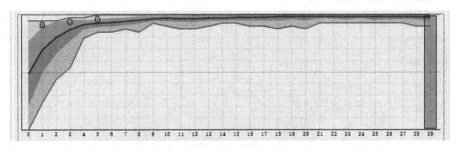

Fig. 7. Calculation of P_2 by GA ALU

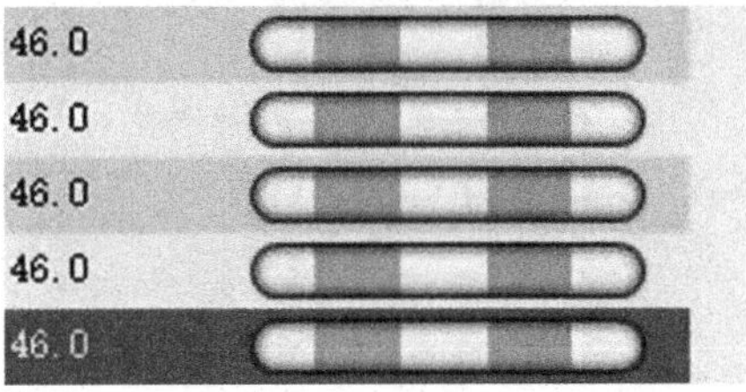

46.0

46.0

46.0

46.0

46.0

Fig. 8. Calculation of N for P_2 by GA ALU

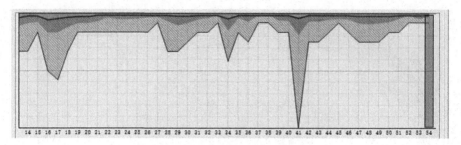

Fig. 9. Calculation of P₃ by GA ALU

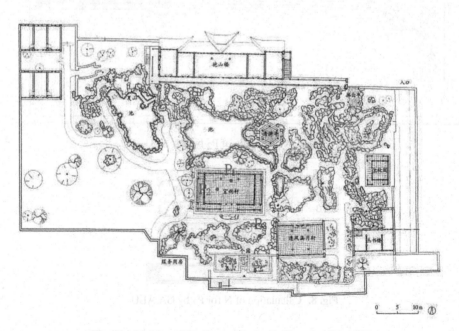

Fig. 10. Calculation of N for P₃ by GA ALU

Mark P_1, P_2 and P_3 in the plane (Fig. 11) and calculate the intersection N of the four scenes (N_1 for artificial hills, N_2 for ponds, N_3 for buildings and N_4 for plants) to obtain the following table (Table 1):

Fig. 11. Position of P_1, P_2 and P_3 in the Plane by GA ALU

Table 1. Intersection N for P_1, P_2 and P_3, and sub-item N for the 4 scenes

Perception range radius R of the elderly P	S/N for the optimal perception point P	N_1	N_2	N_3	N_4	N
50 m	P_1	9	4	4	12	29
25 m	P_2	4	1	2	5	12
80 m	P_3	9	4	6	27	46

P_1 is about 5 m from P_3, and P_2 is about 15 m from P_1 and P_3.

The computed result is artificially corrected as the case maybe to conform to the reality. In the 3 points, 2 are inside the "Yiyu Pavilion" and 1 at the artificial hill by its south. Indoor scenes are not the research objects in this paper. The artificial hills can't be a stop point for the elderly due to its rough terrain. In real life, better perception effect can be obtained by taking activities around the optimal recreational point. Therefore, the areas close to the 3 points are optimal for the elderly.

3.5 Examination and Analysis of the Computed Results

By field investigation, the Four-season Artificial Hills have 9 elegant scenes in addition to the area around the "Yiyu Pavilion", which may fit for the elderly. To validate the computed result of GA, the location (X_p, Y_p) of the elderly P is input and the elderly is placed in the 9 spaces (Fig. 12) to calculate the number of intersections between the elderly's perception range and the scene model. The results are shown in the table below (Table 2):

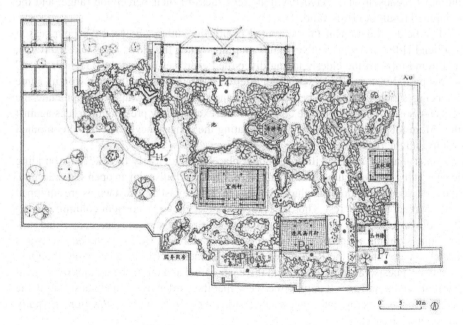

Fig. 12. 12 Other 9 recreational points

Table 2. N and sub-item N of the elderly P at other 9 recreational points

Elderly no.	Intersection N (N_1, N_2, N_3 and N_4) with the Perception Radius of 50 m	Intersection N (N_1, N_2, N_3 and N_4) with the Perception Radius of 80 m	Intersection N (N_1, N_2, N_3 and N_4) with the Perception Radius of 25 m
P_4	25 (7, 4, 4, 10)	44 (9, 4, 7, 24)	6 (2, 2, 3, 5)
P_5	27 (7, 3, 6, 11)	45 (10, 3, 6, 26)	8 (3, 1, 2, 2)
P_6	17 (4, 0, 6, 7)	34 (11, 0, 6, 17)	4 (2, 0, 1, 1)
P_7	19 (6, 0, 6, 7)	32 (8, 0, 6, 18)	8 (2, 0, 3, 3)
P_8	27 (7, 3, 5, 12)	38 (9, 4, 6, 19)	11 (2, 2, 2, 5)
P_9	26 (7, 0, 5, 14)	38 (13, 0, 6, 19)	11 (2, 0, 2, 7)
P_{10}	28 (7, 0, 4, 17)	45 (9, 6, 6, 24)	9 (2, 0, 2, 5)
P_{11}	28 (7, 4, 4, 13)	45 (10, 4, 4, 27)	11 (3, 2, 2, 6)
P_{12}	21 (2, 0, 2, 17)	40 (5, 4, 3, 28)	7 (1, 1, 1, 4)

From Tables 1 and 2:

The Area Around the "Yiyu Pavilion" Fits for the Elderly. P_1, P_2 and P_3 neighbor the "Yiyu Pavilion". Arguably, the area around the "Yiyu Pavilion" is the optimal recreational point for the elderly by GA. According to artificial observation and the intersection value N, the total number of intersections N between the elderly and the scene model from P_4 to P_{12} are less than these at P_1, P_2 and P_3, suggesting that the elderly can perceive the most scenes around "Yiyu Pavilion" regardless of their perception range, and the computed result of GA is valid.

For field validation of the computed result, the author observed the Four-season Artificial Hills on 3 consecutive winter mornings when the elderly less take exercises, and found most of the elderly taking diversified exercises around the "Yiyu Pavilion" in this period of time. Some sat in the "Meiren Kao" (a bench with back won its name for being sit on by ancient beauties and leaned along their waist) to appreciate the scenery. Some walked along the corridor. Some exercised by pressing their legs against the "Meiren Kao" (Figs. 13, 14, 15), indicating the consistency between the computed results and the reality.

What makes "Yiyu Pavilion" an ideal place for the elderly to rest? This building locates at the central south of the Four-season Artificial Hills with an open space around, and is circled by corridors, of which, the corridors at the east and west wings are equipped with "Meiren Kao" for rest. There is a pair of couplets hung on corridor columns, saying that "playing Guqin in the morning and Se when the sun sets; old rain comes and new rain joins". In this couplet, "rain", quoted from Qiu Shu by Du Fu, signifies guests and friends. According to the Records of Geyuan Garden by Liu Fenggao from the Qing Dynasty: "guests gather here to spend the leisure time and enjoy the tranquility in great harmony and kindness". It depicts the scene that the garden owner and guests enjoy the scenery for endless joy, and suggests the historical function of "Yiyu Pavilion" for party and appreciation.

Fig. 13. Activity scene 1 for the elderly

Fig. 14. Activity scene 2 for the elderly

Fig. 15. Activity scene 3 for the elderly

By analyzing the design of the "Yiyu Pavilion" from the perspective of the elderly, it can be seen that:

The Pavilion is Arranged at the Center with a Broad Perception Angle. The "Yiyu Pavilion" is located in the middle of the Four-season Artificial Hills and embraced by landscapes, such as the "Hill Spring", the "Hill Summer", the "Mountain-embracing Tower", the "Qingyi Pavilion", the "Hill Autumn", the "Wind and Moon Pavilion" and the "Zhuqiu Pavilion", which offer a wide perception angel for elderly around the "Yiyu Pavilion".

The Attractions are Arranged in Multiple Layers to Adapt to Various Perceptions. Different attractions form multiple layers around the "Yiyu Pavilion", including low ponds, hills, pavilion and trees" about 10 m to 20 m away, high visual landscapes enclosed by artificial hills at 20 m to 30 m; behind the artificial hills, there is the "Mountain-embracing Tower", which is higher and bigger. The close, middle and remote features spread in sequence to improve abundance for the elderly with various perceptions.

The Features are Diversified. The "Four-season Artificial Hills" of Geyuan Garden are so named since its features can reflect the characteristics of the four seasons. Looking around from the "Yiyu Pavilion", many feature portfolios come into our eyes, including plants and waterscape, artificial hills and waterscape, artificial hills and plants, buildings and artificial hills, which change over the four seasons and weather, like birds singing and flower fragrance in Spring, raindrops drumming rhythmically against the banana leaves in Summer, red maples and falling leaves in Autumn and white snow in Winter, brining rich and changeable perception experience to the elderly.

Though the "Yiyu Pavilion" is not dedicated to the elderly, its design meets their demands to appreciate features and fits for stay and rest.

Characteristics of Other Recreational Points. From Table 2, the "Yiyu Pavilion" is followed by P_{11}, P_8, P_5 and P_4 in terms of N value. In addition to high N values, the 4 spaces also have sub-item N for artificial hills, ponds, buildings and plants, indicating that the elderly can perceive the four features in the four spaces at the same time (Figs. 13, 14, 15, 16, 17, 18, 19).

P_{11} and P_4 are next to the pond of the "Hill Summer" in the Midwest of the garden, where the elderly can perceive more features of mountains and water; P_8 and P_5 are close to the "Hill Autumn", "Books Tower" and "Wind and Moon Pavilion" in the east part, where the elderly has less chance to ponds but features of buildings and artificial hills.

In comparison, amongst the five spaces (P_6, P_7, P_9, P_{10} and P_{12}), some (P_7, P_{10} and P_{12} for example) has 0 sub-item N regardless of the high N value, which means that the elderly can't perceive some garden features therein. A 0 sub-item N doesn't mean that the spatial design of the garden is defective. "Seeing big things through small ones" is a practice in garden landscaping to purposely restrict our perception range so that we focus on certain scenery. An example is appreciating the artificial hill bonsai in the courtyard through the lattice window. However, in the context of this paper, these spaces are possibly not the most ideal recreational points for the elderly.

Fig. 16. P$_{11}$

Fig. 17. P$_8$

Fig. 18. P$_5$

Fig. 19. P₄

4 Conclusions

Based on the Four-season Artificial Hills in Yangzhou Geyuan Garden, this paper applied the GA to calculate the optimal recreational points for the elderly and analyzed their design characteristics. The design intelligence in traditional gardens can inspire the design of today's public spaces in cities. Nowadays, many cities have public spaces for the citizens to take exercise and rest, and most of them can meet the basic activity demands of the elderly, such as rest, exercise and walking pets, etc. However, little consideration is given to their higher levels of demands for landscape appreciation. Limited by space, this paper only concludes some data rules from the landscape design of Geyuan Garden and puts forward the following modification suggestions:

Add the landscape level of urban public space to at least 3. Difference shall be embodied between different levels in feature type, depth and volume, so as to meet the perception demands of elderly with different perceptions.

Arrange rockery, water bodies, buildings and plants around the preset optimal recreational point so that the elderly can perceive the four types of features at the same time. The ratio of the number of perceived intersections N and the perception range radius of the elderly shall be close to or greater than 1:2, namely, $N/R \geq 1/2$.

Categorize and proportionally arrange features around the best recreational points. As an example, for the best recreational point around the natural landscape of rockery and water body, the ratio of rockery, water body, building and plant shall be close to 2:1:1:3; in case of humanistic landscape of buildings and plants, the proportions of rockery and water bodies shall be reduced properly while the ratio of building to plant shall be increased. In such a way, different types of perceptive stimulation are developed and the perception activities of the elder are enriched.

Acknowledgements. This research is financial supported by the Philosophy and Social Science Foundation of Jiangsu (No. 19YSC009).

References

1. Chen, C.: About Gardens, Tongji University Press, Shanghai, p. 8 (2017)
2. Hu, Z., Lin, Y.: Environmental Psychology, China Architecture and Building Press, Beijing, p. 6 (2008)
3. Yunsheng, B., Yunhe, G.: Parameterized Non-linear Design of Grasshopper. Huazhong University of Science and Technology Press, Wuhan (2018)
4. Yigang, P.: Analysis of Classical Gardens in China. China Architecture and Building Press, Beijing (1986)
5. Marcus, G.C., Yu, K., Wang, Z., Sun, P.: People Places: Design Guidelines for Urban Open Space. Beijing Science and Technology Press, Beijing (2020)

Accessibility Evaluation of E-Government Web Applications: A Systematic Review

Daniela Cisneros, Fernando Huamán Monzón$^{(\boxtimes)}$ ⓘ, and Freddy Paz ⓘ

Pontificia Universidad Católica del Perú, Av. Universitaria 1801, San Miguel, Lima, Peru
{cisneros.daniela, fpaz}@pucp.pe, fhuamanm@pucp.edu.pe

Abstract. For this study a systematic literature review was conducted in order to establish how accessibility evaluations of E-Government Web applications are performed. The search was carried out in two of the most relevant databases in the Software Engineering field, obtaining 421 results. Once the previously defined inclusion and exclusion criteria were applied, 36 articles were selected as relevant. Likewise, the Pontifical Catholic University of Peru (PUCP) thesis digital repository was reviewed in order to find evaluations within the Peruvian context. In this way, it was possible to determine that: (1) most of the studies which include an accessibility evaluation are carried out in countries within the Americas region, (2) the most widely used Web accessibility guidelines are the Web 2.0 Content Accessibility Guidelines, (3) the most frequently used evaluation method is automated evaluation, (4) the most used tool is AChecker, and (5) accessibility studies generically address disabilities. Concerning the research found in the PUCP digital thesis repository, even if it did not specifically deal with a government entity, it provided an idea on the execution of Web accessibility evaluations in Peru.

Keywords: Human-computer interaction · Accessibility · Systematic review · E-government · Web applications

1 Introduction

The Internet has become a priceless tool in society as it facilitates development and innovation through the access and exchange of massive amounts of information [1]. Although access to the Internet is vital to any individual there are still conditions that prevent its use without barriers. Currently, one billion people in the world have some kind of disability, and as such, web accessibility takes a central role in providing them the same opportunities as the rest of the population [2]. This concept was defined to ensure that everyone is able to understand, navigate, and contribute to the Web [3]. Therefore, it is essential to consider Web Accessibility in the development of software applications of all domains, from recreational websites to ones from educational, financial, and government entities. The last-mentioned category is, within the scope of E-government, understood as the use of information and communication technologies (ICT) to provide state services more effectively and efficiently to citizens and companies [4]. Given the relevance of government tools for citizens, it was deemed necessary to explore how the specialists in

© Springer Nature Switzerland AG 2021
M. M. Soares et al. (Eds.): HCII 2021, LNCS 12780, pp. 210–223, 2021.
https://doi.org/10.1007/978-3-030-78224-5_15

Human-Computer Interaction (HCI) are covering accessibility in this specific context. In this article, a systematic literature review was conducted in order to establish how accessibility evaluations of E-Government Web applications are performed.

2 Planning the Review

2.1 Definition of Research Questions

As the systematic review was aimed at finding out where and how e-government web application accessibility evaluation research has been performed, the following research questions were posed:

Q1: In which countries has research been reported on web application accessibility evaluation in the framework of e-government?
Q2: What are the most used guidelines or directions in web application accessibility evaluation studies in the e-government framework?
Q3: What are the most widely used evaluation methods in web application accessibility evaluation studies in the e-government framework?
Q4: What are the most used tools in e-government framework accessibility evaluation studies?
Q5: What type of disability is targeted in e-government web application accessibility evaluation research?

The PICOC criteria (Population, Intervention, Comparison, Outcome and Context) was used to structure the research questions and define the general concepts of the systematic review. The Comparison criterion was not applied because the results found were not to be contrasted with any specific evaluation method. The outcome of the application of the PICOC criteria was:

- **Population**: E-government web applications.
- **Intervention**: Accessibility evaluation.
- **Comparison**: Not applicable.
- **Results**: Accessibility evaluation case studies in the field of e-government.
- **Context**: Academic and empirical.

2.2 Elaboration of Research Strategy

The search strategy was defined based on the selection of the sources and the construction of the search string.

Source Selection. The primary search was performed at SCOPUS and Web of Science (WoS). These databases were selected taking into consideration that they are the most relevant in the area of informatics engineering and that professors with experience in research projects recommended them.

Construction of the Search String. The results from the PICOC Criteria were used to elaborate the search string. It was also taken into consideration that the English Language is the most used in scientific articles and that the use of synonyms of the terms will enrich the search.

Furthermore, only the publications of the last 5 years (2015–2019) were examined in order to obtain the most updated information under a similar context to the present one.

The search strings used in each database were:

SCOPUS: ABS (e-government OR e-gov OR government OR public) AND TITLE-ABS (website* OR (web AND site*) OR (web AND application*)) AND TITLE-ABS (study OR evaluation OR assessment) AND TITLE-ABS (accessibility) AND (PUBYEAR > 2013).

WEB OF SCIENCE (WOS): TS = ((e-government OR e-gov OR government OR public) AND (website* OR (web AND site*) OR (web AND application*)) AND (study OR evaluation OR assessment) AND (accessibility)) AND PY = (2014–2019).

2.3   Elaboration of Selection Strategy

The results obtained from the search string were reviewed to determine whether they answered the research questions posed. The inclusion criteria defined were:

- It is written in the English or Spanish language.
- It is an accessibility study or one of the dimensions it explores is accessibility in e-government web applications.

On the other hand, the exclusion criteria were:

- It is not an accessibility study. The definition of accessibility from the Web Accessibility Initiative (2005) will be taken into consideration.
- It is not conducted within the scope of e-government explicitly.
- It is not executed in a web application.

3   Execution of the Review

Initially, 421 results were obtained when entering the search string in the two databases. After applying the inclusion and exclusion criteria, 36 relevant articles were selected for review. Table 1 shows the results found during the search and selection process, and Table 2 shows the detail of the articles selected as relevant.

Table 1. Results of the systematic search process

Data base	Search results	Repeated articles	Relevant articles
SCOPUS	244	0	33
Web of science	177	64	3
Total	**421**	**64**	**36**

Table 2. Relevant articles for the systematic review

ID	Authors	Publication year	Article title
A01 [5]	Kamoun, F., Almourad, M.B.	2014	Accessibility as an integral factor in e-government web site evaluation: The case of Dubai e-government
A02 [6]	Luján-Mora S., Navarrete R., Peñafiel M.	2014	Egovernment and web accessibility in South America
A03 [7]	Darmaputra I.G.B.N.E., Wijaya S.S.	2017	Evaluating the accessibility of provinces' e-government websites in Indonesia
A04 [8]	AkgÜL Y., Vatansever, K.	2016	Web content accessibility of municipal web sites in Turkey
A05 [9]	Verkijika S.F., De Wet L.	2018	Quality assessment of e-government websites in Sub-Saharan Africa: A public values perspective
A06 [10]	Ismailova R.	2017	Web site accessibility, usability and security: a survey of government web sites in Kyrgyz Republic
A07 [11]	Agbozo E., Spassov, K.	2018	Evaluating metropolitan assembly web sites in Ghana: Accessibility, compatibility and usability
A08 [12]	Yaokumah W., Brown S., Amponsah, R.	2015	Accessibility, quality and performance of government portals and ministry web sites: a view using diagnostic tools
A09 [13]	Acosta-Vargas P., Luján-Mora S., Salvador-Ullauri L.	2017	Quality evaluation of government websites
A10 [14]	Barricelli B.R., Sciarelli P., Valtolina S., Rizzi, A.	2018	Web accessibility legislation in Italy: a survey 10 years after the Stanca Act

(*continued*)

Table 2. (*continued*)

ID	Authors	Publication year	Article title
A11 [15]	Brooks L., Persaud A	2015	Comparing local e-government websites in Canada and the UK
A12 [16]	Al-Bataineh A.F., Mustafa S.H	2016	How Jordanian e-Government websites respond to the needs of people with disabilities
A13 [17]	Dollie M., Kabanda S.	2017	e-Government in Africa: Perceived concerns of persons with disabilities (PWDs) in South Africa
A14 [18]	Moreno L., Martínez P., Muguerza J., Abascal J.	2018	Support resource based on standards for accessible e-Government transactional services
A15 [19]	Al-Khalifa H.S., Baazeem I., Alamer R.	2017	Revisiting the accessibility of Saudi Arabia government websites
A16 [20]	Ansari R.F., Baqar A., Hassan H., Saeed F.	2016	Heuristic, accessibility and usability evaluations of Pakistan's e-government websites
A17 [21]	Ahmi A., Mohamad R	2016	Evaluating accessibility of Malaysian ministries websites using WCAG 2.0 and Section 508 Guideline
A18 [22]	Leist E., Smith D.	2014	Accessibility issues in e-government
A19 [23]	Zitkus E., Brigatto A.C., Ferrari A.L.M., Bonfim G.H.C., Carvalho Filho I.F.P., Reis T.D., Medola F.O., Paschoarelli L.C.	2016	Accessibility and usability of websites intended for people with disabilities: A preliminary study
A20 [24]	Ismailova R., Inal Y.	2017	Web site accessibility and quality in use: a comparative study of government Web sites in Kyrgyzstan, Azerbaijan, Kazakhstan and Turkey
A21 [25]	Ismail A., Kuppusamy K.S., Nengroo A.S.	2018	Multi-tool accessibility assessment of government department websites: a case-study with JKGAD
A22 [26]	Angélico M.J., Silva A., Teixeira S.F., Maia T., Silva A.M	2017	Web accessibility and transparency for accountability: The Portuguese official municipal websites

(*continued*)

Table 2. (*continued*)

ID	Authors	Publication year	Article title
A23 [27]	Tashtoush Y.M., Darabseh A.F., Al-Sarhan H.N.	2016	The Arabian E-government websites accessibility: A case study
A24 [28]	Herrera J.A.R., Ricaurte J.A.B.	2015	Web accessibility: Study web accessibility in public places of the Colombian State
A25 [29]	Balaji V., Kuppusamy K.S.	2016	Accessibility evaluation of indian railway websites
A26 [30]	Karaim N.A., Inal Y..	2019	Usability and accessibility evaluation of Libyan government websites
A27 [31]	Acosta T., Acosta-Vargas P., Lujan-Mora S..	2018	Accessibility of eGovernment Services in Latin America
A28 [32]	De Souza I.M., Maciel C., Cappelli C.	2016	The model of accessibility to electronic Government: Applicability in DATAPREV
A29 [33]	Sam-Anlas C.A., Stable-Rodríguez Y	2016	Evaluating accessibility in Peruvian Government websites
A30 [34]	Youngblood N.E.	2014	Revisiting Alabama state website accessibility
A31 [35]	Gharbi I., Bouraoui A., Bellamine Ben Saoud N.	2018	Multilevel accessibility evaluation of institutional websites in Tunisia
A32 [36]	Gopinath S., Senthooran V., Lojenaa N., Kartheeswaran T.	2016	Usability and accessibility analysis of selected government websites in Sri Lanka
A33 [37]	King B.A., Youngbloob N.E.	2016	E-government in Alabama: An analysis of county voting and election website content, usability, accessibility, and mobile readiness
A34 [38]	Mtebe J.S., Kondoro A.W.	2017	Accessibility and Usability of Government Websites in Tanzania
A35 [39]	Piñeiro-Naval, V., Mangana, R., & Serra, P.	2018	Validation of the Formal Quality Index as a model for assessing websites: The case of the local Portuguese e-Administration
A36 [40]	Noh K.-R., Jeong E.-S., You Y.-B., Moon S.-J., Kang M.-B.	2015	A study on the current status and strategies for improvement of web accessibility compliance of public institutions

4 Results of the Systematic Review

4.1 Research Question 1

Research in 96 countries was reviewed. Since the list was extensive, we worked with regions in order to better analyze the data obtained (Table 3). Table 4 provides more detail on the Americas region, as it presented the largest number of accessibility studies.

Table 3. Accessibility research papers by region

Region	Number of studies in that region	Papers
Americas	42	A02, A09, A19, A24, A27, A28, A29, A30, A33
Africa	37	A05, A07, A13, A23, A31, A34
Asia	27	A01, A03, A04, A06, A09, A15, A16, A20, A21, A23, A26, A32, A36
Europe	24	A02, A09, A10, A11, A14, A18, A22, A35

The largest number of Web accessibility studies has been conducted in countries located in the Americas (Table 3) and Brazil is the country with the largest number of studies reported in the region (Table 4). It is important to note that Brazil ranks fifth in the Americas in the 2018 United Nations e-Government survey [41] and that this version of the ranking gave greater importance to accessibility in general [41].

4.2 Research Question 2

It was shown that the most used guidelines in research of accessibility evaluations of e-government web applications are the Web Content Accessibility Guidelines 2.0, Web Content Accessibility Guidelines 1.0, Section 508, E-Government Accessibility Model, Korean Web Content Accessibility Guidelines 2.0, and Researchers' own Proposals.

Web Content Accessibility Guidelines 2.0. Guidelines published in 2008 by the Web Accessibility Initiative. It consists of 4 basic principles (Perceptible, Operable, Understandable and Robust), 12 guidelines and 61 success criteria [42].

Web Content Accessibility Guidelines 1.0. Guidelines published in 1999 by the Web Accessibility Initiative. It consists of 14 guidelines, each with a series of checkpoints with an assigned priority level [43].

Section 508. Section of the U.S. Rehabilitation Act. It focuses on protecting the rights of people with disabilities and details 16 standards for achieving Web accessibility [21].

Own Proposal. The first is a support resource for transactional services and is based in part on the Web 2.0 Content Accessibility Guidelines [5]. The second is based on another author and proposes four criteria for web accessibility analysis: use of valid HTML and CSS, accessible navigation, description of images and structure of data tables [33].

Table 4. Accessibility research papers by country.

Country	Number of studies in that country	Papers
Brazil	4	A02, A19, A27, A28
Colombia	3	A02, A24, A27
Peru	3	A02, A27, A29
United States of America	3	A09, A30, A33
Argentina	2	A02, A27
Bolivia	2	A02, A27
Chile	2	A02, A27
Ecuador	2	A02, A27
French Guiana	2	A02, A27
Paraguay	2	A02, A27
Suriname	2	A02, A27
Uruguay	2	A02, A27
Venezuela	2	A02, A27
Costa Rica	1	A27
Cuba	1	A27
El Salvador	1	A27
Guatemala	1	A27
Haiti	1	A27
Honduras	1	A27
Mexico	1	A27
Nicaragua	1	A27
Panama	1	A27
Dominican Republic	1	A27
Canada	1	A11

Accessibility Model of Electronic Government. This model, developed by the Brazilian government, provides technical recommendations for the construction and adaptation of accessible web applications for users with some type of disability [32].

Korean Web Content Accessibility Guidelines 2.0. South Korean standard based on version 2 of the Web Content Accessibility Guidelines. It includes technical specifications for improving Web accessibility and consists of three steps: Principles, guidelines and requirements [40].

Table 5. Papers reporting the use of Web Accessibility guidelines.

Guideline	Number of times used	Papers
Web Content Accessibility Guidelines 2.0	30	A01, A02, A03, A04, A05, A07, A08, A09, A10, A11, A13, A15, A16, A17, A18, A19, A21, A22, A23, A24, A25, A26, A27, A29, A30, A31, A32, A33, A34, A35
Web Content Accessibility Guidelines 1.0	5	A02, A06, A12, A21, A29
Section 508	3	A17, A33, A34
Own Proposal	2	A14, A29
Accessibility Model of Electronic Government	1	A28
Korean Web Content Accessibility Guidelines 2.0	1	A36

The Web Content Accessibility Guidelines 2.0 were the most used, being present in 30 cases (Table 5). Considering that the studies reviewed have a publication year after 2013, it was expected that the majority used the international standard proposed in 2008 [42]. The first version of the guidelines has been replaced as it does not contemplate the new technologies and tools that support Web access nowadays [37]. Regarding the other guidelines, the e-Government Accessibility Model and the Korean Web Content Accessibility Guidelines 2.0 are used only in their home countries [32, 40]. On the other hand, Section 508 is considered valid around the globe and is used to measure the web accessibility of other countries [21, 38]. Finally, the new proposals were built on the basis of some of the guidelines mentioned above or based on the proposals of other authors [18].

4.3 Research Question 3

It was shown that the most used evaluation methods for accessibility were: Evaluation with Experts, Evaluation with Users and Automated Evaluation.

Expert Evaluation. A method that involves the manual analysis of web applications in order to verify their compliance with certain guidelines [19].

User Evaluation. A method that involves a group of users systematically going through the web application and testing its accessibility from their point of view [19].

Automated Evaluation. A method that involves the use of Web Accessibility Evaluation Tools (WAET) (Al-Khalifa et al. 2017), defined as software programs or online services that determine whether web content meets accessibility guidelines [44].

Table 6. Papers reporting the use of Web Accessibility guidelines.

Guideline	Number of times used	Papers
Expert evaluation	61	A01, A02, A03, A04, A05, A06, A07, A08, A09, A10, A11, A12, A13, A14, A15, A16, A17, A18, A19, A20, A21, A22, A23, A24, A25, A26, A27, A29, A30, A31, A32, A33, A34, A35, A36
User evaluation	7	A14, A15, A28, A29, A31, A33, A36
Automated evaluation	4	A13, A16, A19, A31

The most used method in accessibility evaluations was automated evaluation, being applied in 61 of the cases (Table 6). The reason for the preference of this method is that it is fast, simple, and often free of charge [32, 5]. As such, it is especially useful when you want to evaluate a large number of web applications. However, it is not as accurate or captures the perspective of a user with a disability in the way that an expert or user evaluation might do even if it requires more time and effort [5]. In summary, the use of a combination of these evaluation methods would be the best.

4.4 Research Question 4

The most widely used accessibility evaluation tool was AChecker, being used in 16 of the cases (Table 7). AChecker is a free Web site that allows classification of accessibility problems into three categories: known, probable, and potential problems, the last two requiring human judgment [45].

The preference of this tool mainly results in this classification, which allows accessibility evaluation to become a continuous and interactive process, often requiring the opinion of the evaluator [5]. AChecker also provides detailed and highly accurate results, although it is criticized for its coverage [19, 14]. Regarding the Web Accessibility Test (TAW) and WAVE, their success is based on a similar philosophy in requiring human intervention in some way [6].

4.5 Research Question 5

The only studies that specify what type of disability they are targeting are the research of Zitkus, Dollie, and Kabanda [17, 23]. These focus on the blind or visually impaired population, with the justification that this disability affects a greater number of individuals [17, 23]. The remaining articles deal with disabilities in a generic way.

Most of the accessibility studies reviewed do not seek to emphasize a particular condition. Thus, they are aligned with the concept of Web accessibility [3] which is aimed at all types of disabilities that affect an individual's opportunity to navigate and contribute to the Web regardless of the number of people who have them.

Table 7. Papers reporting the use of Web Accessibility guidelines.

Automation tool	Number of times used	Papers
AChecker	16	A02, A03, A10, A11, A13, A17, A18, A20, A21, A22, A23, A25, A26, A30, A31, A33
Test de Accesibilidad Web (TAW)	11	A02, A04, A08, A09, A12, A15, A16, A23, A26, A29, A35
WAVE	11	A02, A07, A14, A16, A17, A19, A21, A23, A25, A27, A32
SortSite	4	A07, A16, A23, A34
Total Validator	3	A02, A03, A15
EvalAccess 2.0 Web Service tool	3	A06, A12, A25
HERA-FFX	3	A21, A24, A29
Web browser plug-ins	2	A24, A31
Web Accessibility Assessment Tool (WaaT)	1	A01
Examinator	1	A02
Functional Accessibility Evaluator 2.0 (FAE)	1	A05
Siteimprove Accessibility Checker	1	A14
Cynthia Says	1	A21
Tenon	1	A21
MAUVE Accessibility Validator	1	A21
A-Tester	1	A31

5   Conclusions

From the systematic review of the literature, it was possible to determine the current situation of web accessibility studies in the framework of e-government. Thus, it is concluded that:

1. Evaluation studies are conducted more frequently in countries within the Americas region (Table 4).
2. The most widely used Web accessibility guidelines are the Web Content Accessibility Guidelines 2.0 (Table 5).
3. The most frequently used accessibility evaluation method is Automated Evaluation (Table 6).
4. The most used accessibility evaluation tool is AChecker (Table 7).
5. Accessibility studies address disabilities in a generic way.

Analyzing the exposed results, it is observed that Web Accessibility is a topic of interest. It is being explored by multiple countries and has at its disposal a wide range of guidelines, methods, and tools for its evaluation. However, the analysis, adoption and implementation of Web accessibility is still scarce or deficient.

References

1. Human Rights Council: The promotion, protection and enjoyment of human rights on the Internet (2016). https://www.article19.org/data/files/Internet_Statement_Adopted.pdf. Accessed 02 Feb 2021
2. World Bank: Disability Inclusion Overview (2019). http://www.worldbank.org/en/topic/disability. Accessed 02 Feb 2021
3. Web Accessibility Initiative: Introduction to Web Accessibility (2005). https://www.w3.org/WAI/fundamentals/accessibility-intro/. Accessed 02 Feb 2021
4. Division of Public Institutions and Digital Government: E-Government (2021). https://publicadministration.un.org/egovkb/en-us/About/UNeGovDD-Framework. Accessed 02 Feb 2021
5. Kamoun, F., Almourad, M.B.: Accessibility as an integral factor in e-government web site evaluation : the case of Dubai e-government. Inf. Technol. People 27(2), 208–228 (2014). https://doi.org/10.1108/ITP-07-2013-0130
6. Luján-Mora, S., Navarrete, R., Peñafiel, M.: Egovernment and web accessibility in South America. In: 2014 First International Conference on eDemocracy & eGovernment (ICEDEG), pp. 77–82 (2014). https://doi.org/10.1109/ICEDEG.2014.6819953
7. Darmaputra, I.G.B.N.E., Wijaya, S.S., Ayu, M.A.: Evaluating the accessibility of provinces' e-government websites in Indonesia. In: 2017 5th International Conference on Cyber and IT Service Management (CITSM), pp. 1–6 (2017). https://doi.org/10.1109/CITSM.2017.8089322
8. AkgÜL, Y., Vatansever, K.: Web content accessibility of municipal web sites in Turkey. J. Adv. Inf. Technol. 7(1), 43–48 (2016). https://doi.org/10.12720/jait.7.1.43-48
9. Verkijika, S.F., De Wet, L.: Quality assessment of e-government websites in Sub-Saharan Africa: a public values perspective. 84(2), e12015 (2018). https://doi.org/10.1002/isd2.12015
10. Ismailova, R.: Web site accessibility, usability and security: a survey of government web sites in Kyrgyz Republic. Univ. Access Inf. Soc. 16(1), 257–264 (2015). https://doi.org/10.1007/s10209-015-0446-8
11. Agbozo, E., Spassov, K.: Evaluating metropolitan assembly web sites in Ghana: accessibility compatibility and usability. Webology 15(1), 46–60 (2018)
12. Yaokumah, W., Brown, S., Amponsah, R.: Accessibility, quality and performance of government portals and ministry web sites: a view using diagnostic tools. In: 2015 Annual Global Online Conference on Information and Computer Technology (GOCICT), pp. 46–50 (2015). https://doi.org/10.1109/GOCICT.2015.18
13. Acosta-Vargas, P., Luján-Mora, S., Salvador-Ullauri, L.: Quality evaluation of government websites. In: 2017 Fourth International Conference on eDemocracy & eGovernment (ICEDEG), pp. 8–14 (2017). https://doi.org/10.1109/ICEDEG.2017.7962507
14. Barricelli, B.R., Sciarelli, P., Valtolina, S., Rizzi, A.: Web accessibility legislation in Italy: a survey 10 years after the Stanca Act. Univ. Access Inf. Soc. 17(1), 211–222 (2017). https://doi.org/10.1007/s10209-017-0526-z
15. Brooks, L., Persaud, A.: Comparing local e-government websites in canada and the UK. In: Tambouris, E., et al. (eds.) EGOV 2015. LNCS, vol. 9248, pp. 291–304. Springer, Cham (2015). https://doi.org/10.1007/978-3-319-22479-4_22

16. Al-bataineh, A.F., Mustafa, S.H.: How Jordanian e-Government websites respond to the needs of people with disabilities. In: 2016 7th International Conference on Computer Science and Information Technology (CSIT), pp. 1–6 (2016). https://doi.org/10.1109/CSIT.2016.7549447

17. Dollie, M., Kabanda, S.: e-Government in Africa: perceived concerns of persons with disabilities (PWDs) in South Africa. In: Proceedings of the European Conference on e-Government, ECEG, pp. 63–70 (2017)

18. Moreno, L., Martínez, P., Muguerza, J., Abascal, J.: Support resource based on standards for accessible e-Government transactional services. Comput. Stand. Interfaces **58**, 146–157 (2018). https://doi.org/10.1016/j.csi.2018.01.003

19. Al-Khalifa, H.S., Baazeem, I., Alamer, R.: Revisiting the accessibility of Saudi Arabia government websites. Univ. Access Inf. Soc. **16**(4), 1027–1039 (2016). https://doi.org/10.1007/s10209-016-0495-7

20. Ansari, R.F., Baqar, A., Hassan, H., Saeed, F.: Heuristic, accessibility and usability evaluations of Pakistan's e-government websites. Electron. Gov. **12**(1), 66–85 (2016). https://doi.org/10.1504/EG.2016.074247

21. Ahmi, A., Mohamad, R.: Evaluating accessibility of Malaysian ministries websites using WCAG 2.0 and Section 508 Guideline. J. Telecommun. Electron. Comput. Eng. **8**(8), 177–183 (2016)

22. Leist, E., Smith, D.: Accessibility issues in e-government. In: Kő, A., Francesconi, E. (eds.) EGOVIS 2014. LNCS, vol. 8650, pp. 15–25. Springer, Cham (2014). https://doi.org/10.1007/978-3-319-10178-1_2

23. Zitkus, E., et al.: Accessibility and usability of websites intended for people with disabilities: a preliminary study. In: Marcus, A. (ed.) DUXU 2016. LNCS, vol. 9747, pp. 678–688. Springer, Cham (2016). https://doi.org/10.1007/978-3-319-40355-7_66

24. Ismailova, R., Inal, Y.: Web site accessibility and quality in use: a comparative study of government Web sites in Kyrgyzstan, Azerbaijan, Kazakhstan and Turkey. Univ. Access Inf. Soc. **16**(4), 987–996 (2016). https://doi.org/10.1007/s10209-016-0490-z

25. Ismail, A., Kuppusamy, K.S., Nengroo, A.S.: Multi-tool accessibility assessment of government department websites:a case-study with JKGAD. Disabil. Rehabil. Assist. Technol. **13**(6), 504–516 (2018). https://doi.org/10.1080/17483107.2017.1344883

26. Angélico, M.J., Silva, A., Teixeira, S.F., Maia, T., Silva, A.M.: Web accessibility and transparency for accountability: the Portuguese official municipal websites. In: Information Resources Management, A. (ed.) Open Government: Concepts, Methodologies, Tools, and Applications, Hershey, PA, USA, pp. 1579–1605. IGI Global (2020)

27. Tashtoush, Y.M., Darabseh, A.F., Al-Sarhan, H.N.: The Arabian E-government websites accessibility: a case study. In: 2016 7th International Conference on Information and Communication Systems (ICICS), pp. 276–281 (2016). https://doi.org/10.1109/IACS.2016.7476064

28. Herrera, J.A.R., Ricaurte, J.A.B.: Web accessibility: Study web accessibility in public places of the Colombian State. In: 2015 Latin American Computing Conference (CLEI), pp. 1–7 (2015). https://doi.org/10.1109/CLEI.2015.7360037

29. Balaji, V., Kuppusamy, K.S.: Accessibility evaluation of indian railway websites. In: Proceedings of the International Conference on Informatics and Analytics, pp. Article 59. Association for Computing Machinery, Pondicherry, India (2016). https://doi.org/10.1145/2980258.2980393

30. Karaim, N.A., Inal, Y.: Usability and accessibility evaluation of Libyan government websites. Univ. Access Inf. Soc. **18**(1), 207–216 (2017). https://doi.org/10.1007/s10209-017-0575-3

31. Acosta, T., Acosta-Vargas, P., Luján-Mora, S.: Accessibility of eGovernment services in Latin America. In: 2018 International Conference on eDemocracy & eGovernment (ICEDEG), pp. 67–74 (2018). https://doi.org/10.1109/ICEDEG.2018.8372332

32. de Souza, I.M., Maciel, C., Cappelli, C.: The model of accessibility to electronic government: applicability in DATAPREV. Proceedings of the 17th International Digital Government Research Conference on Digital Government Research, Shanghai, China, pp. 287–292. Association for Computing Machinery (2016). https://doi.org/10.1145/2912160.2912212
33. Sam-Anlas, C.A., Stable-Rodríguez, Y.: Evaluating accessibility in Peruvian Government websites. Revista Espanola de Documentacion Cientifica **39**(1) (2016). https://doi.org/10.3989/redc.2016.1.1213
34. Youngblood, N.E.: Revisiting Alabama state website accessibility. Gov. Inf. Q. **31**(3), 476–487 (2014). https://doi.org/10.1016/j.giq.2014.02.007
35. Gharbi, I., Bouraoui, A., Bellamine Ben Saoud, N.: Multilevel accessibility evaluation of institutional websites in Tunisia. In: Miesenberger, K., Kouroupetroglou, G. (eds.) ICCHP 2018. LNCS, vol. 10896, pp. 43–46. Springer, Cham (2018). https://doi.org/10.1007/978-3-319-94277-3_8
36. Gopinath, S., Senthooran, V., Lojenaa, N., Kartheeswaran, T.: Usability and accessibility analysis of selected government websites in Sri Lanka. In: 2016 IEEE Region 10 Symposium (TENSYMP), pp. 394–398 (2016). https://doi.org/10.1109/TENCONSpring.2016.7519439
37. King, B.A., Youngblood, N.E.: E-government in Alabama: an analysis of county voting and election website content, usability, accessibility, and mobile readiness. Gov. Inf. Q. **33**(4), 715–726 (2016). https://doi.org/10.1016/j.giq.2016.09.001
38. Mtebe, J.S., Kondoro, A.W.: Accessibility and usability of government websites in Tanzania. Afr. J. Inf. Syst. **9**(4), 261–279 (2017)
39. Piñeiro-Naval, V., Mangana, R., Serra, P.: Validación del Índice de Calidad Formal como modelo para la evaluación de websites: el caso de la e-Administración local portuguesa. Transinformação. **30**(2), 153–165 (2018)
40. Noh, K.-R., Jeong, E.-S., You, Y.-B., Moon, S.-J., Kang, M.-B.: A study on the current status and strategies for improvement of web accessibility compliance of public institutions. J. Open Innov. Technol. Market Complex. **1**(1), 1–17 (2015). https://doi.org/10.1186/s40852-015-0001-0
41. United Nations Department of Economic and Social Affairs: United Nations E-Government Survey (2018). https://publicadministration.un.org/egovkb/en-us/Reports/UN-E-Government-Survey-2018. Accessed 02 Feb 2021
42. Web Accessibility Initiative: Web Content Accessibility Guidelines (WCAG) 2.0 (2008). https://www.w3.org/TR/WCAG20/. Accessed 02 Feb 2021
43. Web Accessibility Initiative: Web Content Accessibility Guidelines 1.0 (1999). https://www.w3.org/TR/WAI-WEBCONTENT/. Accessed 02 Feb 2021
44. Web Accessibility Initiative: Web accessibility evaluation tools list (2006). https://www.w3.org/WAI/ER/tools/. Accessed 02 Feb 2021
45. AChecker: Web Accessibility Checker (2021). https://achecker.ca/documentation/index.php?p=checker/index.php. Accessed 02 Feb 2021

Emergence of Polarization and Marginalization in Online Education System of Bangladesh Due to COVID-19: Challenges and Policies to Ensure Inclusive Education

Md Montaser Hamid[1], Tanvir Alam[1], Md Forhad Rabbi[1], Khalad Hasan[2], Anastasia Kuzminykh[3], and Mohammad Ruhul Amin[4(✉)]

[1] Shahjalal University of Science and Technology, Sylhet, Bangladesh
montaser_cse@rpsu.edu.bd, frabbi-cse@sust.edu
[2] University of British Columbia at Okanagan, Kelowna, Canada
khalad.hasan@ubc.ca
[3] University of Toronto, Toronto, Canada
anastasia.kuzminykh@utoronto.ca
[4] Fordham University, New York, USA
mamin17@fordham.edu

Abstract. Before COVID-19, online learning was almost non-existent in the educational institutions of Bangladesh. Unavailability of Internet and proper devices among the students, lack of training, and the unwillingness of the institutions in integrating a new way of providing education were the main reasons behind the less prevalence of online education in Bangladesh. Due to their lack of experience, design policies, and infrastructural incapacity, educational institutions struggled enormously to make the transition to online learning from face-to-face teaching during this ongoing pandemic. Primary and secondary educational institutions are the major victims of this hasty transformation. Although universities in Bangladesh are trying to continue their regular academic curriculum, the real scenario is far from perfect. To understand the problems of the online education system of Bangladeshi universities, we conducted a survey among 184 students. The user responses were analyzed in two different ways: unsupervised clustering that revealed socio-economic polarization among the students; and feature specific statistical analysis that identified the emerging marginal student groups. Our analysis shows that the factors behind the polarization and marginalization of students include locality, living conditions, primary device for attending class, Internet connectivity etc. Based on these factors, we lay out an inclusive design policy with three action plans that would reduce the polarization and marginalization of university students in online education.

Keywords: Polarization in online education · Emerging marginal student groups · COVID-19 pandemic · Inclusive education in Bangladesh

© Springer Nature Switzerland AG 2021
M. M. Soares et al. (Eds.): HCII 2021, LNCS 12780, pp. 224–238, 2021.
https://doi.org/10.1007/978-3-030-78224-5_16

1   Introduction

During the COVID-19 pandemic, online learning is considered the most effective and safest way of providing education in universities [1]. However, for many countries, especially for the lower middle income countries, the digital transformation of higher education is bringing additional challenges. To evaluate the appropriateness of online learning compared to face-to-face teaching, many socioeconomic factors need to be considered [2]. For example, a known societal issue for female students is the lack of family support [3]. This lack of support becomes even more intense during the pandemic and crisis [4]. According to UNESCO, 5.2 million female students are at risk of not returning to classes when the schools will reopen after the COVID-19 pandemic [5]. From an economic point of view, many students are struggling financially due to the economic damage imposed by COVID-19 [6,7]. In many cases, these students are unable to afford the necessary device and Internet connection for participating in online classes [8]. These issues are causing disparities among the students and worsening their psychological condition which is already vulnerable due to COVID-19 [9].

In a low-middle-income country like Bangladesh, the socio-economic disparity among the students has always been highly prevalent. Lack of sustainable policies and government investments are the major factors behind the inequalities in the education system of the country [10]. According to a report published by the World Bank, in 2019, Bangladesh spent only 1.3% of its GDP on education [11]. This is one of the lowest education expenditure rates in the entire world. Even after increasing the expenditure on public education, almost 50% of the benefits are enjoyed by the people coming from the high-income group due to policy failures [10]. Moreover, the association between the education policy designed by the government and the budget allocation is extremely inadequate [12]. Altogether, the aforementioned factors are segregating the students into several groups which are ultimately causing polarization in the overall education system of Bangladesh. In addition to these factors, the students also get further marginalized based on demographic properties such as gender (male vs female) and residence (rural vs urban areas) [13]. Due to the current pandemic situation, the inequalities in the education system of Bangladesh are becoming even more prominent [14,15].

By the term polarization in online education, we mean the division of students into two or more groups based on their differences related to demography and opinions. When a polarized student group gets even more ostracized due to the deprivation of certain amenities, we call this marginalization in education. In this paper, we tried to find out the reasons behind the polarization and marginalization of students in the online education system of Bangladesh during COVID-19. For this purpose, we conducted a survey with Bangladeshi university students who are participating in online classes since the lockdown. We performed cluster-based and feature specific statistical analysis on the survey data to investigate the reasons behind both the polarization and marginalization. To further isolate the key factors of polarization and marginalization, we divided the students into several categories such as male vs female, public university vs private university, and rural residence vs urban residence. During the analysis of each category, we focused on features such as primary device usage, type of Internet connection, employment status, support from family, and the capability to pay Internet bills. This analysis helped us in understanding the set of properties that are causing the polarization and marginalization in online education. Lastly, we discussed the immediate action plans that are needed to be taken for an inclusive online education system design policy so that the inequalities in online education among the students become less prevalent.

2 Related Works

Before COVID-19, online education in Bangladesh was mostly at the complementary and experimental level [16]. Most of the online courses contained pre-recorded video lectures with supporting presentation slides [17]. The non-interactive nature of the classes was found to be less intriguing among the students and could not motivate them to communicate with the teachers [17]. Poor Internet connection of users was another obstacle in the overall online class experience. Such pre-existing limitations intensified the consequences of COVID-19 in education and made it even more difficult for the educational institutions to go online entirely. As a result, educational institutions had to go through a rapid transition. In most of the cases this transition was implemented without formulating any sustainable policies [20]. The lack of policy as well as the infrastructural incapacity imposed enormous challenges on both students and teachers [19]. Many students in Bangladesh do not have the proper devices and Internet connections required to ensure their participation in online education [21]. Moreover, the economic burden imposed by COVID-19 is making it even more difficult for the students coming from low-income group to bear the additional expenses associated with online education [14]. As a result, 42 million students are considered to be affected by the consequences imposed by the COVID-19 pandemic in the education sector of Bangladesh [21].

From the very beginning of the lockdown, universities in Bangladesh have taken initiatives to continue their academic curriculum by going online [22]. However, different adversities are interrupting such initiatives of universities in making online education uniformly accessible to their students. The students are no longer able to stay at their university residence. Many of them had to go back to their family residences in village areas where there is lack of high-speed Internet connection [18]. The only alternative is to buy data packs from mobile companies. In many cases, students need to attend 2–3 classes each day which can require data packs worth 3 dollars [23]. It is nearly impossible for most of the rural students to attend online classes regularly with such overly expensive mobile data [18]. Moreover, many of these students lost their income from private tutoring, on-campus and part-time jobs due to the relocation and the lockdown [22]. This imposed a new economic burden on many disadvantaged students who bear their own educational expenses. Prevalence of such socio-economic disparities are affecting the participation and interaction of students in online

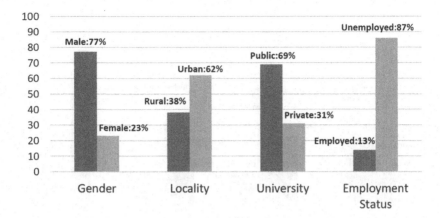

Fig. 1. Demographics of survey responses.

classes. According to a report published by Biotechnology, Enhancement, and Development (BioTED), only 23% of university students from Bangladesh can participate in online classes regularly [24]. The irregular students who are facing the aforementioned socio-economic issues are ultimately getting polarized and in some cases even marginalized in the online education system.

3 Data Collection

For understanding the challenges of online education in Bangladesh, user opinions have been collected from online surveys and key informant interviews (KIIs).

3.1 Online Survey

The surveys have been conducted with the online survey platform Qualtrics [25]. At the beginning of the survey, the objective of the study and question settings were explained, and then an informed consent of the study was taken from the participants. The criteria of selecting the participants were that each participant must be a current student at a private or public university anywhere within Bangladesh. To start filling out the questionnaire, participants were needed to choose the "agree" option; otherwise, the questionnaire could not be filled out. Confidentiality was managed by placing anonymous coding of for each self-report questionnaire. So far, 480 students have participated in this survey. After removing the incomplete and incorrect responses, 184 responses have been selected for data analysis.

The questionnaire of the survey contains 45 questions. These questions are divided into two broad categories: factual questions and opinion-based questions. The factual questions ask user about 8 demographic information such as gender, age, locality, employment status etc. The major demographic information of the survey is depicted in Fig. 1.

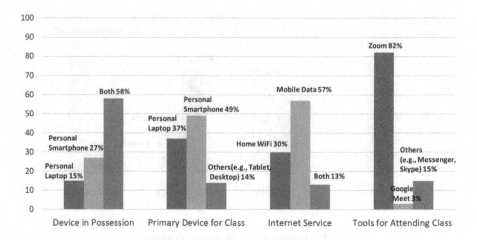

Fig. 2. Device and Internet usage related information of survey responses.

This category also contains 9 questions related to device and Internet usage, type of Internet connection etc. The general information of the survey about these questions are demonstrated in Fig. 2.

In addition to this category, 28 opinion-based questions are also added to the questionnaire to know about different issues of online education such as privacy, comparison and personal preferences. The responses of the opinion-based questions of our survey are in likert scale.

3.2   Key Informant Interview (KII)

We have taken 8 one-to-one key informant interviews (KIIs). All the participants of these interviews are university students who are participating in online classes from rural areas. Among them, 5 of the participants are studying in undergraduate level and 3 are in graduate level. In terms of gender, 3 of the participants are female and the rest of them are male. All of them use mobile data for attending online classes.

The main objective of this interview was to investigate and validate the presence of polarization and marginalization in online education. Another objective was to learn about the perception of the underprivileged students regarding the overall online class experience. The interview was semi-structured and the students were given the opportunity to express their own opinions freely. The interviews were conducted over phone calls and the participation of the students were completely voluntary. The findings of our interviews are discussed in the Sect. 4.3.

4 Results

The analysis of the survey data has been done in two ways: 1) Cluster analysis on user responses, and 2) Feature specific statistical analysis. We discuss the details of these analyses below:

4.1 Cluster Analysis

To understand the socio-economic polarization in online education, we performed unsupervised clustering on the survey data and identified the prominent student groups. Clustering helped us in finding the student groups who have differences in terms of their responses in the survey. To perform clustering, each student response has been represented as a vector of 17 demographic, device, and Internet access related attributes from the survey. These 17 attributes are all the factual questions of our survey. The elbow method based on the within-cluster sum of errors (WCSS) has been implemented to find out the optimum number of clusters in the survey responses. However, for our dataset, this technique did not produce any conclusive results. Therefore, we tried clustering for $K = 2, 3, 4, 5$, and analyzed each individually. Finally, based on manual inspection, the dataset has been divided into two clusters with the help of Principal Component Analysis (PCA) and K-means algorithm. Figure 3 demonstrates the visual representation of these two clusters (*Red* and *Blue*).

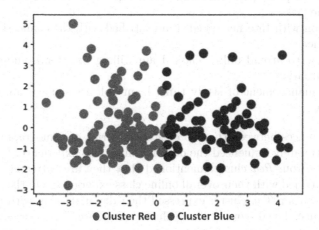

Fig. 3. Two clusters of student survey responses. (Color figure online)

The responses of the students in these two clusters have significant differences for most of the attributes including living condition, locality, average time spent online, primary device for attending class, Internet connection, willingness to attend class, and satisfaction on overall online class experience. There are 112 students in the *Red* cluster and 72 students in the *Blue* cluster.

Table 1. Significant attributes related to factual questions.

Attributes with $p < 0.05$	Primary response of *red* cluster	Primary response of *blue* cluster
Average time spent online per day	5.94 h	3.4 h
Locality	Urban areas (80%)	Rural areas (67%)
Living condition	personal room (63%)	Shared room (74%)
Primary device for online class	Personal laptop (55%)	Smartphone (71%)
Internet connection	Home Wi-Fi (45%)	Mobile data (88%)

We conducted a t-test analysis and the results of the test revealed the attributes of the dataset which have significantly different responses ($p < 0.05$) for the two clusters. In Table 1, we mention a set of attributes that yielded significantly different responses from students based on factual questions of the survey. Figure 4 shows the significantly different attributes from opinion-based questions in a comprehensible way. Followings are the 5 attributes mentioned in that figure:

- Easy Internet access: I am able to easily access the Internet as needed for my online classes.
- Capability of paying Internet bills: I am capable of paying Internet bills to attend the classes.
- Satisfaction with Internet speed: I am satisfied with the connection speed of the Internet.
- Willingness to attend online class: I am willing to attend online classes in current situation
- Effective management of study time: I am able to manage my study time effectively

The differences between the two clusters in terms of demography and opinions have ultimately influenced the overall online class experience. For example, 58% students from *Red* cluster mentioned that they are extremely or at least somewhat satisfied with their overall online class experience. On the other hand, 79% students from *Blue* cluster expressed their dissatisfaction with their online class experience. The discovery of two clusters from user responses and the stark differences that we observed among the members of those clusters indicate that the students are getting polarized in the online education system of Bangladesh.

Socio-Economic Polarization. The results of the t-test with *Red* and *Blue* clusters demonstrate the key factors behind the polarization in the online education system of Bangladesh. Here, we observe that in terms of demographic properties, students from the *Red* cluster predominantly came from urban areas. Most of them have home Wi-Fi and use personal laptops as their primary device

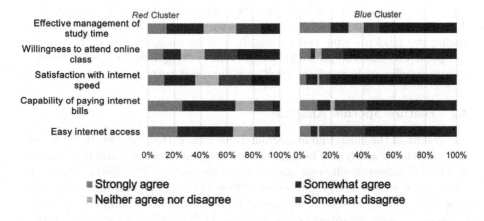

Fig. 4. Comparison of responses from opinion-based attributes.

to attend online classes. Also, a large proportion of them has a personal room. On the other hand, students from the *Blue* cluster represent a very different demographic and socio-economic spectrum. For instance, they are mostly from rural areas. Unlike the students from the *Red* cluster, the majority of them share a room with other family members. Their primary device for attending online classes is mostly smartphones and almost all of them use mobile data for Internet connectivity.

Such demographic contrasts between the two student groups have strong impacts on their opinion-based survey responses. As represented in Fig. 4, we can see that most of the students from the *Red* cluster have easier access to the Internet due to their urban locality and their economic capacity to pay the Internet bills. As a result, a large proportion of them is satisfied with their Internet connection. This scenario is different in the *Blue* cluster. As most of the students from the *Blue* cluster live in rural areas, it is difficult for them to get access to a broadband Internet connection. As an alternative, most of them (88%) try to use mobile data which is very expensive. In the rural areas of Bangladesh, about 35% people live below the poverty line [26]. Therefore, it is difficult for many students from rural areas to manage the high expenses of mobile data. We can validate the prevalence of this issue from our cluster analysis where 77.78% students from the *Blue* cluster said that they are not capable of paying the Internet bills to attend the online classes. Moreover, even after buying highly expensive mobile data, students can not use the Internet properly due to poor network coverage. As a result, almost all the students from the *Blue* cluster (87.8%) have expressed their dissatisfaction with the Internet service.

Altogether, the demographic features are influencing the overall willingness and satisfaction to attend online classes. Due to their superior Internet connection, better devices, and personal space, students from the *Red* cluster are more willing to attend online classes and their satisfaction on overall online class experience is also more positive than the students from the *Blue* cluster. Such deprivation of essential amenities indicates the possibility of further segregation among the students that can eventually lead to marginalization. To validate this possibility and the probable reasons behind marginalization, we conducted feature specific analysis whose results are discussed next.

4.2   Feature Specific Analysis

The results of the cluster analysis from Table 1 show that for some demographic factors such as locality and living condition, students from *Red* and *Blue* clusters provided significantly different answers from one another. The effects of these differences in demographic properties are reflected in their opinions regarding online education. In Fig. 4, we can see that students from two clusters provided very different opinions regarding accessibility to the Internet, the capability of paying Internet bills, ability to manage study time effectively, satisfaction regarding Internet services and online class, and willingness to attend online class during the pandemic. The table and the figure indicate that there are associations between the demographic properties and the opinions of the students regarding online education. The results also indicate the prevalence of polarization in the online education system of Bangladesh.

In feature specific analysis, we checked whether the aforementioned factors that are creating polarization can further lead to marginalization or not. For these purposes, we divided the dataset into several categories based on the attributes or features mentioned in Table 1 and Fig. 4. The attributes that extracted the most prominent differentiating characteristics of the survey are: 1) Gender (Male vs Female), 2) Locality (Rural vs Urban), and 3) Internet Connection (Home Wi-Fi vs Mobile Data). For each of these attributes, the dataset was divided into two categories. Then we performed t-test ($p < 0.05$) to find out the attributes which have significantly different responses for these categories. The findings of this feature specific analysis is given in Table 2. The results of this analysis helped us in finding out the marginalized groups of the online education system of Bangladesh as well as the set of features that are causing this marginalization. The detailed findings of this analysis are discussed in the results and discussion section.

Identification of Marginal Groups in Online Education. The feature-specific analysis of the survey data potentially identifies the marginal student groups within our communities. Based on the findings of previous literature and our cluster analysis, we have selected three features from our dataset to check the presence of marginalization in online education. One of the features of this analysis is gender. Gender-based marginalization is common in developing and underdeveloped countries during any pandemic and crisis [4]. The lack of family support and economic burden imposed by the pandemic ultimately results in an increased number of dropouts among the female students [4]. In the education sector of Bangladesh, gender inequality is highly prevalent. Even before this

Table 2. Significant attributes related to factual questions.

Features	Significant attributes	Primary response	
		Column 1 (C1)	Column 2 (C2)
Gender: Male (C1) vs Female (C2)	Living condition	Personal room (52.55%)	Shared room (66.67%)
	Cooperation of family members	Strongly or somewhat agree (68%)	Strongly or somewhat agree (52.75%)
Locality: Rural (C1) vs Urban (C2)	Living condition	Shared room (66%)	Personal room (53.3%)
	Device in possession	Personal smartphone (74.46%)	Personal Laptop (54%)
	Primary device to attend online class	Personal smartphone (68%)	Personal Laptop (46%)
	Comfort level if camera is on during class	Extremely or somewhat uncomfortable (74.46%)	Extremely or somewhat uncomfortable (65.6%)
	Easy access to Internet	Strongly or somewhat disagree (63.77%)	Strongly or somewhat agree (47.44%)
	Satisfaction with the Internet	Strongly or somewhat disagree (80.85)	Strongly or somewhat agree (56.21%)
Internet connection: Home WiFi (C1) vs Mobile data (C2)	Daily average time spend online	6.01 h	4.1 h
	Locality	Urban and Semi-urban (95%)	Rural (43%)
	Living condition	Personal room (67.5%)	Shared room (66%)
	Primary device to attend online class	Personal laptop (52.5%)	Personal smartphone (63%)
	Easy access to Internet	Strongly or somewhat agree (70%)	Strongly or somewhat disagree (73%)
	Capable of paying Internet bill	Strongly or somewhat agree (70%)	Strongly or somewhat disagree (62%)
	Satisfaction with the Internet	Strongly or somewhat disagree (46.25%)	Strongly or somewhat disagree (77%)
	Satisfaction level regarding overall online class experience	Strongly or somewhat dissatisfied (42.5%)	Strongly or somewhat dissatisfied (70%)
	Willingness to attend online class	Strongly or somewhat disagree (46.25%)	Strongly or somewhat disagree (76%)

pandemic, female students were marginalized in education [3, 27]. By conducting a t-test with all the attributes between male and female students, we further explored whether the female students are also getting marginalized in online education or not. In the same way, we have conducted a t-test for two other features: locality and type of Internet connection. The results of cluster analysis indicate the influence of these two features on overall online education. Therefore, in the feature-specific analysis, we wanted to see if these features can also lead to marginalization.

In Table 3, we present a comparison between different user groups based on features such as gender, locality, and Internet connection. For each of these groups, we also present the attributes for which the corresponding t-test obtained a significant p-value ($p < 0.05$). From the table, we observe that two marginal groups emerge, such as female student groups and rural student groups. Female student groups have severe problems in participating in online classes due to the lack of family support and living condition. On the other hand, the online class experience of the rural student groups gets compromised due to their inappropriate primary device for attending class and Internet connectivity issues such as speed and high expenses.

4.3 Findings of the KIIs

The KIIs gave us the opportunity to know more about the real-life scenario of polarization and marginalization in the online education system of Bangladesh. In these interviews, we get the reflection of the findings of our cluster analysis and feature specific analysis.

From the results of cluster analysis, we have seen that internet connectivity and locality of a student plays a vital role in polarization. In KIIs, practical impacts of such issues became visible to us. For example, one student said *"To get mobile network, I have to walk 2 km to go to the market of my village. There I attend my classes inside a relative's shop where all the noises around the market make it very difficult to concentrate in my classes. Moreover, it becomes even more difficult during rainy season to go there and attend classes."* Like this student, most of the participants informed us about the difficulties they face with mobile data, lack of proper devices to attend class, and their financial incapacity to afford the additional cost of online education. They feel like they are falling behind from their classmates who are in an advantageous position in terms of Internet and devices.

Table 3. Significant attributes of feature specific analysis.

Features	Results with $p < 0.05$
Gender: Male vs Female	Female shares living room and has less cooperation of family members to participate online class
Locality: Urban vs Rural	Rural students share living room and use mobile devices as the primary device for attending online class
Internet connection: Home Wi-Fi vs Mobile data	Most of the mobile data users live in the rural area, share living room, suffer from Internet speed and are unable to pay the Internet bills

In feature specific analysis, we found that female students are getting marginalized due to lack of cooperation from their family members regarding online education. All the female participants of our KIIs were outspoken in this issue. They even stated their fear of getting dropped as their family members are reluctant to their education. One female participant said *"My family does not like the idea of going outside of my house to attend classes online. They also feel that participating in online classes is not as important as real-time classes."*

From our interviews, it is clear that female students and the students from rural areas are having hard-time to cope up with the online education system. Factors such as Internet connectivity, lack of proper devices, lack of family support, and financial incapacity are creating obstacles in their online class experience. In designing the action plans, we have to ensure that the online education is inclusive especially for the students coming from marginalized groups.

5 Discussion

For taking the edge off polarization and marginalization in online education, we propose three immediate action plans. These action plans are targeted specifically at the marginalized student groups such as female and rural students. With these action plans, we also address another important factor of polarization- the Internet connectivity issue. To resolve this issue, alternative solutions have been suggested where the dependency on high-speed Internet for a better online class experience will be minimized. The action plans are discussed in detail here.

5.1 Subsidized Mobile Phone Internet Packages

From the feature specific analysis, female and rural students can be identified as the marginalized student groups of online education. The female students suffer from a lack of family support and the rural students can not afford the high expenses of mobile data. Both of these groups require additional support to ensure their participation in online classes. Subsidized mobile Internet packages designed specifically for these student groups can alleviate the financial burden associated with online education. Moreover, the participation of these student groups will help the educational institutions in continuing their academic curriculum.

5.2 Asynchronous Online Education System

In Bangladesh, the infrastructural capacity required for operating a nationwide online education program is extremely inadequate [28]. It is very difficult to improve this situation overnight. For ensuring maximum participation in online education, we propose that the online education system in Bangladesh should be asynchronous. This will enable the immediate inclusion of marginalized students by avoiding the necessity of improving lots of infrastructural and socio-economic issues. For instance, in rural areas, poor electricity supply makes it difficult for the students to participate in live classes and exams. If the recorded classes and supporting materials are shared on online platforms, they can check these out at their convenient time. In this way, an asynchronous education system can increase the participation of marginalized student groups.

5.3   Low-Bandwidth Teaching Materials

In the current online education system of Bangladesh, students need to check recorded class lectures, supporting materials such as YoutTube tutorials, presentation slides, etc. They also need to give presentations and submit assignments. To download or upload these materials, a user may require a high-speed Internet connection which is very rare in Bangladesh. This problem can be solved by integrating low-bandwidth technology and strategies such as discussion board with texts/images, optimized video lectures, mobile view friendly class presentation, low-bandwidth platforms (Google Classroom), etc. These strategies can improve the online class experience of mobile data users as well as users with Internet connectivity issues.

6   Conclusion

In the education sector of Bangladesh, the aftermaths of the damages done by COVID-19 will be prevalent for a long time. Prolonged academic years are looming large over universities, students are dropping out, teachers are loosing their jobs, and the educational institutions are struggling financially. Moreover, the pandemic is widening the socio-economic gap among students even further. To ensure an all-inclusive online education, it is necessary to isolate the causes that are segregating students during this current pandemic. The results of our cluster analysis demonstrate the demographic and socio-economic factors behind the polarization in online education. Further, the feature specific analysis helped us in understanding the factors that are eventually leading to marginalization of certain student groups such as female students and students coming from rural areas. Our proposed action plans for solving this current situation target the marginalized student groups specifically. The marginalized students require support in terms of the expenses associated with online education. The universities should be more flexible by integrating an asynchronous education system. Lastly, the dependency on high-speed Internet for better online class experience should be eliminated by providing low-bandwidth teaching materials. Implementation of these action plans requires collective efforts from universities and the government. To lessen the long term impacts of a global pandemic, we need to invest our time, energy, and resources in improving the education sector more than ever.

References

1. Rapanta, C., Botturi, L., Goodyear, P., et al.: Online university teaching during and after the Covid-19 crisis: refocusing teacher presence and learning activity. Postdigit. Sci. Educ. **2**, 923–945 (2020). https://doi.org/10.1007/s42438-020-00155-y

2. Kamenetz, A.: 'Panic-gogy': teaching online classes during the coronavirus pandemic, 19 March 2020. https://www.npr.org/2020/03/19/817885991/panic-gogy-teaching-online-classes-during-the-coronavirus-pandemic. Accessed 4 Dec 2020

3. Salahuddin, M., Khatun, R., Bilkis, S.: Present situation of female education in Bangladesh: an overview of last decade. BPDM J. Res. 1(2) (2014). Available at SSRN: https://ssrn.com/abstract=3372022

4. What is the effect of Covid-19 on girls' education? (2020). https://reliefweb.int/report/world/what-effect-covid-19-girls-education. Accessed 5 Dec 2020

5. Acosta, A.M., Evans, D.: Covid-19 and girls' education: what we know so far and what we expect, 2 October 2020. https://www.cgdev.org/blog/covid-19-and-girls-education-what-we-know-so--and-what-we-expect-happen. Accessed 5 Dec 2020

6. Hoque, E., Islam, M.S., Das, S.M., Mitra, D.K., Amin, M.R.: Adjusted dynamics of Covid-19 pandemic due to herd immunity in Bangladesh (2020)

7. Islam, M S., Hoque, M.S., Amin, M.R.: Integration of Kalman filter in the epidemiological model: a robust approach to predict Covid-19 outbreak in Bangladesh. medRxiv (2020)

8. Anwar, K., Adnan, M.: Online learning amid the Covid-19 pandemic: students perspectives. J. Pedag. Res. 1, 45–51 (2020). https://doi.org/10.33902/JPSP.2020261309

9. Covid-19 Raises Anxiety Levels for College Students by Presenting Extraordinary Health and Financial Challenges, 11 November 2020. https://www.businesswire.com/news/home/20201111005413/en/COVID-19-Raises-Anxiety-Levels-for-College-Students-by-Presenting-Extraordinary-Health-and-Financial-Challenges. Accessed 4 Dec 2020

10. Karim, M.: Public education spending and income inequality in Bangladesh. Int. J. Soc. Sci Hum. 5, 75–79 (2015). https://doi.org/10.7763/IJSSH.2015.V5.425

11. Government Expenditure on Education, Total (% of GDP) - Bangladesh (n.d.). https://data.worldbank.org/indicator/. Accessed 18 Jan 2021

12. Al-Samarrai, S.: The impact of governance on education inequality: evidence from Bangladesh (2009). http://lst-iiep.iiep-unesco.org/cgi-bin/wwwi32.exe/[in=epidoc1.in]/?t2000=026962/(100).29.10.1002/pad.529

13. Matin, K.A.: Measuring education inequality: Gini coefficients of education for Bangladesh. In: 20th Biennial Conference on Economics and Ethics of the Bangladesh Economic Association (2017)

14. Choudhury, F.M.: OP-ED: can education help reduce inequality during the pandemic? 6 August 2020. https://www.dhakatribune.com/opinion/op-ed/2020/08/06/op-ed-can-education-help-reduce-inequality-during-the-pandemic. Accessed 18 Jan 2021

15. Ajansı, A.: Covid-19: Bangladesh shuts all educational institutions (2020). https://www.aa.com.tr/en/asia-pacific/covid-19-bangladesh-shuts-all-educational-institutions/1767425. Accessed 18 Jan 2021

16. Asad. A.-U.-Z.: E-Learning in Bangladesh: a New Era in the Field of Education. Bangladesh Educ. Article, 7 April 2020. https://bdeduarticle.com/e-learning-in-bangladesh-a-new-era-in-the-field-of-education/

17. Sarker, M.F.H., Mahmud, R.A., Islam, M.S., Islam, M.K.: Use of e-learning at higher educational institutions in Bangladesh: opportunities and challenges. J. Appl. Res. Higher Educ. 11 (2), 210–223 (2019). https://doi.org/10.1108/JARHE-06-2018-0099

18. Shama, S.: Education during a pandemic: a feasibility study of online classes in Bangladesh to counteract potential study gaps caused by Covid-19 related lockdowns (2020). https://doi.org/10.31235/osf.io/p6mws

19. Emon, E.K., Alif, A., Shahanul, I.M.: Impact of Covid-19 on the institutional education system and its associated students in Bangladesh. Asian J. Educ. Soc. Stud. **11**, 34–46 (2020). https://doi.org/10.9734/ajess/2020/v11i230288

20. Esani, M.: Moving from face-to-face to online teaching. Clinical laboratory science. J. Am. Soc. Med. Technol. **23**, 187–190 (2010). https://doi.org/10.29074/ascls.23.3.187

21. Bangladeshi children share experiences of remote learning and the challenges they face. UNICEF Bangladesh, 8 December 2020. https://www.unicef.org/bangladesh/en/stories/bangladeshi-children-share-experiences-remote-learning-and-challenges-they-face

22. Begum, F.S., Hossain, S., Alam, S., Islam, U., Lemon, H., Omar, N.: Combating the impact of COVID-19 on Public University Students Through Subsidized Online Class: Evidence from Bangladesh (2020). https://doi.org/10.7176/JEP/11-27-17

23. Jasim, M.M., Eyamin, S.: Costly data, poor connection key challenges for online classes in public universities, 23 June 2020. https://tbsnews.net/bangladesh/education/costly-data-poor-connection-key-challenges-online-classes-public-universities. Accessed 3 Feb 2021

24. Islam, D.: Online classes for university students in Bangladesh during the Covid-19 pandemic- is it feasible? 01 June 2020. https://tbsnews.net/thoughts/online-classes-university-students-bangladesh-during-covid-19-pandemic-it-feasible-87454. Accessed 5 Dec 2020

25. Qualtrics XM - Experience Management Software, 28 January 2021. https://www.qualtrics.com/. Accessed 3 Feb 2021

26. Agricultural Development in Bangladesh. https://www.ifad.org/en/web/operations/country/id/bangladesh. Accessed 3 Feb 2021

27. Ferdaush, J.: Gender Inequality in Bangladesh. Unnayan Onneshan - The Innovators, Dhaka (2019)

28. Rahman, M.M., et al.: Covid-19 responses among university students of Bangladesh: assessment of status and individual view toward Covid-19. J. Hum. Behav. Soc. Environ. (2021). https://doi.org/10.1080/10911359.2020.1822978

Performing a Disembodied Mind: Neurotechnology Between Empowerment and Normalization

Johannes Kögel(⊠)

Institute of Ethics, History and Theory of Medicine, LMU Munich, Munich, Germany
johannes.koegel@med.uni-muenchen.de

Abstract. Given that a brain-computer interface (BCI) operates by circumventing the peripheral nervous system, i.e. functions in virtue of one's mind only, does it exemplify the acting of a disembodied mind? Illustrating BCI use by means of a qualitative interview with a user shows that performing a disembodied mind can bring about the experience of empowerment. Taking into account the social context of technology use, the practice and discourse of neurosciences, and the role of technology among marginalized communities, the risk of a continued normalization arises. Neurotechnology such as the BCI may thus bring about beneficial as well as detrimental consequences for disabled users. How the respective future will look like may also depend on our understanding and the social attribution of agency.

Keywords: Brain-computer interface · Disembodied mind · Dis/ability · Empowerment · Normalization

1 Background

Brain-computer interfaces (BCIs) have come a long way. Their history can be traced to the invention of the electroencephalography (EEG) a hundred years ago [1]. By now the brain-computer interface allows people to communicate or enables movement to individuals who would not have the opportunity for it otherwise or supplements therapy for those who are in need of rehabilitation medicine. As technology and science do not operate in isolation from broader context, but are always embedded in society and interact with and affect each other in various ways, also the neurotechnology of brain-computer interfaces can be identified within a web of social relations and determinants. Technologies come along with potential risks and benefits which, as we will see, can neither always be separated from each other nor clearly classified as one or the other. In addition, the social question arises regarding who develops what for whom and with which purposes or to what ends. At the same time social reality often carves its own ways disregarding the original intentions, purposes and applications involved. By applying the concept of the disembodied mind to BCI use, possible implications and consequences, in particular empowerment and normalization, are assessed. Performing a disembodied mind can be regarded as a social norm, the standard of an unbounded and unmediated

© Springer Nature Switzerland AG 2021
M. M. Soares et al. (Eds.): HCII 2021, LNCS 12780, pp. 239–251, 2021.
https://doi.org/10.1007/978-3-030-78224-5_17

competent actor that appears to be acting without any contributing entities that would be essential to the actor's doing.

The line of argumentation is illustrated by passages drawn from an interview with Nicole.[1] Nicole, being in her mid-40s, was diagnosed with spinocerebellar ataxia 25 years ago. Since then she had to rely on technology by an increasing level such as a wheelchair, a computer with voice recognition, or a respiration apparatus. 15 years later she joined an experimental study with an invasive BCI for the purpose of which she received two electrodes that were implanted on her motor cortex. She engaged in various applications of BCI training, i.e. steering a robotic arm. The method of all these applications was based on motor imagery, i.e. she needed to imagine body movements which were translated into computer generated output. Nicole describes her BCI experience to have been very empowering. In the following I will argue that her feeling of empowerment[2] is partly due to the ability to perform a disembodied mind.

Starting with a short summary of BCIs and user studies, followed by a conceptualization of the disembodied mind, the discourse and practice of neurosciences, and the role of the brain as an influential signifier shall set the context for the application of the disembodied mind to the case of brain-computer interface use. Lastly, the theoretical gain from brain-computer interfaces shall be compared with practical challenges.

1.1 Brain-Computer Interfaces: Studying the User Perspective

A brain-computer interface is a system that measures brain activity and converts it into artificial output that replaces, restores, enhances, supplements, or improves natural central nervous system output [3]. It consists of directing external devices such as personal computers, wheelchairs or prostheses, or activating a person's muscles [4–9]. BCIs are directed either to the purpose of enhancement and entertainment or to medical reasons. Among the latter, BCI training intends to restore or increase communication and motor skills of persons with physical impairments, as neurorehabilitation to improve the neurological condition of persons that suffered stroke or spinal cord injuries, to regulate epilepsy, and to treat psychiatric conditions [10–14]. BCIs promise nothing less than increased agency, autonomy, self-determination, and quality of life [15–23].

The peculiar aspect of BCIs is that their operations bypass the peripheral nervous system. As a consequence, the BCI user does not move at all and may look like doing nothing to an external observer.

---

[1] For the whole interview study, see Kögel/Jox/Friedrich 2020 [2].

[2] Note that I will not provide a particular definition of empowerment. "Empowerment" is something Nicole experienced during the course of but also after BCI training. I do not want to take anything away from it by comparing it to some theoretical concept. Furthermore, empowerment can apply to individuals or collectives. It may refer to an individual succeeding in doing something by its own means which is normally not easy to do or has not been done before and may be accompanied by a permanent increase of capabilities or autonomy. For collectives, especially ones that are marginalized or discriminated against, it may refer to an accomplished gain in self-consciousness, self-determination, control, standing, or rights. While Nicole experiences empowerment as an individual one cannot preclude that her case denotes also a collective or structural phenomenon.

A recent interview study with users with physical impairments that were enrolled in experimental studies to test therapeutical BCIs renders insights of the experiences, evaluation, and self-perceptions of the BCI users [2, 24, 25]. Three main effects can be identified that BCI training can bring about [2]. BCIs can establish agency and grant a sense of agency to the users and at least temporarily can restore or enable communication, mobility, or motor functions. Furthermore, BCI can lead to changes or reinforcements when it comes to one's self-definition or self-image. It can foster pride, self-esteem, and feelings of empowerment. It can also help to build coherent life narratives and identities with one's past, at least among persons that experienced severe life changes due to car accidents or outbreaks of degenerative diseases. At last, BCI training also provides opportunities for social participation. It denotes a meaningful occupation to some users who cherish the opportunity to play their part in the scientific and technological progress. Some enjoy the environment of having something like a job, working in a team, having colleagues, a structured day, etc. At the same time BCI use can lead to public competitions or showings, even artwork that can be exhibited. This brings about publicity, social recognition and the possibility to raise awareness.

In addition, particular "ability expectations" [26], abilities that are required or pre-supposed, apply to BCIs and their users [24]. There are explicit ability expectations, such as having some particular physical impairment in addition to being BCI "literate", i.e. having the cognitive abilities as well as meeting further conditions to match the BCI setup. Among the implicit expectations are the disposal of various resources such as time, mobility or staff (driver, care-giver), high motivation, a very high level of concentration, being tolerant towards discomfort and pain as well as frustration, and lastly emotion control. Getting frustrated or getting distracted by emotions lead to a poor BCI outcome and hence need to be avoided. As a consequence, users can get the impression that they need to pitch for training with their cognitive functions being ready while having to suppress their affective and emotional self. Especially the psychological components turn BCI training into a highly demanding mix of abilities.

1.2 Disembodied Mind and Agency

The disembodied mind denotes a philosophical point of contention in the first place [27]. Assuming a Cartesian dualism that grants its ontological status of an independent substance to both, mind and body, the question arises whether there is something like an immaterial *res cogitans*. Opponents to this view stress that the mind or conscious-ness presupposes some material substrate on which it depends on some form (causality, correlation, instantiation, constitution, emergence, supervenience, etc.). The possibil-ity of a disembodied mind would cause a problem for principles of identification and individuation in particular [28].

In psychology the disembodied mind can be seen as a psychotic state referring to a state of schizophrenia: "Whereas melancholics are imprisoned in their corporealized centricity, the schizophrenic patient is lost 'in the orbit', in a disembodied, imaginary, and delusional view from the outside" [29]. In this regard individuals feel like a "Cartesian machine", acting according to a perceived "divorce of the self from its body" [29].

The socio-political legacy of the Cartesian dualism comprises binary attributions that are ascribed according to a distinct power structure, whereby the conceptual pair of disembodied-embodied conflates with pairs such as unmediated – mediated, transcendent – immanent, rational – emotional, male – female, etc.

According to Donna Haraway [30], "[t]he imagined 'we' are the embodied others, who are not allowed not to have a body, a finite point of view, and so an inevitably disqualifying and polluting bias in any discussion […]" while at the same time "[o]nly those occupying the positions of the dominators are self-identical, unmarked, disembodied, unmediated, transcendent".

In Haraway's case the "we" refers to women in particular but may hold true for all (other) marginalized or subaltern positions. The point at stake is the one of universalistic objectivity. Claiming an impartial and neutral standpoint conceals its underpinning bias, which is White, Western, male, and among others able-bodied. Only a subject of those characteristics can appear to be disembodied. Everyone else is determined by their sexualized, racialized, or impaired body.

Following this line of thought, Ingunn Moser [31–33] utilizes the concept of the disembodied mind in describing dis/ability and agency within an "order of the normal", according to which "[t]o perform as a 'disembodied mind' is a required form of embodiment in normalization" [32]. This is because we uphold a "norm which locates agency, mobility and a centred subjectivity in a naturalised and given human body" [34].

In our common understanding and everyday language we tend to ignore contributing entities (relations, things, technology, other people) and to address as subject of an action only whose objective the overall action serves [35]. Hence, we say "I'm flying to the US", even though I'm not a pilot, or "I'm building a house", even though I'm neither a construction worker nor a handyman. My actual involvement in these doings may be confined to paying some money to some agency or firm. "The point, then, is that centredness, autonomy, discretion, and also independence and active agency, are achievements which rest upon distribution –but where the distribution usually, and ideally, disappears into the background" [32]. In other words, agency rests on the ability to perform a disembodied mind., i.e. act according to a Cartesian imagination: "To perform a disembodied mind implies to enact a boundary between body and mind, to disconnect from, censor, and master the body and other forms of embodiment"[32]. According to Moser, performing a disembodied mind means being credited with agency whereby one's body as well as other embodiments (technology, artefacts, other people, or other distributed and contributing entities) become invisible as if one's action would be in virtue of one's mind only. This ability is regarded as a common disposition to able-bodied actors, but denied to disabled people: "whereas the standardized environments and forms of embodiment of abled normal subjects seem to become invisible, and have the ability to perform 'disembodied mind', non-standard, disabling, and even normalizing and so enabling networks usually do not. With disabled subjects materiality resists: there are always bad passages, missing links and problematic bodies which mean that the distributions remain visible and present in the situation" [32]. It is important to stress that to regard performing a disembodied mind as a disposition means that this ability is socially attributed and only granted to be at one's disposal when one qualifies as a "normal", abled-bodied actor.

2 Performances of the Body and the Brain

2.1 The Brainification of the Mind

The disembodied mind is a Cartesian fiction[3], given we assume that there is no human consciousness without an integrated organism interacting with its internal and external environment. Nevertheless, BCI-mediated actions may come as close as possible to humans acting as (if) disembodied. This is simply for the reason that there are no movements of the body that could be recognized. BCI actions are as bodiless as mental arithmetic, the difference being that the BCI renders some visible output while the results of mental arithmetic may remain opaque.

The power of the Cartesian fiction lies upon the circumstance that one may seek to live up to and behave as if the disembodied mind is something we can achieve and perform as such.

For now, the standpoint of a naïve observer shall be occupied to whom BCI use appears – due to the absence of detectable motions on the side of the user – as the performance of a disembodied mind. Consequently, performing as such indeed may be seen as an object of aspiration for BCI users.

Nicole gradually mastered BCI use until she reached a level where she managed to "let instinct take over". She explains this process:

> "[…] in the beginning, I was concentrating very hard. Then I was thinking 'Move right, move right, move right'. As I stopped concentrating so hard, I just trusted that I knew how to do it and started to just do it without thinking about how I was doing it, then it became much easier. I realized I didn't have to try as hard as I was trying, that my brain had not forgotten."

It is noteworthy to highlight Nicole's use of words. It is not her that has not forgotten, but her brain. In fact, she adopted what may be called "brain talk" that is prevalent within the field of neuroscience and -technology whereby "brain" is used as a metonymy for mind. This occurs multiple times during the interview where one rather – at least in common or everyday speech – would expect the word "mind" or "I". She talks about implants that "read the intentions of the brain" or states that "I would just look at which way I wanted it to go, then my brain automatically made it go that way."

"Mind", in contrast, is only used once when discussing computer assistance: "The more we did it, the less they turned down the computer, then the more my mind was doing it."

Of course, Nicole is not wrong because what is measured during BCI use is her brain activity. We also may grant intentions to the brain, which may be to think, just as we may say that our intestines have the intention to digest or a bench the intention for people to sit on it. Yet, this is not how we normally speak. As a consequence, using "brain" instead

---

[3] Fictions do not necessarily mean to be less real and there are good reasons to assume some mind or spirit beyond the boundaries of the individual [36]. Here, I am only concerned with the intra-individual disembodied mind (disembodied mind as an individual's disposition, even though socially attributed).

of "mind" or as *pars pro toto* for the "I" or one's self or person, we may indicate signs of the "creed" of being brains that shall be discussed in a bit.

For Nicole the realization that her brain had not forgotten causes a change of her self-perception:

> "Oh God, it really changed my self-image. It changed, as I said, the empowerment. The feeling, 'I did this, look what I can do.' It helped me realize that – I have a saying up on my wall, 'You are more than the body you live in.' I just realized the truth of that statement, that my brain was the most important part of me, and that working meant I could do a lot."

We called this redefinition based on a centering of oneself in favor of one's brain "brainification" [2]. This may be read in the broader context of neuroscience and its discourse.

Vidal and Ortega [37] identify in the discourse of the neurosciences (but not confined to it) the tendency to establish the notion of a "cerebral subject" accompanied by the "creed" of understanding ourselves as our brains in the first place. The brain becomes the *pars pro toto* for humans. This, however, only denotes a preliminary point of culmination of a "cerebralisation" of humans, a process that has developed for a good 200 years by now [38]. Rose and Abi-Rached [39, 40] are reluctant whether the "neurobiological complex" has replaced the "psychological complex" that used to shape the twentieth century. Nevertheless, they identify areas where the "neuro" establishes new ways of "government of the living" [40].

Melike Şahinol (33) examined brain-computer interfaces in particular. Making sense of the mutual adaptive or cybernetic processes of human-machine interaction, Şahinol arrives at the notion of the "techno-cerebral subject". Within her research she recognized how neuroscientists isolate brain processes and detach them from the rest of the body. By separating cerebral entities from bodily movements in order to delegate cerebral motion activities to the computer also the bodily experiences of the users change, possibly leading to an altered "Leiberfahrung", (lived) body experience. The worldview behind the neuroscientific practices she studied can be identified as Cartesian "cerebro-centrism" that reduces humans to cerebral functions. In this context we may read Nicole's remarks on changing her self-image towards a brain-centered understanding of herself.

2.2 Performing a Disembodied Mind

Disregarding her self-image, Nicole experienced BCI use as empowering, as she had stressed at another point before:

> "It felt very exciting, but very empowering. It made me feel like, 'Look what I can do'. I can't do this on my own, but I can make a machine do it because my brain, the only part of my body that's working now, my brain still works. It was, as I said, empowering."

She does not say that the empowerment is due to being able to feed oneself or move things herself or perform particular acts (this seemed to be the most obvious interpretation which, however, begs to be supplemented). A lot speaks for the empowerment being due to performing a disembodied mind. Her brain – or we may read "mind" – is the only part of her still functioning, as her body – or we shall say the rest of her body as the brain is also part of the body (unless read as "mind") – is not responsive to voluntary control, and can make a machine do things. Disregarding the kind of embodiment she can perform actions. BCI use allows for a sense of agency and agency is also granted by others [2]. Looking what she can do, for the external observer her physical body or the state it is in is of no concern here. Hence, performing a disembodied mind is experienced as empowering.

The transformation from embodied and technically restrained movements to disembodied motions during the course of training and increasing routinization also reflects in Nicole's own account. In the beginning, she was "concentrating very hard" and thinking single commands such as"right, left, go up, go down" while trying to follow motions of the computer steered robotic arm. After a while Nicole took over control:

> "Then I started saying 'I moved my arm'. Not 'Look what the arm did', but 'Look at what I did'. Instead of saying 'I moved the computer right', I would say 'I moved right' because it became my arm."

Consequently Nicole simply started doing things:

> "I started grasping things, closing my fingers around an object, and then moving it, and then putting it down."

Or in the flight simulator:

> "I spent two days flying, and having a great time, and taking off from different airports around the world. I went to Paris and flew through the Eiffel Tower. I flew through the pyramids of Egypt."

Certainly, Nicole also appreciates the particular tasks she could do via BCI, may it be fetching, grasping, and moving things with the robotic arm, steering a virtual plane in a flight simulator, or other tasks. Nevertheless, she states:

> "What I miss more is having the job. I went to the office three days a week. I had co-workers, people I worked with and became close to. I missed the camaraderie of working with the group. I miss having a place to go and something to do every day."

What Nicole misses the most is the daily routine, the environment of a workplace, including pursuing a common goal with colleagues, social interaction and team spirit, as well as finding a meaningful task in doing so.

> "I'm left with a feeling of I achieved a lot, but more importantly, I was able to make a contribution. I used to do charity work and I had to stop that when I lost my physical abilities. To be able to do something to make a contribution again was very important to me, very meaningful."

We may also say that what Nicole cherishes is what we tend to call a "normal" life or some degree of "normalcy". This underlines the aforementioned interpretation that empowerment lies not only in doing particular tasks but also in performing a disembodied mind, as this is regarded as a presupposed standard or norm.

3   Theory vs. Practice: Normalization Continued?

Technology such as BCIs can empower disabled people. The empowerment is not only due to restoring or enabling communication, mobility or motor functions, but also by being able to perform a disembodied mind because having the disposition to perform a disembodied mind is the standard for "the normal competent actor" [32]. The consequence then may be to grant BCI users the access to a (home-based) BCI, also after the experimental studies have been completed [41]. This has been stressed in the ethical literature before [42], but may deserve additional emphasis, given that performing a disembodied mind is regarded as a disposition of abled-bodied actors. Therefore, to bridge the gap between abled-bodied and disabled users, the latter need to have the technology at their permanent disposal.

If BCI use may be understood as performing a disembodied mind, BCIs enable disembodied agency disregarding its user, i.e. it does not make a difference whether the user has any physical impairments or not.

In theory, this can be regarded as being the biggest promise of BCIs: granting the ability of performing a disembodied mind ignorant of the user's subjectivization (i.e. its subject status according to sex, race, dis/ability, age, etc.), which would be empowering to those who have been barred from this disposition before. Yet, the time where BCIs will be a technology of everyday life is yet to come.

In any event, existing societal norms and inequalities are likely to apply and play out also in and through new technologies. "Neuroscientific ideas do not necessarily transform self-understandings in any radical manner but combine with existing perceptions and sometimes reinforce current norms" [37].

In fact, disabled users and their technology often are medicalized. When it comes to technology, disabled people are depicted by means of a medical narrative and an ability-deficient language [43]. As a consequence, disabled people are exclusively portrayed as therapeutic BCI users and not as non-medical BCI users. Technologies they use automatically turn into "assistive devices" or "assistive technology", while technology for non-disabled users is referred to as "enhancing".

Hence, we may expect users with disabilities to be seen as acting a disembodied mind only in regard to their own body which may become invisible, while the operated device, computer, prosthesis, or something else, will be seen as an essential embodiment, turning it into an "assistive" technology and restraining their (claims of) agency. At the same time, users without disabilities will be seen as steering devices that are not regarded as being essential to their actions, i.e. as "enhancing".

In addition, the gulf that is intended to be bridged may even increase, given that there are several factors at play that give non-disabled BCI users an advantage over disabled users. First of all, the criteria for eligibility, i.e. BCI "literacy" [44], are lower due to the absence of involuntary body movements such as spasms or epileptic reactions. In addition, residual muscle functions that can be controlled often exist among disabled users and can prove detrimental for BCI use. Medication such as muscle relaxants also can have an impact on BCI performance. Sometimes, the underlying causes for better BCI performance among non-disabled users in some BCI applications are still contested [45, 46].

The attempt to provide disabled people with new technology to bring them to the level of what able-bodied people can do, to get to the standard of "the normal competent actor", is at risk of perpetuating "the order of the normal" [32]. Given the social context within which technology use takes place, it does not come as a surprise that in particular marginalized groups pointed out that technologies often do not bring about the enabling or empowering effects that were originally intended.

Shulamith Firestone stated that "in the hands of our current society and under the direction of current scientists [...] any attempted use of technology to 'free' anybody is suspect" [47], which certainly applies to the present as well. This skepticism resonates also in today's feminism (or some strands of it), stressing "that technologies are not inherently beneficial – indeed, they are not even inherently neutral – but are in fact constrained and constituted by social relations" [48].

In fact, technologies can further societal divide due to unequal distributions of access or catalyze societal inequalities across the globe [49] (even more so in the wake of dig-italization [50]). Especially new technologies such as big data and artificial intelligence bring about new ways of discrimination in terms of class and/or race [51–54]. They "reflect and reproduce existing inequities but [...] are promoted and perceived as more objective or progressive than the discriminatory systems of a previous era" [54].

Also among disabled people technology is seen controversially [55]. What may be beneficial for some, can be detrimental for others (curbstones require walking/stepping, telephones require hearing, internet (mostly still) requires sight, etc.). In technology research disabled people report of "epistemic violence" [56] or are included at best as "knowledge producer" regarding usability aspects of advanced technology [57].

As a consequence, new technologies on their own will not solve the problems they propose to tackle. For them to be able to live up to the hopes and promises they offer, they need to be developed, managed, and directed into the right channels. This applies equally to the neurosciences as they "seem an unlikely ally of progressive social thought" [39].

4 Conclusion: What Now?

Applying the concept of performing a disembodied mind to interview data, there are indications that the empowerment that users experience when operating a BCI may not be limited to the enabling or restoring of motor functions. It may also be due to being able to be active with one's mind only and detach one's actions from one's body. Hence, at least when it comes to one's own body we may talk of performing a disembodied mind in these temporary instances. However, acting a disembodied mind as a social attribution that originates from the standard of what qualifies as a "normal" agential subject perpetuates social inequality and discrimination.

As a consequence, technological change cannot bring about a better future on its own. There needs to be societal change as well. For the case put forth in this text the task at hand would be to come to a different understanding of agency, one that operates independently of the notion of a disembodied mind or actor as the norm. Agency supposedly needs to be acknowledged as a social attribution rather than being treated as the disposition of an individual (or a brain).

For Haraway, disembodiment is not an objective that is aspired as it stands for a false sense of objectivity. "Feminist" and, we may add again, any other emancipatory "embodiment, then, is not about fixed location in a reified body […] but about nodes in fields, inflections in orientations, and responsibility for difference in material-semiotic fields of meaning. Embodiment is significant prosthesis" [30]. The goal therefore cannot be to seek for the disembodied mind as it is ignorant of the various and manifold reality of situatedness and embodiment and perpetuates the status quo of reigning norms. The body of the BCI user and the embodiment of the BCI subject (which has been described as a techno-cerebral subject) manifest their very own particular objectivity. This, also for us as researchers, is the starting point.

References

1. Kübler, A.: The history of BCI: from a vision for the future to real support for personhood in people with locked-in syndrome. Neuroethics 13(2), 163–180 (2019). https://doi.org/10. 1007/s12152-019-09409-4
2. Kögel, J., Jox, R.J., Friedrich, O.: What is it like to use a BCI? – Insights from an interview study with brain-computer interface users. BMC Med. Ethics 21(2) (2020). https://doi.org/ 10.1186/s12910-019-0442-2
3. Wolpaw, J.R., Wolpaw, E.W.: Brain-Computer Interfaces: Principles and Practice. Oxford University Press, Oxford (2012)
4. Bouton, C.E., et al.: Restoring cortical control of functional movement in a human with quadriplegia. Nature 533(7602), 247–250 (2016)
5. Graimann, B., Allison, B., Pfurtscheller, G.: Brain-computer interfaces: a gentle introduction. In: Graimann, B., Pfurtscheller, G., Allison, B. (eds.) Brain-Computer Interfaces, pp. 1–27. Springer, Berlin, Heidelberg, Heidelberg (2009). https://doi.org/10.1007/978-3-642-02091-9
6. Mak, J.N., Wolpaw, J.R.: Clinical applications of brain-computer interfaces: current state and future prospects. IEEE Rev. Biomed. Eng. 2, 187–199 (2009). https://doi.org/10.1109/rbme. 2009.2035356
7. Marchetti, M., Priftis, K.: Brain–computer interfaces in amyotrophic lateral sclerosis: a met-analysis. Clin. Neurophysiol. 126(6), 1255–1263 (2015). https://doi.org/10.1016/j.clinph. 2014.09.017
8. Wolpaw, J.R., Birbaumer, N., McFarland, D.J., Pfurtscheller, G., Vaughan, T.M.: Brain–computer interfaces for communication and control. Clin. Neurophysiol. 113(6), 767–791 (2002)
9. Daly, J.J., Wolpaw, J.R.: Brain–computer interfaces in neurological rehabilitation. Lancet Neurol. 7(11), 1032–1043 (2008)
10. Chaudhary, U., Birbaumer, N., Ramos-Murguialday, A.: Brain-computer interfaces for communication and rehabilitation. Nat. Rev. Neurol. 12(9), 513–525 (2016). https://doi.org/10. 1038/nrneurol.2016.113
11. Salisbury, D.B., Parsons, T.D., Monden, K.R., Trost, Z., Driver, S.J.: Brain-computer interface for individuals after spinal cord injury. Rehabil. Psychol. 61(4), 435–441 (2016). https://doi. org/10.1037/rep0000099

12. Maksimenko, V.A., et al.: Absence seizure control by a brain computer interface. Sci. Rep. **7**, 2487 (2017)
13. McFarland, D.J., Daly, J., Boulay, C., Parvaz, M.A.: Therapeutic applications of BCI technologies. Brain-Comput. Interf. **4**(1–2), 37–52 (2017)
14. Zafar, M.B., Shah, K.A., Malik, H.A.: Prospects of sustainable ADHD treatment through brain-computer Interface systems. In: Innovations in Electrical Engineering and Computational Technologies (ICIEECT), 2017 International Conference on 2017, pp. 1–6. IEEE (2017)
15. Glannon, W.: Neuromodulation, agency and autonomy. Brain Topogr. **27**(1), 46–54 (2013). https://doi.org/10.1007/s10548-012-0269-3
16. Friedrich, O., Racine, E., Steinert, S., Pömsl, J., Jox, R.J.: An analysis of the impact of brain-computer interfaces on autonomy. Neuroethics **1**, 13 (2018). https://doi.org/10.1007/s12152-018-9364-9
17. Holz, E.: Systematic Evaluation of Non-Invasive Brain-Computer Interfaces as Assistive Devices for Persons with Severe Motor Impairment Based on a User-Centred Approach – in Controlled Settings and Independent Use. Universität Würzburg, Würzburg (2015)
18. Holz, E.M., Botrel, L., Kaufmann, T., Kübler, A.: Long-term independent brain-computer interface home use improves quality of life of a patient in the locked-in state: a case study. Arch. Phys. Med. Rehabil. **96**(3 Suppl), S16-26 (2015). https://doi.org/10.1016/j.apmr.2014.03.035
19. Holz, E.M., Botrel, L., Kübler, A.: Independent home use of brain painting improves quality of life of two artists in the locked-in state diagnosed with amyotrophic lateral sclerosis. Brain-Comput. Interf. **2**(2–3), 117–134 (2015)
20. Nijboer, F., Birbaumer, N., Kübler, A.: The influence of psychological state and motivation on brain-computer interface performance in patients with amyotrophic lateral sclerosis - a longitudinal study. Front. Neurosci. **4**, 55 (2010). https://doi.org/10.3389/fnins.2010.00055
21. Holz, E.M., Höhne, J., Staiger-Salzer, P., Tangermann, M., Kübler, A.: Brain-computer interface controlled gaming: evaluation of usability by severely motor restricted end-users. Artif. Intell. Med. **59**(2), 111–120 (2013). https://doi.org/10.1016/j.artmed.2013.08.001
22. Cincotti, F., et al.: Non-invasive brain-computer interface system: towards its application as assistive technology. Brain Res. Bull. **75**(6), 796–803 (2008). https://doi.org/10.1016/j.brainresbull.2008.01.007
23. Zickler, C., Halder, S., Kleih, S.C., Herbert, C., Kübler, A.: Brain painting: usability testing according to the user-centered design in end users with severe motor paralysis. Artif. Intell. Med. **59**(2), 99–110 (2013)
24. Kögel, J., Wolbring, G.: What it takes to be a pioneer: ability expectations from brain-computer interface users. NanoEthics **14**(3), 227–239 (2020). https://doi.org/10.1007/s11569-020-00378-0
25. Kögel, J.: Brain-computer interface use as materialized crisis management. In: Friedrich, O., Wolkenstein, A., Bublitz, C., Jox, R.J., Racine, E. (eds.) Clinical Neurotechnology Meets Artificial Intelligence. AN, pp. 101–116. Springer, Cham (2021). https://doi.org/10.1007/978-3-030-64590-8_8
26. Wolbring, G.: Citizenship education through an ability expectation and "ableism" lens: the challenge of science and technology and disabled people. Educ. Sci. **2**, 150–164 (2012). https://doi.org/10.3390/educsci2030150
27. Chong-Fuk, L.: On the possibility of a disembodied mind. Yearb. East. West. Philos. **2017**(2), 338–352 (2017)
28. Steinberg, J.R., Steinberg, A.M.: Disembodied minds and the problem of identification and individuation. Philosophia **35**(1), 75–93 (2007)
29. Fuchs, T.: Corporealized and disembodied minds: a phenomenological view of the body in melancholia and schizophrenia. Philos. Psychiatry Psychol. **12**(2), 95–107 (2005)

30. Haraway, D.: Situated knowledges: the science question in feminism and the privilege of partial perspective. Fem. Stud. **14**(3), 575–599 (1988). https://doi.org/10.2307/3178066
31. Moser, I.: On becoming disabled and articulating alternatives. Cult. Stud. **19**, 667–700 (2005). https://doi.org/10.1080/09502380500365648
32. Moser, I.: Disability and the promises of technology: technology, subjectivity and embodiment within an order of the normal. Inf. Commun. Soc. **9**(3), 373–395 (2006)
33. Moser, I.: Sociotechnical practices and difference: on the interferences between disability, gender, and class. Sci. Technol. Hum. Values **31**(5), 537–564 (2006). https://doi.org/10.1177/0162243906289611
34. Moser, I.: Against normalisation: subverting norms of ability and disability. Sci. Cult. **9**, 201–240 (2000). https://doi.org/10.1080/713695234
35. Schulz-Schaeffer, I.: Technik und Handeln. Eine handlungstheoretische Analyse. In: Schubert, C., Schulz-Schaeffer, I. (eds.) Berliner Schlüssel zur Techniksoziologie, pp. 9–40. Springer, Wiesbaden (2019). https://doi.org/10.1007/978-3-658-22257-4_2
36. Žižek, S.: Less Than Nothing: Hegel and the Shadow of Dialectical Materialism. Verso, London (2012)
37. Vidal, F., Ortega, F.: Being Brains Making the Cerebral Subject. Fordham University Press, New York (2017)
38. Hagner, M.: Homo cerebralis: Der Wandel vom Seelenorgan zum Gehirn Suhrkamp, Frankfurt/Main (2008)
39. Rose, N., Abi-Rached, J.: Neuro: The New Brain Sciences and the Management of the Mind. Princeton University Press, Princeton (2013)
40. Rose, N., Abi-Rached, J.: Governing through the brain: neuropolitics, neuroscience and subjectivity. Camb. Anthropol. **32** (2014). https://doi.org/10.3167/ca.2014.320102
41. Kögel, J., Schmid, J.R., Jox, R.J., Friedrich, O.: Using Brain-computer interfaces: a scoping review of studies employing social research methods. BMC Med. Ethics **20**(1), 18 (2019). https://doi.org/10.1186/s12910-019-0354-1
42. Sample, M., et al.: Brain–computer interfaces and personhood: interdisciplinary deliberations on neural technology. J. Neural. Eng. **16**(6), 063001 (2019). https://doi.org/10.1088/1741-2552/ab39cd
43. Wolbring, G., Diep, L.: Cognitive/neuroenhancement through an ability studies lens. In: Jotterand, F., Dubljevic, V. (eds.) Cognitive Enhancement, pp. 57–75. Oxford University Pres, Oxford (2016)
44. Thompson, M.C.: Critiquing the concept of BCI iliteracy. Sci. Eng. Ethics (2019). https://doi.org/10.1007/s11948-018-0061
45. Friedrich, E.V.C., Scherer, R., Neuper, C.: User-appropriate and robust control strategies to enhance brain-computer interface performance and usability. In: Guger, C., Allison, B.Z., Edlinger, G. (eds.) Brain-Computer Interface Research: A State-of-the-Art Summary, pp. 15–23. Springer, Heidelberg (2013). https://doi.org/10.1007/978-3-642-36083-1
46. Novak, D.: Biomechatronic applications of brain-computer interfaces. In: Segil, J. (ed.) Handbook of Biomechatronics, pp. 129–175. Academic Press, London (2019)
47. Firestone, S.: The Dialectic of Sex: The Case for Feminist Revolution. Morrow, New York (1970)
48. Hester, H.: Xenofeminism. Polity Press, Cambridge (2018)
49. Mirza, M.U., Richter, A., van Nes, E.H., Scheffer, M.: Technology driven inequality leads to poverty and resource depletion. Ecol. Econ. **160**, 215–226 (2019). https://doi.org/10.1016/j.ecolecon.2019.02.015
50. Van Dijk, J.A.G.M.: The evolution of the digital divide: the digital divide turns to inequality of skills and usage. Digit. Enlight. Yearb. **2012**, 57–75 (2012). https://doi.org/10.3233/978-1-61499-057-4-57

51. O'Neil, C.: Weapons of Math Destruction: How Big Data Increases Inequality and Threatens Democracy. Crown Publishers, New York (2016)
52. Eubanks, V.: Automating Inequality: How High-Tech Tools Profile, Police, and Punish the Poor. St. Martin's Press, New York (2018)
53. Noble, S.U.: Algorithms of Oppression: How Search Engines Reinforce Racism. New York University Press, New York (2018)
54. Benjamin, R.: Race After Technology: Abolitionist Tools for the New Jim Code. Polity Press, Cambridge (2019)
55. Roulstone, A.: Disability and Technology: An Interdisciplinary and International Approach. Palgrave Macmillan, London (2016)
56. Ymous, A., et al.: "I am just terrified of my future" — Epistemic violence in disability related technology research. Paper presented at the Extended Abstracts of the 2020 CHI Conference on Human Factors in Computing Systems, Honolulu, HI, USA (2020)
57. Lillywhite, A., Wolbring, G.: Coverage of artificial intelligence and machine learning within academic literature, Canadian newspapers, and twitter tweets: the case of disabled people. Societies **10**(1), 23 (2020)

Studying the Phenomenon of Verbal Bullying in High School Students for Video Experience Design: A Case of an International School in Guangzhou, China

Zhen Liu[1] [ORCID] and Yue Cai[2]([✉])

[1] School of Design, South China University of Technology, Guangzhou 510006, People's Republic of China
[2] Nansha College Preparatory Academy, Nansha, Guangzhou 511458, People's Republic of China

Abstract. Bullying is always a serious problem in schools. An occurrence of a bullying can cause a series of consequences, which consume money, time, and deteriorate interpersonal relationships between people. With the development of different technologies, more kinds of bullying emerged, and instead of physically, those bullying tend to be done on verbal ways. Different than physical bullying, verbal bullying is easier to be ignored by the community, including schools, parents, peers, even the victims themselves, due to its characteristics. In this way, raising the public awareness of verbal bullying is absolutely urgency. This paper aims to explore the phenomenon of verbal bullying in high school students with the consideration of their backgrounds, particularly in China, and to find out the unique parts of the phenomenon in the target region. The research method of this paper is divided into four steps. An online Questionnaire is adopted in the first step, which gathers the opinions about verbal bullying from high school students of an international school in Guangzhou, China. Following on is a video experience design for anti-verbal bullying in high school, which reflects the problems described and pointed out in the questionnaire. Then the first draft of the video will be presented to the students who were once experienced in the process of verbal bullying. The last step is to optimize the video according to the suggestions from the students who participate in the reflection process, and publish the video to the public. The result of this research shows several unusual points: firstly, countering on the problem that if students will laugh at people right in front of them, different gender shows a significant gap; secondly, particularly in the target region, the uncommonness of the victims' interests caused students to bully them. Other than these, physical appearance and personality can also be the reason for students to bully others, and bullying was done both on the internet and in real world.

Keywords: High school · Verbal bullying · Appearance · Internet · Personality · Interests · Questionnaire · Experience design · Video

© Springer Nature Switzerland AG 2021
M. M. Soares et al. (Eds.): HCII 2021, LNCS 12780, pp. 252–269, 2021.
https://doi.org/10.1007/978-3-030-78224-5_18

1 Introduction

Whether in the past or now, bullying is always a serious issue in schools. Bullying can cause many negative consequences on the victims. First of all, evidences have shown that the average academic performance of the victims is lower than students who didn't involve in bullying behaviors [1]. Health problems are also appeared alongside with bullying, that more psychosomatic problems are being reported from the victims comparing with other groups, and children who can clearly remember the bullying processes usually have a high level of post-traumatic stress [1]. Anti-social behaviors were also being commonly found in victims of school bullying [2, 3]. Furthermore, due the development of today's technology, the internet had also become a place where bullying frequently happens [4]. According to a study conducted in a Turkish high school, as cyber bullying increases, victims' self-esteem decreases [5]. Not only the victims are being hurt in bullying, who need to spend time and energy to solve the problem, but also the schools; and even the perpetrators, those future obstacles might emerge when they are building interpersonal relationship with others [1].

Bullying is still a phenomenon that widely influenced Chinese students. In the September of 2019, five college students were being sentenced by the court in Ningbo, China [6]. These students were the bullies of a serious school bullying event happened in the November of 2018, that they insulted another student by stuffing tissues in her mouth, binding her body with leather belts, taking off her clothes while shooting videos, pour alcohols into her mouth, forcing her to smoke, cutting her hair and writing disrespectful words on her body. The victim was largely hurt by this experience, which she refused to go out in the next several months, and completely seal her up. This is not the only case. On April 27th, 2018, Yulin, China, a man used a dagger to stick the students of a middle school, and caused 9 deaths and 12 injuries [7]. The reason he did that is because he was bullied by the students of that middle school at the time he was still a student, and after that he began to hate students, which eventually led to his anti-social behavior. On April 4th, 2019, a video spread out on WeChat, a social media platform in China, in which a girl was slapped by a few other girls in the bathroom of a school. On the second day, the local Bureau of Education proves that it was a true event [8].

From these cases, it can be seen that they are mostly fell into the category of physical bullying, which is the kind of bullying that most of the school bullying-related news reports focused on. However, in the author's daily observation, the type of school bullying that happens most frequently is actually verbal bullying. This has been proved by a committee which dedicated to solve the safety problem of teenagers, that in a survey they conducted national wide, it is shown that 81.45% of the participants claimed that solving verbal bullying is in urgent. This ratio outnumbered all the other types of school bullying [9].

Verbal bullying here refers to behaviors that cause mental and psychological injuries through ridicule, irony, disgust, harshness, contempt, indifference, etc. The reason why verbal bullying is more common in schools might be the following: first, verbal bullying is not limited by the factors of time, location, space, and even language, it basically can happen any moments at any places; secondly, the punishment of verbal bullying is always lighter than that on physical bullying, in most cases, students often only get teachers' verbal warning when they are verbally bullying their peers; thirdly, verbal bullying is easier to become a group action, that students tend to support their friends more even if their friends are the perpetrators.

Due to its characteristic, verbal bullying is something people usually pay little attention on. This paper aims to explore the phenomenon of verbal bullying specifically in the international high schools in China. It will discuss several factors that might differentiate the verbal bullying behaviors between individuals, including gender, age, and the previous learning environment students got involved in. As the result is clear, a promotion video will be produced accordingly to increase people's awareness of verbal bullying.

2 Research Method

2.1 Questionnaire

An online Questionnaire was designed to explore the phenomenon of verbal bullying among students in Nansha College Preparatory Academy (NCPA), an international school in Guangzhou, China. As shown in Fig. 1, the questionnaire was divided into three parts: the basic information of the subjects, subject's experience about verbal bullying, and subject's opinions about potential solution of verbal bullying. The questions in the second portion were designed based on the observation in NCPA in the past three years. The questionnaire has been uploaded to wjx.cn and distributed to NCPA students via WeChat, a popular social media in China. 34 students responded to the questionnaire within a week, including 17 males and 17 females. The quantitative data analysis was conducted via SPSS (Statistical Product and Service Solutions) software.

2.2 Video Design Experiment

A video design experiment was conducted in the second part of this study. The experiment contains three steps. First, a conceptual video was being produced, that the plot, characters and scenes within the video were designed according to the results from the previous questionnaire. Following on, this conceptual video was being presented to five students who studied in NCPA separately. After watching the video, each student had a one-to-one interview, which they answered three questions about the clarity and the truthfulness of the video. The final step is the refinement of the conceptual video that scenes and plots were being optimized based on the suggestions and concerned raised by the students in their interviews. Lastly, the video was being published on the internet to serve for a promotion purpose.

Survey about Verbal Bullying in High School

The purpose of this survey is to explore the phenomenon of verbal bullying (causing mental and psychological problems to a person through ridicule, irony, disgust, harshness, contempt, and indifference) among high school students. Your answer will be submitted anonymously. Thank you for your support!

* 1. What Grade are you in?

○ 9

○ 10

○ 11

○ 12

* 2. What is your gender?

○ Male

○ Female

* 3. Which following middle/secondary school did you attend before NCPA?

○ Traditional middle school in China

○ International department of a traditional middle school in China

○ International school

○ Local middle school outside China

* 4. Which following occasions of verbal bullying have you ever seen or experienced?

☐ Posting sarcastic languages about someone on the internet

☐ Laugh at someone right in front of her or him

☐ Speaking ills of someone behind her or his back

☐ Others

* 5. Which following types of appearance-related verbal bullying have you ever seen or experienced?

☐ Sarcasm about appearance (ex. calling a relatively fat person as fat swine)

☐ Purposely make difficulties for someone due to her or his appearance

☐ Others

* 6. Which following types of personality-related verbal bullying have you ever seen or experienced?

☐ Sarcasm about personality or personal interests (ex. calling a boy sissy because he like to dance K-POP from female idol groups)

☐ Purposely make difficulties for someone due to her or his personality or personal interests

☐ Others

7. What else verbal bullying do you know?
Verbal bullying refers to actions that cause mental and psychological problem to a person through ridicule, irony, disgust, harshness, contempt, and indifference. Verbal bullying doesn't include physical assault.

8. What kind of actions do you think we can take to diminish verbal bullying in high school?
You may consider from different perspectives, such as schools and individuals.

9. If you have ever verbal bullied others or been verbal bullied by others, would you like to be interviewed?
If you would like to do so, please leave your email address below. Thank you for your participation!

Fig. 1. The structure and questions of the questionnaire for exploring the phenomenon of verbal bullying among high school students in NCPA.

3 Result

3.1 Gender and Grade

As shown in Fig. 2, most of the 34 questionnaire respondents that are 17 boy and 17 girls are from Grade 11 (41.18%) and Grade 12 (32.35%).

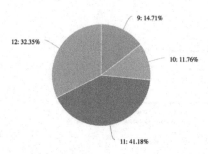

Fig. 2. The distribution of grade levels among students who finished the survey.

3.2 Former Education Background

As shown in Fig. 3, over half (64.71%) of the questionnaire respondents studied in traditional school in China, about a quarter (26.47%) of respondents were once studied in international school, 5.88% respondents were from international department of a traditional school in China, and 2.94% respondents studied in local school outside China. Since the sample from the last two kinds of middle/secondary school is too small comparing with the other two, so the researcher decided to sort respondents who studied in the international department of a traditional school in China into the traditional school in China branch, and sort the respondent who studied in local school outside China into the international school branch for the analysis later on.

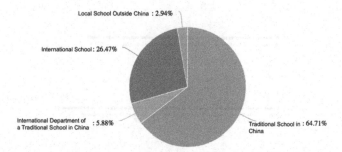

Fig. 3. Respondents' former education background information.

3.3 Verbal Bullying Experience

Respondents were asked to choose all the options that fit on them. As shown in Fig. 4, over four fifths (85.29%) of the questionnaire respondents responded that they have seen or experience the verbal bullying occasion that "Speaking ills of someone behind her or his back", while 67.65% of the questionnaire respondents have seen or experience "Laughing at someone right in front of her or him", and 61.76% have seen or experience "Posting sarcastic language about someone on the Internet". The responses provided in "Others" didn't provide useful information for this study, so their results won't be included in the analysis.

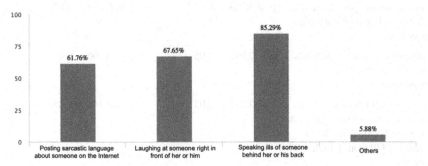

Fig. 4. Respondents' verbal bullying experience.

Regarding gender distribution (see Fig. 5), a little more male respondents chose the "Posting sarcastic language about someone on the Internet" option, while slightly more female respondents chose "Speaking ills of someone behind her or his back". According to the results of the T-test of the groups of boys and girls, as shown in Table 1, significant difference between female and male's answer is presented in the "Laughing at someone right in front of her of him" option, that much less female chose this option then male.

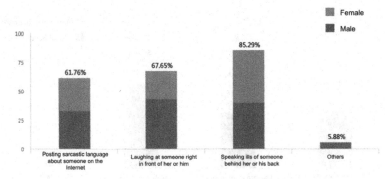

Fig. 5. Respondents' verbal bullying experience in terms of gender.

Table 1. Results of T-test of the respondent groups of boy and girl.

Verbal bullying experience	Boy vs. Girl	International school vs. local school
Posting sarcastic language about someone on the Internet	p = 0.304 > 0.05	p = 0.521 > 0.05
Laughing at someone right in front of her/him	p = 0.010** = 0.01 < 0.05	p = 0.461 > 0.05
Speaking ills of someone behind her/his back	p = 0.158 > 0.05	p = 0.102 > 0.05
Sarcasm about appearance (ex. calling a relative fat person as fat swine)	p = 0.303 > 0.05	p = 0.258 > 0.05
Purposefully make difficulties for someone due to her or his appearance	p = 0.082 > 0.05	p = 0.706 > 0.05
Sarcasm about personality or personal interests (ex. calling a boy sissy because he like to dance K-POP from female idol groups)	p = 0.257 > 0.05	p = 0.241 > 0.05
Purposefully make difficulties for someone due to her or his personality or personal interests	p = 0.467 > 0.05	p = 0.608 > 0.05

Regarding the kinds of middle/secondary school respondents have attended, the distribution of the responses is shown in Fig. 6. According to the T-test (see Table 1), no significance difference was being seen between students from international schools and students from local schools.

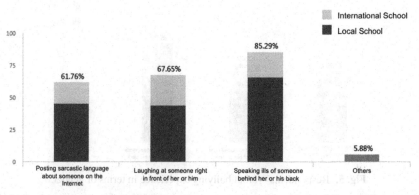

Fig. 6. Respondents' verbal bullying experience in terms of the kinds of the middle/secondary school the respondents attended.

3.4 Types of Appearance-Related Verbal Bullying Respondents Have Seen or Experienced

Respondents were asked to choose all the options that fit on them. As shown in Fig. 7, almost 90% (88.24%) of the questionnaire respondents responded that they have seen or experience the appearance-related verbal bullying that "Sarcasm about appearance (ex. Calling a relative fat person as fat swine)", while 61.76% of the questionnaire respondents have seen or experience "Purposefully make difficulties for someone due to her or his appearance". The responses provided in "Others" didn't provide useful information for this study, so their results won't be included in the analysis.

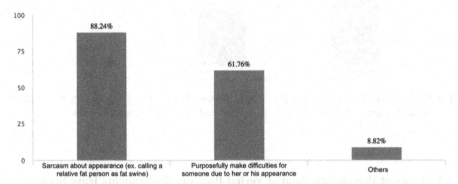

Fig. 7. Respondents' overall choices on types of appearance-related verbal bullying they have seen or experienced.

Regarding gender distribution (see Fig. 8), the number of female and male respondents who chose the "Posting sarcastic language about someone on the Internet" option is about the same, while slightly more male respondents chose "Purposefully make difficulties for someone due to her or his appearance". According to the T-test (see Table 1), no significance difference was being seen between female and male respondents.

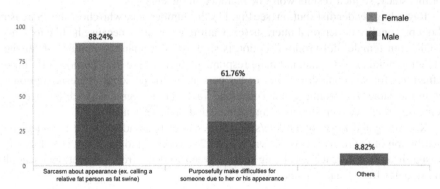

Fig. 8. Respondents' choices on types of appearance-related verbal bullying they have seen or experienced in terms of gender.

Regarding the kinds of middle/secondary school respondents have attended, the distribution of the responses is shown in Fig. 9. According to the T-test (see Table 1), no significance difference was being seen between students from international schools and students from local schools.

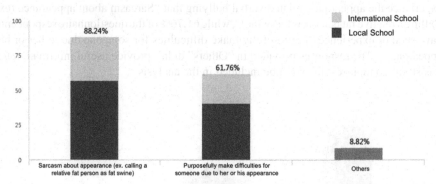

Fig. 9. Respondents' choices on types of appearance-related verbal bullying they have seen or experienced in terms of the kinds of the middle/secondary school students attended.

3.5 Types of Personality-Related Verbal Bullying Respondents Have Seen or Experienced

Respondents were asked to choose all the options that fit on them. As shown in Fig. 10, almost three quarters (73.53%) of the questionnaire respondents responded that they have seen or experience the appearance-related verbal bullying that "Sarcasm about personality or personal interests (ex. Calling a boy sissy because he like to dance K-OP from female idol groups)", while 70.59% of the questionnaire respondents have seen or experience "Purposefully make difficulties for someone due to her or his personality or personal interests". The responses provided in "Others" didn't provide useful information for this study, so their results won't be included in the analysis.

Regarding gender distribution (see Fig. 11), the number male who chose the "Sarcasm about personality or personal interests (ex. Calling a boy sissy because he like to dance K-OP from female idol groups)" option is slightly more than the number of female, while the number of female and male respondents who chose the "Purposefully make difficulties for someone due to her or his personality or personal interests" option is about the same. According to the T-test (see Table 1), no significance difference was being observed between students from female and male respondents.

Regarding the kinds of middle/secondary school respondents have attended, the distribution of the responses is shown in Fig. 12. According to the T-test (see Table 1), no significance difference was being seen between students from international schools and students from local schools.

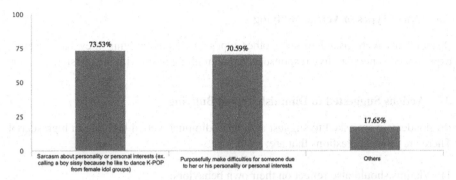

Fig. 10. Respondents' overall choices on types of personality-related verbal bullying they have seen or experienced.

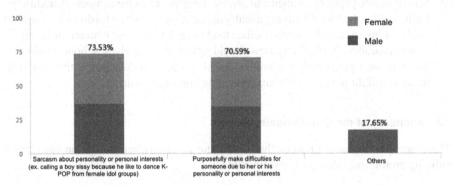

Fig. 11. Respondents' choices on types of personality-related verbal bullying they have seen or experienced in terms of gender.

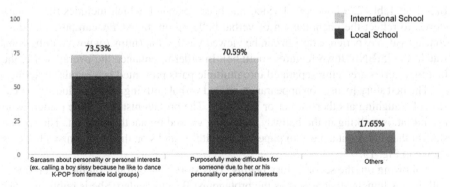

Fig. 12. Respondents' choices on types of personality-related verbal bullying students have seen or experienced in terms of the kinds of the middle/secondary school they attended.

3.6 Other Types of Verbal Bullying

Respondents were asked to state other types of verbal bullying they have seen or experienced. There are five responses that had nothing to do with the question.

3.7 Actions Suggested to Diminish Verbal Bullying

Respondents were asked to suggest actions to diminish verbal bullying in high school. There are three suggestions that are:

1) Victims should also reflect on their own behaviors;
2) School should enhance anti-bullying education, and set up psychological counseling for students; and
3) School should promote an open and diverse atmosphere on the campus. In traditional Chinese schools, verbal bullying usually happens on students who don't have a good grade; in international schools, bullies tend to target on those who are different on their appearance. While the victims should reflect on themselves, school should also intervene and guide both the bullies and the victims. Education is the first step, though it might not have obvious effect, it is important to do so.

3.8 Summary of the Questionnaire Results

There are questionnaire findings that contribute to experience design an anti-verbal bullying promotion video, as shown in Table 2.

4   Video Experience Design

Based on Table 2, a conceptual video has been designed, which includes three small stories to reflect the phenomenon of verbal bullying on the NCPA campus. The draft concept video experience design can be viewed via the link (https://www.youtube.com/watch?v=z75tBNtDJbw&feature=youtu.be). In order to enhance the overall sense, the first two stories are being separated into multiple parts presented in a regular timeline.

The first story focuses on appearance-related verbal bullying which include the occasion of "laughing at others at her or his back". The protagonist A, a male student who is a bit fat, is walking in the hallway and being viewed by another student. The second student then takes out a piece of paper and stealthily sticks on the protagonist's back, as shown in Fig. 13.

Following on, the second story begins. This story concentrates on the cyber-verbal bullying. A female student acts as the protagonist B in the video. She is publishing her selfie on the social media at this scene, as shown in Fig. 14.

Then it comes to the third story, which is a coherent story that doesn't separate into parts, also the turning point of the video. This story addresses the personality-related verbal bullying, in an occasion of "laughing at someone right in front of her or him". In this scene, a male student, the protagonist C, is practicing a dance, while a few other students passed by and saw him, then they stopped at the gate and watched him. After a

Table 2. Questionnaire findings for experience design of an anti-verbal bullying promotion video.

Questionnaire findings	Corresponding for an anti-verbal bullying promotion video experience design
Although cyber-verbal bullying and face-to-face verbal bullying are not as frequent as verbal bullying that happen behind victims' back, there are still more than 65% of respondents indicate them, which shows that those two occasions should also gained enough attention	All three types of bullying occasions will be included in the video, as their proportion varies, that "verbal bullying behinds the victims back" will have the largest portion, following by "cyber-verbal bullying", and "face-to-face verbal bullying" will have the smallest portion
Female students are less likely to verbally bully others or be bullied by others in face-to-face situations comparing with male students; rather, they are more likely to have verbal bullying experiences in places that are more private	According to this finding, the protagonist (victim) of the "face-to-face verbal bullying" case will be a male student, and the person who mainly leads the bullying behavior will also be male
The verbal bullying experiences of students who have Chinese educational backgrounds don't differentiate much with that of students who have non-Chinese educational backgrounds	Due to this result, the plot won't emphasize or present the educational background of the characters in the video
The data collected for 3.5 (appearance-related verbal bullying) and 3.6 (personality-related verbal bullying) prove the author's previous observation that appearance, personality, and personal interests are actually the points bullies target on the victims	In this way, the reason why victims in the video are being bullied will also focus on these two areas, while "appearance-related bullying" will have a larger portion since about 15% more students chose this option in the questionnaire comparing with the response for "personality-related bullying"

Fig. 13. The scene that protagonist 1 has been stealthily stuck a piece of paper on his back.

moment, they began to laugh at the protagonist, which caused him fell into depression, as shown in Fig. 15.

Moving on, it goes back to the second story, which Protagonist B is eating in the cafeteria. At the same time, her phone notified her for new message. When B happily opens up the social media, what she found is some bad comments, as shown in Fig. 16.

Lastly, the first story continues, and it got two more scenes. In the second scene of the first story, Protagonist A is studying in the library with the note still on his back, as

Fig. 14. The scene that protagonist 2 posts a selfie on the social media.

Fig. 15. The scene that protagonist 3 was being laughed by a group of bullies while dancing.

Fig. 16. The scene that protagonist 2 received some vicious comments on the social media. In the middle, the three comments mean "It hurts my eyes", "What a weirdo" and "Please block me when you post photos" respectively.

few students walked by and saw the note, and they started to titter beside A. Protagonist A thoughts those are kind smiles and felt joy, as shown in Fig. 17.

Fig. 17. The scene that protagonist 1 was being laughed by a bunch of students without knowing.

Then Protagonist A went back to his dorm. As he was telling his experiences to his roommate, his roommate noticed the paper and took it off. When A saw that, and the word on the paper, he fell silent and was depressed by it, as shown in Fig. 18.

Since the video will eventually serve for promotion purpose, a slogan appears at the end in Fig. 19 to highlight the purpose of the video that is Embrace Differences.

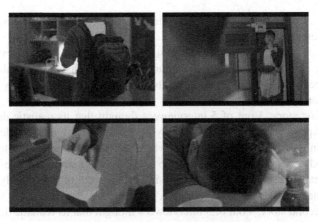

Fig. 18. The scene that protagonist 1 finally realized he was being bullied.

Fig. 19. The slogan 'Embrace Differences' for the conceptual video.

5   Validation Follow-up Interview

The conceptual video was being presented to five questionnaire respondents who currently studying in NCPA separately. Each of them accepted a one-to-one interview, during which they answered and discussed three content-related questions for validation and improvement.

Interviewees were asked to answer questions that are 'Do you think the story is clear? Could you understand the story immediately? Please to rate the clarity of the three stories separately from 1 to 4 (1-Extremely unclear, 2-Unclear, 3-Clear, 4-Extremely clear)'. For the first story, all the interviewees gave the rate of either clear or extremely clear. For the third story, all the interviewees thought it is extremely clear. As for the second story, 3 out of 5 interviewees claimed that it is extremely clear. Interviewee, who gave a rate of 2, explained that he cannot see the content on the screen in the first scene, which prevents him from understanding the story.

Interviewees were asked to answer questions that are 'Do you think the logic of the plot is clear? In the video, the plot is developing from setting, which shows what the protagonists are like and the things they are doing, to the process of verbal bullying, to finally to the result of verbal bullying, which are the reactions of the protagonists. Do you think this is true? Rate the clarity of the whole video from 1 to 4 (1-Extremely unclear, 2-Unclear, 3-Clear, 4-Extremely clear)'. All the interviewees gave a rate of 4, which is extremely clear.

Interviewees were asked to answer questions that are 'How do you view the realistic degree of the story? Do you think these three events will happen in reality? Rate the realistic degree of the three stories separately from 1 to 4 (1-Extremely low, 2-Low, 3-High, 4-Extremely high)'.

For the first story, 3 out of 5 interviewees thought that its realistic degree is low, because: a) Appearance-related verbal bullying won't happen right beside the victims; instead, it is more common to do at places where victims don't present (Interviewee M); b) If somebody sees others are laughing to him or herself strangely, one won't feel it is compliments (Interviewee S1); and c) Using sticky notes to verbal bullying others is rarely happened nowadays (Interviewee C).

For the second story, 4 out of 5 interviewees thought that its realistic degree is high. The Interviewee M claimed that when people verbal bullying others on the internet, the language should be more ironic.

For the third story, 4 out of 5 interviewees thought that its realistic degree is high, and 3 out of these 4 interviewees gave a rate of 4. The Interviewee S2 believed that the bullies should also laugh at the protagonist's back.

Table 3 presents the issues interviewees indicated for each scene and the response actions toward them.

Table 3. Follow-up interview results with taken actions.

Scene	Issues indicated by interviewees	Actions
A male student was bullied by another student who stuck a paper on the victim's back due to his appearance, while other students also laughed at him when they saw the paper. The victim didn't realize until his roommates pointed it out	Appearance-related verbal bullying won't happen right beside the victims; instead, it is more common to do at places where victims don't present	According to the observation, appearance-related verbal bullying does happen in the occasions where victims present, the main point should be that the victims don't realize she or he is being bullied. No action taken
	If somebody sees others are laughing to him or herself strangely, one won't feel it is compliments	The video will be adjusted based on the issue
	Using sticky notes to verbal bullying others is rarely happened nowadays	Due to time limitation, it is hard to re-design the whole story, while using sticky notes in verbal bullying still exists today although the frequency decreased
A female student posts a selfie onto the social media, and as she checked it later, she received some vicious comments	The content on the female student's phone screen is unclear, which prevent the interviewee from understanding the story	The video will be adjust based on the issue
	In cyber-verbal bullying, the language will be more ironic	The author believes the real situation M suggested doesn't fit in this video. To understand the true meaning of the ironic languages, there must be a certain context. Without that, the audiences will easily misinterpret the words

(continued)

Table 3. (*continued*)

Scene	Issues indicated by interviewees	Actions
A male student was being directly laughed by a group of students who passed by when he was practicing dancing K-POP dance from female idol group	The bullies should also laugh at the protagonist's back	For this concern, the author believe it will be better in the original way. If the bullies laugh at the Protagonist C's back, a lot more scenes are needed in order to clear show the idea. However, as a promotion video, it cannot be too long, or the audiences' attention will be easily dispersed. Due to this reason, direct interactions between characters are necessary

6 Refinement

In line with results and actions in Table 3, two refinements have been made in the final video (https://www.youtube.com/watch?v=4HNjsazMo8M&feature=youtu.be), which are:

I) Scene 1 of Story 2: Enlarging the screen of the posting page, in order to clearly show the content of the post, which help the audiences with clearly understanding the plot, as shown in Fig. 20.

Fig. 20. Original scene (left) and scene after refinement (right) for Action I.

II) After the interview, Interviewee S1 further suggested an alternate scene that can fit in story 1. Combining with her opinion, a substituting the library scene has been added into the following: the male student notices that others are strangely smiling to him, so he goes up and asks them what are they laughing at. Those bullies deceive the male student that they thought him looks good, and then tap his back to make the notes stick more firmly. The male student trusts their words and really considers those smiles as complements, as shown in Fig. 21.

Fig. 21. Original scene (left) and scene after refinement (right) for Action II.

7   Conclusion

7.1   Significance of This Study

A conclusion can be drawn from the results above, that verbal bullying is actually happening so frequently to a point that immediate actions need to be taken to diminish the effects. This study explores several new aspects that might influence the verbal bullying behaviors in high school, which include differences between distinguish backgrounds of secondary education and between genders. This study also considered video experience design as a possible tool to increase students' awareness of verbal bullying, and examines three occasions verbal bullying might take place, and two qualities of victims that might cause them to become the target of bullies, which are countering on the problem that if students will laugh at people right in front of them, different gender shows a significant gap; particularly in the target region, the uncommonness of the victims' interests caused students to bully them; and physical appearance and personality can also be the reason for students to bully others, and bullying was done both on the internet and in real world.

The result of this study and the data included in it can be used for future studies that focus on similar aspects of bullying in schools, and served as reference for comparisons which might reveal a broader message about the phenomenon of bullying in China and the world.

7.2   Limitation and Future Study

There are some limitations of this study. First, the sample size of the questionnaire is small, and the questionnaire has not been responded by all the students in the school, thus the result may only represent the students who finished the questionnaire but not the whole NCPA. Secondly, when answering the questionnaire, the subjects were self-directed, that errors might be produced during the process. In addition, the numbers of subjects who attended international middle/secondary schools are much less than that of the subjects who attended Chinese traditional middle/secondary schools, the comparison regarding the educational backgrounds might be biased.

As for the video, the performers and time are very limited due to school schedule. There may be a lack of professional video editing skill of the research team as well. Hence, it is hard to achieve the best impact of video experience design effect of anti-verbal bullying to the respondents.

In the future, several aspects can be further investigated from the current status. As this study explores the phenomenon of verbal bullying in high school students, and the causes of verbal bullying have not been revealed, as well as the possible solutions for verbal bullying. More research and experiments can be conducted by using different research method, such as direct interviews with the victims and the bullies, for digging in those areas. New promotion means can also be implemented to diminish the verbal bullying behaviors.

Acknowledgements. The authors wish to thank all the people who provided their time and efforts for the investigation. This research was funded by Guangzhou Philosophy and Social Science Planning 2020 Annual Project, Guangzhou, China, grant number 2020GZYB12.

References

1. Houbre, B., Tarquinio, C., Thuillier, I., Hergott, E.: Bullying among students and its consequences on health. Eur. J. Psychol. Educ. **21**(2), 183–208 (2006)
2. Grell, B.S., Meyer, R.C.: Perceived connections between anti-social gateway behaviors and school bullying and culture. High. Educ. Stud. **6**(4), 190–196 (2016)
3. Hemphill, S.A., Tollit, M., Herrenkohl, T.I.: Protective factors against the impact of school bullying perpetration and victimization on young adult externalizing and internalizing problems. J. Sch. Violence **13**(1), 125–145 (2014)
4. Hase, C.N., Goldberg, S.B., Smith, D., Stuck, A., Campain, J.: Impacts of traditional bullying and cyberbullying on the mental health of middle school and high school students. Psychol. Sch. **52**(6), 607–617 (2015)
5. Aliyev, R., Gengec, H.: The effects of resilience and cyberbullying on self-esteem. J. Educ. **199**(3), 155–165 (2019)
6. Say No to School Bullying! Five College Students in Ningbo Were Sentenced, http://www.chinanews.com/sh/2019/09-05/8948132.shtml. Accessed 21 Jan 2020
7. 9 Students Died and 10 Students Were Injured in Shanxi. It's School Bullying Again, Are Your Children Really Safe? http://dy.163.com/v2/article/detail/DH6P98V40516VS91.html. Accessed 21 Jan 2020
8. Officers of Liuzhou Responded to the Junior High School Girl Who Has Been Slapped by 20: The Situation Is True, and Will Be Dealt Seriously. https://www.thepaper.cn/newsDetail_forward_3263873, Accessed 21 Jan 2020
9. Du, X.H.: A brief analysis of campus soft violence. Mod. Women (in Chin.) **5**, 252–254 (2014)

A Study of Teaching Aids Design for Autistic Children with Focus on Hand-Eye Coordination

Zaixing Liu[1](✉), Lijun Jiang[2], Xiu Wang[2], and Zhelin Li[2]

[1] Guangzhou Academy of Fine Arts, Guangzhou, Guangdong, China
[2] South China University of Technology, Guangzhou, Guangdong, China

Abstract. To improve the usability of teaching aids for children with autism, this paper study the key features of designing teaching aids aiming for training hand-eye coordination of children with autism. The corresponding design strategy is derived base on the principle of inclusive design and two design proposals are proposed. And following the rationality and effectiveness evaluation of those design schemes, which including the comparison to existing teaching aids. The analysis results show that the design scheme with newer training methods﹑sensory stimulation and gamification design gave a better performance.

Keywords: Teaching aids design · Autism · Hand-eye coordination

1 Introduction

Autism is a generalized neurodevelopmental disorder, which is usually noticed by parents at the age of 3 [1]. At present, rehabilitation intervention and treatment methods for autism have covered many fields, including medicine, psychology, special education, etc. [2]. The effective implementation of rehabilitation training for autism must rely on the corresponding rehabilitation teaching aids, which can effectively improve the rehabilitation effect [3, 4]. There is very little research on teaching aids for children with autism. The teaching aids on the market are mainly for normal children, and children with autism cannot use them properly due to their abilities. Take hand-eye coordination rehabilitation training as an example. Most of the teaching aids used in institutions are hand-made by autism rehabilitation teachers. Teaching aids have become a satisfactory tool to support the rapid rehabilitation of autistic patients [5]. Children with autism can only be intervened effectively if they are accompanied by appropriate teaching aids due to their impairments [6]. At present, there is little research on designing teaching aids for children with autism, and there is a serious imbalance with the current urgent need for rehabilitation aids in autism rehabilitation institutions.

The 'Autism Resource Network' is a very popular website for purchasing autism aids abroad, but there are only 15 models of hand-eye coordination aids showing on the site, which is far below the actual demand for rehabilitation. In research at educational institutions, it was found that some of the available teaching aids for autistic children exceed the hand-eye coordination of children with autism, and they are not able to play with them well. As result, institutions are more likely to use teachers' home-made manual aids. Furthermore, most rehabilitation teachers are not professionally trained in design, the teaching aids they made are lacking in terms of safety, variety, fun, training effectiveness, and systematic graded training.

At present, many teaching aids on the market have "design exclusion" for children with autism and are intolerant of the actual abilities of children with autism. The "design exclusion" means that the ability requirement of the teaching aid exceeds the child's ability and cannot be used normally. Rehabilitation teaching aids currently available on the market do not match the ability of children with autism, mostly are deficiencies in diversity, fault tolerance, and equal use. In response to this phenomenon, this paper is a practical approach to the design of teaching aids for hand-eye coordination rehabilitation of children with autism from an inclusive design perspective. Inclusive design aims to make a product or service available to as many people as possible without special adaptations. It provided reasonable and effective product design for ordinary users and special users at the same time by making the product easier to use. Inclusive design principles include diversity, fault tolerance, simplicity of using, equal use, and flexibility [7–9].

2 Proposed Solution

Hand-eye coordination is the ability to produce goal-directed gestures that are guided by visual information from the eyes [10]. Hand-eye coordination operation is based on visual attention. The visual attention of children will greatly affect the practicality of teaching aids. Individuals with autism have impaired skills in communication, interaction, emotion recognition, joint attention, and imitation [11]. Patients with autism will have defects in executive function, and a large part of executive function defects is due to poor hand mobility. The hand mobility of autistic children is much lower than that of normal children of the same age [12]. Repetition of monotonous tasks during executive function training decreases motivation and increases attrition rates, adding an element of play will increase motivation and may improve training results [13].

To address the above-mentioned problems of children with autism, teaching aids for hand-eye coordination rehabilitation training must have the appropriate features and functions to better meet the requirements of hand-eye coordination rehabilitation training for children with autism. The research found that the main features and functions of the hand-eye coordination rehabilitation aids are as follows:

1. Visual focus. Only when the teaching aids are visually appealing can the child be guided to establish the visual focus for the subsequent procedure.
2. Dynamic visual tracking. Visual perception practice is the basis of hand-eye coordination training and can be designed to take into account the dynamic appeal of the teaching aids during manipulation so that the child can continue visual tracking.
3. Manipulability. To Achieving a better recovery, hand-eye coordination teaching aids must be maneuverable to a certain degree, engaging children in releasing their hands. And should be designed according to the target of finger movement training.

4. Hand-eye synergy. The tasks must be set to be completed by relying on visual guidance to operate. Any task that can be completed without vision could not improve the ability of hand-eye coordination.

3 Design Strategy

In this study, children who participated in hand-eye coordination rehabilitation training were followed up for one month. Questionnaire surveys and user interviews were conducted among teachers and parents of rehabilitation institutions, and competitive products were systematically analyzed. Summarize the problems in the use process, and then put forward the corresponding design strategy according to the inclusive design principle, which is shown in Table 1.

Table 1. Problems and corresponding design strategies.

	Problem	Design strategy
1	Too difficult	– Combine visual attention, manual dexterity, and hand-eye coordination to design operation difficulty grading
2	Risky	– Adopt the whole assembly mode, reduce small parts – Consider the characteristics of children with autism who prefer to engage in common risky movements – Strictly designed under the safety standards for young children's playthings
3	Fragile	– Using durable materials – Structural design to carry falls and resist blows
4	Boring	– Integration of game elements – Innovating newer ways to play – Combining sensory preferences in children with autism
5	Monotonous appearance	– Extracting design materials from multiple angles – Free from the constraints of existing design
6	Need for intensive stimulation	– Adding interactive feedback – Immediate feedback after completing tasks

4 Proposed Solution

According to the design strategy combined with key features and inclusive design principles, two design proposals of teaching aids for hand-eye coordination training were carried out.

4.1 Sensory Reward Exploration

Compared with normal children, children with autism have some fundamental differences in the perception and attention preferences of different sounds [14, 15]. Ma and

Lee [16] found that the visual characteristics of light have an emotional soothing transfer effect on children with autism. Through the study of specific sound and light attribute materials, it is found that the impact sound has the best effect on improving the performance of children's task completion, and it can exist in the form of teaching aids as a common reinforcement. At the same time, it was found that children with autism were extremely happy after hearing the sound of music and showed active social interaction. After soliciting the opinions of rehabilitation teachers, consider using music as a staged reinforcement.

4.2 Introduce Smart Hardware Modules

The intelligent hardware part is introduced into the design of hand-eye coordination rehabilitation teaching aids, and sound and light rewards are made possible through intelligent hardware. This article will choose Arduino for the design of intelligent modules. The functions required by the smart sensor module are as follows:

1. The intelligent module has the function of sensing whether the steel ball currently operated accurately falls into the intelligent sensing box and can provide enhanced feedback for the current correct behavior in time.
2. The intelligent module judges whether the number of steel balls entering the box is a multiple of 5, and the device will provide a stage reward when the child has completed every 5 times.

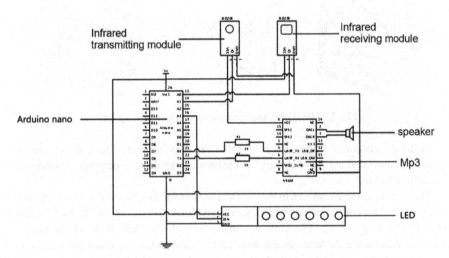

Fig. 1. Circuit connection diagram of the sensor system

The sensor module includes Arduino nano V3.0, laser sensor module (laser transmitter and laser receiver tube), LED light strip, N9100 MP3 module, speaker (8-Ω, 0.5 W), SD card, rocker switch (MTS-102), power supply. When the laser sensor module detects that there is a steel ball passing through, it transmits the signal to the Arduino board. When the number of times is not a multiple of 5, the speaker plays the pre-stored collision sound in the SD card. When the number of passes is a multiple of 5, a staged reward will be given. The speaker will play music pre-stored in the SD card, and the LED strip will have dynamic flashing lights. The circuit connection of the intelligent induction part is shown in Fig. 1.

4.3 Appearance and Structure Design

Design #1
Combine the hand operation "twisting" with the gamification elements of Pac-Man. There are 5 turntables in the interface with the assistance of the parents, the child will align the turntable to the slide, put the ball into the hole, and then turn the turntable to make the ball successfully falls into the box. The turntable has three opening sizes, 15°, 30°, and 45°, representing three levels of difficulty. The cover is a transparent PVC mask and can be opened by removing the knob to replace the turntable. The color setting is based on the visual preference of children with autism, mainly green and blue. The sketch and the rendering effect are shown in Fig. 2.

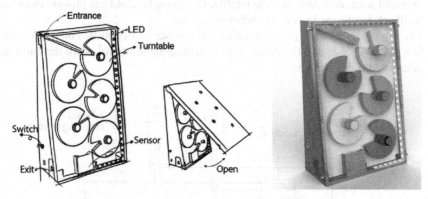

Fig. 2. The sketch and the rendering effect of design #1

In the experimental stage, it is found that the improvement effect of the hand-eye coordination-related ability of option 1 is the most significant, so here is a more detailed description below.

The exploded view is shown in Fig. 3. The cover and the main body of the teaching aid are connected by convex points and concave positions, and the cover cannot be opened when the knob is setting. The slide is connected with the main body of the teaching aid by a buckle, the Arduino board and the toy main body are fixed by screws, and the power supply and the toy main body are fixed by a square limiting plate to prevent displacement. The outer cover of the steel ball box is tightly matched with the toy body, and the backplate and the toy body are fixed by screws. As shown in Fig. 3, the turntable passes through the double bearings to achieve rotation and is connected and fixed with the main body through a nut. The rotation achieved by the bearing makes it more friendly to children with autism who have weak hand flexibility and hand strength and can easily rotate.

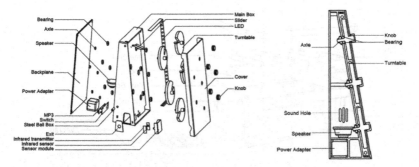

Fig. 3. Exploded and side sectional figure of design #1

Design #2

This design is mainly based on the magnetic ball transfer and hand movement "plugging". The teaching aid is innovative based on the maze. It provides five difficulty levels of puzzle sheets. The plug-in module is set with three different lengths. During the splicing process, children's awareness of quantity and length can also be exercised. With the assistance of the parents, the child puts the steel ball into the hole on the right side and holds the magnet into the middle operation area of the teaching aid, and uses the magnet to absorb the steel ball to control the movement of the steel ball. When crossing all obstacles and entering the induction box on the left, the induction device can be triggered to give immediate feedback as a reward. The obstacle difficulty can be set according to the provided drawings, or parents can define by themselves. The device mainly helps children to establish a sense of hand-eye association, and at the same time establish a macro-consciousness, learn to overcome obstacles, and not focus too much on the part. And continuously increase the strength of the small muscles of the child through continuous hanging and grasping operations. The sketch and the rendering effect are shown in Fig. 4.

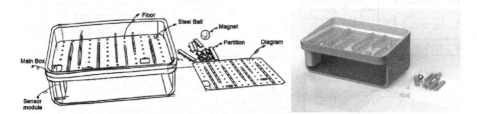

Fig. 4. The sketch and the rendering effect of design #2

The main body of design 2 is integrally formed and is connected with the induction box through a buckle. The inner side of the main body is provided with a convex edge to receive the partition, and the splicing plate is directly inserted into the circular hole of the partition through the convex point. The cover of the device is a transparent PVC mask and is fixed with the body through a tight fit. And providing a grip for easy access. Remove the cover to change the position of the splicing board and change the difficulty of the puzzle.

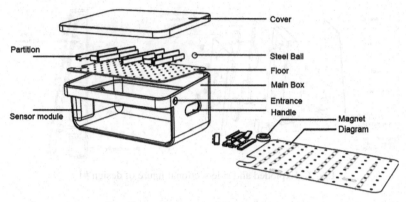

Fig. 5. Exploded view figure of design #2

5 Testing and Results

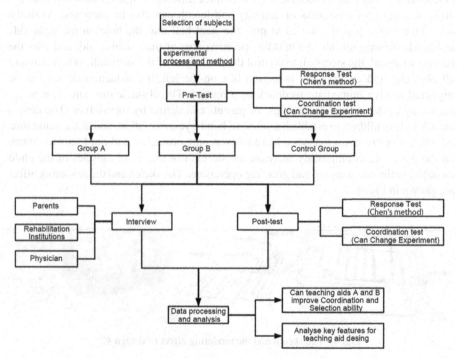

Fig. 6. Flow chart of the experiment

5.1 Experimental

We use the experimental research method to evaluate the usability of the teaching aids for children with autism in this study. Focus on the effects of the rehabilitation of children's hand-eye coordination and selective response-ability after a period of training compared to traditional models (Group C). The independent variables are three different teaching aids, and the dependent variable is the hand-eye coordination related scores measured after training with different teaching aids. 36 children participated in the test and were divided into three groups. Each group practiced for 15 min a day for 15 days, totaling 15 times. The operation process of this experiment is shown in Fig. 6.

Fig. 7. Usage scenarios for design A (left) and design B (right)

There are two measurement items in this study, which are the selective response-ability test and hand-eye coordination test. Chen's hand-eye coordination method and the 'can change test' was used in the experiment. Data were collected in two phases, pre-test and post-test. The training scenario for design A and design B is shown in Fig. 7. The pre-test and post-test scores of design A (Group A) are shown in Table 2, the pre-test and post-test scores of design B (Group B) are shown in Table 3, the pre-test and post-test scores of the existing device (Group C) are shown in Table 4.

Table 2. Pre-test and post-test results of Group A (Unit: second)

Group A	Selective response-ability		Hand-eye coordination	
	Pre-test	Post-test	Pre-test	Post-test
A1	133.59	121.13	29.56	20.23
A2	122.74	116.06	23.48	19.32
…	…	…	…	…
A12	138.55	120.89	37.21	28.46
Avg	130.91	114.46	31.95	24.37

Table 3. Pre-test and post-test results of Group B (Unit: second)

Group B	Selective response-ability		Hand-eye coordination	
	Pre-test	Post-test	Pre-test	Post-test
B1	136.70	120.51	33.45	26.12
B2	108.26	100.03	23.45	20.33
...	...	...	...	...
B12	97.78	92.55	28.56	24.29
Avg	128.50	120.68	32.71	27.85

Table 4. Pre-test and post-test results of Group C (Unit: second)

Group C	Selective response-ability		Hand-eye coordination	
	Pre-test	Post-test	Pre-test	Post-test
AC	99.44	95.62	30.12	25.26
AC	90.49	88.36	24.35	20.13
...	...	...	...	...
C12	139.88	132.89	34.56	28.91
Avg	128.81	122.76	31.96	27.63

The data above led to the following conclusions:

1. The new design can effectively improve the child's hand-eye coordination and selective response-ability

A one-way ANOVA on the pre-test scores of selection response-ability showed no statistically significant differences between groups ($P > 0.05$), and the results of the analysis are shown in Table 5, which proved that the grouping was reasonable. The results of the paired t-test on the post-test scores of hand-eye coordination selective response-ability are shown in Table 6: the post-test scores (completion time) of all three groups were lower than the pre-test scores (completion time), and the difference was statistically significant ($P < 0.05$), indicating that all three exercise methods could improve the hand-eye coordination selective response-ability of the subject children. The results of the homogeneity test with regression coefficients for the pre and posttest data showed F $= 2.775$ ($p > 0.05$), which did not reach the significance level and was consistent with the assumption of homogeneity of regression coefficients, and the results are shown in Table 7, allowing the use of analysis of covariance. A one-way analysis of covariance on the post-test scores of hand-eye coordination selective responsiveness showed a significance level (F $= 26.271$ ($p < 0.05$)), and the results are shown in Table 8, indicating a difference in hand-eye coordination responsiveness between experimental groups A and B and control group C after adjusting the pre-test scores.

Based on the previous test, to control the influence of the pre-test data on the post-test data, the post-test results are adjusted and averaged. From the adjusted average Table 9 and the paired comparison result Table 10: Group A was 8.449 S (95% CI: −experimental group A had a better lifting effect than experimental group B. Group A was 10.244 S (95% CI: −13.318–7.170, P < .001) lower than group C, indicating that experimental group A had a better lifting effect than the control group; group B was 1.794 S (95% CI: −4.867–1.278, P > 0.05) lower than the Group B was 1.794 S (95% CI: −4.867–1.278, P > 0.05) lower than the control group, and the difference was not statistically significant. The results of this study showed that the teaching aids in all three groups were effective in improving the children's hand-eye coordination and choice of response, but group A showed the best improvement, and there was no significant difference between groups B and C.

Table 5. Pre-test single-factor analysis of variance for select reaction ability

Group	Avg. (s)	Std. deviation	F	P
A	130.91	28.82	0.026	0.975
B	128.50	28.57		
C	128.81	27.55		

Table 6. Pre- and post-test paired t-test for selection response-ability (Unit: second)

Group	Chen's pre-test (s)		Chen's post-test (s)		F	P
	Avg.	Std. deviation	Avg.	Std. deviation		
A	130.91	28.82	114.46	25.08	9.745	<.001
B	128.50	28.57	120.68	28.07	7.845	<.001
C	128.81	27.55	122.76	26.21	8.102	<.001

Table 7. Homogeneity test of pre-test and post-test regression coefficients of selection response-ability

	Type III SS	DF	MS	F	Sig.
Modify model	23216.202[a]	5	4643.240	377.915	<.001
Intercept	.583	1	.583	.047	.829
Group	13.053	2	6.527	.531	.593
Chen's pre-test(S)	22711.228	1	22711.228	1848.476	<.001
Error	368.594	30	12.286		
Grand	535959.208	36			
Grand after Modify	23584.796	35			

[a]$R^2 = .984$ (After: $R^2 = .982$).

Table 8. One-way covariance results for posttest performance of selection response-ability

	Type III SS	DF	MS	F	Sig.
Modify model	23148.018[a]	3	7716.006	565.304	<.001
Intercept	.467	1	.467	.034	.854
Group	717.155	2	358.577	26.271	<.001
Chen's pre-test(S)	22701.090	1	22701.090	1663.168	<.001
Error	436.778	32	13.649		
Total	535959.208	36			
Total after modify	23584.796	35			

[a]$R^2 = .981$ (After: $R^2 = .980$).

Table 9. Selection response-ability post-test adjustment average

Group	Avg.	Standard error	95% Confidence interval	
			Lower limit	Upper limit
A	113.069[a]	1.067	110.896	115.243
B	121.519[b]	1.067	119.346	123.692
C	123.313[c]	1.067	121.141	125.486

a = 3.487 + 0.926 * 129.40 – 10.244.
b = 3.487 + 0.926 * 129.408–1.794.
c = 3.487 + 0.926 * 129.40.

Table 10. Results of comparisons of pre-test and post-tests of selective response-ability

Group	Group	Mean difference	Std. deviation	Sig.	95% Confidence interval	
					Lower limit	Upper limit
A	B	−8.449	1.509	<.001	−11.524	−5.375
	C	−10.244	1.509	<.001	−13.318	−7.170
B	A	8.449	1.509	<.001	5.375	11.524
	C	−1.794	1.508	.243	−4.867	1.278
C	A	10.244	1.509	<.001	7.170	13.318
	B	1.794	1.508	.243	−1.278	4.867

2. The new design can effectively improve the hand-eye coordination

Hand-eye coordination data were analyzed in the same way as above and are omitted. From the adjusted mean and pairwise comparison result: Group A was 2.852 S (95% CI: −4.247–1.458, P < .001) lower than group B, indicating that group A improved better than group B. Group A was 3.243 S (95% CI: −4.636–1.850, P < .001) lower than the control group, indicating that group A improved better than the control group; group B was 0.391 Slower than the control group (95% CI: −1.786–1.003, P > 0.05), and the difference was not statistically significant. The results of this study showed that the teaching aids in all three groups were effective in improving the hand-eye coordination of the children, but group A had the best improvement, and there was no significant difference between groups B and C.

5.2 Conclusion of the Evaluation

1. **Effects of different teaching aids on hand-eye coordination-related abilities.** Under this experimental condition, the results showed that all three teaching aids improved the children's hand-eye coordination selective response and hand-eye coordination, and device A had the most significant effect. The result may be related to the training method. In future designs, more consideration can be given to how to innovate in the play method to design teaching aids that can better exercise hand-eye coordination-related skills.

2. **The effects of different teaching aids on the training cooperation of children with autism.** Children with autism prefer sensory toys, and the use of dynamic reflections and immediate audio feedback as reinforcement rewards can better motivate children to train and cooperate with teachers. By comparison, device A's cooperation is higher. The main reason is that device B need for holding a magnet suspended close to the partition to adsorb the steel ball. Therefore, it's better to have a break after each phase.

3. **The effect of different teaching aids on the social interactivity of rehabilitation training for children with autism.** The use of sensory rewards has positive implications for the social initiative of the child. The design of future teaching aids can consider the use of sensory feedback to gradually help children change from food reinforcement to interest reinforcement.

4. **The effect of different teaching aids on the initiative of rehabilitation training for children with autism.** Device A adds more gamification elements, and each operation will have a corresponding physical collision sound, it's the reason why it has more appeal. It can be seen that the design of teaching aids can be more considered to integrate gamification elements, while the operation process can make full use of the characteristics of play. Furthermore, material selection to take full account of the sound properties, for example, here the turntable to choose a hard material can be better to send a collision sound.

6 Discussion

In the process of hand-eye coordination rehabilitation training for children with autism, the rationality of the design of the teaching aids will have a great impact on the motivation, cooperation, and enjoyment of the children, which will affect the rehabilitation effect. This paper summarizes the functions and features of hand-eye coordination rehabilitation teaching aids for children with autism. Based on the full consideration of its functional factors (e.g., visual focus, visual tracking, operability, etc.) and inclusive design principles (e.g., diversity principle, fault tolerance principle, simplicity, and ease of use principle, equal use principle, etc.), the corresponding design strategies for hand-eye coordination rehabilitation teaching aids for children with autism are derived, and the corresponding design practices are carried out based on the strategies. Experiments were conducted based on the sketch models of the two schemes, and the rationality and effectiveness of the design were verified by quantitative assessment of selection response-ability and hand-eye coordination after stage training. This study also explores the product needs of special populations from an inclusive perspective and translates them into specific product designs follow by validation for product effectiveness. The process provides a methodological reference for similar product design studies.

The application and design strategies of other rehabilitation aids such as social, cognitive, and expressive language aids in the corresponding rehabilitation training contexts can be investigated in the future, and to improve other aspects of rehabilitation aids for children with disabilities. Other more insightful issues can also be investigated, such as assistive rehabilitation devices with a capacity assessment.

Acknowledgent. At the end of the paper, we would like to thank Prof. Lijun Jiang and other teachers for their guidance and help in the whole research process. And we are grateful to all the scholars involved, without the help and inspiration of their research results, it would have been very difficult for us to complete this paper. Finally, we would like to thank the Science and Technology Planning Project 2017B030314169 of Guangdong Province of China for funding the publication of this paper.

References

1. Thapar, A., Pine, D.S., Leckman, J.F.: Rutter's Child and Adolescent Psychiatry, 5th edn. Child and Adolescent Psychiatry in Europe, Steinkopff (1999)
2. Zhao, B., Ma, X.W.: Review of research on educational rehabilitation for autistic children. J. Teach. Educ. 2(2), 104–110 (2015)
3. Mcmurray, K., Pierson, M.R.: The importance of assistive technology in the classroom for males and females with autism spectrum disorder. J. Gender Power 5(1), 59–143 (2016)
4. O'Neill, S.J., Smyth, S., Smeaton, A.: Assistive Technology: Understanding the Needs and Experiences of Individuals with Autism Spectrum Disorder and/or Intellectual Disability in Ireland and the UK. Assistive Technology, pp. 1–9 (2019)
5. Valadão, C.T., Alves, S.F.R., Goulart, C.M., Bastos-Filho, T.F.: Robot toys for children with disabilities. In: Tang, J.K.T., Hung, P.C.K. (eds.) Computing in Smart Toys. ISCEMT, pp. 55–84. Springer, Cham (2017). https://doi.org/10.1007/978-3-319-62072-5_5
6. Golan, O., Ashwin, E., Granader, Y.: Enhancing emotion recognition in children with autism spectrum conditions: an intervention using animated vehicles with real emotional faces. J. Autism Dev. Disord. 40(3), 269–279 (2010)
7. Zhao, C.: Design for ageing: an inclusive stance and critical attitude. Art Des. 9, 16–21 (2012)
8. Li, F., Dong, H.: Development and challenges of universal design and inclusive design principles. Fine Arts Des. 5, 71–78 (2018)
9. Li, S.: Application of inclusive design in daily products. Design 19, 124–126 (2018)
10. Lee, K., Junghans, B.M., Ryan, M.: Development of a novel approach to the assessment of eye-hand coordination. J. Neurosci. Methods 228, 50–56 (2014)

11. Charman, T., Swettenham, J., Baron-Cohen, S.: Infants with autism: an investigation of empathy, pretend play, joint attention, and imitation. Dev. Psychol. **33**(5), 781(1997)
12. Vries, M., Prins, P.J., Schmand, B.A.: Working memory and cognitive flexibility-training for children with an autism spectrum disorder: a randomized controlled trial. J. Child Psychol. Psychiatry **56**(5), 566–576 (2015)
13. Prins, P.J., Davis, S., Ponsioen, A.: Does computerized working memory training with game elements enhance motivation and training efficacy in children with ADHD? Cyberpsychol. Behav. Soc. Netw. **14**(3), 115–122 (2011)
14. Ceponiene, R., Lepisto, T., Shestakova, A.: Speech-sound-selective auditory impairment in children with autism: they can perceive but do not attend. Proc. Natl. Acad. Sci. U S A **100**(9), 5567–5572 (2003)
15. Kuhl, P.K., Coffey-Corina, S., Padden, D.: Links between social and linguistic processing of speech in preschool children with autism: behavioral and electrophysiological measures. Dev. Sci. **8**(1), F1–F12 (2005)
16. Ma, M.Y., Lee, Y.H.: Children with autism and composite tactile-visual toys during parent-child interaction. Interact. Stud. **15**(2), 260–291 (2014)

A Video Experience Design for Emotional Bullying in Public High School in Guangzhou, China

Zhen Liu[1] (iD) and Zihao Zhuang[2]([✉])

[1] School of Design, South China University of Technology, Guangzhou 510006,
People's Republic of China
[2] Guangzhou No.2 Middle School, Guangzhou 510040, People's Republic of China

Abstract. In Guangzhou, a region boasts advanced economy and education, campus bullying still exist. One hidden form of campus bullying is emotional bullying, which is difficult to identify and take precaution against. First, both the victims and the victimizers may not be aware of the occurrence of bullying. Second, the hazard of emotional bullying tends to be underestimated, which is responsible for the overall absence of care and protection for the victims. To address these issues, this paper adopts video experience to educate students, teachers, and parents on the existence and hazards of emotional bullying is necessitated. The design process of the video includes the following steps. First, questionnaires were designed to investigate emotional bullying in high school class within Guangzhou, and volunteers who participated the questionnaire were selected to share experience. Second, interviews with the volunteers were conducted to acquire information and story of emotional bullying on campus, which was used to develop video content. Third, based on information obtained from the interviews, a video was created about high school campus bullying. The results show that 1) there are no significant gender difference in emotional bullying; 2) the most common forms of emotional bullying are rumor and isolation; and 3) the most people are not sure whether they should seek help in the face of emotional bullying.

Keywords: Public high school · Emotional bullying · Rumor · Internet · Questionnaire · Video experience · Interview

1 Introduction

In western countries, campus bullying has received due attention. As time passes, researches into campus bullying have been developed and expanded [1]. Recently, Chinese Ministry of Education has launched a campaign to tackle campus bully [2]. Primarily, campus bully takes two different forms, namely, psyche means and physical means [3, 4]. Physical bullying has received more public attention and research efforts, yet verbal or emotional bullying has only been recognized recently. As China undergoes dramatic modernization, the campus bullying in high schools in China's first-tier and second-tier cities has been characterized by verbal and emotional bullying, instead

© Springer Nature Switzerland AG 2021
M. M. Soares et al. (Eds.): HCII 2021, LNCS 12780, pp. 284–299, 2021.
https://doi.org/10.1007/978-3-030-78224-5_20

of physical bullying. According to an investigation by China Youth Research Center among 5864 students across ten provinces in China, 36.3% students were once beaten, 22.5% were extorted, and the rest 41.2% were verbally abused, which in particular, compared with male students, female students are more inclined to become victims to campus bullying [5]. These were statistics collected a decade ago. It could be presumed that in modernized societies, non-physical campus bullying accounts for more proportion. In the best schools in first-tier cities, such as Guangzhou, physical abuse is largely absent, but it does not follow that campus bully does not exist. It has only become more indiscernible. As such, what this paper seeks to probe into is one of non-physical form of bullying, i.e. emotional bullying. Emotional bullying is a type of bullying that causes mental and emotional damage [6, 7]. It is usually characterized by malicious rumors, ganging up on others, ignoring, provoking, belittling and humiliating [8]. It is predictable that emotional bullying is more common and concealed, thereby hampering preventative efforts. The reasons for this are manifold. First, emotional bullying may not involve physical confrontation or even verbal attack, which causes it to be indiscernible. For example, "ignoring one on purpose", one form of emotional bullying, is difficult to identify. Because it does not involve physical bully or verbal abusing, the guilt of the victimizer tends to be smaller. Second, the harm caused by emotional bullying has not been recognized by parents or teachers. Consequently, there is a lack of adequate and timely protection for victims. Thirdly, emotional bullying becomes more difficult to prevent when it is helped by the Internet. Compared with bullying in the classroom or campus, online emotional bullying is far more undetectable. Considering these, this paper aims to investigate emotional bullying, including its circumstances and the usual forms it takes, in one class in a public high school in Guangzhou, China. The information from this investigation and its analysis contribute to an anti-bullying video that help with educating the public about emotional bullying's existence and harm.

2 Research Method

2.1 Questionnaire

This paper designed an online questionnaire to investigate the emotional bullying in one Grade 12 class in Guangzhou Number Two High School, a first-rate public high school in Guangzhou, China. As is shown in Fig. 1, the content of this questionnaire constitutes two parts. The first part investigates the common forms of emotional bullying. The questions were based on information from Wikipedia and a website of anti-bullying on campus [9]. The second part seeks to gain insight into students' attitude towards and opinions of emotional bullying, thereby helping to select several interviewees. The questionnaire was designed with the help of Questionnaire Star and delivered to participants through WeChat. The data were analyzed via SPSS.

2.2 Interview

After finishing the questionnaire, four participates expressed interest in providing more details. In order to elicit more details from them, the questions in the following interview

Questionnaire about Emotional Bullying in High School

The purpose of this questionnaire is to research the situation of emotional bullying in our class. The answer will be submitted anonymously. Thank you for filling the questionnaire.

*1. What is your gender?
- ○ Male
- ○ Female
- ○ Others

*2. Which kind of emotional bullying have you or your friends experienced? [请选择1-4项]
- ☐ Saying hurtful things
- ☐ Spreading malicious rumors about people
- ☐ Getting certain people "gang up" on others
- ☐ Others

*3. Which kind of hurtful words have you or your friends heard? [请选择1-4项]
- ☐ Commenting negatively on someone's looks or body
- ☐ Directing foul language
- ☐ Taunting on someone's interest or dreams
- ☐ Others

*4. Which kind of rumors have you heard? [请选择1-4项]
- ☐ About relationship status
- ☐ About classmates committing wrongdoings
- ☐ About family condition
- ☐ Others

*5. Which kind of package bullying have you or your friends experienced? [请选择1-4项]
- ☐ Denying one in any kind of conversation
- ☐ Refusing to be teamed up with one
- ☐ Not informing a student of any group activity
- ☐ Others

*6. Do you think it is necessary to seek help from adults in the face of emotional bullying?
- ○ Total unnecessary
- ○ Unnecessary
- ○ Unknown
- ○ Necessary
- ○ Total necessary

7. How can high school students fight against emotional bullying?

Fig. 1. Questionnaire on emotional bullying in one class in Guangzhou Number Two High School.

with them were designed based on the analysis of the results from the questionnaire. The face-to-face interviews with them provided real cases of emotional bullying. The essay adopts a content analysis approach to analyze the information from the interview.

2.3 Video Production

Based on the results of questionnaire and interview, a video has been produced in line with story board. After video shooting, the material was edited and placed for the emphasis of the interview results.

3 Results

3.1 Results of Questionnaire

Gender Distribution in This Investigation. As is shown in Fig. 2, of the 34 responses to this questionnaire, near three fifth of responses were from female participants, whereas two fifth of responses were from male participants.

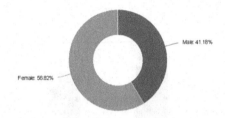

Female: 58.82%   Male: 41.18%

Fig. 2. Gender distribution in this investigation.

Types of Emotionally Bullying Witnessed or Experienced (in Contrast to Physical Bullying). As indicated in Fig. 3, approximately four fifths of participants experienced or witnessed emotional bullying in the form of "belittling" or "saying hurtful things". Over three quarters of participants experienced or witnessed malicious rumors being spread. Over two thirds of participants experienced or witnessed "ganging up" on others. From these statistics, it could be concluded that spreading rumors, belittling, and ganging up on others are common forms of emotional bullying, among which rumors and belittling are the most prevalent forms.

Negative Comments Witnessed or Experienced by Participants. As shown in Fig. 4, over two thirds of participants have experienced or witnessed emotional abuse in the form of commenting negatively on someone's appearance or body. Nearly three fifths of participants have experienced or witnessed taunting on someone's interest or dreams. Over half of participants have experienced or witnessed foul language or profanity directed at the victim. Based on these statistics, it could be inferred that attacking one's appearance is the most frequent form of verbal emotional abuse. Other forms, including taunting or foul language directed at the victim, are also common.

Rumors. As shown in Fig. 5, statistics indicate that an overwhelming majority (94.12%) of participants have heard rumors about relationship status. Roughly two third of participants have heard rumors about classmates committing wrongdoings. Over two fifths of participants have heard rumors regarding family conditions. These statistics support the conclusion that rumors about relationship are the most frequent, far more than any other types of rumors.

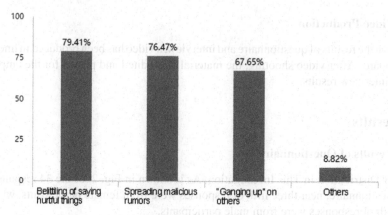

Fig. 3. Types of emotional bullying witnessed or experienced by participants.

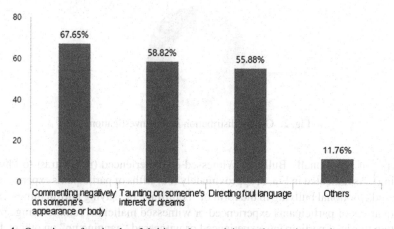

Fig. 4. Occasions of saying hurtful things that participants have witnessed or experienced.

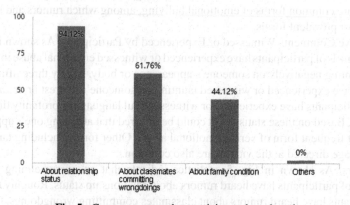

Fig. 5. Campus rumors that participants have heard.

Package Bullying That Participants Have Witnessed or Experienced. As shown in Fig. 6, a majority of participants (70.59%) have suffered or heard about package bullying or isolation in the form of denying one in any kind of conversation. Over two thirds of participants suffered or experienced such package bullying during which a student is refused to be teamed up with. Over a fifth of participants experienced or heard of isolation by not informing a student of any group activity. These statistics indicate that the two common types of package bullying are denying one in a conversation and refusing to team up with a student.

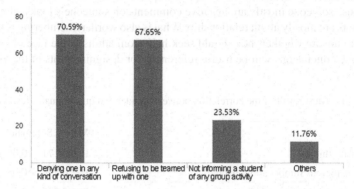

Fig. 6. Package bullying that participants have heard or experienced.

Seeking Help from Adults for Emotional Bullying. As shown in Fig. 7, approximately half of the participants are not sure whether they should seek help from adults. Over a fifth of them believe that they should turn to adults for help. Nearly a fifth of the participants strongly believe that it is necessary to ask help from adults. Nearly a tenth of them regard it unnecessary for students to seek help from adults. Few participants (2.94%) consider it completely unnecessary to turn to adults for emotional bullying. It can be concluded that most participants are unsure whether they should seek help from adults. Also, a larger proportion of participants believe that help from adults is necessary.

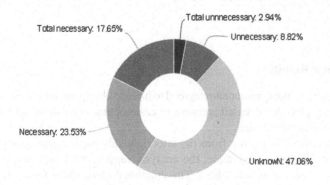

Fig. 7. Participants' choices on whether they should seek help from adults.

Participants' Advice about How to Fight Against Emotional Bullying. There are eighteen suggestions from the open question. Four suggestions are concerned with seeking help from adults. Another four pieces of advice are about asking help from friends. Three suggestions regard school regulation and law as solutions. The rest four suggestions are irrelevant.

Summary of the Questionnaire Results. According to the T-test, as shown in Table 1, no significant difference is found between male participants' responses and female participants' responses. In addition, the statistics suggest that the commonest form of emotional abuse is belittling or saying hurtful things and spreading malicious rumors. The words used to abuse someone mostly are negative comments on someone's looks, clothes, and body; rumors are mostly about relationship. What is also worth remembering is that most students are unsure whether they should seek help from adults in the face of emotional abuse. These conclusions will be useful references for designing plots of the video.

Table 1. T-test result of the correlation between gender and questionnaire response.

Answer	Male V.S. female
Saying hurtful things	$P = 0.171 > 0.05$
Spreading malicious rumors about people	$P = 0.736 > 0.05$
Getting certain people "gang up" on others	$P = 0.736 > 0.05$
Commenting negatively on someone's looks or body	$P = 0.704 > 0.05$
Directing foul language	$P = 0.134 > 0.05$
Taunting	$P = 0.601 > 0.05$
About relationship between boys and girls	$P = 0.235 > 0.05$
About bad things classmate did	$P = 0.655 > 0.05$
About family background of classmates	$P = 0.212 > 0.05$
Ignoring someone on purpose	$P = 0.112 > 0.05$
Not willing to group with someone	$P = 0.736 > 0.05$
Not informing someone to participate in group activities	$P = 0.171 > 0.05$

3.2 Interview Results

Four participants of the questionnaire agreed to have a subsequent interview. As is shown in Table 2, they provided detailed accounts of cases of emotional abuse according to the questions in the questionnaire.

To analyze the information from the interview, this paper adopts content analysis to analyze. Regarding verbal abuse, the analysis suggests that such abuse comes not only from students but also teachers. The emotional abuse done by teachers may be long overlooked, so a story was designed in which a teacher humiliates a student verbally. In responses about rumors, the most detailed answers can be found. This suggests

Table 2. Interviewee responses to questions on real cases of emotional bullying.

Question	Interviewee 1	Interviewee 2	Interviewee 3	Interviewee 4
Have you ever been attacked by negative comments on your appearance? If not, is there anyone you know who has been attacked in this way? What was the scenario? What was the cause?	Yes. They called me squirrel, because I have big front teeth. They called me this in different scenarios. For instance, when they see me in a corridor, they call me squirrel. Though I've complained many times, they insist on calling me in this way.	No. But I believe this happens a lot around us, though I cannot recall any specific instances.	There is an overweighed boy in our class. He is over 100 kilograms. It is said that gene problem causes him to have this problem. When we were shooting a photo on graduation ceremony, no classmates wanted to stand beside him. They sneered and shoveled, taunting that it was too crowded. Though these comments were not directed towards the boy, he must have suffered.	There was a boy in our class not as tall as everyone else. He is 162 cm in height probably. So, some male students like to call him little man or dwarf. He looked very upset but kept silent.
Have you ever experienced vicious personal attack? What was the scenario? What was the cause?	Yes. When I made mistakes playing video games with my friends, some would curse me, saying that I was good for nothing. This hurt a lot. Their vicious attack may be attributed to their over excitement	No.	Yes. But it was not my classmates but my physics teacher and English teacher. My GPA was among the worst in the class. The headteacher said that I was hopeless and that he would	No.

(continued)

Table 2. (*continued*)

during the game. Also, it was because on the Internet, people show less constraints on what they say.		leave me alone. He said that I could do anything as long as I did not disrupt other students. Physics teacher added that I was a loser. I felt so angry and upset that I would not forgive them for a lifetime.	
Have you ever been mocked for your dream or hobby? If not, do you know anyone who has such experience? What was the scenario? What was the cause?	No.	No.	No.	No.
Is there any rumor about your relationship? If not, do you know anyone who has such experience? What is the rumor? Why does it spread?	There is no rumor about me, but I've heard many about my friends. Interestingly, there are often contradictory rumors around. For instance, one moment I heard that they broke up. The very next moment, I heard rumor that they were back together. Perhaps, these rumors cause troubles for them; but fur us,	I once had a crush on a girl from neighboring class, so I started to learn more about her. This was when I found out that there were many rumors about her. Rumor had it that she had a crush on a senior student from the Model Airplane Society; another rumor claimed that she had been in rela-	I have a male bestie from neighboring class and hang out with him a lot. So, my classmates assume that we are lovers. No matter how I explain to them that we are not lovers, they simply ignore my explanation. Perhaps it is because they do not believe true friendship between opposite genders.	I have a friend who ends up in a relationship with someone she does not like because of rumors. They are in the same class. The boy courted her first, but while she had not said yes, he spread rumors around that they were already in a relationship. Later on, with him constantly courting her with other

(*continued*)

Table 2. (*continued*)

some rumors are interesting topics of conversations.	tionship with many students from our school; another rumor spread that she had a boyfriend from outside the school. The reason for all these rumors about her may be attributable to her popularity.		classmates, she agreed under pressure. He deliberately spread the rumor to push her to accept him.
	There is a rumor in our school that a student sneaked into the Ladies and took photos. It is certain that someone spotted him with a cellphone that night near the Ladies but there is no evidence that he has committed that misbehavior. But online, people claim that he is a habitual "criminal" and humiliate him online. Many "busybodies" even deliberately shout out his names to humiliate him offline.		
	Such rumors are common in dorms. They are usually about "misbehaviors" like forgetting to turn down the light, steal someone else's shampoo, or forget to flush the toilet. There are two reasons. First, it starts with someone who has terrible memory. Second, the rumor is invented to avoid being punished.		
Is there any rumor of a wrongdoing that you actually never commit? If not, do you know any such rumors of others? What is the rumor exactly? Why does it spread?		My friend's boyfriend has depression and now is absent from school for treatment at home. She is very attentive to her boyfriend, but rumor has it that my friend caused this boy to become depressed. This rumor hurt her to such an extent that she severed ties with many of the rumor spreaders.	When my dormmates lambast a girl they do not like, they tend to find fault with everything. Whatever the girl has done, they exaggerate, distort, and maliciously question the motive. They fabricate many rumors of this girl doing terrible things. When I ask them for evidence, they replied very ambiguously

(*continued*)

Table 2. (*continued*)

Is there any rumor about your family? If not, do you know any such rumor about your classmates? What is it? Why does it spread?	No.	There is a rumor about a girl who many people believe to be coquettish and pretentious. The rumor is that her parents have cerebral palsy. The reason for this rumor is that everyone thinks she is bizarre and thus finds a reason to explain her bizarreness. Or perhaps the rumor is intended to humiliate her.	Rumor has it that the father of one of my friends has been sent to jail. I am not sure about the authenticity of this rumor.	No.
Have you been excluded or ignored intentionally? If not, do you know anyone who has such experience? What is the scenario? What is the cause?	There is one classmate who everyone else refuse to talk with. It is because he is extremely annoying. In a self-study class when everyone is supposed to be silently studying, he likes to sing and disrupts us. Also, he likes to quarrel with our teacher during the class, thereby interrupting the class. This is why we dislike him.	No.	One girl in our class likes to ask questions to which the answer seems obvious, for instance, how to draw a certain function. In grade 3, these questions are easy and basic. But this girl asks these simple questions relentlessly and never seem to figure them out. So eventually, we are not willing to answer her questions.	No.

(*continued*)

Table 2. (*continued*)

| Have you been excluded from group activity or been denied in any form of social events? If not, do you know anyone who has such experience? What is the scenario? What is the cause? | There is an overweight boy in our class. No one wants to share a desk with him, because he takes up too much room, and he talks loudly. | No. | There is one classmate that she likes to turn to (who sits behind her). Eventually, the boy wrote on a piece of paper these words: I am not available. An example is the overweight boy who we refused to stand beside when taking a group photo upon graduation. | One girl in our class is a loner. She seems to have no friend. She has strange hobbies and talk in a really weird way. She is not ugly looking. I am not sure she is excluded, but for sure, few want to be in a group with her. |

Note: The texts in green color are words intended to hurt; the texts in blue are contents of specific rumors; the texts in yellow are about social exclusion.

that rumors may be the commonest form of emotional abuse. The rumors listed in the responses are widely spread in grade 12, which indicates that it is representative. Hence, based on this information, a further two stories were designed. One story is about a rumor of relationship, and the other is about rumors of wrongdoing. Also, the interview suggests that the spread of rumors often involves the impact of Internet, which causes large-scale of spreading. This would also be reflected in the story. From responses about social exclusion, the commonest form is to exclude any activity with a certain student. Thus, based on this, another story was designed in which no one wants to sit with a specific student.

3.3 Video Production

Story Board. Based on the responses from the interview and questionnaire result, a story board consisting of six short stories has been drawn for helping with shooting a video. The first story, as shown in Fig. 8, is about exclusion on campus. The inspiration is derived from a personal experience shared in the interview. The protagonist sits at the desk quietly reading a book, yet two girls passing by wears an expression that indicates strong aversion. They refuse to sit beside the protagonist. Though the whole process is silent, it causes damage to the protagonist's self-esteem. The second story, as shown in Fig. 9, is about rumor on relationship. The male protagonist walks out from the classroom with the female protagonist. This is noticed by their classmate, who then takes a photo of them walking together and upload it online, which lead their circle to believe that they are in a relationship. The third story, as shown in Fig. 10, is also about rumor. It is a rumor of one student's misbehavior. The inspiration is derived from a true incident in the high school. The secondary lead is memorizing English vocabulary near the bathroom. It is then rumored that he sneaked into the Ladies and take photos. The fourth story, as shown in Fig. 11, is a continuation of the second story. The female protagonist learns the rumor and gossip spreading online. This upsets her. The fifth story, as shown in Fig. 12, is the continuation of the second and third story. The male protagonist is dining at the cafeteria when he hears girls gossiping about his romance with the female protagonist and the secret shooting by the secondary lead. As the protagonist of the rumor, he is embarrassed but pretends that he has not heard about the rumor and goes on dining. The sixth story, as shown in Fig. 13, is about hurting someone with negative comments. Unlike other emotional bullying, this is committed by teachers instead of students. The teacher is scolding the protagonist with humiliating words because of his poor performance in exams and rumors about his romance with another students. This agonizes him.

Fig. 8. The 1st scene of story board when the protagonist is excluded.

Fig. 9. The 2nd scene of story board of being sneaked and taken a photo without permission.

Fig. 10. The 3rd scene of story board the secondary lead memorizing vocabulary.

Video Production. Based on above story board, video Scenes, as shown in Fig. 14, were shot and edited. The finished video is uploaded on YouTube (https://youtu.be/asWhra bLKsk.) The video with its slogan, as shown in Fig. 15, has been shown for the high school class where questionnaire and interviews have been conducted.

Fig. 11. The 4th scene of story board the female protagonist being upset.

Fig. 12. The 5th scene of story board male protagonist being gossiped about.

Fig. 13. The 6th scene of story board the male protagonist being humiliated by a teacher.

Fig. 14. Scenes from the video.

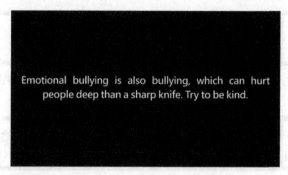

Emotional bullying is also bullying, which can hurt people deep than a sharp knife. Try to be kind.

Fig. 15. Slogan for this anti-emotional bullying video.

4   Discussion and Conclusion

This investigation concludes that emotional bullying is far more prevalent than participants assumed. It sheds light on its forms and characteristics, which may contribute to future preventive efforts. The statistics and conclusion based on the questionnaire will be important reference for future research. The questionnaire and anti-emotional bullying video have made positive influence, at least, on high school class, making students realize that emotional bullying exists. Predictably, they will pay more attention to such incidents in their life and avoid becoming the victimizer in the future. Though it is conducted within a class, it helps shed light on the essence of emotional bullying. The investigation serves as an exploration into the status of emotional bullying, so the relatively small sample size will not influence the production of the video. The video content is mostly based on the interview. This research into emotional bullying can be continued in a university campus in a foreign country in the future, and conduct comparison analysis across different races in order to obtain more generalized conclusion.

Acknowledgements. The authors wish to thank all the people who provided their time and efforts for the investigation. This research was funded by Guangzhou Philosophy and Social Science Planning 2020 Annual Project, Guangzhou, China, grant number 2020GZYB12.

References

1. Burger, C., Strohmeier, D., Spröber, N., Bauman, S., Rigby, K.: How teachers respond to school bullying: An examination of self-reported intervention strategy use, moderator effects, and concurrent use of multiple strategies. Teach. Teach. Educ. **51**, 191–202 (2015)
2. Notice of the General Office of the Ministry of Education on the Issuance of the Special Action Plan for Preventing Bullying Among Primary and Secondary School Students. http://wap.moe. gov.cn/srcsite/A06/s3325/202101/t20210126_511115.html. Accessed 21 Jan 2021
3. Nansel, T.R., Overpeck, M., Pilla, R.S., Ruan, W.J., Simons-Morton, B., Scheidt, P.: Bullying behaviors among U.S. youth: prevalence and association with psychosocial adjustment. J. Am. Med. Assoc. **285**, 2094–2100 (2001)
4. Nansel, T.R., Craig, W., Overpeck, M.D., Saluja, G., Ruan, W.J.: Cross-national consistency in the relationship between bullying behaviors and psychosocial adjustment. Arch. Pediatr. Adolesc. Med. **158**, 730–736 (2004)

5. Liu, T., Gong, L.: Characteristics, causes and countermeasures of current school bullying. J. Shandong Youth Manage. Cadre Inst. (2009)
6. So what is bullying? https://web.archive.org/web/20090220222902/http:/stopbullyingnow. hrsa.gov/index.asp?area=whatbullyingis. Accessed 21 Jan 2021
7. Bolton, J., Graeve, S.: No Room for Bullies: From the Classroom to Cyberspace. Boys Town Press, Nebraska (2005)
8. The Effects of Belittling. https://www.ccpa-accp.ca/blog/?p=3021. Accessed 21 Jan 2021
9. Bullying Statistics Anti-Bullying Help, Facts, and More. http://www.bullyingstatistics.org. Accessed 21 Jan 2021

Adapting Participatory Design Activities
for Autistic Adults: A Review

Rachael Maun⬤, Marc Fabri(⊠)⬤, and Pip Trevorrow⬤

Leeds Beckett University, Leeds LS6 3QS, UK
{r.maun,m.fabri,p.trevorrow}@leedsbeckett.ac.uk

Abstract. This paper presents a literature review investigating the suitability of participatory design when conducted with autistic adults. Six relevant papers were discovered, with key information extracted prior to analysis. A thematic analysis revealed six core themes of adaptations and considerations to be made when working with autistic adults: (1) appropriate approaches and methodology, (2) individual differences, (3) flexibility, (4) communication, (5) environment and sensory issues and (6) challenge assumptions. Overall, it was found that participatory design is a suitable method for use with autistic adults, providing careful adjustments are made to some or all of the design activities to ensure their accessibility and effectiveness. It is important that researchers and practitioners have sufficient autism understanding to make these adjustments, and that they invest time to get to know the autistic people involved in their study.

Keywords: Autism · Participatory design · Human-centered design · Co-design · User-centered design

1 Introduction

Participatory design (PD) has been a focal point of many scholarly articles on the effective conception or re-design of technology. This is partly attributed to the success of design firms such as IDEO and Continuum who specialize in the innovation of new products, services and experiences derived from user-centered design methods (Continuum 2019; IDEO 2019). UCD refers to design approaches which consider end users as sources of innovation, with their insights heard, behaviors observed, and needs met (Lowdermilk 2013). This then informs the iterative development of new products, services and experiences (Bordin and Angeli 2017; Dell'Era and Landoni 2014; Rogers et al. 2011).

In traditional UCD, users are not active participants in the research process, rather they are used as a testing and evaluation service for designers. Participatory design builds on the premise of UCD by involving users more actively in the design process, from conception of an idea through to prototype testing at the end of the design process (Roberston and Simonsen 2012a, b). Users are empowered to make decisions and contribute as partners throughout the design process, offering contributions and expert knowledge. (Anthony et al. 2012; Constantin et al. 2019; Roberston and Simonsen 2012a, b).

© Springer Nature Switzerland AG 2021
M. M. Soares et al. (Eds.): HCII 2021, LNCS 12780, pp. 300–314, 2021.
https://doi.org/10.1007/978-3-030-78224-5_21

In this paper, we investigate how autistic people can be involved in the participatory design of technology for this user group. This considers characteristics, preferences and strengths as well as the suitability of established PD methods and potentially the conception of new methods.

1.1 Terminology

For the purpose of this paper, the terms "autistic adult" and "adult on the autism spectrum" will be adopted. This is based on recent research by Kenny et al. (2016), showing that most autistic adults prefer 'identity first' language as opposed to 'person first' terminology i.e. 'adult with autism'. This has also been mirrored by autistic people who took part in the Autism&Uni project (Fabri et al. 2016).

2 Autistic Characteristics

Autism spectrum condition (ASC) is a lifelong pervasive neurodevelopmental condition, characterized by impairments in social communication. Other characteristics of autism include repetitive and restrictive behaviors, which can impact on both the individual and their family's lives (APA 2013). Autism is also considered a spectrum condition, with some individuals showing mild symptoms while others display more severe symptoms (Anderson et al. 2014; Dillenburger et al. 2015). It is estimated that around 1 in 100 people in the UK are autistic (Baird et al. 2006), and autism can occur with or without other intellectual disabilities with 69% of autistic people having no intellectual disabilities, and around 46% with average or advanced intellect (Anderson et al. 2018).

For this paper, we focus on autistic adults without intellectual difficulties as this is a group that has traditionally been under-researched, with participatory design research in autism often involving children with learning difficulties and/or communication impairments (Aresti-Bartolome and Garcia-Zapirain 2014). The work is done in the context of a research project that aims to create technology to support and inform autistic university students.

3 Participatory Design with Autistic People

The use of PD with autistic people has grown over recent years, with autistic children between the ages of 8 and 12 being the most often researched group (Börjesson et al. 2015). The use of PD with autistic children has spawned a variety of new technologies, with outputs ranging from learning aids (Guldberg et al. 2017), social communication tools (Abdullah and Brereton 2017; Harrold et al. 2014), mental health aids (McGowan et al. 2017; Simm et al. 2016), to language tools (Weisblatt et al. 2019).

Several researchers, including Benton et al. (2011) and Frauenberger et al. (2012), have acknowledged that standard PD methods may not be suitable for autistic children for a variety of reasons, and techniques may need to be modified to meet individual needs and abilities (Francis et al. 2009). The primary reason that traditional PD methods may not be suitable is due to the key need for collaboration between design team members, something which autistic children may struggle with due to a lack in communication and social skills (Benton et al. 2011). Generating ideas can also be challenging for autistic children (Benton et al. 2014).

Additionally, there is a heightened fear of failure in autistic children, which can serve as a barrier to creativity and participation (Francis et al. 2009). When comparing the use of PD with typically developing children, adults are involved in the process more intensively, with adults including; users, proxies, experts and facilitators (Börjesson et al. 2015).

3.1 PD Methods for Working with Children

Responding to the concern about involving autistic children, a series of new participatory design methods have been researched and developed. These include IDEAS (Benton et al. 2011), an Interface Design Experience for the Autistic Spectrum, which amends existing participatory design methodologies with a quiet environment to reduce distractions, an initial explanation of the proposed session, a visual timeline, demonstrations of existing software and the integration of hobbies and interests of the target group as identified in previous questionnaires (ibid).

Others identified a need to build a relationship with the children prior to embarking on the design process, with some researchers spending months building rapport with the students (Börjesson et al. 2015). The ECHOES project also used a specifically designed participatory design approach with both typically developing children and those with special needs. Their research concluded that the use of non-digital formats was found to be imperative to overcoming barriers to creativity, especially in autistic children (Frauenberger et al. 2011).

3.2 PD Methods for Working with Adults

In contrast, research into the use of participatory design with autistic adults is under-represented, with very few papers investigating its use. Examples of research include; the development of serious games for autistic teenagers (Bossavit and Parsons 2016a, b; Mohd et al. 2019), the development of self-tracking tools for tracking their everyday lives (Kim et al. 2019; Ryu et al. 2017), the development of an online peer support network (MacLeod 2010) and the development of an online toolkit to aid with the transition into higher education (Fabri et al. 2016).

Crucially, there is limited literature surrounding suitable preparations and adaptations when conducting participatory design with autistic adults. The assumption has been made that these will be similar to those adaptations applied when involving autistic children (Nicolaidis et al. 2019). However, this assumption needs to be challenged. Previous work has indicated that visual preferences and interaction preferences may well be different with this group (Fabri et al. 2016).

A gap in knowledge surrounding autistic adults has been uncovered in recent years. Large cohorts of children were diagnosed as autistic in the 1990's and early 2000s, with research and interventions for autistic children and adolescences forming the majority of research on autistic people (Piven et al. 2011; Warner et al. 2019). Those autistic children have now reached adulthood and would benefit from increased research on issues that affect them as autistic adults, yet this has not been a focal point of research thus far (ibid).

Research has also shown that autistic people, regardless of cognitive abilities, still benefit from support and accommodations to succeed in gaining independence or progress with their education (Glennon 2001), yet there is still limited information on how to meet the specific needs of this group (VanBergeijk et al. 2008).

This leads to the current paper, where the focus is on evaluating the suitability of participatory design with autistic adults with no intellectual disabilities, something that thus far appears to have been neglected.

4   Method

Literature was reviewed from a number of online scientific databases including; ACM, ERIC, MEDLINE, PsychINFO, Academic Search Complete, NAS and Scopus. The search strategy included terms (and synonyms) for; autism, participatory design, co-design, design thinking, co-creation, human-centered design, human-centered computing, computing and technology. Given the advent of Design Thinking as a generalizable approach to participatory design in the mid-2000s (Plattner et al. 2012), peer reviewed papers from the past 15 years were included. Upon completion of the literature search, 17 papers were identified as relevant.

Papers using PD with adolescents or teens were removed as research has shown that the preferences of children and young people differ from those of adults (Chevalier et al. 2017; Fabri and Andrews 2016), leaving a total of 7 papers focusing specifically on the use of PD with autistic adults. Upon reading the papers, a further paper was removed (Kim et al. 2020) as there was no reference to adaptations made to the PD approach to better meet the needs of autistic adults. Table 1 summarizes the papers included in this review.

From each of the remaining 6 papers, key information was extracted prior to analysis, following the approach by Börjesson et al. (2015):

- name and description of the developed technology,
- details about the autistic participants,
- details about any other participants, e.g. facilitators, designers, coders, mentors
- the phases of inclusion in the design process,
- the methods and techniques used with the target group in each phase,
- any autism-specific adaptations made to methods, techniques or phases
- any adaptations recommended on completion of the study

Table 1. Summary of papers included

Author	Summary of paper
Aslam et al. (2019)	PD was used to empower autistic adults to design their own social robot. The process incorporated building blocks to guide autistic participants through an iterative co-design process and incorporated scaffolding to bridge imaginative and communication-related gaps
Cascio et al. (2020)	PD was used to design a bio-music smartphone application with a wearable sensor for measuring physiological signals to translate to auditory output. Strategies developed from researchers and the autistic community were used to create a space which was more accessible for autistic participants
Fabri et al. (2016)	PD was used to develop an online toolkit to help with the transition into higher education. A 5-step design thinking approach was applied, with various stakeholders involved at various points. Participants in PD activities included; autistic students, parents and friends of autistic people
Fletcher-Watson et al. (2018)	UK based seminars were organized in collaboration with autistic and non-autistic people. These seminars focused on considerations to be made when conducting PD research with autistic adults. 5 core themes were identified; respect, authenticity, assumptions, infrastructure and empathy
MacLeod (2010)	PD was used to develop an online 'AS Portal' for peer-to-peer support for autistic higher education students. The project was student-led, with the design and development steered by the students involved
Nicolaidis et al. (2019)	PD guidelines were created, based on research using PD methods with autistic adults between 2006–2018. These guidelines were developed in collaboration with autistic adults and academics. 7 key themes were identified; transparency, clearly defined roles, clear processes for communication and power sharing, building and maintaining trust, collaboratively disseminate findings, actively encourage community capacitation and fairly compensate participants for their work

5   Results

Six core themes emerged from the extracted information, highlighting important considerations when planning and conducting PD with autistic adults. Table 2 highlights the themes and sub-themes that were extracted from the papers, following the approach by Börjesson et al. (2015). The themes will be described in more detail in the following sections.

Table 2. Themes and Subthemes Identified

Theme	Subthemes
Appropriate approaches and methodology	Methods Defining stakeholders involved PD stages Planning
Individual differences	Unique experiences Adjustments
Flexibility	Flexible contributions Accessibility Understand preferences Allow freedoms
Communication	Academic jargon Consideration amongst group members Discussions/Open dialogue Give all group members opportunity to contribute Listen Offer opportunities to ask questions Define group roles Build trust Respond to feedback
Environment and sensory issues	Autism-friendly spaces Accessibility Sensory concerns Stimming Physical space
Challenge assumptions	Challenge stereotypes Allow participants to flag assumptions

5.1 Appropriate Approaches and Methodology

Across the papers reviewed, a number of different PD approaches were identified including; a 'design after design approach' (Cascio et al. 2020), a five-step design thinking method (Fabri et al. 2016), a four-phase iterative design method (Kim et al. 2020), an entirely student-led approach (MacLeod 2010), a community-based participatory research method (Nicolaidis et al. 2019), and a bottom-up participatory approach (Aslam et al. 2019). Though these approaches all have different names and descriptions, they all follow traditional design thinking methodologies commonly used in PD. Below we will explore the adjustments made to these established methodologies.

Aslam et al. (2019) stated that successfully collaborating with autistic participants in PD is fundamentally about managing, facilitating and guiding interplay between freedom and structure. It was also highlighted that encouraging autistic participants to open up about their emotions, continuously co-constructing the groups understanding of the technology and its' functioning, embedding researchers into the research space a few weeks prior to commencement, choosing appropriate approaches to meet partnership goals, considering the abilities and preferences of the participants and considering who should be included on the team were all vital to the success of PD (Cascio et al. 2020; MacLeod 2010).

The inclusion of participants in all phases of the design was also considered important. Cascio et al. (2020) facilitated this by allowing autistic participants to organize the workshops themselves. Nicolaidis et al. (2019) involved participants in the dissemination of findings and MacLeod (2010) gave participants roles of responsibility within the group and offered participants a draft of the final report to make comments should they wish. This full involvement of participants throughout all stages of the PD process is not often seen in research and shows that fully involving autistic participants in the design process can be achieved. This was also noted in reflections from Fabri et al. (2016) who felt that users could have been involved in earlier stages of the design, creating an uninterrupted continuum of user involvement.

A number of reflections were also made on the PD approaches used. Aslam et al. (2019) realized that simply providing participants with the 'building blocks' was not sufficient in fostering creativity. Instead, a narrative had to be added to the design sessions to encourage technological familiarity, imaginative skills and collaborative and social skills. Participants needed further encouragement to make decisions, reconsider their ideas, mix ideas, reflect on their ideas and diverge and reframe iteratively. Fabri et al. (2016) found that combining the 'prototype' and 'test' stages worked well as it did not require careful structuring but still produced useful feedback. Other methods such as focus group interviews and 'day in the life of...' diaries and data collection needed further consideration, as some participants were able to verbally recount relevant experiences but were unable to type them into an online form, despite wishing to do so.

5.2 Individual Differences

Four of the papers highlight the need to address individual differences. Some autistic participants may need structure and guidance within a PD workshop as they may struggle with imaginative and abstract thinking. It can help to give these participants examples and explicit demonstrations. Other autistic participants may find it easier to be 'naturally' creative (Aslam et al. 2019).

Individual differences may also include adjustments to the materials for accessibility, for example Nicolaidis et al. (2019) had to adjust materials to be suitable for a blind participant in their workshops, they integrated braille materials and offered 3D raised graphs so that they could be included in the workshops. By acknowledging and understanding participants' individual differences, ideas of what adjustments may be needed can be highlighted and offering these adjustments can help them feel a part of the workshops, and in turn allow them to contribute effectively. There may also be individual differences that are considered positives, for example Fabri et al. (2016) found participants who appeared to cope better than others despite starting from the same situation. These were labelled as 'positive deviants' which can provide valuable insights into how these individuals managed to succeed, and positive strategies can be shared with the group.

5.3 Flexibility

While addressing individual differences, it is also important to be flexible in an approach to meet the needs of those with individual differences or preferences. Cascio et al. (2020), for example, highlights the importance of allowing participants to make contributions to the workshop in a way of their choosing. This may include stereotypical methods such as short videos, interviews, questionnaires, discussions, audio recordings, but may also include more abstract methods such as; poetry, art work, different types of recording and even abstract dance (in the case of their workshops focusing on bio-music).

This focus on flexibility was also highlighted as important by MacLeod (2010) who suggests that there should be options for participants to choose from when engaging in interviews, this may include; face-to-face interviews, telephone interviews, real-time email interviews and the use of instant messenger chat, this can maximize the inclusion of autistic participants with different strengths and needs. Maintaining flexibility at all times, paying close attention to individualized needs and making accommodations can help with participation. Aslam et al. (2019) mirrored the sentiment of having a flexible approach, by allowing participants the freedom to discover their own pathway, letting their creativity unfold with a balance between creative freedom and structure.

5.4 Communication

When considering good communication within a PD group, Cascio et al. (2020) and Nicolaidis et al. (2019) offer some initial recommendations:

- Being transparent
- Defining roles within the group from the outset
- Communicating and offering channels for communication (e.g. offering participants the opportunity to ask questions or share concerns, either via email, on the phone or face-to-face)
- Share power
- Build and maintaining trust
- Sharing findings and building a community
- Communicating how participants may be fairly compensated, should this be the case

Many of these are arguably general "good practice" and would be part of a research study's ethical considerations. This makes them particularly relevant to design practitioners conducting activities outside of an institutional ethics framework. Fletcher-Watson et al. (2018) mirrors these recommendations by highlighting the importance of openly communicating about the research focus and methods from the offset to help contextualize the work and educate participants about the research process, the dialogue should also be open, not constrained by specific research questions.

Creating a shared language has also been highlighted as important, this involves introducing academic jargon selectively, allowing a shared understanding of terminology to be built over the course of the workshops and allowing the participants to create their own shared language (Cascio et al. 2020; Nicolaidis et al. 2019).

It is also pertinent to highlight the importance of respectful communication between group members. This consists of asking for consideration from each of the members. An example of considerate communication between group members is to ask a team member to stop banging on the table as other members may find this distracting or overwhelming (Cascio et al. 2020; Fletcher-Watson et al. 2018). Respectful communication can also consist of giving all project members an opportunity to communicate, in a judgement free environment. Participants have commented on how it feels good to be listened to and been given the space and time to share experiences (Fabri et al. 2016). Differences should also be recognized, and an acceptance that there may not always be agreement should be established, this can generate a mutual respect between autistic and non-autistic members of the group (Fletcher-Watson et al. 2018).

Open discussion is also important, though this needs to be achieved by both the participants and the facilitators. This can allow for the development of a common shared experience facilitators (Cascio et al. 2020). Fletcher-Watson et al. (2018) builds on this by also stating that facilitators should also be prepared to learn from workshop participants and be prepared to make changes in response to feedback. Power imbalances should also be addressed although it is not always possible to avoid this.

It is also important to maintain communication channels throughout the entire project, this means allowing participants to ask questions even when the workshops are completed (Fletcher-Watson et al. 2018). MacLeod (2010) suggests offering participants a draft of the report upon completion of the research and asking for comments or feedback on the report, this ensures participants are involved until the end of the research project.

5.5 Environment and Sensory Issues

Considering the environment in which the workshops are being facilitated is another important aspect of designing with autistic participants. Cascio et al. (2020) highlights the importance of autism friendly spaces, a space in which autistic participants feel safe and can access, where autistic participants can be themselves, accomplish their goals and navigate more easily. It may also be worth considering meeting autistic participants in a place of their choosing (Fletcher-Watson et al. 2018).

Having used a number of different sites for their workshops, Cascio et al. (2020) were able to see the impact the environment can have on autistic participants. Most workshops took place within Spectrum Productions, a specifically co-designed space for autistic people. Aside from an initial complaint about the facilitator's cologne, not liking being touched, not liking loud noises and not liking a specific guitar riff within the researched bio-music, the use of Spectrum Productions proved to be a successful space to conduct PD. When the research was moved to a university classroom, problems arose, one participant left the room and was unable to return due to the strong perfumes worn by students, to crowdedness of the room and closed windows.

Aslam et al. (2019) highlighted an interesting use of the physical space within workshops. The left-hand side of the room was a 'problem space' where participants started blueprinting ideas. Once participants were happy with their blueprints, they moved to the right-hand side of the room to actively build their technology. These spaces were used iteratively, with continuous and rapid movement between the spaces, where the problems and solutions could co-evolve, allowing for the problem to be reframed and solutions to diverge into a variety of novel combinations.

Other aspects to consider include, allowing participants to stim during the workshops (Cascio et al. 2020) and the need for a quiet space where participants can retreat if they feel they need to (Fletcher-Watson et al. 2018).

5.6 Challenge Assumptions

Challenging assumptions was also considered an important aspect of PD, especially when working with autistic participants. Fabri et al. (2016) highlighted the importance of challenging stereotypes surrounding autism spectrum condition. For example, there is an assumption that autistic people think visually, which was not found to be true. Instead, autistic participants preferred well-structured text over infographics or videos and only preferred visual information when it depicted real people or places, or when it specifically added to the text information being presented.

Examples of what was considered an appropriate use of visual information included the use of photographs of landmarks for directions, photographs of people they would be meeting and photos of the buildings and rooms in which the workshops were being carried out. Another example of an assumption that was challenged was that autistic people lack creativity and imaginative thinking. Participants were able to contribute to the design process creatively and imaginatively providing the environment and situation was comfortable for them. Fletcher-Watson et al. (2018) mirrored the need to challenge assumptions, as there are diverse patterns of autism, and also highlighted the importance of allowing autistic participants to flag these assumptions should they arise within the workshops.

Nicolaidis et al. (2019) also highlighted that it cannot be assumed that survey instruments that have been validated with the general population will work with autistic participants. Surveys and interview guides may need to be adapted to be more accessible to autistic participants.

6 Conclusions

Based on this review, we argue that participatory design can be a suitable design methodology for autistic adults. Despite the challenges outlined, participatory design is considered vital when aiming to design tools that meets end-users' needs and are usable. Excluding members of society from the design process because current design practice is not a good fit for this group is clearly unethical. There is an obligation on the designer's part to adapt the methods employed, so that the desired outcome can be achieved. Or in other words, the obligation is to make design practice more inclusive. Any autism characteristics which may pose as a barrier to involvement in participatory design activities need to be fully understood and the activities adapted. Researchers and practitioners will have to ensure they have the time and are willing to put in the effort to make these adjustments.

Key issues of choosing appropriate methodologies and approaches can be easily overcome by considering the ability and preferences of participants. Varying degrees of participation can also be successful, providing the correct adjustments are made. Entering into PD with autistic adults blindly may result in some initial teething issues but providing workshop facilitators take the time to listen to the wants, needs and preferences of participants, and take the time to address any issues or feedback, any challenges should be easily rectified.

Challenges surrounding individual differences can also be easily overcome with a selection of adjustments, some encouragement to promote abstract thinking and acknowledgement of these individual differences rather than ignorance towards them.

Flexibility is key in PD, particularly when collaborating with autistic adults. An inclusive approach where participants are given options for how to contribute their experiences and preferences is needed. For example, data does not have to be collected in stereotypical ways, e.g. questionnaires and interviews, and participants should be encouraged to contribute in a way which they feel is appropriate and safe for them. It is important to consider the overall aims and objectives of any study. Some studies may benefit from online only questionnaires, where others may require methods such as interviews, focus groups etc. and these can be adapted to meet individual needs e.g. phone interviews, email interviews, large focus groups, smaller focus groups and one-to-one design sessions.

Another important aspect is communication: communicating effectively from the outset, with defined roles, rules and communication channels, can ground the design project effectively. Being clear with participants about what is expected of them, what can be expected of the facilitators and what is expected from the group can negate early disagreements. This includes giving participants the opportunity to communicate their preferences and strengths prior to any activities. Allowing participants to develop their own language can generate a feeling of belonging, and all communication within the group should be respectful and open.

Considering the environment is something that must not be overlooked when working with autistic individuals. Sensory issues are prevalent in autistic individuals (Kojovic et al. 2019) and ensuring there are no strong smells, loud noises or overcrowded areas can help autistic people feel safe in an environment. As highlighted by Cascio et al. (2020), autism-friendly spaces should be considered as the chosen environment for PD workshops with autistic adults, but if this is not possible, selecting a quiet area, away from crowds, is recommended.

Finally, researchers should challenge assumptions of autism when working with autistic adults. Despite previous literature stating that autistic people prefer visual information, Fabri et al. (2016) found this was not the case when working with a group of autistic university students. With autism being such a diverse condition, with each case being unique (Chapman 2020), it could create a barrier to participation if making assumptions on the autistic population as a whole. By the same token, however, assumptions should not be made that the use of standard measures used with neurotypical groups will also apply to groups of autistic adults.

It is important that anyone wanting to conduct participatory design activities with autistic adults requires an understanding of autism that goes beyond a general level of awareness. This includes the understanding that each autistic person must be considered individually when planning design activities, so that adjustments can be made on an individual basis.

References

Abdullah, M.H.L., Brereton, M.: MyCalendar: supporting children on the autism spectrum to learn language and appropriate behaviour. In: Proceedings of the 29th Australian Conference on Computer-Human Interaction, pp. 201–209 (2017). https://doi.org/10.1145/3152771.315 2793

Anderson, A., Carter, M., Stephenson, J.: Perspectives of university students with autism spectrum disorder. J. Autism Dev. Disord. **48**(3), 651–665 (2018). https://doi.org/10.1007/s10803-017-3257-3

Anderson, K.A., Shattuck, P.T., Cooper, B.P., Roux, A.M., Wagner, M.: Prevalence and correlates of postsecondary residential status among young adults with an autism spectrum disorder. Autism **18**(5), 562 (2014)

Anthony, L., Prasad, S., Hurst, A., Kuber, R.: A participatory design workshop on accessible apps and games with students with learning differences. In: Proceedings of the 14th International ACM SIGACCESS Conference on Computers and Accessibility, pp. 253–254 (2012). https://doi.org/10.1145/2384916.2384979

APA: Diagnostic and Statistical Manual of Mental Disorders: DSM-IV-TR, 5th edn. American Psychaitric Association (2013)

Aresti-Bartolome, N., Garcia-Zapirain, B.: Technologies as support tools for persons with autistic spectrum disorder: a systematic review. Int. J. Environ. Res. Public Health **11**(8), 7767–7802 (2014)

Aslam, S., van Dijk, J., Dertien, E.: CoCoCo: co-designing a co-design toolkit for co-bots to empower autistic adults. In: 4th RTD Conference: Design United, Issue 4, pp. 1–16 (2019). https://doi.org/10.6084/m9.figshare.7855904.v2

Baird, G., et al.: Prevalence of disorders of the autism spectrum in a population cohort of children in South Thames: the Special Needs and Autism Project (SNAP). Lancet **368**(9531), 210–215 (2006)

Benton, L., Johnson, H., Brosnan, M., Ashwin, E., Grawemeyer, B.: IDEAS: an interface design experience for the autistic spectrum. In: CHI 2011 Extended Abstracts on Human Factors in Computing Systems, pp. 1759–1764 (2011). https://doi.org/10.1145/1979742.1979841

Benton, L., Vasalou, A., Khaled, R., Johnson, H., Gooch, D.: Diversity for design: a framework for involving neurodiverse children in the technology design process. In: Proceedings of the SIGCHI Conference on Human Factors in Computing Systems, pp. 3747–3756 (2014). https://doi.org/10.1145/2556288.2557244

Bordin, S., De Angeli, A.: Inoculating an agile company with user-centred design: an empirical study. In: Baumeister, H., Lichter, H., Riebisch, M. (eds.) XP 2017. LNBIP, vol. 283, pp. 235–242. Springer, Cham (2017). https://doi.org/10.1007/978-3-319-57633-6_15

Börjesson, P., Barendregt, W., Eriksson, E., Torgersson, O.: Designing technology for and with developmentally diverse children: a systematic literature review. In: Proceedings of the 14th International Conference on Interaction Design and Children, pp. 79–88 (2015). https://doi.org/10.1145/2771839.2771848

Bossavit, B., Parsons, S.: Designing an educational game for and with teenagers with high functioning autism. In: Proceedings of the 14th Participatory Design Conference: Full Papers, vol. 1, pp. 11–20 (2016a). https://doi.org/10.1145/2940299.2940313

Bossavit, B., Parsons, S.: "This is how i want to learn": high functioning autistic teens co-designing a serious game. In: Proceedings of the 2016 CHI Conference on Human Factors in Computing Systems, pp. 1294–1299 (2016b). https://doi.org/10.1145/2858036.2858322

Cascio, M., Grond, F., Motta Ochoa, R., Tembeck, T., Veen, D., Blain-Moraes, S.: Working together: ethnographic observations on participatory design involving adults with autism. Hum. Organ. **79**, 1–12 (2020). https://doi.org/10.17730/0018-7259.79.1.1

Chapman, R.: The reality of autism: on the metaphysics of disorder and diversity. Philos. Psychol. **33**(6), 799–819 (2020). https://doi.org/10.1080/09515089.2020.1751103

Chevalier, P., Martin, J.-C., Isableu, B., Bazile, C., Tapus, A.: Impact of sensory preferences of individuals with autism on the recognition of emotions expressed by two robots, an avatar, and a human. Auton. Robots **41**(3), 613–635 (2017)

Constantin, A., et al.: Expecting the Unexpected in Participatory Design. Extended Abstracts of the 2019 CHI Conference on Human Factors in Computing Systems, (2019). https://doi.org/10.1145/3290607.3311758

Continuum: The Future. Made Real.™ (2019). https://www.continuuminnovation.com/en/

Dell'Era, C., Landoni, P.: Living lab: a methodology between user-centred design and participatory design. Creat. Innov. Manage. **23**(2), 137–154 (2014). http://10.0.4.87/caim.12061

Dillenburger, K., Jordan, J.-A., McKerr, L., Keenan, M.: The Millennium child with autism: Early childhood trajectories for health, education and economic wellbeing. Dev. Neurorehabil. **18**(1), 37–46 (2015). https://doi.org/10.3109/17518423.2014.964378

Fabri, M., Andrews, P.C.S.: Human-centered design with autistic university students: interface, interaction and information preferences. In: Marcus, A. (ed.) DUXU 2016. LNCS, vol. 9747, pp. 157–166. Springer, Cham (2016). https://doi.org/10.1007/978-3-319-40355-7_15

Fabri, M., Andrews, P.C.S.S., Pukki, H.K.: Using design thinking to engage autistic students in participatory design of an online toolkit to help with transition into higher education. J. Assistive Technol. **10**(2), 102–114 (2016)

Fletcher-Watson, S., et al.: Making the future together: shaping autism research through meaningful participation. Autism **23**(4), 943–953 (2018). https://doi.org/10.1177/1362361318786721

Francis, P., Balbo, S., Firth, L.: Towards co-design with users who have autism spectrum disorders. Univ. Access Inf. Soc. **8**(3), 123–135 (2009). https://doi.org/10.1007/s10209-008-0143-y

Francis, P., Mellor, D., Firth, L.: Techniques and recommendations for the inclusion of users with autism in the design of assistive technologies. Assistive Technol. **21**(2), 57–68 (2009)

Frauenberger, C., Good, J., Alcorn, A., Pain, H.: Supporting the design contributions of children with autism spectrum conditions. In: Proceedings of the 11th International Conference on Interaction Design and Children, pp. 134–143 (2012). https://doi.org/10.1145/2307096.2307112

Frauenberger, C., Good, J., Keay-Bright, W.: Designing technology for children with special needs: bridging perspectives through participatory design. CoDesign **7**(1), 1–28 (2011). https://doi.org/10.1080/15710882.2011.587013

Glennon, T.J.: The stress of the university experience for students with Asperger syndrome. Work **17**(3), 183–190 (2001)

Guldberg, K., Parsons, S., Porayska-Pomsta, K., Keay-Bright, W.: Challenging the knowledge-transfer orthodoxy: knowledge co-construction in technology-enhanced learning for children with autism. Br. Educ. Res. J. **43**(2), 394–413 (2017). https://doi.org/10.1002/berj.3275

Harrold, N., Tan, C.T., Rosser, D., Leong, T.W.: CopyMe: an emotional development game for children. In: CHI 2014 Extended Abstracts on Human Factors in Computing Systems, pp. 503–506 (2014). https://doi.org/10.1145/2559206.2574785

IDEO: IDEO | ideo.com (2019). https://www.ideo.com/eu

Kenny, L., Hattersley, C., Molins, B., Buckley, C., Povey, C., Pellicano, E.: Which terms should be used to describe autism? Perspectives from the UK autism community. Autism **20**(4), 442–462 (2016)

Kim, B., et al.: PuzzleWalk: a theory-driven iterative design inquiry of a mobile game for promoting physical activity in adults with autism spectrum disorder. PLoS ONE **15**(9), e0237966 (2020). https://doi.org/10.1371/journal.pone.0237966

Kim, S.-I.I., et al.: Toward becoming a better self: understanding self-tracking experiences of adolescents with autism spectrum disorder using custom trackers. In: Proceedings of the 13th EAI International Conference on Pervasive Computing Technologies for Healthcare, pp. 169–178 (2019). https://doi.org/10.1145/3329189.3329209

Kojovic, N., Ben Hadid, L., Franchini, M., Schaer, M.: Sensory processing issues and their association with social difficulties in children with autism spectrum disorders. J. Clin. Med. **8**(10), 1508 (2019)

Lowdermilk, T.: User-centered design: a developer's guide to building user-friendly applications. " O'Reilly Media, Inc." (2013)

MacLeod, A.: 'Welcome to my first rant!' Report on a participatory pilot project to develop the 'AS portal', an online peer support network for higher education students on the autism spectrum. J. Assistive Technol. **4**(1), 14–24 (2010). https://doi.org/10.5042/jat.2010.0041

McGowan, J., Leplâtre, G., McGregor, I.: CymaSense: a novel audio-visual therapeutic tool for people on the autism spectrum. In: Proceedings of the 19th International ACM SIGACCESS Conference on Computers and Accessibility, pp. 62–71 (2017). https://doi.org/10.1145/313 2525.3132539

Mohd, C.K.N.C.K., Shahbodin, F., Jano, Z., Azni, A.H.: Visual perception games for autistic learners: design & development. In: Proceedings of the 2019 Asia Pacific Information Technology Conference, pp. 5–11 (2019). https://doi.org/10.1145/3314527.3314533

Nicolaidis, C., et al.: The AASPIRE practice-based guidelines for the inclusion of autistic adults in research as co-researchers and study participants. Autism **23**(8), 2007–2019 (2019). https://doi.org/10.1177/1362361319830523

Piven, J., Rabins, P., Group, A. A. W: Autism spectrum disorders in older adults: Toward defining a research agenda. J. Am. Geriatr. Soc. **59**(11), 2151–2155 (2011)

Plattner, H., Meinel, C., Leifer, L. (eds.): Design thinking research. Springer, Berlin, Germany (2012)

Roberston, T., Simonsen, J.: Participatory design: an introduction. In: Routledge International Handbook of Participatory Design, pp. 21–38. Routledge (2012a)

Robertson, T., Simonsen, J.: Challenges and opportunities in contemporary participatory design. Des. Issues **28**(3), 3–9 (2012b)

Rogers, Y., Sharp, H., Preece, J.: Interaction design: beyond human-computer interaction. John Wiley & Sons (2011).

Ryu, M., Jo, E., Kim, S.-I.: COSMA: cooperative self-management tool for adolescents with autism. In: Proceedings of the 19th International ACM SIGACCESS Conference on Computers and Accessibility, pp. 409–410 (2017). https://doi.org/10.1145/3132525.3134825

Simm, W., Ferrario, et al.: Anxiety and autism: towards personalized digital health. In: Proceedings of the 2016 CHI Conference on Human Factors in Computing Systems, pp. 1270–1281 (2016). https://doi.org/10.1145/2858036.2858259

VanBergeijk, E., Kiln, A., Volkmar, F.: Supporting more able students on the autism spectrum: college and beyond. J. Autism Dev. Disord. **38**(7), 1359–1370 (2008). https://doi.org/10.1007/s10803-007-0524-8

Warner, G., Parr, J.R., Cusack, J.: Workshop report: establishing priority research areas to improve the physical health and well-being of autistic adults and older people. Autism in Adulthood **1**(1), 20–26 (2019)

Weisblatt, E.J., et al.: A tablet computer-assisted motor and language skills training program to promote communication development in children with autism: development and pilot study. International J. Hum. Comput. Interact. **35**(8), 643–665 (2019). https://doi.org/10.1080/10447318.2018.1550176

A Case Study of Augmented Physical Interface by Foot Access with 3D Printed Attachment

Tatsuya Minagawa[✉] and Yoichi Ochiai

University of Tsukuba, Tsukuba, Japan
mina.tatsu@digitalnature.slis.tsukuba.ac.jp, wizard@slis.tsukuba.ac.jp

Abstract. We propose an attachment creation framework that allows foot access to existing physical interfaces designed to use hands such as doorknobs. The levers, knobs, and switches of furniture and electronic devices are designed for the human hand. These interfaces may not be accessible for hygienic and physical reasons. Due to the high cost of parts and initial installation, sensing or automation is not preferable. Therefore, there is a need for a low-cost way to access physical interfaces without hands. We have enabled foot access by extending the hand-accessible interface with 3D-printed attachments. Finally, we proposed a mechanism (component set) that transmits movement from a foot-accessed pedal to an interface with attachments. And we attached it to the doorknob, water faucet, and lighting switch interface. A case study was conducted to verify the system's effectiveness, which consisted of 3D-printed attachments and pedals.

Keywords: Health · Covid-19 · DUXU · Fabrication · 3D printer

1 Introduction

There are many physical interfaces in our lives. A physical interface is a contact point between a user and a system that can be physically contacted to control a system, change the state of the system, and notify the system of information. For example, a doorknob controls the opening and closing of a door, a switch that controls the on/off state of lighting, and a button that notifies a microwave oven of a warming command. The human hand is a sophisticated effector that can handle, make, and manipulate many things and the most complex movements of any living thing on earth. Therefore, these physical interfaces are designed to be operated by human hands. We can usually access these interfaces by hand without barriers. However, the physical interface is not accessible by hand for two main reasons. 1) Physical reasons: Physical reasons are the inability to use one's hands. For example, it is difficult to turn the doorknob or turn on the light switch with luggage in both hands. The hand interface relies on the freedom of movement of at least one hand or one finger. Therefore, access to the interface is difficult if both hands are not free for any reason. 2) Hygienic reasons: Although

© Springer Nature Switzerland AG 2021
M. M. Soares et al. (Eds.): HCII 2021, LNCS 12780, pp. 315–332, 2021.
https://doi.org/10.1007/978-3-030-78224-5_22

not conscious in a personal environment, hygienic issues are a concern in a public environment. When an unspecified number of people are in contact with the physical interface, or when it is in an unsanitary condition, access to the interface must be avoided from infection prevention. Also, when one's hands are dirty and do not want to touch the interface and get it dirty, we have to refrain from accessing the interface. Because if you open the faucet with your hands dirty, you have to clean the faucet.

In general, the method has been established by using a non-contact sensor or using an automation trigger. One example is an automatic door triggered by a motion sensor that uses infrared rays. If it is an automatic door, the door can be opened without using a hand. However, sensing and automation are expensive for development into components, and they may rely on continuous electrical energy. Therefore, there is a need for a low-cost and feasible method of accessing the physical interface without the use of hands.

We have created an attachment with a 3D printer that allows foot access to a physical interface intended to be used by hand. 3D printers have been used to solve various real-world problems [8,9]. A 3D printer is suitable for making physical enhancements to existing objects. Therefore, we made foot access capable on a hand-accessed interface by extending the interface with 3D printed attachments. The group of attachments we created is divided into components with different functions. This allows us to create the most suitable components for each function. By using industrial components for some of the components, we were able to reduce the printing time of 3D printed attachments and made the attachments more robust. For the hand-accessed interfaces, the interfaces are usually installed away from the ground since the interface is devised to be accessible by hands. Therefore, we devised a mechanism with our implemented component set that is capable of transmitting the motion from the foot through the devised pedal, which is attached to the interface.

2   Related Work

This research extends the accessibility of existing physical interfaces by utilizing digital fabrication technology. This section will show the usefulness of 3D printers based on examples of efforts for interfaces using fabrication technology, and we will describe the relationship with them.

2.1   Digital Fabrication Technology

Digital fabrication centered on 3D printers is becoming familiar to us. This is due to computer 3D graphics development over the last 60 years and the expiration of Stratasys' patents for 3D printers. Digital fabrication technology aims to create designable and reproducible objects. Research is being conducted to create a physical interface using that technology. There are two approaches to creating a physical interface. One of the approaches is the definition and creation of shapes. Ion et al. created an interface for switches and doorknobs with a dynamic structure created from a combination of cells with deformation rules defined [5]. They also created a key-lock interface that could be created with an only 3D printer by adding a spring shape that could record the binary state in a cell or transmit the state to other cells [7]. It suggests that electronic devices can be replaced with designed structures. It is possible to create an interface as a single object as well as a combination of cell shapes. Schmitz *et al.* have realized a flexible 3D-printed interface that operates on a capacitive touch screen with a single-pass printable structure [20]. Ion *et al.* also proposed a texture-variable surface geometry created with origami-inspired structures [6]. The structure has made it possible to create interfaces with properties not found in the original material. Methods have also been developed to extend the interface possibilities depending on the properties of the material. Wessely *et al.* proposed an inexpensive manufacturing method, a highly elastic user interface that combines sensing and visual output using polydimethylsiloxane (PDMS) [23]. It made it possible to attach the interface to objects and hands with complex surfaces. This research does not create attachments for interfaces using special shapes or materials. Considering the low manufacturing cost, the attachment can be made with a general Fused Deposition Modeling (FDM) printer.

Digital fabrication technology provides a way to bring designable structures to the real world. The shapes of many products in circulation are optimized for mass production and the average human being. Therefore, it is difficult for each individual to be delighted with the shape. Fabrication technology has the potential to optimize the product for individual needs. For example, physiotherapists have modified or created standardized assistive technologies to suit the needs of their patients. Introducing a 3D printer into this process became more comfortable to adapt the grips and tips of crutches to individual needs, demonstrating the apparent potential of fabrication technology in assistive technology [13]. Many 3D printable shapes that match the actual product are shared on the website[1]. However, Kim *et al.* focused on the lack of customizability for personal needs. So they proposed a way to insert the buffer, which is adjustable after printing the shape of the model, into an existing 3D model [8]. Savage *et al.* have devised a system that combines existing mechanical hinges and electronic components with custom-designed shapes [19]. In this way, how to optimize the shape for the actual product is one of the topics of fabrication technology. Koyama *et al.* create an automated method to create customized 3D printable connectors that hold and secure free-geometry objects such as smartphones and mugs to structured objects such as desk and chair boards and pipes [9]. This research creates attachments to physical interfaces but does not propose an automatic attachment generation scheme.

Researchers are also working to improve interface performance and accessibility by using fabrication technology to overlap existing interfaces. For example, Guo *et al.* created tactile buttons by 3D printing to give visually impaired people access to physical interfaces [4]. In contrast, Chen *et al.* worked on extending the physical interface involved in mechanical operation rather than the

---

[1] https://www.thingiverse.com/.

physical interface in which information is digitized. It is possible to increase the tightness of the grip, increase the torque of rotation, and increase the base for stability for existing objects according to the needs of the user [2]. Ramakers *et al.* have devised an end-to-end design and manufacturing environment that allows non-experts to modify the physical interface [18]. It allows access from external software by extending the physical interface with electronic devices. In response, Li *et al.* proposed expanding physical mechanisms (slider, link), not limited to physical interfaces such as switches [11]. That made it possible to control the mechanism by software using an actuator. Fabrication technology using 3D printers is shown to be useful in extending these interfaces. In this research, we will generate attachments using a 3D printer because of its flexible design and low manufacturing cost. The work is an extension of the hand interface and has been expanded by an electric actuator. This research is an extension of the hand interface with a non-electronic mechanism, and it is a new proposal for the concept of a 3D printable module capable of transmitting motion from foot motion to the interface.

2.2   Mechanical Mechanism with Digital Fabrication Technology

Fabrication technology makes it possible to realize not only housings and interfaces but also mechanical gears and link structures. Many researchers are interested in semi-automatic or automatic mechanism generation and placement from data such as motion paths or selected movements for animatronic use in entertainment or personal creation of toys [3,24]. The problem with mechanical mechanics can be the complexity of the parts produced. Research is also being conducted on the mechanism based on the link mechanism of the components [1,22]. Megaro *et al.* also proposed a method that can design arbitrary movements using compliant mechanisms that can be integrally modeled by a 3D printer while being a link mechanism [15]. The ideal fabrication has few components and does not require the user to assemble after processing by the fabrication device. However, this isn't easy with a general 3D printer. Creating a mechanical mechanism is not limited to using a 3D printer. Research is also conducted to realize two-dimensional or three-dimensional functional mechanical objects using a laser cutter [10,14]. When using a laser cutter, the processing time is shorter than that of a 3D printer. However, compared to desktop-sized 3D printers, laser cutters have a larger installation area, so installation costs are higher. Creating a mechanism with a 3D printer is more useful as the modeling volume is smaller. Song *et al.* create Wind-up toys using a 3D printer [21]. Interest in mechanical mechanisms in the field of fabrication is not limited to entertainment. Li *et al.* Created a framework to create a movement based on a real task using a cable-driven mechanism [12]. The mechanism generated by the framework cannot be dealt with any task when the task's physical size becomes more extensive than the build size of the 3D printer. To transmit the physical interface's motion, it is desirable that parts that can be printed by an appropriate 3D printer and components that are industrially standardized coexist. The problem to be solved in this research is to transmit the movement required for the physical interface for the hand from the foot. Therefore, a complicated link mechanism is not assumed.

2.3 Componentization and Digital Fabrication Technology

Before the advent of 3D printers, basic manufacturing combines standardized industrial products to realize the desired structure and mechanism. Focusing on fabrication technology using 3D printers, an integrated shape that does not require assembly is ideal. However, creating the shape mainly requires a Stereolithography (SLA) or Selective Laser Sintering (SLS) 3D printer, which is difficult to realize at low cost and requires high-precision output and much time. Also, the integrated mechanism must be completely rebuilt due to damage to the parts. Even in fabrication technology, parts and modularization for each function and shape are practical in rapid prototypes. Peek *et al.* conducted a workshop using modules using cardboard frames, stepper motors, and electronic parts programmable by Python. They demonstrated the modular approach's effectiveness [17]. There is also a proposal to use standardized Brick to reduce the time it takes to complete the structure [16]. Modularization or componentization has many benefits for us. It is possible to correct or improve each part and replace it if it is damaged. Therefore, the modeling time and the manufacturing cost is reduced, and the productivity is improved. In this study, the interface's attachment does not integrate the physical interface for the foot. That is, the design is done for each module. Also, by using already standardized industrial parts, the connection of parts is strengthened, and motion transmission is facilitated.

3   Implementation

This section details the configuration of 3D-printed attachments for foot access to the physical interface. The expansion attachment designed in this research has three points to pay attention to reduce production costs.
1) The attachment can be 3D printed: The attachment can be printed with a standard FDM 3D printer. SLA/SLS/Inkjet 3D printers, which are expensive to install, are not a requirement. All models are printable with a stacking pitch of 0.2 mm. **2)** The attachment is power independent: Electronic parts are not included in the attachment configuration. We do not need to prepare a power supply or battery for the attachment. Therefore, the installation cost is low. **3)** The attachments do not consist of particular parts: It does not require specialized knowledge because it does not depend on particular electronic parts. Therefore, the assembly cost is low.

3.1 Physical Interface

A physical interface is defined as a contact point between a user and a system that can be physically contacted to control a system, change the system's state, and notify the information to the system. The contacts are attached to functional objects such as furniture, appliances, machines, and electronic devices. Many physical interfaces are designed to be operated by human hands.

3.2 Pedal

The pedal is known as a representative interface among the physical interfaces using the foot. This is an essential interface if a user needs to enter while using him/her hands to operate the system or if a user wants to access three or more physical interfaces at the same time. For example, the accelerator pedal of a car adjusts the speed while holding the handle with both hands. The kick pedal allows a user to hit the bass drum while hitting the hi-hat and snare with both hands. The sustain pedal allows a user to control the sound while hitting the keyboard with both hands. There are many examples of use. The pedal is an interface prepared in case a user cannot use both hands. However, it is also for when he/she does not want to use both hands. Before COVID-19, there is a pedal to open a trash can with a lid, addressing hygiene concerns. The foot interface effectively prevents infections from a public health perspective, as the foot is in constant contact with the ground and is farthest from the pathogen entry route of the eye/nose/mouth. In fact, in Japan, a pedal interface[2] has been developed for spraying disinfectant alcohol from a bottle without using hands.

We chose the pedal as the physical interface for inputting motion into the attachment. With the pedal, a high torque can be obtained using the human foot, and a sufficient length for linear motion can be obtained. There is a footswitch as an interface that uses the foot. However, the footswitch is not suitable for this study because it has a short distance for linear motion and is often an electrical part. The foot pedal transmits the movement to the components explained in the next section as a vertical linear motion by stepping on the foot without electricity.

We have developed a pedal capable of sufficient linear motion to transmit motion to attachments to doorknobs, toggle switches, and levers. The pedal is consists of a wall-mountable rail for sliders (Fig. 1(1)), a slider that connects with wires or rigid linkages to transmit movement from the foot (Fig. 1(2)),a pedal with a rotating shaft that comes into direct contact with the foot (Fig. 1(3)), and a cap for attaching the rotating shaft of the pedal to the rail (Fig. 1(4)). The slider moves linearly by receiving force from the pedal. Since the foot's stepping force vector is not parallel to the rail, the design is such that the parts that connect to other components and the features that come into contact with the foot are separated. The sliders and pedals can be improved in various ways depending on the attachment. For example, an attachment pedal for a toggle switch is a flat pedal because it does not require a hook to apply force in front. In addition, the cap is fixed with screws, so the slider and pedal can be easily replaced.

---

[2] https://www.monotaro.com/p/5530/4288/.

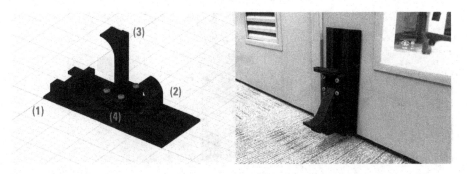

Fig. 1. Pedal designed for attachments: Pedal developed in Autodesk Fusion 360 (left), 3D printed and assembled pedal (right); **(1)** Rail, **(2)** Slider, **(3)** Pedal, **(4)** Cap

3.3 Component

In this study, the existing interface is overlapped by a mechanism divided into components with high flexibility about installation and improvement. This subsection adds a description of components other than pedals.

Attachment. The attachment overlaps the physical interface and transmits the motion transmitted through the link or motion conversion component to the interface. In this study, the same automatic generation as the AutoConnect system [9] is not performed. Therefore, designs are required for various interfaces such as doorknobs (Fig. 2), switches, levers, handles, sliders, and valves. The attachment is secured to the interface by tightening screws for greater replaceability.

Link. Links are the parts that transmit motion between each component. This component is preferably off-the-shelf to reduce strength and production costs. The user chooses rigid linkages, wires, and belts according to the movement. The wire can transmit motion in any path with a silicone tube inspired by the release cable for the camera shutter and the brakes on the bicycle.

Motion Conversion Component. Knobs, levers, handles, and valves have axes of rotation. Therefore, it is necessary to convert between rotational motion and linear motion. This component transforms rotational and linear motions into each other. In this case, a slider-crank mechanism is used to convert motion (Fig. 3).

Fig. 2. 3D printed attachments designed for each doorknob.

Fig. 3. Motion conversion component combined with doorknob attachment and rigid linkage

4   Case Study

The effectiveness of the proposed attachment was investigated from tasks performed on the actual physical interface. This section details the interface with the proposed attachments and the tasks performed.

4.1   Doorknob

Doorknobs are held firmly in the hand when used, so there are concerns about public health. It is also difficult to access the doorknob when the user has to carry the user's luggage with both hands. For private homes, hygiene concerns are less than for public doors. We also thought that the situation where both hands could not be used due to luggage would not occur at home. Therefore, we designed a task that assumes the door inside a public building used by an unspecified number of people.

System Setup. The door used for the task is Panasonic's SMJE1[3]. It is a right-handed in-swing/left-handed out-swing door. The height of the door is 1995 mm, and the width is 780 mm. Both sides of the door frame are fixed with scaffolding pipes. The physical attachment is attached to the end of a lever-type knob. The pedals are fixed at the bottom of the door using a 3M Scotch KPS-12[4]. A stainless wire with a load capacity of 70 kg and a diameter of 1.5 mm connected the attachment and pedal.

Fig. 4. System setup for case studies; **(A)** Overall view, **(B)** Room and doors used in the experiment and lines for tasks.

Participants. This study involved 7 participants (2 females, 5 males) aged between 20 and 23 years (M = 21.3, SD = 1.25). Two of the seven participants own a 3D printer. We recruited general participants from the members of our laboratory for COVID-19. They have not been injured in their hands or feet since a week ago and can fully use both hands.

Study Process. We have prepared two types of tasks to evaluate the doorknobs system that uses the foot to access the interface. Each participant was free to pass through the door for about 5 min using our attachment so that participants could get used to the attachment. The tasks were then assigned to each participant in a random order, and the participants performed the tasks. In Task 1, participants moved through the door from line to line drawn 1 m from the door (Fig. 4(B)), with no restrictions on both hands. In Task 2, participants carried the load through the door from area to area 1.2 m from the door (Fig. 4(B)), with a container (530 × 366 × 283 [mm]) that limits both hands. We have prepared tasks with different attachments and movement direction conditions.

---

[3] https://www.monotaro.com/g/01344534/#op_1=SMJE1&op_2=PA&op_3=D&op_4=N&op_6=01&op_7=B&op_10=A2&op_14=R&op_16=7&op_17=4&op_20=CY (last accessed : February, 12th, 2021).

[4] https://www.monotaro.com/p/3953/9053/ (last accessed : February, 12th, 2021).

Subjects passed through the door three times for each task, for a total of 24 times. To evaluate our developed attachment with understanding how satisfying, easy, or comfortable participants felt when they run a task, we asked them to rate each question. These questions were created by reference to NASA-TLX. In addition, we asked for details with free-description questions. We analyzed the scores of each question on a 7-point Likert scale, which was analyzed using one-tailed paired T-tests evaluated at an alpha level of 0.05.

Results. To understand the usefulness of our attachment for the door knob, we asked participants four questions in each task. Satisfaction: "Did you complete the specified task smoothly or smartly, or to your satisfaction?", Easiness: "Did you get the task done without the difficulty of thinking and remembering?", Comfortable (Physical) "Did you get the task done without frustration?", Comfortable (Psychological) "Did you get the task done without feeling tired?".

Figure 5(A) showed results of four questions when participants used the left-handed out-swing door with and without our attachment in task1. The T test for each question showed that no significant difference between "without" and "with" attachment was observed. Satisfaction: $p = 0.26 > 0.05$, Easiness: $p = 0.37 > 0.05$, Comfortable (Physical): $p = 0.26 > 0.05$, Comfortable (Psychological): $p = 0.22 > 0.05$.

Some participants gave some opinions about the durability of the attachment pedals.

P2 *"I heard a creaking noise when I stepped on the pedal with my foot, and I was a little worried that it wouldn't break. I felt like I wanted to step on the pedal smoothly with a smooth feeling."*
P7 *"It is more difficult to adjust the force to open the door with the feet than with the hands, but I thought that I could exert a large force (even a heavy door can be opened)"*
P3 *"The moment the bar goes down, the resistance becomes stronger, so I hesitated for a moment thinking that I had broken it."*

Figure 5(B) showed results of four questions when participants used the right-handed in-swing door with and without our attachment in task1. No significant difference between "without" and "with" attachment was observed at using the right-handed in-swing door either. Satisfaction: $p = 0.13 > 0.05$, Easiness: $p = 0.26 > 0.05$, Comfortable (Physical): $p = 0.22 > 0.05$, Comfortable (Psychological): $p = 0.39 > 0.05$. Some participants noted that there are some caveats regarding the use of attachment pedals.

P2 *"I found it a little more difficult to balance myself when pulling the door than when pushing the door with my foot."*
P1 *"I had to consciously look down (to pedals) to accomplish the task."*
P7 *"Compared to opening and closing by hand, I had to put the pivot foot on the outside of the door frame, and I felt that it was a hassle (to use the attachment)."*

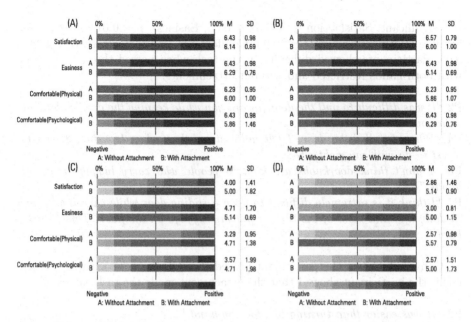

Fig. 5. (**A**) Rating the usefulness at task1 using our attachment compared to no attachments with the left-handed out-swing door, (**B**) Rating the usefulness at task1 using our attachment compared to no attachments with the right-handed in-swing door, (**C**) Rating the usefulness at task2 using our attachment compared to no attachments with the left-handed out-swing door, (**D**) Rating the usefulness at task2 using our attachment compared to no attachments with the right-handed in-swing door.

Figure 5(C) showed results of four questions when participants used the left-handed out-swing door with and without our attachment in task2. No significant difference between "without" and "with" attachment was observed at using the left-handed out-swing door except for questions about Comfortable (Psychological). Satisfaction: $p = 0.19 > 0.05$, Easiness: $p = 0.22 > 0.05$, Comfortable (Physical): $p = 0.21 > 0.05$. The T test for Comfortable (Psychological) showed that the difference was significant ($p = 0.02 \leq 0.05$). When passing through the door without an attachment, participants operated the doorknob with their elbows, fingers, or the container that we prepared. When using the attachment, participants expressed positive or negative opinions about their posture.

P2 *"It was easier because I could pass through the door without changing the posture of my upper body, unlike when I pushed the doorknob with my elbow."* (positive)
P5 *"It's hard to stand on one leg."* (negative)

Figure 5(D) showed results of four questions when participants used the right-handed in-swing door with and without our attachment in task2. The T test for all questions at using the right-handed in-swing door showed that the difference was significant. Satisfaction: $p = 0.02 \leq 0.05$, Easiness: $p = 0.01 \leq 0.05$, Comfortable (Physical): $p = 0.00 \leq 0.05$, Comfortable (Psychological): $p = 0.03 \leq 0.05$. Participants showed difficulty in the task when passed through the door with both hands restricted and without attachments.

P2 *"It was difficult to pull the door toward you while keeping the doorknob turned with your elbow."*
P4 *"When I pulled the door, I felt more stress than when I pushed it. It's the worst to do with my right elbow."*
P5 *"I don't think doorknobs are kind to people who carry luggage with both hands."*
P7 *"I think it is extremely difficult to open a sliding door while carrying luggage in daily life, and most of the time, I put my luggage on the floor. This (task) is hard."*

Conversely, when the participant passed through the door with the attachment, the participant showed that the attachment made the task easier.

P2 *"It was easier than turning the door by hand."*
P4 *"I was surprised that not having to cross the posture would make me so comfortable. The pedal hook is very convenient."*
P5 *"I'm glad I had two legs."*
P7 *"It was overwhelmingly easier to open than when using your hands."*

4.2 Toggle Switch

An attachment was installed on the interface for switching the lighting on and off. We don't frequently turn room lights on and off. However, in public facilities, there is no doubt that it is a switch that an unspecified number of people come into contact with.

System Setup. The switch used for evaluation is a single-pole switch whose shape is defined in JIS C 8304: 2009. The attachment consists of a part that pushes the switch according to the wire's pull, a jig that holds it down (with a guide that changes the direction of the force transmitted to the wire), and a frame that fixes them to the switch (Fig. 6(A)). The pedals are fixed at the bottom of the wall near the switch using 3M's Scotch KPS-12 (Fig. 6(C)). A stainless wire with a load capacity of 70 kg and a diameter of 1.5 mm connected the attachment and pedal.

Participants. This study involved 5 participants (1 females, 4 males) aged between 19 and 25 years (M = 23.4, SD = 2.50). No participant has a 3D printer. We recruited general participants from the members of our laboratory for COVID-19. They have not been injured in their hands or feet since a week ago and can fully use both hands.

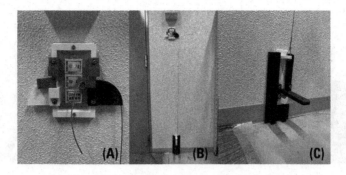

Fig. 6. System setup for case studies; **(A)** Attachments installed on the physical interface, **(B)** Overall view, **(C)** Installed pedals.

Study Process. We have prepared a simple question to evaluate the system for toggle switches that use their feet to access the interface. Each participant was free to press the toggle switch using our system. Understanding whether it is easy for participants to use the system to press the toggle switch, feel tired, frustrated, or hygienic, and the attachment is sufficient. We asked them to rate each question.

Results. Figure 7 showed results of four questions when participants used the toggle switch door with our attachment.

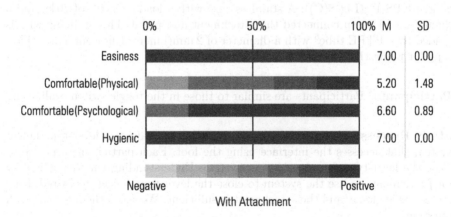

Fig. 7. Rating the usefulness using our attachment with toggle switch.

Fig. 8. System setup for case studies; **(A)** Attachments installed on the physical interface, **(B)** Overall view, **(C)** Installed pedals.

4.3   Lever-Type Faucet

The attachment was installed on the interface to control the amount of water. After washing your hands, it is not hygienic to touch the lever the user touched with dirty hands to stop the water.

System Setup. The lever-type faucet used for the evaluation is TOTO's TKWC35E. The attachment consists of a part that attaches the wire to the lever and a jig that fixes the tube that guides the wire near the lever (Fig. 8(A)). The pedal is attached to the bottom of the side of the washbasin using 3M's Scotch KPS-12 (Fig. 8(C)). A stainless wire with a load capacity of 70 kg and a diameter of 1.5 mm connected the attachment and pedal. This stainless wire is guided by a PTFE tube[5] with a diameter of 2 mm(inner)/3 mm(outer). Besides, a jig for fixing the tube is attached near the pedal.

Participants. Participants are similar to those in the toggle switch evaluation.

Study Process. We prepared a simple question to evaluate a lever-type faucet system that accesses the interface using the foot. Each participant was free to close the lever-type faucet using our system. Understanding whether it is easy for participants to use the system to close the lever-type faucet, feel tired, frustrated, or hygienic, and the attachment is sufficient. We asked them to rate each question.

Results. Figure 9 showed results of four questions when participants used the lever-type faucet with our attachment.

---

[5] https://www.monotaro.com/p/3760/8322/ (last accessed: February, 12th, 2021).

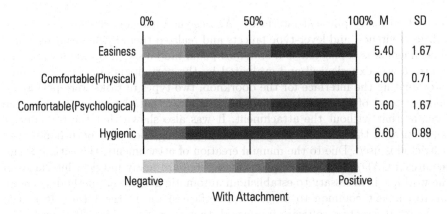

Fig. 9. Rating the usefulness using our attachment with lever-type faucet.

5 Discussion

We demonstrated a case study for the usefulness of the attachment system. Both tasks used two door-passing methods. Since pushing the door and pulling the door are fundamentally different, we separated the cases and conducted the case study. In Task 1, no significant difference was observed between the right-handed in-swing door and the left-handed out-swing door using T-test with and without attachment. Focusing on each item's average, the results with the attachment decreased by 0.14 points at the minimum and 0.57 points at the maximum from the results without the attachment. Some participants mentioned their experience with attachments. Operating with the attachment that developed the doorknob, which is usually handled by hand, is an unfamiliar movement for the participants, which affected the average decrease. The lack of significant difference is by no means a negative result. Since it is a paired one-sided t-test, there is no difference means that the evaluation results with attachments are neither good nor bad compared to those without attachments. In other words, the attachment system is likely to be accepted by many users because the evaluation is similar to the movement of the hand. In Task 2, which restricted both hands' use, significant differences were observed in one item when the participants used the left-handed out-swing door and in all items when they used the right-handed in-swing door. The average point increased for all items for which significant differences were observed. From this, the usefulness of the attachment installed in the right-handed in-swing door is high. It is clear from the results that the attachment system is evaluated as equal to or better than the hand type interface. However, there are many improvements to the attachment.

6 Conclusion

With a 3D printer, we create a low-cost, non-electronic mechanism, which allows the feet to operate the interface. No standard attachment is created that can connect to many physical interfaces. We designed attachments for doorknobs, lighting switches, and lever-type faucets and realized them by 3D printing. Each attachment was connected to a standard pedal module with stainless wire. The interface was experienced and evaluated by the participants of the case study. In evaluating the interface for the doorknob, two types of tasks were performed under a total of four conditions. It became clear that the evaluation was the same as that without the attachment. It was also shown that the attachment is practical in the case of the right-handed in-swing door with both hands that restricted is used. Due to the manual creation of attachments, the actual design requires a CAD/3D printer expert. Since there are many physical interfaces in the world, it is necessary to establish an automatic generation method or create an attachment common to a specific interface shape in the future. It is also necessary to create a software framework that users can design. It is necessary to search for the optimum module with various designs to improve UX and appearance. Participants showed that they felt frustrated when standing on one leg and tired when raising their legs. For this reason, it is necessary to design a better installation position and a more stable pedal structure. Participants also mentioned the durability of the pedals and the experience of the pedals. Users are frustrated when they feel uneasy about durability or when they feel friction when pedaling. Therefore, it is necessary to design a pedal with high UX that proves sufficient strength and does not feel friction.

Acknowledgment. We would like to thank the members of the Digital Nature Group for support in our research activities.

References

1. Bächer, M., Coros, S., Thomaszewski, B.: Linkedit: interactive linkage editing using symbolic kinematics. ACM Trans. Graph. **34**(4), 1–8 (2015). https://doi.org/10.1145/2766985
2. Chen, X.A., Kim, J., Mankoff, J., Grossman, T., Coros, S., Hudson, S.E.: Reprise: a design tool for specifying, generating, and customizing 3d printable adaptations on everyday objects. In: Proceedings of the 29th Annual Symposium on User Interface Software and Technology, UIST 2016, pp. 29–39. Association for Computing Machinery, New York (2016). https://doi.org/10.1145/2984511.2984512
3. Coros, S., et al.: Computational design of mechanical characters. ACM Trans. Graph. **32**(4), 1–12 (2013). https://doi.org/10.1145/2461912.2461953
4. Guo, A., et al.: Facade: auto-generating tactile interfaces to appliances. In: Proceedings of the 2017 CHI Conference on Human Factors in Computing Systems, pp. 5826–5838 (2017)
5. Ion, A., et al.: Metamaterial mechanisms. In: Proceedings of the 29th Annual Symposium on User Interface Software and Technology, UIST 2016, pp. 529–539. Association for Computing Machinery, New York (2016). https://doi.org/10.1145/2984511.2984540
6. Ion, A., Kovacs, R., Schneider, O.S., Lopes, P., Baudisch, P.: Metamaterial textures. In: Proceedings of the 2018 CHI Conference on Human Factors in Computing Systems, pp. 1–12 (2018)

7. Ion, A., Wall, L., Kovacs, R., Baudisch, P.: Digital mechanical metamaterials. In: Proceedings of the 2017 CHI Conference on Human Factors in Computing Systems, pp. 977–988 (2017)
8. Kim, J., Guo, A., Yeh, T., Hudson, S.E., Mankoff, J.: Understanding uncertainty in measurement and accommodating its impact in 3d modeling and printing. In: Proceedings of the 2017 Conference on Designing Interactive Systems. DIS 2017, pp. 1067–1078. Association for Computing Machinery, New York (2017). https:// doi.org/10.1145/3064663.3064690
9. Koyama, Y., Sueda, S., Steinhardt, E., Igarashi, T., Shamir, A., Matusik, W.: Auto-connect: computational design of 3d-printable connectors. ACM Trans. Graph. 34(6), 1–11 (2015). https://doi.org/10.1145/2816795.2818060
10. Leen, D., Peek, N., Ramakers, R.: Lamifold: fabricating objects with integrated mechanisms using a laser cutter lamination workflow. In: Proceedings of the 33rd Annual ACM Symposium on User Interface Software and Technology. UIST 2020, pp. 304–316. Association for Computing Machinery, New York (2020). https://doi.org/10.1145/3379337.3415885
11. Li, J., Kim, J., Chen, X.A.: Robiot: a design tool for actuating everyday objects with automatically generated 3d printable mechanisms. In: Proceedings of the 32nd Annual ACM Symposium on User Interface Software and Technology. UIST 2019, pp. 673–685. Association for Computing Machinery, New York (2019). https://doi.org/10.1145/3332165.3347894
12. Li, J., Andrews, S., Birkas, K.G., Kry, P.G.: Task-based design of cable-driven articulated mechanisms. In: Proceedings of the 1st Annual ACM Symposium on Computational Fabrication. SCF 2017, Association for Computing Machinery, New York (2017). https://doi.org/10.1145/3083157.3083161
13. McDonald, S., et al.: Uncovering challenges and opportunities for 3d printing assistive technology with physical therapists. In: Proceedings of the 18th International ACM SIGACCESS Conference on Computers and Accessibility. ASSETS 2016, pp. 131–139. Association for Computing Machinery, New York (2016). https://doi.org/10.1145/2982142.2982162
14. Megaro, V., Thomaszewski, B., Gauge, D., Grinspun, E., Coros, S., Gross, M.: Chacra: an interactive design system for rapid character crafting. In: Proceedings of the ACM SIGGRAPH/Eurographics Symposium on Computer Animation. SCA 2014, pp. 123–130. Eurographics Association, Goslar (2015)
15. Megaro, V., Zehnder, J., Bächer, M., Coros, S., Gross, M., Thomaszewski, B.: A computational design tool for compliant mechanisms. ACM Trans. Graph. 36(4), 84 (2017). https://doi.org/10.1145/3072959.3073636
16. Mueller, S., Mohr, T., Guenther, K., Frohnhofen, J., Baudisch, P.: Fabrickation: fast 3d printing of functional objects by integrating construction kit building blocks. In: Proceedings of the SIGCHI Conference on Human Factors in Computing Systems. CHI 2014, pp. 3827–3834. Association for Computing Machinery, New York (2014). https://doi.org/10.1145/2556288.2557005
17. Peek, N., Coleman, J., Moyer, I., Gershenfeld, N.: Cardboard machine kit: modules for the rapid prototyping of rapid prototyping machines. In: Proceedings of the 2017 CHI Conference on Human Factors in Computing Systems, pp. 3657–3668 (2017)
18. Ramakers, R., Anderson, F., Grossman, T., Fitzmaurice, G.: RetroFab: a design tool for retrofitting physical interfaces using actuators, sensors and 3D printing. In: Proceedings of the 2016 CHI Conference on Human Factors in Computing Systems, pp. 409–419 (2016)

19. Savage, V., Follmer, S., Li, J., Hartmann, B.: Makers' marks: physical markup for designing and fabricating functional objects. In: Proceedings of the 28th Annual ACM Symposium on User Interface Software and Technology. UIST 2015, pp. 103–108. Association for Computing Machinery, New York (2015). https://doi.org/10.1145/2807442.2807508
20. Schmitz, M., Steimle, J., Huber, J., Dezfuli, N., Mühlhäuser, M.: Flexibles: deformation-aware 3D-printed tangibles for capacitive touchscreens. In: Proceedings of the 2017 CHI Conference on Human Factors in Computing Systems, pp. 1001–1014 (2017)
21. Song, P., et al.: Computational design of wind-up toys. ACM Trans. Graph. **36**(6), 1–13 (2017). https://doi.org/10.1145/3130800.3130808
22. Thomaszewski, B., Coros, S., Gauge, D., Megaro, V., Grinspun, E., Gross, M.: Computational design of linkage-based characters. ACM Trans. Graph. **33**(4), 1–9 (2014). https://doi.org/10.1145/2601097.2601143
23. Wessely, M., Tsandilas, T., Mackay, W.E.: Stretchis: fabricating highly stretchable user interfaces. In: Proceedings of the 29th Annual Symposium on User Interface Software and Technology. UIST 2016, pp. 697–704. Association for Computing Machinery, New York (2016). https://doi.org/10.1145/2984511.2984521
24. Zhu, L., Xu, W., Snyder, J., Liu, Y., Wang, G., Guo, B.: Motion-guided mechanical toy modeling. ACM Trans. Graph. **31**(6), 1–10 (2012). https://doi.org/10.1145/2366145.2366146

Towards a Conceptual Model for Consideration of Adverse Effects of Immersive Virtual Reality for Individuals with Autism

Matthew Schmidt(✉) and Nigel Newbutt

University of Florida, Gainesville, FL 32611, USA
matthew.schmidt@ufl.edu

Abstract. Interest in the use of virtual reality (VR) technologies for individuals with autism has been increasing for over two decades. Recently, research interest has been growing in the area of immersive virtual reality (IVR) technologies thanks to increased availability and affordability. Affordances and theorized benefits of IVR for individuals with autism are quite promising, with the majority of research reports overwhelmingly presenting positive outcomes. Notably absent in the dominant research discourse, however, are considerations of how leveraging the affordances of IVR might lead to unintentional, unexpected, and perhaps deleterious outcomes. This is a particular concern in light of documented adverse effects associated with IVR, such as cybersickness, increased anxiety, and sensory disturbances. Given known characteristics of autism, the impact of adverse effects potentially could be even more pronounced for people with autism than for the general population. In the current paper, we present a conceptual process model for minimizing potential adverse effects of IVR for individuals with autism. Specifically, we highlight the notion of gradual acclimation and detail how gradual acclimation unfolds in a stage-wise manner across implementation contexts and technologies. When working with vulnerable populations, researchers have a special ethical obligation and greater responsibility to actively take precautions to help minimize real or potential risks. Correspondingly, we assert that application of the implementation procedures detailed in the current paper can contribute to researchers minimizing and controlling for potential adverse effects of IVR for individuals with autism.

Keywords: Autism · Immersive virtual reality · Head-mounted displays · Implementation · Adverse effects

1 Introduction

The promise of virtual reality (VR) technology has long been acknowledged for education and training [1, 2]. VR can promote learning along cognitive, affective, and psychomotor dimensions in a manner that is particularly motivating and engaging [3, 4]. Further, VR can provide learners highly realistic experiences in potentially dangerous, impossible, counter-intuitive, or expensive situations (DICE) [5] without potential real-world consequences [6–8]. VR also can situate learners in contexts that would not be

© Springer Nature Switzerland AG 2021
M. M. Soares et al. (Eds.): HCII 2021, LNCS 12780, pp. 333–342, 2021.
https://doi.org/10.1007/978-3-030-78224-5_23

possible in the real-world, such as exploring space, experiencing the inside of a painting, examining the interior of a human heart, or taking a tour of neural connections within a human brain [9, 10]. VR environments have been effectively implemented across a multitude of learning domains, including medicine [11], nursing [12], engineering [13], second language acquisition [14], and vocational training [15].

The increasing rate of technological advancement in the area of VR introduces profound opportunities to create highly engaging and effective educational, training, and therapeutic interventions [16]. However, VR technologies are typically developed by and for people who are neuro- and physio-typical—not for those with disabilities [17]. Technology features and affordances that might lead to effective learning experiences for Abled people could have unanticipated effects when used with disabled people, particularly when disabled people are not included in the design and evaluation of the technologies. This is especially relevant when working with autistic people. Autism is a lifelong condition that is characterized by differences in social communication/interaction and restricted, repetitive patterns of behavior [18]. As a spectrum condition, manifestations of autism present substantial heterogeneity across affected individuals [19]. Therapeutic supports have been shown to lead to improvements in quality of life [20]; however, access to and consistency of these supports are known barriers. As such, viable and effective supports are in high demand. One potential support modality is VR, which has been steadily gaining attention in the field [21, 22].

VR is considered to be a promising and useful technology for autistic people due to technological affordances which align closely with instructional needs [23], including abilities to encounter and practice useful skills in highly realistic and customizable contexts, have input stimuli intentionally manipulated, and have real-world consequences mitigated or removed. Early research studies on the acceptability and possibility of VR for autistic people suggested that the technology could hold tremendous potential for delivering training, education, and therapy [24]. However, the prohibitive costs of fully immersive VR head-mounted displays (HMD) and the nascent state of VR technologies in the mid-1990s hindered subsequent research from focusing inquiries specifically on the use of headset-based VR [25]. As a result, the field focused for nearly two decades on more readily available immersive technologies, such as virtual worlds like Second Life or bespoke desktop-based VR experiences and interventions [26]. More recently, and largely due to the increasing availability and affordability of high-quality HMD (e.g., Oculus Quest 2, Valve Index, Playstation VR), research on fully immersive VR (IVR) for individuals on the autism spectrum has begun to see a resurgence [27].

1.1 Accelerating Interest in IVR

IVR systems are high-fidelity VR systems that have the potential to immerse users along spatial, sensorimotor, cognitive, and emotional dimensions [28]. IVR presents interesting and novel opportunities for researchers to continue and extend a research tradition that until recently has been conducted predominantly in the domain of desktop-based immersive technologies. These VR technologies are advancing at an exponential rate. According to Moore's Law, computing power doubles every 1.5 years, meaning that the processors that power the current generation of VR devices could be superseded by processors that are up to 16 times more powerful in just 6 years. Correspondingly,

Kurzweil's Law of Accelerating Returns suggests that the increasing rate of technological advancement itself leads to even more rapid technology acceleration, resulting in increased efficiencies, economies of scale, and reduced costs in ever-decreasing timespans. Extrapolating from Moore's Law and Kurzweil's law regarding technological progress in VR, it seems reasonable that advances of the past 20 years will be eclipsed multiple times over in just the next few years, and that highly sophisticated IVR systems soon will be widely available at a fraction of their current cost.

The user experiences and interaction possibilities provided by modern, hyper-realistic, deeply immersive IVR systems present fertile ground to explore and test how these more modern technologies might be leveraged to influence the lives of autistic people in positive and productive ways. However, given the exponential rate of technological advancement, it is simply not feasible for researchers to keep pace. As such, it is very likely that technologies will be adopted and implemented by and for autistic people before those technologies are fully understood. Compounding this is the limited attention to and understanding of how to best implement IVR for individuals with autism [22]. Further, researchers seeking to design studies using IVR are presented with an apparent quandary in that the majority of extant research has been performed using technology tools with considerably different features and affordances than contemporary IVR systems. That is, research evidence suggesting VR is a particularly promising technology for autistic people [26, 29, 30] draws primarily from studies that use rather primitive VR tools. Questions of how autistic people might perceive and react to the hyper-stimulating, immersive experiences provided by modern IVR systems remain largely unanswered.

1.2 IVR, Autism, and the Risk of Adverse Effects

Implementing technologies with vulnerable populations before those technologies are well understood introduces a number of risks. Of particular concern when working with autistic groups is the risk of adverse effects associated with HMD usage [31]. These adverse effects include, but are not limited to, negative effects such as sweating, nausea/motion-sickness, dizziness, headache, eye fatigue, safety concerns (e.g., static balance, transient reduced depth perception), increased anxiety, sensory disturbances, and disorientation [32–35]. The literature exploring VR for individuals on the autism spectrum largely ignores potential adverse effects, with consideration being cursory at best [21, 30, 36–38]. This is perhaps because the majority of research studies have been conducted using less immersive or non-immersive VR systems, which are less likely to cause adverse effects [39]. Further consideration is therefore warranted, as people with autism could be more likely to experience adverse effects in fully immersive VR systems, and with greater severity, than neuro- and/or physio-typical individuals.

The question of how individuals with autism might be particularly impacted by adverse effects is informed by sensory conflict theory and postural instability theory. According to sensory conflict theory, humans gather sensory cues from multiple channels to present a continually updated model of the world and one's body [40]. However, the use of VR can introduce conflicts between what is experienced and what is expected, and this mismatch can lead to adverse effects such as nausea and dizziness [41]. Such mismatches could be even more pronounced for individuals on the autism spectrum due to diminished multisensory integration [42] and hyper-reactivity to sensory input

[43]. Sensory processing and sensory integration differences in individuals on the autism spectrum could potentially generate conflicts between visual and proprioceptive information in a virtual environment, which would increase the potential for adverse effects to present. Adding to this are the difficulties that many autistic people have maintaining postural stability—referred to as atypical postural reactivity [44]—due to reduced perceptions of body movements and shifts relative to their body's orientation and equilibrium. According to postural instability theory, extended postural instability in VR environments can lead to adverse effects [45, 46]. Since some individuals on the autism spectrum can have difficulties related to postural stability, adverse effects may be particularly acute for them when using IVR. Perceived adverse effects are well established in the VR literature for general users; however, given the known characteristics of autism, adverse effects could be particularly acute.

2 Towards a Conceptual Model for Minimizing Adverse Effects

Problematically, researchers have yet to meaningfully and systematically approach questions related to people with autism experiencing adverse effects when using immersive VR [27]. Assuming a continued trend of interest in IVR for individuals with autism, we argue that consideration of the affordances of the technology must include systematic attention to potential adverse effects and how to mitigate them. According to Kellmeyer [33], "very little systematic discussion of the neurophilosophical and ethical challenges from the clinical use of these new VR systems is available" (p. 2). These issues raise ethical concerns, as when working with vulnerable populations, researchers have a special obligation and greater responsibility to actively take precautions to help minimize real or potential risks [47, 48]. This extends to possible adverse effects associated with the use of IVR for individuals with autism. A significant gap exists, therefore, related to exploring and reporting potential adverse effects [27]. We argue that with rapid technological advancements in this area, professionals working with people with autism have an urgent responsibility to confront these issues [49].

2.1 Proposed Conceptual Model

In prior published research, we proposed a framework for addressing adverse effects when using HMD-based VR with autistic groups [49]. The purpose of this work was to foreground the need for IVR implementation guidelines to minimize adverse effects for autistic people. This framework came about as a result of two studies [23, 50] synthesizing approaches in working with autistic groups at two different research sites. Our efforts resulted in a synthesis of methods and processes for deploying IVR in a stage-wise manner, with the primary aim of minimizing adverse effects for participants. The methods we used to develop the resulting framework are detailed in the research published by Schmidt and colleagues [49]. In that work, we describe an iterative analysis process in which we collaboratively compared the approaches separate researchers adopted for implementing IVR with autistic groups. By deconstructing our techniques and critically analyzing them, we were able to identify points of convergence and divergence and subsequently distill and synthesize a set of common practices, principles, and procedures.

We present these in a graphical format that is designed to be simple enough that anyone could implement it, including both researchers and practitioners (Fig. 1).

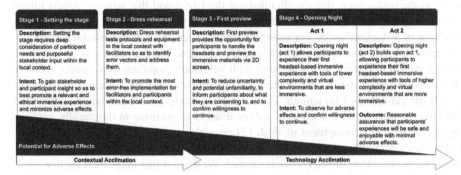

Fig. 1. Stage-wise process model promoting gradual acclimation to minimize potential adverse effects of IVR for individuals with autism.

Central to our stage-wise process is the notion of gradual acclimation, that is, the process through which the VR experience is continually optimized within and across implementation stages. Gradual acclimation begins with contextual acclimation (Stages 1 and 2). Contextual acclimation seeks to identify the local variables that potentially could impact successful implementation. The gradual acclimation process continues through technology acclimation (Stages 3 and 4). Technology acclimation provides opportunities for participants to handle and experience the technology. Importantly, by technology, we refer not only to the VR headset, but also to the virtual environment. Gradual acclimation is utilized due to known characteristics of autistic groups, such as anxiety, a preference for sameness and routine, sensory differences, etc.

Turning now to the specific stages in the model, *Stage 1: Setting the Stage* includes front-end analysis and intervention design. In addition, intentional solicitation of collaborative and meaningful input from all stakeholders during this stage ensures the voices of those who matter the most are heard [17]. *Stage 2: Dress Rehearsal* tests in-situ the IVR technology used to deliver the intervention, thereby allowing teams to collectively examine the space where the technology will be used. Importantly, dress rehearsal is not technology testing; it is preparing for social-behavioral human subjects research [43]. *Stage 3: First Preview* provides structured opportunities to communicate the project to participants. Participants can examine the technology and learn about the virtual environment they will experience. This helps provide concrete and real examples of what they will be experiencing, thereby enhancing communication. An additional benefit of this relates to informed consent, as concrete examples and hands-on activities are well aligned with known autistic traits. In *Stage 4: Opening Night Act 1*, the equipment and experience is delivered in a limited manner so as to promote gradual acclimation. This is achieved by limiting the amount of time that participants engage in the VR experience and using lower tech versions of the technology to reduce complication and promote usability [23, 51], as well as reducing the potential for frustration or confusion [52].

Finally, *Stage 4: Opening Night Act 2* provides opportunities for participants to fully engage in the IVR experience using high-fidelity HMDs (i.e., Oculus Quest, HTC Vive).

By following the stage-wise approach, we assert that participants will gradually acclimate to the technology, thereby diminishing the likelihood that adverse effects might unfavorably impact participants. Efforts to minimize risk should continue across the duration of VR experiences; for example timely check-ins with stakeholders to determine comfort and willingness to continue. As we have highlighted above, researchers have a special obligation when working with vulnerable populations to reduce risks. A dearth of guidance exists for researchers and practitioners seeking to harness the promise of VR for individuals with autism. The conceptual model we present here is a first step towards an operational reflection of values that (1) is sensitive to the rapidly advancing technological development of IVR, (2) promotes inclusion of autistic voices, and (3) recognizes our special ethical obligation as researchers when working with autistic populations. However, further work is needed. We discuss this in the next section.

3   Discussion and Implications

The current paper argues and positions the need for considering adverse effects when using IVR with autistic populations. The work is both timely and relevant, as interest in using IVR for individuals with autism is growing in areas such as: supporting attention, communication, daily living skills, emotional skills, and social skills, as well as addressing phobias and fears and promoting physical activity [30]. Although many of the procedures in our stage-wise process model arguably could extend to the general population, they were articulated for autistic populations in particular due to known autistic characteristics. Related to general audiences, 3D virtual learning environments (which include VR) provide a number of affordances that are considered to be particularly beneficial for promoting meaningful learning, including specifically (1) representational fidelity and (2) opportunities for learner interaction [53]. Examples include realistic display of the environment, user representation, embodied actions, and embodied verbal and non-verbal communication. Related to individuals with autism specifically, researchers have further considered affordances of VR that are promising, such as predictability, lack of real-world consequences, ability to experience new places in a safe and structured manner, ability to simplify the environment and tasks, etc. To date, the manner in which VR affordances have been presented in the literature has been overwhelmingly positive. Notably absent in the dominant research discourse, however, are considerations of how leveraging these affordances might lead to unintentional, unexpected, and perhaps deleterious outcomes.

Given known characteristics of autism, many of the affordances presented by others as promising also have the potential to result in adverse effects. We present here examples connected with realistic display of environments and smooth display of view changes and object motion, as well as HMD devices themselves. First, a highly realistic virtual environment can provide concrete representations, which in theory, could promote generalization from the virtual world to the real world [54]. However, the hypersensitivity to visual stimuli that some individuals with autism experience could lead to feeling overwhelmed and overstimulated. Next, IVR can allow for smooth display of view changes and object motion, which can promote a positive and engaging user experience. However, the degree to which this can be achieved is determined by the quality of the IVR system. Even with some of the most advanced HMDs, most end-users will experience some degree of cybersickness [32, 55]. As stated previously, given the sensory differences associated with autism, these virtual experiences could be particularly acute. In addition to this, some autistic users could have difficulties bringing these experiences to the attention of researchers due to known communication challenges associated with autism. Finally, the HMD systems that are believed to make possible these affordances could themselves be problematic for some. Donning HMDs can be an extraordinarily visceral experience, including (1) having someone who is presumably a stranger fit the HMD to the user, (2) physical sensations related to the HMD's weight, size, and the pressure of the tight-fitting straps, and (3) the sudden transition into a high-fidelity, hyper-realistic visual and auditory environment. Taken together, these factors potentially could trigger heightened anxiety and associated behaviors. If researchers and practitioners are to effectively are to apply IVR technologies with autistic populations, then the known characteristics of autism must be carefully considered alongside potential technology affordances. However, anticipating and accounting for all potentialities a-priori is neither practical nor feasible. Because our process model derives from our own practice, many of the challenges that we have experienced implementing IVR with autistic populations are embedded within the various stages. However, the model is also flexible in that unanticipated contextual or technological challenges that emerge can be identified and minimized or corrected through collaboration with stakeholders and participants.

4 Conclusion

The work presented herein explores an unmet and arguably critical need in the new and emerging field of IVR for individuals with autism concerning the meaningful and systematic consideration of adverse effects. We proffer the stage-wise implementation framework (Fig. 1) as a conduit for both considering and minimizing potential adverse effects associated with these technologies. This framework draws its importance not only because it addresses a known gap in the literature, but also because it could potentially guide future implementation in design of research studies and deployment and utilization in practice of IVR for individuals with autism. While no evidence exists currently to suggest that the proposed framework results in reduced adverse effects, what is presented here is the first phase of framework development—an important first step. Future research will seek to evaluate the framework empirically and incorporate subsequent refinements.

We offer this provisional framework in a space and time when there is very little known about how wearable technology like HMD might adversely affect individuals with autism. Practitioners, researchers and other professionals will benefit from this clear, simple and informed framework for implementing IVR with individuals with autism in a safe and ethical manner.

References

1. Girvan, C., Savage, T.: Identifying an appropriate pedagogy for virtual worlds: a communal constructivism case study. Comput. Educ. **55**, 342–349 (2010)

2. Merchant, Z., Goetz, E.T., Cifuentes, L., Keeney-Kennicutt, W., Davis, T.J.: Effectiveness of virtual reality-based instruction on students' learning outcomes in K-12 and higher education: a meta-analysis. Comput. Educ. **70**, 29–40 (2014)
3. Hew, K.F., Cheung, W.S.: Use of three-dimensional (3-D) immersive virtual worlds in K-12 and higher education settings: a review of the research: use of 3-D in K-12 and higher education. Br. J. Educ. Technol. **41**, 33–55 (2010)
4. Jensen, L., Konradsen, F.: A review of the use of virtual reality head-mounted displays in education and training. Educ. Inf. Technol. **23**, 1515–1529 (2018)
5. Bailenson, J.: Experience on Demand: What Virtual Reality Is, How It Works, and What It Can Do. WW Norton & Company (2018)
6. Lele, A.: Virtual reality and its military utility. J. Ambient Intell. Humaniz. Comput. **4**, 17–26 (2013)
7. Moglia, A., et al.: A systematic review of virtual reality simulators for robot-assisted surgery. Eur. Urol. **69**, 1065–1080 (2016)
8. Sacks, R., Perlman, A., Barak, R.: Construction safety training using immersive virtual reality. Constr. Manag. Econ. **31**, 1005–1017 (2013)
9. Eklund, M., Christensen, M.: Art plunge: experiencing the inner worlds of famous artworks. In: SA 2018, pp. 1:1–1:2. ACM (2018). https://doi.org/10.1145/3275495.3275510
10. Howard, M.C.: Investigating the simulation elements of environment and control: extending the Uncanny Valley Theory to simulations. Comput. Educ. **109**, 216–232 (2017)
11. Gurusamy, K., Aggarwal, R., Palanivelu, L., Davidson, B.R.: Systematic review of randomized controlled trials on the effectiveness of virtual reality training for laparoscopic surgery. Br. J. Surg. **95**, 1088–1097 (2008)
12. Jenson, C.E., Forsyth, D.M.: Virtual reality simulation: using three-dimensional technology to teach nursing students. CIN Comput. Inform. Nurs. **30**, 312–318 (2012)
13. Potkonjak, V., et al.: Virtual laboratories for education in science, technology, and engineering: a review. Comput. Educ. **95**, 309–327 (2016)
14. Lin, T.-J., Lan, Y.-J.: Language learning in virtual reality environments: past, present, and future. J. Educ. Technol. Soc. **18**, 486–497 (2015)
15. Freina, L., Ott, M.: A literature review on immersive virtual reality in education: state of the art and perspectives. In: The International Scientific Conference eLearning and Software for Education, vol. 1 (2015) (133. 'Carol I' National Defence University)
16. Garrett, B., et al.: Virtual reality clinical research: promises and challenges. JMIR Ser. Games **6**, e10839 (2018)
17. Parsons, S., Yuill, N., Good, J., Brosnan, M.: 'Whose agenda? Who knows best? Whose voice?' Co-creating a technology research roadmap with autism stakeholders. Disabil. Soc. **35**, 201–234 (2020)
18. DSM-5 American Psychiatric Association. Diagnostic and Statistical Manual of Mental Disorders. American Psychiatric Publishing (2013)
19. Masi, A., DeMayo, M.M., Glozier, N., Guastella, A.J.: An overview of autism spectrum disorder, heterogeneity and treatment options. Neurosci. Bull. **33**, 183–193 (2017)
20. Estes, A., et al.: Long-term outcomes of early intervention in 6-year-old children with autism spectrum disorder. J. Am. Acad. Child Adolesc. Psychiatry **54**, 580–587 (2015)
21. Bellani, M., Fornasari, L., Chittaro, L., Brambilla, P.: Virtual reality in autism: state of the art. Epidemiol. Psychiatr. Sci. **20**, 235–238 (2011)
22. Parsons, S.: Authenticity in Virtual Reality for assessment and intervention in autism: a conceptual review. Educ. Res. Rev. **19**, 138–157 (2016)
23. Schmidt, M. et al.: Evaluation of a spherical video-based virtual reality intervention designed to teach adaptive skills for adults with autism: a preliminary report. Interact. Learn. Environ. 1–20 (2019). https://doi.org/10.1080/10494820.2019.1579236

24. Strickland, D., Marcus, L.M., Mesibov, G.B., Hogan, K.: Brief report: two case studies using virtual reality as a learning tool for autistic children. J. Autism Dev. Disord. **26**, 651–659 (1996)
25. Newbutt, N., Schmidt, M.M., Riva, G., Schmidt, C.: The possibility and importance of immersive technologies during COVID-19 for autistic people. J. Enabling Technol. (2020). https://doi.org/10.1108/JET-07-2020-0028
26. Lorenzo, G., Lorenzo-Lledó, A., Lledó, A., Pérez-Vázquez, E.: Application of virtual reality in people with ASD from 1996 to 2019. J. Enabling Technol. (2020) (ahead-of-print)
27. Bradley, R., Newbutt, N.: Autism and virtual reality head-mounted displays: a state of the art systematic review. J. Enabling Technol. **11** (2018)
28. Bjork, S., Holopainen, J.: Patterns in Game Design (game development series). Charles River Media, Inc. (2004)
29. Karami, B., Koushki, R., Arabgol, F., Rahmani, M., Vahabie, A.: Effectiveness of Virtual Reality-based therapeutic interventions on individuals with autism spectrum disorder: a comprehensive meta-analysis (2020). https://doi.org/10.31234/osf.io/s2jvy
30. Mesa-Gresa, P., Gil-Gómez, H., Lozano-Quilis, J.-A., Gil-Gómez, J.-A.: Effectiveness of virtual reality for children and adolescents with autism spectrum disorder: an evidence-based systematic review. Sensors **18** (2018)
31. Palmisano, S., Mursic, R., Kim, J.: Vection and cybersickness generated by head-and-display motion in the Oculus Rift. Displays **46**, 1–8 (2017)
32. Cobb, S.V., Nichols, S., Ramsey, A., Wilson, J.R.: Virtual reality-induced symptoms and effects (VRISE). Presence. Teleoper. Virtual Environ. **8**, 169–186 (1999)
33. Kellmeyer, P.: Neurophilosophical and ethical aspects of virtual reality therapy in neurology and psychiatry. Camb. Q. Healthc. Ethics **27**, 610–627 (2018)
34. Kolasinski, E. M. Simulator Sickness in Virtual Environments, vol. 1027. US Army Research Institute for the Behavioral and Social Sciences (1995)
35. Park, S., Lee, G.: Full-immersion virtual reality: adverse effects related to static balance. Neurosci. Lett. **733**, (2020)
36. Fletcher-Watson, S.: A targeted review of computer-assisted learning for people with autism spectrum disorder: towards a consistent methodology. Rev. J. Autism Dev. Disord. **1**, 87–100 (2014)
37. Irish, J.E.N.: Can I sit here? A review of the literature supporting the use of single-user virtual environments to help adolescents with autism learn appropriate social communication skills. Comput. Hum. Behav. **29**, A17–A24 (2013)
38. Wong, C., et al.: Evidence-based practices for children, youth, and young adults with autism spectrum disorder. Compr. Rev. J. Autism Dev. Disord. **45**, 1951–1966 (2015)
39. Holden, M.K.: Virtual environments for motor rehabilitation. Rev. Cyberpsychology Behav. **8**, 187–211 (2005)
40. Stein, B.E.: The New Handbook of Multisensory Processing. MIT Press (2012)
41. Rebenitsch, L., Owen, C.: Review on cybersickness in applications and visual displays. Virtual Real. **20**, 101–125 (2016)
42. Stevenson, R.A., et al.: Evidence for diminished multisensory integration in autism spectrum disorders. J. Autism Dev. Disord. **44**, 3161–3167 (2014)
43. American Psychiatric Association: Diagnostic and Statistical Manual of Mental Disorders. American Psychiatric Association (2013)
44. Doumas, M., McKenna, R., Murphy, B.: Postural control deficits in autism spectrum disorder: the role of sensory integration. J. Autism Dev. Disord. **46**, 853–861 (2016)
45. Arcioni, B., Palmisano, S., Apthorp, D., Kim, J.: Postural stability predicts the likelihood of cybersickness in active HMD-based virtual reality. Displays **58**, 3–11 (2019)
46. Murata, A.: Effects of duration of immersion in a virtual reality environment on postural stability. Int. J. Hum.-Comput. Interact. **17**, 463–477 (2004)

47. American Educational Research Association: Code of ethics (2011). https://www.aera.net/Portals/38/docs/About_AERA/CodeOfEthics(1).pdf
48. Behavior Analyst Certification Board: Professional and ethical compliance code for behavior analysts (2014). https://www.bacb.com/wp-content/uploads/2020/05/BACB-Compliance-Code-english_190318.pdf
49. Schmidt, M., Newbutt, N., Schmidt, C., Glaser, N.: A process-model for minimizing adverse effects when using head mounted display-based virtual reality for individuals with autism. Front. Virtual Real. 2 (2021)
50. Newbutt, N., Bradley, R., Conley, I.: Using virtual reality head-mounted displays in schools with autistic children: views, experiences, and future directions. Cyberpsychol. Behav. Soc. Netw. 23, 23–33 (2020) (31502866)
51. Parish-Morris, J., et al.: Immersive virtual reality to improve police interaction skills in adolescents and adults with autism spectrum disorder: preliminary results of a phase I feasibility and safety trial. Annu. Rev. CyberTherapy Telemed. 2018, 50–56 (2018)
52. Rojo, D., Mayor, J., Rueda, J.J.G., Raya, L.: A virtual reality training application for adults with asperger's syndrome. IEEE Comput. Graph. Appl. 39, 104–111 (2019)
53. Dalgarno, B., Lee, M.J.W.: What are the learning affordances of 3-D virtual environments? Br. J. Educ. Technol. 41, 10–32 (2010)
54. Schmidt, C., Schmidt, M.: Three-dimensional virtual learning environments for mediating social skills acquisition among individuals with autism spectrum disorders. In: Tartaro, A., Hayes, G.H. (eds.) Meeting of the 7th International Conference on Interaction Design and Children (2008)
55. Dennison, M.S., Wisti, A.Z., D'Zmura, M.: Use of physiological signals to predict cybersickness. Displays 44, 42–52 (2016)

Usability of a Digital Elder Mistreatment Screening Tool for Older Adults with Visual and Hearing Disabilities

Sarah J. Swierenga[1(✉)], Jennifer Ismirle[1], Chelsea Edwards[2], and Fuad Abujarad[2]

[1] Michigan State University, East Lansing, MI 48824, USA
sswieren@msu.edu
[2] Yale University, New Haven, CT 06510, USA

Abstract. Elder mistreatment (EM) is a public health problem that affects 10% of Americans aged 60 or older. As the number of older adults increases due to national demographics, instances of elder mistreatment are also likely to increase without services in place to prevent it. The goal of our study was to evaluate the usability and feasibility of the VOICES tablet-based elder mistreatment screening tool with older adults who have visual and hearing disabilities. VOICES is a tablet-based self-administrated digital health tool that screens, educates, and motivates older adults to self-report elder mistreatment. Study participants included older adults who were blind, had low vision, were deaf, or were hard of hearing. Findings from this study will inform geriatricians, user interface designers, digital health professionals, and the general public on the specific needs of older adults with disabilities and universal design considerations for digital health applications intended to be used by older adults with visual or hearing disabilities.

Keywords: Healthcare UX · Usability · Elder mistreatment

1 Introduction

Elder mistreatment is a persistent, national issue that affects approximately 1 in 10 Americans aged 60 or older, which is an estimated 5 million older adults every year [1, 2]. The Centers for Disease Control and Prevention defines elder mistreatment, also known as elder abuse, as "the intentional act, or failure to act, by a caregiver or trusted person that causes or creates a risk of harm to an adult age 60 or older [3, 4]." The six commonly reported categories of elder mistreatment are: physical abuse, financial exploitation, emotional abuse, sexual abuse, neglect, and abandonment [1, 3]. It is estimated that only 1 in 24 cases of elder mistreatment become known to authorities [5].

Older adult victims are not likely to self-report that they are being mistreated due to several barriers that limit help-seeking behaviors. These barriers include fear of nursing home placement, fear of losing autonomy, and fear that if the abusive caregiver is removed, no one will take care of them. There are also concerns regarding involving an abusive family member with legal trouble [6–8].

© Springer Nature Switzerland AG 2021
M. M. Soares et al. (Eds.): HCII 2021, LNCS 12780, pp. 343–360, 2021.
https://doi.org/10.1007/978-3-030-78224-5_24

Existing methods to increase the identification of elder mistreatment focus on educating healthcare professionals and developing screening tools to be administered by providers with limited input from older adults themselves. We developed a different and unique approach to address the lack of identification of victims of elder mistreatment for community dwelling and cognitively intact older adults. In our approach, we include the older adults in the screening process and help them be their own advocate.

1.1 Overview of VOICES Tool

VOICES is a digital health screening tool designed to place the process of elder mistreatment screening in the hands of the older adult and to motivate them to self-report mistreatment [5, 9, 10]. VOICES is self-administered by a digital coach and runs on a tablet device to deliver elder mistreatment screening content targeting attitudes, subjective norms, and perceptions of control. The tool provides educational content, as well as resources and services available, to older adults along with information on the Adult Protective Services (APS) response to disclosure. VOICES uses a digital coach, called Vicky, to guide the user through a customized pathway depending on the user's needs. Vicky uses an automated text-to-speech feature to narrate the text presented on the screen or the audio contained in the animated educational videos. If suspicion of mistreatment is identified, the tool will attempt to motivate the user to identify with being mistreated and disclose their mistreatment to a healthcare professional.

The development of the VOICES tool consisted of content and application development. The content of the VOICES tool was based on existing literature on elder mistreatment, theories of planned behavior and self-determination [11, 12], the technological needs of older adults and subject matter expert interviews, including clinical researchers in geriatrics, psychology, and intimate partner violence. The application development of the VOICES tool was based on the User-Centered Design (UCD) approach, which involved requirement gathering, conceptual model design, focus groups and interviews, prototyping and mockups, tool development, and an initial evaluation with a representative sample from potential end users [9, 10, 13]. We conducted focus groups to test and validate the concept of elder mistreatment electronic screening and we have validated the usability of our tool using formal usability evaluation [5]. The focus group results showed a willingness to use a tablet for elder mistreatment screening and the initial usability results suggested that older adults are capable, willing, and comfortable with using a tablet-based screening tool.

1.2 VOICES Tool Screening Process

VOICES is presented to the older adult on a tablet device by the provider who will remain in the vicinity to assist with initial tool orientation and to answer any questions. Before initializing the tool, the older adult is informed that their provider will be notified if any suspicion of elder mistreatment is identified. The VOICES tool starts with an educational module, utilizing evidence from multidisciplinary fields to introduce the topic of elder mistreatment and emphasize that elder mistreatment is rarely an isolated incident, which can escalate in severity and intensity if left undisclosed. The VOICES tool then continues to the elder mistreatment screener, which assesses the user's mistreatment risk. The older adult is then shown an educational module consisting of a brief animated video that provides a general summary of mistreatment. Afterward, the user is invited to watch up to five short (1–2 min) animated videos detailing each common category of elder mistreatment, along with its respective risks, signs, and consequences.

The results from the previous screener will determine whether the VOICES tool ends without suspicion of mistreatment or continues to a motivational Brief Negotiation Interview (BNI) module (suspicion of mistreatment), which will then encourage the user to reflect on and understand their experience as having been mistreated. A key component of the motivational BNI module is to prompt the user to consider the benefits or motives for self-identifying as being mistreated [14, 15]. If the user decides not to identify as mistreated, the VOICES tool will end. Otherwise, the user will be motivated to self-report and seek professional help. At this point in the tool, VOICES will privately notify the provider if a suspicion of mistreatment was identified to prompt the provider to follow up with a more comprehensive mistreatment screening.

1.3 Current Study

In addition to the common barriers for elder mistreatment identification, older adults with disabilities who are blind, have low-vision, or are deaf or hard of hearing are at a greater risk of elder mistreatment compared to those without, and face further limitations in communicating their needs with health professionals and disclosing mistreatment [1, 16]. The goal of our study is to make the VOICES tool more inclusive and usable by older adults with vision and hearing disabilities. We are aiming to reduce disparities and empower this segment of older adults to be their own advocates and to help increase the coverage of the VOICES tool to include persons with disabilities. Digital screening of elder mistreatment can produce significantly higher rates of elder mistreatment reporting. Digital tools that offer the opportunity to confidentially self-report risky or stigmatizing behavior should not exclude persons with disabilities.

In this paper we describe how we performed a preliminary evaluation of the usability of the VOICES screening tool for older individuals with visual or hearing disabilities. Specifically, we describe how we evaluated the ease of use and usefulness of VOICES as a screening tool for older adults who are blind, have low vision, are deaf, or are hard of hearing, to assess the degree to which this tool is appropriate for these potential populations of users. We also describe how we used the findings and recommendations from the usability evaluation and the User-Centered Design (UCD) approach to enhance and refine the VOICES tool to be more usable and acceptable by older adults with visual or hearing disabilities.

The objective in this paper is to describe our approach to increase the scope of the user population of the VOICES tool to include adults with disabilities and to present our findings from the usability evaluation that we conducted during the enhancement of our tool.

2   Methodology

We conducted one-on-one usability evaluation sessions with (n = 14) cognitively intact older adults age 60 or older who are blind, have low vision, are deaf, or are hard of hearing. In the usability evaluation sessions participants used the VOICES tool on an iPad tablet to perform elder mistreatment screening scenarios. We then analyzed audio and video recordings, and participant feedback from the evaluation sessions. Usability was evaluated in terms of its three constituent components: effectiveness, efficiency, and satisfaction. The International Organization for Standardization defines usability as, "the extent to which a system, product or service can be used by specified users to achieve specified goals with effectiveness, efficiency and satisfaction in a specified context of use" [17].

2.1 Usability Testing Configuration

Participants used an Apple ® iPad Pro with a 12.9-in. screen size while seated at an adjustable drafting table with height and angle options (see Fig. 1), allowing the user to change the angle and position of the table to their liking. The tablet rested on the surface of the table to avoid any strain caused by holding the device, and the table was angled to reduce glare [18]. In addition, the adjustable table was used to provide necessary support for older adults who may have dexterity limitations to assist with accuracy of button presses and reduce unintended inputs [19, 20].

Fig. 1. Mobile testing configuration.

A non-slip matting was also placed on the table to keep the iPad from sliding, and participants could move the position of the tablet within an approximately 40 × 40 cm area that was taped off. If needed, overhead fluorescent lights were turned off, and a lamp with a 60 W lightbulb was placed next to the table to eliminate glare for each participant.

Video of the iPad screen was captured with a Logitech C525 USB Webcam mounted on a tripod and TechSmith's Morae (v3.3.4) software, and a separate back-up audio recorder was used (Olympus WS-821). We also used the screen recording feature on the iPad.

2.2 VOICES Tool Modes and Interface

VOICES Modes. Participants used either the coach Vicky Mode (hard of hearing and low vision participants) or VoiceOver Mode (blind and low vision participants) to attempt the two task scenarios.

Vicky Mode. This mode is intended for either users without accessibility requirements, low vision users, or users who are hard of hearing or deaf. By default, this mode uses automated text-to-speech with a female voice, called the Vicky digital coach. Users have the ability to mute the audio via a volume button on the bottom menu bar or allow the Vicky coach to auto-play and read the text with each slide. Videos automatically display closed captioning. The speech rate of the Vicky voice was 155 WPM.

Digital coach Vicky reads from a separate text track similar to what is shown on the screen which allows for customizable pronunciation of words that the automated text-to-speech coach may not properly pronounce by default. For example, while the word "caregiver" may be shown as one word to the user, in the text track it is displayed as "care giver" so the Vicky coach can pronounce the appropriate hard ⟨g⟩, rather than the text-to-speech default soft ⟨g⟩ pronunciation (similar to pronouncing the 'g' in "gym").

VoiceOver Mode. This mode is intended for users without vision, or with some degree of vision impairment. The iPad's internal accessibility feature, VoiceOver (which is a gesture-based screen reader), is activated on the device and when a new user is created in the tool, accessibility requirements can be toggled for the user's profile. The user's interface will have slight adjustments to accommodate the iPad's VoiceOver functionality. For example, the Vicky coach text-to-speech functionality will be disabled, and the VOICES's volume button will be hidden since it is not needed. For this study, the default speech rate of 175 WPM for VoiceOver was used.

Interface Design. The VOICES tool was designed with a simple layout, large buttons to minimize selection errors, and large high-contrast text (using Arial font and size of 32pt in black against a white background) with limited text on each screen. For example, Fig. 2 shows an example of a screen from the Vicky version with a top and bottom banner and a large content area; the bottom bar includes a "Play"/"Pause" button, volume control, and the "Continue" button (which becomes active after the narration has finished or after a selection has been made for a question). The VoiceOver version of this screen did not include the "Play"/"Pause" or volume control buttons.

2.3 Procedure

Usability evaluation sessions were conducted at the facilities of Michigan State University Usability/Accessibility Research and Consulting (UARC) laboratory. All procedures

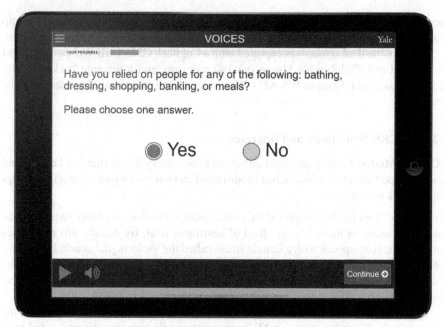

Fig. 2. Example of VOICES tool page from Vicky mode.

were approved by the Michigan State University Human Investigation Committee (IRB). Participants used an Apple ® iPad Pro (12.9-in.) tablet that had the VOICES tool loaded onto it. Each one-on-one usability session lasted approximately 90 min. Participants were given a brief overview of the study, asked to sign the Informed Consent Form, fill out a brief demographic questionnaire, attempt the task scenarios, and fill out post-study surveys.

Task Scenarios. During the usability sessions, participants were asked to use pre-prepared scenarios and assume a certain persona for each task. This did not impact participants' understanding or use of the tool, but it did cause users to focus on evaluating VOICES. Therefore, participants were asked to use the VOICES tool on the iPad to go through a step-by-step screening process using a specific set of instructions that were provided and talk-out-loud to share their thoughts and insights as they moved through the process. Participants were verbally given specific instructions on which selections to make during the step-by-step screening process tasks, but they were not instructed on how to use the tool. Participants were specifically instructed not to disclose any personal experiences with elder mistreatment and were reminded several times that they would be performing task scenarios from different perspectives, i.e., "It is important to know that this study is not about your personal experience. We will ask you to use the tool from the perspective of a specific person described in the task."

Before each task, the facilitator explained the participant's role or persona they needed to assume and what they hoped to accomplish. The first task scenario involved having participants use the VOICES tool as if they were a completely independent, older adult who did not have a caregiver, and who did not rely on anyone to take care of them.

They were instructed to indicate that no one was treating them poorly or in a way that they did not want to be treated. The second task explored a scenario where the participant responded as if they had been positively screened as someone with a caregiver who was mistreating them. They indicated that they believed that they had been mistreated by this caregiver, and they also felt that this mistreatment may have led to some problems in their life. As a result, they were somewhat ready to disclose this information to someone that day using the VOICES tool.

Metrics. The VOICES tool's usability was evaluated quantitatively and qualitatively through effectiveness, efficiency, and satisfaction metrics. Usability effectiveness was measured as the percentage of tasks completed successfully. Usability efficiency was measured as the average time to perform a task and assessed based on issues observed during performance of the tasks. Usability satisfaction was measured by user satisfaction ratings (i.e., from post-task and post-study questionnaires) and written or verbal feedback on the questionnaires, and verbal comments from each session. While effectiveness and efficiency measures were quantitative, satisfaction was measured qualitatively.

The surveys collected demographics, usability perceptions, ease-of-use questions, familiarity and comfortability with technology, current emotional state, understanding of elder mistreatment principles, and open-ended qualitative feedback. The System Usability Scale (SUS), an industry standard, asked participants to rate their level of agreement to 10 user satisfaction statements; the SUS has been proven to be accurate for small sample sizes of 8–14 [21–23]. The Computer Efficacy Scale, a 10 question, validated survey for measuring comfortability with technology, was administered to assess participant's level of technological competency [24]. Emotional reactions to VOICES were assessed using the 10-item International Positive and Negative Affect Schedule Short Form (I-PANAS-SF) [25]. A five-question comprehension survey tested participants' knowledge of mistreatment after using VOICES. Open-ended questions provided an opportunity for participant recommendations and targeted potential challenges.

2.4 Recruiting Strategy

A significant challenge in conducting this study was reaching and recruiting potential participants. While recruiting participants for a typical usability study can take 2–3 weeks, reaching potential participants with specific disabilities can take considerably more time. Additionally, the eligibility requirements for the current study required locating participants with visual and hearing disabilities who were 60 years or older, which took more than 2 months.

Successful recruiting efforts are primarily built on establishing relationships with individuals within the specific communities. Finding "champions" within the user communities who can spread the word about the study and are credible voices is the most effective and efficient way to find potential participants. For example, individuals who are deaf may also identify as "uppercase Deaf," meaning that they share a language

– American Sign Language (ASL) – and a culture; members of this group use sign language as a primary means of communication and hold a set of beliefs about themselves and their connection to the larger society [26].

Sources. Participants for the current study were recruited in a variety of ways, including through flyers on information boards (physical and virtual); local and professional organization newsletters and listservs; social media; disabilities offices within universities and colleges; and our organization's own professional and personal networks and websites. Suggestions for finding older participants who are blind, have low vision, are deaf, or are hard of hearing include: Centers for independent living, disability rights coalitions, nursing homes and assisted living facilities. For individuals who are blind or have low vision, contact local blind and low vision organizations and associations, e.g., National Federation of the Blind, American Council for the Blind, or Braille Institute. For deaf and hard of hearing associations, try local chapters of the National Association of the Deaf or Hearing Loss Association of America.

Scheduling. Individuals with disabilities, including older adults who are using assistive technologies, may require extra time to complete the usability evaluation. For example, based on prior findings [27] and anecdotal evidence from other researchers and practitioners, it is recommended that a 1:4:4 (no visual disabilities:low vision:blind) rule of thumb be used for estimating how much time to allow for individuals with visual impairments. If an individual who is sighted takes 10 min. to complete the task, then it is reasonable to anticipate that an individual who is blind and using a screen reader may require 40 min. This is not because individuals with visual impairments are less capable than those without, but rather because assistive technology and different ways of interacting can take more time, particularly as most products are designed or optimized for individuals who do not have disabilities.

To help with planning for sessions, it is suggested to find out during the recruiting process what assistive technology the participant typically uses and/or requires to be able to participate in the study. Anticipating how frequently a potential participant uses assistive technology, and their level of confidence is important for understanding if they are a novice or are a more expert user. When scheduling, participants should be informed about the duration of their session ahead of time, and it may be helpful to build in a buffer of a least 30 min between sessions (e.g., allow time for any technical issues that may have happened during the previous session, to account for a participant who is late, time for recordings to finish saving after a session has finished, time to set up for next participant, time to take a break to use the bathroom, etc.).

2.5 Participants

The (n = 14) participants in this study included three user groups, with seven participants who were blind (in both eyes), three with low vision (20/70 to 20/200, corrected vision), and four who were hard of hearing (bi-lateral hearing loss). Although invited, no deaf participants completed the online recruiting eligibility screener before the data collection was suspended due to COVID-19 research restrictions. All blind participants and two low vision participants used the iPad's native VoiceOver screen reader mode, while all hard of hearing participants and one low vision participant used the VOICES Vicky coach mode. Participants with low vision were asked whether they typically would use VoiceOver. Eight participants were male and six were female. Twelve participants identified as White, while two identified as Black or African American. Age ranged from 62 to 80 (average age, 67; median age, 68). General Internet use was uniformly high with 12 participants reporting using the Internet daily and two at least weekly, accessed on either a desktop computer, laptop, tablet, or smartphone. Ratings for confidence in their abilities to use new technology was relatively high, average of 7.7 (Scale: 10 = "Very confident" to 0 = "Not confident at all"). Participants received a $75 gift card for participating in the usability session as a thank-you for their time.

3   Results

Our iterative enhancement and usability evaluation of the VOICES tool was conducted in two phases. First, we conducted Phase 1 of the usability evaluation with six participants. Then, some enhancements were made to the VOICES tool to improve the reading sequence and focus order (e.g., to try to ensure the screen reader/virtual coach would start at the top of a screen, focus would stay within a pop-up region, etc.), especially for participants using VoiceOver mode. Later, Phase 2 was conducted with 8 participants to complete the usability evaluation after the Phase 1 enhancements.

The following tables (see Tables 1 and 2) provide a summary of the results by phase, including the participant group, which mode of the VOICES tool was used, whether they were successful on their own for each task, and each participant's System Usability Scale (SUS) score and Computer Efficacy Scale (CES) response average. Overall, five participants used the Vicky coach mode and eight participants used the VoiceOver mode.

Table 1. Summary of Phase 1 of usability evaluation

Participant*	Group	Mode of VOICES tool	Task 1: completed successfully on own?	Task 2: completed successfully on own?	SUS scores	CES avg.
P1	Hard of hearing	Vicky coach	Yes	Yes	90	10
P3	Blind	VoiceOver	No	No	55	9.6
P4	Low vision	Vicky coach	Yes	No	77.5	7.1
P5	Blind	VoiceOver	No	Yes	55	9.5
P6	Hard of hearing	Vicky coach	Yes	Yes	100	9.4
%/Avg.			60%	60%	76	9.1

*The data from P2 (a blind participant) was dropped in this case because they had only used an Android device (i.e., this particular evaluation was focused on participants who already use an iPad).

Table 2. Summary of Phase 2 of usability evaluation

Participant	Group	Mode of VOICES tool	Task 1: completed successfully on own?	Task 2: completed successfully on own?	SUS scores	CES avg.
P7	Hard of hearing	Vicky coach	Yes	Yes	87.5	8.5
P8	Low vision	VoiceOver	Yes	No	80	7.2
P9	Blind	VoiceOver	No	No	90	6.4
P10	Hard of hearing	Vicky coach	Yes	Yes	100	8.9
P11	Blind	VoiceOver	Yes	Yes	92.5	9.2
P12	Blind	VoiceOver	Yes	Yes	90	7.3
P13	Blind	VoiceOver	No	Yes	90	5.4
P14	Low vision	VoiceOver	No	No	95	6.8
%/Avg.			63%	63%	91	7.5

Across the two phases, six participants completed the tasks successfully on their own; seven participants (mostly participants using VoiceOver) completed the tasks with some intervention or help from the moderator. The help or slight prompts given to participants was related to the focus or reading order not always starting at the top of a screen (e.g., participant may not have realized they were on a new screen), lack of instructions/feedback or focus in relation to available buttons (e.g., "Continue" button on first screen, "Play" button and "Close" button for a video dialog), or lack of confirmation after an option had been selected or unselected (e.g., number on the interactive ruler prompt or an answer to a question). Overall, participants using VoiceOver mode with the VOICES tool had longer task times across the phases.

The SUS scores were promising in relation to the usability of the tool: The majority of participants had SUS scores in the acceptable range (above 70) across the phases and most of the participants in Phase 2 had SUS scores of 90 or above.

Based on the responses to the CES [11, 24], there was a range of overall confidence with new technology across participants. Most participant responses to the CES were on the higher end with an average of 8.1 across the phases, although three of the participants (two blind and one with low vision in Phase 2) had CES response averages below 7, indicating somewhat less comfort with navigating digital tools independently.

Of all the participants, 12 (92%) stated that they would recommend the VOICES tool to others. However, five participants also thought a user would need some familiarity with this type of technology (or VoiceOver for that version of the tool). Participants also suggested a "coach" who could explain how to use the technology and provide assistance if needed, as well as help with an older adult's potential anxiety or fear in relation to technology (i.e., as stated earlier, most of the participants in this particular study had high levels of confidence with technology and had used an iPad before). One participant who used the VoiceOver mode thought that this type of screening should be done with a real person due to older adults having potential aversion toward or lack of experience with this type of technology.

The majority of participants had positive reactions to using the VOICES tool. Most found VOICES easy to use and easy to navigate (although most participants using the VoiceOver mode did receive some form of help during the tasks). In relation to recommending the tool, most thought this would be an important tool for mistreatment screening (e.g., educational and helpful in conveying information, useful option for people to express themselves, less intimidating or judgmental if dealing with a real person for this topic, etc.). Participants who were hard of hearing or had low vision appreciated the larger text size, color choices, and high contrast (see Fig. 3). Some of the low vision participants suggested the inclusion of additional options for preferences (e.g., switch between contrast modes, enlarge text).

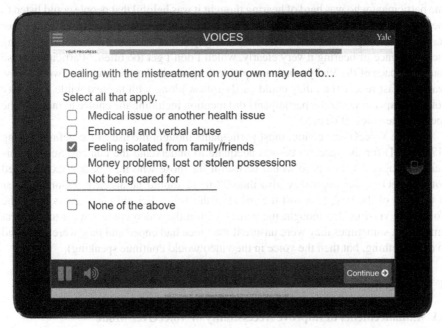

Fig. 3. Example of VOICES tool page with checkbox selection options.

Although the VOICES tool was intuitive to most, some participants suggested adding content or other features to help with getting started and to check on an answer, if needed. For example, some participants were unclear at first that they needed to use the "Continue" button after the first screen was read out (especially for the VoiceOver users) and the addition of brief introductory instructions for the tool would be helpful. Additionally, VoiceOver users suggested the inclusion of in-tool help or optional instructions at the beginning for those who may be infrequent VoiceOver users or needed a refresher. The inclusion of a "Back" button for each slide would also provide a way to correct an earlier mistake for a question or to check an answer.

Across the modes and phases, most participants thought the content was easy to understand (e.g., clear wording for questions and choices, helpful illustrations/graphics, brief amount of text on each screen). Additionally, most participants liked (or were not bothered by) the use of first person (e.g., "I'm sorry to hear you've been mistreated. You're a strong person to admit this...") throughout the VOICES tool; several participants thought this type of language could be helpful by making the tool feel more personable, and some VoiceOver users thought this type of approach would be familiar to VoiceOver users already. For the 5-question comprehension survey that tested the participants' understanding of the information after using the VOICES tool, 10 of the 13 participants scored 100% and 3 of the participants scored 80%. However, some of the participants did think the reading level of the language was still a bit high and one participant suggested indicating that further explanations will be given for terms throughout the use of the tool to reassure users.

Participants who used the Vicky mode appreciated the voice narration. For example, one participant who was hard of hearing thought it was helpful that people could listen to the voice instead of reading as well as follow along with the text if preferred, and another stated: "Normally I'd just use the text, but I enjoyed the voice so much. I was enjoying the experience of hearing it very clearly, which I don't get too often." Participants also found the pace of the Vicky coach acceptable despite whether they felt they were a slow reader or fast reader (i.e., they could easily follow along with the text while the Vicky voice was speaking); some participants did mention including the choice to increase the speed of the voice, if desired.

For the VoiceOver version, most participants thought the use of the default setting (175 WPM) for the speech rate was adequate to understand the content. Several participants suggested this pace would be useful for those who may be less experienced with VoiceOver, although they also thought there should be an easy option, such as at the start of the tool, to adjust the speed of the voice. Several participants using the VoiceOver version also thought the pauses within the video content were too long at times (e.g., sometimes they were unsure if the video had ended and they were supposed to do something, but then the voice in the video would continue speaking).

4   Discussion

4.1   Enhancements to Improve Accessibility of VoiceOver Mode

Most of the issues that participants encountered that required help from the moderator occurred in Phase 1 with the VoiceOver mode of the VOICES tool which included: inconsistent and unclear reading sequence, focus order, and screen reader feedback, as well as unclear button labels. Overall, this evaluation demonstrated the importance of ensuring that a tool works with the standard screen readers (i.e., VoiceOver on the iPad in this case) and does not interfere or overwrite how the assistive technology works. VoiceOver may not always pronounce words as intended either (e.g., caregiver), and therefore it is important to listen through all content beforehand to note if any adjustments are needed to ensure understanding for users. Also, as one participant stated, "I think it's wonderful that you've brought me in and bringing other people in to test at this point. I think it's a mistake not to have people with disabilities on your development team… get people with disabilities embedded at all stages of product development."

Consistent and Correct Reading & Focus Order. Across the tasks, the reading order (i.e., the order in which a screen reader provides content) and the focus order were not consistent or clear (e.g., reading did not always start automatically when a new screen loaded and did not always start at the top of the content, and the focus did not always stay within a video dialog that had opened), which led some participants to explore screens further to figure out whether all the content had been read aloud and where the focus was on the screen. To ensure a consistent and accurate experience, reading sequence and focus order need to advance to the correct location on the next screen (e.g., consistently start at the top of the content without forcing the user to find the beginning of the content), and reading order and focus should immediately move to a dialog when it is opened and focus should be restricted to the dialog's content while it is open (i.e., focus should not reach the page behind the dialog). For decorative images (such as within the banner area), use null alt text to ensure these will be ignored by the screen reader. Structural information should also be appropriately conveyed to users (e.g., headings should be appropriately structured, list items should be consistently coded as programmatic lists, etc.).

Clear and Consistent Feedback. Throughout the tasks, appropriate feedback was not always provided to the screen reader, which made it unclear to participants whether they had moved to a new screen at times (e.g., whether the page had updated to a new question to answer), when a video dialog had opened, and when a selection had been made on the screens with an interactive ruler (see Fig. 4). Screen readers and other assistive technologies should be clearly and consistently notified after completing an action and/or when page content has changed or updated (e.g., after moving to a new screen/page, when a dialog has opened or closed, after making a selection, etc.) to ensure users receive audio feedback via VoiceOver.

In addition, information or feedback should not be conveyed through the use of color alone (e.g., after selecting a number on the ruler, see Fig. 4), and videos should also not start playing automatically without warning and without an option to pause or stop the video, especially if the audio of the video interferes with the feedback from the screen reader (e.g., participants were confused about what was happening when VoiceOver and a video were speaking at the same time).

Descriptive and Associated Labels. Participants encountered some difficulties when trying to use the controls within the video dialogs due to unclear button labels. For example, the label for the "Play" button included additional information regarding the length of the video which obscured the specific button purpose and led some participants to miss the button entirely and require help. Interactive controls (e.g., buttons, form elements, etc.) require associated and clear labels to ensure a screen reader recognizes and provides the label with type of input to the user.

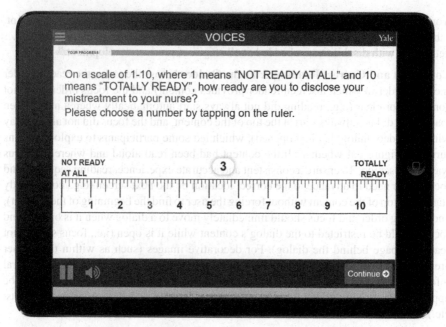

Fig. 4. VOICES selection 'ruler' with 3 selected.

4.2 Importance of Flexibility for Universal Design

During our sessions with participants, we observed their usage of the VOICES tool and asked post-study interview questions to learn more about their experiences with the tool and their broader experiences. Overall, the observations and comments gathered from this study demonstrated the importance of flexibility and agility [28, 29] in the universal design of the VOICES tool to support a range of functional and technical needs across disabilities. Most importantly, the default design of the tool should be equally usable for older adults with or without disabilities and be flexible enough to allow for a range of abilities (e.g., easily accessible instructions) and preferences (e.g., easily accessible setup options at the start of the tool to make adjustments based on their needs, if desired) to facilitate further ease of use.

As already described in the results, participants recommended adding options to adjust the text (e.g., text size or contrast options). In addition, although having captions for videos turned on as a default is useful to easily provide this option, one participant mentioned that they are a slow reader and therefore find video captions distracting; therefore, providing an option to easily turn off captions if desired is also helpful.

Participants described adding options to easily adjust the volume and speech rate, although most thought the default speech rate should still be close to a speaking rate to work well for a broad audience (i.e., a "kiosk voice"). Two participants thought there should be an option to choose between female or male voices. As one participant brought up, for older adults, high-frequency hearing loss occurs first [30]. Sounds at a higher pitch can be more difficult for older adults to hear and difficulties related to frequency can also vary depending on whether a person is using hearing aids or has cochlear implants (e.g., lower frequency sounds may be more difficult to hear with cochlear implants); therefore, providing easily accessible options at the start to adjust the gender, pitch, and the speed of the voice used for either mode of the VOICES tool would be helpful to meet the range of hearing needs of older adults [31].

Participants who used the VoiceOver mode of the VOICES tool mentioned a range of preferences regarding the size of the device. For example, some of these participants prefer a smaller device (e.g., iPhone or iPad mini) because they are more familiar with or used to the screen size and felt like they had to adjust to the layout being more spread out (e.g., inadvertently touching the screen at times). One participant also mentioned having a condition in which their hands shake a little, which can cause them to accidentally touch other parts of the screen on a larger size device versus an iPhone size. Another participant mentioned that although a larger screen size could be helpful for some with low vision, a smaller screen size could be more helpful for some conditions, such as tunnel vision (i.e., vision is constricted to a central, tunnel-like field of vision). However, some participants also thought the larger size was helpful so the layout was not as crowded together on the screen (versus on an iPhone) and could allow for even larger text size if needed. Another participant suggested considering the option of an external Bluetooth keyboard to use with the iPad. Overall, a range of potential options for users could be helpful to meet a variety of needs or preferences.

When asked whether they would be comfortable using the VOICES tool without headphones in a public setting, most participants agreed that having headphones would be very important to them to preserve their privacy while using this mistreatment screening tool. However, preferences regarding the type of headphones that would work varied across the participants, indicating that a range of headphones options should be offered. For example, users who are hard of hearing may wear some form of traditional hearing aid(s) (e.g., in-the-canal, in the ear, behind the ear) or have cochlear implant(s), and their hearing aids may have additional features such as telecoils and/or Bluetooth compatibility to pick up audio from a phone or other type of device [32]. Most of the participants who were hard of hearing would prefer to use over-ear headphones versus earbuds to avoid having to take out their hearing aids and/or to help block out background noise. One participant said they cannot wear headphones due to feedback issues and they instead prefer to use a neck or induction loop, and another said they have found it difficult to use headphones due to their cochlear implant and would prefer to read the text on the screen (and the option to turn off the voice narration) for privacy if in a public setting. Although one participant suggested the possibility of using Bluetooth capability if a person's hearing aid(s) included this feature instead of using headphones, they also thought it would depend on whether the person was familiar with how this feature would work.

In terms of privacy, some participants also described the issue of the screen being visible and the need for a private setting when using this type of tool. Some of the participants who used the VoiceOver version described the issue of being unaware if someone is looking at your screen when you are blind, and therefore recommended an option at the start of the tool to have the display turned off while they are using VoiceOver (i.e., "Screen Curtain") to hear the audio with headphones.

Across the versions, some participants also thought a user should use the VOICES tool in a private room or booth-type situation along with headphones and without the presence of a caregiver or family member to ensure their privacy. Additionally, although participants with dexterity impairments were not included in this particular study, we determined considerations from previous research related to the environment of a private room: A tablet should not be fully attached to a surface (such as a fixed stand) to allow the user to hold the device or move it around on a surface if needed, and an adjustable surface allows for various height and angle options for ease of viewing and arm support for users with dexterity limitations [19].

The VOICES tool is still in the early stages of development and further evaluation with older adults with other types of disabilities (e.g., cognitive, physical, etc.) and abilities or experiences (e.g., little or no familiarity with an iPad or any type of tablet or smartphone device) is needed to ensure ease of use, as well as flexibility to support diverse users.

Acknowledgements. The authors acknowledge Ossama Ali, MSU UARC user experience intern, for his assistance with data collection and preliminary analysis.

Funding Source. This project is funded by a National Institute on Aging of the National Institutes of Health grant to Yale University (3R01AG060084-02S1), and a supplemental award from Yale University to Michigan State University (3R24OD016474-07S1). The content is solely the responsibility of the authors and does not necessarily represent the official views of the National Institutes of Health.

References

1. Rosen, T., et al.: Review of programs to combat elder mistreatment: focus on hospitals and level of resources needed. J. Am. Geriatr. Soc. **67**(6), 1286–1294 (2019). https://doi.org/10.1111/jgs.15773
2. Lachs, M.S., Pillemer, K.: Elder abuse. Lancet **364**(9441), 1263–1272 (2004). https://doi.org/10.1016/s0140-6736(04)17144-4
3. Centers for Disease Control and Prevention: Understanding Elder Abuse (2016)
4. Ejaz, F.K., Rose, M., Reynolds, C., Bingle, C., Billa, D., Kirsch, R.: A novel intervention to identify and report suspected abuse in older, primary care patients. J. Am. Geriatr. Soc. **68**(8), 1748–1754 (2020). https://doi.org/10.1111/jgs.16433
5. Abujarad, F., et al.: Development and usability evaluation of VOICES: a digital health tool to identify elder mistreatment. J. Am. Geriatr. Soc. 1–10 (2021). https://doi.org/10.1111/jgs.17068
6. Dong, X.Q.: Elder abuse: systematic review and implications for practice. J. Am. Geriatr. Soc. **63**(6), 1214–1238 (2015). https://doi.org/10.1111/jgs.13454
7. Ziminski Pickering, C.E., Rempusheski, V.F.: Examining barriers to self-reporting of elder physical abuse in community-dwelling older adults. Geriatr. Nurs. **32**(2), 120–125 (2014). https://doi.org/10.1016/j.gerinurse.2013.11.002
8. Burnes, D., et al.: Prevalence of and risk factors for elder abuse and neglect in the community: a population-based study. J. Am. Geriatr. Soc. **63**(9), 1906–1912 (2015). https://doi.org/10.1111/jgs.13601

9. Lees-Haggerty, K., Rosen, T., Fulmer, T.: The national collaboratory to address elder mistreatment: coordinating networks of care. Innov. Aging **3**(Suppl 1), S74–S74 (2019). https://doi.org/10.1093/geroni/igz038.288

10. De Vito, D.A., et al.: User-centered design and interactive health technologies for patients. Comput. Inform. Nurs. **27**(3), 175–183 (2009). https://doi.org/10.1097/ncn.0b013e31819f7c7c

11. Abujarad, F., et al.: Building an informed consent tool starting with the patient: the patient-centered Virtual Multimedia Interactive Informed Consent (VIC). AMIA Annual Symp. Proc. **2017**, 374–383 (2017). PMCID: PMC5977640 PMID: 29854101

12. Ng, J.Y., Ntoumanis, N., Thøgersen-Ntoumani, C., Deci, E.L., Ryan, R.M., Duda, J.L., Williams, G.D.: Self-determination theory applied to health contexts a meta-analysis. Perspect. Psych. Sci. **7**(4), 325–340 (2012). https://doi.org/10.1177/1745691612447309

13. D'Onofrio, G., Pantalon, M.V., Degutis, L.C., Fiellin, D.A., O'Connor, P.G.: Development and implementation of an emergency practitioner-performed brief intervention for hazardous and harmful drinkers in the emergency department. Acad. Emerg. Med: Official J. Soc. Acad. Emerg. Med. **12**(3), 249–256 (2005) https://doi.org/10.1197/j.aem.2004.10.021

14. Dow, B., Gahan, L., Gaffy, E., Joosten, M., Vrantsidis. F., Jarred, M.: Barriers to disclosing elder abuse and taking action in Australia. J. Fam. Violence **35**(8), 853–861 (2020). https://doi.org/10.1007/s10896-019-00084-w

15. D'Onofrio, G., Degutis, L.C.: Integrating Project ASSERT: a screening, intervention, and referral to treatment program for unhealthy alcohol and drug use into an urban emergency department. Acad. Emerg. Med: Official J. Soc. Acad. Emerg. Med. **17**(8), 903–911 (2010). https://doi.org/10.1111/j.1553-2712.2010.00824.x

16. Lachs, M.S., Pillemer, K.A.: Elder abuse. New England J. Med. **373**(20), 1947–1956 (2015). https://doi.org/10.1056/nejmra1404688

17. International Organization for Standardization: Ergonomics of human-system interaction—Part 11: Usability: Definitions and concepts (ISO Reference No. 9241-11:2018) (2018)

18. Pierce, G.L., Jackson, J.E., Swierenga, S.J.: Enhanced User Interface and Interaction Design Standards for Accessible Mobile Voting Systems. Technical Report, Michigan State University, Usability/Accessibility Research and Consulting, East Lansing, MI (2014)

19. Ismirle, J., O'Bara, I., Swierenga, S.J., Jackson, J.: Touchscreen voting interface design for persons with disabilities: insights from usability evaluation of mobile voting prototype. In: Proceedings of the Human Factors and Ergonomics Society 2016 Annual Meeting, vol. 60, no. 1, pp. 780–784 (2016). https://doi.org/10.1177/1541931213601179

20. Jackson, J.E., Ismirle, J., Swierenga, S.J., Blosser, S.R., Pierce, G.L.: Joystick interaction strategies of individuals with dexterity impairments: observations from the smart voting joystick usability evaluation. In: Antona, M., Stephanidis, C. (eds.) LNCS, vol. 9178, pp. 192–203. Springer International, Switzerland (2015). https://doi.org/10.1007/978-3-319-20687-5_19

21. U.S. Department of Health & Human Services: System Usability Scale (SUS). https://digital.gov/2014/08/29/system-usability-scale-improving-products-since-1986/

22. Brooke, J.: SUS: a retrospective. J. Usab. Studies **8**(2), 29–40 (2013)

23. Bangor, A., Kortum, P.T., Miller, J.T.: An empirical evaluation of the system usability scale. Int. J. Human-Comp. Interact. **24**(6), 574–594 (2008). https://doi.org/10.1080/10447310802205776

24. Laver, K., George, S., Ratcliffe, J., Crotty, M.: Measuring technology self efficacy: reliability and construct validity of a modified computer self efficacy scale in a clinical rehabilitation setting. Disab. and Rehab. **34**(3), 220–227 (2012). https://doi.org/10.3109/09638288.2011.593682

25. Thompson, E.R.: Development and validation of an internationally reliable short-form of the Positive and Negative Affect Schedule (PANAS). J. Cross-Cult. Psych. **38**(2), 227–242 (2007)

26. National Association of the Deaf: Community and culture – Frequently asked questions. https://www.nad.org/resources/american-sign-language/community-and-culture-frequently-asked-questions/

27. Swierenga, S.J., Propst, D.B., Pierce, G.L., Sung, J.E.: Impact of visual impairments on the duration of usability tests. Poster presentation at the Usability Professionals Association International Conference 2011, Atlanta, GA (2011)

28. Harte, R.P., et al.: Human centred design considerations for connected health devices for the older adult. J. Pers. Med. **4**(2), 245–281 (2014). https://doi.org/10.3390/jpm4020245

29. Story, M.F.: Maximizing usability: the principles of universal design. Assist. Tech. **10**(1), 4–12 (1998). https://doi.org/10.1080/10400435.1998.10131955

30. U.S. National Library of Medicine: Age-related hearing loss. https://medlineplus.gov/genetics/condition/age-related-hearing-loss/#diagnosis

31. Blair, J., Abdullah, S.: It didn't sound good with my cochlear implants: understanding the challenges of using smart assistants for deaf and hard of hearing users. Proc. ACM Interact. Mobile, Wear. Ubiquit. Tech. **4**(4), 1–27 (2020). https://doi.org/10.1145/3432194

32. Mayo Clinic Staff: Hearing aids: how to choose the right one. https://www.mayoclinic.org/diseases-conditions/hearing-loss/in-depth/hearing-aids/art-20044116

Ergonomic and Usability Analysis of Platform for Communication of People with Limited Talk

Caroline Torres[1](✉) and Marcelo M. Soares[1,2](✉)

[1] Federal University of Pernambuco, Recife, Brazil
[2] School of Design, Hunan University, Changsha, People's Republic of China

Abstract. The educational applications developed for smartphones inaugurate a new form of interaction, since the experience of use happens with the touch of the fingers on the screen, allowing a greater control on the interface. However, because it is a recent equipment, it still needs studies that lead to the adequate development of these applications, especially when these involve the internalization of knowledge beyond the operational level. Therefore, they involve conducting usability tests and analyzing the results.

Previously, projects were carried out for certain segments of the population today, designers should think about the wide variety of existing consumers and their limitations. Thus, a design project must contain features that can encompass as many users as possible; what we call universal design. These types of concerns aim to improve the usability of the product and facilitate its use for the largest number of people, including left-handed people, elderly people, people with disabilities and/or people with special needs, always observing their daily lives.

In this context, this research aimed to study the most appropriate way to present educational content on smartphones, starting from the methodological analyzes of Leventhal and Barnes (1998), regarding three applications: LetMeTalk, Aboard and Jade Autism. This work will not only focus on the ergonomic and usability analysis of platforms for alternative communication, but above all on the learning efficiency and skills of people with speech limitations, such as autistic individuals.

Keywords: Communication media · Users · Limitations · Universal design · Usability · Autism

1 Introduction

Design has always been related to various areas of knowledge, such as psychology, engineering, art, and lately it is increasingly related to usability, where product design has shifted from being object-centric to user-centric (Iida and Buarque 2016).

From the advances in technology, the market for consumer products was characterized by constant changes, including more user interaction and practicality with tools such as smartphones and tablets, which appeared in the market in 2007. Combining this advance in technology, With the number of people who somehow need to use an alternative medium to communicate, digital tools have increased in importance. As a result,

© Springer Nature Switzerland AG 2021
M. M. Soares et al. (Eds.): HCII 2021, LNCS 12780, pp. 361–372, 2021.
https://doi.org/10.1007/978-3-030-78224-5_25

content production also had to be rethought and adapted to these new ways of relating to learning, always thinking about the user and how he will handle the artifact in his daily life and how it will positively influence in their learning development (Traxler 2007).

Every day millions of people still seek full inclusion in society, as they have difficulty communicating, moving around, shopping, using transport, and still suffer from it. One alternative that many researchers have been working on and refining for years is the use of digital technologies to improve communication for this group of people, such as mobile apps. An entire path had to be trod to achieve the goal of creating a mobile app that could greatly benefit the treatment of children with autism, for example. Initially, it was necessary to establish milestones in order to define the necessary steps for the construction of an efficient and effective tool. The first step outlined was to understand the particularities of the autistic universe. Knowledge of the symptoms, characteristics of the autism spectrum, specificities, peculiarities, variants and other details of this universe was fundamental, after all, all software needs to adapt to the real needs of its target audience, which in this particular case are children with autism (Farias and Cunha 2013).

2 Methodological Procedures

For this study we analyzed applications that could be evaluated by usability principles. These are: Jade Autism, LetMeTalk, and Aboard, which are available for free from App Stores accessed by people around the world to seek information, entertainment, and other content that can help the everyday lives of people with disabilities. speaks. The principles studied here and led to analyze the applications in question were proposed by Leventhal and Barnes (1998), for the evaluation of their interfaces.

The methodology of this research is qualitative and quantitative, composed of two phases: the first, theoretical and analytical, aims to identify the methods, techniques and/or tools directed to an ergonomic and usability evaluation of communication applications; The second part consists of a field study, divided into similar steps, with questionnaires, interviews and observations on the handling of the applications studied by the research subjects on smartphones, in order to verify the effectiveness of these applications.

The research is initially grouped into 20 subjects: 5 autistic children, aged 2–8 years; 5 fathers or mothers of these autistic; 5 speech-language and 5 occupational therapy professionals; recommended by Nielsen (2006) for quantitative studies.

Regarding the methodology itself, for this project was chosen the methodology of Leventhal and Barnes (1998), because it presents more complete principles in relation to systems interface and welcomes other methodologies for itself, such as the models developed by Shackel (1991), Nielsen (1993), and Eason (1984) for usability analysis on software and websites.

According to Falcão and Soares (2013), the proposed model is an attempt to put together the most important factors of the three models that were considered, and assumes that a number of variables that are taken together will determine if the interface has good usability. These variables are divided into: situational variables and user interface variables, as illustrated in the Fig. 1.

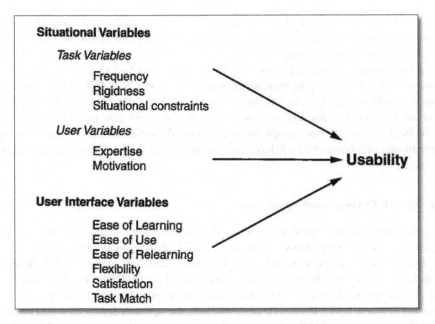

Fig. 1. Usability model proposed by Leventhal and Barnes (1998). Source: Falcon and Soares (2013).

According to the situational variables, the frequency was recognized by Eason (1984) as a usability influencing variable, since if a task is performed too often, it becomes easy to perform later due to the memorization of the sequence by the user. user. Rigidness is linked to the amount of options that are available to the user to perform the same task. If many options are available to the user to complete a task, the level of stiffness is low. In this case, an interface that offers a simple and clear sequence should be friendlier than one that has an unclear sequence. Situational constraints refer to more specific constraints, such as knowing whether the task has unusual characteristics or whether a safety procedure must be performed before it can be executed, for example. Regarding situational variables related to the user, Eason (1984) realized that experience and motivation can directly influence the usability of a product or system. The user who has previous experience with a similar activity, will certainly be easier to use a product. Assuming the same assumption, a user who is more motivated to perform a task will certainly do it more easily and successfully (Araújo et al. 2017).

3   Applied Study

Aware that technology has proven beneficial in many sectors, including health and education, as it enables the automation of various tasks and facilitates the accounting of treatment outcomes, it is believed that the use of computer resources will generate positive impacts on the treatment of people with disabilities, since it has an increasingly ubiquitous character in the everyday life of society (Farias and Cunha 2013).

The significant evolution of mobile technologies has expanded the options of digital inclusion strategies and features as they allow interaction anytime and anywhere without the limitations of time and space as they are connected to wireless networks. integrate mobility, communication and processing power (Hassan and Al-Sadi 2009). Visual stimulation, as it is worked on in training methods such as PECS and TEACCH, tends to ensure a child with ASD - Autistic Spectrum Disorder, for example, to better express their feelings, such as discomfort or need for something. For this, many professionals in the field of occupational therapy and speech therapy prefer the use of these learning mechanisms, where the child will have more freedom and options in social development, for example.

3.1 Speech Development Applications

The following are the three applications that will be used in this dissertation for ergonomic and usability analysis. They are: LetMeTalk, Aboard and Jade Autism.

LetMeTalk is an app that originated in Berlin, Germany, and is funded through donations, so it's free. People can easily find it for download from the Play Store or the official app page: https://www.letmetalk.info/download.html and can be used for Android or Apple IOS. On first use of LetMeTalk, the app will download a data packet with all images (about 70 Mb), then no need to stay connected anymore (LETMETALK - https://www.letmetalk.info/en).

LetMeTalk's proposal allows you to align images so that your set consists of meaningful sentences. Image alignment is known as ISPC (Pictographic Symbol Interchange for Communication, PECS) or CAA (Alternative and Augmentative Communication, AAC). The interface (Fig. 3) consists of several categories, where the professional, family member or even the user with preserved movements can navigate and assemble phrases according to their needs. The application comes pre-configured for children with autism spectrum disorders and has voice support for the images and phrases already established and for those that can be added later by the user and/or professional who helps with the use of LetMeTalk, in the languages: English, Spanish, French, Italian and German. Other languages supported without voice support: Chinese, Portuguese, Brazilian Portuguese, Arabic, Russian, Polish, Bulgarian, Romanian, Galician, Catalan, Basque (LETMETALK - https://www.letmetalk.info/) (Fig. 2).

Fig. 2. LetMeTalk – screen. Source: LetMetalk (https://www.letmetalk.info/)

Jade Autism is an application for stimulation and development of autistic and down syndrome children. According to its developers, it is a game that stimulates cognitive development, memory, reasoning, skill and performance, and reports on the child's performance during the game, providing valuable data for the therapists involved to apply the game. best therapeutic plan and address the difficulties/deficiencies presented (JADE AUTISM). This game that was designed by Ronaldo Cohin, father of an Autistic child, and a student of Computer Science, from the University of Vila Velha - ES, had the validation and collaboration of APAE-ES speech therapist, Adriana Mallini. The idea for the creation of JADE came from his experience as a parent of a child with autism and immersions made at the Association of Parents and Friends of the Exceptional (APAE-ES), to elaborate the concept of the application. Any child can use Jade as long as they need cognitive stimulation. The example of: Neurotypic children; Autistic Children (ASD); Children with Down Syndrome (T21); Children with Attention Deficit Disorder, with or without Hyperactivity Disorder (ADHD and ADHD); Children with any unspecified syndrome with cognitive comorbidities (JADE AUTISM).

The following figure (Fig. 4) shows the Jade Autism application home screen. Note that for a better assessment by professionals who help autistic, for example, has the option of "results", thus, it is possible to have a better analysis of user development against the application.

Fig. 3. Jade home screen. Source: Google Play - Jade Autism

Finally, the "ABoard" Software (or Portuguese "Prancha Assistive") is an Augmentative and Alternative Communication (CAA) application for tablet (Fig. 5), whose differential is its ability to give suggestions, which speed up the production of meaningful sentences (ASSISTIVE GROUP). It was developed by researchers from the education and computer centers of the Federal University of Pernambuco - UFPE, in order to benefit people with some speech limitation. With the use of this app, people with stroke sequelae; head trauma; children with cerebral palsy; autism; people with intellectual disabilities; Down's syndrome; are having the ability to communicate better (ASSISTIVE GROUP - https://www.facebook.com/AssistiveCAA/).

Fig. 4. Aboard. Source: Assistive CAA

"The app is based on the use of symbols, images, which are easier to understand. Therefore, when choosing a symbol or image, he or she is choosing a word or set of words that will express that person's desire and interest. And the set of these symbols form a sentence, where this sentence will express what he wants to communicate." Robson Fidalgo (ABorad Project Coordinator).

The high technology of the vocalizers (boards with voice production) or the computer with specific software, guarantee the communicative function great efficiency (Promines Institute 2017). This is how applications today seek to adapt their settings to this type of feature, aiming at the development of user speech, such as LetMeTalk, Aboard and Jade Autism.

4   Analysis

There are several types of product usability assessment that can be classified by subject, data collected, and purpose. For this research, the following methods were selected: Interviews Observation, Thinking Out Loud, Cognitive Walkthroughs Method, Questionnaires, that fit the methodology of Leventhal and Barnes (1998).

4.1   Interviews

Initially, 5 autistic parents and/or family members were asked to participate - direct users of the applications mentioned here. These volunteer family members were interviewed informally to find out: 1) the age of the autistic child, 2) the degree of autism, 3) other characteristics of autism that this child could have, 4) when diagnosed, 5) if you use medication, 6) if you have professional supervision, 7) if you go to school, and 8) if you use some method of training/speech development and skills. All interviews were conducted with the responsible parents of the autistic child, where they have direct contact with the child; which is included in the research as an inclusion factor for this method. In addition, both parents and autistic children conducted interviews at their homes, without the need for movement or distance from their usual place, which helped in the development of the task. All parents reported that their children have professional supervision; This corresponds to 100% of the autists observed. This same totality goes to school, however, an important point to note is that only 70% have this same monitoring in schools. That is, the child has access to education but, in the classroom, does not have adequate help for daily activities. Regarding the use of assistive technologies, to aid in the development of speech, skills and socialization of children, 90% answered that their children have the habit of using smartphones for games and other applications that help in this process.

4.2 Observation

According to Gil (2006) the observation "constitutes a fundamental element for the research", because it is from this that it is possible to delineate the stages of a study: formulate the problem, construct the hypothesis, define variables, collect data and so on. It was following this line of reasoning that the field observation method was one of the first to be performed. On the same day that interviews were conducted with relatives of autistic children, these users were observed with the applications under analysis in this study. It is noteworthy that there are different levels of participation, and the researcher can, from just watching, to acting in the situation object of observation. Thus, the observation presented here was semi-structured, given that the researcher has already arrived at the site with a table, previously prepared, about the methodology of Leventhal and Barnes (1998), in order to make the observations. Based on the same, where the observations were made 100% at the usual place of the autistic, that is, in their homes, with the prior permission of the parents. During the presentations or parent responsible for the child, each application and its functions are displayed, so that a child familiar with a technology and an interest in showing their emotions and uses it on the spot. I have always followed the same order: LetMeTalk, Aboard and Jade Autism. It was requested to register images of the child manipulating the applications, however, without showing the face, as shown in the following images.

4.3 Thinking Out Loud Method

The Thinking Out Loud Method was performed with all 10 (ten) volunteer professionals: 5 (five) Occupational Therapy and 5 (five) Speech Therapy. For inclusion criteria in the accomplishment of the methods it was necessary that the professionals had at least some experience with training methods and/or applications to aid in the communication of people with speech difficulties. For this method, each participant was asked, while handling the application (Fig. 6a, b), to report their experience and actions, in order for the researcher to acquire more information.

At the professionals' first contact with the LetMeTalk and Aboard applications, they all referred to the PECS training method. For those who had not handled the PECS, but had visual memory made by studies in their profession, they also found the application

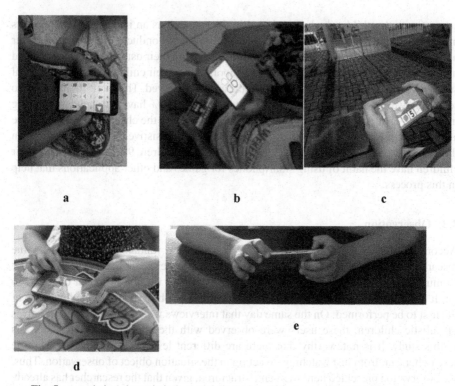

Fig. 5. a: autistic 1, b: autistic 2, c: autistic 3, d: autistic 4, e: autistic 5. source: Author

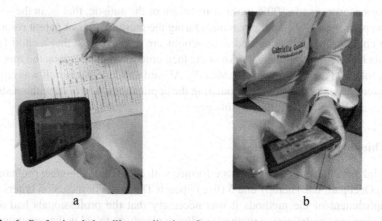

Fig. 6. Professionals handling applications for comparative analysis. Source: Author

very similar to the method. What they also didn't like about the app was the robotic voice that the app emits when clicking on an image or forming phrases.

4.4   Cognitive Walkthroughs Method

This technique was performed in conjunction with the Thinking Out Loud Method. An evaluator or group of evaluators inspects the interface of a product and/or system to assess the ease of understanding and direct user learning of that product which, in this case, it's autistic (Fig. 7).

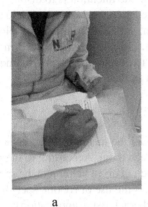 

a   b

Fig. 7. Professionals handling applications for comparative analysis. Source: Author

Faced with the combination of two methods: Thinking Aloud and Cognitive Walk-throughs Method, as occupational therapy professionals, who responded to research, concluded 100% of autistic children, when the LetMeTalk manuscript is very easy to use. app. Thus, an assimilation of information contained in the application, very easily. One variable that questioned professionals a little more was the Nomenclature used. They explain that the application is very good, has a lot of information, but the terms used are not entirely allowed for children, with words that are difficult to pronounce.

4.5   Questionnaires

A questionnaire is not an official type of form, nor is it a list of questions gathered without prior planning. Rea and Parker (2000) define a questionnaire as a series of unstructured and well-structured questions that will systematically obtain the information sought by the researcher. Thus, this method gathered 4 opens questions for each professional, occupational therapy and speech therapy, in order to, together with the other methods already performed, better evaluate the LetMeTalk, Aboard and Jade Autism applications, against Assistive Technology and the development of speaks of autistic children. They were:

1. "Point out situations where you found the system easy to use"
2. "Point out situations where you had difficulties"
3. "Given the test, do you think the program has achieved the goal for which it was developed?"

4. "The space below is reserved for you to express your opinion and suggest system improvements"

As it was possible to observe while asking all the questions, the LetMeTalk and Aboard applications have a lot of similarities between them. Both reach their goals of helping in the speech development of autistic children, but, a pertinent characteristic is, as most professionals said, the use of robotic speech. As the intention is to distance the autistic person from this characteristic, applications aimed at communication should emit a more personified voice. The Jade Autism application, which was initially developed for the communication of people with limited speech, did not meet this need in this regard. As the professionals already mentioned, if it is to develop skills, environmental perception, etc., that's fine; another function would not fit the application.

5 Results and Discussions

As it was possible to observe during the realization of all the methods, the LetMeTalk and Aboard applications have a lot of similarities between them. According to the professionals who participated in this study both achieve their goals of helping in the speech development of autistic children, but a relevant feature is the use of robotic speech. As the intention is to distance the autistic person from this characteristic, applications aimed at communication should emit a more personified voice.

An important point in the Cognitive Walkthroughs Method that was made by one of the professionals was the need to include images and words with the way of speaking in some regions. It is understood that the applications are for worldwide use, anyone, from anywhere in the world can download and use perfectly, but this idea of getting closer to the environment in which the child is inserted helps even more in the development of communication.

A relevant fact about the layout of the applications is the size of the images and the way they are arranged on the device. As well as, the rotation of the screens. According to the Thinking Out Loud Method, performed by professionals, the LetMeTalk can be handled vertically or horizontally, but Aboard cannot. And this is a factor that makes it difficult at times when teaching autistic children, as some speech The Jade Autism application, which was initially developed for the communication of people with limited speech, did not meet this need in this regard. As the professionals have already mentioned in the questionnaires, if it is to develop skills, environmental perception, etc., that's fine; another function would not fit the application. It has different types of game categories, but it does not have many levels, which makes it a repetitive and tiring task. It draws the user's attention due to colors, animals, etc., but does not have the corresponding sound. So, some details that can be easily adjusted, are the ones that can make the application a very good tool for autistic children to develop a better perception of the things around them.

6 Conclusions

When it comes to Assistive Technology and Augmented Communication, it is very difficult not to encompass design. He is the one who will be part, from the creation of platforms that will help in the development of people with speech limitations, to the environment that the user will be inserted. An example of this is the participation of one of the applications analyzed here at the REC'n'Play Festival, held in the city of Recife, in 2018. "Held by Porto Digital", the Festival aims to transform and connect people of different backgrounds and intellectual backgrounds. to think about solutions to city and society problems.

Because the issues covered about autism are so intense and there are several communication failures between parents and schools, government, etc., graphic design is becoming a part of this world as it begins to bring information to everyone, whether through social networks, that are full of content, whether by books. And one of those very helpful books is, "Ten Things Every Child with Autism Wishes You Knew," by Ellen Notbohm. The version released in 2012 comes with in-depth updates and analysis on communication and social skills issues (Focus Intervention 2019).

Another major contribution to design is the awards apps have won, such as Jade Autism, which won first place in the BioInnovation Challenge 2019 (JADE AUTISM).

When talking about universal design care must be taken when referring to products and/or objects that can be used by all types of people. What is not true. What will exist is a series of criteria to be analyzed when developing a certain product so that it is cheaper to develop it with characteristics to accompany certain groups of people, with limitations or not, than, over time, adding special apparatuses to shape the object for use by this same segment of the population. Each person has their specific characteristics and when joining a group of people with similarities in these characteristics, such as intellectual disabilities, we need to analyze their daily life and how this user will deal with the product in which they are inserted.

References

Araujo, J., Pereira, M., Sousa, V.G., Campos, L.F.: User-Centered Design and Usability: A Proposal for a Mobile Application, pp. 1943–1954. Blucher, São Paulo (2017). ISSN 2318-6968. https://doi.org/10.5151/16ergodesign-0205

Assistive Group, Assistive CAA. https://www.facebook.com/AssistiveCAA/. Accessed 05 Oct 2017

Falcão, C.F., Soares, M.M.: Usability of Consumer Products: an analysis of concepts, methods and applications. Design Studies (2013)

Farias, E.B., Cunha, M.X.C.: Prototype of a software tool to support the treatment of children with Autism. In: Brazilian Symposium on Information Systems, vol. 9, pp. 332–342. João Pessoa - PB. Annals ... John Pessoa: SBSI, 2013 (2013)

Focus Intervenção. Focus tip. Rio Grande do Norte (2019). Instagram: @focusintervencao. https://www.instagram.com/focusintervencao/. Accessed 08 July 2019

Gil, A.C.: Methods and Techniques of Social Research. Atlas, São Paulo (2006)

Hassan, M.H., AL-Sadi, J.A.: New mobile learning adaptation model. Int. J. Interact. Mobile Technol. 3(4) (2009). ISSN: 1865-7923

Iida, I., Guimarães, Lia Buarque de Macedo.: Ergonomics: Design and Production. Edgard Blücher, Sao Paulo (2016)

Jade Autism. https://jadeautism.com/home. Accessed 04 April 2019

Letmetalk. Aplicação Grátis CAA. https://play.google.com/store/apps/details?id=de.appnotize.let metalk&hl=pt. Accessed 04 Mar 2018

372   C. Torres and M. M. Soares

Leventhal, L., Barnes, J.: Usability Engineering: Process, Products and Examples. Pearson, London (1998)

Promines Institute: Assistive Technology Single College (2017)

Rea, L.M., Parker, R.A.: Research methodology: from planning to execution. Trad. Nivaldo Montingelli Jr. Pioneer, Sao Paulo (2000)

Traxler, J.: Defining, discussing, and evaluating mobile learning: the moving finger writes and having writ... Int. Rev. Res. Open Distance Learn. 8(2) (2007)

Design Your Life: User-Initiated Design of Technology to Support Independent Living of Young Autistic Adults

Thijs Waardenburg[1,2]([⊠])(iD), Niels van Huizen[2], Jelle van Dijk[2](iD),
Maurice Magnée[1](iD), Wouter Staal[3,4,5](iD), Jan-Pieter Teunisse[1,6],
and Mascha van der Voort[2](iD)

[1] HAN University of Applied Sciences, Nijmegen, The Netherlands
{thijs.waardenburg,maurice.magnee,janpieter.teunisse}@han.nl
[2] University of Twente, Enschede, The Netherlands
{j.c.vanhuizen,jelle.vandijk,m.c.vandervoort}@utwente.nl
[3] Karakter Child and Adolescent Psychiatry University Centre,
Nijmegen, The Netherlands
w.staal@karakter.com
[4] Department of Cognitive Neuroscience, Donders Institute for Brain, Cognition and
Behavior, Radboud University Nijmegen Medical Centre, Nijmegen, The Netherlands
[5] Institute for Brian and Cognition, Leiden University, Leiden, The Netherlands
[6] Dr. Leo Kannerhuis, Oosterbeek, The Netherlands

Abstract. This paper describes the development of and first experiences
with 'Design Your Life': a novel method aimed at user-initiated design
of technologies supporting young autistic adults in independent living.
A conceptual, phenomenological background resulting in four core principles is described. Taking a practice-oriented Research-through-Design
approach, three co-design case studies were conducted, in which promising methods from the co-design literature with the lived experiences and
practical contexts of autistic young adults and their caregivers is contrasted. This explorative inquiry provided some first insights into several
design directions of the Design Your Life-process. In a series of new case
studies that shall follow, the Design Your Life-method will be iteratively
developed, refined and ultimately validated in practice.

Keywords: Autism · Assistive technology · Phenomenology ·
Participatory design · Research-through-Design · Independent living

1 Introduction

An estimated one in hundred people worldwide have been diagnosed with autism
[1]. While many autistic people have both the motivation and intellectual capacity to contribute fully to society, the group shows a relatively large percentage
of school dropout and unemployment, especially if a suitable support network
is lacking [2]. In recent years, participatory design has become of interest in

© Springer Nature Switzerland AG 2021
M. M. Soares et al. (Eds.): HCII 2021, LNCS 12780, pp. 373–386, 2021.
https://doi.org/10.1007/978-3-030-78224-5_26

the context of designing technologies that could support autistic people in daily life [3,4]. The motives for adopting a participatory design approach range from "addressing a pragmatic need to increase the fit between features and users' requirements" to "idealistic agendas related to empower people, democratise innovation and designing alternative futures" [5].

Morally, a call for empowerment through participation has been advocated more broadly within what is called the 'neurodiversity movement' [6]. According to Frauenberger, Makhaeva and Spiel, there is "consensus that participatory design is particularly powerful when creating technologies for groups who are typically marginalised in design and have life-worlds which are far removed from those of designers and researchers" [5].

The epistemic value of participatory design has been invoked as well: without a proper understanding of autistic experiences, designers may be at risk to end up creating technologies that are both stigmatising and ineffective [7]. Yet, evidence for the effectiveness of technology-based interventions remains limited [8,9]. One reason may be that it is inherently difficult for (non-autistic) designers to empathise with the lived experience of autism. Incorporating one's lived, subjective experiences into the design process is difficult, but this is especially complex in the context of autism due to differences in perceptions between autistic and non-autistic people. This is something Milton refers to as the 'double empathy problem' [10]. Another reason may be that the autistic population is itself highly heterogeneous, with each person having both individual support needs as well as highly personal and sometimes quite specific interests and capabilities. Estimates of intellectual capacities are highly variable in the autism spectrum as well, varying from intellectual disability in about forty percent of the autistic population to normal and (very) high IQ ranges [1].

Finally, many assistive technologies tend to be developed within the context of professionals and health care organisations seeking possibilities for technologically augmenting (or even partly replacing) existing therapeutic methods. This means that the function of the resulting living space, device or app will be grounded in the logic of formal therapy structures and objectives. As a result, such technologies may come to reflect a frame in which the autistic person is at the core seen as a person who displays dysfunctional behaviour, which needs somehow to be corrected, with the 'healthy' neurotypical person as the target model. In such cases, it can be argued that the main user of the product is in some sense not the autistic person but, for instance, the therapist, who uses the product to bring about a desired normative change in the patient. It is precisely this medical frame that autistic people may find disempowering.

Starting with these challenges in mind, a first iteration of the 'Design Your Life-method' (hereafter DYL) is developed: a co-design method that helps young autistic adults (hereafter YAA[1]) and their caregivers in designing a personalised,

---

[1] There appears to be no clear consensus on the naming of 'a person with an autism spectrum disorder' [11]. There are several variations, for instance: 'autistic person','person with autism', 'person who has autism', 'person on the spectrum', etc. In this research, the term 'young autistic adult' (abbr. as 'YAA', also in plural form) is used, without the intention to disregard various conceptions of the designation.

supportive, technological environment that contributes to independent living. Its purpose is two-fold. First, DYL brings creative forms of shared sense-making to the care practice. Second, DYL signifies the next step in reaching autistic empowerment by providing autistic individuals not just participation in a designer's project, but to instead provide them with tools to design and implement their own supportive interventions. This is guided by a phenomenological perspective on autistic experience as being fundamentally embodied, holistic and contextual in nature [12,13].

The rest of this article is organised as follows: With the challenges and values described in this introduction in mind, four core principles are described. These were brought in practice and further refined during three case studies described in the subsequent chapter. Reflecting on the cases studies, a first version of the DYL process is developed. Conclusions are discussed in the remainder of the article.

2 Four Core Principles

DYL underscores the phenomenological nature of (autistic) experiences. At its essence, phenomenology is the philosophical study of experience. It premiered in the transcendental phenomenology of German philosopher Edmund Husserl. Dourish explains that "Husserl was frustrated by the idea that science and mathematics were increasingly conducted on an abstract plane that was disconnected from human experience and human understanding" [14]. In other words, Husserl believed that abstract reasoning and idealised conceptualisation of world phenomena would severely gloss over everyday experiences.

Phenomenology is not new to the field of human-centred design. In the 1980s, a study by Winograd and Flores [15] invoked the work of phenomenologist Martin Heidegger to shed a new light on human-computer interaction. Later, Weiser [16] would build upon phenomenological insights to explore his vision for ubiquitous computing. Dourish places endeavours as such in a historical perspective. According to him, the very emergence of tangible and social computing signifies an appreciation of phenomenological thought. He writes:

> Instead of drawing on artefacts in the everyday world, it draws on the way the everyday world works or, perhaps more accurately, the way we experience the world. Both approaches draw on the fact that the ways in which we experience the world are through directly interacting with it, and that we act in the world by exploring the opportunities for action that it provides to us – whether through its physical configuration, or through socially constructed meanings. In other words, they share an understanding that you cannot separate the individual from the world in which that individual lives and acts [14].

Usually, 'young adult' refers to an age category of 16–30 years. In this study, a broader definition is used, namely 16–35 years, because the development towards more independence may occur on a later age.

Inspired by this phenomenological background, the four core principles for DYL are presented.

2.1 Focus on Experience

Although it is already entailed by a phenomenological approach itself, experience is the focal point of DYL. In the context of autism, one must observe that the design challenge is too often described in terms of functional and psycho-social limitations. Frauenberger, Makhaeva and Spiel explain that such a "reductionist model of disabilities" glosses over the importance of experience that autistic individuals have with technologies [17]. A mismatch ensues in which autistic individuals may abandon technologies that they find ineffective. This observation comes close to Husserl's aforementioned criticism of abstraction. By describing autism in terms of 'technical limitations', one may expect that many technologies related to autism come in the shape of a 'technological fix'. Or, to put it in words of Husserl: "Merely fact-minded sciences make merely fact-minded people" [17]. In light of technology abandonment, better incorporation of autistic experiences is one of the core principles of DYL. To this end, DYL builds upon phenomenology as the philosophical study of experience to comprehend and articulate autistic experiences as valuable input in the design process. In this regard, phenomenologists have emphasised the cognitive, social, cultural and biological constituents of a user experience [12,18,19]. These constituents must be well-understood before a technology can become successfully integrated in autistic life-worlds. To stay in phenomenological terminology: the technology must become properly 'embodied'.

2.2 Action-Oriented Tinkering

DYL encourages 'action-oriented tinkering'. This builds on what Svanæs [19] calls 'the feel dimension': "[in] the same way as you see a rose, not a collection of petals, and hear a musical theme, not a sequence of notes, you perceive the interactive behaviour of an interactive artefact not as a collection of action/reaction pairs, but as a meaningful interactive whole". In this regard, Svanæs argues that it would be nonsensical trying to articulate an experience in terms of logical analysis. Rather, an experience must be lived through; it must be tried and felt. Its implications for design are clear: prototypes must evolve 'on stage' by acting out future scenarios rather than "defining design as a separate activity" [19]. Only then, Svanæs claims, the lived experience of the user is properly reflected in the design outcome.

2.3 User-Initiated Design

DYL promotes user-initiated design (UID). This is in contrast with most co-design methods that do involve stakeholders during the design of a product or service, but do not equip them with the tools to design own, specific solutions [18]. Choosing your own technology means that the design process departs from your own lived experience with technology. This may represent a state of empowerment in its own right. UID steps away from the concept of 'one-size-fits-all' solutions that are designed for the masses.

2.4 Off-the-Shelf Technologies

To enable user-initiated design, DYL promotes using already available technologies, ranging from non-digital low-tech to digital high-tech, instead of developing new ('assistive') technologies. The reason for this is two-fold. On one hand, generating design ideas proved to be challenging as YAA have difficulties with conceptualising a concrete, technological intervention 'out of nothing'. By introducing off-the-shelf technologies already at the start of the design process, it is easier to envisage the design possibilities. A more practical consideration is that off-the-shelf technologies are relatively low-cost and "present opportunities for applications that can be individualised at lower costs than using the more traditional custom hardware solutions" [20].

3 Case Studies

Three case studies were conducted between March and September 2020, following the tradition of 'Research-through-Design', focusing not so much on the end result, but on insights gained during the design practice [21]. These case studies were conducted for this study to explore several design directions of the underlying DYL process: the steps to be taken during the design of solutions.

All case studies involved working with stakeholders embedded in a real care practice and consisted of designing and trialling a prototype of a concrete DYL toolkit. This toolkit represented the underlying DYL process and provided hands-on guidance for a YAA and caregiver to move through the design process one or more times (so-called 'iterations'). The prototypes were designed, developed and tested by Industrial Design Engineering students from the University of Twente. In all cases, Stanford's d.school design thinking process was used as a basis. This model assumes five phases, which can be repeated in various orders: Empathize (i.e. observing, engaging, immersing), Define (i.e. understanding a useful challenge), Ideate (i.e. exploring solutions), Prototype (i.e. realising ideas) and Test (i.e. gathering feedback, refining solutions) (Fig. 1) [22].

For each phase it was further explored how to support the YAA and caregiver with concrete tools (instruction cards, visual materials, expressive tools, a representation of state and process and so on) to move through this basic process, and how to concretely give form to this phase. This meant on the one hand selecting and adapting various promising tools and techniques from the co-design literature as well as getting to know the YAA and caregiver that were participating in the case, being informed and inspired by their lived experiences and practices, and subsequently bringing theory and practice together in concrete design choices for the method and toolkit.

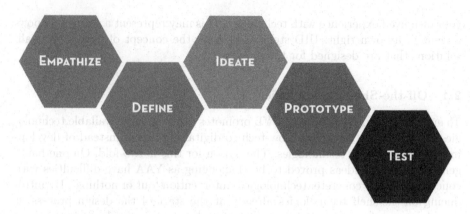

Fig. 1. Stanford's d.school design thinking process [22], CC BY-NC-SA 4.0.

3.1 First Case Study

The first case study involved Tim[2], a 14-year-old adolescent and his mother (Tim lives at home). Although Tim is not a young adult, it was chosen to carry out a case study with him, mainly because the development to independence begins at a younger age than adulthood. Tim's mother feels responsible for the development in independence of her son. However, Tim seems to find that less urgent. For instance, at one moment he remarked something along the lines of 'Why should I learn to tie my laces? My mother is much better at it than I am'. Also, "[i]f he wants to do something, he wants someone to be with him" [23].

Three different prototype forms were explored: tangible, digital and a tangible-digital combination. Although tangible co-design tools have been argued to provide a shared space for sense making and open up a rich freedom of expression for co-design participants, in this case Tim actually preferred the digital form, due to his affinity with ICT and his reluctance to write with a pen. Eventually an interactive PowerPoint prototype was developed and tested (Fig. 2). It offers a step-by-step guidance in designing a solution. The various phases were translated to fit the life world of Tim and his mother. The 'Empathize' phase, for instance, was translated to 'Discover who you are' and 'Prototype' was translated to 'Make your tool'. This prototype did not appeal sufficiently. For instance, it turned out to be too textual and too much effort to fill in all the text boxes. Commitment declined and no tool was designed by Tim and his mother (however, as said, this was not the primary goal of these case studies).

3.2 Second Case Study

The second case study involved Paul, a 33-year-old YAA, and his caregiver. Paul lives at a mental healthcare institution that is involved in this research

---

[2] To protect the privacy of participants, pseudonyms are used.

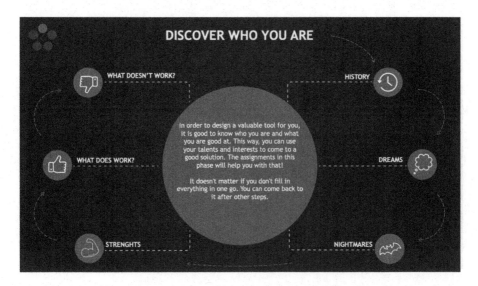

Fig. 2. One of the phases of an interactive prototype made with PowerPoint [23]

project. Slowly but steadily, he is working towards more independence. Again, three different forms were explored: A game board, an adaptable online guide and a physical toolkit. Low-fi prototypes were used as input ('probes') for a co-design session with Paul and his caregiver. During this session, they interacted with the prototypes to discover preferences and difficulties in the designs. It resulted in a new prototype design that consists of a set of 'prompt cards' that is aimed at stimulating, inspiring and guiding the design process. "The cards spark creativity or provides the users with new prompts to follow when they stagnate in the design process" [24] (Fig. 3). Due to time limitations of the case study, no tool was developed. However, useful insights were gained that could possibly be translated into a useful solution. For example, they thought it would be useful if Paul could have a 'little voice on his shoulder' to help him every now and then. Recording, sending (by a caregiver) and playback of messages can provide such functionality [25].

3.3   Third Case Study

The third case study involved Vincent, a 23-year-old YAA, and his caregiver. Just as Paul, he lives at one of the involved mental healthcare institutions. In this case, a game-like prototype was developed (Fig. 4). This really appealed to Vincent, because he likes to play board games. He had no trouble with the metaphors used. The prototype "consists out of six islands, five of which belong to the design thinking phases understand, define, ideate, prototype, and test. The final island includes the goal of the YAA" [26]. The goal that they chose was to stimulate a better sleep-wake rhythm. Vincent's caregiver already had a specific technology in mind beforehand: a care robot called Tessa (this robot

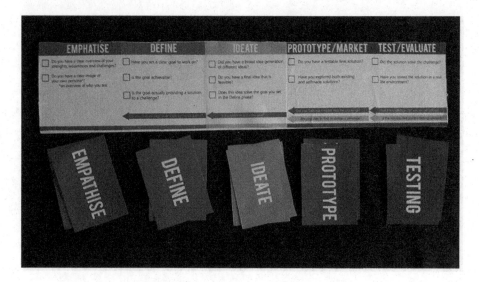

Fig. 3. A set of physical prompt cards to guide the design process [24].

reads out messages and agenda items). She hoped that this project would justify the purchase. How-ever, they found out that Vincent has a clear preference for non-auditory modalities (i.e. sounds). So, they ended up with a different, better fitting and simpler solution that was also much cheaper and easier to use: a wake-up light.

4   Design Your Life Process

The various proposed design processes of the three pilot studies were analysed and discussed with the involved researchers in an online Mural environment. This led to the first iteration of the DYL-process (Fig. 5). Notably, these kinds of processes are not unique to participatory design projects: both in the digital and the tangible sphere, iterative processes with similar stages have become conventional to include stakeholders and make effective use of their expertise - also in the context of autism [3,8]. The DYL-process and the four core principles together are called the DYL-method. The process presented here encompasses six design stages: Understand, Define, Ideate, Prototype, Test and Evaluate. They revolve around the development of goals and products.

4.1   Design Stages

Goals and Products. At the centre are the goals and products, that will develop during the process. The bidirectional arrow indicates that they influence each other, meaning that a product can also lead to the insights and development of one's goals and vice versa.

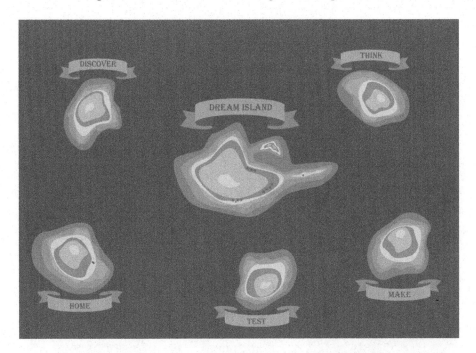

Fig. 4. A game-based prototype called "Good Trip!" [26].

Understand. The focus here is on establishing a self-understanding ("Who am I?", "What is the world that I live in?"), starting from the fact that a YAA and a carer already know each other, at least to a certain degree. So, the goal is to make the insights into one-self and one's world more explicit. Not for a designer or researcher, but for oneself, to unlock design ideas and make them actionable.

Define. This phase focuses on defining a specific purpose for the solution ("What should the technology support?") as relative to a larger life goal that a YAA and caregiver define as well.

Ideate. The ideation phase is about broadening the solution-space. It is aimed at stimulating creativity to come up with possible (non-obvious) directions for a solution.

Prototype. In this phase products are acquired or realised. Depending on the available resources, possibilities and affinity with technologies, choices are made how to realise product(s). These conditions influence the extent to which technology can be adapted for its own application. Most people will be able to use technology, but fewer will (be able to) configure, modify or even create technologies themselves. This observation is visualised in the form of what is called here the 'Pyramid of technological personalisation' (Fig. 6).

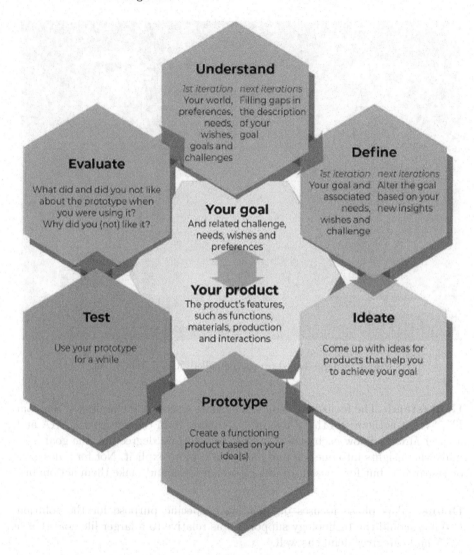

Fig. 5. The Design Your Life process that resulted from the first three case studies.

This was inspired by the four levels of creativity described by Sanders and Stappers [29].

Test. Here, products are being used in everyday life. It will be determined if and how it works and to what extent it contributes to the independence of the YAA.

Evaluate. It was chosen to create an extra phase to evaluate the whole process. It is aimed at gaining insights to refine self-understanding.

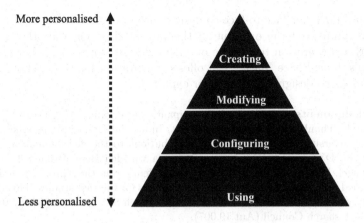

Fig. 6. Pyramid of technological personalisation: most people use technology, fewer configure, modify or create technology.

5   Conclusion

This paper offers the first version of the Design Your Life-method: a novel approach that is aimed at increasing the effectiveness of technologies that support young autistic adults in independent living. It is based on three case studies and inspired by phenomenology synthesised into four core principles: 'focus on experience', 'user-initiated design', 'action-oriented tinkering' and 'off-the-shelf technologies'. These principles will put the design process firmly into both the lived experience of young autistic adults as well as being integrated into the daily practice of care.

The added value of this method lies not so much in the 'designerly approach', but mainly in its phenomological foundations. This will be given a more prominent role in the next iterations of the method. Furthermore, the extent to which the findings are generic or unique will be explored in more detail. The question is to what extent the method itself should be adaptable to meet users' preferences (i.e. Should the DYL-method itself be personalised?).

As described in the last part of this paper, users of the method will only be able to personalise technology to their own needs to a certain extent. So, the effectiveness of the method will probably depend on the willingness and capacities of the users. Another important factor is that applying the proposed method will have an impact on the caregivers and organisations who provide care to YAA. To anticipate a better collective understanding and support throughout the organisation, multi-stakeholder co-reflection sessions will be organised [27], in which the results of the case studies are interpreted from the different perspectives. This gives a more robust reflection of the insights: it identifies the challenges faced and forms the starting point for the co-design case studies that will follow.

The case studies were conducted between March and November 2020. It was therefore necessary to anticipate the Covid-19 circumstances. For example, shorter and far fewer face-to-face co-design gatherings could be organised. This may have influenced the outcome of the case studies. On the other hand, it also sparked inspiration to explore other 'modes of cooperation'. For example, Johansen's Time-Space Matrix [28] offered inspiration for this: remote and/or asynchronous co-design will be further explored.

Acknowledgements. We thank all participants and organisations who took part in this research. Thanks to Nathalie Overdevest, Industrial Design Engineering student from the University of Twente, for her contributions to the development and visual design of the DYL-model. We also thank Laura van den Berg, Brian Schipper and Jasmijn Sagel, Industrial Design Engineering students from the University of Twente, who designed the models and realised the prototypes for the case studies. This research is funded by the Dutch Taskforce for Applied Research SIA (RAAK.PRO.03.045) and the Dutch Research Council (Aut.19.007).

References

1. Idring, S., et al.: Autism spectrum disorders in the Stockholm Youth Cohort: design, prevalence and validity. PLoS ONE **7**(7), 9 (2012). https://doi.org/10.1371/journal.pone.0041280
2. Scheeren, A.M., Geurts, H.M.: Research on community integration in autism spectrum disorder: recommendations from research on psychosis. Res. Autism Spectr. Disord. **17**, 1–12 (2015). https://doi.org/10.1016/j.rasd.2015.05.001. https://linkinghub.elsevier.com/retrieve/pii/S1750946715000458. ISSN 17509467
3. Fabri, M., Andrews, P.C.S., Pukki, H.K.: Using design thinking to engage autistic students in participatory design of an online toolkit to help with transition into higher education. J. Assist. Technol. **10**(2), 102–114 (2016). https://doi.org/10.1108/JAT-02-2016-0008. https://www.emerald.com/insight/content/doi/10.1108/JAT-02-2016-0008/full/html. ISSN 1754-9450
4. Wilson, C., Brereton, M., Ploderer, B., Sitbon, L.: Co-design beyond words: 'moments of interaction' with minimally-verbal children on the autism spectrum. In: Proceedings of the 2019 CHI Conference on Human Factors in Computing Systems, Glasgow Scotland UK, May 2019. ACM, pp. 1–15. https://doi.org/10.1145/3290605.3300251. https://dl.acm.org/doi/10.1145/3290605.3300251. ISBN 978-1-4503-5970-2
5. Frauenberger, C., Makhaeva, J., Spiel, K.: Blending methods: developing participatory design sessions for autistic children. In: Proceedings of the 2017 Conference on Interaction Design and Children, Stanford California USA, June 2017. ACM, pp. 39–49. https://doi.org/10.1145/3078072.3079727. https://dl.acm.org/doi/10.1145/3078072.3079727. ISBN 978-1-4503-4921-5
6. Fletcher-Watson, S., et al.: Making the future together: shaping autism research through meaningful participation. Autism **23**(4), 943–953 (2019). https://doi.org/10.1177/1362361318786721. http://journals.sagepub.com/doi/10.1177/1362361318786721. ISSN 1362-3613, 1461-7005
7. Fletcher-Watson, S., Happé, F.: Autism: A New Introduction to Psychological Theory and Current Debate. Routledge (2019). ISBN 978-1-351-58983-3
8. Zervogianni, V., et al.: A framework of evidence-based practice for digital support, co-developed with and for the autism community. Autism **24**(6), 1411–1422 (2020). https://doi.org/10.1177/1362361319898331. https://www.ncbi.nlm.nih.gov/pmc/articles/PMC7376625/. ISSN 1362-3613

9. Frauenberger, C., Makhaeva, J., Spiel, K.: Designing smart objects with autistic children: four design exposès. In: Proceedings of the 2016 CHI Conference on Human Factors in Computing Systems, San Jose California USA, May 2016. ACM, pp. 130–139. https://doi.org/10.1145/2858036.2858050. https://dl.acm.org/doi/10.1145/2858036.2858050. ISBN 978-1-4503-3362-7

10. Milton, D.E.M.: On the ontological status of autism: the 'double empathy problem'. Disabl. Soc. **27**(6), 883–887 (2012). https://doi.org/10.1080/09687599.2012.710008. Publisher: Routledge. ISSN 0968-7599

11. Kenny, L., Hattersley, C., Molins, B., Buckley, C., Povey, C., Pellicano, E.: Which terms should be used to describe autism? Perspectives from the UK autism community. Autism **20**(4), 442–462 (2016). https://doi.org/10.1177/1362361315588200. http://journals.sagepub.com/doi/10.1177/1362361315588200. ISSN 1362-3613, 1461-7005

12. Klin, A., Jones, W., Schultz, R., Volkmar, F.: The enactive mind, or from actions to cognition: lessons from autism. Philos. Trans. Royal Soc. Lond. Ser. B Biol. Sci. **358**(1430), 345–360 (2003). https://doi.org/10.1098/rstb.2002.1202. https://royalsocietypublishing.org/doi/10.1098/rstb.2002.1202. ISSN 0962-8436, 1471-2970

13. De Jaegher, H.: Embodiment and sense-making in autism. Front. Integr. Neurosci. **7** (2013). https://doi.org/10.3389/fnint.2013.00015. http://journal.frontiersin.org/article/10.3389/fnint.2013.00015/abstract. ISSN 1662-5145

14. Dourish, P.: Where the Action Is: The Foundations of Embodied Interaction. MIT Press, Cambridge (2001). ISBN 978-0-262-54178-7

15. Winograd, T., Flores, F.: Understanding Computers and Cognition: A New Foundation for Design (1986). ISBN 978-0-201-11297-9

16. Weiser, M.: The computer for the 21st century. SIGMOBILE Mob. Comput. Commun. Rev. **3**(3), 3–11 (1999). https://doi.org/10.1145/329124.329126. Place: New York, NY, USA Publisher: Association for Computing Machinery. ISSN 1559-1662

17. Husserl, E., Carr, D.: The Crisis of European Sciences and Transcendental Phenomenology: An Introduction to Phenomenological Philosophy. Northwestern Univ. Press, Evanston (2006). ISBN 978-0-8101-0458-7

18. Sarmiento-Pelayo, M.P.: Co-design: a central approach to the inclusion of people with disabilities. Revista de la Facultad de Medicina **63**(3Sup), 149–154 (2015). https://doi.org/10.15446/revfacmed.v63n3sup.49345. https://revistas.unal.edu.co/index.php/revfacmed/article/view/49345. Number: 3Sup. ISSN 2357-3848

19. Svanæs, D.: Interaction design for and with the lived body: some implications of Merleau-Ponty's phenomenology. ACM Trans. Comput. Hum. Interact. **20**(1), 8:1–8:30 (2013). https://doi.org/10.1145/2442106.2442114. ISSN 1073-0516

20. Hayes, G.R., Yeganyan, M.T., Brubaker, J.R., Hosaflook, S.W.: Using Mobile Technologies to Support Students in Work Transition Programs. Twenty-First Century Skills for Students with Autism (2013)

21. Zimmerman, J., Forlizzi, J., Evenson, S.: Research through design as a method for interaction design research in HCI. In: Proceedings of the SIGCHI Conference on Human Factors in Computing Systems - CHI 2007, San Jose, California, USA, pp. 493–502. ACM Press (2007). https://doi.org/10.1145/1240624.1240704. http://dl.acm.org/citation.cfm?doid=1240624.1240704. ISBN 978-1-59593-593-9

22. Doorley, S., Holcomb, S., Klebahn, P., Segovia, K., Utley, J.: Design Thinking Bootleg — Stanford University and School (2018). https://dschool.stanford.edu/resources/design-thinking-bootleg

23. van den Berg, L.: Designing a toolkit that supports autistic young adults in creating a personalized contribution to their independence. Library Catalog: essay.utwente.nl Publisher: University of Twente, August 2020. http://purl.utwente.nl/essays/84061

24. Schipper, B.: Design of a Co-design Toolkit for Young Adults With Autism Spectrum Disorder to Support Their Independence (2020). http://purl.utwente.nl/essays/84061

25. Bouck, E.C., Bartlett, R.S.W.: Promoting Independence through Assistive Technology: Evaluating Audio Recorders to Support Grocery Shopping, p. 13 (2021). https://www.jstor.org/stable/23879639

26. Sagel, J.: Designing 'Good Trip!': A Co-design Toolkit for Young Autistic Adults and Their Carers to Promote Independence, p. 122 (2021). http://purl.utwente.nl/essays/85588

27. Tomico, O., Lu, Y., Baha, E., Lehto, P., Hirvikoski, T.: Designers initiating open innovation with multi-stakeholder through co-reflection sessions. In: Roozenburg, N.F.M., Chen, L., Stappers, P.J. (eds.) Delft, The Netherlands, pp. 317–329. Technische Universiteit Delft (2011)

28. Johansen, R.: Groupware: Computer Support for Business Teams. Series in Communication Technology and Society. Free Press, New York (1988). ISBN 978-0-02-916491-4

29. Sanders, E.B.-N., Stappers, P.J.:: Co-creation and the new landscapes of design. CoDesign **4**, 5–18 (2008). https://doi.org/10.1080/15710880701875068

Design for Health and Well-Being

Building a Digital Health Risk Calculator for Older Women with Early-Stage Breast Cancer

Fuad Abujarad[1]([✉]), Shi-Yi Wang[2,3], Davis Ulrich[1], Sarah S. Mougalian[1,3], Brigid K. Killelea[2,3], Liana Fraenkel[1], Cary P. Gross[1,3], and Suzanne B. Evans[1,3]

[1] Yale School of Medicine, New Haven, CT 06519, USA
fuad.abujarad@yale.edu
[2] Yale School of Public Health, New Haven, CT 06519, USA
[3] Cancer Outcomes, Public Policy, and Effectiveness Research (COPPER) Center, New Haven, CT 06519, USA

Abstract. Thousands of older women diagnosed with early-stage breast cancer receive adjuvant radiation treatment therapy that can be safely omitted. The decision to undergo radiation treatment therapy is based upon several factors unique to the individual. Understanding the patient-specific relative risk and benefit of radiation therapy—and making the right decision for the patient's health—is a complex process that often fails to follow the shared-decision model between patient and clinician. The use of digital health tools to support and navigate complex and personalized healthcare focused decisions have been shown to increase patient comprehension and reduce decision-based conflict. In this paper we describe how we designed, developed, and tested an electronic, tablet-based decision aid tool to provide patient-specific, risk-benefit information with the goal of helping older women determine whether to receive radiation therapy. Our decision aid tool, Radiation for Older Women (ROW), utilizes user-centered design principles to facilitate evidence-based treatment decisions.

Keywords: User centered design · Breast cancer · Decision aid · Digital health · Oncology

1 Introduction

For women in the United States, breast cancer is the most common cause of death from cancer [1]. Older women are particularly vulnerable: nearly half of new diagnoses occur at age 65 and older and one-quarter occur after age 75 [2]. Fortunately, over 62% of diagnoses are found during stage I when the cancer remains localized and highly curable, and most patients undergo lumpectomy or breast-conserving surgery [3, 4]. While the use of adjuvant radiation therapy (RT) alongside lumpectomy has been shown to reduce the risk of local recurrence, radiation therapy does not improve overall survival for the majority of older women [5, 6]. This is due to older women often having comorbidities that predispose them to non-cancer-related death, thus minimizing

© Springer Nature Switzerland AG 2021
M. M. Soares et al. (Eds.): HCII 2021, LNCS 12780, pp. 389–402, 2021.
https://doi.org/10.1007/978-3-030-78224-5_27

radiation therapy benefits [7]. Side effects of radiation therapy, such as fatigue, breast pain, and pneumonitis, and burden of treatment (e.g., travel to undergo radiation therapy) are important considerations before receiving radiation therapy [8–11]. Indeed, national guidelines recommend that radiation therapy could be omitted for women ages 70 and older with low-risk, early-stage breast cancer. Despite these recommendations, more than two-thirds of this population undergo radiation therapy [12, 13].

The discrepancy between guidelines and actual clinical treatment for older women underscores the challenges in radiation therapy decision-making. Effective treatment plans for older women with breast cancer are highly individualized and require consideration of a multitude of factors—patient age, tumor size, patient preferences, comorbidities, functional status, and potential benefit and harm. Consequently, it may be difficult for physicians to accurately estimate an individual patient's risk for cancer recurrence as well as the benefits from radiation therapy. As a result, patients will not be able to make informed decisions that align with their preferences and values. Patients are also prevented from participating in the shared decision-making process, despite research supporting their desire to become more involved [14]. Even women who seek a more passive role in their treatment decision want to be as informed as possible [15]. Therefore, physicians are too often left to make these determinations on their patient's behalf.

Across the health care field, digital risk calculators and decision aids have been developed to support complex decision-making. These digital decision aids—electronic tools used to improve patient understanding, participation, and decision-making in health care—have been shown to improve patient satisfaction and reduce decisional conflict [16–18]. Decision aids support patients' knowledge allow for informed decision-making, and lead to better health outcomes [19, 20], making them valuable tools for promoting informed discussion between patients and providers.

Additionally, the User-Centered Design (UCD) approach stipulates that the targeted ender user provide feedback and criticism during every phase of the design process [21, 22]. In doing so, the tool or product may better serve and match the needs of the end user. Problems may be identified earlier, and with feedback from the user, each iteration of the product will improve upon the one before it. In the context of decision aids, applying these principles ensures that the final product features functions, a display, and an interface that accounts for the particular needs of the end user.

To assist the decision process of whether or not to pursue radiation therapy for breast cancer, we sought to develop a patient-centered, risk-based digital risk calculator. By providing patients with an easily interpretable, graphic-based risk-benefit analysis of radiation therapy, individuals could better understand their options and align their goals with expected treatment outcomes.

While many decision aids use risk calculators to simplify medical decisions in oncology, to our knowledge, no risk calculator for women with breast cancer ages 65 and older exists that accounts for personal comorbidities and functional status and estimates the benefits of radiation therapy to support shared decision-making in the clinical setting. In this paper we describe how we used the User-Centered Design (UCD) approach to design, develop and evaluate the usability and acceptability of the risk calculator, Radiation for Older Women (ROW), the tool's potential to improve decision-making, and treatment satisfaction for breast cancer patients.

2 Methods

This research study focused on the acceptability and usability of the ROW digital risk calculator amongst potential users. ROW was created to improve shared decision-making between providers and older women with breast cancer who underwent lumpectomy and were considering radiation therapy. By providing individualized risk estimates with and without radiation therapy, ROW could help patients make informed decisions about their health.

Our methods followed an iterative UCD process that emphasized relevant stakeholder feedback to assess, inform, and refine the ROW tool at each development stage [21, 22]. This approach ensured ROW's interface and functionality would meet the needs of the patients in the clinical environment. Major stages of ROW's development process included: building a risk calculator, developing a prototype, usability and acceptability testing, and field testing and piloting.

We used two prediction models to create a risk calculator that could estimate local cancer recurrence and all-cause mortality with and without radiation therapy. We used the Early Breast Cancer Trialist Collaboration Group (EBCTCG) model to forecast both five- and ten-year outcomes for stage I and stage II breast cancer [23]. Breast cancer specific inputs included a woman's age, tumor size, tumor grade, surgical margin status, lymph node involvement, and estrogen receptor status, which are important predictors for recurrence. To estimate an older woman's life expectancy, we utilized the ePrognosis model, frequently used as a survival prediction tool in geriatric assessment [24]. Specific risk inputs for the ePrognosis model included a woman's age, sex, body mass index (BMI), smoking status, functional status, and four selected comorbidities (lung disease, congestive heart failure, diabetes, and other cancer). To account for additional health factors beyond the included 18 variables in ROW, we built in an option for clinicians to use their expertise and adjust a patient's risk based upon other known health or tumor characteristics. We conducted 56,700 model simulations using each combination of the 18 input parameters to generate risk outcomes. Further detail regarding the statistical analysis and methodology of the prediction calculator has been previously described [25].

For the tool's iterative design process, we first put together an advisory committee consisting of breast cancer survivors (n = 6), advocates of breast cancer care and aging (n = 7), oncology clinicians (n = 4), and researchers (n = 4). The advisory committee assessed user needs and limitations to inform the tool's functional and technical requirements. Following requirement gathering, we developed the screen mockups of the ROW tool using Balsamiq® [\cite: https://balsamiq.com/]. We presented multiple series of prototype mockups to the advisory committee. The committee provided feedback around visual presentation, interface, functionality, text, usability, and acceptability.

The ROW digital tool is divided into three sections: (1) patient data input, (2) clinician data input, and (3) risk estimate results. First, patients enter demographical, health, and lifestyle information, including age, height, weight, smoking status, comorbidities, and functional status. These characteristics are used to calculate a patient's mortality risk. Figure 1 below is an early black-and-white sample mockup draft, which was presented to the advisory committee for feedback and comments.

Following the patient section, the clinician is required to enter data. The clinician inputs patient-specific tumor characteristics and reviews the patient's data input for accuracy. The clinician has the option to edit and update any patient entry errors. Following the input obtained from the patient and clinician sections, the tool then generates a graphical risk estimate of the patient's five- and ten-year breast cancer local recurrence and mortality, with and without radiation therapy.

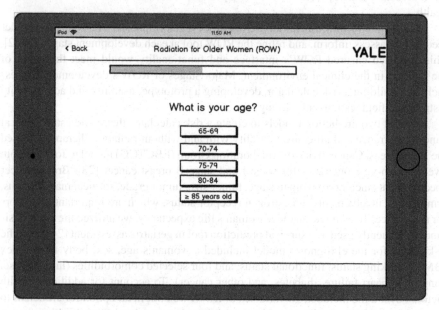

Fig. 1. Early black and white ROW mock-up using Balsamiq software.

We recruited two groups of participants in the pilot study to evaluate the usability and acceptability of the tool. While we initially sought to include only patients with stage I-II breast cancer receiving breast-conserving surgery who were candidates for adjuvant radiation therapy, there was an insufficient number of women who fit the specific qualification criteria. Therefore, we also recruited a separate group of women volunteers who did not have breast cancer. The number of participants between both groups would provide us with a sufficient number of participants for qualitative feedback. All participants were required to be women ages 65 and older who could read and understand English and provide informed consent.

Yale IRB approved the study, and volunteers were recruited from the local New Haven, Connecticut community using IRB approved flyers posted publicly in New Haven, CT. Patients were recruited from the Smilow Cancer Center at Yale New Haven Hospital using authorized access to patient EPIC medical health records. Each participant was compensated $20 for her time. Interested volunteers complete the tool in a non-clinical setting, while patient volunteers were asked to complete ROW in an actual clinical setting prior to meeting with their oncologist to discuss their diagnosis and treatment.

During pilot testing of ROW and completion of the evaluation survey, the research assistant observed patients' and volunteers' use of the tool, noting any challenges or difficulties collecting all qualitative feedback, and assisting with technical obstacles. In the process of completing the decision aid, volunteers and patients entered their actual demographical and health information. For the clinician section, the research assistant entered in preset, standardized tumor and cancer characteristics for the volunteer group. For patients, their oncology provider entered in the patient's actual tumor and cancer characteristics during the patient's clinical appointment.

Following the entry of the participants' health data into ROW, volunteers were shown the results of their input with the research assistant, while patients viewed their results alongside their clinician. Results compared ten-year mortality and local cancer recurrence risk with and without radiation therapy. For volunteers, the risk estimates were for example purposes only, which the research assistant explained. The risk estimates for patients reflected actual clinical prognostic outcomes. The clinician discussed the local recurrence outcomes with the patient and used these results to arrive at a shared decision of whether to pursue adjuvant radiation therapy.

We focused on evaluating the usability and acceptability of ROW, as well as other qualitative perceptions of the tool, through a paper survey that was completed by both volunteers and patients. The survey for volunteers gathered feedback from a controlled, simulated clinical experience with the ROW tool. The patients' survey reflected use of the ROW tool in an actual clinical setting with an oncologist.

All participants completed the following survey sections:

- "Experience Using the Tool": evaluated usability, acceptability, and perception of the ROW tool
- "Radiotherapy Benefits": evaluated knowledge of breast cancer survival with and without radiation therapy treatment
- "Health and Demographics": collected race, ethnicity, education level, marital status, income, and other characteristics
- "Computer Experiences": evaluated familiarity with everyday technology

The "Experience Using the Tool" portion of the survey measured usability—or the ease in which participants interacted with ROW—through the system usability scale (SUS), a validated, ten-question Likert-scale tool that may be applied to small sample sizes [26–28]. Open-ended questions also provided an opportunity for participant recommendations on the tool's design and features and to measure acceptability, or the degree to which ROW served its intended purpose. The "Radiotherapy Benefits" section surveyed participants about the impact of radiation therapy on survival and whether or not they planned to receive radiation therapy. "Health and Demographic Information" collected information on participants' marital, race, income, and education status as well as emotional responses to ROW. These questions were intended to understand any limits, biases, or preferences in the design of ROW. The Computer Efficacy Scale (CES) was used in the "Computer Experiences" section to determine participants' familiarity and confidence with everyday technology [29]. Additionally, the patient group was asked to respond to the "Decision-Making Process", which used a five-point Likert scale to assess patient decisional satisfaction of whether to pursue radiation therapy. This section of the survey evaluated ROW's ability to influence patient decision-making around treatment. All participant survey feedback was aggregated and analyzed as numerical indicators and summarized using common descriptive statistics appropriate for discrete and continuous data.

3 Results

Outcomes of our work included in-depth feedback on ROW prototypes from targeted end users and advisory committee members about ROW's design and usability, leading to a polished and user-friendly final product. The finalized tool features a large font size, sensitive language, a streamlined process for inputting user information, and a simplified pictographic for risk estimates, enabling ROW to meet the specific needs and challenges of older women. To be mindful of older population needs, the interface and screens display prompts for one question at a time in large, clear, and simple font with minimal text and graphics. A sample screenshot displaying the final high-contrast, large text interface is shown in Fig. 2.

A text-to-speech function supports read-aloud functionality for patients with vision difficulty or low literacy. A progress bar displays how far a patient has advanced through the tool, allowing the user to anticipate the time required for completion. Core features of the tool include:

- Clean design with patient prompts displayed clearly and individually on each screen in large font
- Older adult friendly interface
- Straightforward patient input features
- One-click screen navigation
- Automated text-to-speech translation, with headphone support
- Design for seamless use in a clinical workflow
- A web-based platform, providing an easily accessible platform for both patients and clinicians that can be updated rapidly and disseminated broadly
- A visual pictograph of prognostic estimates
- Cancer recurrence and mortality outcomes, with/without radiation therapy

Following the patient's data entry, the clinician may enter and review the data entered by the patient as well as include specific characteristics of the cancer. This review includes correcting patient responses of 'unknown' to questions about health conditions or diagnoses. This screen display is shown below in Fig. 3.

ROW was optimized as a web-based application for any internet-capable device, including a desktop, tablet, or smartphone. Figure 4 shows the final risk estimate picto-graph, a colorful, side-by-side design displaying risk estimates with and without radiation therapy that are specific to the individual patient's health and cancer characteristics. This display facilitates comparison and interpretation for both patients and clinicians.

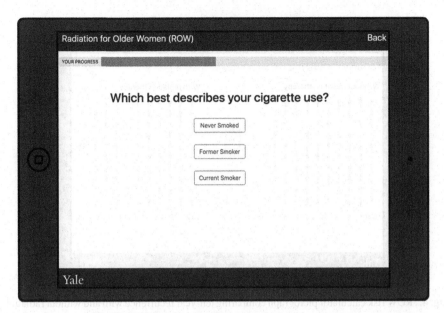

Fig. 2. ROW patient health – patient data entry prompt.

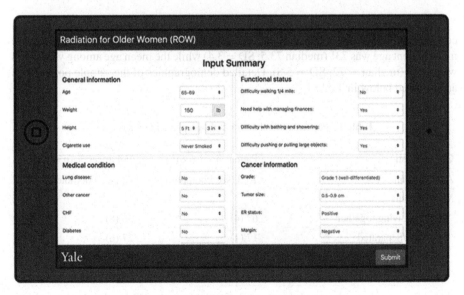

Fig. 3. ROW clinician data input screen.

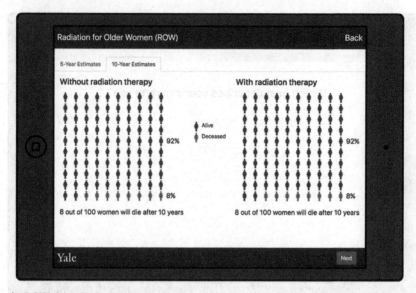

Fig. 4. ROW risk calculator pictograph comparing ten-year recurrence with and without radiation therapy.

Field testing was conducted with all participants, 22 volunteers and 6 patients, who completed ROW in the pilot study. Averages between the two groups were similar: the mean patient age was 73[1] (median 73.5, SD = 3.4) while the mean age among volunteers was 73.2[2] (median = 72, SD = 5.8). Detailed demographics of the sample populations are included below in Table 1.

Table 1. Patient and volunteer demographic characteristics.

Characteristic	Patient % (n = 6)	Volunteer % (n = 22)
Age, Median	73.5 (see Footnote 1)	72 (see Footnote 2)
Marital status		
Married/Living together	67 (4)	36 (8)
Divorced/Separated	17 (1)	27 (6)
Never married/lived together	0	9 (2)
Widowed	17 (1)	27 (6)
Race		
African American	17 (1)	5 (1)
White	83 (5)	95 (21)

(*continued*)

---

[1] Only 4 patients provided their age.

[2] Only 21 volunteers provided their age.

Table 1. (*continued*)

Characteristic	Patient % (n = 6)	Volunteer % (n = 22)
Ethnicity[a]		
Not Hispanic/Latino	67 (4)	95 (21)
Education		
Some high school; did not graduate	33 (2)	0
High school degree or equivalent	17 (1)	14 (3)
Associates' degree	0	23 (5)
Undergraduate degree	33 (2)	27 (6)
Master's degree	17 (1)	36 (8)
Income		
< $30,000	17 (1)	9 (2)
$30,000–$49,999	0	18 (4)
$50,000–$69,999	17 (1)	27 (6)
$70,000–$89,999	17 (1)	18 (4)
$90,000 and above	17 (1)	9 (2)
Decline to answer	33 (2)	18 (4)

[a]Two patients and one volunteer declined to answer

The mean System Usability Scale score of the ROW tool was 84.7 (SD = 15.6), classifying its usability as 'excellent' [26]. Volunteers (n = 22) scored the ROW tool an average of 88.4, while patients (n = 5) gave the tool a 68.5 (SD = 22.9)[3]. Survey responses from one patient were omitted, as her responses of '1' to every question indicated that she did not adequately understand the SUS questions. For all participants who provided their age and a SUS score (n = 24), the median age was 72.5 while the mean SUS score was 87.3. Participants who were younger than the median age scored ROW an average of 87.1, while participants older than the median age scored ROW an average of 87.5. Table 2 below lists the SUS questions.

Table 2. Patient and volunteer ROW questions.

System Usability Scale Question
I think that I would like to use this system frequently
I found the system unnecessarily complex
I thought the system was easy to use

(*continued*)

---

[3] One patient's survey responses were omitted, as she did not adequately understand the SUS questions.

Table 2. (*continued*)

System Usability Scale Question
I think I would need the support of a technical person to be able to use this system
I found the various functions in this system were well integrated
I thought there was too much inconsistency in this system
I would imagine that most people would learn to use this system very quickly
I found the system very awkward to use
I felt very confident using the system
I needed to learn a lot of things before I could get going with this system

With the exception of one 'no' response, all participants (n = 26) indicated that they would recommend the ROW tool to others (one respondent did not answer this question). On a scale of 1 (meaning 'very dissatisfied') to 7 (meaning 'very satisfied'), all pilot study participants rated the ROW tool a mean of 6.4 (n = 27; one respondent did not answer this question); patients rated the tool a 5.7 (n = 6) while volunteers rated the tool a 6.7 (n = 21). Fourteen participants provided verbal or written feedback that ROW would help their decision of whether to pursue radiation therapy treatment. One patient commented that she did not like the "strange robotic voice" of the audio narrator. Other suggestions included having a stand to support the iPad and better differentiation of on-screen colors.

Twenty-seven participants responded to the statement, "the chance that my breast disease will come back after treatment is the same for lumpectomy with radiation as it is for lumpectomy without radiation." Of the five patient responses, four correctly answered "false" while one reported "don't know." Only one volunteer correctly reported "false"; thirteen reported "true" and eight reported "don't know." When asked whether they would elect to receive radiation therapy, all twenty-eight participants responded: twelve responded "no", four responded "yes", and twelve responded "don't know." Of the patient group, three responded "no", two responded "don't know", and one patient indicated she would receive radiation therapy.

Only patients responded to the statement, "the chance of being alive 5 years after treatment is generally the same for lumpectomy with radiation as it is for lumpectomy without radiation." Three patients correctly answered "yes," and there was one response each to "no" and "don't know" (one did not respond). The six patients also reported their plans to pursue radiation therapy: one reported plans to receive radiation therapy, three reported no plans to pursue radiation therapy, and two reported uncertainty. Of the six patients, four were satisfied with their radiation therapy decision, though one of these four individuals also reported 'not sure' about whether to pursue radiation therapy treatment. Of the six patients, four reported 'strongly agree' when asked if they felt adequately informed about the issue important to their decision; one reported 'neutral' and another 'strongly disagree.'

All participants were asked about their emotional state after viewing their cancer recurrence risk estimates. Answers were rated on a scale of 1 to 4, with 1 corresponding to 'not at all' and 4 corresponding to 'very much.' Patients reported a median of 3.5 (SD = 1.7) in terms of feeling calm after completing ROW, indicating a high degree of calm. Volunteers reported a median 3.8 (SD = 1.2) when asked the same question. Patients also reported a median of 1.3 (SD = 0.5) when asked if they felt upset, and volunteers reported a median of 1.2 (SD = 0.8). All patients except one reported only a 1 or 2 when asked if they were worried. Nineteen volunteers reported a 1 when asked if they were worried; one participant answered 2 and another answered 4.

All participants completed the Computer Efficacy Scale (CES) with a mean score of 7.6 out of 10 (SD = 0.9), indicating a relatively strong degree of confidence amongst study participants.

4 Discussion

Electronic decision aids have already proven tremendously beneficial in promoting shared decision-making and patient education for breast cancer treatment, but the vast majority of these published decision aids rely on general averages that do not consider actual estimated clinical outcomes for patients. Research has demonstrated an increasing desire amongst older women with early-stage breast cancer to have input and agency in their treatment decisions, and ROW empowers these women by providing highly-individualized and straightforward estimates [30]. ROW is a significant advancement for integrating a patient-specific breast cancer risk calculator and decision aid into the clinical setting. Future research is now needed to determine ROW's accuracy to project clinical outcomes among a larger scale study amongst older women with breast cancer.

Both patients and healthy volunteers gave ROW high marks for usability and acceptability, with participants finding the tool easy to use and well-integrated into the clinical workflow. Designing technology to fit the specific needs of older adults is multilayered and requires special cognitive, visual, language, and dexterity considerations. Participants' overwhelming recommendation of ROW and high degree of satisfaction signaled the strength of the tool's design, presentation, and content for this population. Incorporating an extensive user-centered design process from ROW's inception allowed for manipulation of important design and display features to best convey the sensitive and complex information of early breast cancer treatment options for older women. While patients did score ROW lower on average than volunteers for SUS, the scored average remains above the expected SUS average score of 68. Additionally, comparisons between the groups must be made with caution: the number of cancer patients was significantly fewer than volunteers. The tremendous variability in distribution of SUS scores amongst the patient group also reflects the smaller sample size. With the sensitive and emotionally driven content of ROW, it was encouraging to see that neither patients nor volunteers found ROW to cause undue emotional distress. These responses implied that the majority of participants, both patients and volunteers, maintained calmness after completing ROW and while observing their cancer recurrence risk estimates.

ROW was not designed to be used as a stand-alone tool. There was a greater consensus among the patient group: almost all understood that while radiation therapy changed the likelihood of recurrence, the risk of mortality remained unchanged. These patients likely benefitted from the provider's explanation of the ROW pictograph estimates. Ultimately, only one patient chose to pursue radiation therapy, and it was clear from her survey responses that she recognized how radiation therapy would impact local recurrence but not overall survival. In our study, patients likely may have needed more time to make a final decision. Choosing a breast cancer treatment is a critical medical decision for anyone and carries an enormous emotional burden. Patients in our study were asked about their treatment decision only minutes after receiving their risk estimate and prognosis. However, delaying assessment of decisional satisfaction may be more accurate.

Limitations of this study included few patient group participants. There may be other considerations amongst breast cancer patients that are only revealed with larger sample sizes. Future research should expand on mixed-method evaluation of ROW amongst a larger sample of breast cancer patients to better understand how patients may use ROW to understand their diagnosis and guide treatment options. As the tool was only offered in English, this resulted in a homogenous participant pool that was predominantly white, educated, and of higher socioeconomic status. Further, we did not test ROW's usability and acceptability amongst clinicians to understand whether it would be well received.

That said, ROW serves as a strong example of how to successfully build a risk-based electronic decision aid to improve shared decision-making in the clinical environment.

5 Conclusion

Older women found the ROW risk calculator to be a helpful, easy-to-use decision aid with important clinical implications. By providing personalized risk estimates, ROW can deliver information to a patient population that desires knowledge and shared decision-making. The usability and acceptability of ROW among older women demonstrates the promise of using a personalized prediction model to facilitate patient-provider conversations around breast cancer treatment. ROW serves as an exemplar for future electronic, risk-based decision aids.

References

1. Siegel, R.L., Miller, K.D., Jemal, A.: Cancer statistics. CA. Cancer J. Clin. **69**(1), 7–34 (2019). https://doi.org/10.3322/caac.21551
2. Brandt, J., Garne, J.P., Tengrup, I., Manjer, J.: Age at diagnosis in relation to survival following breast cancer: a cohort study. World J. Surg. Oncol. 13(1) (2015). https://doi.org/10.1186/s12 957-014-0429-x
3. Society AC. Cancer Facts & Figures (2019). http://www.cancer.org/content/dam/cancer-org/research/cancer-facts-and-statistics/annual-cancer-facts-and-figures/2019/cancer-facts-and-figures-2019.pdf
4. Pollock, Y.G., et al.: Adjuvant radiation use in older women with early-stage breast cancer at Johns Hopkins. Breast Cancer Res. Treat. **160**(2), 291–296 (2016). https://doi.org/10.1007/s10549-016-4005-7
5. Hughes, K.S., et al.: Lumpectomy plus tamoxifen with or without irradiation in women 70 years of age or older with early breast cancer. N. Engl. Med. **351**(10), 971–977 (2004). https://doi.org/10.1056/NEJMoa040587

6. Kunkler, I.H., Williams, L.J., Jack, W.J., Cameron, D.A., Dixon, J.M.: Breast-conserving surgery with or without irradiation in women aged 65 years or older with early breast cancer (PRIME II): a randomised controlled trial. Lancet Oncol. **16**(3), 266–273 (2015). https://doi. org/10.1016/s1470-2045(14)71221-5

7. Patnaik, J.L., Byers, T., DiGuiseppi, C., Denberg, T.D., Dabelea, D.: The influence of comorbidities on overall survival among older women diagnosed with breast cancer. J. Nat. Cancer Inst. **103**(14), 1101–1111 (2011). https://doi.org/10.1093/jnci/djr188

8. Davidoff, A.J., et al.: Out-of-pocket health care expenditure burden for medicare beneficiaries with cancer. Cancer **119**(6), 1257–1265 (2013). https://doi.org/10.1002/cncr.27848

9. Demirci, S., Nam, J., Hubbs, J.L., Nguyen, T., Marks, L.B.: Radiation-induced cardiac toxicity after therapy for breast cancer: interaction between treatment era and follow-up duration. Int. J. Radiat. Oncol. Biol. Phys. **73**(4), 980–987 (2009). https://doi.org/10.1016/j.ijrobp.2008. 11.016

10. Whelan, T.J., Levine, M., Julian, J., Kirkbride, P., Skingley, P.: The effects of radiation therapy on quality of life of women with breast carcinoma: results of a randomized trial. Cancer **88**(10), 2260–2266 (2000). https://doi.org/10.1002/(SICI)1097-0142(20000515)88:10%3c2 260::AID-CNCR9%3e3.0.CO;2-M

11. Yi, M., et al.: Other primary malignancies in breast cancer patients treated with breast conserving surgery and radiation therapy. Ann. Surg. Oncol. **20**(5), 1514–1521 (2013). https:// doi.org/10.1245/s10434-012-2774-8

12. Rutter, C.E., et al.: The evolving role of adjuvant radiotherapy for elderly women with early-stage breast cancer. Cancer **121**(14), 2331–2340 (2015). https://doi.org/10.1002/cncr.29377

13. Soulos, P.R., et al.: Assessing the impact of a cooperative group trial on breast cancer care in the medicare population. Clin. Oncol. **30**(13), 1601–1607 (2012). https://doi.org/10.1200/ JCO.2011.39.4890

14. Stacey, D., Samant, R., Bennett, C.: Decisionmaking in oncology: a review of patient decision aids to support patient participation. CA Cancer J. Clin. **58**(5), 293–304 (2008). https://doi. org/10.3322/ca.2008.0006

15. Neuman, H.B., Charlson, M.E., Temple, L.K.: Is there a role for decision aids in cancer-related decisions? Crit. Rev. Oncol./Hematol. **62**(3), 240–250 (2007). https://doi.org/10.1016/j.critre vonc.2006.12.006

16. Syrowatka, A., Krömker, D., Meguerditchian, A.N., Tamblyn, R.: Features of computer-based decision aids: systematic review, thematic synthesis, and meta-analyses. J. Med. Internet Res. **18**(1), e20 (2016). https://doi.org/10.2196/jmir.4982

17. Qiao, S.: Predicting downstream effects of high decisional conflict: meta-analyses of the Decisional Conflict Scale. Thèses, 1910–2010 (2005). https://doi.org/10.20381/ruor-18514

18. Gattellari, M., Ward, J.E.: Men's reactions to disclosed and undisclosed opportunistic PSA screening for prostate cancer. Med. J. Aust. **182**(8), 386–389 (2005). https://doi.org/10.5694/ j.1326-5377.2005.tb06756.x

19. Stacey, D., et al.: Decision aids for people facing health treatment or screening decisions. Cochrane Database Syst. Rev. (4) (2017). https://doi.org/10.1002/14651858.CD001431.pub5

20. Woodhouse, K.D., et al.: A review of shared decision-making and patient decision aids in radiation oncology. J. Cancer Educ. **32**(2), 238–245 (2017). https://doi.org/10.1007/s13187-017-1169-8

21. Goldberg, L., et al.: Usability and accessibility in consumer health informatics: current trends and future challenges. Am. J. Prev. Med. 40(5, Supplement 2), S187–S197 (2011). https:// doi.org/10.1016/j.amepre.2011.01.009

22. Witteman, H.O., et al.: User-centered design and the development of patient decision aids: protocol for a systematic review. Syst. Rev. **4**(1), 11 (2015). https://doi.org/10.1186/2046-4053-4-11

23. Early Breast Cancer Trialists' Collaborative Group (EBCTCG), Darby, S., et al.: Effect of radiotherapy after breast-conserving surgery on 10-year recurrence and 15-year breast cancer death: meta-analysis of individual patient data for 10,801 women in 17 randomised trials. Lancet **378**(9804), 1707–1716 (2011). https://doi.org/10.1016/S0140-6736(11)61629-2

24. Yourman, L.C., Lee, S.J., Schonberg, M.A., Widera, E.W., Smith, A.K.: Prognostic indices for older adults: a systematic review. JAMA **307**(2), 182–192 (2012). https://doi.org/10.1001/jama.2011.1966

25. Wang, S.-Y., et al.: "Radiotherapy for older women (ROW)": a risk calculator for women with early-stage breast cancer. J. Geriatr. Oncol. **11**(5), 850–859 (2019). https://doi.org/10.1016/j.jgo.2019.12.010

26. Brooke, J.: SUS: a retrospective. J. Usability Stud. **8**, 9–40 (2013). https://doi.org/10.5555/2817912.2817913

27. Bangor, A., Kortum, P.T., Miller, J.T.: An empirical evaluation of the system usability scale. Int. J. Hum.-Comput. Interact. **24**(6), 574–594 (2008). https://doi.org/10.1080/10447310802205776

28. Bangor, A., Kortum, P., Miller, J.: Determining what individual SUS scores mean: adding an adjective rating scale. J. Usability Stud. **4**(3), 114–123 (2009). https://doi.org/10.5555/2835587.2835589

29. Laver, K., George, S., Ratcliffe, J., Crotty, M.: Measuring technology self efficacy: reliability and construct validity of a modified computer self efficacy scale in a clinical rehabilitation setting. Disabil. Rehabil. **34**(3), 220–227 (2012). https://doi.org/10.3109/09638288.2011.593682

30. Wang, S.-Y., et al.: Information needs of older women with early-stage breast cancer when making radiation therapy decisions. Int. J. Radiat. Oncol. Biol. Phys. **98**(4), 733–740 (2017). https://doi.org/10.1016/j.ijrobp.2017.02.001

Design of Form and Motion of a Robot Aimed to Provide Emotional Support for Pediatric Walking Rehabilitation

Jaime Alvarez[1]([✉]), Eriko Hara[2], Toshihiko Koyama[2], Koji Adachi[3], and Yoshihito Kagawa[3]

[1] Department of Design, Faculty of Engineering, Takushoku University, Tatemachi 815-1, Hachioji-shi, Tokyo 193-0985, Japan
a-jaime@id.takushoku-u.ac.jp
[2] Graduate School of Engineering, Takushoku University, Tokyo, Japan
[3] Department of Mechanical Systems Engineering, Faculty of Engineering, Takushoku University, Tokyo, Japan

Abstract. In Japan, increasing number of elderly who need care and shrinking workforce has driven the introduction of robotic technology for medical and nursing-care tasks. Despite the emergence of robots that provide physiological and mental care, in the walking rehabilitation field, this research could not find a robot that offers emotional support to patients, who usually experience stress, worry and anxiety during therapy due to pain and tiredness. In this paper, we present the design of a robot aimed to provide emotional support to children attending walking rehabilitation, essentially by "cheering" them during therapy. We first assessed walking rehabilitation procedures and summarized a general outline of a typical rehabilitation therapy. Then, we investigated the positive and negative emotions that children experience during each step of the rehabilitation therapy outline, and proposed roles that the robot must fulfill to deal with those emotions. Based on the established emotional roles, the robot morphology, design and motion were concurrently defined. The central design intention is to create a robot with a simple morphology and abstract form (less anthropomorphic or biomorphic) that is soft, gentle and characterized by not having face features. Two prototypes were built and prelaminar evaluations were performed with adult respondents, including healthcare professionals. The overall impressions of the robot design, motion and effectiveness was favorably evaluated, and validation with pediatric patients will be implemented as a next step.

Keywords: Emotional support robot · Walking rehabilitation · Form design

1 Introduction

Presently, the medical and nursing-care sectors face a severe labor shortage. In Japan, the Ministry of Health, Labor and Welfare has announced that this scarcity will dramatically increase by 2025 due to advancing aging society and declining birth rate [1]. As

© Springer Nature Switzerland AG 2021
M. M. Soares et al. (Eds.): HCII 2021, LNCS 12780, pp. 403–419, 2021.
https://doi.org/10.1007/978-3-030-78224-5_28

one of the solutions to overcoming this situation, industries place expectations on the introduction of robots that can take care of patients' needs [2]. In the nursing-care sector, the development of robot technology was initially focused on providing physiological assistance (see Fig. 1), but usage scope has been widening to mental care tasks (Fig. 2), such as psychological, social and emotional support.

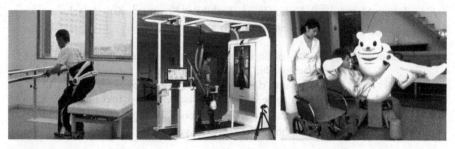

Fig. 1. Examples of robots that provide physiological support (from the left: HAL2, Wellwalk and ROBEAR4).

Fig. 2. Examples of robots that provide mental care (from the left: Telenoid R1, QTrobot, PARO and Qoobo).

In the specific field of walking rehabilitation for children, providing emotional support has a particular importance for effective pain management [3], dealing with stress and anxiety [4] and therapy engagement [5]. Furthermore, research has shown that children are more emotionally sensitive than adults because they are less able to regulate their emotions, so they tend to feel in a stronger way those emotions experienced during rehabilitation [6–8]. Additionally, recent research has remarked increasing negative effects in children mental health due to social isolation resulting from the COVID-19 worldwide epidemic [9].

In this paper, we present the main outcomes of the analysis and design process of a robot aimed to provide emotional support for walking rehabilitation pediatric patients. Section 2 describes a general outline of a typical walking rehabilitation therapy, from which patients' emotions were clarified and the robot specific roles towards those emotions were defined. Section 3 explains the design process of the robot morphology, form and motion, and Sect. 4 summarizes prototyping and validation of the design proposal. The work is concluded in Sect. 5.

2 Analysis of Walking Rehabilitation

2.1 General Outline of Walking Rehabilitation

In order to define the robot roles for providing emotional support, firstly it was necessary to clarify the specific phases of rehabilitation therapy, as well as the emotions that children experience on each one. The walking rehabilitation process was studied by carrying out literature review, observation of walking rehabilitation therapies and interviews with physical therapists with experience in pediatric walking rehabilitation. Based on the results, a walking rehabilitation general outline was defined. The outline covers the following four steps (Table 1):

(1) "Preparation" step: A physiotherapist performs stretching and preparation exercises,
(2) "Immediately before the start" step: Patient transfers to the rehabilitation area or equipment and gets ready,
(3) "During rehabilitation" step: Patient performs walking rehabilitation, usually with auxiliary equipment (parallel bars, crutches, walker, etc.) and must complete a defined set of repetitions of a certain exercise or to walk a specific distance,
(4) "End" step: Therapy finishes when patient has completed the designated number of exercises or walking distance, or as indicated by therapist.

2.2 Child's Emotions and Robot Roles

With the aim of defining the specific roles of the robot, the emotions of pediatric patients present in every step of the walking rehabilitation outline were clarified by carrying out interviews with a physiotherapist member of the Japanese Physical Therapy Association, who has experience in pediatric walking rehabilitation. Emotions experienced by patients were classified into negative and positive categories, since the purpose of our robot is not limited to mitigate negative emotions, but also aims to enhance positive ones. Once main emotions the patients experience at every rehabilitation step were clarified, the robot emotional role towards each emotion was defined. Table 1 summarizes the steps of the walking rehabilitation outline, patient emotional state at each step and the robot emotional role towards patient emotions.

As can be seen in Table 1, the patient's negative emotional states during rehabilitation are dominated by anxiety, worry and stress mainly related to pain and tiredness that the patient experiences during therapy. The positive emotional states are more related to optimistic emotions for self-encouraging. From these findings we concluded that the main emotional role of our emotional support robot should be to "cheer" the patient through the whole rehabilitation therapy and recovery process, in ways that help to reduce or eliminate negative emotions and stimulate the positive ones.

Table 1. Steps of walking rehabilitation outline, patient's emotions and robot's roles.

	① Preparation ② Immediately before start ③ During rehabilitation ④ End
Step	

Patient's emotional state	➕ Positive emotion	I will do my best!	It doesn't hurt, half more!	I worked hard
	How was last time?	I will complete it soon	It doesn't hurt anymore	I achieved today's goal
	Will I fell down? Will I feel pain?	I hope it won't hurt	It hurts, I'm getting tired	It hurted
			Must do it for another half	I don't like it anymore
	➖ Negative emotion			
Robot's role towards patient	Remove anxiety	Let's do it soon	I sympathize with your difficulty of walking	You did your best
	Calm down	I will support you to do your best	Affirm that this is okay Support to the goal Show the final point and encourage	To affirm To congratulate

3   Design of Walking Rehabilitation Support Robot

The robot design process started by defining its general concept, based on the findings obtained in the previous analysis of walking rehabilitation. After that, the definition of robot basic morphology, form design and ideation of its motion were performed in a concurrent way (not linearly, as reported in the structure of this paper). Different ideas of the robot form and movements were evaluated using numerous models and working prototypes, taking decisions but sometimes discovering something new and looping back to explore other ideas. By this iterative process we gradually defined the different characteristics of the design of the robot and its behavior.

3.1   Concept

The target users of this robot are pediatric patients of walking rehabilitation. Although presently the robot is operated by remote control, this research envisions an autonomous robot that plays a role as a "cheering" third party (it does not intend to replace rehabilitation therapist or family members), and accompanies the child during rehabilitation therapy, providing emotional support by its body movements, which can be reinforced by voice or melody. The ideal flow of interaction between the patient and the walking rehabilitation support robot is as follows: (1) The robot detects the emotions of the patient by means of automated emotion recognition (AEE) technology. Next, (2) it determines the specific emotional support role that must be performed as well as the motion that can fulfill that role. Then, (3) when the patient is walking, the robot moves alongside him/her to show empathy and build a sense of unity, as well as to encourage to achieve the goal. (4) After patient completed a partial goal (a set of exercise repetitions, walking through a certain distance), the robot celebrates the achievement and encourages patient to continue doing his/her best. We speculate that, by repeating steps (1) to (4), the interaction between the robot and the child will be strengthened, and the child's willingness to rehabilitate will improve.

3.2 Appearance Assessment of Existing Nursing-Care Robots

A first step for the design of our robot was to analyze the form of existing nursing-care robots presently available in the market, by building a product positioning map (see Fig. 3). On the horizontal axis robots are classified according to their function (Mental support-Physiological support). On the vertical axis the classification (anthropomorphic/biomorphic/abstract) proposed by Bartneck and Forlizzi [10] was used, in which they classify robot forms in anthropomorphic, biomorphic and abstract Robots providing physiological support, at the right side of the map, present all types of forms according to the specific function they perform. On the opposite side, robots that provide mental support are biomorphic and anthropomorphic, which can be explained by the requirement of having a high degree of familiarity in order to facilitate cognitive, social and emotional interaction. At the center of horizontal axis of the map are located robots whose main functions are walk guiding, therapy coaching or having communication with user.

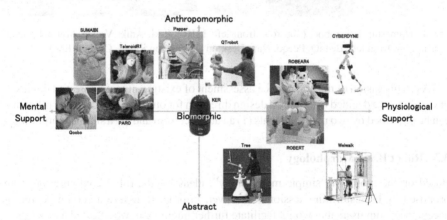

Fig. 3. Product positioning map for nursing-care robots.

An important finding of the positioning map analysis was the absence of robots in the map's bottom left quadrant, which comprises robots for mental support having an abstract form. This finding became a first motivation to explore this design direction for our robot. We speculate that, since the main function of our robot is to cheer and encourage children undertaking walking rehabilitation, it does not require the same level of familiarity as highly anthropomorphic and biomorphic robots used for other mental therapeutic purposes.

Having in mind a design direction which points towards an abstract form, we widened the scope and gathered information of robots used for purposes other than nursing-care tasks. In the category of domestic or home desk robots we found products that clearly resemble a person, animal o vehicles (Fig. 4, top row) but also found robots with abstract appearance (Fig. 4, bottom row). Despite having a simple morphology the simplicity of home desk robots' morphology called our attention, since we speculated that a robot without limbs can offer a safer operation in a rehabilitation environment. Another reason is that a simple morphology would tend to produce movements that are also simple so, for this research in early stages, it is more appropriate to explore communicating emotion first with simple movements, and later to gradually examine more complex motions.

Fig. 4. Domestic desk robots (Top row, from left: LIKU, Kiki, Aniki Vector, MyDeskFriend. Bottom row, from left: BeanQ, Peeqo, Hub, Desktop Companion Robot, Clicbot, Jibo).

As a conclusion of the appearance assessment of existing nursing-care and domestic desk robots, we decided to explore a design direction for our emotional support robot that can be described by two main elements (1) an abstract form and (2) a simple morphology.

3.3   Robot Basic Morphology

Based on the motto of "simple morphology", ideas for the robot configuration were proposed by brainstorming sessions. However, in order to assure a certain degree of acceptance from users that would facilitate further interaction, we selected a robot morphology composed by body (without limbs) and head. We sustained this decision in the conclusions of the research of Wirtz et al. [11], who assert that service robots aimed to perform social and emotional interactions require a certain level of "perceived human-ness" (p. 917) in order to facilitate trust and comfort during interaction. Although they affirm that both robot appearance and behavior influence in perceived humanness, they noticed that users prefer human-like features than human-like behaviors. From the design point of view, in one hand, we want a simple morphology that avoids safety risks and produces simple but effective movements. On the other hand, we speculate that body-head configuration may promote some familiarity in users' perception, hence giving us some level of freedom for the design of the robot form and its behavior (motion).

Another important decision regarding robot morphology was to make it face-less. A first reason for that is regarding safety. We considered that a robot with face would make patient to focus on its eyes, and this distraction could interfere with therapy or even represent a risk. A second reason is that evaluation of users' impressions towards the robot motion can be more accurately assessed by considering only robot motion, without the influence of expressions resulting from face features. A third reason is that we noticed a strong trend in robot design to include face features, so we became interested in exploring a different direction, in which the robot form is more abstract and less anthropomorphic or biomorphic. However, we speculate that our robot can be able to effectively perform its emotional functions by means of its design and motion, without requiring face expression.

3.4 Design of Robot Form

In order to define basic features of the robot form, several images that match our design intention were gathered, analyzed and some of them selected and used for building a mood board (see Fig. 5) that captures the key elements of intended design direction of the robot form. We defined four main formal elements: (1) "Symmetry": we think that a symmetric robot is more likely to move easily in different directions, and also that it matches the attribute of being faceless, (2) "Rounded tension": rounded surfaces transmit a gentle image but having surface tension can also transmit a modern appearance and the "abstract" image we are pursuing, (3) "Dynamism": for safety reasons the robot cannot move very quickly, however its design can transmit more dynamism even at low speed, and (4) "Edge & Surface": To explore a more active role of edges in the robot form, rather than merely being a connection between surfaces.

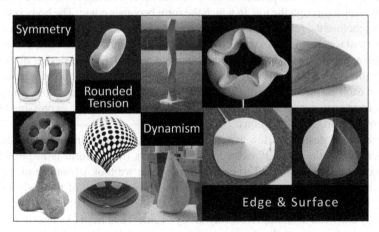

Fig. 5. Design mood board of robot intended form key elements.

Based on the design mood board, we carried out an ideation process by drawing thumbnail and idea sketches, then building rough models with cardboard and blue foam to evaluate different sizes and forms, and once final design was selected it was gradually improved through the same process of model making and evaluation by the design team. Once the final design was selected, a 3D CAD model was also built (Fig. 6).

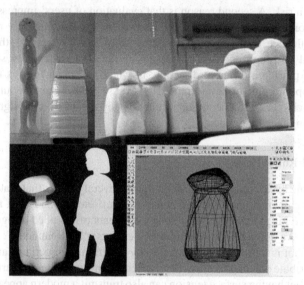

Fig. 6. Robot design process (from top-left: Full-size cardboard model, blue foam rough models, styling model and 3D CAD model). (Color figure online)

The robot enclosure consists of three elements: body, head and neck (see Fig. 7). The body has a form that is pyramidal in its bottom base, with highly rounded edges that gradually vanish through the top, in which the form becomes conic. The body is wider in its base to enclose the robot omni-wheels and to increase stability. Surfaces and edges of the body twist together in clockwise direction with a 75° angle to enhance the dynamism of the robot, as well as to emphasize its rotational movement. The design of the body aims a gently image that feels soft just by looking at it. At the body bottom base, in the middle of each surface or side of the pyramid, there is a small depression, which aims to break form monotony and also to hint the presence of the wheels, expressing that the robot moves in different directions.

For the head design, its lower part is cylindrical, harmonizing with the shape of the upper part of the body. If viewed from above, its overall form is inspired in the Reuleaux triangle or "spherical triangle", from which we took advantage of its three-sided morphology and sense of roundness. Since the lower part of the body has four sides, by having a head with just three sides, we can effectively combine the symmetries of the body and head in an imperfect way. Body (4 sides) and head (3 sides) don't match perfectly, so it becomes difficult to perceive one part of the robot as the "front" or the "rear", therefore increasing its sense of symmetry, and also its freedom to move towards any direction, without triggering any feeling of strangeness to users. From side view, the head has a form that tends to be oval or almond-shaped, depending on the angle. It is divided by an edge in lower and bottom parts.

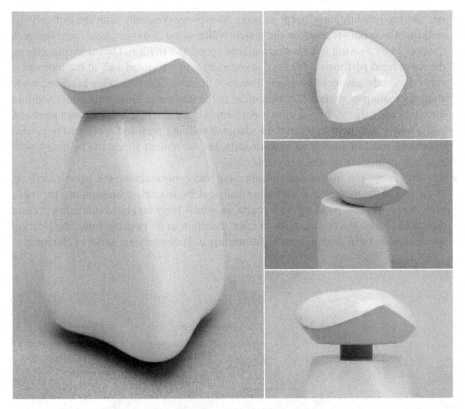

Fig. 7. Robot final design model.

White was selected as the color for the robot. It is vastly used in robots and, since it is perceived as neutral, in evaluation of robot design and motion the color will not influence results.

3.5 Design of Robot Motion

Considering the patients' emotions on each step of the rehabilitation general outline described in Sect. 2.2, the following robot basic actions (movements) for emotional support were defined (see Fig. 8).

- At "Preparation" step: The robot performs a "slow up and down" head reciprocating movement. When the head moves slowly upwards and downwards, resembles the expansion and contraction of a living being while breathing pacefully, so we speculate that it may help to decrease patients' anxiety by transmitting them a sense of calmness.
- At "Immediately before start" step: Aiming to encourage and boost positive emotions, the robot performs a "quick up and down" reciprocating movement. We think it may resemble the gesture of nodding enthusiastically, or an energetic gesture of raising the fist while cheering.

- At "During rehabilitation" step: In order to express sympathy with the difficulty of walking, the robot –located on the patient's side some distance ahead- accompanies the patient by moving at his same walking speed and rhythm. During displacement, the robot head performs a "sliding" movement going forward and, at the moment it stops, the body advances a certain distances in same direction. This head and body slide alternating movement can be similar to the way some birds walk while nodding forward. Since this sliding motion is performed in an alternate way between head and body, it may also help to support an adequate walking pace and motivate the patient to achieve rehabilitation goal. Additionally, the movement appears to be funny, so it also may contribute to alleviate stress.
- At "End" step: For the purpose of affirming and congratulating the patient's efforts at the end of the therapy and enthusiastically celebrate goals achievements, the robot performs a "reverse rotation" movement, in which body and head rotate in opposite directions. Since the body rotates in same direction as its twisting form, the rotation speed appears to be higher, hence transmitting a more energetic sense of cheering.

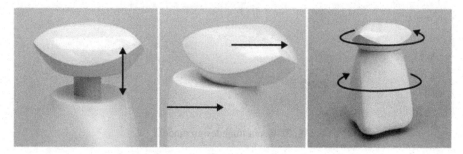

Fig. 8. Robot motion (left: up and down, center: sliding, right: reverse rotation).

Based on defined robot structure, enclosure design and intended motion, prototypes of the robot were built and tested.

4 Prototyping and Verification

Aiming to evaluate the proposed robot design and motion, two prototypes were built (Fig. 9). The first prototype has medium size (313 mm Width × 313 mm Depth × 600 mm Height) and was used for assessing impression towards robot motion. After this evaluation we considered this prototype size may be intimidating for small children, so we decided to adjust robot dimension and build a smaller prototype. The dimensions of the second prototype were reduced to 230 mm Width × 230 mm Depth × 435 mm Height. During the making process of the robot enclosure, the body shape of the first prototype had to be changed in order to decrease costs related to 3D printing, becoming flatter and more squared. Internal mechanisms (Fig. 10) and parts of both prototypes are basically the same, having slight differences in size and motors specifications. The robot has four omnidirectional wheels, arranged with a 90° angle between them. Robot motion is enabled by 7 stepping motors and it has proximity sensors for obstacle detection. Motion is controlled by an Arduino microcontroller board and, as it has been stated before, at the present stage of this research the prototypes are operated by remote control.

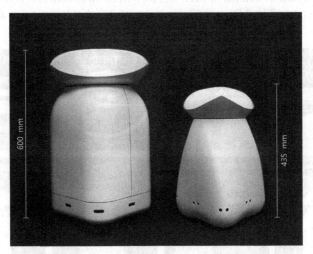

Fig. 9. Robot mid-size and small-size prototypes.

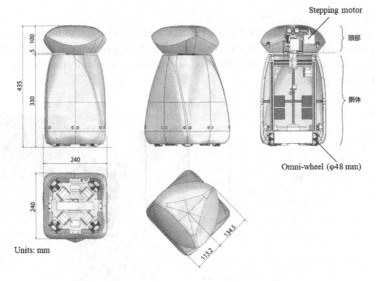

Fig. 10. Robot's omni-wheels and motors layout.

4.1 Evaluation of Impression Towards Robot Motion

Since involving children in the validation process of this research became increasingly difficult due to the Covid-19 situation in Japan, prototype evaluations had to be carried out with adult subjects. For evaluation of impression towards motion, the subjects were 20 healthy university students (12 males and 8 females) who were randomly selected at campus. The walking rehabilitation outline was first explained and then mid-size robot performed the motions defined in Sect. 3.5, as well as more conventional displacement and rotation actions (Fig. 11); users' impression while robot is static was also assessed.

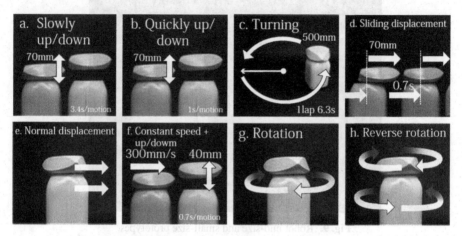

Fig. 11. Evaluated types of robot motion.

The evaluation was performed using the SD method (11 pairs of impression words, 7-points scale). The layout of the experiment and robot trajectories is shown in Fig. 12. Table 2 describes each movement of the robot, as well as detailed information of operating speed and moving distance.

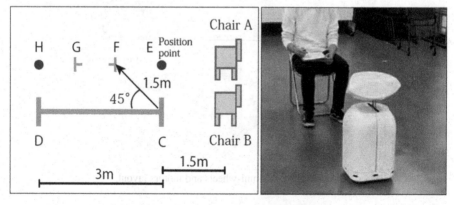

Fig. 12. Layout and aspect of the experiment.

Table 2. Description of robot motion.

Rehabilitation step		Robot motion
Before therapy		Static state
① Preparation	a	Reciprocating movement that slowly raises and lowers the head (3.4s / reciprocation).
② Immediately before start	b	Reciprocating movement that quickly raises and lowers the head (approx. 1s/reciprocation).
	c	Turning motion (6.3 s/lap) with point C in Fig. 3 as the rotation axis.
③ During rehabilitation	d	The head slides and the torso moves forward (moves 70 mm each for the head and torso in 0.7 s).
	e	Normal displacement that moves forward while stopping irregularly at the operator's timing.
	f	It moves from point E to point H at a constant speed (300 mm / s), stops at point H, and then reciprocates up and down. This vertical reciprocating operation has a height of 40 mm (0.7s / reciprocating).
	g	As an operation for repetition, a rotation operation with the center of the robot body as the rotation axis.
④ End	h	Body and head rotates in opposite directions at the same time. (Body: 0.5 rotation/s, Head: 1 rotation/s with respect to the body).

The main results of the evaluation of impression towards robot motion can be summarized as follows:

- Stationary state, "slow up and down" reciprocating movement and "slow sliding displacement" were associated to an impression of [being calm].
- The movements of "quick up and down" reciprocating movement and "reverse rotation" movement transmitted an impression of [being energetic and excitement].
- The "up and down" reciprocating movement -regardless of speed- were associated to an impression of [cheering].
- "Sliding displacement" was indicated as transmitting a [cuddling] impression.
- "Reverse rotation" was linked to an impression of [being happy].

From the results of this first evaluation it can be concluded that the movements defined for the robot's behavior are capable of transmitting feelings that can be associated to the desired emotions for each of its support roles.

4.2 Evaluation of Impression Towards Robot Form

An online questionnaire was conducted with the aim of clarifying the impression of the robot exterior design. In this evaluation, the small-size prototype with the original design (Fig. 9) was used. The questionnaire was responded by a total of 71 persons, with a great majority of university students and some persons from general public (46 men and 25 women). Respondents were asked to evaluate robot images according a set of impression words, which were extracted from past robot sensitivity evaluation experiments found in literature review [12–16]. The evaluation included comparison of the form of both medium and small size prototypes. The answer method is the SD method (12 pairs of impression words, 7-step scale) and free questions.

As a result of histogram analysis, it became clear that the overall impression towards the robot form was associated to the following expressions: "good", "gentle", "cute", "I like it", "sense of stability", "interesting" and "mechanical". Comparison of the two prototypes revealed that the smaller robot was higher evaluated as "friendly", and it became clear that form elements that mainly affect this evaluation are the robot curved lines, rounded form and smaller size. On the question "Do you think the small prototype has a face?" 43 people (60.6%) answered positively. For such cases, we asked to select the robot area that looks like a face, and most of these respondents selected the area in the head with protrusions. Among them, few respondents had a negative impression of this protruding ("mechanical", "unfriendly", and "scary"), but there at the same time few persons said that protruding elements makes the head to look "cute", "as an animal". As a conclusion of this evaluation it can be said that the majority of respondents had a positive overall impression of the robot form, with an image associated to positive adjectives that match the intended robot emotional roles. However, regarding the robot face, the fact that more than half or respondents perceived the robot as having a face requires further analysis. Regarding this matter, it may be inferred that, some respondents found scary to perceive a face in the robot while not having explicit face attributes.

4.3 Evaluation of Overall Impression by Healthcare Professionals

The purpose of this evaluation is to clarify the impression regarding the robot form and the effectiveness of the robot movement for each role. A total of 10 medical professionals (6 nurses, 2 medical universities professors, 1 nursing teacher and 1 physiotherapist) participated in this evaluation, carried out by a web questionnaire. As for the evaluation method, the concept of the robot and the defined outline of walking rehabilitation were explained, together with the design intention of the robot form and motion. Short videos of every motion of the robot were included for evaluation (Fig. 13). These videos were shown in an order according to the rehabilitation outline steps discussed in Sect. 4.

Fig. 13. Video of the prototype motion used in the evaluation study (screen capture).

The analysis method was SD and free questions. For the impression of the robot form, 5 pairs of impression words were evaluated on a 7-points scale, and for the effectiveness of each movement, evaluation was done with a 7-points scale. Although 10 respondents are not an adequate statistical sample, the study results are summarized as follows:

- In evaluation of the overall impression of the robot form, impressions tended to "good", "I like it" and "mechanical". Although there were favorable opinions such as "its unique shape can help to call kid's attention" and "I think it may be easier to get along with the robot without a face than having one", a contrasting opinion such as "it might be a little scary for kids" was also obtained.
- On the evaluation of the 8 proposed robot motion, 7 movements were satisfactorily evaluated, with more than half of respondents considering each movement to be effective for its intended emotional role. Only "sliding displacement" was considered not effective for the role of expressing empathy with the difficulty of walking.
- The usefulness of the robot in its present state (operated by remote control, without automated functions) was favorably evaluated by more than half of respondents. Similar results were obtained regarding the willing to use a robot incorporating automated functions.

5   Conclusions

This study aimed the realization of an emotional support robot for children walking rehabilitation by first clarifying the emotional roles that the robot must perform during rehabilitation, designing the form and motion of the robot that can fulfill these roles, and finally performing validation of these elements by using prototypes.

Although a final goal of this research is to develop a robot with a high level of automation, presently the robot prototype is operated by remote control. At this state, the overall impressions of the robot design, motion and effectiveness have been favorably evaluated. These results may allow concluding that using the proposed robot for emotional support for pediatric walking rehabilitation could be effective.

It is clear that, at this moment, the weakest point of this research is that children have not been formally participated evaluation studies, due mainly to difficulties related to Covid-19 pandemic. Additionally, due to this situation the evaluation studies of the robot form and effectiveness were performed online. However, although the number of medical professionals who participated in the evaluation was low, their opinions tended to be as favorable as the one obtained by other respondents. Overall, obtained results have been encouraging, and not favorable opinions also shed light on issues that can further verified or improved. One example is regarding the design of the head, since more than half of respondents indicated that it looks as having face.

From a design perspective, a valuable contribution of this research has been working toward a direction in which the robot does not mimic a human or animal. Despite the strong tendency of robots with anthropomorphic and biomorphic forms, this research explored a direction aiming to achieve good acceptance by a balance between a more abstract form and motion that can be seen with some familiarity. The proposed robot's form and motion in this research has been generally evaluated with satisfactory results.

Nevertheless, a more comprehensive validation requires involving children and performing a quantitative evaluation with more statistical power, as well as on-site qualitative observation.

As tasks for further research, the robot development must incorporate integration of sensing, intelligence and other technological systems leading to achieve some autonomous behavior, as well as to explore additional ways for interaction with patients, such as voice or physical contact.

References

1. Ministry of Health, Labour and Welfare: 2025-Estimated supply and demand for long-term care personnel toward 2025. Nen ni muketa kaigo jinzai ni kakaru jukyū suikei (kakutei-chi) ni tsuite. https://www.mhlw.go.jp/file/05Shingikai-12601000SeisakutoukatsukanSanjikansh itsu_Shakaihoshoutantou/270624houdou.pdf.pdf. Accessed 26 October 2019
2. Ministry of Economy, Trade and Industry. New JIS as Safety Standards for Robot Services Established. https://www.meti.go.jp/english/press/2019/0520_003.html. Accessed 14 November 2019
3. Mazur, A., Radziewicz, I., Szczepański, T.: Pain management in children. Ann. Agric. Environ. Med. 1(1), 28–34 (2013)
4. Gerik, S.: Pain management in children: developmental considerations and mind-body therapies. South. Med. J. 98(3), 295 (2005)
5. Pritchard, L., et al.: Child, parent, and clinician experiences with a childdriven goal setting approach in paediatric rehabilitation. Disabil. Rehabil. 1–8 (2020). https://doi.org/10.7210/jrsj. Accessed 20 August 2019
6. Ryugo, C.: Review of children's stress reduction in painful procedures. J. Jpn. Soc. Child Health Nurs. 13(1), 77–82 (2004). Kodomo no shochi ni okeru sutoresu kanwa ni kansuru bunken kentō. https://doi.org/10.20625/jschn.13.1_77. Accessed 6 August 2019
7. Yamazaki, Ch., et al.: A study of stress in hospitalized children and assistance in relieving it. J. Child Health 65(2), 238–245 (2006). Nyūin-chū no kodomo no sutoresu to sono kanwa no tame no enjo ni tsuite no kenkyū. https://www.jschild.medall.net/Contents/private/cx3child/2006/006502/025/0238-0245.pdf. Accessed 2 August 2019
8. NHK Educational Corporation: Why are children more likely to change their mood than adults? Kodomo no kata ga otona yori mo kibun ga kawari yasui no wa naze? https://www.sukusuku.com/contents/qa/58467. 15 February 2020
9. Morrissette, M.: School closures and social anxiety during the COVID-19 pandemic. J. Am. Acad. Child Adolesc. Psychiatry 60(1), 6–7 (2021)
10. Bartneck, C., Forlizzi, J.: A design-centred framework for social human-robot interaction. In: 13th IEEE International Workshop on Robot and Human Interactive Communication (IEEE Catalog No. 04TH8759), RO-MAN 2004, pp. 591–594. IEEE (2004)
11. Wirtz, J., et al.: Brave new world: service robots in the frontline. J. Serv. Manag. 29(5), 907–931 (2018)
12. Kanda, T., Ishiguro, H., Ono, T., Imai, M., Makatsu, R.: An evaluation on interaction between humans and an autonomous robot Robovie. J. Robot. Soc. Jpn. 20(3), 315–323 (2002). Ningen to sōgo sayō suru jiritsu-gata robotto Robovie no hyōka. https://doi.org/10.7210/jrsj.20.315. Accessed 19 October 2019
13. Kanda, T., Ishiguro, H., Ishida, T.: Psychological evaluation on interactions between people and robot. J. Robot. Soc. Jpn. 19(3), 362–371 (2001). https://doi.org/10.7210/jrsj. Accessed 19 October 2019

14. Inoue, H.: Impression evaluation for motions of pet type robot based on "Large-small" and "Fast-slow". In: Proceedings of the 29th Fuzzy System Symposium, pp.136–138 (2013). 'Ōkī - chīsai' 'hayai-osoi' ni motodzuita petto-gata robotto no dōsa ni taisuru inshō hyōka. https://doi.org/10.14864/fss.29.0_31. Accessed 21 October 2019

15. Mori, Y., Ota, K., Nakamura, T.: Motion generation of interactive robot considering KANSEI of human. J. Jpn. Soc. Kansei Eng. 4(1), 17–20 (2004). Hito no kansei o kōryo shita intarakushonrobotto no kōdō seisei. https://doi.org/10.5057/jjske2001.4.21. Accessed 22 October 2019

16. Shibata, R., Kojima, T., Sato, K., Hashikura, Y., Ozeki, M., Oka, N.: Effects of personal characteristics on an impression of a robot. In: Proceedings of the 26th Annual Conference of the Japanese Society for Artificial Intelligence (2012). Kojin no tokusei ga robotto no inshō ni ataeru eikyō efekuto of pāsonaru.https://doi.org/10.11517/pjsai.JSAI2012.0_3 K1R116. Accessed 24 October 2019

Exploring the Factors Aiding Speech-to-Text Emotional Restoration

Xin Chen and Qingxin Deng[✉]

Shenzhen University, Guangdong 518060, China
xinchen@szu.edu.cn

Abstract. In recent years, with the development of artificial intelligence technology, speech recognition technology can perform high-precision interpretation and transcription on voices in various complex environments, improving typing efficiency. However, the text obtained by speech translation is only composed of text and simple punctuation, which hinders the real emotion expression of users. The pale translated text hinders the formation of context, affects the emotional transmission of semantics, and lead to a poor user experience when users communicate with others. Based on user experience and emotion, this article discusses the factors that assist the speech-to-text emotional restoration. Through the qualitative and quantitative study, this research compares four emotional effects of information texts composed by different elements: emoticon, punctuation, interjections, and speech-to-text function of WeChat, and further studies the factors that assist speech-to-text emotion restoration. The research results reveal that emoticon and punctuation have a positive effect on the speech-to-text emotional restoration. The addition of the above two factors can restore the emotional effect of speech in text mode with lower loss, fully improve the user experience in mobile communication, and make the online communication smoother.

Keywords: Emotional restoration · Speech-to-text · Emotion · User experience

1 Introduction

1.1 A Subsection Sample

Intelligent speech recognition is the first step of human-machine voice interaction. In instant messaging, computers assist humans through voice interaction, speech recognition is closely related to user experience. Voice information contains many non-verbal cues, including pitch, pause, etc. The effectiveness of verbal interaction among people is closely related to the rhythm [1]. Voice is closest to natural language, and the efficiency of voice input speed is significantly better than text typing, making human-computer interaction more efficient and natural [2]. The manual typing process is more cumbersome and inconvenient for the rapid transmission of information. Based on Chinese and English, Ruan et al., finds that the speed of voice input is almost three times faster than that of keyboard input with fewer errors [3]. However, compared with voice information, text information can be continuously combed and integrated in the editing

© Springer Nature Switzerland AG 2021
M. M. Soares et al. (Eds.): HCII 2021, LNCS 12780, pp. 420–433, 2021.
https://doi.org/10.1007/978-3-030-78224-5_29

process. The content will be more logical, and the author's emotions can be reflected by editing methods, so that the recipient can understand the content more quickly which makes the dialogue more effective. Therefore, speech-to-text function needs to be more accurate and restore non-verbal information other than the speech content as much as possible. In order to promote the accuracy of speech-to-text and real-time speech translation, researchers have used Multimodal Machine Learning with vision to conduct text translation in 1986 [4]. The former speech recognition technology needs users to make pause deliberately for sentence breaking [5]. With the development of artificial intelligence, the current research on speech recognition is to improve the details such as the user experience, and the recognition accuracy and personification of users' emotions, etc. Researchers like Kwon et al., are actively conducting research on speech emotion recognition [6]. The recognition technology of speech emotion has made great progress.

Nowadays, speech recognition technology can extract the text information of speech with high accuracy in various complex environments, but the content of the output text generally only consists of simple punctuation marks and text. Therefore, in the absence of information such as tone and intonation, awkward text can easily lead to the omission of important non-verbal clues (such as emoticon, punctuation, interjections, etc.). From the perspective of emotional attributes, such stereotyped text expressions are pale and seriously lack individualized emotions which greatly reduces the emotional restoration of information. The cold machine language hinders the formation of context and thus affects semantic transmission. Texts that lack emotions are not conducive to the user experience of information transmission between the two parties that are likely to cause the ineffectiveness of verbal interaction. Therefore, exploring the factors that aids the speech-to-text emotional restoration helps to retain the voice content and enhance the user experience.

With the development of deep learning technology, such as multimodal sentiment analysis, the speech recognition technology has obtained certain achievements. In terms of user experience, there are still gaps in the research on related factors of emotional restoration in speech-to-text recognition on how to optimize the experience from the speech to text output content, allowing users to receive information with the lowest loss. From the perspective of the user experience, this study identifies three non-textual factors through qualitative and quantitative research: emoticon, punctuation, and interjections. By obtaining the interviewees' chat data in WeChat to construct a semi-structured situational dialogue, a small corpus is built according to the interviewee's input habits, and four types of text are obtained through manual transcription. The interviewees evaluate the emotional restoration of the text. This article verifies the impact of emoticon, punctuation and interjections in non-text factors on speech-to-text emotional restoration, and proposes output targets that help information transmission for speech recognition technology which further promotes the user experience in voice typing.

2   Research Method

The research object of this experiment is 43 young Chinese, including 14 men and 29 women at the age of 18–37. They use personal communication software WeChat daily. The shortest period for the interviewees using WeChat is 4 years, and the longest reaches

9 years. In order to obtain more realistic data, the interviewees are asked to use their mobile devices to accept online interviews with the most natural state in their familiar spaces. Qualitative and quantitative research methods are used in experiment of the research.

Part of the interviewees (21 in total) are randomly invited to conduct qualitative research so that the we could basically grasp the interviewees' usage of speech-to-text function, emoticon, punctuation, and interjections of WeChat which helps prepare for the quantitative interviews. With the interviewees' permission, the using data of the classic small yellow face emoticon and interjections in WeChat are extracted. Multiple interview questions are designed to understand the interviewees' usage of punctuation in WeChat. The duration of each interview is approximately16 min.

Based on the users' usage data obtained by the qualitative research, we carry out the construction and labeling of the corpus, the scenario design, and the manual transcription. Moreover, we design 21 long questions for the questionnaire. A total of 43 valid questionnaires are obtained in this study.

3   Experiment Procedure

3.1   Build a Corpus

Due to the large number and types of custom stickers, this research mainly analyzes WeChat's classic yellow face emoticons. In the qualitative study, the usage of non-text elements in WeChat of 21 interviewees are recorded. First, the yellow face emoticons of the interviewees in the "most frequently used" section are recorded. The context and emotions of yellow face emoticons used by the interviewees are viewed by the "search" function, and then combined with interviews, and the corresponding emoticons used by users to express different emotions in WeChat are summarized. Second, the interviewees are asked about the usage habits of interjections in different contexts. Through the "search" function, the interviewees' chat records under the corresponding interjections are consulted, and the emotions at that time are recorded. Third, because the data on the use of punctuation cannot be easily obtained, the researchers directly interview the interviewees. The interview questions include: "Under what circumstances will this punctuation be used? Please give an example", "Will the same punctuation be use multiply? What kind of emotion do you think this is to express?" etc., and we design multiple sentences with obvious emotions and continuous text without any pauses. Interviewees insert punctuation, and then record punctuation that they use frequently as well as the symbols and their corresponding emotions. With the active cooperation of the 21 interviewees, this study manually obtains the usage of emoticon, punctuation and interjections, and constructs a small corpus with high usage rate by the interviewees.

3.2 Corpus Annotation

This article refers to the sentiment classification model of Ekman [7], which classifies the corpus as a total of six categories, like anger, disgust, fear, happiness, sadness, and surprise. Since interviewees express that there are many moments without obvious emotion in the instant messaging, this research expands the category of a neutral state (no obvious emotion). Under the seven emotion categories, the only annotator in this study makes the corresponding annotations for emoticon, punctuation, and interjections which are frequently used by interviewees in the corpus under seven emotion classifications (Table 1).

Table 1. Corpus annotation.

Emotion	Emoticon	Punctuation	Interjection
HAPPINESS		"!", "!!", "."	"啊-a", "哦-o", "呢-ne", "啦-la", "吧-ba", "喽-lou"
ANGER		"?!", "???", "…"	"啊-a", "唉-ai", "了-le"
SURPRISE		"!", "?"	"啊-a", "哇-wa", "呐-na"
SADNESS		"…", "."	"啊-a", "吧-ba", "了-le"
FEAR		"…", "??", "…"	"啊-a", "呀-ya"
DISGUST		"!!", "…", "!", "?!"	"啊-a", "呢-ne", "吧-ba"
NEUTRAL		"~", "!", "."	"哦-o", "咧-lie", "吧-ba"

3.3 Scenario Design

In order to represent the real scene of the online conversation as much as possible, this research includes 21 real dialogue obtained from the conversation content of the interviewees (Table 2). For the 7 categories of emotions, each class is designed for 3 scenarios. There are a total of 21 online chat dialogues. Each scene has only one voice content. By semi-structure chat content, the interviewees would quickly enter the context and prepares for the follow-up interviewees to evaluate the emotional restoration to the four texts.

Table 2. Chat content excerpts in 21 scenes.

Emotion	Scene	Speech content
HAPPINESS	Eat	"The Korean food of the restaurant is really good! Come on, haha. Wait for you"
	Shopping	"I have finally bought a very nice pair of pants"
	Joke	"Then the classmates next to him actually beat him. They beat him so hard that he was about to cry, haha"
ANGER	Online shopping	"It took me more than a month to wait for the arrival of the goods and it is still bad"
	Noise	"I just can't fall asleep. It's so annoying"
	Late	"Have you done it yet?"
SURPRISE	Chance encounter	"And I can't believe that he came with the baby in his arms"
	Winning	"Really? You are so lucky"
	Stock	"Wow, haha, it increases so much and it is good"
SADNESS	Near death	"What can I do, can I save it"
	Epidemic	"You haven't come back for two years, but you really can't help it"
	Overtime	"It's really bad, and I hate working overtime"
FEAR	Sick	"I'm so scared, and I don't know if there is anything wrong"
	Accident	"Oh my God, this is too scary"
	Danger	"No, I keep the door of the dormitory open, and I don't know it's so dangerous"
DISGUST	Smell unpleasant	"This smell is really unbearable"
	Game	"What is this stuff and I will definitely not play this week"
	Advertising	"The advertising is so confident. It's pretty awesome"
NEUTRAL	Notice	"Before going home, everyone must understand the relevant policies and prepare in advance"
	Suggest	"If there is anything you don't understand, you just need to search the official account. It takes you relatively little time but you can learn more"
	Discuss	"I'm going to the supermarket to buy it. I a little bit want to eat beef balls and gluten"

3.4 Manual Transcription

Multimodal sentiment analysis that uses manual transcription is a precedent for fully automatic sentiment classification [8]. The application of artificial transcription in this research effectively simulates deep learning technology. According to the corpus, we annotate the only voice of the 21 scripts and process them into four types of text (Table 3):

1. Text directly output by the voice translation function of WeChat; 2. Text only with emoticon; 3. Text only with special punctuation; 4. Text only with special interjections.

Table 3. Four types of text processing methods (Scene 5).

Type	Text (The smell is really unbearable)
WeChat speech-to-text	这味道真的受不了了(zhe wei dao zhen de shou bu liao le)
Emoticon	这味道真的受不了了 😵 (zhe wei dao zhen de shou bu liao le 😵)
Punctuation	这味道真的受不了了!!(zhe wei dao zhen de shou bu liao le! !)
Interjection	这味道真的受不了了啊(zhe wei dao zhen de shou bu liao le a)

3.5 Evaluation

In a text environment, sentiment analysis can be conducted from the perspective of the authors, or the readers. The former refers to the emotion of the authors when writing messages, and the latter refers to the users' reaction to the emotions caused by the emotional text [9]. As describing emotions is a complex problem, and in this study, interviewees do not need to classify emotions. Through the survey of the questionnaires, interviewees are asked to evaluate the emotional restoration of the four types of transcribed texts. 21 different dialogue contexts are randomly arranged. Interviewees are asked to make subjective evaluation of the four texts manually transcribed by the annotator through the semantic differential scale with 7 points (-3 indicates that the emotional restoration of the text is extremely low; 3 indicates that the text has a high degree of emotional restoration).

3.6 Data Analysis

This research is based on 7 basic emotions. According to each emotion, 3 dialogues in different scenarios are established which construct 21 dialogue context in total. The interviewees in each dialogue are asked to evaluate the four processed texts. A total of 43 online questionnaires are obtained with 3612 scores.

According to the degree of text emotion restoration, the scores of the four text types are compared by SPSS, and the scores of the emotion restoration under different factors are analyzed. Moreover, the factors that affect the emotion restoration of text information are explored, and the factors with higher scores and lower scores of the interviewees are summarized and analyzed. In addition, the scoring preferences of interviewees in different genders for text types are also explored.

4 Empirical Study

4.1 Findings

Usage of the Emoticon. Only Introduction The annual report of WeChat data in 2019 [10] reveals that the yellow-face emojis used frequently are [Facepalm], [Grin], and

[Chuckle]. Com-pared with the annual report of WeChat data in 2018 [11], the most frequently used emoticons are basically the same. Several interviewees agree in the interviews that the three emojis mentioned above are the three yellow-face emojis they use and receive information most frequently. When they are asked what kind of yellow-face emoji would be used in happy emotions, [Grin], [Chuckle], and [Lol] are the three most frequently used emoticons by interviewees. Interviewee (P1) expresses that he will not use any emoji when he is extremely angry. In addition to that, he expresses his angry by [Angry] and [Smile]. When they are asked about the emoticons they would use when they were surprised, several interviewees express that they would use [Lol], but some interviewees say that there is no suitable yellow-face emoji to express surprise emotions. In a sad mood, the interviewees express they would use [Facepalm] and [Frown]. WeChat launched the new yellow-face emoticon in November, 2020, among which, [Hurt] and [Broken] become new yellow-face emojis for young interviewees to express sad emotions. The newly launched emoticons are more exaggerated with stronger emotions, and are more accepted by teenagers. In the fear mood, the interviewees often use often [Panic] and [Grimace]. In the disgust mood, the interviewees say that they would use [Smile], [Facepalm], and [Broken] to express dissatisfaction. In neutral emotions, the interviewees' expressions vary greatly. In this context, interviewees tend to use emoticons with ambiguous emotions, such as [Smirk]. A interviewee (P2) who likes to prefer to use in neutral emotions by [Emm] states that she could not accurately describe the specific meaning of [Emm], but her purpose is to reduce the sense of seriousness.

In qualitative research, [Grin], [Chuckle], and [Facepalm] are received good feedback among the interviewees, and they are used in happy emotions. The new version of the yellow-face emojis is also favored by young interviewees due to the strong emotions. There are differences in the expressions of interviewees under neutral emotions.

Usage of Punctuation. Punctuation is used for text's pause. Interviewees express that most of the time in instant messaging, messages are sent multiple times in short sentences. Generally, there is only little punctuation that indicate pauses and express questions or special emotions in the end of sentences, and only in rare cases, large texts will be sent. However, it is worth noting that speech input generally contains relatively long sentences, so there will be a lot of long sentences in the text of speech translation. Whether the punctuation at this time can express the degree of emotional restoration to a certain extent is worthy of our exploration. In the interviews, a total of 16 interviewees say that multiple identical punctuation in succession can increase the tone, enhance emotional expressions, and make it easier for the receivers to understand the senders' emotions.

Compared with the text in the general environment, the interviewees use fewer punctuation in instant messaging, and it is difficult to summarize the rules of the use of punctuation. The use of continuous punctuation may have an impact on emotional restoration.

Usage of Interjections. Through the interviewees' WeChat data, we can see that some young female users prefer to use some emerging interjections such as the onomatopoeia of "害-hai", "鸭-ya", "捏-nie". The interviewees believe that this kind of new interjections will accompany the emotion of acting like a baby, and some interviewees say that they can't understand this kind of interjections. On the other hand, some interviewees state that the use of interjections is due to the expression of dialects, such as "Suo", "Sai" which are with great Chinese characteristics. The interviewees say that such interjections are generally used in the communication of fellows from same village. The exchange between the two parties will help bring them closer together. In addition, interviewees say that the expressions of interjections in daily spoken language, such as "哈-ha" and "呐-na", would also be used in online communication. Researchers find that the only interjections currently translated by WeChat are the regular interjections, like "呢-ne", "啊-a", and "吧-ba". When there is other interjections, it will directly omit or replace them with the ones that are close to the basics. Such transcribed text will certainly cause ambiguity.

Since the scope of this research is not conducted in a specific region, interjections with local characteristics are not analyzed, but the more conventional interjections used by the interviewees are analyzed. Interjections are lacking in the current speech-to-text function of WeChat.

Usage of Speech-to-Text Function. Among the 21 interviewers, there are 18 people who indicate that they have used speech-to-text function. The other 3 users say they do not know this feature. Some interviewees state that the accurate speech translation can only be achieved under standard mandarin, which leads to a high probability of errors in the text they obtain in most cases. The accuracy of speech-to-text function has now become a hot research direction in deep learning, and it is expected to be realized in high-accuracy translation in the near future, it will not be discussed in this article. Some interviewees also say that the lack of integrated voice functions affects the user experience. The use of voice input reduces the time for thinking, and many contents is not filtered. For example, pauses and modal particles that indicate hesitation, and words that are wrong and repeated are completely recorded. In this case, the text obtained by speech translation is confusing, which will cause the inconvenience for the recipient to read. Speech-to-text function is not as accurate as text input in terms of repeated modification and logical integration, which is also a meaningful research direction. Other interviewees state that they would use the voice input function when they want to express their fullest emotions directly, but the speech-to-text function would ignore these tones, which would greatly affect the user experience.

4.2   Data Analysis

The Influence of Emoticon on Emotional Restoration   Comparing scores of the emotional restoration of the text obtained by voice transcription of WeChat and the text with emoticons (Table 4), it is concluded that the degree of the text emotion restoration of emoticons is significantly higher than that of the voice transcription of WeChat. The interviewees believe that text with emoticons can restore emotions better than the default text translated by WeChat. Therefore, adding the appropriate emoticons to the text of speech translation will help improve the user experience.

Table 4. Paired-sample in T-test of emotional restoration obtained from WeChat speech-to-text translation and the emoticon.

	t	df	Sig. (2-tailed)
WeChat speech-to-text - emoticon	−11.357	902	.000

Note: There is a difference under the significance level of 0.05.
P = 0.000 < 0.005. There is a big difference in the emotional restoration between WeChat speech-to-text translation and the emoticon. The evaluation of the emotion restoration of emoticon is higher than that of the original text, and the difference is significant.

This article further analyzes whether the emoticon's performance in speech emotional restoration is related to emotional context. The analysis finds (Table 5), the score of the emotional restoration of the emoticon under happiness mood is significantly higher than that of surprise. Similarly, the score of the emotional restoration of the emoticon under fear and disgust mood are also significantly higher than that of surprise, which indicates that the yellow-face emojis in this study do not have a high restoration of surprise emotions, and from the other side, it is also confirms the conclusions obtained in the previous interviews: At current stage, WeChat's expressions of surprise emotions are poorly restored, which need to be redesigned. Compared to the surprise emotion, the current emoticons of happy, fear, and disgust are more recognized at this stage, and users are more likely to have empathy on them. In addition, the emotional restoration of emoticons in the fear emotion is obviously higher than that of sadness and neutral. In other words, for the WeChat emoticons in the corpus, when the emotion of the voice belongs to happiness, fear, and disgust, adding the corresponding yellow-face expressions to the transcribed text will help restore the emotion and improve the user experience.

Table 5. The scores of the emotional restoration of three types of scenes under seven types of emotions

Emotion	Scene1	Scene2	Scene3	Mean
Happiness	1.37	1.98	1.74	1.70
Anger	1.74	1.09	1.77	1.55
Surprise	1.35	1.58	1.05	1.33
Sadness	1.86	1.56	0.95	1.46
Fear	1.93	1.42	2.12	1.82
Disgust	2.07	1.81	1.14	1.67
Neutral	1.49	1.81	1.49	1.49

The score of the emotional restoration is 1.82 for fear, 1.70 for happiness, and 1.67 for disgust. The lowest score for surprise is only 1.33.

This study also compares the scores of the emotion restoration of emoticons used in three different scenes under the same emotion. It is worth noting that in the three scenes of anger emotions, the score of the scene 9 is significantly lower than the other two scenes (p < 0.05), so [Facepalm] (be used in scene 9) does not perform well in expressing anger emotions. In addition, [Facepalm] used in the scene 19 to express sad emotions and in the scene 11 to express disgust emotion reduction has also low degree of emotional restoration, which can be explained from the side that [Facepalm] is more restrictive to accurately convey emotions, and its user acceptance is not high. Therefore, it is not recommended to use [Facepalm] in the voice transcribed text. On the other hand, in the scene10, the use of [Grin] which means happiness, gets a high score of 1.98, and the emotional restoration is very good. At the same time, in the emotionless scene 8, [Smart] gets a high score of 1.81. Therefore, [Grin] and [Smart] can better restore voice emotions in the happy and neutral speech-to-text translations respectively.

The Influence of Punctuation on Emotional Restoration. After the analysis, the scores of the emotional restoration of punctuation are also significantly higher than that of the original text (Table 6). Its score is slightly lower than the emoticons, but significantly higher than the original text. Therefore, in the speech-to-text output, adding punctuation appropriately will help improve user experience.

Table 6. Paired-sample in T-test of emotional restoration obtained from WeChat speech-to-text translation and the punctuation

	t	df	Sig. (2-tailed)
WeChat speech-to-text - punctuation	−10.443	902	.000

Note: There is a difference under the significance level of 0.05.
P = 0.000 < 0.005. There is a big difference in the emotional restoration between WeChat speech-to-text translation and the punctuation. The evaluation of the emotion restoration of punctuation is higher than that of the original text, and the difference is significant.

This study also explores whether there is a difference in the influence of punctuation on text emotional restoration in different emotions. According to the data analysis, the emotional restoration of the text of the punctuation under neutral and sad is significantly lower than that under other emotions. Therefore, in this study, "…" that interviewees use in sadness and "~" in neutral are not highly recognized. The punctuation in anger has the highest score of emotional restoration (1.88). The punctuation used in anger is "!!", where continuous exclamation marks can restore the emotion of anger. In addition, the score of emotional restoration in surprise is low. The three punctuation under surprise all use exclamation marks, so the use of exclamation marks to express surprise is not very effective. The use of multiple consecutive symbols under strong and clear emotion will strengthen the tone. In addition, there is no obvious regularity in the performance of punctuation in other emotions.

Punctuation is compared in different scenes. In the insensible emotions, the score of the emotional restoration of applying "~" to the "notification" scenario is significantly lower than the other two scenarios. One interviewee (P5) comments - 2 states that "~" has a lively feeling, and it is slightly frivolous when used in the serious occasion of notification. In happiness emotion, the score of the emotional restoration of using "…" in 21 scenarios is very low, and some interviewees express that they do not like to add "…". Such emotions have hesitating and contrived effects. In disgust emotion, the score of the emotional restoration of using "!" in 15 scenarios is worse than the other two scenarios.

In conclusion, in anger emotion, appropriate use these punctuation with strong emotion, such as multiple question marks in rhetorical questions and exclamation marks in the text obtained by speech translation can help improve the emotional restoration. The punctuation with soft emotions like "…"and "~" can easily cause the lack of emotional restoration.

The Influence of Interjections on Emotional Restoration. The emotional restoration of interjections is not significantly different from the original text (Table 7), so interjections have little effect on emotional restoration in this study. Due to the large number of interjections, and the same interjection has different effects in different contexts, it is difficult to divide emotions for the standardization of interjections. Emoticon have clear emotions, and punctuation help to strengthen the tone, and interjections have completely different usages in different contexts, such as "Come here quickly" : "你快点来哦-ni kuai dian lai o", "你快点来吧-ni kuai dian lai ba", "你快点来喔-ni kuai dian lai wo", "你快点来啦-ni kuai dian lai la", the above four modal particles have no obvious difference in emotional expression. The rules of using interjections vary greatly from person to person. For example, girls like to use coquettish modal particles such as "快点哦-kuai dian o" ("hurry up") and "好好吃哦-hao hao chi o" ("very delicious"), but the frequency with which men use such interjections is very low. Therefore, it is difficult to summarize the usage rules of users' interjections at this stage. In the current speech-to-text function, it is not recommended to add too many special interjections, which may cause negative effects.

Table 7. Paired-sample in T-test of emotional restoration obtained from WeChat speech-to-text translation and the interjection

	t	df	Sig. (2-tailed)
WeChat speech-to-text - interjection	−.998	902	.319

Note: There is a difference under the significance level of 0.05.
P = 0.319 > 0.005, There is no big difference in the emotional restoration between WeChat speech-to-text translation and the interjection.

WeChat Speech-to-Text Emotional Restoration. The emotional restoration of the WeChat speech-to-text translations is obviously worse than that of emoticons and punctuation, but there is no significant difference compared with the degree of emotional restoration of interjections. It means that in today's speech-to-text situation, appropriate addition of emoticon and punctuation in speech translation text will have a significant effect on the increase of emotional restoration, but adding interjections has no obvious effect. At this stage, in WeChat and other communication software, adding expressions or punctuation to the text output by voice transcription can significantly improve the emotional restoration of the voice, which is beneficial to improve the efficiency of speech-to-text emotion restoration and improves user experience.

Under different emotions, the degree of speech emotional restoration is obviously different. The emotional restoration of the text translated from WeChat under neutral emotions scores significantly higher than any other emotions. Based on this, it can be explained that under neutral emotions, the text obtained from WeChat voice translation can restore certain emotions.

Difference of the Scores of Emotional Restoration on Genders. This study also analyzes the difference of the scores of emotional restorations on gender, and the results show that males and females have significant differences in the scores of the three text types, WeChat speech translation text, emoticons, and punctuations. The category scores of males in the original text are lower than females, but the emotional restoration scores of emoticons and punctuation are higher than females (Table 8), based on this, it can be shown that men are more likely than women to think that compared with the WeChat speech-to-text texts, the emoticon or punctuation can restore voice emotions better.

Table 8. Independent sample T-test of emotional reduction scores of interviewees of different genders

	Group	Mean	T	p-Value
WeChat speech-to-text	Male	.61	−2.096	.036*
	Female	.85		
Emoticon	Male	1.83	4.415	.000**
	Female	1.45		
Punctuation	Male	1.80	4.665	.000**
	Female	1.38		
Interjection	Male	.91	.873	.383
	Female	.81		

Note: *It indicates there is a difference under the significance level of 0.05. **It indicates there is a difference under the significance level of 0.01.

In the WeChat speech translation text, P = 0.036 < 0.005, men's restoration scores for this type of text are significantly lower than that of women. In the emoticon text, P = 0.000 < 0.005, the scores of males on this type of text are significantly higher than females. In punctuation, P = 0.000 < 0.005, men's restoration scores for this type of text are significantly higher than that of women. In Interjection, P = 0.383 > 0.005, there is no significant difference between male and female scores.

5 Conclusion

In face-to-face communication, gestures, facial expressions, and speech are jointly called to express an expected message, which includes not only verbal information, but also nonverbal information that enriches human communication. It is worth noting that these clues is emotional information, which plays a vital role in daily communication [12]. The text transcribed from speech lacks actual body signals (including actions, facial expressions, eye movements, etc.) and voice signals (including volume, pitch, pauses, etc.). The current speech translation text only retains the basic text content and simple punctuation. As a result, a large number of non-discourse clues are incomplete and cannot effectively restore the senders' emotions.

Facial expressions are related to the expression of emotions [13]. Graphic emoticon in instant messaging software is a very valuable supplement. It can communicate specific information online [14]. Punctuation is called "the rhythm of online communication", because prosody (for example, intonation) is an important clue of emotion in a face-to-face context [15]. Interjections can be compared to the facial expressions of people in actual communication, which can convey specific emotions [16]. From the perspective of user experience, this research studies three non-text factors through qualitative research: emoticons, punctuation, and interjections. The research results show that emoticons and punctuation have a positive effect on the emotional restoration of speech, while interjections have no obvious effect on the emotional restoration of speech. Therefore, adding emoticons or punctuation appropriately in the speech-to-text conversion helps to enrich the emotion of the text and restore the emotional information in the speech, thereby enhancing the user experience. While realizing high-efficiency information typing, it can also restore the emotional clues in the voice to make up for the missing non-speech information of the current WeChat speech-to- text function.

When the intelligent speech recognition technology further optimizes the speech-to-text function, the output of the two non-text languages of emoticon and punctuation is rich in emotional expression, which is beneficial to the transmission of information in user communication. In recent years, due to the development of artificial intelligence technology, the application scenarios of voice transcription have become more abundant, such as intelligent voice robots, car driving, Google Glass which use voice and interface to let users give instructions to products and receive information [17]. With the increase in user requirements for interactive experience, this type of products will have higher needs for emotional restoration of the voice translation. In addition to emoticons and punctuation, more factors that assist emotional restoration are worthy of further study. The interaction of multiple elements should make the information loss of the translated text lower to fully improve the user experience in mobile communication, allow users to be more efficient in information transmission, and make online communication smoother.

Acknowledgments. We thank the Foundation for Young Talents in Higher Education of Guangdong, China [Project Batch No. 2020WQNCX061] for the research support. Part of the study was supported by Shenzhen Educational Science Planning Project (zdfz20015).

References

1. Shneiderman, B.: The limits of speech recognition. Commun. ACM **43**(9), 63–65 (2000)
2. Basapur S, Xu S, Ahlenius M, et al.: User expectations from dictation on mobile devices. In: International Conference on Human-Computer Interaction, pp. 217–225 (2007)
3. Ruan, S., Wobbrock, J.O., Liou, K., et al.: Comparing speech and keyboard text entry for short messages in two languages on touchscreen phones. Proc. ACM Interact. Mob. Wearable Ubiquit. Technol. **1**(4), 1–23 (2018)
4. Kumar, A., Paek, T., Lee, B.: Voice typing: a new speech interaction model for dictation on touchscreen devices. In: Proceedings of the SIGCHI Conference on Human Factors in Computing Systems, pp. 2277–2286 (2012)
5. Karat, C.M., Halverson, C., Horn, D., et al.: Patterns of entry and correction in large vocabulary continuous speech recognition systems. In: Proceedings of the SIGCHI Conference on Human Factors in Computing Systems, pp. 568–575 (1999)
6. Kwon, O.W., Chan, K., Hao, J., et al.: Emotion recognition by speech signals. In: Eighth European Conference on Speech Communication and Technology (2003)
7. Ekman, P.: Facial expression and emotion. Am. Psychol. **48**(4), 384 (1993)
8. Morency, L.P., Mihalcea, R., Doshi, P.: Towards multimodal sentiment analysis: harvesting opinions from the web. In: Proceedings of the 13th International Conference on Multimodal Interfaces, pp. 169–176 (2011)
9. Yadollahi, A., Shahraki, A.G., Zaiane, O.R.: Current state of text sentiment analysis from opinion to emotion mining. ACM Comput. Surv. (CSUR) **50**(2), 1–33 (2017)
10. Report of WeChat data (2019). https://mp.weixin.qq.com/s/gi_3xSDWBie-fgg76XXJCg
11. Report of WeChat data (2018). https://support.weixin.qq.com/cgi-bin/mmsupport-bin/getopendays
12. Busso, C., Narayanan, S.S.: Joint analysis of the emotional fingerprint in the face and speech: a single subject study. In: 2007 IEEE 9th Workshop on Multimedia Signal Processing, pp. 43–47 (2007)
13. Arya, A., Jefferies, L.N., Enns, J.T., et al.: Facial actions as visual cues for personality. Comput. Anim. Virtual Worlds **17**(3–4), 371–382 (2006)
14. Huang, A.H., Yen, D.C., Zhang, X.: Exploring the potential effects of emoticons. Inf. Manage. **45**(7), 466–473 (2008)
15. Kalra, A., Karahalios, K.: TextTone: expressing emotion through text. In: IFIP Conference on Human-Computer Interaction, pp. 966–969 (2005)
16. Motley, M.T.: Facial affect and verbal context in conversation: facial expression as interjection. Hum. Commun. Res. **20**(1), 3–40 (1993)
17. Bailey, D.V., Dürmuth, M., Paar, C.: "Typing" passwords with voice recognition: how to authenticate to Google Glass. In: Proceedings of the Symposium on Usable Privacy and Security, pp. 1–2 (2014)

Reprojecting a Fitness App Regarding Retention and Usability Using Nielsen's Heuristics

Renata Faria Gomes(✉)⑩ and Maria de Fátima Costa de Souza(✉)⑩

Federal University of Ceará, Fortaleza, CE, Brazil
renata.faria.gomes@hotmail.com, fatimasouza@virtual.ufc.br

Abstract. The increasing use of wearable devices, associated with sports practices, served as a motivation for the researchers of this work analyzed the app called Fitness, developed for iOS platform. The choice for iOS was due to the fact that Apple Watch is considered the best selling smartwatch in the world. Besides that, during their physical activities Apple watch users have the possibility to have their data captured by the biosensors in the watch. Such data can be transferred to the iPhone, processed and the result presented to the user to a structured report. However, it was identified serious problems of design in the generated report, probably because it disregards the user's context. Thus, the objective of this research is to identify the existing limitations in Fitness using the evaluation heuristic, in addition to proposing solutions to the referred problems identified through the restructuring of the application interface based on Nielsen's heuristics. To the identification of the limitations and the consequent restructuring of the interface, the research used qualitative and quantitative methods. The results showed a great improvement in usability, with more than 20 points on the SUS scale. In addition, it was noted that heuristics minimize user memory loads, shortcuts and speak the user's language were those that most brought benefits to the interface.

Keywords: Fitness app · Nielsen heuristics · Usability improvement

1 Introduction

Health, exercise and well-being are getting more relevant issues for the mobile app development market, in [1] it is evident a high growth of those applications. These data have relationship with new wearable technologies evolution that has an important role because of their biosensors which are able to precisely measure data from the body [2].

Thus, the most purchased smartwatch in the world is the Apple Watch, with 4 million new active owners in just the first 4 months of 2020 [4]. This gadget has a very close integration with Apple smartphone and with many applications developed by Apple. One of these applications is the Fitness, an app exclusively

© Springer Nature Switzerland AG 2021
M. M. Soares et al. (Eds.): HCII 2021, LNCS 12780, pp. 434–449, 2021.
https://doi.org/10.1007/978-3-030-78224-5_30

designed for sports and physical fitness. This application stores data during exercise in the biosensors of the watch. The data is transferred to the mobile and then, processed in order to show a report to the user.

However, the report generated by the app has visible design drawbacks. For example, as repeating totally or partially the data layout to all available sports, the user context might not have been considered [12]. Besides that, different visual elements from the interface are too close; making the user believes that they form information from the same group [6] and making the search for any specific element more difficult. These problems may negatively affect the application retention, and this as it was previously seen in [1] is one of the greatest challenges found in the health apps. Therefore, this factor is highly relevant for the context of this work.

As an evidence, an experiment carried out by Tison, Hsu et al. [10] has shown that when three design techniques in an Apple Watch app are applied the retention grows significantly. These techniques were: feedback – warn about changes; efficiency – raise the daily frequency of the data updating; and minimalism – simplification of the interface in order to make visualization of the tendencies easier. Such techniques are notable shown in the heuristics done by Nielsen [7]. However, would it be possible to use this and other heuristics to find out new drawbacks and enhance the application interface?

Thus, this work aims to identify problems in Fitness application and how to solve them in order to enhance its usability and retention through heuristics shown by Nielsen.

2   Related Works

Taking into account that one of the pillars of this research is related to the user engagement factor in wearable devices, this section aims to present other works that seek to identify that factors that favor the engagement or disengagement of the user when using the app and the device, regardless the area.

In this sense, Keseberg [15] developed a research in which he sought to understand what favored user engagement with the health app. In it, the definition of engagement adopted was smartwatch Kim, Y. H., Kim, D. J., Wachter, K. [16] who says that engagement is expressed by the user through satisfaction, intention and a perceived value. It was also mentioned that engagement was related to three types of motivation, where the first would be of a utilitarian nature, which can be understood as the ability to complete a task, the second of a hedonic nature, which refers to "feeling entertained" and finally, the third refers to a social order that corresponds to "connecting with others".

In this research, personal and technological factors that favored engagement were identified. Regarding those of a personal nature, it is possible to mention: intrinsic motivation, bond and personal adjustment. Regarding the technological ones, what stood out the most was monitoring, through reminders, goals, among others.

However, another highlight in Keseberg's research is related to identifying the factors that contributed to the user's disengagement in an application. Among them, lack of perception and reliability were mentioned as factors that served as a stimulus for discontinuing the use of the application or wearable. This is because of the perception, regarding the understanding in the form of the functions or understanding of the measures, was not clear.

It was also perceived as important, on a technological level, the presence of factors that make people feel engaged, both in the app and in the wearable. In this sense, the most cited factor is the function of monitoring one's behavior. This is experienced as a motivator, as people are continually encouraged to achieve their goals and thus adjust their behavior.

In the same direction, Asimakopoulos, Asimakopoulos and Spillers [3] conducted a survey with wearables to understand the factors that contributed to motivate and, consequently, engage users, in an application. The research isolated inherent motivational and engagement factors with fitness tracking participants, over time, in an attempt to investigate the reasons for abandonment and, consequently, the barriers outlined for engagement.

One of the barriers identified was related to the lack of application customization. Thus, some declared the need for applications to balance autonomy with the creation of more self-directed goals to support their engagement.

In this sense, the results revealed three main areas of UX that directly impact the motivation and effectiveness of users: data, gamification and content. With this result, it was possible to propose a set of heuristics focused on mobile health, which included a strategy of challenges and tests to motivate the user to interact with their device.

However, just engaging is not enough, what interests us is a cycle that was described by O'Brien and Toms [8], which starts with a phase of interests, which remains and ends, and it can return to the starting point depending on certain factors.

Therefore, the following section will present the problem and the proposal for this research.

3   Methodology

In order to assess the level of commitment of users with the Fitness app, this research made use of a qualitative method and it was organized in three main stages, namely: heuristic assessment, redesign of the application and usability assessment. Next, each of the steps mentioned will be described.

3.1   Heuristic Evaluation

In the first part of the research, a bibliographic survey was made in order to identify works with similar objectives to this research. One of them was the research by Tison, Hsu et al. [10], where they applied techniques related to a series of positive characteristics contained in [7]. Such characteristics were mapped and organized in ten heuristics, which are guidelines that contain desired characteristics in the interaction and in the interface of an application.

Knowing these rules, it is possible to inspect if a certain application contains interaction problems. This inspection method is called heuristic evaluation. Taking into account the context of the researchers, the main reasons for choosing this methodology were due to low cost, agility in data collection, in addition to being used by [10] and showing good results.

After the assessment was made, the results found were organized into three categories. They are: Not applicable, needs investigation with users, detected failures. All categories mentioned here will be detailed in the result section. However, it is important to explain that the heuristics classified as "needs researches with users" were those in which the researchers were unable to identify the presence or absence of each heuristic in the application without the prior help of the users. For this reason, an auxiliary questionnaire for heuristic evaluation was developed to be applied to an audience to be defined later in order to evaluate information found in the application interface.

In the following subsection, the questionnaire will be detailed.

Auxiliary Questionnaire for Heuristic Assessment. The development and application of a questionnaire with users was necessary to confirm whether some heuristics were consistent with the metrics raised by Nielsen [7]. For a better understanding, it is possible to cite as an example, the equivalence between a data presented by the Fitness app, in the swimming activity, called "Average rhythm per stroke" and how a real user uses it in their daily lives. For the results not be mistaken, a specific target audience was defined, which in this case were characterized by people who swim.

The first part of the questionnaire asked for authorization on the use of participants' anonymous responses, followed by questions that assessed the user's profile such as, "how long have you been swimming?", "Do you have an Apple Watch?" among others. The purpose of this first part of the questionnaire was to understand how familiar the user was with the sport and the app.

The second part is related to the evaluation of the information itself. For that, each data that existed on the Fitness app screen was separated into an image. Each image had the same task as in this case, to evaluate the relevance of this information for monitoring its results during training. The respondent then had five options, based on the likert scale [13] and to extra to assess whether the user understood the meaning of the information.

With the results extracted with the aid of the questionnaire, it was possible to proceed to the next step, which in this case was the second and was related to the redesign of the interface. About this redesign it is possible to obtain more details in the following subsection.

3.2   Redesign of the Interface

With the results of the heuristic evaluation stage, it was possible to start the application redesign. The changes were evaluated in order to add the missing characteristics discovered by the user in the previous step. In addition, the interface of other sports applications was taken into account, such as: *Runstatic*,

Nike run club and *My Swimming Pro*. Associated with such sports applications, other applications were considered, but of a non-sports nature, such as *Telegram, Reminders, Settings and Notes*, present in the cell-phone, so that the result was friendly for iPhone users.

In view of the above, a prototype was developed using the *Figma* digital design platform, but it was found that the result would not be interactive enough. For this reason, a new prototype was developed using the Swift language, which is a small application containing only the redesigned screen, with static data. This new application was inserted in the official Apple testing service, *Testflight*, for the exclusive use of the research participants, needing a code to be made available, by the researchers involved in this work, to download and, consequently, its use.

The results of using the new prototype were analyzed in the third and last stage of the methodology, which in this case is the usability evaluation of the redesign detailed in Subsect. 3.3.

3.3   Evaluation of the Redesign

The objective of this phase is to evaluate, with real users, the original Apple application and the redesign proposed during the research. The evaluation phase is essential to understand whether users are able to carry out the proposed interactions and correctly understand the information passed by applications.

The first step was to seek evaluation methods that would meet the demands of the search. Considering that usability is the main metric of the research, it was chosen the use of the System Usability Scale (SUS) system [14], as it is a simple and well-known. However, this method is ideally quantitative and to obtain more information about the results. A previous step was added to the questionnaire: an evaluation communicability.

The communicability assessment, as described in Barbosa [11], is a method that assesses the quality of the interface communication. Thus, users are invited to perform a set of tasks within the application, while evaluators pay attention to how the participant feels when interpreting the information. With this type of methodology, it is possible to observe points of doubt. If the user takes a long time to find any information, and also the opposite, when information is easily found.

Thus, the participant first performed the communicability assessment and, after completing it, answered a questionnaire based on the SUS system, with answers in Likert [11]. Besides that, subjective responses were added to the questionnaire, so that the user could highlight points he liked and disliked within the application. Each step was performed in the original application and redesigned application. The results section provides, in detail, the explanation how the usability test was applied.

4   Results

Likewise the methodology section, this section will be divided into three other ones: heuristic evaluation, application redesign and usability evaluation. At the end, an overview of the result as a whole will be presented.

4.1   Heuristic Evaluation

When doing the heuristic evaluation, each studied point was classified as one of the three options: absent, it can affect the system and the others were not applicable in that context. The heuristics, classifications and justifications are listed below.

For better visualizing the interface problems, an example of the application, which swimming was selected as a sport, will be used as shown in Fig. 1.

Fig. 1. Evaluated Screen interface using swimming as the sport.

Feedback. This heuristic is about keeping users informed about what is happening through feedback. However, as the interface has data that has already been registered, this heuristic is not applicable in this research.

Speak the User Language. According to Nielsen, the terminology of the interface needs to be based on the terms used by the user. In other words, the system needs to use words that are easy to understand. For example, see in image 1 that some terms may not be understandable to the user, such as total active calories or average pace. However, there is no way to be sure of this, as the heuristic evaluation was carried out with two researchers who are not frequent practitioners of the sport and thus do not know the terms. That is why this heuristic was classified as "needs investigation".

Clearly Mark Exits. The interface must have emergency exits to leave the unwanted state without having to go through an extensive dialogue. In addition, the interface needs to allow the user to undo and redo their actions. However, the interface has no interaction that makes the user undo his actions and for this reason it was classified as "not applicable".

Consistency. We can divide the concept of consistency into actions and appearance of the interface, both are related to what the user is used to do. For example, in Apple's standard interfaces, tabulated information usually appears organized as in Fig. 2.

Fig. 2. Detail of a common table, inside Apple's Settings App

Usually, the information is presented in a row, divided into two columns. For example, the title "Videos" appears in the left column and the information contained in it "244" appears on the right. In addition, the lines occupy the entire horizontal extent of the screen.

However, in the application interface, as seen in Fig. 3, the information is not divided in the standard way of the platform. If we look at one of them, for example, the title "*Tempo total*" is located in the second column of a line, dividing space with "*Distância*", the information "0:31:24" is in another line.

In addition, the lines do not use the full length of the screen, causing very large titles to join with others, such as, "*Batimentos médios*" and "*Voltas*" (this occurs only when platform is in Portuguese language). As a consequence, there is a difficulty for users to find the information they want, considering that the platform layout makes them search for the title on the left and the content on the right.

Minimize User Memory Loads. This heuristic deals with the ease of memorizing elements on the screen. If the interface works well with these characteristics, the user can recognize the elements without having to memorize the location of the information. In the application, the titles are very close to each other, making it difficult to read them individually [6].

However, this difficulty can be overcome by the presence of data that are in a larger font size and that also have strong colors that draw attention. Despite

Fig. 3. Detail of Fitness app in Portuguese language

this, the colors compete with each other, making the user almost to have to look at all of them before finding the information he seeks, an aspect that also hinders the recognition of the elements.

Shortcuts. The interface should provide the user with options to streamline their interaction, such as offering a mechanism for frequent actions. In addition, the system should rescue potential customizations based on past interactions. In the Fitness app, in addition to not having an option to rank the most relevant data for each user, as a way to streamline their search, there is also the aggravation that different exercises, which have some data in common, are organized in identical ways, disregarding the user context (Fig. 4).

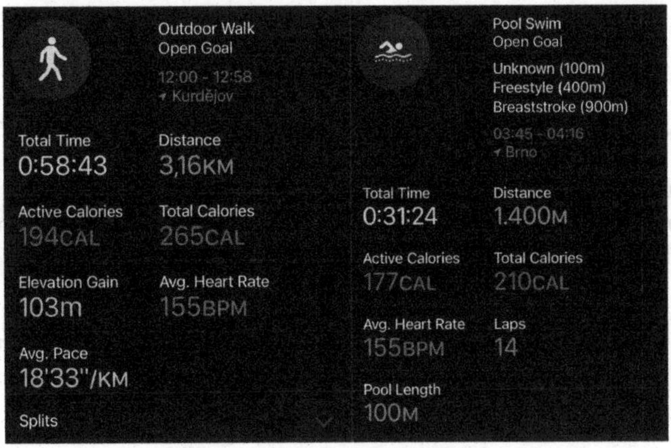

Fig. 4. Comparison between outdoor walk screen and pool swim screen

Simple and Natural Dialogue. Some evidence of the above characteristics is shown in image 4 where we compare the interface for two different exercises. Considering [12], it is necessary to consider the context of who will use the system, such as the location, exercise characteristics and user objective. Possibly, the goals of those who practice swimming and those who practice walking are different. For example, perhaps a map for an outdoor walking is very important, as the person moves between different locations, but it may be irrelevant for a person who swims, since the pool will be in a static location. However, before removing or changing the information hierarchy, it is necessary to understand the user needs.

Prevent Errors. This heuristic says that a problem should be avoided, as the interface has no active interactions, there is no way for users to make mistakes when using it.

Good Error Messages. In this heuristic, error messages should be expressed in simple language, indicate the problem precisely and suggest a solution in a constructive way. As in the previous one, there is no way for users to experience this type of problem.

Help and Documentation. Finally, there is a help and documentation heuristic. Nielsen states that this heuristic is not always applicable, however, there are nomenclatures in the interface that are understandable only to practitioners of the sport, that is, users who do not have sports knowledge do not understand. For example, "Average cadence" is information that appears in an outdoor race and the researchers only managed to understand after an internet search. Because it is not necessarily the fault of the interface, but because of the relationship between information and exercise, it was considered that this heuristic was important and the application should contain a documentation section.

4.2   Redesign

The redesign was divided into two main phases: design and development. The design was made based on the findings of the previous step, for each missing heuristic, something was designed for the new interface to correct.

Speak the User's Language. Since it was found that most users understood what the terms were being used for, only a button named "Glossary" was added. This button led to a screen where all the data was listed.

Consistency. As previously mentioned, the organization of the screen in the previous app was not consistent because it used two and a half columns for information. In the redesign, the organization was changed to a consisted list with the iOS platform (Fig. 5).

In addition, the header has been modified to look similar to Telegram, a widely used messaging app.

Fig. 5. Comparison between the redesign and app Telegram

Minimize User Memory Loads. The solution to this problem was made by making the standardized list with the platform, since the titles are always positioned on the left and the content always on the right, with adequate spacing. In addition, information that previously consumed almost the entire screen, such as, "Automatic Series", in the image below, was taken to a new screen. The goal of the exercise was not very visible, as this is a relevant data, more emphasis was given on this information. After the summary, the goal and its related data are in two columns above the other information.

Shortcuts. One of the shortcuts that can speed up the reading of information is the hierarchy, in other words, the order in which the information appears. For this, an edit button was added to the screen, when pressed, it activates the edit mode, which adds a "drag and drop" option to change the order of the data. This button has been consistently added to the platform, based on Apple's reminders application, in Fig. 6.

Fig. 6. Edit functionality in Reminders app.

Simple and Natural Dialogue. Along with the "drag and drop" action, it was also added in the functionality to edit a button to show and hide information. Thus, the user can customize which information interests him or not. The result is in the Fig. 7.

Fig. 7. Redesign with the edit functionality activated

Help and Documentation. For this heuristic, a glossary has been added, as stated in speak the user's language.

4.3   Development

The development of the application was necessary because it was easier to be tested by the user than the prototype built on the figma platform. This was due to the author having a good command of development for iOS systems, the functionality of editing was very complex to be done using design tools and the distribution of the application is relatively simple using the Apple test platform testflight.

The application was developed in three days, using the Swift language and the SwiftUI framework. The information contained in it was static, inserted into the code so that it was always the same regardless whether the user used the application before.

4.4   Evaluation

The usability assessment step was done with the intention of validating the study proposed by this article. However, it goes beyond that, it will not only show if the usability of an application is better in one than in the other, it will indicate whether the way the heuristic applied resulted in increased usability, in addition to answering the reasons for such result.

Based on this motivation, the first step of this stage was making the material that would be used. In addition to the prototype mentioned in the previous point, two forms were also developed based on the SUS system and material with questions to guide the assessment of communicability.

Profile. With materials in hand, seven Apple Watch users were invited. From this group, only one did not know the Apple application. Two of them knew, but did not use it to record exercises and the others knew and used the application. The participants were heterogeneous in relation to the main sport they practiced using the watch.

App Fitness Review. At the beginning of the evaluation, the researcher explained the research, the terms and how the dynamics of the application would work. A script of tasks was elaborated that the participant needed to perform, at this point, it is important to emphasize that the participant was told he could perform any action he wanted to perform the task.

In the assessment of communicability, the participants demonstrated a certain facility in finding some information, but a great deal of difficulty in finding other information. In addition, there was a task in which the interviewer described one of the data and asked the user to find, in this task, only one of the participants stated with certainty what was the correct information. The others used questions, such as "Is that information?" or dubious statements "I think this is it, but I'm not sure."

Regarding the goal of the exercise, which is at the top of the interface, all participants were able to successfully find the places where the goal was. However with the exception of a single participant, all the others had difficulty in relating which information would be related to the goal. Most chose data that they found most important for themselves, while others stated that it was the information that had the same color as the graph located around the image, but when there were two pieces of information with the same color (for example, total calorie and active calories) the user was unable to answer the question correctly.

At the end of the evaluation, the user was asked to answer a form that contained open and closed responses. The open questions were related to an adaptation of the SUS scale, while the closed questions were for the user to say what they liked or disliked in the application. The result of the first part, referring to the SUS scale resulted in average of 51 points, which is considered as "poor" below the recommended, which is an average of 68.

In the result of the second part, the positive points raised by the users were that the application was simple, had pleasant colors and contained important data. Some drawbacks are about confusing information, irrelevant information and lack of emphasis about the sports' most important information.

Redesign Evaluation. The evaluation of the redesign followed the same methodology as the evaluation of the Apple app, so it would be simpler to make a comparison between the two. The only difference was in the questionnaire, to make future improvements, an extra open question was added, asking for suggestions for improvement in the prototype.

In the assessment of communicability, the interviewees easily located the information. There was no difficulty regarding the search for data. However, in the task of locating data based on its meaning, only four out of the seven respondents accessed the glossary to find out which information was being questioned. It was also noted that in other tasks users entered the glossary and were surprised and asked to return to the task mentioned above.

In addition, there were tasks that asked users to reorder information and hide those that were unnecessary, in both they performed quite easily. When asked which information was related to the goal, the participants responded quickly and confidently.

After the evaluation, the interviewees answered the questionnaire containing the SUS scale and the open questions. The result of the scale was an average of 75, which is equivalent to a "good" index, above the recommended average of 68. The result of the responses on positive points showed that all participants liked the power to reorder and hide information. They were also praised for new hierarchy and the presence of the glossary. On the negative side, several users did not like the graphics being moved to a new screen and commented that they preferred how it was being done in the original application.

Finally, in relation to the improvements, the participants indicated that they felt they lacked what was the total goal. In the app only the percentage and how much was achieved is shown. As in the previous paragraph, it was also mentioned at this point that the graphics should be on the same screen as the information. In addition, one of the interviewees complained that the glossary was not visually striking, that because it is an important part of the redesign it should be somewhere more visible. The last point indicated on the form was the possibility to move information from the table below to the table above, where the goal is.

The comparison between the two applications, the conclusion and possible future work will be discussed in the next section.

5   Results Analysis

Regarding the result from the SUS scale, the redesign of the application screen obtained 24 points more than the original application, which shows a positive aspect of the application of heuristics in the interface design. However, this result is only indicative. In order to obtain more information regarding the improvements, it is also necessary to examine the other artifacts, such as open responses and also the perceptions of the evaluations of communicability. With that in mind, in this section, the results will be discussed in order to reach a conclusion.

In both interfaces, a certain easy search for information was perceived, but being slightly slower in Apple software. In this context, it is important to remember that most users already had prior knowledge of the original application, while none knew the redesigned interface and for that reason it is valid to state that the performance of the redesign was superior.

Regarding confusing data, the glossary helped many users to understand better data and also being one of the features praised by the participants in the forms answered. However, this component would have a greater effectiveness if it were better positioned on the screen or if it was implemented other way. However, in relation to the original app, thanks to the glossary, the redesign had a superior performance, evidencing a successful heuristic "speak the user's language".

Regarding the goal, in the app, participants were confused with which data it was related to the goal of the exercise, which did not happen with the redesign. That positive result is attributed to the consistency heuristic since it follows the pattern of the interfaces that users are used to seeing. In return, it was perceived in both systems that users missed the total goal value, since only the achieved value was displayed and how much it was worth, in percentage of the total.

In addition to comparatives, the redesign stood out for giving the power to edit the information list. The participants commented several times during the evaluation of communicability and also in the open responses that was a fundamental functionality within the application. This fact shows the importance of one of the heuristics cited by [10], the minimalism (minimize memory User memory loads) and also another heuristic: shortcuts.

However, the preference of the participants for the original application in relation to the exercise graphs, such as the beat map, was clear. This change was done following the heuristic minimize user memory loads, however the effect was obtained reverse, since users needed to move from one screen to another.

6   Conclusion and Future Work

This article has analyzed the growing use of mobile devices, specifically wearables, associated with health and practices related to physical activities. In this sense, the research sought to analyze the application called Fitness, developed for iOS platform and which aims to practice sports in search of physical conditioning. The choice for iOS was due to the fact that the wearable device Apple Watch be considered the best selling smartwatch in the world.

Fitness is a native application from Apple, dedicated exclusively to sports and physical conditioning. Apple Watch users, during their physical activities, have their data captured by the biosensors present in the watch. Such data is transferred for the iPhone, processed and the result presented to the user through a structured report. However, the generated report by the mobile application presented serious problems with related design, probably by disregarding the user context.

In this sense, the objective of this research was to identify the problems in Fitness, in addition to seeking solutions in order to improve its usability and engagement by through the heuristics presented by Nielsen. The solution to such problems was presented from a restructuring of the design.

For this, three steps were performed. The first step was the heuristic, in which one of the researchers analyzed whether the interface had certain characteristics in order to meet the quality that each demanded. However, it was noticed that some of them needed investigation with some specific profile. Thus, an additional questionnaire was made, which included 51 people with a swimming profile. At the end of the questionnaire, it was possible to complete the heuristic and move on to the next phase.

Then, the second stage began, which consisted of the redesign. This step used input from the last stage. For example, the absence of a mechanism that met the shortcut heuristic was thus added to the redesign a button for the user to be able to reorder that most important information, in order to read it before any other information, thus being a shortcut to its use.

With the redesign in hand, it was then possible to proceed to the third phase, which aims to evaluate comparatively the two interfaces, the original and the redesigned. That phase was carried out in two phases: a communicability assessment and a form containing objective and subjective questions. The objective questions were based on the SUS system to measure usability.

The results showed a great improvement in usability, with more than 20 points of SUS scale. In addition, it was noted that the heuristics minimize user memory loads, shortcuts and speak the users' language were the ones that most brought benefits to the interface. However, when applying user memory loads, an error was noticed by the redesign, which resulted in an inverse effect.

As future work, it is intended to implement and apply the same methodology in the version of the Fitness app for smartwatch, and thus seek heuristics that best serve the platform.

References

1. Research2Guidance mHealth Economics 2017 - Current Status and Future Trends in Mobile Health (2017). https://research2guidance.com/product/mhealth-economics-2017-current-status-and-future-trends-in-mobile-health/
2. Rawassizadeh, B.R., Price, A., Petre, M.: Wearables: has the age of smartwatches finally arrived? Commun. ACM **58**, 45–47 (2014). https://doi.org/10.1145/2629633
3. Asimakopoulos, S.; Asimakopoulos, G., Spillers, F.: Motivation and user engagement in fitness tracking: heuristics for mobile healthcare wearables. In: Informatics, vol. 4 (2017). https://doi.org/10.3390/informatics4010005
4. Laurel, B.: Computers as Theatre. Addison-Wesley, Reading (1993)
5. CANALYS: Worldwide smartwatch shipments grew 12% in Q1 2020 despite coronavirus, 17 June 2020. https://www.canalys.com/newsroom/canalys-worldwide-smartwatch-shipments-q1-2020
6. Schlatter, T., Levinson, D.: Visual usability: principles and practices for designing digital applications. Newnes (2013)
7. Nielsen, J.: Usability Engineering. Academic Press, New York (1993)

8. O'Brien, H.-L., Toms, E.-G.: What is user engagement? A conceptual framework for defining user engagement with technology. J. Am. Soc. Inform. Sci. Technol. **59**(6), 938–955 (2008)
9. Chapman, P.: Models of engagement: intrinsically motivated interaction with multimedia learning software. Unpublished master's thesis, University of Waterloo, Waterloo, Canada (1997)
10. Tison, G.-H., et al.: Achieving high retention in mobile health research using design principles adopted from widely popular consumer mobile apps. Circulation **136**, A21029–A21029 (2017)
11. Barbosa, S.-D.-J.: Interação Humano-Computador. Elsevier, Rio de Janeiro (2010)
12. Sharp, H., Rogers, Y., Preece, J.: Interaction Design: Beyond. Human-Computer Interaction. Wiley, New York (2019)
13. Likert, R.: A Technique for the Measurement of Attitudes, vol. 22, pp. 5–55 (1932–1933)
14. Brooke, J.: SUS - a quick and dirty usability scale **189**(194), 4–7 (1996)
15. Keseberg, M.: Understanding engagement with health-apps: an evaluation of user experiences with the long-term usage of health-apps and wearables (2018)
16. Kim, Y.H., Kim, D.J., Wachter, K., Spillers, F.: A study of mobile user engagement (MoEN). Engagement motivations, perceived value, satisfaction, and continued engagement intention. Decis. Support Syst. **56**, 361–370 (2013). https://doi.org/10.1016/j.dss.2013.07.002

Lessons Learned in Developing a Patient-Centered Website to Support Stroke Patients and Caregivers During Transitions of Care

Michele C. Fritz[1]([✉]), Sarah J. Swierenga[1], Paul P. Freddolino[1],
Constantinos K. Coursaris[2], Amanda T. Woodward[1], and Matthew J. Reeves[1]

[1] Michigan State University, East Lansing, MI 48824, USA
fritzmi2@msu.edu
[2] HEC Montréal, Montréal, Canada

Abstract. Stroke is one of the leading causes of adult disability in the United States, affecting almost 800,000 United States citizens annually. Inadequate care during the transition back to home can lead to poor outcomes and delayed recovery. Although the transitional care period is often complex and multifaceted, providing patients and caregivers with timely, relevant education and informational resources remains an important foundation to any transitional care service. Utilizing technology to enhance post-stroke transitional care services and provide unlimited access to information may increase survivors' understanding and ability to manage their stroke recovery during the transition period.

The Michigan Stroke Transitions Trial (MISTT) was a two-phased clinical trial study that engaged stakeholders in developing and refining two patient-centered post-stroke transitional care interventions intended to improve 90-day stroke survivor and caregiver outcomes. This case study describes the Patient-Centered Design approach used to develop the MISTT website intervention, which is a curated, patient-oriented website containing information and resources relevant to lived, post-stroke transitional care experiences.

Lessons Learned: Substantial time, support, and funding is required for a multi-stage approach to creating and building a patient-centered website. Stakeholder engagement was crucial to the final content, design, and functionality of the MISTT website. Stakeholders were instrumental for determining how to apply best practice universal design guidelines to meet needs and preferences for stroke survivors and their caregivers.

Keywords: Aging and UDUX · Stroke · Transitional care · Website development · Health information · Patient education · Patient-centered design

1 Background

Stroke affects close to 800,000 people in the United States every year, and the number is growing, especially as the population ages [1]. Two-thirds of stroke survivors return

© Springer Nature Switzerland AG 2021
M. M. Soares et al. (Eds.): HCII 2021, LNCS 12780, pp. 450–466, 2021.
https://doi.org/10.1007/978-3-030-78224-5_31

home, some after complex transitions between acute hospital, rehabilitation, and nursing care settings [2, 3]. Inadequate care during this critical transition period contributes to hospital readmissions, delayed recovery, and decreased quality of life for patients and caregivers. The cumulative effect of these challenges results in substantial treatment burden [4], which is exacerbated by the poor coordination of existing post-acute care services [2, 3].

Patient and caregiver education remain a cornerstone to increasing engagement and self-management [5, 6]. Similarly, education is an essential, underlying aspect of all transitional care components [5]. Providing access to high quality patient-centered educational information during the transitional care period has the potential to be a cost-effective intervention to improve transitions for both patients and caregivers.

Technology, often labelled as tele-health, tele-medicine, e-health, or m-health for mobile device-related applications and services, offers great potential for improving the medical care and outcomes of patients transitioning across care settings and after returning home [7–11]. However, the implementation of these technologies is complex because they need to 'fit' the specifics of the clinical purpose and population; more research is required so that these technologies deliver on their promise. [12, 13]. While studies describing the effectiveness of online tools in support of chronic disease self-management have been undertaken [14, 15], they do not address these online tools' usability or information quality. O'Reilly et al. [16] found that a potentially useful web-based tool for chronic disease management was poorly adopted by health care providers, in turn making an assessment of its utility and value to patients unattainable.

Access to reliable, accurate, trusted, and easy-to-digest information is consistently identified as a critical need by patients and caregivers recovering from acute stroke and is a critical component of self-management strategies [17]. In the area of stroke, there is limited literature evaluating technology tools, including websites and mobile apps, to promote patient engagement and self-management among stroke patients. For example, a set of reports by Pierce and her colleagues [18, 19] describe a web-based stroke intervention with communication and information resources for family caregivers. Eames et al. [20] found that patients and caregivers were often dissatisfied with the information available. Through interviews Eames et al. [21] learned that patient and caregiver preferences for methods of conveying information after discharge varied, suggesting the need for a variety of formats when offering assistance to this population. Cameron et al. [22] demonstrated the need to have interventions, including information, reflect the changing care environment of stroke patients and caregivers, from the acute stage to long term adaptation to the illness. Thus, information needs will change during the course of the illness and recovery [23] and an adaptable online resource is an ideal.

To address the ongoing need for post-stroke transitional care resources and support, the Michigan Stroke Transitions Trial (MISTT) research team proposed a two-phased clinical trial study – comprised of Development and Trial phases - to develop and test two interventions intended to improve 90-day outcomes for stroke survivors and caregivers [24, 25]. All study-related activities were approved by Biomedical Institutional Review Boards. The MISTT study interventions involved access to a 60-day Social Work Case Management program (SWCM) alone or in combination with access to a patient-centered information website, referred to as the MISTT website. During the Development Phase of the study, stroke survivors, their caregivers, and stroke-related health professionals were engaged in developing and refining the two study interventions to ensure that they were patient-centered and designed to address a variety of post-stroke patient needs during the transition back to home [26]. In the Trial Phase, efficacy of the two interventions was formally tested in a 3-group randomized controlled trial (see Fig. 1) [24]. Randomized controlled trials are considered as the highest standard study design for determining the efficacy of different interventions on an intended outcome because they compare the intervention groups to a "control" (or unaltered) group, which accounts for additional variables that may also contribute to or influence the outcome of interest [27].

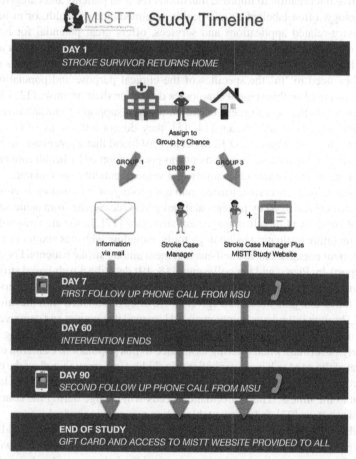

Fig. 1. Michigan Stroke Transitions Trial (MISTT) randomized controlled trial design and timeline.

The aim of this paper is to present a case study describing the development of the MISTT website, a curated patient-centered, mobile-friendly website designed to provide information and support resources for stroke patients and caregivers during their transitional care period following discharge to home. Decisions about the visual design and interaction design, including embedded functionality, and how these aspects were informed by stakeholder input will be described. Lessons learned about project-related time, complexity, technical support, funding, content, and stakeholder engagement will also be shared. Development of the SWCM intervention [26] and results of the trial are reported elsewhere [24].

2   The MISTT Website Development Process

The MISTT website development process, undertaken during the MISTT study Development Phase, was guided by several key goals, including: 1) meeting stakeholder-identified needs by creating a patient-centered website informed by lived experiences and 2) applying evidence-based guidelines for healthcare web design to ensure usable and accessible informational website resources for stroke survivors and their caregivers. From inception, development of the MISTT website involved an interactive process among the MISTT research team, stakeholder groups, and a creative design team. The technical construction was undertaken by the research team in collaboration with its university's creative design team. The research team prepared all website content and approved all final decisions regarding visual and interactive design. The originally-proposed concept for the website (see Fig. 2) was based on a broad review of technology-based applications available in medical, health care, and social service fields, together with initial suggestions from stroke patients, caregivers, and health care professionals.

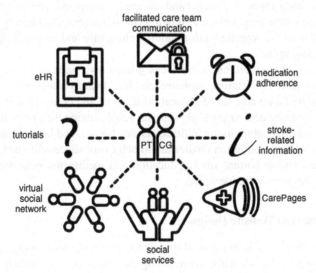

Fig. 2. Originally-proposed conceptual design of the MISTT website.

The development process involved a 10-month, 3-staged approach where, in Stage 1, the original conceptual design was fashioned into a non-functional prototype website. In Stage 2, the prototype website was converted into a stakeholder-informed, functional beta website, and in Stage 3, the beta version was iteratively modified into the final production version of the MISTT website. Each stage involved modifications in response to input from patient, caregiver, and healthcare professional stakeholders (see Fig. 3). The prototype was a wireframe design (consisting of preliminary content and initial page layouts) of the original website concept, while the beta version was a functional website implementation. The efficacy of the final MISTT website was subsequently tested in the randomized controlled trial [24].

2.1 Stakeholder Engagement

Stakeholder engagement during the MISTT Development Phase involved stroke survivors (i.e., patients) and their caregivers, as well as stroke-related healthcare professionals. Focus groups were chosen as the primary method to gain a better understanding about the 'lived experience' of stroke survivors and caregivers during the transitional care period and to generate ideas for refining the MISTT website content and design preferences. Stroke survivors and their caregivers were the intended end users for the MISTT website. Three different pairs of patient-caregiver focus groups were conducted throughout Stage 1 and Stage 2 in each of two geographic locations, resulting in six total patient-caregiver focus group sessions (see Fig. 3). Eighteen patients and nine caregivers participated, with many attending more than one session. Participants in the first two sessions identified major themes related to the post-stroke transition to home [26], while participants in the third and fourth sessions reported their likelihood of using various potential online resources to address needs associated with these major themes. In the last two focus group sessions, patients and caregivers interacted with a prototype of the MISTT website where they participated in a series of exercises to identify their preferences in relation to the website's information architecture and visual design including style, fonts, and graphics.

In addition to the patient-caregiver focus groups, two pairs of focus groups were also conducted with 34 different stroke-related healthcare professionals. The professionals represented a diverse set of clinical professions and clinical settings, including social workers, nurses, neurologists, physiatrists, rehabilitation therapists, hospitals, and administrators from rehabilitation facilities, nursing homes, and home healthcare agencies. At these sessions, common challenges to achieving successful stroke transitions were discussed, and important stroke education and medication education topics for patients and caregivers were identified.

2.2 User-Centered Website Design

User-centered design (UCD) is a formal approach to the product (i.e., website) design and development process that prioritizes conducting user experience research from end users throughout an iterative product lifecycle. Incorporating end user input throughout the website's design and development is critical to the UCD approach [28]. UCD considers user characteristics, tasks, user interface features/functionality, and the environmental context during the user-driven design process. The process typically includes context of use, user requirements analysis, design, user experience evaluations (and then iterating back to design), followed by implementation, launch and maintenance [29]. Patient-centered design is a specific type of UCD where the end user is the patient (rather than the provider or clinician), and patients have a voice in the design and development process, helping to design the website or care intervention collaboratively with healthcare providers, medical staff, and design teams [30, 31]. The MISTT study approached website design and development with a patient-centered design process where the end users were stroke survivors and their caregivers.

Throughout the development phase, the MISTT team relied extensively on user interface design guidelines and best practices, along with the Web Content Accessibility Guidelines (international standard for designing inclusive websites) [32], to inform each step of the MISTT website design and development. The website design was intended to make content easy to locate and to consume, with simple navigation, multiple options for users, and an appropriate reading level [33]. The core design goals were organization and navigation (information architecture and flow of the pages), page layout, and content. Stakeholder feedback was imperative to understanding how to feasibly and practically implement each element to meet post-stroke capabilities and preferences. The following sections will outline the three stages employed for developing the MISTT website using a patient-centered design process (see Fig. 3), as well as discuss the impacts and contribution of stakeholder feedback on iterative content and design creation.

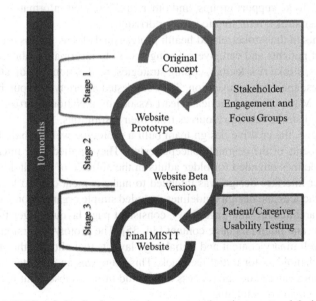

Fig. 3. The MISTT website development phase: a staged, patient-centered design approach.

2.3   Stage 1: Original Concept to Prototype Website

The primary focus in Stage 1 was to develop a prototype website from the original design concept. This involved identifying patient-centered content topics relevant to the in-home transitional care period, gathering feedback on the original content topics compiled by the research team, and then creating a prototype website consisting of wireframes with preliminary content and initial page layouts. Discussions during the first two pairs of patient-caregiver focus groups revealed common post-stroke informational and transitional care needs, which were summarized into four core themes: 1) practical and emotional support, 2) preparedness, 3) identifying and addressing unmet needs, and 4) addressing actions and interventions related to stroke prevention [26]. MISTT website content was subsequently written to align with these themes, addressing several care domains that participants indicated were important to them during their transition, including physical and mental function, stress, quality of life (QOL), quality of care, stroke knowledge and prevention strategies, and integration back into community roles.

Patient and caregiver focus group participants also emphasized the importance of solid, reputable content that could be easily accessed from a single location. The creative design team implemented the MISTT website content by obtaining content from existing authoritative sources and linking to existing websites, where possible, to avoid re-creating already available authoritative information. Linking to established online resources minimized the need for ongoing content revisions, as revisions would generally be managed by the original authors and institutions. Discussions during the second pair of patient-caregiver focus groups revealed priority topics that patients and caregivers reported they were most likely to access online, including information about medications, joining stroke support groups, and other stroke-related information (i.e., how to prevent another stroke, returning to work or driving, etc.).

Participants in the stroke-related health professionals focus groups emphasized the importance of patients and caregivers having access to information about stroke signs and symptoms, stroke risk factors, coping strategies, medications, medication management strategies, and stroke prevention. They suggested a variety of reputable resources including the Mayo Clinic, American Heart Association, National Stroke Association, and also shared stroke-related resources from their institutions.

At this stage, the creative design team built a prototype website based on the proposed components of the original concept design. They applied their interpretation of universal guidelines intended for older adults in the absence of stakeholder input. The prototype user interface design was intended to make content easy to locate and consume. Best practices and design guidelines included simple organization and navigation (information architecture and page flow), consistent page layout, larger font sizes and color contrast, and plain language content [34, 35]. The prototype version was a wireframe with preliminary content and initial page layouts that allowed the study team to share with stakeholders for initial feedback. This stage was an important aspect of the iterative patient-centered design process that would inform subsequent revisions of the website's design and development.

2.4   Stage 2: Prototype to Beta Version

Stage 2 of the development phase was focused on understanding patient and caregiver preferences for website design and content, and on building a functional beta version of the website based on their preferences and best design practices. A preliminary website prototype design and set of content topics were presented in the third pair of patient-caregiver focus groups, using the original conceptual design outlined in Fig. 1. These focus group discussions assisted the team's understanding of end user preferences and influenced the tone used in identifying, preparing, and refining content. The prototype was then converted into a beta version, which was an early functional website with substantial stakeholder-informed content. The beta version presented content in multiple formats (i.e., text, graphics, videos) to respond to different learning and access styles. Videos were identified as an essential feature, specifically for survivors with post-stroke deficits impacting their ability to read text. Content organization was improved to move from elementary or summary-level information to more in-depth details for each topic.

Content developed by the MISTT research team focused on introducing the topic at hand, explaining its importance to the context of stroke and stroke recovery, providing an overview of the selected links and materials, and providing videos with helpful hints for navigating the website. A short introduction to each external link/resource was provided, acknowledging its original source. Based on stakeholder suggestions, messages were presented with an active voice of hope, and the content was intended to provide a comprehensive scope of material to address physical/functional health, mental/emotional health, social, lifestyle, and environmental aspects of stroke.

Ultimately, stakeholder feedback informed which content topics of the original website concept to retain and which to discard in the beta website. Table 1 summarizes modifications made to the original concept topics based on this feedback, along with the subsequent content topics used to develop the beta version and ultimately retained in the final MISTT website. To determine the most relevant content topics, patients and caregivers were asked during the second pair of focus groups how likely they were to interact with each of the eight originally proposed content components. Patients were least interested in e-mailing their care team and interacting with a caregiving social networking tool, while caregivers were more likely overall to interact with various aspects of the website. Both stakeholder groups identified a significant need for caregiver-related resources, which resulted in creating a separate section dedicated to caregiver needs.

The stroke information section was expanded and a separate section for stroke recovery and prevention information was created based on evidence that stakeholders view stroke, stroke recovery, and stroke prevention as related but distinct topics. Thus, "stroke information" was revised to focus on the disease pathology, symptomatology, and treatment of stroke, while the "stroke recovery and prevention" section was focused on post-acute deficits, care, recovery, and rehabilitation, as well as risk factors and ways of preventing stroke recurrence. The medication information section was expanded beyond the original concept of medication adherence to include information about common post-stroke medications and how they work, how to talk with their doctors and pharmacist about medications, drug interactions, medication-related financial resources, and other medication-related resources.

Post-stroke support is crucial to successful transitions of care and the website intervention addressed support at two levels – social support and social services. Due to minimal interest by patients and caregivers in utilizing a social networking tool, the research team dropped the original concept of building a project-supported networking tool and the social networking section was eliminated. Instead, established resources for

Table 1. Results of stakeholder feedback on the initial website concept and how these influenced the final MISTT website components.

Original components of the initial concept	Final MISTT website components informed by stakeholder feedback
Stroke-related information (e.g., disease pathology, symptomatology, and treatment of stroke; stroke recovery and prevention)	Very strong interest, especially from caregivers; retained, expanded, and reorganized into two separate topic sections: 1) Stroke Education and 2) Stroke Prevention and Recovery
Medication information to prevent another stroke (e.g., medication management, health literacy, complexity of dosing, patient-physician communication, etc.)	Very strong interest, especially from caregivers; retained and expanded as the Medication Information section
Electronic health record (provides access to patients records through hospital portals)	Some interest, especially from caregivers; modified content and renamed section to My Providers to encourage portal benefits and use
E-mail your care team (a 'facilitated care team communication tool' that supports direct patient-caregiver contact with providers)	Very little interest; discarded initial concept of creating a study-specific communication tool. Content within the My Providers section encouraged patients to organize a list of their provider contact information and communicate through their patient portal
Link to social services in your area (e.g., meals, transportation, respite care, access to durable medical equipment, etc.)	Some interest; retained as Community Resources section focused on Michigan 2-1-1, a free 24/7 confidential resource to provide information about local services to help with transportation, medical supplies, respite care, etc.
Social networking (project-supported networking tool)	Some interest; revised and expanded as Stroke Support Groups section to include caregiver social support resources; discarded project-supported tool
Family support websites (free websites pages that help family and friends communicate when a loved one is receiving care)	Very little interest; support-related resources moved to social support section. Original section replaced with the Caregiver Resources section to provide a variety of resources relevant to post-stroke caregiving roles

social networking tools were identified and combined with other support resources into the Stroke Support Group section. The Stroke Support Group section included information for several local, regional, and national face-to-face support groups, as well as telephone and e-mail-based support groups or networks. In response to focus group discussions, support resources relevant to stroke survivors under the age of 50 were added. The social services section was renamed Community Resources to help stakeholders better understand its content. Community-based social services vary across communities and often shift in availability or range of services due to funding and competing priorities. To decrease the efforts required in maintaining an up-to-date list of local community services, the website referred users to Michigan 2-1-1. Michigan 2-1-1 is a free confidential state-wide resource, available 24 hours a day, seven days a week, that provides information about a broad range of local services, including services addressing needs associated with transportation, medical supplies, housing or housing repairs, respite care, etc.

Healthcare providers deemed the idea of a facilitated care team communication tool impractical; thus, the originally proposed concepts for the facilitated care team communication tool and electronic health record sections were significantly modified and merged into a new section entitled My Providers. This modified section focused on encouraging and supporting patients to use their hospital-based patient portal to communicate with their providers. Simple, introductory information was created to help patients understand how to access and navigate their hospital-specific patient portals along with the associated benefits of utilizing their portal. In addition, the creative design team developed a structure within the MISTT website for documenting a contact list of the patient's providers/services, thereby creating a single repository for organizing this information.

Overall, the feedback from both the patient-caregiver and healthcare professional focus groups directly informed the scope and depth of content as well as the visual and interaction design of the beta version of the website.

2.5   Stage 3: Beta Version of the MISTT Website

In Stage 3, a usability evaluation was undertaken on the beta version of the website. Usability was evaluated quantitatively and qualitatively in terms of its core components: Effectiveness, efficiency, and satisfaction [36]. To obtain feedback on how well the website met user expectations for content, visual design, and interaction design, four stroke survivors and three caregivers completed 60 to 75-min individual sessions that involved a series of information-seeking tasks. Results indicated that the website needed significant improvement to meet the needs of stroke survivors and caregivers. While the participants were able to find basic information, e.g., types of strokes (100% task success) and local face-to-face support groups (100%), finding more detailed information on other websites that the MISTT website linked out to was much more difficult. For example, only one out of seven participants was able to find information on drug interactions, and none were able to locate transportation resources. The System Usability Scale (SUS) score for the MISTT website was 51.8 for the combined patient-caregiver participant group, which is below average and considered only marginally acceptable [37].

Recommendations from the usability evaluation were incorporated into the final stage of website development to prepare the MISTT website for the randomized controlled trial during the Trial Phase of this research project (which is outside of the scope of this paper and will not be discussed here). Modifications were undertaken to simplify the website's structure, content, and navigation to make it more user-friendly and appropriate for post-stroke users based on guidelines for designing websites for older adults [34, 35, 38]. Specific changes included adding a Home option on the far-left side of each page, as participants often tried to click the Main Menu header (flat text) to get back to Home. Each major section of the website was also given a specific accent color to help orient users. Also, the primary navigation menu was re-formatted, a table of contents was added at the top of webpages containing four or more headings, and the navigation menu was replicated at the bottom of the page for mobile users.

Content-heavy categories were broken up into separate categories or shorter sections to alleviate how much information users needed to process within each overall category, and the overall number of pages was reduced to ensure the fewest possible clicks to get to information [33, 34, 38]. The team also spent considerable time working with the content applying best practices and design guidelines, such as using plain language to aid users in comprehending text, use, and simplifying and shortening sentences to their main points [33, 34]. Also, speaking to stroke survivors directly with an encouraging tone instead of talking about them (e.g., directly state the actions patients should take, instead of what not to do) was a key takeaway from the user tests.

Changes to the page layout included moving the search box closer to the main content to help users notice it; ensuring the search box (and other main-level navigation) was located in the same place on every page of the website [34]; and simplifying the format of the results page. Related content was visually grouped together, descriptive headings were added to provide better context [34], and the most useful resources were placed first on the page [33, 34].

Other page-level enhancements included increasing the prominence and visibility of links and buttons within the pages (e.g., creating specific content type icons/colors and created callout boxes), revising the link text to match the page title of the landing page, and having all external links open a new browser tab. Font sizes were enlarged, spacing was increased, and color contrasts were increased to support accessibility (using darker, heavier weight fonts) [34, 35, 38]. Meaningful text descriptions were added to images (via alt text), so that screen reader assistive technology could read it out for users with visual disabilities [33, 34]. Finally, during this final stage the core stroke and medication content was revised and finalized, a Caregiver Resources section was added, and videos, with closed captions, were produced for several content sections.

2.6   Final Version of MISTT Website Intervention

The final MISTT Website was a curated, patient-centered website that provided information and resources addressing stroke education, prevention, recovery, and community services (see Fig. 4). It was designed to encourage patient activation and self-management. The final seven main sections of the MISTT website (mistt.org) included: 1) Stroke Education, 2) Stroke Prevention and Recovery, 3) Medication Information, 4) My Providers – including a section that allowed patients to organize a contact list of their various providers and information promoting and encouraging use of the patient's hospital patient portal, 5) Community Resources – access to community resources for social services, 6) Stroke Support Groups, and 7) Caregiver Resources – to assist caregivers with their role. Additionally, the MISTT website included a welcome video, account details page, search function, help/FAQ page, and a contact form. To allow data collection of website utilization during the randomized controlled trial, access to the MISTT website required a username and password.

Fig. 4. Screenshot example of the MISTT Stroke Information landing page, which showcases the navigation structure, page layout, and plain language content.

3 Lessons Learned

The experience of designing and developing the MISTT website as an intervention to be tested in a randomized controlled trial provided several lessons learned. These lessons, which may be valuable to website development efforts in other transitional care studies, healthcare contexts, or populations, can be categorized under the headings of time, complexity, technical support, funding, content, and stakeholder engagement.

3.1 Time

It quickly became apparent that everything related to website design and development required more time than expected. From participant recruitment and organizing the stakeholder focus groups used to guide content creation, to the actual process of creating and editing text and video content, time was a constant challenge. Despite having planned a discreet phased approach to the overall MISTT project, the initial Development Phase timeline was insufficient for conducting a formal accessibility audit and limited the amount of video production and usability testing sessions that were conducted. Fortunately, videos were produced along with a high-level accessibility review and usability testing with seven stakeholders. Research funders and investigator teams should plan substantial time (>10 months) when developing and testing a technology-related intervention, even when planning to utilize existing content and resources.

3.2 Complexity

The process of designing and developing the MISTT website was more complicated than originally envisioned. For example, locating and/or creating content at the appropriate reading level, packaged in a way that met best practices for user interface design and was appropriate for a post-stroke population, was quite challenging. The design process was more complex and required more time than initially anticipated due to the extent of team interaction needed to create and revise user interface requirements, design the website structure (information architecture), integrate the content into appropriately-sized pages, and incorporate media including graphics, videos, and links to external websites. It is critical to recognize the number of moving pieces and the complexity that each piece assumes in planning and executing the development of a website intervention using a patient-centered approach. Consideration and anticipation of alternative plans are recommended for each aspect of the development process to accommodate flexibility in achieving project goals.

3.3 Technical Support

Reflecting a typical approach within an academic setting, the MISTT creative design team included an internal university-based website development group. They were tasked with developing a website from content provided by the MISTT research team and implementing evidence-based guidelines for healthcare web design. Although the team had expertise in instructional website design and development within learning management systems, they were not as familiar with designing public-facing websites for general, non-academic or patient audiences. Unfortunately, this misalignment of expertise became clear only after website construction was well underway. As an example of how this impacted the development timeline, the navigation structure within each of the content topic sections had to be reorganized several times because there were too many sub-sections or the individual pages were too long without adequate navigation aids and longer text management (e.g., 'back to top' links). Additional personnel were hired to fulfil visual design, videography, and video production needs because the web developers lacked these skills and expertise. Partnering with an internal or external vendor who has the capacity and expertise to respond to a full range of technological needs is extremely important. In addition, having a technology project manager is recommended for ensuring process efficiency and effectiveness of deliverables that meet project objectives.

3.4 Funding

The budget allocation for website design and development was insufficient for the total scope of activities related to website design and development and the production of materials. As an example, funding for video creation was not included in the original budget; however, videos turned out to be an essential aspect of the website based on stakeholder feedback. As a result, re-budgeting required identifying low-cost or "free" resource solutions, even if the final solutions were not the most effective or preferred options. Fortunately, the University environment provided access to students with relevant skills. The MISTT project offered an opportunity for interested students to participate in research while gaining experience in their field of study, which included media and information studies. Careful planning, including realistic budgeting, is crucial for conducting a successful website design and development project because available funds may impact the scope, timeline, and quality of the finished product.

3.5 Content

The MISTT website was ultimately designed to complement social work case management services and to encourage patient activation and self-management. One constant challenge during content development was to resist the temptation of providing material that was too in-depth and comprehensive, rather than summarizing critical facts. It was also important to use authoritative resources that would not require constant updating by the project team.

Reducing the content available from multiple authoritative sources into manageable and accessible web pages was a much greater challenge than finding relevant material. The amount of information potentially useful to patients and caregivers was immense and required careful selection, followed by careful editing to simplify language and reduce total volume. Dedicating time and resources to gathering stakeholder feedback on content topics, scope and depth of information, and preferences for the way content is formatted and presented are essential in ensuring a patient-centered development process. Substantial modifications were made to content topics and concepts in response to stakeholder feedback.

3.6 Stakeholder Engagement

Although the original concept for the MISTT website reflected limited stakeholder input at the time the original proposal was written, these discussions merely provided a starting point for what information and resources stroke patients and caregivers might need after returning home. Engaging a larger group of patients, caregivers, and healthcare professionals, especially patients and caregivers who recently experienced their post-stroke transition of care, expanded the scope of ideas related to gaps in post-stroke healthcare services and post-stroke needs. The emerging lesson revealed the importance of engaging a larger group of stakeholders. Focus group discussions highlighted the lesson that because stroke and stroke recovery are complex and variable, individual post-stroke experiences and needs are even more complex and diverse. In order to create a comprehensive intervention targeted to the broader stroke population, it is crucial to ensure it addresses the wide-ranging scope of patient-caregiver experiences and needs. Regarding patient-centered website design, patients and caregivers were crucial in understanding how to implement universal design principles relevant to post-stroke capabilities and preferences. In addition to content, stakeholder input critically impacted decisions about organization, navigation, and page layout.

In summary, substantial time, support, and funding is required for a multi-staged approach to creating and building a patient-centered website. Stakeholder engagement was crucial to the final content, design, and functionality of the MISTT website. Stakeholders were instrumental for determining how to apply best practice universal design guidelines to meet needs and preferences for stroke survivors and their caregivers. The methodologies and lessons learned in the MISTT study Development Phase may be valuable for planning the design and development of websites or digital tools more broadly in other transitional care populations and in other healthcare contexts.

Acknowledgments. The authors acknowledge and thank the stroke survivors, caregivers, and healthcare professionals who participated in Phase 1 of the MISTT study. We acknowledge Dr. Anne Hughes and the creative design team – Mr. Nathan Lounds, Mr. Joseph Fitzgerald, and Mr. Izak Gracy – and those featured in the MISTT website videos, including Mrs. Daneille Rhodes. We also acknowledge Ms. Jennifer Ismirle for co-leading the usability evaluation.

Funding. This research was funded through a grant to Michigan State University from the Patient-Centered Outcomes Research Institute (PCORI). *Improving Care Transitions for Acute Stroke Patients through a Patient-Centered Home Based Case Management Program.* Award # IHS-1310-07420-01. Grant # R-D2C-1310-07420. The content is solely the responsibility of the authors and does not necessarily represent the official views of the Patient-Centered Outcomes Research Institute.

References

1. Virani, S.S., et al.: Heart disease and stroke statistics—2020 update: a report from the American Heart Association. Circulation **141**, e139–e596 (2020). https://doi.org/10.1161/cir.000 0000000000757
2. Cameron, J.I., Tsoi, C., Marsella, A.: Optimizing stroke systems of care by enhancing transitions across care environments. Stroke **39**, 2637–2643 (2008). https://doi.org/10.1161/STR OKEAHA.107.501064
3. Wissel, J., Olver, J., Sunnerhagen, K.S.: Navigating the poststroke continuum of care. J. Stroke Cerebrovasc. Dis. **22**, 1–8 (2013). https://doi.org/10.1016/j.jstrokecerebrovasdis.2011.05.021
4. Gallacher, K.I., May, C.R., Langhorne, P., Mair, F.S.: A conceptual model of treatment burden and patient capacity in stroke. BMC Fam. Pract. **19**, 9 (2018). https://doi.org/10.1186/s12875-017-0691-4
5. Naylor, M.D., Shaid, E.C., Carpenter, D., Gass, B., Levine, C., Li. J., et al.: Components of comprehensive and effective transitional care. J. Am. Geriatr. Soc. **65**, 1119–1125 (2017). https://doi.org/10.1111/jgs.14782
6. Lorig, K.R., Holman, H.: Self-management education: history, definition, outcomes, and mechanisms. Ann. Behav. Med. **26**, 1–7 (2003). https://doi.org/10.1207/S15324796ABM260 1_01

7. Farley, H.: Promoting self-efficacy in patients with chronic disease beyond traditional education: a literature review. Nurs. Open **7**(1), 30–41 (2019). https://doi.org/10.1002/nop2.382

8. Cameron, J.E., Voth, J., Jaglal, S.B., Guilcher, S.J., Hawker, G., Salbach, N.M.: "In this together": social identification predicts health outcomes (via self-efficacy) in a chronic disease self-management program. Soc. Sci. Med. **208**, 172–179 (2018). https://doi.org/10.1016/j.socscimed.2018.03.007

9. Cottrell, M.A., Galea, O.A., O'Leary, S.P., Hill, A.J., Russell, T.G.: Real-time telerehabilitation for the treatment of musculo-skeletal conditions is effective and comparable to standard practice: a systematic review and meta-analysis. Clin. Rehabil. **31**(5), 625–638 (2017). https://doi.org/10.1177/0269215516645148

10. Fors, A., et al.: Effects of a person-centered telephone-support in patients with chronic obstructive pulmonary disease and/or chronic heart failure – a randomized controlled trial. PLoS ONE **8**, e0203031 (2018). https://doi.org/10.1371/journal.pone.0203031

11. Kennedy, C.A., et al.: A prospective comparison of telemedicine versus in-person delivery of an interprofessional education program for adults with inflammatory arthritis. J. Telemed. Telecare **23**(2), 197–206 (2017). https://doi.org/10.1177/1357633X16635342

12. Bhaskar, S., Bradley, S., Chattu, V.K., Adisesh, A., Nurtazina, A., Kyrykbayeva, S., et al.: Telemedicine as the new outpatient clinic gone digital: position paper from the Pandemic Health System REsilience PROGRAM (REPROGRAM) International Consortium (Part 2). Front. Public Health **8**, 410 (2020). https://doi.org/10.3389/fpubh.2020.00410

13. Peeters, J.M., Wiegers, T.A., Friele, R.D.: How technology in care at home affects patient self-care and self-management: a scoping review. Int. J. Environ. Res. Public Health **10**(11), 5541–5564 (2013, October 29). https://doi.org/10.3390/ijerph10115541. PMID: 24173139; PMCID: PMC3863859

14. Fortin, M., Chouinard, M.C., Diallo, B.B., Bouhali, T.: Integration of chronic disease prevention and management services into primary care (PR1MaC): findings from an embedded qualitative study. BMC Fam. Pract. **20**(1), 7 (2019). https://doi.org/10.1186/s12875-018-0898-z

15. Contant, É., Loignon, C., Bouhali, T., Almirall, J., Fortin, M.: A multidisciplinary self-management intervention among patients with multimorbidity and the impact of socioeconomic factors on results. BMC Fam. Pract. **20**, 1–8 (2019). https://doi.org/10.1186/s12875-019-0943-6

16. O'Reilly, D.J., et al.: Evaluation of a chronic disease management system for the treatment and management of diabetes in primary health care practices in Ontario: an observational study. Ont. Health Technol. Assess. Ser. 1 **14**(3), 1–37 (2014, April). PMID: 24748911; PMCID: PMC3991329

17. Forster, A., Brown, L., Smith, J., House, A., Knapp, P., Wright, J.J., et al.: Information provision for stroke patients and their caregivers. Cochrane Database Syst. Rev. **11**, CD001919 (2012). https://doi.org/10.1002/14651858.cd001919.pub3

18. Pierce, L.L., Steiner, V.: Usage and design evaluation by family caregivers of a stroke intervention web site. J. Neurosci. Nurs. **45**(5), 254–261 (2013). https://doi.org/10.1097/JNN.0b013e31829dba61

19. Pierce, L.L., Steiner, V.L., Khuder, S.A., Govoni, A.L., Horn, L.J.: The effect of a web-based stroke intervention on carers' well-being and survivors' use of healthcare services. Disabil. Rehabil. **31**(20), 1676–1684 (2009). https://doi.org/10.1080/09638280902751972

20. Eames, S., Hoffmann, T., Worrall, L., Read, S.: Stroke patients' and carers' perception of barriers to accessing stroke information. Top Stroke Rehabil. **17**(2), 69–78 (2010). https://doi.org/10.1310/tsr1702-69

21. Eames, S., Hoffmann, T., Worrall, L., Read, S.: Delivery styles and formats for different stroke information topics: patient and carer preferences. Patient Educ. Couns. **84**(2), e18–23 (2011). https://doi.org/10.1016/j.pec.2010.07.007

22. Cameron, J.I., Gignac, M.A.: "Timing It Right": a conceptual framework for addressing the support needs of family caregivers to stroke survivors from the hospital to the home. Patient Educ. Couns. **70**(3), 305–314 (2008). http://doi.org/S0738-3991(07)00441-7 [pii] https://doi.org/10.1016/j.pec.2007.10.020

23. Hanger, H.C., Walker, G., Paterson, L.A., McBride, S., Sainsbury, R.: What do patients and their carers want to know about stroke? A two-year follow-up study. Clin. Rehabil. **12**(1), 45–52 (1998). https://doi.org/10.1191/026921598668677675

24. Reeves, M.J., et al.: Michigan stroke transitions trial. Circ. Cardiovasc. Qual. Outcomes **12**(7), e005493 (2019). https://doi.org/10.1161/circoutcomes.119.005493

25. Reeves, M.J., et al.: Improving transitions in acute stroke patients discharged to home: the Michigan Stroke Transitions Trial (MISTT) protocol. BMC Neurol. **17**(1), 115 (2017). https://doi.org/10.1186/s12883-017-0895-1

26. Hughes, A.K., Woodward, A.T., Fritz, M.C., Reeves, M.J.: Improving stroke transitions: development and implementation of a social work case management intervention. Soc. Work Health Care **57**(2), 95–108 (2018). https://doi.org/10.1080/00981389.2017.1401027

27. Pocock, S.J.: Clinical Trials: A Practical Approach, pp. 1–13, 50–65. John Wiley & Sons, Chichester, West Sussex, England (2013)

28. International Organization for Standardization: Ergonomics of human-system interaction – Human-centred design for interactive systems. ISO Reference No. 9241-210:2010 (2010)

29. U.S. General Services Administration: user-centered design basics. https://www.usability.gov/what-and-why/user-centered-design.html

30. Stichler, J.F.: Patient-centered healthcare design. J. Nurs. Adm. **41**(12), 503–506 (2011, December). https://doi.org/10.1097/nna.0b013e3182378a3b. PMID: 22094612

31. Morales Rodriguez, M., Casper, G., Brennan, P.F.: Patient-centered design: the potential of user-centered design in personal health records. J. AHIMA **78**(4), 44–46 (2007, April). PMID: 17455846

32. International Organization for Standardization: Information technology – W3C Web Content Accessibility Guidelines (WCAG) 2.0 (ISO/IEC 40500:2012) (2012)

33. Centers for Disease Control and Prevention (CDC): Simply Put: A Guide for Creating Easy-to-Understand Materials, 3rd edn. Report, Health and Human Services, National Institute on Aging (2010, July)

34. National Institutes on Aging: Making your website senior friendly tips from the National Institute on Aging and the National Library of Medicine. National Institutes of Health, Department of Health and Human Services (2009)

35. Nahm, E.-S., Preece, J., Resnick, B., Mills, M.E.: Usability of health web sites for older adults: a preliminary study. Comput. Inform. Nurs. **22**(6), 326–334 (2004). https://doi.org/10.1097/00024665-200411000-00007

36. International Organization for Standardization: Ergonomics of human-system interaction — Part 11: Usability: Definitions and concepts. (ISO Reference No. 9241-11:2018) (2018)

37. Brooke, J.: SUS: a retrospective. J. Usab. Stud. **8**(2), 29–40 (2013)

38. Saludin, F.A., Maarop, N., Zainuddin, N.M.M., Mohammad, R., Shariff, S.A.: A conceptual model on websites design features for self-management of chronic-diseases patients. Int. J. Eng. Technol. **7**(4.36), 479–483 (2018). http://dx.doi.org/10.14419/ijet.v7i4.36.23922

Usability Evaluation of Music Applications for Stress Reduction

Moushume Hai, Ariana Lacue, Yuwei Zhou, Yogesh Patel, Asturias Roncal,
and Patricia Morreale[✉]

School of Computer Science and Technology, Kean University, Union, NJ 07078, USA
{haim,lacuea,zhouyuw,patyogeh,roncala,pmorreal}@kean.edu

Abstract. People use music applications to provide comfort and to help keep their minds relaxed and stress-free . During times of reduced social activity, with corresponding increases in social distancing for health and public safety, many people face high levels of anxiety, loneliness, depression, and stress. Music applications can relive these concerns, by providing access to personal music libraries. However, many users make mistakes while using music applications. These mistakes include not noticing an element, taking a long time to complete a specific task, or failing to complete a task altogether. This can make the product difficult to use and challenging to learn, while failing to provide a pleasant, enjoyable experience. In this research, a comparative analysis was conducted with 20 users between 18–24 years old to investigate the interface design and functionality of the Spotify and Apple Music using human computer interaction methods and tools. The findings indicate the differences and similarities between the two user interfaces, indicating which music application platform provides a better user experience, particularly for users seeking stress reduction.

Keywords: Usability evaluation · Music application · Mobile applications

1 Introduction

While stress is a common occurrence within society, some individuals face extreme stressors that can negatively impact their physical and psychological health. College students are a subset of the community that meets extreme stress daily. One of the most common forms of coping among college students is listening to music. The current research examines the effects of music looking on college student's stress levels. There are numerous examples of media players within the market, but it is debatable that very few that try to establish a compromise between all different classes of users effectively.

Many students would most likely agree that to stay sane, they must take some mental break throughout their homework or study period. Whether this break is meditation, listening to music, exercising, or internet scrolling, these are all things that help combat the negative impact of stress on physical and psychological well- being. Clinicians examined college student's cognitive coping strategies and levels of stress and established that accommodation or accepting the stressor for what it is, and facing the stressor one step

© Springer Nature Switzerland AG 2021
M. M. Soares et al. (Eds.): HCII 2021, LNCS 12780, pp. 467–476, 2021.
https://doi.org/10.1007/978-3-030-78224-5_32

at a time, were two most common forms of cognitive coping mechanisms [1]. Using this type of information is useful in understanding how college students can self-regulate their chronic stress through their cognitive abilities. In regard to external avenues, other common coping strategies include discussing with close friends, exercising, and leisure activities [2]. Though these specific categories under 'leisure activities' were not explicitly denoted, it could be assumed that activities, like reading or actively listening to music, could fall under this category.

2 Prior Work

Constant information on the radio and television news channels stating that students are feeling more stressed-out than ever before. The American College Health Association [3] found that approximately 30% of students reported that their stress levels affected their academic and personal lives; furthermore, more than 50% of students said that they experienced an overwhelming or above-average amount of stress within the last year. Daily stress can be caused and magnified by multiple personal and environmental factors. These could easily include mental health diagnoses, financial problems, or relationship problems. Though these issues can be quite debilitating at times, research has shown that there are effective coping mechanisms to handle our stress.

A study was conducted in which a list was compiled of ten coping strategies that typical functioning college students used to deal with stress [4]. The study found that the number one coping strategy for participants was listening to music. Music is a convenient coping mechanism to come by due to the overwhelming majority of the population continually being on their phones every day. Using music as a coping mechanism does not have any drawbacks as music, particularly music application, are easily accessible. Assessment of the usability of mobile applications has been done before, frequently assessing application, [5] or the hardware as well as the software [6]. The research presented here evaluated the usability of music applications, considering that their role may be to provide distraction and entertainment to relive stress.

3 Methodology

In the research methodology, two mobile music applications were used. Both applications were analyzed in their desktop version as well as their mobile version. Most research was focused to the mobile aspect. Accessibility and portability make smartphones and their applications a necessity in today's environment, and music applications are a go-to for most users. While there has been an increase in popularity for both Spotify and Apple music applications, this research concentrates on breaking down the applications to the point that user interaction with both apps can be evaluated.

With both music applications defined, a user-friendly survey was developed to collect data. The first part of the survey consisted of open and closed questions about both applications. Data were collected from a sample size of 20 test subjects. To retrieve more data and have a better understanding of user behavior, usability testing, heuristic evaluations [7], interviews, user interface (UI) tenets and traps [8], and observational studies were also conducted. Finally, methods such as triangulation were used to derive results and assumptions from the collected data using System Usability Scales (SUS) [9] and Radar Plots. A keystroke-level model (KLM) was also used to analyze the music apps in this experiment. The KLM model was used to predict five task execution times, and each task had a specified task scenario. The KLM analysis was modified to simulate the touch screen slide [10].

4 Data Gathering and Analysis

For data gathering, qualitative data collection methods were used because this helped obtain answers from users by conducting 'yes or no' answers using semi-structured and structured questionnaires. Open-ended responses from users were also incorporated to get in-depth answers. After collecting all the data, the tenets and trap methodology was used to determine which user interface provided good interface design and which interface possessed traps, which led to bad user experience and design problems.

For further insights, a SUS questionnaire was sent to twenty subjects, with ages ranging from 18 to 24 years. The user responses were then analyzed and triangulated with the previously gathered research. In total, the research consisted of tenets and traps, heuristic review, KLM analysis, and a radar plot to help determine which user interface provided good user interaction and which one did not.

4.1 Heuristics Review - Nielsen's 10 Heuristics: Spotify

Visibility of System Status: When opening up the Spotify application, users can see the status of the system. When the user clicks on their favorite artist and the album the artist created for listeners, they can see that the system's services are fulfilling all of the users' requests. When they download the album, system shows "Downloading…" telling users the system is up and running. The download tab shows a green bar with "Downloading…" on the side, telling the user the system is running and fulfilling the request.

Match Between System and Real World: The Spotify application meets with the user's needs with the GAMs feature. GAMs are short for Genres and Moods. Spotify has incorporated this feature into the app to match with the user's moods for every activity, whether it is meditation, cleaning, or cooking. With the GAMs feature, Spotify can relate to its listeners by creating an album for the different moods and activities in the Real World. These descriptors help users figure out what they are looking for in an engaging approach.

Consistency and Standards: The Spotify application provides consistency throughout its entire UI. It has specific colors for its call-to-action icons and unique colors for genres and plays buttons. When picking a particular genre, users can select any type knowing that there will be a white icon that says "Play Radio" for every genre they choose. The call-to-action button "Play Radio" is the color white throughout the entire UI for every type of genre on the application.

Help Users Recognize, Diagnose, and Recover from Errors: Spotify provides users a diagnosis whenever they encounter a problem while using the app, telling users correctly what they can do to fix the error if they receive it. Mistakes are portrayed with a red window and a red flag or in white with bold letters.

Help and Documentation: The mobile version of the app does not have any help or documentation, which is what needs most improvements and fixes. However, the desktop version of the application does provide assistance and documentation for users. If novice users have specific questions or need help to support their tasks, they would need to refer to the desktop version of the Spotify application. The desktop version has advice and documentation, while the mobile app does not.

4.2 Heuristic Review - Apple Music

Visibility of System Status: When opening the apple music application, the system status is visible to the users. The tab bar at the bottom of the app tells users what part of the app they are on or what music is are playing. When offline, users cannot view different music but can listen to whatever songs they have downloaded.

Match Between System and Real World: The language in the app is natural and consistent with the real world. The app personalizes the content within the app, so it is more targeted towards the user and no one else. The lack of distinction in terminology can get confusing when being in the radio tab of the application.

Flexibility and Efficiency of Use: Apple added support for different controls and gestures which the Apple Music application uses as well. The tap and hold gesture allows a user to see more options within the albums or the playlist. Users can also drag down the player to compress it to its smallest version.

Error Prevention: Apple helps protect the play queue that has been created to play in order. When adding songs to the "Up Next" section and playing a song, a message pops up asking if the user is sure she wants to play the next few songs in order.

Help and Documentation: Similar to Spotify, there is no help and documentation on the mobile version of Apple Music. Instead, if the user is using the desktop version, the app does have help plus documentation.

4.3 Key Level Model

In order to add more insights about the usability of both apps, a keystroke-level model (KML) study was done on the same tasks for each application, respectively. For this exercise, the user was expected to have already created an account, and he or she was already logged in. All tasks started from the home screen. The users were asked to record the operations they did for every task by making screen recording videos. The data was gathered from eight different users, four users for each app respectively, such that each user had a different level of experience. The tasks were as follows:

Task 1: Create a Playlist.
Task 2: Search and add a song to the playlist created in Task 1.
Task 3: Search for Playlist in Task 1 and search for a song inside the playlist.

Task 4: Search for an artist; add a song from the artist to playlist from Task 1.
Task 5: Search for an artist; play the artist's shuffle playlist.

While KLM was designed for desktop systems, it is also useful in producing models for evaluating mobile applications and comparing them. To simulate the touch screen slide, a combination of KpressPKrelease was used to indicate the press, slide, and release [7]. The operators which were used, and times are listed in Table 1.

Table 1. Operators table for use in keystroke-level model (KML)

Operator	Description	Time (Seconds)
P	Pointing with a pointing device	1.10
K	Key or button press and release	0.20
H	Move from the mouse to keyboard (or back)	0.40
R(t)	Waiting for the system to become responsive	t
M	Mental preparation and thinking time	1.35
KpressRKrelease	Press, slide, and release	1.5

Key Level Model - Spotify: Data was retrieved from four users (Table 2), where User A was Beginner Level, Users B and C were Intermediate Level, and User D was Expert.

Table 2. KLM time result table - Spotify

Time (s)	Task 1	Task 2	Task 3	Task 4	Task 5
Predict	8.75 s	12.9 s	10.95 s	19.70 s	11.4 s
User A	11.20 s	16.04 s	12.15 s	15.45 s	14.25 s
User B	9.94 s	17.15 s	8.12 s	15.97 s	16.4 s
User C	9.70 s	16.23 s	9.97 s	12.43 s	9.60 s
User D	9.21 s	15.96 s	11.01 s	13.61 s	8.19 s

The results in Table 2 Testing Spotify's functionality revealed that all the tasks worked as expected. There is a progression of time efficiency as the user gets familiar with the user interface. Regardless of the level of experience, users were able to accomplish all tasks. The system is habituating with time reflecting the efficiency as the level of expertise progresses.

Key Level Model - Apple Music: For Apple Music, data was gathered from four users (Table 3), where User E was Beginner Level, Users F and G were Intermediate Level, and User H was Expert.

From the results in Table 3, the detailed action sequence for every task from the user listing the calculated KLM times. The results follow expectations. Overall, User H

Table 3. KLM time result table - Apple Music

Time (s)	Task 1	Task 2	Task 3	Task 4	Task 5
Predict	8.75 s	12.90 s	10.95 s	19.70 s	11.4 s
User E	12.89 s	19.62 s	11.20 s	19.79 s	11.65 s
User F	11.47 s	18.75 s	8.55 s	21.02 s	7.98 s
User G	10.51 s	13.20 s	7.98 s	25.15 s	8.85 s
User H	9.08 s	9.15 s	8.16 s	23.21 s	8.50 s

(Expert Level) took less time to finish the tasks than others. Regardless of which level the users are in, tasks are completed in a brief period of time, indicating that the system is efficient to use.

4.4   User Interface Tenets and Traps

Tenets and traps in user interface (UI) design commonly refer to attributes of good design (tenets) and common detectable problems that downgrade good design (traps) [8]. Using the UI Tenets and Traps heuristic approach, common problems with a user experience can be identified and resolved. Using the UT Tenets and Traps heuristic, the music applications were evaluated.

User Interface (UI) Tenets and Traps (Spotify)
Tenets:

– **Discreet:** Devices and UIs are social by nature. Humans use mobile devices in social contexts. In fact, with computing trending to more miniaturized form factors, UIs are found more often in social situations because of device portability. Spotify has an option to make a playlist public or private to the community.
– **Understandable:** The system provides informative feedback to the user, on the left image Spotify prompts the user with the question "Are you sure?", making sure the user is one hundred percent sure of his or her decision. On the second screen, Spotify lets the user know that the app is being used on a different device and shows a prompt with the device name.

Traps:

– **Irreversible Action:** The user is unable to "undo" an incorrect step they have taken. In Spotify users have accidentally clicked "Ok we won't play this again". By clicking these options users will not be able to listen to the song or artist radio/album anymore.
– **Ambiguous Home:** There is no single place the user can return to at any time to begin a new task or get re-orientated. In Spotify, every time a user loads up the home screen, it is filled with recommended playlists and radio channels.
– **Unnecessary Step:** When the UI is used as intended, the amount of actual or perceived UI navigation needed to achieve a goal is too high. Spotify had an update that made the player less intuitive by making the user unnecessarily click around to get to their queue and genius lyrics.

– **Invisible Element:** Spotify has invisible elements laid throughout its entire UI. Many inexperienced users will not be able to tell that there are invisible elements present in the interface, as there are no clear signs that let the users know. When a user is listening to a particular song on the account, the user will not know that if the current tab is slide down, then the user can continue looking at the album's song collections. This feature is an advantage for experienced users. New Spotify users may not be aware of this element.

UI Tenets and Traps (Apple Music)
Tenets:

– **Understandable:** The system seems to be easy to use for users, as navigating different parts is not troubling. The system provides informative feedback when using certain aspects. When searching for specific songs or playlists, Apple Music gives specific details of the different playlists selected (length, artists, quantity). It is easy to understand and navigate through the application.

– **Responsive:** Apple Music has a very fast response time and does not make users wait as long as the user is connected to Wi-Fi. When offline, users can listen to downloaded content which has been saved. This response time helps users regularly access and listen to music.

Traps:

– **Invisible Element:** In the Apple music application, invisible elements are included in the UI which only experienced users would be familiar with. The UI does not tell let users know that by tapping on the bolded title of the song or the red highlighted album name users can see a collection of songs from the same album. This element is considered to be an invisible element and poses a disadvantage for inexperienced users.
– **Bad Prediction:** When listening to a playlist that friends have created and shared with a user, Apple will start to suggest music based on who or what the user listens to. Under the "For you" tab of Apple music, all of the music that Apple has suggested for a user based on the individual's search history and listening history is listed. This feature may not always be accurate when a user is listening to random artist's music. This feature may get the user frustrated as the user may not want these songs or artists on the suggested feed.

4.5   Radar Plots

Radar plots were used to give a visual representation of the data collected from the users through surveys and questionnaires.

The radar plot created for Spotify (see Fig. 1), shows how the Spotify music application excelled in almost every category with help, feedback, and error tolerance being the least outstanding category. When compared to Apple Music's radar plot (see Fig. 2), a few UI design elements did not meet the Apple standard. Page Layout & Design and Accessibility & Technical Design were both evaluated on the low end of the UI design elements which is unusually for Apple products. When comparing both radar plots together (see Fig. 3), Spotify appears to have the better UI design elements throughout its application, based on this evaluation.

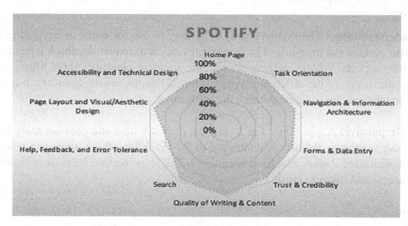

Fig. 1. Radar plot for Spotify music application

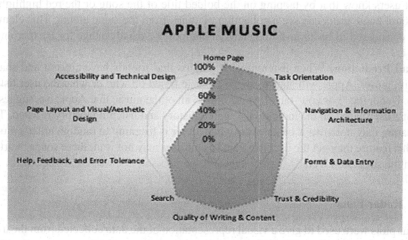

Fig. 2. Radar plot for Apple Music application.

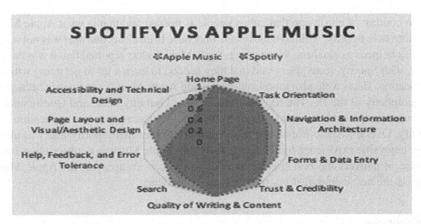

Fig. 3. Radar plot for Spotify and Apple music applications, superimposed.

5 Results

This research provides a clear view of how the user interface of both applications works in practice and how people view the applications. Music applications are very important in the world today and relied upon by users for relaxation and entertainment. Spotify is an application that is widely used as it can be free for users. Additionally, the Spotify application is flexible, providing support for both experienced and novice users. New users are able to easily work with this UI as 90% of the users' Help, Feedback, and Error Tolerance section has the lowest percentage of the 10 sections evaluated at only 75% (see Fig. 1). One hundred percent of the users have said that Spotify provided an enjoyable experience. When using the KLM study for this app, users performing certain tasks have varied times while most users were under the predicted times. This shows how the Spotify app was developed keeping user orientation in mind.

Apple Music is also another application that is widely used. Apple Music is not free for the public but is available by subscription only. While gathering information through users, Apple Music seemed to be simple and easy to use as well. Ninety percent of surveyed users mentioned the simplicity of Apple Music and the ease of use. One hundred percent of the users said that Apple Music provided an enjoyable experience. When using the KLM study for the Apple Music app, users performing the tasks accomplished many tasks under the predicted time, identifying the speed and efficiency of the Apple Music app. Apple Music is a popular application that is widely used.

6 Conclusion

With the information gathered from usability evaluation both of the applications, comparisons that can be made. Both Spotify and Apple Music have superior features which appeal to users. Spotify has been reported easier to use than Apple Music from the surveys administered to users. In addition to music, Spotify includes features such as podcasts that are very popular in the app.

In contrast, a music app that calms people is needed and that is what Apple Music provides over Spotify. Although the results may have been close, one user was not sure if Spotify helped to calm him. When using Apple Music, users reported that it was easy to learn, with Spotify, many users said that they needed to learn a lot to get going with the application. Users were also more confident using Apple Music over Spotify because of the simplicity of the UI. The results of the System Usability Scale and Questionnaires that were completed by users identified Apple Music as an easier-to-use application than Spotify. Overall, Apple Music has fewer usability issues than Spotify and was also a more enjoyable experience for the users. Although Apple Music is a subscription-based service, it delivers the best user experience to users from ages 18–24. Apple Music delivers the best calming, stress-reducing user experience.

References

1. Brougham, R.R., Zail, C.M., Mendoza, C.M., Miller, J.R.: Stress, sex differences, and coping strategies among college students. Curr. Psychol. **28**, 85–97 (2009)
2. Pierceall, E., Keim, M.: Stress and coping strategies among community college students. Community Coll. J. Res. **31**, 703–712 (2007)
3. American College Health Association: National College Health Assessment II: Spring 2015 Reference Group Summary. American College Health Association, Hanover, MD (2015)
4. Bland, H., Melton, B., Gonzalez, S.: A qualitative study of stressors, stress symptoms, and coping mechanisms among college students using nominal group process. J. Georgia Public Health Assoc. **5**(1), 24–37 (2010)
5. Chorianopoulos, K., Spinellis, D.: Affective usability evaluation for an interactive music television channel. ACM Comput. Entertain. **2**(3), 14 (2004). https://doi.org/10.1145/102 7154.1027177
6. Moumane, K., Idri, A., Abran, A.: Usability evaluation of mobile applications using ISO standards. SpringerPlus **5**, 548 (2016). https://doi.org/10.1186/s40064-016-2171-z
7. Nielsen, J.: "10 Heuristics for User Interface Design" Nielsen Norman Group (2020). www.nngroup.com/articles/ten-usability-heuristics/ (2020, April)
8. Medlock, M., Herbst, S.: UI Traps. www.uitraps.com (2020, April)
9. Brook, J.: SUS: a quick and dirty usability scale. In: Usability Evaluation in Industry. Taylor and Francis Pub., UK (1996). https://hell.meiert.org/core/pdf/sus.pdf (2020, April)
10. Schulz, T.: Using the keystroke-level model to evaluate mobile phones (2008). https://norweg ianrockcat.com/assets/iris31 (2020, April)

The Art Therapy Experience Based on Online Education System for Higher Education During the COVID-19 Pandemic: A Case Study of Communication Method

Zhen Liu⬭, Lingfeng Ren(✉), and Ke Zhang

South China University of Technology, Guangzhou 510006, People's Republic of China

Abstract. During the epidemic period, students' mental health needs more attention. Art therapy based on school can help students deal with psychological problems. However, with the implementation of online education, traditional art therapy needs to make changes to adapt to the current situation. Therefore, the purpose of this paper is to explore the way of integrating art therapy communication into university online education system under the background of the pandemic, to clarify the significance and value of art therapy to defend the novel coronavirus pneumonia and to explore the problem and improvement of a kind of online group art therapy for higher education. This paper conducted an exploratory case study, which carried out an online group art therapy communication project on an English course provided by the school of design, the South China University of Technology for first-year postgraduates. 15 Chinese students participated in the project and they were interviewed after the project. The results show that this kind of online group art therapy project can help students to get a more positive emotional experience. Communication is the key to the success of this kind of art therapy, and network technology is the main challenge. In the future, it is necessary to establish an art therapy framework in the online education system and to explore more therapy programs and methods.

Keywords: Art therapy · Online education · Higher education · COVID-19 · Mental health · Communication · University students

1 Introduction

Since the outbreak of COVID-19, the pandemic has caused tremendous negative impacts on people's lives. The virus brings risks to people's safety, which makes people refrain from going outdoors as much as possible. During this difficult period, people's mental health would more likely be in trouble. Especially for some university students, the occurrence of such magnitude outburst public health incident may cause the psychological disease of PTSD and depression in a short time. The extreme fear is the biggest risk factor for psychological distress, followed by shortened sleep time [1]. Besides, anxiety is a relatively common psychological problem. The study found that living in an epidemic environment, about 24.9% of university students experience anxiety.

M. M. Soares et al. (Eds.): HCII 2021, LNCS 12780, pp. 477–489, 2021.
https://doi.org/10.1007/978-3-030-78224-5_33

The infection of acquaintances, financial pressure, changes in daily life, and delays in studies may aggravate their anxiety [2]. Unfortunately, the global epidemic of the virus will continue for a long time. The consequence is that students' behavioral and emotional functioning, particularly externalizing and attention problems will get persistent negative effects. Therefore, in addition to ensuring educational achievements, universities need to be fully prepared to deal with the continuing impact of the pandemic on students' mental health [3]. However, preliminary findings focus on the multiple factors leading to students' distress during the pandemic. There are still many things to discuss about the psychological impact that students affected and how to reduce the negative impact [4].

Art therapy is considered to be an effective way to deal with psychological problems, it is an integrative mental health and human services profession that enriches the lives of individuals, families, and communities through active art-making, creative process, applied psychological theory, and human experience within a psychotherapeutic relationship [5]. Researches of art therapy focus on depression, borderline personality disorder, schizophrenia and post-traumatic stress disorder [6]. Art therapy enables people to express themselves through different forms of artistic creation. Individuals can provide outlets for their emotions based on self-compassion and mindfulness, which helps to improve individuals' mental health with depressive mood and depressive symptoms [7]. In the context of public event pressure, art therapists are rapidly acting: they hope to support the proposed public health psychological guidance by disseminating information, promoting expression and inspiration, challenging stigma, modulating media input, securing family connections, monitoring secondary traumatic stress, developing coping and resilience, maintaining relationships, and amplifying hope [8].

Based on the positive effect of art on mental health, traditional art therapy has been used in the school education system. To meet the educational needs of different groups of students, schools will set up some projects to help solve students' educational difficulties, whether social, intellectual, physical or emotional problems [9]. Art therapy based on school environment has specific characteristics: schools are often equipped with a special art therapy classroom and employ special art therapists. Students receive some art therapy outside of the stressful school hours, which gives them a chance to relax. The art therapy room is regarded as a shelter by students. When therapists play a supporting role for students, the whole experience of students in school tends to be positive, so these experiences are easier to be accepted by students [10]. And art therapy can effectively reduce students' learning pressure. Because of its simplicity and economy, it is a promising intervention for the higher education system. It doesn't waste time and doesn't require any training or special manpower [11]. Compared with psychotherapy in a special environment (such as art therapy clinic), art therapy in school is feasible and accessible, without too much pressure on students, However, the current situation of art therapy practice in the school system is far from the full potential of art therapy. Moreover, there may be conflicts between the educational purpose and the Therapeutic goal [12]. Therefore, how to ensure the achievement of educational purpose and give full play to the advantages of art therapy is a problem worthy of study.

Although under the epidemic situation, more and more university students have psychological problems, and art therapy for the students seems to be more necessary, another serious problem is that with the normalization of the epidemic situation, most universities have begun to use online education, which will continue for a long time. Using digital technology to build an education system is no longer a choice, but necessary, and in such special circumstances, and school should play a more important role in society [13]. This makes the traditional school-based art therapy mode no longer applicable. Therefore, how to integrate art therapy with the online education system for higher education in the context of epidemic needs to be discussed. The purpose of this paper is to explore the way of integrating art therapy communication into university online education system under the background of the pandemic, to clarify the value of art therapy to defend the novel coronavirus pneumonia and to explore the problem and improvement of a kind of online group art therapy.

2 Method

The case study method was used in this paper

2.1 Case Introduction

This case is based on the course offered by the school of design of South China University of technology for first-year postgraduates, and the course name is *usability research design*. The course was equipped with a Chinese professor, a British professor and a teaching assistant, a total of 15 Chinese graduate students participated in the course. They are all from the school of design, but they have different bachelor's degrees including engineering and art, Teachers and students communicated in English in the course. Therefore, this course has a cross-cultural, cross-professional background. During the course, the academic teaching part was completed under the guidance of the Chinese professor, and the main content was usability academic research. The art therapy part was mainly completed under the guidance of the British professor from the Royal Academy of Arts (RCA), which main content was the artistic creation project with the theme of "timeline". This paper focuses on the art therapy part. Due to the impact of the epidemic, the British scholar took the way of online education, using the platform Zoom. The art therapy part lasted for three weeks, and 3-h online courses were set up twice a week. Students were required to complete a work of art with the theme "timeline", In the creative process, the professor and the students maintained close communication. The students were encouraged to fully express their ideas, and with the help and suggestions of the professor, they refined their ideas and implemented artistic creations. At the end of the project, the students presented their artworks individually.

2.2 Project Detail

Artwork-Sharing and Project Theme Release. The RCA professor showed the students a wealth of artworks, including graphic design, photography, painting, collage, and art installation. It allowed students to experience the creativity of different media arts. The RCA professor proposed that art is to find a voice to communicate with others. Then the theme of art therapy was announced: timeline. The RCA professor believes that the timeline is a trace of the passage of time, which can be expressed in a variety of ways, including the soundtrack of music playback, annual rings, and light and shadow left by time-lapse photography. The RCA professor suggested that the students should set out on their own to think about ideas for timeline projects.

Art Creation Process Sharing and Question Answering. The RCA professor showed the students a large-scale public art project and proposed that artists should be good at collecting materials and finding the connection between materials. As for the creation of "timeline". The RCA professor thought that everyone should find their way of expression and encouraged students to focus on the divergence of thinking and find interesting creative inspiration at the beginning of the inspiration capture stage instead of considering the methods of realization.

Communication of Initial Ideas. During these two courses, The RCA professor discussed with the students about artistic creation. The students found the creative inspiration for the visualization of the "timeline" according to their personal experience and hobbies and explained their ideas to The RCA professor, and then The RCA professor gave encouragement and suggestions for improvement. The RCA professor said that the presentation of the timeline is not only to show the passage of time but also to show personal attributes. Making the "timeline" meaningful and meaningful is the key to artistic creation.

Further Communication and Exchange. The RCA professor again gave encouragement and suggestions for the students' new ideas. The RCA professor suggested that students use their familiar artistic creation techniques to present their ideas.

Personal Artworks Exhibition and Professor's Comments. In the last class, each student spent ten minutes presenting the artwork. The RCA professor made detailed comments on student's artworks, affirmed the progress of the students, and gave some forward guiding suggestions on the defects of these artworks.

2.3 Semi-structured Interview

At the end of the course, this paper carries out one-to-one interviews with the students participating in the course. The interview theme is divided into five parts, which are the source of inspiration, the reasons for choosing artistic forms, the emotional experience of the course, project communication and the psychotherapy effect of artistic creation.

3 Result

3.1 Project Achievement

In the later stage of the project, all the 15 students completed their artworks independently. Their works are arranged as follows in Table 1. Students' artworks all started from the theme of the timeline, showing their different perspectives on the change of time. Most of the students put more personal ideas into their works, most of which focus on the relationship between personal growth and the passage of time. Some of the students' works aim to show the importance of family affection. In addition, some students pay attention to physical health and environmental pollution. From the point of view of the most artistic forms used by students, the most popular form used by students is video, followed by image and installation.

Table 1. Art therapy design works of students.

Students	Title	Form	Description
Student 01	Impact of lifestyle on individuals	Video	In a video, the time wasted and the time won are represented by comparing the clockwise and counterclockwise rotation of the pointer. The author wants to express that the bad body state caused by bad living habits, and the time spent is wasted, but a good lifestyle leads to a good body state, and the time spent at this time is the time won
Student 02	Somewhere in time	Video	This video combines forward and backward modes to records his college life from a different perspective, more humorously to show a positive attitude towards the passage of time
Student 03	Invisible line	Video	The author uses the video to record the different life track between herself and her mother, hoping to remind herself that time will pass, love will always exist, and people need to care more about their mother
Student 04	Hair	Image	The author uses hair as the creative element to create different paintings to represent different stages of life. The author wants to express that we grow up in love, strive to survive, take responsibility, and finally learn to pass the love on. In this process, life can be passed on and the timeline can be extended
Student 05	Blackening	Video	This is an experimental art film. Colored plastic particles golden powder, watercolor pigments and water were used in the experiment. The colored plastic particles represent plastic pollution, and gold powder represents human benefits. The constant use of watercolors in the film represents an increase in plastic pollution. Eventually, the clean water is replaced by sewage, and plastic waste floats on the water
Student 06	Tea	Video	This is a video about tea in the water. As time goes by, tea blooms and sends out fragrance, which gives the water color. Although it will leave eventually, the trace that tea leaves are the proof that once existed

(*continued*)

Table 1. (*continued*)

Students	Title	Form	Description
Student 07	COSMOS	Image	This is a painting about the universe. It depicts the universe we use to explore time through painting, to arouse people's more thinking about time
Student 08	TAG TREE	Installation	The author found that in the process of growth, we are constantly given new tags, and the old tags may also fall off, which is the inevitable process of growth. So the author uses cards, wire and other materials to make a "tag tree" to encourage people to face themselves bravely
Student 09	Everything change, but love	Video	The video clip shows the change and conflict between parents and children on the way of growing up. The author wants to express that we may be indifferent and quarrel with our parents, but the love between us and our parents has never changed. Time has changed, the family will not change
Student 10	Life is a pendulum	Video	This is a video of the pendulum clock. The author thinks that life is like a pendulum clock. A child is a pendulum ball in it. He is born at home and gets along with his parents day and night. With the increase of new pursuits, the boundary of the swing is expanding and the time to go home is decreasing. If every time we go home, we turn into a grain of sand. When we finish our life, we will sigh that we have so little sand in our hands
Student 11	Ink mark	Video	This is a video recording paper covered with speckles. The author thinks that our life gradually becomes dull due to repetition, just like this paper covered with speckles. What impresses us is always a different color in the uniform picture. The author hopes to encourage people to try to find new experience and add color to their life
Student 12	Life of cigarette	Video	This work combines the burning process of a cigarette with the sound of an electrocardiogram and compares the life of a smoker through the burning of a cigarette, to persuades the smoker to quit smoking as soon as possible

(*continued*)

Table 1. (*continued*)

Students	Title	Form	Description
Student 13	The sandwich melts and time flows out	Installation	This art installation uses a ball made of pigment to represent candy, which slowly melts and drops on a piece of white paper. The author thinks that every good memory is like a sandwich candy, and time is the stuffing wrapped. Countless memories form a unique time stream, reflecting a person's unique life experience. When we began to recall the beauty at that time, time began to flow again, just like candy melting, adding different color and taste to our "time flow"
Student 14	The song of light	Light painting	In modern physics, the wave-particle duality of light determines the nature of light which is difficult to observe. However, if we put it in four-dimensional space (space + time), we can see the trace of light flow. Similarly, the production of music depends on the change of sound wave in the time dimension. Through the technique of extending exposure, the work captures the changing track of light in space, and uses it as the cover of the album, making light and music interweave in the dimension of time
Student 15	The sound of time	Installation	This work records all kinds of sounds during the day, such as alarm bells, birds, water when washing hands, calls, supermarket sounds and so on. In an enclosed space, the author placed a speaker and played the recorded sound towards the lighted candle, recording the change of candle flame

3.2 Interview Findings

All 15 students participated in the interview after the project.

Inspiration Source. Students have a wide range of sources of inspiration for their artistic creation. Five artworks come from the author's experience, for example, *The impact of life on individuals* comes from the subjects the author has studied in the past, *Life of cigarette* comes from the author's painful experience of smoking people around him. Six artworks are inspired by specific things, for example, *Somewhere in time* comes from the movie *Creed*; *Invisible line* comes from the old telephone line; *Blackening* comes from plastic contaminants floating on the surface of the water. Another part of the inspiration is related to the author's observation of personal growth, for example, *Hair* comes from the author's observation of hair changes at different life stages, and *Tag tree* comes from the author's observation that people are constantly labelled in the process of growing up. Through artistic creation, students begin to observe life with a more positive attitude,

Student 15 said that art may bring him some thinking and observation of life, and he will pay more attention to some things and phenomena in life. Student 08 said that this project will let him take the initiative to recall the past and rethink, which will inspire him to study and live better now.

Artistic Form Choosing. Video is the most popular form (9 out of 15) of artistic expression used by students. Students who created videos think that video will show their ideas more intuitively, clearly and strongly, and they think that video has both visual and auditory dimensions, which will be more attractive and more operable. At the same time, three students think that video itself has the property of timeline, which can record the state of time changes well, and can more easily achieve the interpretation of the theme of "timeline", so it will be more convenient to express. In addition to video creation, three students are using the image method. The author of hair mentioned that the use of the image is simple and fits the idea she wants to express, Student 14 chose light painting photography. He thinks that the image combined with the sense of space has a strong visual impact. Another student who uses image mentioned that the main reason for choosing is to be good at it. Finally, three students adopted the form of installation. The author of *Tag tree* thinks that installation is three-dimensional and more expressive, and this kind of form will make people more involved in artistic creation. The author of *The sound of time* mentioned that her work should belong to installation, because she wanted to show the change of the candle fire, but she had to record it with video.

Project Communication. Students generally reflected that they got practical bits of help in the process of communicating with the professor. The help was mainly some specific suggestions to guide them to express their ideas reasonably. At the same time, through gradual and heuristic discussion, students were easily encouraged by the professor, Student 11 said that most of the time the professor would encourage them, And the professor would ask about their daily work and encourage them to look for material from their own experience. When talking about the difficulties of online art communication. Four students mentioned that the most important technical problem is network jam, which caused the voice was not clear enough, Student 11 mentioned that our communication seems to be separated by a barrier. Sometimes they can't pay attention to the communication between teachers and other students. Besides, nine students believe that this kind of art therapy using the online course mode is often unable to provide enough communication. Student 05 pointed out that the biggest disadvantage of this kind of online art therapy is that it can't communicate with the professor in time, because there will be problems in the process of creation, but it can only wait until class to ask questions. Student 02 said that if we can communicate face to face, we may have more ideas. For artistic creation, online communication can't convey the details of the artwork. Student 13 said that some works may convey information through texture, so we must feel it in front of it. Shooting may weaken the feeling and atmosphere created by the whole work, and they hope to discuss our work face to face with the professor.

Emotional Experience. In terms of emotional experience in the process of art therapy communication project, most students (11 out of 15) have some changes. Before the project, the main emotion of students was to expect. Four students said that they were excited about this new form of course because they had never been exposed to art courses.

At the same time, three students were worried that non-native language teaching would cause certain pressure. In the ideation stage, the main emotions of students were anxiety and doubt. Anxiety came from their inability to quickly determine the purpose and idea of creation. The doubt lied in the inability to understand the boundaries of art and how to choose the right form of artistic expression. In the creative stage, the two opposite emotions of happiness and pain appeared at the same frequency. Six students pointed out that they enjoyed the process of creation. Student 02 thinks that the creation process is very interesting for him, and the first contact with art-related projects is a breakthrough in his school experience. Five students pointed out that there were a lot of negative emotions in the creation process, the main reason for which was the lack of self-confidence in the work. Student 06 said that she always thought her ideas were not good enough, and she was assured to complete her work only when she got the affirmation of the professor during the communication. Besides, the negative emotions seem to be related to the audience's background experience, Student 15 said that she had only received an engineering education in the past, so it was very difficult for her to engage in artistic creation. She had difficulties making clear which ideas she wanted to express, and she encountered lots of problems in the creation process. Moreover, academic pressure may also aggravate negative emotions. Student 13 mentioned that when she thought that this creation was a kind of homework and it will be graded and evaluated, she would think about whether her work had met the requirements. But after finishing the work, most of the negative emotions have been alleviated. Student 04 mentioned that although there some pressure in the process of creation, she was very happy when finishing the work.

Psychotherapy Effect. After the completion of the artworks, the main experience of the students was to relax, Student 02 said that it's an interesting thing because it allowed them to do something they like in the way they enjoy. Most students (8 out of 15) got the feeling that art comes from life, and they think that artistic creation is a good emotional outlet, Student 11 said that expressing his thoughts and emotion through an artwork makes him feel better. Although it can be interpreted differently in different people's eyes. Artistic creation can also bring more positive emotions, Student 13 said that after using art to express her ideas, that will be full of curiosity and provide an impulse to communicate. Student 14 believes that art can bring people a sense of identity, especially when others are curious and sympathetic to her work, and she would get some inner rewards. However, three students were in a low mood after finishing their works. Originally, it came from dissatisfaction with the work. Student 04 said that the expressiveness of the work was good not enough, which made her feel a little sad. Although it was gratifying to complete the work in a new way. This kind of group art creation may also bring peer pressure. Student 03 thinks that there is a big gap between herself and other students and that she had done well in the project, which made her very disappointed.

4 Discussion

This paper summarizes a case study of integrating an art therapy communication project into the university online education system under the background of the pandemic. The project has a cross-cultural background and using English to teach (learners' second language). The theme of the project "timeline" is to help students improve their mental health during the epidemic through artistic creation.

Under the influence of the epidemic situation, the art therapy communication project, in this case, was carried out online, and integrated into the online education system, with the participation of 15 students, therefore it was a kind of online group art therapy project. The results show that this art therapy communication project is successful that all the students involved in the project have completed the artworks, and it has a positive impact on students' mental health. From the perspective of students' works, self-expression is a key part of artistic works. The choice of forms of expression can fully illustrate this point. Most students used digital video to present their ideas because the digital video is more intuitive. Digital video has been successfully used as a tool for artistic creation, analysis and research, and providing behavioral feedback for students and teachers [14], Moreover, expressiveness seems to be positively related to the positive experience of creation. Students who think that the expressiveness of works meets the expectations have a higher evaluation of art therapy communication project and more positive emotions. This may be because expressive art therapy can make the participants know more about themselves, and then create artworks with more personal significance and emotional effects, which can often turn their negative emotions into positive energy [15]. Also, for the students who have completed the artistic creation, some students expect to communicate with others and get feedback from others after showing their works, Collie et al's research points out that it is important for the participants gave not to making art but to discussing their art together and how this contributed to a sense of connection [16]. Additional peer communication during the project may improve the effect of art therapy, which will give full play to the advantages of group art therapy since This can provide an opportunity to demonstrate continuity, enhance participants' self-worth and identity, and increase the joy of accomplishing challenges and achievements [17].

Group art therapy in the online education system should ensure communication to enhance the emotional experience of the whole processes. On the one hand, more communication can make students get some practical suggestions that make it easier for them to express their ideas, Communication on creative techniques will not only reduce students' confusion about art but also reduce the difficulty of artistic creation. Such participants and therapists and/or groups discuss art together, which is the most prominent helping event in art therapy because the joint observation of art products is regarded as an intimate moment. The therapist can help the participants to find the connection between the internal experience reflected in the work and the parallel process in the external reality [18]. On the other hand, giving students enough encouragement through communication will help them to experience the happiness of artistic creation more easily. And the previous experience of artistic creation is very necessary [19], since students who participate in the creation may be those who have never been in touch with art projects, and art creation is difficult for them. And in the education system, art therapy may lead to some academic pressure on students. At the same time, the way of group art therapy, especially in the education system of art creation, may produce peer pressure, making students feel less confident, and hurting students' self-esteem. In conclusion, creating an atmosphere without judgment is a key part of cultivating students' sense of security in art creation [20]. The art projects in online courses should encourage more open communication and interaction, give more suggestions and encouragement, and consider the difficulties of students with different backgrounds to reduce academic pressure and peer pressure.

However, this kind of online group art therapy also has challenges, especially in the integration of art therapy communication project in university online education system. These challenges are similar to those encountered in online education. The review of ade-doyin and soykan pointed out that the challenges of online learning under the epidemic situation include technical problems, socio-economic impact, human and pet interference, differences in digital ability, difficulties in evaluation and supervision, additional workload and course compatibility [21]. In this case, the communication difficulty caused by network jam is the main technical problem and the communication in the project is insufficient. First of all, the use of online conference communication tools in class will lead to fewer opportunities for communication, which can only be obtained during class. At the same time, the professor can't be on-site for real-time guidance, and can't fully take care of the needs of each student when facing many students in the online class at the same time. Using social media for communication may bring improvement. Students think that social media is a more appropriate communication tool because it is easy to use, useful and interactive [22]. Secondly, to convey artworks through network technology, whether the professor shows them to the students or the students show them to the professor, the experience will be weak due to the lack of telepresence, such as the inability to convey the material and texture of the works, Lecturers need to ensure the accessibility of teaching materials so that students can also master the ability to access teaching materials [23]. More advanced technologies, such as the immersive virtual reality, may improve the effectiveness of online art therapy. VR technology can not only create a therapy environment that meets the specific needs of the participants but also is a form of artistic expression [24].

5 Conclusion

This study tentatively describes an online group art therapy communication case in higher education, which aims to help students receiving online education in the context of the pandemic to deal with their mental health problems. This study found that art creation can make students re-examine their thoughts and life, turning negative emotions into positive emotions, and let them gain happiness from identity. This paper proposes that communication should be emphasized in the use of art therapy in the online education system. Therapists, i.e. university professors, in this case, should give more specific advice to students, and take care of students with different professional backgrounds or peer pressure, to ensure that students with different needs can get a good experience in the whole therapy project. Creating more opportunities for communication after class may promote the success of art therapy. At present, there are some challenges in online art therapy projects, Network jam is the main technical problem, and then how to ensure that the details of art are communicated is worth considering. This study has shown the significance and value of art therapy in the online education system for higher education. Therefore, it is feasible to gradually improve the online education system and integrate art therapy projects, and more ways should be explored to deal with the long-lasting pandemic.

Acknowledgements. The authors wish to thank all the people who provided their time and efforts for the investigation. This research was funded by Guangdong Province Education Science Planning Project, "Research on Youth Psychological/Mind Models and Art Therapy Strategies: Taking Greater Bay Area University as an Example", grant number 2019GXJK196.

References

1. Tang, W., et al.: Prevalence and correlates of PTSD and depressive symptoms one month after the outbreak of the COVID-19 epidemic in a sample of home-quarantined Chinese University Students. J. Affect. Disord. **274**, 1–7 (2020)
2. Cao, W., et al.: The psychological impact of the COVID-19 epidemic on college students in China. Psychiatry Rese. **287**, (2020)
3. Copeland, W.E., et al.: Impact of COVID-19 pandemic on college student mental health and wellness. J. Am. Acad. Child Adolesc. Psychiatry **60**(1), 134–141 (2021)
4. Grubic, N., Shaylea, B., Amer, M.J.: Student mental health in the midst of the COVID-19 pandemic: a call for further research and immediate solutions. Int. J. Soc. Psychiatry **66**(5), 517–518 (2020)
5. American Art Therapy Association homepage. https://arttherapy.org/about-art-therapy/. Accessed 12 Feb 2021
6. Van Lith, T.: Art therapy in mental health: a systematic review of approaches and practices. Arts Psychother. **47** (2016)
7. Braus, M., Brenda, M.: Art therapy in the time of COVID-19. Psychol. Trauma: Theor. Res. Pract. Policy **12**(S1), S267–S268 (2020)
8. Potash, J.S., Kalmanowitz, D., Fung, I., Anand, S.A., Miller, G.M.: Art therapy in pandemics: lessons for COVID-19. Art Ther. **37**(2), 105–107 (2020)
9. Prasad, S., Paula, H., Jennie, K.: Using Art Therapy with Diverse Populations: Crossing Cultures and Abilities. 1st edn. Jessica Kingsley Publishers, 73 Collier Street London ni 9BE. UK and 400 Market Street. Suite 400 Philadelphia, PA 19106, USA (2013)
10. Harpazi, S., Regev, D., Snir, S., Raubach-Kaspy, R.: Perceptions of art therapy in adolescent clients treated within the school system. Front. Psychol. **11**, (2020)
11. Soejanto, L.T., Bariyyah, K., Pambudi, P.R., Yaman, D.M.: Art Therapy for students academic stress. In: Proceedings of the 2nd International Conference on Education and Social Science Research (ICESRE 2019). Atlantis Press, Kota Semarang, Central Java. Atlantis Press, Indonesia (2020)
12. Regev, D., Anat Green-Orlovich, Sharon, S.: Art therapy in schools - the therapist's perspective. Arts Psychother. **45**, 47–55 (2015)
13. Korkmaz, G., Cetin, T.: Are we ready for the Post-COVID-19 educational practice? an investigation into what educators think as to online learning. Int. J. Technol. Educ. Sci. **4**(4), 293–309 (2020)
14. Orr, P.P.: A documentary film project with first-year art therapy students. Arts Psychother. **33**(4), 281–287 (2006)
15. Snyder, B.A.: Expressive art therapy techniques: healing the soul through creativity. J. Hum. Educ. Dev. **36**(2), 74–82 (1997)
16. Collie, K., Hankinson, S.P., Norton, M., Dunlop, C.: Online art therapy groups for young adults with cancer. Arts Health **9**(1), 1–13 (2017)

17. Reynolds, F., Kee, H.L.: Contribution of visual art-making to the subjective well-being of women living with cancer: a qualitative study. Arts Psychother. **34**(1), 1–10 (2007)
18. Shakarov, I., Regev, D., Snir, S., Orkibi, H., Adoni-Kroyanker, M.: Helpful and hindering events in art therapy as perceived by art therapists in the educational system. Arts Psychother. **63**, 31–39 (2019)
19. Stevenson, M., Kayleigh, O.: Art therapy: stimulating non-verbal communication. Nurs. Residential Care **15**(6), 443–445 (2013)
20. Sonnone, A., Jessie, S.R.: Wellness at universities: a group art therapy approach. J. Coll. Couns. **23**(2), 168–179 (2020)
21. Adedoyin, O.B., Emrah S.: Covid-19 pandemic and online learning: the challenges and opportunities. Interact. Learn. Environ. **136**, 1–13 (2020)
22. Sobaih, A.E.E., Ahmed M.H., Ahmed E.A.E.: Responses to COVID-19 in higher education: social media usage for sustaining formal academic communication in developing countries. Sustainability **12**(16), 6520 (2020)
23. Simamora, R.M.: The challenges of online learning during the COVID-19 pandemic: an essay analysis of performing arts education students. Stud. Learn. Teach. **1**(2) (2020)
24. Hacmun, I., Dafna, R., Roy, S.: The principles of art therapy in virtual reality. Front. Psychol. **9**, 2082 (2018)

Spatial Interaction Design for Children's Magnetic Resonance Imaging Examination Based on Embodied Cognition

Bao Quan Luo[1,2][✉]

[1] Guangzhou Academy of Fine Arts, No.257, Changgang East Road, Haizhu District, Guangzhou City, Guangdong Province, People's Republic of China
[2] Faculty of Innovation and Design, City University of Macau, Macau, People's Republic of China

Abstract. To explore the spatial interaction design method for children's MRI examination based on embodied cognition theory, and to construct a design model suitable for the spatial interaction by combining the concepts of image schema and environmental affordance. This study adopted literature analysis and visual analysis tools to analyze research on embodied cognition at home and abroad, and explore the correlation between embodied cognition and spatial interaction design from the perspective of designing. Through observation and in-depth interview, this paper analyzed a series of problems encountered by children in MRI examination, and studied the applicability and feasibility of applying embodied cognition theory to spatial interaction design of children's MRI examination. At the same time, through field survey, users' journey map was drawn to probe into the hidden needs; finally, the feasibility of the theoretical model was verified by combining the design workshop and the design scheme, and the design thinking of children's MRI spatial interaction was put forward. When children undergo MRI examination, they have special psychological characteristics and behavioral needs and show high sensitivity to the space environment. By combining embodied cognition theory with spatial interaction design, four elements of interactive design for children's MRI examination space were obtained. The four elements are the matching degree of embodied cognition, the recognition degree of image schema, the operational degree of environmental affordance and the immersion degree of interactive experience. The design elements were verified by practical practice in workshops, which provides design thinking cases for the interactive design of children's MRI examination space.

Keywords: Children's MRI · Embodied cognition · Environmental affordance · Spatial interaction

1 Introduction

With the development and derivation of nuclear magnetic resonance imaging (MRI) technology, MRI witnesses more extensive clinical application in pediatrics [1]. However, MRI will be accompanied by obvious vibration and noise during examination, and

© Springer Nature Switzerland AG 2021
M. M. Soares et al. (Eds.): HCII 2021, LNCS 12780, pp. 490–505, 2021.
https://doi.org/10.1007/978-3-030-78224-5_34

it needs the absolute cooperation of examinees to be successfully completed, which is a great test for children. Besides, whether it will cause children's claustrophobia, tension, anxiety, resistance, resistance and other psychology in the process of examination is also a problem worth studying. Experiments prove that children with medical fear experience will reduce their compliance with medical care [2]. Apart from the problems in the examination process, the special environment of the hospital and children's strangeness, distance and oppression to MRI space may also cause negative psychological hints, which need further research and test. In the current medical system, each hospital has rare MRI system equipment. Except for a small number of children's hospitals, which have special MRI space for children, the rest basically share equipment and space regardless of age. In case of children's MRI, most of them adopt sedation and psychological intervention assistance [1], and seldom seek solution from the design perspectives of space environment, human-computer interaction, service experience, etc.

In this context, this paper attempted to explore the spatial interaction design for children's MRI based on interdisciplinary research, integrated embodied cognition theory, image schema and environmental affordance concepts, and combined children's physical and mental characteristics during MRI.

2 Embodied Cognition and Spatial Interaction

2.1 Embodied Cognition Theory A Subsection Sample

Embodied cognition is a revolutionary school developed in cognitive psychology since 1980s. It holds that human cognitive mind is formed in the interaction of brain, body and environment, and the formation of cognition is intrinsically related to the behavioral state of the body (i.e. embodied structure) and the empirical schema of physical activities [3]. Embodied cognition theory emphasizes the importance of physical activity participation when people carry out cognitive activities. Human cognition is formed when their physical activity experience matches their behavior patterns [4]. The basic process of cognitive composition is closely related to human physiological structure, and environment is an important factor in shaping human physical and mental structure. Therefore, cognition, as a product of interaction between human and environment, is the result of synergy among body, environment and activities [5]. The development of embodied cognition theory can be seen, which recognizes the role of body in cognitive activities and emphasizes that cognition comes from the interaction between human physical activities and environment, and undoubtedly provides a theoretical basis for reference for the design of specific spatial interaction that requires cognitive behavior participation.

In light of the development of embodied cognition theory, it is clear that since 1884, James and Langer have proposed that people's emotions are influenced by their physical changes. By 1945, Maurice Merleau-Ponty first proposed in his book Phenomenology of Body: The subject of perception is the body. Then, Gibson put forward the concept of functional affordance in 1979, which directly affected Norman's functional affordance in Design Psychology. Wilson put forward six viewpoints of embodied cognition in 2002 and John Baker studied the design framework of embodied learning in 2012. Many scholars are demonstrating and emphasizing the relationship and importance of interaction between human cognition and physical environment, as shown in Fig. 1. In life, we can see such a phenomenon: people who have not ridden bicycles cannot understand how "balance" is controlled; children can recognize abstract mathematical concepts by counting their fingers.

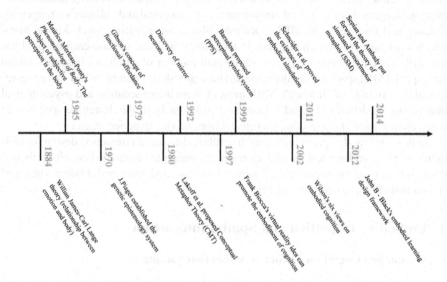

Fig. 1. Development of embodied cognition theory.

Historically, the research on embodied cognition theory has gradually shifted from metaphysical concept discussion to scientific verification based on empirical evidence [6]. A large number of research and experimental data prove that cognition is closely related to physical behavior and environmental situations.

2.2 Application of Embodied Cognition Theory in Design Field

Related Theoretical Research

Since entering the 21st century, scholars at home and abroad have begun to study embodied cognition theory, and have made sound discussions on its academic source, concepts, practical application, etc. Meanwhile, some scholars started to study the application of embodied cognition theory in the field of design. On CNKI database, when searched with the keyword "design + embodied cognition", 659 Chinese documents of related research were found. After statistical visualization of the data, it can be seen that the number of related articles showed an obvious growth trend. Especially after 2019, many experts began to study the relationship between embodied cognition and interactive design, as shown in Fig. 2a. When we carried out literature analysis in CiteSpace, we used keyword co-occurrence visual analysis and merges synonyms (such as virtual reality and VR) to obtain an analysis map showing the relationship between keywords, as shown in Fig. 2b. The keyword clustering information and association shown in the figure, to a certain extent, reveal the theme and development of Chinese scholars in studying embodied cognitive theory, focusing on three major aspects: related theoretical research, various types of instructional design, embodied interaction technology, etc.

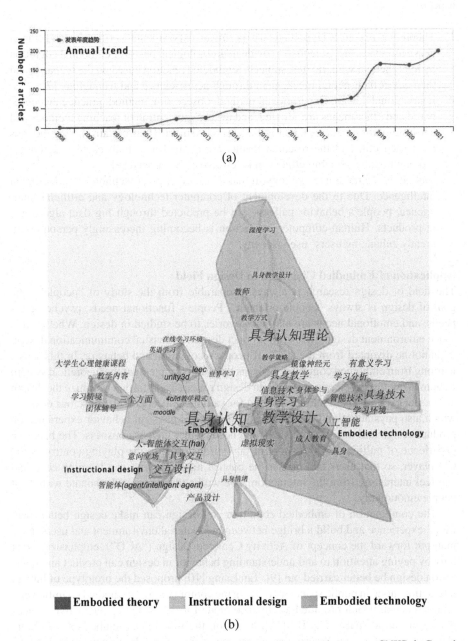

(a)

(b)

Fig. 2. a. Publication trend of embodied cognitive theory literature (data source CNKI). b. Growth trend of published articles and co-occurrence analysis map (CiteSpace).

Through CiteSpace's analysis of the three clustering studies obtained from embodied cognition theory, we can know the research methods of embodied cognition in these aspects.

1. Theoretical research: Hypothetical experiment, experimental verification and cranial nerve forensics, etc. Scientists provide neurobiological basis for embodied cognition by hypothetical scenario, test subjects' embodied reaction based on the scenario, and then detect their neural mechanism through neuroscience and technology [7].
2. Instructional design: Experimental method, observation method, practice evidence-based and other means are adopted, and testees' perception of teaching methods and teaching environment are taken as the research subject. Then, certain guiding theories are teased out, and the research results are applied to actual teaching activities, proving that the teaching effect can be effectively improved [8].
3. Embodied interaction technology: It mainly uses computer technology and artificial intelligence. Due to the development of computer technology and artificial intelligence, people's behavior patterns can be predicted through big data algorithms in products. Human-computer interaction is becoming increasingly personalized, greatly enhancing users' use viscosity.

Application of Embodied Cognition in Design Field

The field of design research is always inseparable from the study of "people". The goal of design is always "people-oriented". People's functional needs, psychological needs, and emotional needs are all the categories to be studied in design. Whether it is space environment design, industrial product design, and visual communication design, it cannot be divorced from the study of people's cognition and behavior. In this sense, learning from embodied cognition theory is helpful to supplement the theoretical system of human cognitive behavior research in design research and further optimize the design effect. For example, Naoto Fukasawa put forward the concept of "unconscious design", which also pays attention to the influence of people's physical behavior experience on product design and meets people's hidden needs under unconsciousness. The behavior experience of pulling down the control fan is transferred to the playing control of the CD player, so that users can master the control mode without any learning cost, and can feel interesting from the interaction. The works thus produced resonate with most people emotionally.

The combination of embodied cognition and design can make design better meet users' experience and build a bridge between the material environment and users. Norman put forward the concept of Activity Centered Design ("ACD"), emphasizing that only by paying attention to and understanding behavior in design can product and inter-action design be better carried out [9]. Tan Liang [10] proposed the prototype of human interaction mode in public space by studying the combination of embodied cognition and image schema, which provided a reference mode for the design of interactive devices placed in public space. Pen Bo [11], based on the research on embodied cognition, clarified the importance of participation and experience in children's education in muse-ums, and deemed that children's cognition mostly came from physical experience, and effective use could deepen children's understanding of exhibits.

2.3 Relationship Between Embodied Cognition and Image Schema

Image schema, as one of the important concepts in cognitive linguistics, was first proposed by American linguists Mark Johnson and Lakoff in 1980 [12]. It refers to the fact that in the long-term life experience, people's behavior, mind and perception all have certain regular patterns and meaning schemas, which enable people to have meaningful and cognitively relevant experiences, and can understand and carry out reasoning learning [13].

Image schema is an abstract cognitive structure formed over time under the repeated interaction experience between human and environment [14]. Its schema determines the embodied expression of cognition and the formation of metaphorical language system. For example, the oral expression "he has great dreams" reflects the degree of "size" in the "nature" schema. Although the degree is a relatively abstract concept, it can affect our cognitive understanding and language system subconsciously. Another example is in behavior activities, when we see "stairs", we naturally associate it with "up and down" actions, which corresponds to the "space" schema. Therefore, the common image schema is the common behavior experience pattern that has been formed in the human brain, as shown in Fig. 3.

种类Type	意象图式 ImageSchema
空间（ORIENTATION）	上-下（UP-DOWN）、中心-边缘（CENTER-PERIPHERY）、远-近（NEAR-FAR）
容器（CONTAINMENT）	容器物（CONTAINER）、满-空（FULL-EMPTY）
历程（PROCESS）	路径（PATH）、起点-路径-终点（SOURCE-PATH-GOAL）、循环（CYCLE）
性质（ATTRIBUTE）	大-小（BIG-SMALL）、轻-重（HEAVY-LIGHT）、直（STRAIGHT）
作用力（FORCE）	推力（COMPULSION）、平衡（BALANCE）、阻碍（BLOCKAGE）
复数物（MULTIPLICITY）	部分-整体（PART-WHOLE）、接触（CONTACT）、连接（LINK）

Fig. 3. Partial classification of image schema.

It can be seen that although "image schema" and "embodied cognition" belong to different conceptual fields, they both focus on human cognition and mental habit models. The former discusses how language is affected by environmental states so as to make corresponding descriptive words; the latter explores how behavior is affected by environmental conditions, so as to make corresponding action inertia. Both of them explain that various interactive behaviors between people and things and between people come from cognition, and cognition is closely related to environmental states. Combining the concepts of "embodied cognition" and "image schema" can provide a theoretical explanation of "motivation" for interactive design.

2.4 Environmental Affordance in Spatial Interactions

Gibson, an American ecological psychologist, put forward the concept of environmental affordance in 1979. In his book The Theory of Affordance [15], he pointed out that "environmental affordance is what the environment provides to animals, whether good or bad" and "the environment is the surface that separates matter from media, and animals live in media (air)". In the field of design, the earliest application of this concept appeared in product interface design. Cognitive scientist Norman's book General Design Rules mentioned that "Affordance" was translated into "functional visibility" [16]. Affordance is the actual attribute that material provides for people to perceive, the basic condition for identifying its functional use, and an important signal for prompting its operability. Affordance theory plays a crucial role in design research and design practice, especially in the interactive design of specific space environments (such as hospitals, schools, gymnasiums and other public places), which is an important indicator for users to evaluate experience satisfaction. This paper mainly studied the design of MRI examination space environment for children, focusing on the psychological suggestion of physical space scenes (including instruments and props) for children, that is, the affordance of interaction between children and the environment in the context of medical space. If this "affordance" is used and transferred to the interactive design of children's MRI examination space to create a medical space that matches children's cognitive level and conforms to their behavior patterns, it is likely to transform the "negative" affordance of the original environment into "positive" affordance and ease their panic and anxiety.

Although the above three theoretical concepts belong to different research fields, they are all intrinsically related to the problems studied in this paper. Embodied cognition emphasizes the influence of human body behavior experience on cognition. Image schema expresses the schematic conceptual structure formed in the interaction between human and environment. Environmental affordance refers to how environmental conditions meet human subconscious needs. The organic integration of these three concepts can provide corresponding guidelines for the interactive design of medical space for children in the early stage of cognition, as shown in Fig. 4.

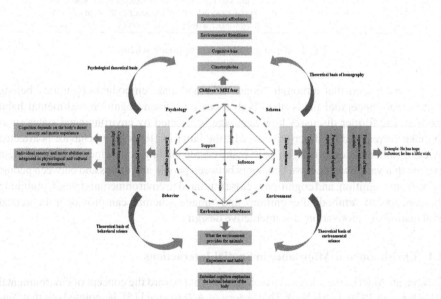

Fig. 4. Theoretical model of spatial interaction design of children's MRI examination based on embodied cognition.

3 Present Situation and Case Analysis of MRI Environment Design for Children

3.1 Status of MRI Environment Design for Children

Currently, most general hospitals in China have set up special pediatrics, but in the design of hospital space environment, the physical and mental needs of children, a special group, are often ignored. Even most professional children's hospitals focus on the superficial needs of children. They add playgrounds, increase bright colors, graffiti and cartoon patterns, etc. Basically, they are pursuing the contrast of superficial visual experience and space atmosphere, and seldom carry out designs from the perspectives of children's cognition, behavior patterns, physiological characteristics and emotional needs. Quite a few researchers explored the design of children's medical environment from the deep needs of children. For example, Peng Boxin [17], starting from the characteristics of children's behavioral psychology, proposed that the design of children's medical space should focus on "biological" needs to "physiological" needs, and hospitals should give more exclusive humanistic care designs to children. Liu Jie and Zhong Yue [18] proposed the best matching scale system for children's ward space design based on children's human factors and behavioral psychology. Besides, there are also studies on the space design of children's hospitals from the perspective of environmental behavior. For example, Rao Hongyue [19] studied the relationship between the affordance of the environment and children's behavior through long-term observation of users of Shenzhen Children's Hospital, and put forward strategies for the design of external public space of Children's Hospital, including barrier-free interesting pavement, flexible regional boundary, and distinguishing amusement space setting according to children's activity ability.

Moreover, some domestic medical experts, from their own professional point of view, studied the problems arising from children's MRI. Hu Yan and Lu Peng [20], professors of the First Clinical Medical College of Three Gorges University, started with the psychological problems of children facing MRI examination, sorted out five psychological problems such as fear, anxiety, resistance, fear of medical treatment and dependence, and put forward countermeasures for nursing intervention: strengthening communication with children, creating an adaptation process, encouraging parents to play their roles, weakening the fear of injection, etc. There are also medical experts who study the solution from the perspective of drug intervention. Peng Yinjuncheng and Tang Wen [1] carried out test on children patients from different ways of sedative drug use, and obtained the sedative intervention methods required by children of different ages.

It can be seen that the research on children's medical environment design still focuses on the design of the hospital's internal and external space environment, and rarely talks about the interaction requirements of special spaces. For example, there is rare research on the design of children's MRI space interaction, from an interdisciplinary perspective, and on comprehensive psychology, cognitive science and design.

3.2 Case Analysis

In foreign countries, especially in Europe and the United States, due to the early popularity of MRI and the fact that many manufacturers of MRI instruments are from Europe and the United States, they have made multiple optimization schemes on the interaction of children's MRI. Especially from the design perspectives of spatial interaction and equipment improvement, a number of excellent cases have emerged that can be used for reference. As reported in the *American College of Radiology* (ACR) in 2019, Siemens and Marvel specially developed an interactive prop system for children's MRI examination for Will Cornell Medical Center of New York Presbyterian Hospital to solve children's fear feeling during MRI and reduce the use of sedatives. It was named "MRI-am-a-Hero" (Fig. 5). The system includes a set of specially adapted comic books, a Superman cloak, a miniature version of MRI instrument toy, dolls of Captain America and Iron Man, and a box of MRI education DVD simulating customs clearance games. Children first watched the educational content of DVD with their parents. The video fictionalized the process of a 10-year-old girl undergoing MRI examination, so that children had a certain understanding of the whole process before undergoing MRI examination. While waiting, children could play with instrument model toys and further know the equipment to be contacted for a while from a macro level. Meanwhile, they can also watch exclusive comic books, which adapt the story of Marvel comic characters Captain America and Iron Man cheering for children. During the examination, children can also hold toys all the time, which plays a good comfort role. Finally, after the examination, children can wear Superman cloaks, which is a reward for their "brave" behavior. The researchers found that after adopting such process, the proportion of outpatients aged 4–15 using magnetic resonance imaging (MRI) sedatives decreased by 5.6% [21].

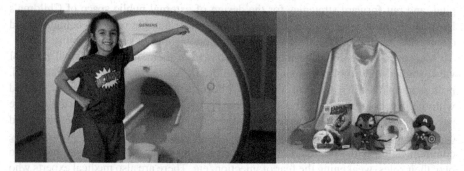

Fig. 5. MRI-am-a-Hero.

From the above successful example, we can see that its design ideas all focus on children's cognitive ability and behavioral characteristics. According to the above theoretical viewpoints and case analysis, this paper teased out the corresponding conceptual design model, as shown in Fig. 6a. That is, the theme was set by embodied cognition (body behavior cognition: MRI process = Superman flight process), psychological suggestion was generated by image schema (nature state suggestion: track forward = Superman bravery), environmental affordance assistance was used (environmental condition provision: space transformation = hero game scene), and finally immersion degree of interactive process (MRI process = hero entry game) was realized, as shown in Fig. 6b.

From more cases, we can see the adaptability and applicability of the above conceptual design model. For example, Character Farms Company has developed a number of

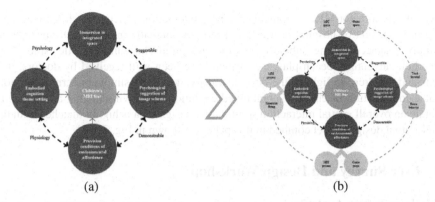

(a)　　　　　　　　　　　　　　(b)

Fig. 6. a. A child MRI spatial interaction model based on embodied cognition. b. Case study using design model.

Themes	Space roaming	Submarine exploration	Pirate ships going to sea

Analysis of design model	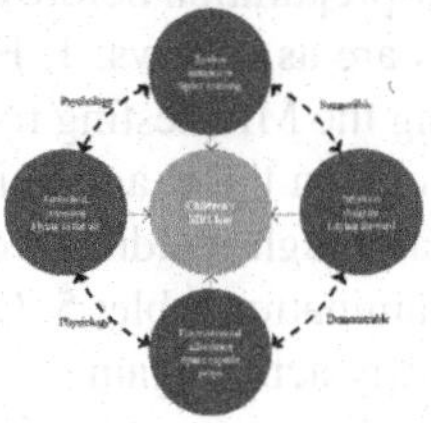	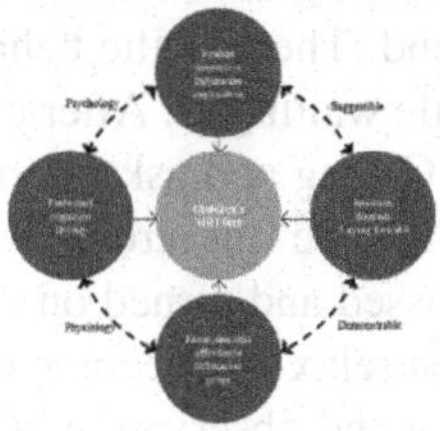	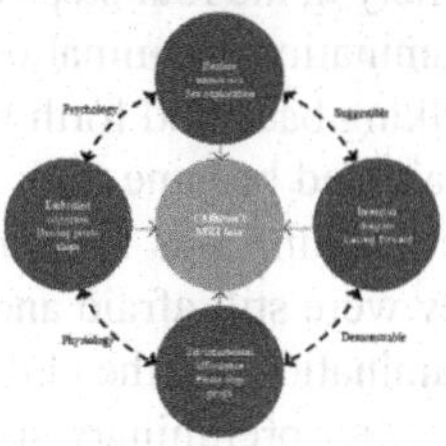
Themes	Castle exploration	Tree hole adventure	Play on the beach

Analysis of design model	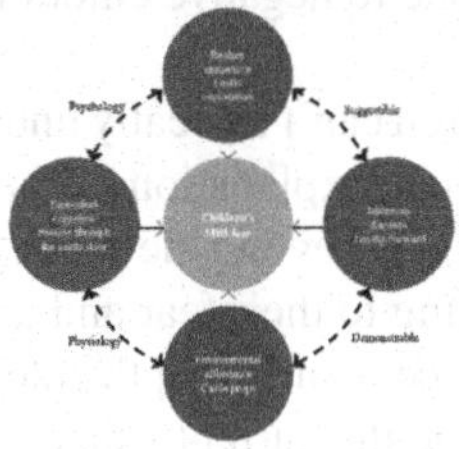	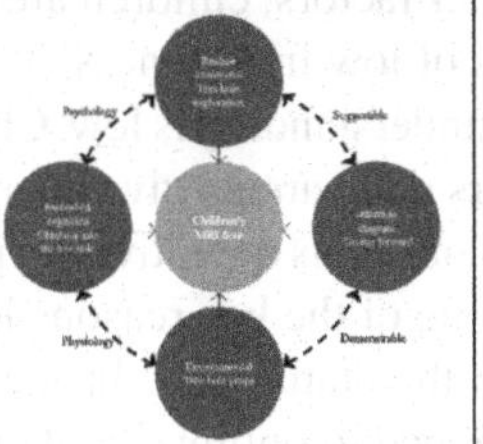	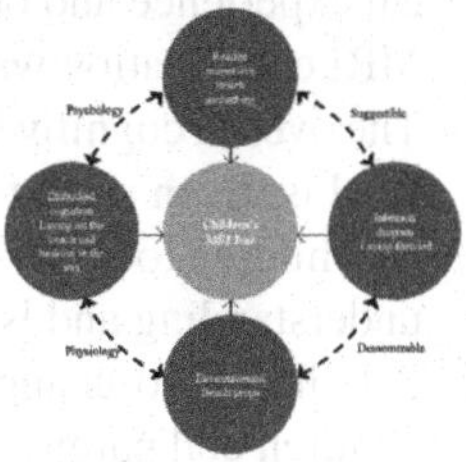

Fig. 7. Case study using design model.

overall solutions for MRI equipment and space interaction systems for children according to the needs of hospital customers. There are thematic interaction forms such as simulated space roaming, submarine exploration, pirate ship sailing, castle exploration, tree hole adventure, beach play, etc., which have been well received by doctors, parents and children. In light of the design strategy, it is not a simple pattern decoration, but a combination of children's embodied cognition and environmental affordance to obtain an overall spatial interaction solution. Its design idea is highly matched with the conceptual design model combed in this paper, as shown in Fig. 7.

4   User Survey and Design Workshop

4.1   User Survey Analysis

According to the theoretical combing and case analysis, after obtaining the spatial interaction design model for children's MRI, this study, supported by the Radiology Department of the First Affiliated Hospital of Sun Yat-sen University in Guangzhou, conducted many field surveys, and employed observation methods, in-depth interviews, user portraits, user journey maps and other methods for research and analysis.

First of all, after many field surveys and careful observation and recording of the whole process of children's MRI, it can be seen that children showed obvious fear and anxiety in the four steps of waiting before examination-preparation before examination-examination-examination-end. The specific behaviors are as follows: 1. Fidgeting and walking back and forth while waiting; 2. After entering the MRI testing room, they felt afraid and became dull; 3. Crying and asking for parents in the examination; 4. When the machine was running, it gave out strong noise; although children wore earplugs, they were still afraid and tossed and turned on the examination table; 5. Only after the examination did the children relax and become obviously active again.

After preliminary survey and observation, the process steps and intuitive problems of children's MRI were clarified, and two of them were interviewed in depth. Eight interview questions were put forward from three directions: intuitive feeling, cognitive understanding and hope vision, as shown in Fig. 8 for details. From the answers of children and parents, we can identify the following key points:

1. The overall experience and feeling is relatively negative. Due to the unfamiliar environment, the strong noise accompanied by the operation of the instrument, the high restriction on the body, certain claustrophobia, inconsistency with children's physical experience and other factors, children are prone to negative emotions. Thus, the MRI examination was of low friendliness;
2. The overall cognitive understanding is low. Children can't basically understand what MRI is. Even if doctors and parents give appropriate explanations, it is still difficult for children to understand. This cognitive deviation is beyond the scope of children's understanding and is one of the key reasons leading to their fear and anxiety;
3. It is hoped to change the status quo. In the process of in-depth interviews, both children and parents hoped to optimize and change the current situation. Especially in the space environment and interaction process, they all expressed their love and

MRI child user journey

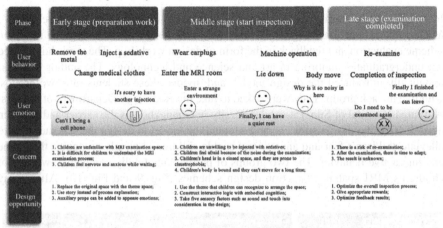

Fig. 8. Child MRI user trip diagram.

yearning for the displayed cases (six groups of schemes of Character Farms Company), and children can accurately recognize the theme and "play method" of the cases, and feel that anxiety and fear can be relieved.

At the same time, according to the preliminary observation and in-depth interview, based on the process of children's MRI spatial interaction, a user journey map was made, as shown in Fig. 9. Through the analysis of each node, the internal needs of users were deeply explored, the main behavioral characteristics and emotional fluctuations of children during the examination process were analyzed, and the concerns of children during the MRI process were identified. In the process line of "early stage (preparation work)-middle stage (start of examination)-late stage (completion of examination)", there are some behavioral points worthy of attention, among which the negative points are: injection of sedatives, entry into MRI room, machine noise and need to be re-examined. These negative emotions are directly related to children's cognition and physical feelings, which further confirms that the aforementioned conceptual models in this paper are highly matched.

To sum up, after field survey, observation records, in-depth interviews and user journey maps, we can see that the actual problems faced by users are similar to the conceptual model mentioned above in this paper, which is of great adaptability and applicability. Starting from embodied cognition, this paper combined image schema and environmental affordance, and constructed a spatial interaction design methodology suitable for children's MRI examination so as to improve the current situation to a certain extent, meet the deep needs of users, reduce the burden on doctors, and achieve a balance and win-win situation.

4.2   Design Workshop

In order to further verify the guiding significance of this design model for children's MRI spatial interaction design, this study used this design model as a guide to obtain scheme evaluation and feedback in the form of design workshop. The workshop invited ten undergraduates majoring in art and science and technology. The author first systematically introduced the design model, and divided these students into two groups, with five in each group. They were asked to take the Radiology Department of the First Affiliated Hospital of Sun Yat-sen University in Guangzhou as the carrier and children aged 3–10 as the design subjects, and adopted the model to design the scheme so as to alleviate children's fear and anxiety and enable children to clearly recognize the theme and interactive behavior. The two groups of participants finally completed two sets of children's MRI spatial interaction design schemes (Fig. 9 and Fig. 10). After many

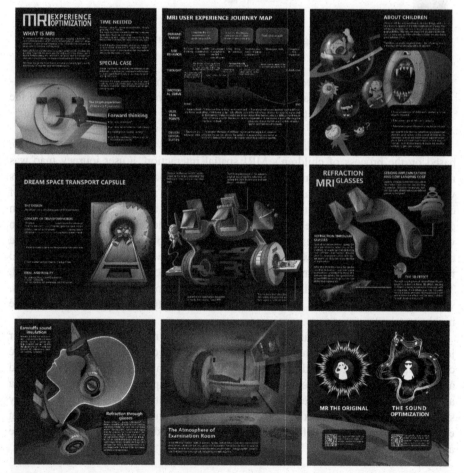

Fig. 9. Design scheme of children's MRI space interaction with the theme of "space transfer warehouse".

arguments, the first group chose the "space transmission warehouse" as the theme and designed the scheme strictly according to the design model: From the perspective of embodied cognition, the theme (MRI process = space transmission)-image schema psychological suggestion (orbit forward = fantasy exploration)-environmental affordance (MRI equipment = transmission props)-immersive interactive experience (MRI space = space space) was designed. At the same time, the scheme also took into account the comprehensive sensory experience design combining visual and auditory factors, and conceived a customized VR glasses and earphone device, which played the video and sound of space roaming, so that children can completely immerse themselves in the content and forget their idea of doing MRI examination. The overall atmosphere of the final scheme was fantastic, the theme was clear, full of children's interest, and the integrity was high. It can attract children's attention, and change the coldness and seriousness of the usual MRI space.

The second group chose "time tunnel" as the theme, and also designed the scheme strictly according to the design model: From the perspective of embodied cognition, the theme (MRI process = time shuttle)-image schema psychological suggestion (track forward = crossing start)-environmental affordance (MRI equipment = shuttle props)-Realize immersion interactive experience (MRI space = time tunnel) was designed.

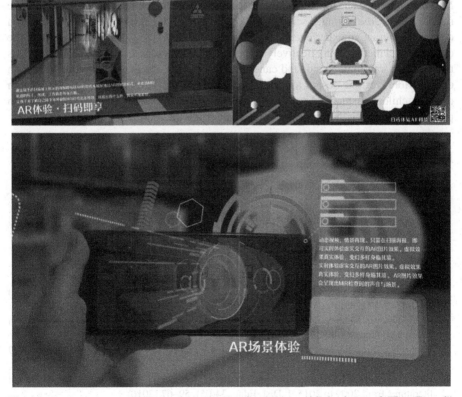

Fig. 10. Design scheme of MRI spatial interaction for children with the theme of "Time Tunnel".

This scheme not only fully considered embodied cognition to spatial interactive applications, but also took into account the digital way of realization. That is, AR (Augmented Reality) and projection imaging technology were used to realize the change of scene theme and the realization of interactive process. Such digital solution greatly reduces the implementation cost and the investment in hospital space equipment. When adults check in the same space, they only need to turn off the projection system to restore the scene, thus realizing the interaction of multiple scenes in one space.

5 Conclusion

With the continuous development and derivation of magnetic resonance imaging (MRI) technology, it has seen wider clinical application in pediatrics. However, due to its serious environment, cold instruments, strong noise, forced body, unfamiliar experience, unknown results, etc., children feel afraid and anxious, and even produce medical fear. The reason is the lack of design and development of MRI system specifically for children. Therefore, starting from children's cognition and behavior, this paper integrated embodied cognition, image schema and environmental affordance theory, and obtained a model based on spatial interaction design of children's MRI examination was obtained. Also, this paper put forward four elements of spatial interaction design for children's MRI examination. The four elements are the matching degree of embodied cognition, the recognition degree of image schema, the operability of environment and the immersion degree of interactive experience. As verified by field survey and design workshop, the design model method can effectively construct spatial themes and interactive operations that children can understand, and can alleviate children's fear and anxiety to a certain extent. Moreover, the design model is also applicable to the special spatial interaction of other children's medical treatment, and has certain mobility and guidance, which provides a reference for the design of special spatial interaction for children.

References

1. Peng, Y.: Current status of sedation in pediatric MRI examination. Clin. Res. Pract. **5**(02), 196–198 (2020)
2. Jin, Y.: Medical fear and its influencing factors of hospitalized school-age children. Chin. J. Nurs. (10), 7–9 (2000)
3. Li, H.: Embodied cognition. Stud. Sci. Sci. (02), 184–190 (2006)
4. Ye, H.: Embodied cognition: a new orientation of cognitive psychology. Adv. Psychol. Sci. **18**(05), 705–710 (2010)
5. Ye, H.: Cognitive psychology: dilemma and turn. J. East China Norm. Univ. (Educ. Sci.) **28**(01), 42–47 (2010)
6. Li, Q.: Discussion on "cognitive revolution" and "second generation cognitive science". Acta Psychologica Sinica **40**(12), 1306–1327 (2008)
7. Zheng, H.: Three theoretical models of embodied cognition. Psychol. Explor. **37**(03), 195–199 (2017)
8. Li, Q.: A review of foreign research and practice of embodied learning-based on SSCI journal literatures from 2009 to 2015. J. Dist. Educ. **34**(05), 59–67 (2016)

9. Cooper, A.: About Face: Essence of Interactive Design 4, 12th edn. Publishing House of Electronics Industry, Beijing (2015)
10. Tan, L.: Constructing embodied interactive design model in public space. Hunan Packag. **34**(03), 34–37 (2019)
11. Pen, B.: Exploring the innovation and practice of children's education in museums from the perspective of embodied cognition. Arch. Cult. (07), 167–168 (2019)
12. Johnson, M.: Metaphors We Live By, 4nd edn. The University of Chicago Press, Chicago (1980)
13. Johnson, M.: The Body in the Mind: The Bodily Basis of Meaning, Imagination, and Reason, 3nd edn. The University of Chicago Press, Chicago (1987)
14. Yin, Z.: Image schema and guiding sign system design-taking shanghai south railway station as an example. Des. Res. **3**(3), 21–27 (2013)
15. Gibson, J.: The Ecological Approach to Visual Perception. 2nd edn. Houghton Mifflin, Boston (1979)
16. Li, Y.: Analysis of affordance and its application in design. Decoration (01), 120–121 (2013)
17. Peng, B.: Influence of children's environmental behavior psychology on the design of visiting space in children's hospital. Arch. Cult. (09), 213–214 (2020)
18. Liu, J.: Space design of hospital children's ward based on human factors. J. Green Sci. Technol. **2020**(22), 171–173 (2020)
19. Rao, H.: Research on Exterior Space Design of Children's Hospital Based on Environmental Behavior. Harbin Institute of Technology (2018)
20. Hu, Y.: Psychoanalysis and intervention of MRI examination in children. Chin. J. Misdiagn. (06), 1347 (2007)
21. Xu, H.: Transforming the imaging experience while decreasing sedation rates. J. Am. Coll. Radiol. **17**(1), 46–52 (2020)

Persuasive Design of a Mobile Application for Reducing Overcrowding in Saudi Hospital Emergency Departments

Khalid Majrashi[(✉)] [iD], Hashem Almakramih, and Mohammed Gharawi

Department of Information Technology, Institute of Public Administration, Riyadh,
Saudi Arabia
{majrashik,almakramih,algharawim}@ipa.edu.sa

Abstract. Overcrowding in emergency departments (EDs) is a critical issue in health sectors worldwide. In Saudi Arabia, EDs experience
this issue because many patients visit EDs seeking treatment even for
a non-emergency health condition. Therefore, in this study, we present
and test a solution to help reduce ED overcrowding in Saudi Arabia—a
mobile application that we developed using persuasive design principles.
The main aims of the application are to discourage patients with non-
emergency conditions from arriving at EDs and, if they have already
arrived, to manage and encourage them to transfer to primary healthcare centers (PHCs) or less-crowded EDs. The application is framed by
eight main design principles (social proof, scarcity, authority, modernity, time-saving, empathy, transparency, and awareness). We tested the
application based on a set of role-play evaluation scenarios through a user
study with 89 participants. The overall result showed that the application
successfully encouraged 73.7% of participants to visit PHCs instead of
EDs, discouraged 55.3% from visiting overcrowded EDs, and encouraged
68.4% to transfer from overcrowded EDs to other health centers. Design
aspects related to the time-saving and empathy principles were the factors that most influenced participants' decisions. Overall, our application
that incorporates design principles can facilitate tackling the ED overcrowding issue, given that it successfully influenced more than half of the
participants. Further, this study has implications for both the human–
computer interaction and the health informatics communities because
it employs a mobile software solution with design principles to tackle
a critical universal issue that affects healthcare quality and patients'
satisfaction.

Keywords: Persuasive design · Overcrowding · Emergency
departments · Saudi Arabia

1 Introduction

The overcrowding of emergency departments (EDs) is defined as "the situation
in which ED function is impeded primarily because of the excessive number of

© Springer Nature Switzerland AG 2021
M. M. Soares et al. (Eds.): HCII 2021, LNCS 12780, pp. 506–518, 2021.
https://doi.org/10.1007/978-3-030-78224-5_35

patients waiting to be seen, undergoing assessment and treatment, or waiting for departure comparing to the physical or staffing capacity of the ED." [29]. Over the past few decades, the number of patients visiting EDs has increased substantially [7,9–12,16,18,21–23]. This situation has led to ED overcrowding becoming a critical issue in many countries [13]. In fact, some countries have identified ED overcrowding as a national crisis [18].

As a major public health problem, ED overcrowding leads to multiple negative consequences, including long waits for diagnosis and treatment, delays in treating seriously ill patients, increased costs owing to unnecessary diagnostic investigations, decreased physician productivity, frustration among medical staff, and patient dissatisfaction [10,14].

In this regard, EDs in Saudi Arabia are overcrowded because of non-urgent visits. A study published in 2020 highlighted that 78.5% of the visits to an ED in a tertiary care center in Saudi Arabia were for non-life-threatening conditions [1]. In 2012, Bakarman et al. [2] used the Canadian Triage and Acuity Scale (CTAS) to assess the emergency levels of ED visits by a sample of patients who attended the ED of King Fahd Hospital, a major hospital in Jeddah city. They found that 65% of the visits were for non-emergency conditions (CTAS IV and V) and that among all ED visits, less than 10% of the patients needed immediate (CTAS I) or emergency care (CTAS II). An earlier study, published in 2002, reported similar results about the percentage of non-emergency cases at a community hospital ED in Saudi Arabia [24]. Further, it was estimated that across the country, EDs received 21.2 million patients in 2015 and that 60% of the cases were non-emergency cases [27]. Similar results were reported for other countries, such as the United States [4] and the United Kingdom [6].

Many factors are associated with non-urgent ED visits. For instance, a study on the United States reported that the younger age of patients, the accessibility of the ED compared with other options, referrals to the ED, and negative perceptions about alternatives such as primary healthcare services were associated with non-urgent ED visits [28]. In Turkey, the reasons for non-urgent ED visits were the need to refill medications, request painkillers, and treat upper respiratory tract infections, as well as the lack of understanding about who should visit an ED and benefit from its services [25]. In South Africa, the reasons for non-urgent ED visits were the lack of benefit from outpatient clinics, the perception that EDs offer better treatment, and the unavailability of PHCs over 24 h [3]. In Saudi Arabia, the main causes for ED visits were the patients' perception that their condition needed urgent medical attention, the ease of access to EDs, and the limited resources and services at PHCs [1]. A study on three Saudi Arabian hospitals found that a significantly high proportion of patients with non-urgent conditions did not attempt to visit PHCs before their ED visits and that patients believe that the ED is the first place to visit in case of illness [8].

Generally, technology and design are less employed to solve ED overcrowding. Since ED overcrowding has been highlighted as a key national challenge, Saudi Arabia has encouraged the innovation of digital solutions to solve this issue [27]. Therefore, to partially contribute to solving this problem, we introduced a mobile software solution with a set of design principles to help discourage patients with non-emergency health conditions from visiting overcrowded EDs and to encourage them to visit PHCs. In this study, we present the mobile software solution, which we named Saleem (an Arabic term for referring to a person who is free from a health issue or at a satisfactory state), and report the results on testing this solution with a group of intended users.

In Sect. 2, we present the mobile application solution and the applied design principles. In Sect. 3, we present the user study method, followed by the results in Sect. 4, and last, the discussion and conclusion in Sect. 5.

2   Designing the Mobile Application

Our application targets two groups of patients, those who have already arrived at EDs and those who have not. The application aims to manage the first group and to encourage those with non-emergency conditions to transit to PHCs or less-crowded EDs. Further, as regards the second group, the application aims to discourage those with non-emergency conditions from visiting EDs (see Fig. 1).

Persuasive design principles are commonly used in different technology domains (see [15,17,19,20,26]) and have been proved to be effective. Therefore, we reviewed the literature and identified a set of persuasive design principles (e.g., social proof) that can be employed in the application to help achieve its goals. We also brainstormed regarding other design principles (e.g., empathy) that can also help achieve the application goals. Figure 1 illustrates the objectives of our mobile application and the design principles applied to it.

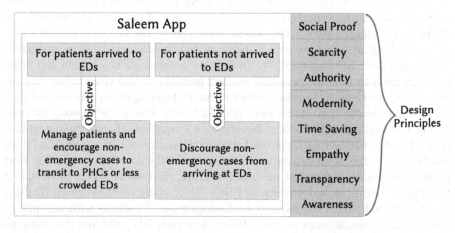

Fig. 1. Saleem application objectives and design principles.

Figure 2, 3, and 4 shows examples of the Arabic interfaces of the application. Figure 2 illustrates a PHC interface and highlights the design principles used to encourage PHC visits. Figure 3 illustrates an ED interface and the design principles used to discourage patients from visiting an overcrowded ED and encourage them to visit PHCs or less-crowded EDs (for patients who have not arrived). Figure 4 shows the ED patient management interface and the design principles applied to the interface to encourage patients with non-emergency conditions to transit from an overcrowded ED to PHCs or less-crowded EDs (for patients who have arrived). The design principles applied to the interfaces are explained in the following subsections.

2.1 Social Proof

If uncertain about something, people usually take cues from others and imitate each other [5]. In interface design, social proof can be represented by providing evidence of other user actions to influence the current user's decision to repeat the same actions. For example, hotel-booking applications show prior customers' rankings and reviews of a hotel to influence the potential users' decisions about booking room(s) in the hotel. The same principle is used in e-commerce: Online shops display the customer recommendations and positive reviews about their products to influence others to buy them. In our mobile application, we employed the social proof principle to encourage patients with non-emergency conditions to visit PHCs (i.e., by displaying patients' rating of PHCs, as shown in Fig. 2b).

2.2 Scarcity

The sense of losing opportunity can significantly influence human decision-making [5]. In the online context, scarcity is used widely across different domains. For example, e-commerce services use phrases such as "available for limited time" or "only two rooms/seats left" when showing offers to users, which can trigger or initiate users to act fast. In our application, we used sentences such as "If you arrive at the PHC within the next 30 min, the waiting time will not exceed 15 min," as shown in Arabic text in Fig. 2c, Fig. 3b, and Fig. 4e, to give them the feeling that the opportunity of a short wait to diagnosis and treatment can be lost if they did not act fast without procrastinating.

2.3 Authority

Information from an authority (e.g., a government organization) can influence decisions on how to act in a particular situation [5]. We expected that providing information in our application from a health authority about PHCs can encourage patients to visit these centers. Hence, we showed such information (five-star quality rating of PHCs in Fig. 2a), indicating that a health authority was its source, to encourage people to visit PHCs. The information was not real and was used for the purpose of evaluating the impact of this design principle on people's decision to visit PHCs.

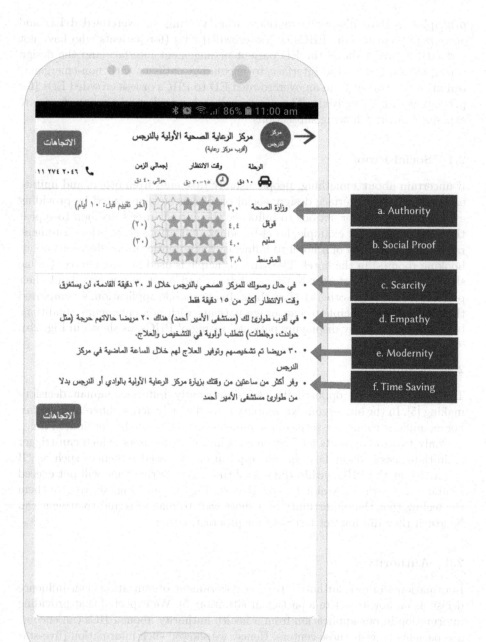

Fig. 2. A PHC interface.

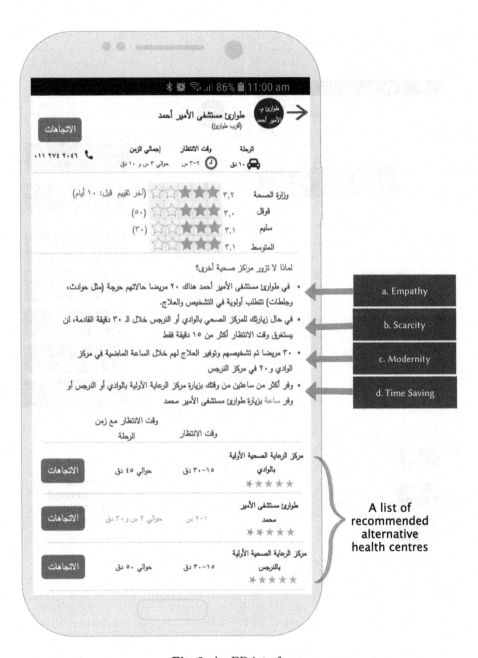

Fig. 3. An ED interfaces.

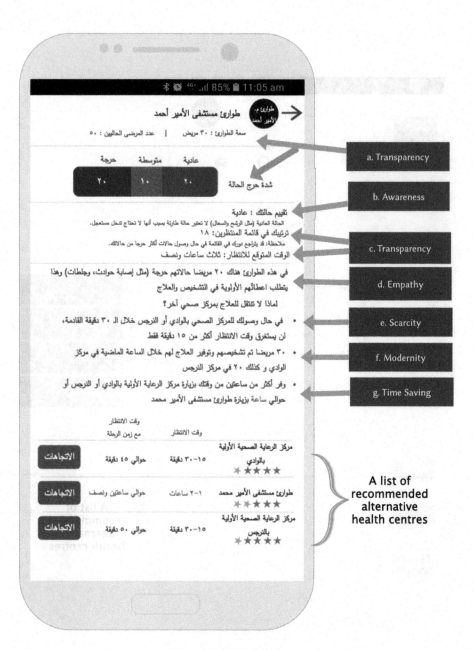

Fig. 4. An ED interface.

2.4 Modernity

The modernity principle has also been used widely in interface design to encourage people to behave in a certain way. For instance, some online services show recent users' actions to motivate other users to perform the same actions. Some hotel-booking websites show data on recent room bookings, such as "latest booking of this kind of room: 30 s ago." In our mobile application, to encourage people to visit PHCs, we used a similar technique by showing phrases such as "In the past hour, 30 patients were diagnosed and received treatment at this center," as shown in Arabic in Fig. 2e, Fig. 3c, and Fig. 4f.

2.5 Empathy, Transparency and Awareness

We also employed the empathy principle. For example, we used phrases to show the numbers and examples of critical cases in the EDs and the priorities for these cases to receive treatment (Fig. 2d, Fig. 3a, and Fig. 4d). We followed this approach to induce patients with non-emergency conditions to empathize with patients with critical conditions. The aim was to motivate the former group to decide to visit PHCs or to transfer from EDs to PHCs to allow the ED medical staff to spend more time with the critically ill patients and hence provide them better care.

We also showed content to improve transparency (e.g., "The capacity of the ED is 30, and the number of current patients is 50"; see Fig. 4a), to encourage patients with non-critical conditions to transfer to PHCs or to less-crowded EDs.

The application was also designed to raise patients' awareness of what is considered an emergency case through using phrases such as "Normal cases, such as a cold, are not considered emergency cases, and they do not need immediate intervention" (see Fig. 4b). One purpose of these phrases was to let patients feel less stressed about their health condition and to visit or transfer to PHCs instead of visiting EDs.

3 Method

3.1 Recruitment, Participants, and Data Collection

We recruited study participants through social media groups. We targeted social media groups in two different regions of Saudi Arabia that have different health-care quality levels. In all, 89 participants (30 female) evaluated our mobile application. They were from different age groups and had various qualifications (see Table 1). They were given a set of evaluation scenarios and instructed to interact with specific interfaces of the mobile application. Then, they were asked to complete a questionnaire with a set of close-ended and Likert questions related to each scenario. We followed the ethical guidelines for research in Saudi Arabia.

Table 1. Age and qualification of participants.

Age	No. of participants	Highest qualifications	No. of participants
≤20	3	High school or less	27
21–29	52	Diploma	9
30–39	28	Bachelor's degree	49
40–49	6	Master's degree	4

3.2   Evaluation Scenarios

In this study, we tested the mobile application based on three main evaluation scenarios.

In Scenario 1, we instructed the participants to assume that they aimed to visit an ED but that before visiting the ED, they need to interact with a specific PHC interface in the mobile application (Fig. 2). We used this scenario to test whether the applied design principles could influence their decision by changing their original aim of visiting the ED to visiting the PHC instead.

In Scenario 2, we instructed the participants to assume that they aimed to visit an ED but that before visiting this ED, they need to interact with the ED page in the application (Fig. 3). We used this scenario to test whether the design discourages users from visiting the ED and encourages them to visit other health centers, and to assess whether the design principles employed in the ED interface had influenced their decision to visit other health centers and to change their original plan of visiting the ED.

In Scenario 3, we instructed the participants to assume that they had already arrived at an ED, that their condition was assessed as a non-emergency, and that while awaiting treatment, they need to use the patient management page for the ED (Fig. 4). We used this scenario to test whether the design encourages participants to transfer from an overcrowded ED to other health centers, and to assess whether the design principles employed in the ED patient management page could influence their decision to transfer from the current ED to other health centers.

4   Results

The results for the first evaluation scenario showed that the design succeeded in encouraging 73.7% of the participants to change their plan from visiting the ED to visiting a PHC presented to them in the scenario. The results also showed that the design principles applied to the PHC interface influenced many participants to make this decision. According to the questionnaire responses, the percentage of participants influenced by the design aspects related to social proof was 68.18%, to scarcity was 72.30%, to authority was 71.6%, to modernity was 63.49%, to time-saving was 73.84%, and to empathy was 76.92%.

The results for the second scenario showed that the design contributed to discouraging 55.3% of the participants from visiting the ED and changing their plan to visit a PHC. In addition, the design principles used in the ED interface influenced many participants to make this decision. That is, 61.53% of them were influenced by scarcity, 64.15% by modernity, 71.69% by time-saving, and 72.54% by empathy.

The results for the third scenario showed that the design succeeded in encouraging 68.4% of the participants to transfer from the overcrowded ED to other health centers. Our analysis of the results also showed that the design principles used in the third scenario influenced these decisions as follows: 86.79% of the participants were influenced by scarcity, 69.64% by modernity, 81.81% by time-saving, 83.01% by empathy, 73.21% by transparency, and 73.68% by awareness.

The design aspects related to each design principle were rated on a 7-point Likert scale ranging from 1 ("not at all important") to 7 ("extremely important"), in terms of how important the aspect was when deciding to visit or not visit a healthcare center. For the first scenario, waiting time, which is related to the time-saving principle, and the text used for the empathy principle were the two most influential design aspects, scoring an average of 5.59 (SD = 1.63) and 5.56 (SD = 1.92) on the scale, respectively. For the second scenario, the text used for empathy (M = 5.40, SD = 1.92) and the explicit text indicating the time to be saved by visiting a PHC instead of an ED (M = 5.39, SD = 1.94) were the two most influential design aspects. For the third scenario, two design aspects, waiting time (M = 5.64, SD = 1.72) and the text indicating the time to be saved by transferring to other healthcare centers (M = 5.61, SD = 1.75), both of which are related to the time-saving principle, were the most influential.

5   Discussion and Conclusion

This study contributed design principles that can be employed in software solutions for tackling the ED overcrowding problem in Saudi Arabia. It also presented the evaluation results of a mobile software solution that employs these design principles to reduce ED overcrowding. The overall result in relation to the objectives of this application showed that it was successful in encouraging many participants to visit PHCs as well as in discouraging many from visiting EDs. The results also showed that all design principles influenced the decision of many participants as follows: to visit PHCs instead of an ED in the first evaluation scenario, to not visit an ED in the second scenario, and to transfer from an overcrowded ED to other centers in the third scenario.

Regardless, this study has some limitations. One is that it is based on role-play scenarios, and participants had been in situations described in the scenarios. Their decisions could differ in real situations when the application is tested "in the wild," given the sensitivity of the situations involved, where people may be fearful for their life. In this case, their behavior is bound to be radically different, which would thus invalidate the presented findings. Hence, we aim to confirm our findings through testing the application with patients in real situations.

The second limitation is that the study involved many variables, making it difficult to establish whether participants were able to remember and report accurately all variables that affected their decisions. Hence, our future studies will involve groups where we will apply only specific design principles to the application, so that we can compare the results for the groups. We intend to design several versions of the application, each with its own design principles, to further confirm the impact of each design principle and to triangulate this study's findings and those of future experiments.

The third limitation is that the study participants were mainly from only two areas in Saudi Arabia. The underlying reasons for the ED overcrowding problem can vary between regions (e.g., a lack of investment in healthcare facilities or the poor distribution of resources in specific regions). Hence, the overcrowding problem in each region must diagnosed before generalizing a solution across different regions.

Last, although the study provided some indications about the potential role of persuasive technology in solving the ED overcrowding problem, it is risky to draw policy decisions based on the experiences of a small number of patients in specific contexts. That is, the number of participants in our study is small considering the large population targeted by the software solution. Therefore, it is necessary to conduct further studies using large samples.

Nevertheless, overall, this study represents the initial step toward employing persuasive technology to tackle ED overcrowding and would encourage further research on this topic.

References

1. Al-Otmy, S.S., Abduljabbar, A.Z., Al-Raddadi, R.M., Farahat, F.: Factors associated with non-urgent visits to the emergency department in a tertiary care centre, western saudi arabia: cross-sectional study. BMJ Open **10**(10), e035951 (2020)
2. Bakarman, M.A., Njaifan, N.K.: Assessment of non-emergency cases attending emergency department at King Fahad General Hospital, Jeddah; pattern and outcomes. Life Sci. J. **11**(8), 20–25 (2014)
3. Becker, J., Dell, A., Jenkins, L., Sayed, R.: Reasons why patients with primary health care problems access a secondary hospital emergency centre. SAMJ South Afr. Med. J. **102**(10), 800–801 (2012)
4. Burt, C.W., McCaig, L.F.: National hospital ambulatory medical care survey: 2003 emergency department summary (2005)
5. Cialdini, R.B., Garde, N.: Influence, vol. 3. A. Michel (1987)
6. of Commons Public Accounts Committee, H., et al.: Department of health: Improving emergency care in England, pp. 1–22. The Stationary Office Limited, London (2005)
7. Crawford, K., Morphet, J., Jones, T., Innes, K., Griffiths, D., Williams, A.: Initiatives to reduce overcrowding and access block in Australian emergency departments: a literature review. Collegian **21**(4), 359–366 (2014)
8. Dawoud, S.O., Ahmad, A.M.K., Alsharqi, O.Z., Al-Raddadi, R.M.: Utilization of the emergency department and predicting factors associated with its use at the Saudi Ministry of Health General Hospitals. Glob. J. Health Sci. **8**(1), 90 (2016)

9. Derlet, R.W.: Overcrowding in emergency departments: increased demand and decreased capacity. Ann. Emerg. Med. **39**(4), 430–432 (2002)
10. Derlet, R.W., Richards, J.R.: Overcrowding in the nation's emergency departments: complex causes and disturbing effects. Ann. Emerg. Med. **35**(1), 63–68 (2000)
11. Derlet, R.W., Richards, J.R.: Emergency department overcrowding in Florida, New York, and Texas. South. Med. J. **95**(8), 846–850 (2002)
12. Derlet, R.W., Richards, J.R., Kravitz, R.L.: Frequent overcrowding in us emergency departments. Acad. Emerg. Med. **8**(2), 151–155 (2001)
13. Di Somma, S., Paladino, L., Vaughan, L., Lalle, I., Magrini, L., Magnanti, M.: Overcrowding in emergency department: an international issue. Intern. Emerg. Med. **10**(2), 171–175 (2014). https://doi.org/10.1007/s11739-014-1154-8
14. Erenler, A.K., et al.: Reasons for overcrowding in the emergency department: experiences and suggestions of an education and research hospital. Turk. J. Emerg. Med. **14**(2), 59–63 (2014)
15. Fogg, B.J.: Persuasive technology: using computers to change what we think and do. Ubiquity **2002**(December), 2 (2002)
16. Henry, M.C.: Overcrowding in America's emergency departments: inpatient wards replace emergency care. Acad. Emerg. Med. **8**(2), 188–189 (2001)
17. Kim, H., Fesenmaier, D.R.: Persuasive design of destination web sites: an analysis of first impression. J. Travel Res. **47**(1), 3–13 (2008)
18. McCabe, J.B.: Emergency department overcrowding: a national crisis. Acad. Med. **76**(7), 672–674 (2001)
19. Oinas-Kukkonen, H., Harjumaa, M.: A systematic framework for designing and evaluating persuasive systems. In: Oinas-Kukkonen, H., Hasle, P., Harjumaa, M., Segerståhl, K., Øhrstrøm, P. (eds.) PERSUASIVE 2008. LNCS, vol. 5033, pp. 164–176. Springer, Heidelberg (2008). https://doi.org/10.1007/978-3-540-68504-3_15
20. Purpura, S., Schwanda, V., Williams, K., Stubler, W., Sengers, P.: Fit4Life: the design of a persuasive technology promoting healthy behavior and ideal weight. In: Proceedings of the SIGCHI Conference on Human Factors in Computing Systems, pp. 423–432 (2011)
21. Richards, J.R., Navarro, M.L., Derlet, R.W.: Survey of directors of emergency departments in California on overcrowding. West. J. Med. **172**(6), 385 (2000)
22. Rowe, B., et al.: Frequency, determinants, and impact of overcrowding in emergency departments in Canada: a national survey of emergency department directors. Canadian Agency for Drugs and Technologies in Health, Ottawa (2006)
23. Schneider, S., Zwemer, F., Doniger, A., Dick, R., Czapranski, T., Davis, E.: Rochester, New York a decade of emergency department overcrowding. Acad. Emerg. Med. **8**(11), 1044–1050 (2001)
24. Siddiqui, S., Ogbeide, D.O.: Utilization of emergency services in a community hospital. Saudi Med. J. **23**(1), 69 (2002)
25. Şimşek, P., Gürsoy, A.: Turkish health care providers' views on inappropriate use of emergency department: who, when and why? Int. Emerg. Nurs. **27**, 31–36 (2016)
26. Toscos, T., Faber, A., An, S., Gandhi, M.P.: Chick clique: persuasive technology to motivate teenage girls to exercise. In: CHI'06 Extended Abstracts on Human Factors in Computing Systems, pp. 1873–1878 (2006)
27. Unit, N.D.: Fekratech: be the creator of digital transformation (2017). https://fekratech.gov.sa/?lang=en#

518   K. Majrashi et al.

28. Uscher-Pines, L., Pines, J., Kellermann, A., Gillen, E., Mehrotra, A.: Deciding to visit the emergency department for non-urgent conditions: a systematic review of the literature. Am. J. Managed Care **19**(1), 47 (2013)
29. Yarmohammadian, M.H., Rezaei, F., Haghshenas, A., Tavakoli, N.: Overcrowding in emergency departments: a review of strategies to decrease future challenges. J. Res. Med. Sci. Official J. Isfahan Univ. Med. Sci. **22** (2017)

Eco-activism, Human-Computer Interaction and Fast Fashion

Antonio Nucci and Matthew Hibberd[⊠]

Università della Svizzera italiana, 6900 Lugano, Switzerland
matthew.hibberd@usi.ch

Abstract. The aim of this paper is to understand the role of social media in organizing environmental protests against the fast fashion industry. The way eco-activist groups talk internally, highlight events, organize protests as well as their networks and platforms is through online communication and, in particular, through social media such as Instagram or Facebook. Using qualitative methodological approaches such as focus groups and qualitative interviews, this paper examines what kind of social platforms activists use in 2021, both for direct communication with fellow activists and in broadcasting their message. How do activists engage with social media and why do they prefer certain platforms to others? What factors play a role in choosing the platforms when analyzing them from a human-computer interaction point-of-view?

The main argument of this paper is that the key social media decisions within climate change groups, what platforms to use, how, when and why, are often determined by a wider peer group pressure rather than according to any strategic plan or design. This allows activists to convey their messages in two ways: to inform and educate publics focusing on debunking fake news or when talking about fashion and greenwashing, etc.

Keywords: Fast fashion · Climate change · Activism · Social Media

1 Introduction

In recent years, the subject of environmentalism has seen a rise in media coverage and public attention, especially from younger generations. Companies and organisations have also implemented more sustainable business models while making sure that their sustainable commitments receive public attention through advertising campaigns, PR and CSR work. Among those businesses making these changes is the fashion world, which is widely recognized, including from those working in the industry, as an extremely wasteful one causing major damage to the world's eco system and contributing to climate change. Among those groups most critical of the fashion industry is the environmental activist lobby, which has stepped up its protests in recent years. The main communication channel for activists is to communicate messages through social media. The aim of this paper is to understand the role of social media in organizing environmental protests against the fashion industry, with particular attention to fast fashion. The way eco-activist

© Springer Nature Switzerland AG 2021
M. M. Soares et al. (Eds.): HCII 2021, LNCS 12780, pp. 519–530, 2021.
https://doi.org/10.1007/978-3-030-78224-5_36

groups talk internally, highlight events, organize protests as well as their networks and platforms is through online communication and, in particular, through social media such as Instagram or Facebook. What kind of social platforms do they use in 2021, both for direct communication with fellow activists and in broadcasting their message? How do activists engage with social media and why do they prefer certain platforms to others? Finally, we will examine key usability factors that determine choice of platform by activists, highlighting the key issues of human-computer interaction in the important area of fashion activism.

The main argument of this paper is that the key social media decisions within climate change groups, what platforms to use, how, when and why, are often determined by peer group pressure rather than according to any strategic plan or design. Group members considered to hold areas of 'expertise' in areas related to social media will often define which social media platforms to use even when, as demonstrated in this article, this expertise extends no further than holding a Twitter or Instagram account. While awareness might exist about targeting certain groups on particular social media and the perceived functionality of some platforms over others, the organisation of social media appears to owe less to technology and rather more to opinion leaders within groups. The reasons why social media are used is to target younger audiences with information and generate debates about fake or misleading information about climate change, so called greenwashing. Activists consider social media as idea platforms for discussing climate change issues and for raising ideological issues related to climate change such as social justice. Our results highlights potential for social media to engage the fashion industry in meaningful dialogue about change and development. This paper will use qualitative methodological approaches through focus group and interviews with activists.

2   Climate Change Activism in Switzerland

This article examines two climate change groups, both based in the Italian speaking part of Switzerland. Sciopero per il Clima (translated here as Climate Strike [CS]), based in the Canton of Ticino, Switzerland, was inspired by another Swiss climate change group, Klimastreik Schweiz. The latter group defines itself as "a political ecological movement fighting for the preservation of biodiversity, nature and against climate change" (Klimastreik Schweiz 2021). Climate Strike is run on a voluntary basis and is decentralized. Affiliated with the Fridays For Future movement led by the prominent activist, Greta Thunberg, it operates on a local, national and international scale. Extinction Rebellion Ticino (XR) is an independently-run offshoot of the British non-violent civil disobedience group Extinction Rebellion. The latter was founded by Roger Hallam and Gail Bradbrook in 2018 as an environmental movement and aims to have national governments across the world declare a climate emergency, reduce greenhouse gas emissions to zero by 2025 and maximize direct participation in democracy in order to prioritize problems caused by the climate crisis. Collaboration exists between the two groups in Ticino not only through joint campaigning, but also at the membership level. One of our focus group participants was a member of both CS and XR.

3 Fast Fashion

The global rise in the earth's surface temperature in coming decades will bring with it increased instances of flooding, drought and volatile weather patterns. One of the main industries causing climate change is fashion, which is responsible for some 5%–10% of current global carbon emissions (Bauck 2017). There is common acknowledgement that every stage in the production and consumption of garments creates increasing pollution and emission problems for the fashion world. From sourcing and use of scarce water resources in the production of cotton to farming processes in the production of leather. From the use of industrial dyes and synthetic textile fibres to the need for ships, planes and lorries to transport the final product globally (Hibberd 2019). These processes have created highly complex supply-chain issues creating contractors and sub-contractors in delivering fashion garments often across continents (Hibberd and Habib 2021). The fashion industry can be defined as the design, manufacturing, distribution, marketing, retailing, advertising, and promotion of all types of apparel from the most expensive *haute couture* and designer fashions to ordinary everyday clothing. Fast fashion is a 'term used to describe clothing designs that move quickly from the catwalk to stores to meet new trends. The collections are often based on designs presented at Fashion Week events. Fast fashion allows mainstream consumers to purchase trendy clothing at an affordable price' (Kenton 2020).

Central to these issues is the role of fast fashion, its importance to modern industry and the waste involved in bringing latest trends to consumers. We asked activists in focus group and interviews about their understanding of fast fashion. The opinion among all participants was one of hostility to various elements of fast fashion and the emphasis on seeking alternative production and consumption patterns:

> "Fast fashion brands are cheap to produce, are super polluting, do not respect human rights in the workplace and there is so much which is bad".

Alternatively, participants sought to draw comparison with 'slow fashion' defined as:

> "an answer to fast fashion, and therefore to the question 'can you buy a sustainable product?'. Slow fashion is recognized as opposite to fast fashion, second hand purchases… repairing older items."

> "For one year I decided to stop buying clothes. Maybe I went to extremes from this point of view, but I reduced all types of consumption".

> "I spend in order not to spend".

Some weight was also given to the concept that smaller is better in the fashion world where big global brands attract much attention. Another key point made by focus group participants was the emphasis they placed on smaller fashion companies being more environmentally aware:

> "Those companies are a little smaller, more eco-sustainable and also more attentive to human rights, to working conditions".

Participants were also keen to stress the difference between slow and the more expensive high or haute couture fashion:

> "High fashion is not considered slow fashion due to 'unjustified prices' and 'unsustainable working conditions', while quality local production emerges as a possible solution to the problem of the climate crisis."

4 Human-Computer Interaction or Peer Group Pressures?

According to the Encyclopedia of Database Systems (2009) the broad definition of human-computer interactions is:

> 'the study of the way in which computer technology influences human work and activities. The term "computer technology" now-a-days includes most technology from obvious computers with screens and keyboards to mobile phones, household appliances, in-car navigation systems and even embedded sensors and actuators such as automatic lighting. HCI has an associated design discipline, sometimes called Interaction Design or User-Centered Design, focused on how to design computer technology so that it is as easy and pleasant to use as possible. A key aspect of the design discipline is the notion of "usability," which is often defined in terms of efficiency, effectiveness and satisfaction.' (Ling and Tamer 2009).

What became very clear in all our discussions with activists was the importance of technology, especially mobile, in developing their communications strategies. The use of smart phones was universal among participants. Most of our participants could be defined as 'millennials', born between 1995 and 2005, and therefore the first generation to be defined as digital natives. Participants understood the issues of human-computer interaction within parameters of defining what the best social media platforms were for the different tasks in hand. So different social media were utilized in different contexts. This was clearly linked too to the usability of different platforms and the efficiency of putting content online quickly. Likewise, there was little explicit awareness of social media as part of the global capitalist infrastructure, perhaps strange for groups that often stress their anti-capitalist credentials. The idea of the social media as part of the platform society, with the commodification of every interaction as a transaction, with the collection of big data, often resold for marketing purposes, and with social media being widely blamed internationally for promoting fake news discourses, was rather an anathema (van Dijck et al. 2018).

So participants related to the issue of human-computer interaction in very practical terms and based choices on effectiveness of each platform. Firstly, the two groups under study operate on the same social media platforms to disseminate messages both internally, to fellow group members, and externally to stakeholders. What set the two groups apart was the range of activities each group promoted and the technical requirements needed to fulfil those activities. As regards Extinction Rebellion, for example, the choice of internal communication took place on two levels:

> "As long as these messages are only to start a discussion as an exchange of knowledge Whatsapp, Signal, Telegram are the ones chosen. In general we use Telegram, as a base forum and in particular for those who want to know more."

"When it comes to organizing actions, we use Signal with partner groups. This means that these are only people we trust".

This last quote is instructive because security was a key point, especially for Extinction Rebellion, which has used non-violence civil disobedience tactics in many countries. Preventing messages from interception, i.e. through encryption, might be useful in retaining secrecy in planning demonstrations, but once those initiatives started, the biggest social media organisations were used to maximize publicity. As an activist argued:

"We (XR) did several actions at H&M where several people had their naked torsos painted red. In that case we use Facebook, Twitter, Instagram and invited journalists. Journalists were invited to all actions and were then given a press release".

Climate Strike seeks to use these social channels but did not have a Twitter account in Italian at the time of writing this article (February 2021). The main idea of using social media was to get the message to as many people as possible.

"The idea is to be as accessible as possible and then use those platforms that our audience uses them. We are a more 'youthful' group than XR so we often use more youthful social networks so maybe more Instagram than Facebook and we also have a Tic Tok account which, however, has never been used, but which will be used regularly at national level soon".

The age of activists and their target publics was also a factor in choosing which social media to use. On this last point, however, XR activists stressed that it is a wrong to think that XR is "for adults" only, indicating that they, too, among their ranks, include young activists. From an individual point of view, one activist said that he does everything possible to be accessible:

"I always try to be as accessible as possible, as central as possible in the discussion on the climate crisis, also because I have faith in my social methods of persuasion and I have also had training, with Climate Strike, on methods to use when talking to people about the climate crisis".

In this case, the activist becomes an access point for publics not only at the level of information, but as an agent of persuasion. It was evident in many discussions we had that activists not only seek to represent themselves and their peers on social media, but also use those platforms as sites of mobilization, very much in line with the model developed by McNair et al. (2003) (see also Hibberd and Nguyen 2013a, b).

Likewise, Climate Strike based their campaigning and social media decisions to align with the fact that their activists were committed to strict adherence to the law rather than committing acts of civil disobedience like XR. As one activist stated:

"Everything we do is legal, so there is no danger of prosecution. This makes us easily reachable on Whatsapp groups. In addition to this we often use Discord which is practical from an organizational point of view".

The use of Discord's was justified in terms of its user-friendly interface that enjoyed significant advantages over other social media sites:

"It is very practical for organizational reasons to divide work and know what messages are written for each recipient. Everything is structured so that others can see. It is transparent. On Whatsapp this would not be possible. If I wanted to know what others in Climate Strike are doing, I can see on Discord".

As important as human-computer considerations might have been to activists from a practical point of view, human-to-human interaction was more important, especially with peer pressure to recognise perceived 'technical' skills among some activists:

"In Switzerland we use Instagram and Facebook equally. But XR Ticino uses more Instagram because we have a person who is very good and who posts there more often than Facebook".

"In addition to wanting to reach audiences on Instagram, we know how to use Instagram better. Many things are not due to rational choices, but to how things are. We stayed on Instagram because we found our audience there. We are not on Twitter because none of us know how to use it".

These quotes found common agreement highlighting the role of social interaction and peer choice, rather than particular forms of human-computer interaction, in making key social media-related decisions among climate change activists. The importance of key players here draws our attention to the work of the Bureau of Applied Research in the USA in the 1940s led by Paul Lazarsfeld. In their analysis of voters in the 1940 and 1944 Presidential elections (published in 1948 as the People's Choice), researchers discovered a small and distinct group referred to opinion leaders. These individuals were distinct from other voters in that they were heavily exposed to media coverage and were seen by other people as having authoritative opinions on politics. Activists in our focus groups identified a small group of their peers as possessing higher levels of expertise in operating social media. This small and select group, so-called opinion leaders, could influence heavily the decision making processes relating to the precise social media platforms used and communication strategies adopted by the group as a whole (Lazarsfeld et al. 1948).

The importance of verifiability in the search for information was also a topic of primary importance for activists. What emerges is that fora and social media are starting points from which to exchange information and ideas or what our participants called 'food for thought'. However, activists emphasized the importance of quality journalism as the most effective and reliable way to retrieve and disseminate information.

"There are newspapers that have a reputation that must be maintained and therefore cannot publish unverifiable news, even if sometimes that happens. If I look at the New York Times, the Washington Post or USA Today sources are cited in their articles, so I look at what the sources are and then from there I judge the reliability of the article. If it's a known source or a scientific article, I'm not going to check it a second time".

"The Guardian can also be a starting point from which to start the search".

"If I have to see the data on companies, I often go to the *Guardian* website, which is the favorite source of every activist, because they focus precisely on pollution, exploitation, etc. ...".

In this last quote, the *Guardian*'s model of journalism is defined by activists as a classic watchdog one, critically analyzing the activity of fashion companies. This investigative form of journalism can highlight both positive and negative roles played by companies in climate change issues as well as highlighting other socio-economic issues related to climate justice. Another point that emerges from the search for information and fact-checking is the large presence of foreign newspapers. Relying on American or British newspapers, according to interviewees, may indicate both a lack of attention to the issues of the climate crisis by local Swiss journalism or might merely emphasize the importance of climate change from an international media point-of-view. This does creates a problem for those who have language barriers and therefore cannot access English-language publications.

Climate change groups also use social media posts to republish official government documents as well as research from other activist groups.

"As a source there are government sites: federal, cantonal and European. Other very interesting source is studies of other movements, for example WWF or Greenpeace which in recent years have collected a lot of data".

Another participant highlighted the importance of dialogue or mutual support facilitated by social media, affirming the importance of having reference figures to rely on in case of doubt. Once again, we see key roles for senior group members and/or our opinion leaders. This continuous exchange of opinions, although conducted on social media and available publicly, formed part of internal communications and often was seen as sources of good advice.

"I have people in the movement that I consider references. When it comes to making a choice, I ask them, for example, when I had to decide whether or not to get a license (because it involved many hours driving) I asked".

"Once at a sushi restaurant and I am vegetarian, some of my friends had left over some food and I called some friends to ask if I should eat it. In the end I called four people to ask for advice and it was also fun to show that there are alternatives".

5   Greenwashing

One area of clear important to activists when stressing the key uses of social media related to greenwashing. The emergence of so-called 'green advertising' in recent decades responding to consumer trends has led to the rise in the number of spurious claims accompanying such adverts – so called greenwash. There is nothing new about instances of greenwash, which is defined here by the Oxford English Dictionary as:

Disinformation disseminated by an organisation, etc., so as to present an environmentally responsible public image; a public image of environmental responsibility promulgated by or for an organisation, etc., but perceived as being unfounded or intentionally misleading (Quoted in Futerra 2008: 3).

In part these complaints come from commercial competitors or the green lobby and groups like Friends of the Earth. But there is increasing evidence of public members intervening to complain about adverts. Given this context it is unsurprising that regulatory authorities around the world have tightened up codes of conduct relating to environmental claims. Complaints relating to greenwash have continued to rise in many countries, including for fashion-linked advertising. We asked activists to describe so-called fashion greenwashing in one or more words. The responses were blunt.

"Masking, lying, dirty, crap, scam".

"Pretending to be ecological despite the fact that the reality is exactly the opposite."

Addressing the issue of greenwashing, the interview shows a sense of distrust and skepticism towards the corporate messages related to sustainability. This mistrust leads all interviewees to check, through the aforementioned sources, the actual truthfulness of the corporate message.

"When I see corporate messages linked to sustainability, I'm reluctant to buy because it tastes like advertising… these messages are also pushed by some online sites. But I can recognise the difference in buying a suit that respects worker rights and one produced under normal conditions".

Once verified and ascertained as greenwashing, some of the interviewees talked about it with people close to them or publish stories on Instagram about the subject.

6 Dialogue with Other Activists and Wider Publics

The topic of fashion is an important one which is discussed within activist groups, although the extent of this discussion depended a lot on the individual activist and their particular interests. Some activists gave the issue a high level of importance saying:

"It is a very heartfelt argument, just look at how certain statistics, certain data, say that pollution from fast fashion or the fashion industry is among the highest".

On the one hand, some activists saw fashion as an important issue which was "under-reported or misunderstood"by general audiences.

"Contrary to that of transport or that of meat, fashion is less exposed, more hidden and not spoken of at the same level. As an activist it is important that this is no longer the case because fashion is often one of the industries that uses greenwashing the most".

Within the activist groups, on the other hand, fashion debates are often not always prioritized as much since it is taken for granted that the topic and key issues are understood in activist circles, although this also depends from case to case:

"It's something we don't talk about that often, or at least I don't talk about it often, because in the environmental movement it's almost a given that we don't buy clothes because everyone is a very sensitive to issues relating to fashion."

During our focus group and interview discussions, two types of conversations emerged between activists and external audiences. One type of debate was with friends and family unconnected to the environmental movement and the second was with general audiences.

"It happened that a friend of mine sent me a picture of a skirt saying" 'look, I bought an environmentally-friendly skirt' because there was no plastic in it, but I had to explain to her that that wasn't the only problem with fashion (plastic), far from it".

From this last quote we can see that fashion-related issues can be general sources of debate between activists and non-activists, with activists operating as gatekeepers or "fact-checkers against greenwashing" even with family and friends.

"On social networks it is a theme that we try to bring with a sort of regularity, even if there are many other themes for debates and therefore it is not always possible to talk only about that".

The dissemination of information and discussion with followers takes place on social media, even if it was emphasized that this is only part of the information campaign that is being carried out. One of our groups under study, Climate Strike, has not yet organized campaigns or events related to fast fashion.

7 Fashion and Social Justice

There was little doubt that many of our activists link their participation in climate change issues to a broader world view that seeks to stress values and principles such as human rights and social justice.

"There can be no climate justice without social justice".

"On a global level, we cannot talk about climate justice without talking about social justice. The exploitation of the most vulnerable countries can also be seen in the context of fashion".

"If the climate crisis is not fought, social justice is unimaginable".

The fashion industry is indeed linked to the various tendencies of global capitalism. According to different political standpoints, fashion can either be seen – positively - as promoting new forms of liberal individual or collective power in contemporary societies or – as we see above - as instrumental in reinforcing economic and social disparities such as poverty and human rights violations in the developing world. While the Bick, Halsey and Ekenga point to environmental engagement by various stakeholders, they conclude by arguing that

Ensuring sustainable consumption and production patterns, seeks to redress the injustices caused by unfettered materialism. Consumers in high income countries can do their part to promote global environmental justice by buying high-quality clothing that lasts longer, shopping at second-hand stores, repairing clothing they already own, and purchasing from retailers with transparent supply chains (Bick et al. 2018: 92).

They also add that:

While fast fashion offers consumers an opportunity to buy more clothes for less, those who work in or live near textile manufacturing facilities bear a disproportionate burden of environmental health hazards. Furthermore, increased consumption patterns have also created millions of tons of textile waste in landfills and unregulated settings. This is particularly applicable to low and middle-income countries (LMICs) as much of this waste ends up in second-hand clothing markets. These LMICs often lack the supports and resources necessary to develop and enforce environmental and occupational safeguards to protect human health (Bick et al. 2018: 92).

Unsurprisingly, perhaps, our activists were skeptical when asked about talking to the fashion industry and the role of social media in that discussion. There was some difficulty in seeing beyond the damage caused to the biosphere and climate change:

"When it comes to fast fashion, they can say what they want, but they don't convince me anyway. Because in principle, what is based on enormous low-cost production is ethically and logically impossible".

"I feel betrayed by these companies. I feel bad when I see this data and I don't want my money to go to them, even if they manage to do everything correctly, I'm not interested in giving these companies a second chance".

"From the moment a company grows in size… there is mistrust. Any brand, if it is large, I do not trust".

On a more positive note, climate activists did see the potential in promoting forms of fashion that spring from local activity:

"I prefer to support someone local, who maybe I know and who I know supports the place where they are".

"When you go to the website of small sustainable shops, they often write their philosophy. You see transparency, where what comes from and where I trust".

And, likewise, there was evidence that should the fashion themselves engage more with climate activists, including through social media, that dialogue could bring rewards in developing understanding between and industry deeply rooted in global capitalism, big brands and fast fashion, and climate change movements that stress their anti-capitalist credentials, localism and the abolition of fast fashion.

"If there was a real intention on their part to establish a dialogue, I would certainly listen to them":

8   Conclusion

This article has examined the role of social media in climate change activism and the fashion industry. Our focus group and interview-based research concluded that human-computer interaction was important to social media choices based on key needs of activists such as efficient, effective, secure and popular platforms. The usability of individual social media was also a key consideration among activists. But in addition to importance of human-computer interaction through selection of social media as opposed to internet blogs, etc., the main finding that struck us was the rather haphazard choice of platforms, at times, dependent on peer selection by perceived social media 'experts'. We found that activists often deferred decisions to opinion leaders within their groups rather than through systematic research or thorough understanding of these platforms. We found that activists chose social media to produce content that best represented their ideas and provided the best chance of mobilizing new participants and activists to the climate change agenda. In that sense, social media provides a vital role in disseminating information vital to discussion in many countries. Climate change activists were more critical about the perceived failure of the fashion industry to stop the dissemination of fake or misleading news, specifically greenwashing, on social media. The article concluded that social media might provide useful spaces for the activists to have dialogue about climate change and biodiversity issues. We recommend further research to look at any such dialogue and understand industry perspectives better.

References

Bauck, W.: The Fashion Industry Emits as Much Greenhouse Gas as All of Russia. Designers, CEOs and a data scientist weigh in on what it will take to change that. In: Fashionista. 22 September 2017. https://fashionista.com/2017/09/fashion-industry-greenhouse-gas-climate-change-sustainability. Accessed on 12 Sept 2018

Bick R,. Halsey, E, Ekenga C.C.: The global environmental injustice of fast fashion. Environ. Health **17**, 92 (2018)

Futerra Greenwash Guide (2008). https://www.slideshare.net/patsario/futerra-greenwash-guide. Retrieved 15 Febuary 2021

Hibberd, M., Nguyen. A.: Communicating climate change: findings from a reception study. Int. J. Media Cult. Pol. **9.1** (2013a)

Hibberd, M., Nguyen. A.: Communicating climate change: introduction. Int. J. Media Cult. Polit. **9.1** (2013b)

Hibberd, M.: Key Challenges for the Fashion Industry in Tackling Climate Change, ScomS, Studies in Communication Sciences special edition on Fashion Communications, vol. 18, no. 2(2018), pp. 383–398 (2019)

Hibberd, M., Habib, M.A.: 'Where Now' for Green Fashion: Impact of COVID-19 on the Ready Made Garments Industry in Bangladesh. SEAJBEL – South East Asia J. Contemp. Bus. Econ. Law **24**(1) (2021)

Kenton, W.: Investopedia, definitions of supply chain and fast fashion (2020). https://www.investopedia.com/terms/s/supplychain.asp Retrieved from 30 August 2020

Klimastreik Schweiz Homepage. https://climatestrike.ch/de. Accessed on 15 Feb 2021

Lazarsfeld, P., Berelson, B., Hazel, G.: The People's Choice: How the Voter Makes Up His Mind in a Presidential Campaign, Legacy edn. Columbia University Press, New York (1948)

Ling L., Tamer O.: Encyclopedia of Database Systems (2009). https://link.springer.com/reference
     workentry/10.1007/978-0-387-39940-9_192. Retrieved from 15 Feb 2021
McNair, B., Hibberd, M., Schlesinger, P.: Mediated Access: Broadcasting and Democratic
     Participation. University of Luton Press, Luton (2003)
van Dijck, J., Poell, T., de Waal, M.: The Platform Society. Public Values in a Connective World.
     Oxford University Press, Oxford (2018)

SeatPlus: A Smart Health Chair Supporting Active Sitting Posture Correction

Zuyu Shen[1], Xi Wan[1], Yucheng Jin[1(✉)], Ge Gao[1], Qianying Wang[1],
and Wei Liu[2]

[1] Lenovo Research, Beijing, China
{shenzy6,wanxi2,jinyc2,gaoge1,wangqya}@lenovo.com
[2] Beijing Normal University, Beijing, China
wei.liu@bnu.edu.cn

Abstract. Nowadays, sedentary and poor sitting postures mainly cause lumbar spine-related diseases for office workers. According to the related medical theory of sitting posture correction, this paper presents a smart chair *SeatPlus* that actively corrects the poor sitting posture. To identify and address the issues in sitting posture correction, we iterated our prototype three times following Lean UX design method. We evaluated *SeatPlus* in terms of system performance and system usability. The accuracy of the sitting posture recognition is higher than 90%, and the effectiveness of correction exceeds 70%. The overall usability of *SeatPlus* is good especially in two usability dimensions, impact and perceived Ease of Use. Furthermore, we find that the effectiveness of correction positively influences some usability dimensions, while the frequency of correction negatively influences the perceived ease of use.

Keywords: Real-time monitoring · Active correction · Smart chair · Healthy sitting posture · Lean UX

1 Introduction

Cervical spondylosis of lumbar vertebra is ranked as the second most persistent ailment in the world by the latest World Health Organization. In China, more than 200 million patients suffer from this disease caused by sedentary and poor sitting postures. Most existing approaches of sitting posture correction work as a reminder, that is users adjust their postures based on the suggestions from the system. By contrast, "active" posture correction takes *dynamical* actions to stimulate users to *subconsciously* adjust poor sitting postures. Figure 1 illustrates the active correction enabled by the inflated airbags.

Following the Lean UX design method, we iterated the design of *SeatPlus* three times based on a minimum viable product (MVP). We use rapid experimentation and measurement to learn quickly how well (or not) our ideas meet

© Springer Nature Switzerland AG 2021
M. M. Soares et al. (Eds.): HCII 2021, LNCS 12780, pp. 531–547, 2021.
https://doi.org/10.1007/978-3-030-78224-5_37

our goals. In specific, we optimized data communication among devices, the algorithm of recognizing sitting postures, and the ergonomic design of the chair. In the end, we evaluated the system performance and system usability of the chair and analyzed relations between them.

Considering the S-shaped spine, the weight of the upper part of the spine will cause the pelvis to turn backward and the shrink of the curvature of the lumbar vertebra. When the body leans forwards the center of gravity moves forwards, which results in excessive pressure on the lumbar vertebra. In order to keep the stability of sitting after a long time, the waist muscles and lumbar muscles are going to be tight and strained. If the pressure cannot be relieved all the time, the intervertebral discs and nerves might be crushed, which will lead to severe pain. The good sitting posture requires users to keep upper body and waist straight, both legs parallel, both feet on the ground, and buttock flat.

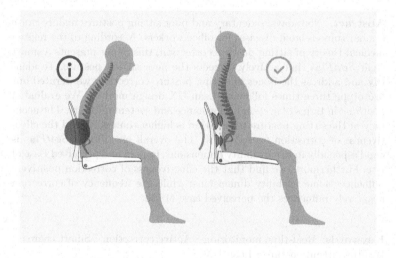

Fig. 1. Illustration of active correction

In this paper, we mainly collected 8 common sitting positions in the office, which includes good sitting posture, humpback, reclining, shallow sitting, cross-leg (left), cross-leg right, inclining to the left and right.

Before designing and developing the prototype, we first elaborated our research motivation from the social, economic and technical aspects by using SET factorial analysis [7].

Social Factors: According to the 2016 edition of the American Diabetes Association (ADA) guidelines, one-time sitting time should not exceed 90 min, and 58.6% of office workers sit for more than one hour at a time, of whom 39.3% sit more than 90 min. The 2019 white Paper on sedentary behaviors in the workplace points out that China has 140 million white-collar workers, of whom only 16.1%

can maintain a good sitting posture. More and more enterprises are paying more attention to employees' sedentary health investments.

Economic Factors: As living standards improve, the demand for health services is shifting from traditional disease treatment to disease prevention. In 2016, the China government issued the "2030" planning framework for a healthy China. It pointed out that the "treatment-oriented" policy should be transformed into a "health-oriented" policy. With prevention as the most important policy, the market of China's health care is estimated to exceed 1.1 trillion USD in 2020, and the market segment for waist care reaches 10 million USD.

Technical Factors: With the rapid advance in sensors and AI algorithm, sitting posture monitoring can be realized with high accuracy and fast response. At present, there are three major techniques for posture recognition: sitting duration monitoring, posture pressure monitoring, and posture image monitoring.

The contributions of this paper are threefold:

1. We proposed a way to integrate active posture correction into a smart chair.
2. We revealed the relationship between the system performance and the system usability. It is found that the accuracy of recognition positively influenced overall usability, while the frequency of correction negatively influences the perceived ease of user.
3. We summarized the practical experience of Lean UX based on research and development in an enterprise environment.

The rest of the paper is organized as follows. We will first discuss the related work followed by the description of the system design, design methodology, and user study. After that, we present the study results and conclude the paper with discussions about the user study and design methodology.

2   Related Work

In this section, we briefly review the related works about sitting posture recognition and correction.

2.1   Sitting Posture Recognition

So far, sitting postures recognition are mainly based on sitting duration, sitting pressure, and sitting posture images. The sitting duration approach reminds users to adjust their postures by sending notifications [10,16,26,29]; however, the users may ignore such an intrusive reminder [23] as it may distract users attention from the primary task. While the pressure-based recognition leverages various sensors to collect sitting pressure data such as load cells [1,3,17,18], accelerometers [19], etc. It is easy to train a good classification model having above 90% accuracy of recognition by using classic machine learning algorithms such as decision trees, SVM (Support Vector Machine), the higher accuracy can be achieved by using deep learning techniques [8,13]. Besides, several systems detect sitting postures by the images captured by an RGBD camera [5, 22, 30], the accuracy of recognition may be subject to the lightness of the environment and the area of body captured by the camera. Therefore, we decide to follow a pressure-based approach to implement the module of detecting sitting posture in our system.

2.2 Sitting Posture Correction

Based on the mechanism of correction, the correction approaches can be categorized into passive correction and active correction. The passive means the system does **not** take direct actions to improve postures. For example, the passive correction can be a reminder or ergonomic sitting back. Most existing correction systems present various ways to remind and guide users to good postures. For example, showing the sitting posture information on different personal devices [4, 6, 15], and providing haptic feedback by vibrators. Since these approaches are all intrusive, some non-intrusive corrections try to avoid distracting users from the primary task while guiding users to good posture, for example, a slowly moving robot arm for unobtrusive posture correction [25]. The representative products of ergonomic design for postures correction are chairs supporting lumbar [11], adjustable desktop platforms [9, 20], and a cushion member for fixing sitting posture [28]. However, the user acceptance of these products may be subjected to the low comfortableness after long time use. By contrast, active correction means a system can dynamically adjust the physical form of a chair when it detects poor sitting postures [21]. As far as we know, most existing approaches of sitting posture correction still work in a passive way.

3 System Design

This section describes the hardware frame design, I/O design, algorithm design, App design, and the practice of Lean UX design method.

Based on the results of user research, *SeatPlus* has the following design requirements:

1. The sitting surface and the backrest need to support the waist and back;
2. The system can detect if the sitting posture of a user is wrong;
3. The system provides a corresponding intervention if a wrong posture lasts longer than a certain time.

3.1 Hardware Frame Design

The design of this hardware frame should be comfortable for sitting and effective for sitting data collection. Moreover, the hardware frame should prevent users from wrong sitting postures. The seat cushion and back cushion are made of memory foam material, which can disperse the pressure on the back, buttocks, and legs to a certain extent. According to the human latissimus dorsi and erector

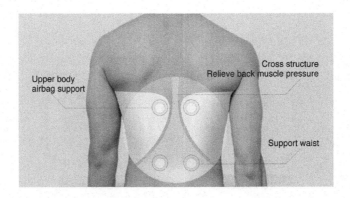

Fig. 2. Design of airbag support

rectus cross-shaped structure shown in Fig. 2, we employed back airbags to keep waist upright. The inflated airbags physically support lumbar spine and prevent lumbar spine from bending. The airbag design is the key to the active correction. We designed a specific action of inflating airbags by adjusting the air volume and inflating time for each of seven poor sitting postures.

3.2 I/O Design

As shown in Fig. 3, the hardware part is mainly composed of the mainboard, WiFi module, air pump, airbags, pressure sensors, ABS base frame. The type of mainboard is Arduino Mega2560, which is suitable for the design of multiple I/O systems, rapid verification, and iteration in the early stage of the product design. The range of the membrane pressure sensor is from 0 to 5 kg. Figure 4 shows the hip pressure map that illustrate the positions of placing 11 membrane pressure sensors on the cushion and back. The positions are determined based on the pressure distribution. After the system is powered on, the mainboard

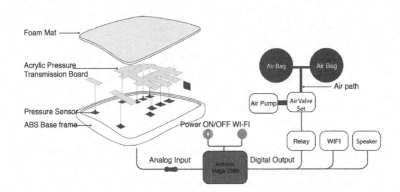

Fig. 3. Hardware frame of the chair

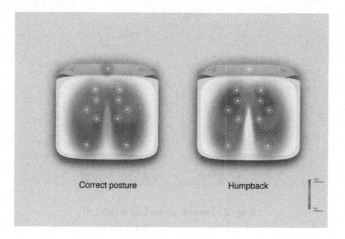

Fig. 4. The pressure distribution map of hip

will continuously receive the pressure data and then send data to the server via WiFi.

3.3   Communication Design

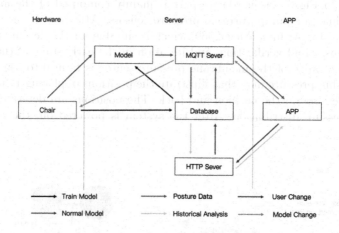

Fig. 5. Communication logic of chair

Data storage and processing are performed on the cloud server. Through WiFi connection, data can be quickly transferred among the chair, server, and App. The neural network algorithm enables the system to recognize different users and store their sitting posture data in the database. Meanwhile, through the Internet of Things network protocol MQTT (Message Queuing Telemetry

Transport) [14], other devices can be connected and controlled. The communication logic is shown in Fig. 5, which can be divided into three parts: hardware, server, and App. The MLP Classifier [27], a multi-layer perceptron, performed well in the classification problem. The chair sends the pressure data to the server for processing and predicts the user's current sitting posture. We stored pressure data and sitting posture data in the database, thus we can analyze and visualize user historical data and the development process of sitting posture habit. Moreover, users can create user profiles, switch working modes, and interact with the chair via a mobile App.

3.4   App Design

As shown in Fig. 6, the user client is an Android App, which can visualize sitting posture data. Continuous data monitoring and analysis facilitates the sitting posture health and provides lifelong health companions.

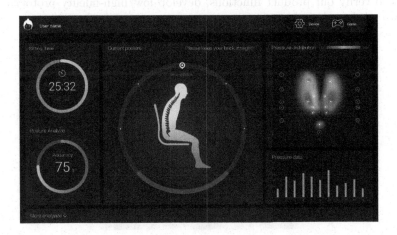

Fig. 6. The user interface of the mobile client

There are four working modes for the user: training mode, correction mode, relaxation mode, and entertainment mode. (1) Training mode: When someone first uses this chair, she/he needs to create an account by the App. At this time, the App will guide the user to switch between different sitting postures, collect the user's sitting posture data, and train a classification model for sitting postures. (2) Correction mode: The chair monitors the user's sitting postures in real-time. When a user maintains a poor sitting posture for a long period of time, the chair actively help the user adjust the current poor sitting posture by inflating airbags. (3) Relaxation mode: the chair will be inflated and deflated at a fixed frequency to give a massage for relaxation. (4) Entertainment mode: There are two ways to activate this mode. One is that when the user has been sitting for more than 45 min, a message will pop-up on the App to remind the user and recommend body exercises for relaxation. Another way is to click the game button on the App, and the a spaceship game will start. Users moves the body to controls the spaceship to catch the falling stars.

4   Design Methodology

Lean UX is the evolution of product design. We chose UX design method rather than other design methods, because of several advantages in product design that are *"1) it helps us remove waste from our UX design process; 2) it drives team members to harmonize our "system" in a transparent, cross-functional collaboration; 3) it is the mindset shift we gain from adopting a model based on experimentation."* [12]. This method is to deeply involve users at each design stage and iteratively optimize products through user testing and user feedback. Besides, following Lean UX method also reduces enterprise development costs and improves development efficiency [12]. We iterated design prototypes three times to verify our product functions, develop low/high-fidelity prototype and finalize product design.

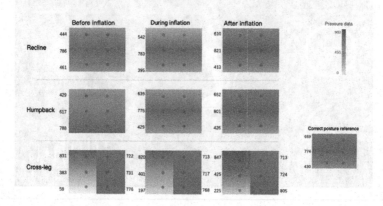

Fig. 7. Pressure distribution for different sitting postures (the first time prototype)

In the first iteration we mainly verified the feasibility of posture recognition and correction enabled by airbag inflation. The early prototype can obtain the average value of pressure distribution on the sitting surface and helped users maintain good sitting posture. Figure 7 shows that the sitting pressures produced by different sitting postures were significantly different. Among them, the sitting pressure graph of the semi-lying sitting posture and the hunched sitting posture after inflation is significantly improved, which is close to the pressure graph of the good sitting posture. It means that airbag inflation can effectively help users change recline and humpback postures. Although it was verified that the inflation reminder is helpful for improving sitting posture, the comfortableness, stability, and accuracy of the chair still need to be improved.

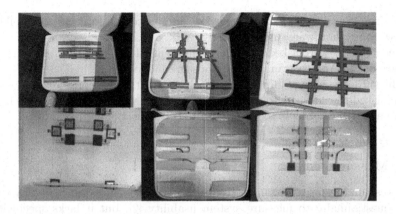

Fig. 8. The placement of pressure sensors (the second time prototype)

In the second iteration, we verified the ID design of the product and hardware system design. The prototypes is more integrated. All components are hidden in the back cover. A built-in rechargeable battery powers the entire system without additional wiring. In order to obtain more accurate sitting pressure data, we increased the sensors from 3 pairs to 5 pairs, as shown in Fig. 8. In order to accurately collect sitting pressures of different body sizes, we enlarged the contact areas by bridging independent touch points. We tried different ways and materials to determine a parallel sensor placement and bridge sensors by ABS material. In the end, we verified the usability of the finalized product. Through three times of iteration, the finalized design can meet the users' requirements and business requirements. On the basis of good system performance of the previous prototypes, we mainly optimized the comfortableness of the chair. The chair cushion is filled with memory foam material to improve comfortableness, and it will not affect the accuracy of the pressure data. The height and backrest of the chair can be adjusted to fit different users. The chair cushion has a triangular curved surface as a whole, which fits the curve of the buttocks and makes legs apart and stabilizes the sitting posture for better support. Besides, the sitting posture prediction algorithm is updated from SVM to MLPClassifier to achieve higher accuracy.

5   User Study

This section shows the system performance test and usability test for the third time of product prototypes.

5.1   Procedure

We recruited participants to test the usability of the chair in a real working environment. The steps of the user study are as follows:

1. We introduced the experiment purpose and process to subjects, then tell them how to use hardware and software.
2. The subjects were asked to perform different sitting postures upon the guidance of the App to train a sitting posture model.
3. The subjects were required to maintain each sitting posture for 30 s.
4. We asked the subjects to use the chair in a real work environment for 15 min.
5. We asked the subjects to fill in a post-study questionnaire.

5.2 Measurements

This test mainly uses a standardized usability questionnaire. SUS is a widely used questionnaire to measure system usability [2], but it lacks specificity in the test of healthcare products. So we employed the Health-ITUES questionnaire [24] that has good reliability and validity indicators. Health-ITUES consists of 20 questions, using a 5-point Likert scale, including four dimensions of influence, perceived usability, perceived ease of use, and controllability (Table 1). The overall score is the average scores of all question items, and each item has an equal weight. Besides, the questionnaire also contains three subjective questions (Table 2) to collect the experience of using the chair.

Table 1. The constructs of Health-ITUES [24]

Dimensions	Questions
Impact	1. I think the chair would be a positive addition for persons living with the issue of being sedentary
	2. I think the chair would improve the Quality of Life of persons living with the issue of being sedentary
	3. I think the chair has an important part of meeting my information needs related to self-management of sitting postures
Perceived Usefulness	4. Using the chair makes it easier to self-manage my sitting postures
	5. Using the chair enables me to self-manage my sitting postures more quickly
	6. Using the chair makes it more likely that l can self-menage my sitting postures
	7. Using the chair is useful for self-management of sitting postures
	8. I think the chair presents a more equitable process for self-management of sitting postures
	9. I am satisfied with the chair for self-management of sitting postures
	10. I self-manage my sitting postures in a timely manner because of the chair
	11. Using the chair increases my ability to self-manage my sitting postures
	12. I am able to self-manage my sitting postures whenever I use the chair
Perceived Ease of Use	13. I am comfortable with my ability to use the chair
	14. Learning to operate the chair is easy for me
	15. It is easy for me to become skillful at using the chair
	16. I find it is easy to use the chair
	17. I can always remember how to log on to and use the chair
User Control	18. The chair gives error messages that clearly and tell me how to fix problems
	19. Whenever I make a mistake using the chair, I recover easily and quickly
	20. The information (such as on-line help, on-screen messages and other documentation) provided with the chair is clear

Table 2. Subjective questions in the questionnaire

SQ1: Which factors do you think probably most influence your intention to use the smart chair, and why?
SQ2: Which situations do you think in which you would like to use the smart chair, and why?
SQ3: What do you want to suggest and ask for the chair?

The evaluation contains both subjective measurement and objective measurement. The subjective measurement employs a questionnaire Health-ITUES; and objective measurement considers three indicators: accuracy of correction[1], frequency of correction[2], and effectiveness of correction[3].

5.3 Subjects

In total, we recruited 12 subjects from a high-tech company. Half of them are female; 11 are between 26 and 35 years old, and one is older than 35 years old. All of them are office workers. Figure 9 shows the sedentary situation realized by the subjects. Besides, three-quarters of users (9) have experience in using the products that remind users of sedentary behaviors.

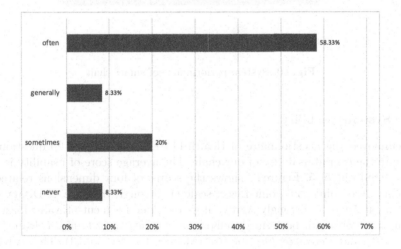

Fig. 9. The subjects' experience of using posture correction products

---

[1] Accuracy of Recognition = number of correctly recognized sitting postures/total number of recognized sitting postures.

[2] Frequency of Correction = the total number of inflations within 15 min.

[3] Effectiveness of Correction = number of the corrections that stimulate users to change the sitting posture/The total number of corrections within 15 min.

6   Experimental Results

This section shows the results of the performance test and usability test and summarizes the subjective feedback of users.

6.1   System Performance

Figure 10 shows the result of system performance. In specific, the accuracy of recognition stands at a satisfying level that is above 90%, and the effectiveness of correction is above 70%, which indicates the usefulness of active correction implemented in our system. The average number of correcting posture is 13.33 (SD = 5.48).

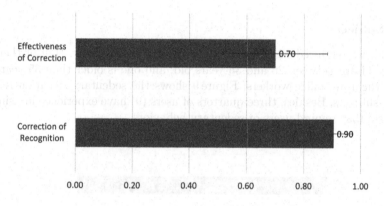

Fig. 10. System performance of smart chair

6.2   System Usability

We employed the questionnaire of Health-ITUES consisting of 20 questions to measure the overall usability of our chair. The average score of usability is 3.81 (SD = 0.68) out of 5. Figure 11 shows the scores of four dimensions related to usability. According to 5 point-Likert scale (1: Strongly disagree, 2: Disagree, 3: Neutral, 4: Agree, 5: Strongly Agree), if we consider 4 is a cut-off value for a satisfying level, our chair performed well on two dimensions of *Impact* (Mean = 4.12 SD = 0.91) and *Perceived Ease of Use* (Mean = 4.11 SD = 0.53). The scores on Perceived Usefulness (Mean = 3.81 SD = 0.95) and User Control (Mean = 3.73 SD = 0.70) are also satisfied.

6.3   Correlation Analysis

Furthermore, we performed correlation analysis between three objective indicators of system performance (accuracy of correction, frequency of correction, and effectiveness of correction) and four subjective indicators of system usability

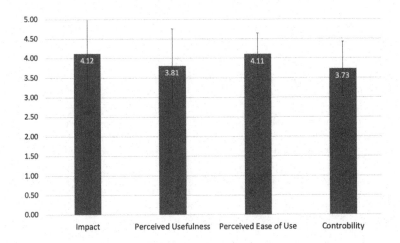

Fig. 11. Scores on four usability dimensions

(Impact, Perceived ease of use, Perceived usefulness, and User control). Figure 12 plots three correlations showing a statistical significance and one correlation that tends to have a statistical significance. In specific, we found correction effectiveness positively correlates with overall usability ($r = 0.600$, $p < 0.05$) and it also positively correlates with two dimensions of usability, Impact ($r = 0.530$, $p = 0.08$) and the Perceived of Ease of Use ($r = 0.692$, $p < 0.05$). Interestingly, we find that correction frequency negatively correlates with perceived ease of use ($r = -0.609$, $p < 0.05$).

6.4   Subjective Feedback

Moreover, the questionnaire contains three subjective questions. For the first question *"SQ1: Which factors do you think probably most influence your intention to use the smart chair, and why?"* One-third of subjects think comfortableness most influences the intention of use, and they also pointed out the importance of safety, noise, and price. For the second questions *"SQ2: Which situations do you think is suitable for using the smart chair, and why?"* 11 out of 12 users say that they tend to use the chair in the office because the sedentary issue often occurs in the office, while one subject thinks she would like to use the chair at home in leisure time rather than in the office because of the noise of pumping air cushion. Toward the last question *"SQ3: What do you want to suggest and ask for the chair?"* Two subjects think the noise of pumping air cushion distracts them from the working task. Besides, user attention to the sitting data and reminders shown on the tablet screen may distract her. Therefore a non-obtrusive way of giving feedback is more desired, for example, reminding by voice in a situation.

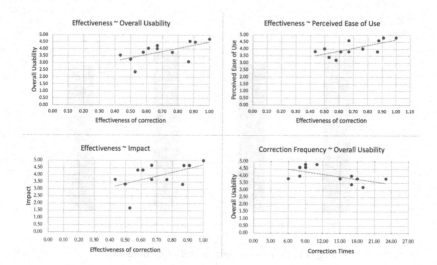

Fig. 12. Correlation analyses between system performance and system usability

7   Discussions

This section mainly discusses the results of user study and the lessons learned from the practice of lean UX methodology in the process of designing and developing the chair.

7.1   System Performance and Usability

The results of the system performance test indicate that the smart chair performs well in terms of accuracy of recognition and effectiveness of correction. The performance can still maintain at a satisfying level when adapting to different body shapes. The high effectiveness of correction (above 70%) proves the advantage of *active correction* over passive correction. The results of Health-ITUES questionnaire show that the overall usability of our chair is good and some dimensions of usability are particularly highly rated by subjects such as Impact and Perceived Ease of Use.

The results of correlation analysis manifest that the effectiveness of correction has a significantly positive impact on overall system usability and two dimensions of usability: Impact and Perceived Ease of Use. Therefore, it may also suggest the positive effects of active correction on system usability. However, the correlation results do not show a significant correlation between accuracy of recognition and system usability. Arguably we suggest that **designers of the smart chair should focus more on increasing effectiveness of correction when the accuracy of recognition reaches a satisfying level.** Also, the negative correlation between the frequency of correction and system usability indicates that frequent correction may undermine system usability. Too frequent actions of correcting sitting postures may aggravate the disturbance of noise made by pumping air cushions. Thus we suggest that **designers of smart chairs should balance the frequency of correction and system usability**.

7.2 Practice of Lean UX

We designed and developed our smart chair following the methodology of Lean UX. We briefly summarize the lessons learned from this practice in our project.

1. Lean UX is particularly suitable for enterprises that follow the bottom-up design approach. It enables the research development team to generate innovative concepts based on the feedback from real customers and then transfer the concepts to product functions.
2. Considering the limited resources of enterprises, the practitioners should prioritize the requirements collected from the communications with customers in production.
3. To ensure the project advances smoothly, we should break down a workflow into fine-grained tasks and set a priority and a deadline for each of them.
4. Compared with software design, the modification in hardware design is much more expensive. Thus, the Minimum Viable Product (MVP) is useful because it allows us to rapidly test our ideas even if the MVP may sacrifice the system performance to a certain extent in the early phase.

8 Conclusion

This paper presents a new smart health chair that supports active correction for the poor sitting postures. The chair can recognize the sitting postures in real-time. We describe how we followed the Lean UX design method in our project and summarized the practical experience of Lean UX. Moreover, we evaluate our smart chair in a real working environment. In specific, we measured the system performance (accuracy of recognition, frequency of correction, and effectiveness of correction) as well as system usability. The correlation analyses reveal that **effectiveness of correction** significantly influences overall usability and several usability dimensions, while the frequency of correction tends to undermine system usability. As we know, developing sitting habits usually takes a long time. To better verify our results, we may need to run a longitude study. Thus, we plan to evaluate our chair by conducting a longitudinal user study with more subjects in a classroom in the future. Overall, we think the approach of active correction and the study results shed light on the design and development of the smart health chair.

References

1. Ahmad, J., Andersson, H., Sidén, J.: Sitting posture recognition using screen printed large area pressure sensors. In: 2017 IEEE Sensors, pp. 1–3. IEEE (2017)

2. Bangor, A., Kortum, P.T., Miller, J.T.: An empirical evaluation of the system usability scale. Intl. J. Hum.-Comput. Interact. **24**(6), 574–594 (2008)
3. Bao, J., Li, W., Li, J., Ge, Y., Bao, C.: Sitting posture recognition based on data fusion on pressure cushion. TELKOMNIKA Indones. J. Electr. Eng. **11**(4), 1769–1775 (2013)
4. Baptista, R., Antunes, M., Aouada, D., Ottersten, B., et al.: Flexible feedback system for posture monitoring and correction. In: 2017 Fourth International Conference on Image Information Processing (ICIIP), pp. 1–6. IEEE (2017)
5. Bei, S., Xing, Z., Taocheng, L., Qin, L.: Sitting posture detection using adaptively fused 3D features. In: 2017 IEEE 2nd Information Technology, Networking, Electronic and Automation Control Conference (ITNEC), pp. 1073–1077. IEEE (2017)
6. Breen, P.P., Nisar, A., ÓLaighin, G.: Evaluation of a single accelerometer based biofeedback system for real-time correction of neck posture in computer users. In: 2009 Annual International Conference of the IEEE Engineering in Medicine and Biology Society, pp. 7269–7272. IEEE (2009)
7. Cagan, J., Cagan, J.M., Vogel, C.M.: Creating Breakthrough Products: Innovation from Product Planning to Program Approval. FT Press, Upper Saddle River (2002)
8. Cho, H., Choi, H.J., Lee, C.E., Sir, C.W.: Sitting posture prediction and correction system using arduino-based chair and deep learning model. In: 2019 IEEE 12th Conference on Service-Oriented Computing and Applications (SOCA), pp. 98–102. IEEE (2019)
9. Edwards, T., Pearsons, E.: Chair with adjustable lumbar support, US Patent 6,981,743, 3 January 2006
10. Estrada, J., Vea, L.: Sitting posture recognition for computer users using smartphones and a web camera. In: TENCON 2017–2017 IEEE Region 10 Conference, pp. 1520–1525. IEEE (2017)
11. Flaherty, D.: Adjustable desktop platform, US Patent 8,671,853, 18 March 2014
12. Gothelf, J.: Lean UX: Applying Lean Principles to Improve User Experience. O'Reilly Media Inc., Sebastopol (2013)
13. Gupta, R., Saini, D., Mishra, S.: Posture detection using deep learning for time series data. In: 2020 Third International Conference on Smart Systems and Inventive Technology (ICSSIT), pp. 740–744. IEEE (2020)
14. Hunkeler, U., Truong, H.L., Stanford-Clark, A.: MQTT-S-a publish/subscribe protocol for wireless sensor networks. In: 2008 3rd International Conference on Communication Systems Software and Middleware and Workshops (COMSWARE 2008), pp. 791–798. IEEE (2008)
15. Kim, M., Kim, H., Park, J., Jee, K.K., Lim, J.A., Park, M.C.: Real-time sitting posture correction system based on highly durable and washable electronic textile pressure sensors. Sens. Actuators, A **269**, 394–400 (2018)
16. Klasnja, P., Pratt, W.: Healthcare in the pocket: mapping the space of mobile-phone health interventions. J. Biomed. Inform. **45**(1), 184–198 (2012)
17. Liang, G., Cao, J., Liu, X.: Smart cushion: a practical system for fine-grained sitting posture recognition. In: 2017 IEEE International Conference on Pervasive Computing and Communications Workshops (PerCom Workshops), pp. 419–424. IEEE (2017)
18. Liang, G., Cao, J., Liu, X., Han, X.: Cushionware: a practical sitting posture-based interaction system. In: CHI 2014 Extended Abstracts on Human Factors in Computing Systems, pp. 591–594 (2014)
19. Ma, S., Cho, W.H., Quan, C.H., Lee, S.: A sitting posture recognition system based on 3 axis accelerometer. In: 2016 IEEE Conference on Computational Intelligence in Bioinformatics and Computational Biology (CIBCB), pp. 1–3. IEEE (2016)

20. Machael, J.R., Hahn, J., Crowell, T.J., Fifield, B.: Flex lumbar support, US Patent 10,064,493, 4 September 2018

21. Martins, L., et al.: Intelligent chair sensor - classification and correction of sitting posture. In: Roa Romero, L. (ed.) XIII Mediterranean Conference on Medical and Biological Engineering and Computing 2013. IFMBE, vol. 41, pp. 1489–1492. Springer, Cham (2014). https://doi.org/10.1007/978-3-319-00846-2_368

22. Min, W., Cui, H., Han, Q., Zou, F.: A scene recognition and semantic analysis approach to unhealthy sitting posture detection during screen-reading. Sensors 18(9), 3119 (2018)

23. Müller, J., et al.: Display blindness: the effect of expectations on attention towards digital signage. In: Tokuda, H., Beigl, M., Friday, A., Brush, A.J.B., Tobe, Y. (eds.) Pervasive 2009. LNCS, vol. 5538, pp. 1–8. Springer, Heidelberg (2009). https://doi.org/10.1007/978-3-642-01516-8_1

24. Schnall, R., Cho, H., Liu, J.: Health information technology usability evaluation scale (health-ITUES) for usability assessment of mobile health technology: validation study. JMIR Mhealth Uhealth 6(1), e4 (2018)

25. Shin, J.G., et al.: Slow robots for unobtrusive posture correction. In: Proceedings of the 2019 CHI Conference on Human Factors in Computing Systems, pp. 1–10 (2019)

26. Thomsen, T., et al.: Motivational counselling and SMS-reminders for reduction of daily sitting time in patients with rheumatoid arthritis: a descriptive randomised controlled feasibility study. BMC Musculoskelet. Disord. 17(1) (2016). Article number: 434. https://doi.org/10.1186/s12891-016-1266-6

27. Windeatt, T.: Accuracy/diversity and ensemble MLP classifier design. IEEE Trans. Neural Netw. 17(5), 1194–1211 (2006)

28. Wu, Y.L.: Structure of a seat of a chair, US Patent App. 11/033,147, 13 July 2006

29. Xu, W., Huang, M.C., Amini, N., He, L., Sarrafzadeh, M.: eCushion: a textile pressure sensor array design and calibration for sitting posture analysis. IEEE Sens. J. 13(10), 3926–3934 (2013)

30. Zeng, X., Sun, B., LUO, W.s., LIU, T.c., Lu, Q.: Sitting posture detection system based on depth sensor. Comput. Sci. (7), 41 (2018)

Potential Usability Design Strategies Based on Mental Models, Behavioral Model and Art Therapy for User Experience in Post-COVID-19 Era

Zulan Yang, Zhen Liu(✉) ⓘ, Ke Zhang, and Chang Xiao

School of Design, South China University of Technology, Guangzhou 510006, People's Republic of China
liuzjames@scut.edu.cn

Abstract. The arrival of the 2019 novel coronavirus (COVID-19) has accelerated the replacement of old lifestyles by new lifestyles. In the post-COVID-19 era, the various behavioral changes, emotional and psychological problems caused by the COVID-19 epidemic may not yet be over, forcing the public to face a variety of experiential changes. Therefore, the purpose of this paper is to summarize the influence of COVID-19 on the psychology, emotion, behavior and experience of the public through literature review, and analyze the causal relationship between them. Then this paper looks for a usability design strategy to solve the user experience from the perspective of design and 'creation of cure'. Finally, the logical framework of the design strategy is summarized to deal with the realistic needs of the post-COVID-19 era. Based on the analysis of the existing literature, this paper proposes: 1) the potential design strategies of mental models and art therapy for psychological and emotional experience, 2) the potential design strategy of behavioral model and art therapy is proposed for behavioral experience, and 3) user experience models in different fields are proposed for the change of user experience.

Keywords: Post-COVID-19 era · Mental models · Behavioral model · User experience · Design strategy

1 Introduction

1.1 The Post 2019 Novel Coronavirus Era (Post-COVID-19 Era)

At the end of 2019, the 2019 novel coronavirus (COVID-19) caused by severe acute respiratory syndrome coronavirus-2 broke out rapidly and spread widely across the world [1]. The arrival of COVID-19 has brought about many earth-shaking changes in people's lifestyle, such as from food, clothing, housing and transportation to study, work and entertainment, which has brought a new lifestyle to the public.

Compared with the original harm caused by the COVID-19 epidemic, the current prevention and control of COVID-19 has achieved important strategic results, ushering

© Springer Nature Switzerland AG 2021
M. M. Soares et al. (Eds.): HCII 2021, LNCS 12780, pp. 548–561, 2021.
https://doi.org/10.1007/978-3-030-78224-5_38

in the post-COVID-19 era for the public. The so-called post-COVID-19 era is not the situation in which the epidemic has completely disappeared and everything has returned as before, but the era in which the epidemic fluctuates from time to time, and may occur on a small scale at any time, returning from foreign countries and seasonal outbreaks, and the duration is relatively long, with far-reaching effects on all aspects [2]. In the post-COVID-19 era, although the status quo in various aspects of life is gradually on track, some people's lifestyle habits, emotional performance, and mental health are gradually changing.

The COVID-19 epidemic poses a number of uncertain threats to populations such as the elderly, children and adolescents. Among them, children, as the vulnerable group in each group, will experience fear, uncertainty, major changes in daily life, physical and social isolation, and high pressure from parents [3]. The panic caused by the rapid spread of COVID-19 may cause lasting psychological problems among the public in all social and economic fields, which may be more harmful than the virus itself in the long run [4]. In this context, Dubey et al. [5] evaluated the relevant psychosocial consequences and impact of COVID-19 in all classes of modern society, they think that the public event of the COVID-19 has produced complex environmental pressures on all sectors of society, and under this environmental pressure, the various experiences of various groups are closely linked. Moreover, the World Health Organization (WHO) counts in real time that the confirmed cases and deaths of the global new crown epidemic are still rising slowly [6]. In general, in the post-COVID-19 era, the various emotional, psychological problems and behavioral changes caused by the COVID-19 pandemic may not be over yet, forcing the public to face a variety of changes in experience.

1.2 The Change of Psychology and Emotion

In January 2020, the World Health Organization (WHO) has declared COVID-19 a 'Public Health Emergency of International Concern', which is the highest level of WHO alert. A study by Wainberg et al. [7] in 2017 showed that the public would have mental health problems after facing major public health emergencies. Therefore, the outbreak of COVID-19 may cause emotional distress and anxiety to the public, thereby exacerbating pre-existing mental health disorders, and causing stress-related disorders in the affected population [8]. It is worth noting that the psychological impact of children and adolescents is easy to be ignored under the pressure of the COVID-19 pandemic environment [9]. Moreover, living in a closed environment during the COVID-19 is a potentially stressful and traumatic experience, which makes children need psychological support from their parents more than ever before [10].

In the post-COVID-19 era, the psychological crisis caused by the COVID-19 is still not over, and may cause a wide range of emotional troubles among children, adolescents, middle-aged and elderly people, such as anxiety, depression, confusion, panic and insecurity [11]. An important factor that causes the change of public mood is the emotional infection brought by the Internet information. Emotional infection is a concept highly related to emotional empathy. It means that observing the emotion of one subject may automatically and primitively trigger the same state and emotion of the second subject [12, 13]. Therefore, when social media spread information containing the infection or death of others, as well as a large amount of misinformation with negative emotions related to the COVID-19, it may lead to excessive empathic response, which intensifies the mood changes of panic and depression in the public [14, 15].

As shown in Fig. 1 through the analysis of keywords in COVID-19 related articles, it is found that many articles have mentioned the topics of mental health, emotion regulation, anxiety, psychological impact and depression. It can be seen that COVID-19 has a significant impact on the mental health and mood of the public.

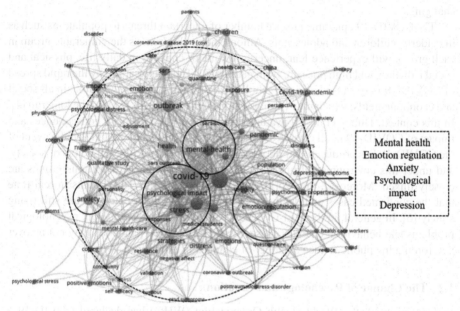

Fig. 1. Keyword analysis of COVID-19 related articles via VOSviewer

1.3 The Change of Behavior

In response to the COVID-19 epidemic, WHO provides basic mitigation and suppression strategies to reduce the harm caused by COVID-19, such as physical distancing, wearing a mask, keeping rooms well ventilated, avoiding crowds, cleaning your hands, and coughing into a bent elbow or tissue [16]. In addition, Wang et al. [17] proposed postponing or canceling personal parties, and Ferguson et al. [18] proposed epidemic prevention measures of working independently at home. In order to overcome this global threat, Manikandan [19] believes that preventive measures such as social distance, hand washing and wearing masks are important and key measures to reduce the spread of COVID-19 in the community. The Center for Disease Control and Prevention also emphasizes: ①Wear a mask to protect yourself and others and stop the spread of COVID-19. ②Stay at least 6 feet (about 2 arm lengths) from others who don't live with you, and avoid crowds. ③Wash your hands with soap and water for 20 s or use hand sanitizer with at least 60% alcohol [20]. In general, prevention and control measures of the COVID-19 such as frequent hand washing, social distancing and wearing masks have become important factors leading to changes in public behavior.

In the post-COVID-19 era, the public has let the 'washing hands frequently' that they used to talk about before have fallen into place, and the number of hand washing has increased. However, washing hands too frequently can cause eczema [21]. Therefore, the correct hand washing behavior can form a good experience process. In addition, under the great environmental pressure of the COVID-19 public incident, necessary social distancing measures and rising unemployment rate may increase the risk of child abuse and neglect [22]. It is worth noting that many studies have investigated behavioral and emotional distress caused by COVID-19 in children and adolescents, of which attachment, distraction, irritability, and fear that a family member will be infected with a fatal disease are the most common behavioral and emotional problems [23].

1.4 The Change of User Experience

The influence of COVID-19 on the psychology, emotion and behavior of the public has caused the change of group experience, and people begin to rethink the meaning of work and life, health and life. During the COVID-19 period, due to restrictions on public access to hospitals and heavy reliance on telemedicine, the medical user experience has gradually changed [24]. Among them, the video consultation experience in telemedicine needs to be improved [25]. The COVID-19 pandemic has also brought challenges of volatility, uncertainty, complexity and ambiguity to the aviation industry, and the experience of users other than passengers, such as employees, airport staff and other stakeholders in airport venues, has also changed dramatically [26]. In the field of education, users of online education platforms have different concerns and needs in the context of COVID-19, forcing many changes between platforms, such as course management, exchanges and interactions, learning and technical support services, all of which have an impact on the user experience of Chinese online education platforms [27]. In short, user experience has gradually penetrated into the service system of various fields following the development of technology. All emotions, preferences, feelings, physical and psychological experiences of users before, during, and after using products and services are also gradually changing in the post-COVID-19 era.

1.5 Summary of Causality

Through the analysis of the source of the event and the impact of the COVID-19, this paper summarizes the causal relationship between the psychological, emotional, behavioral, and experience changes of users in the post-COVID-19 era as shown in Fig. 2.

2 Design Strategy Analysis

In the face of changes in public psychology, mood and behavior, many pediatricians have been committed to cultivating resilience strategies for children and adolescents infected by the COVID-19 virus, among the measures they recommend to parents and family members include: increasing communication with children to address their fears and concerns; playing cooperative games to combat loneliness; encouraging activities that

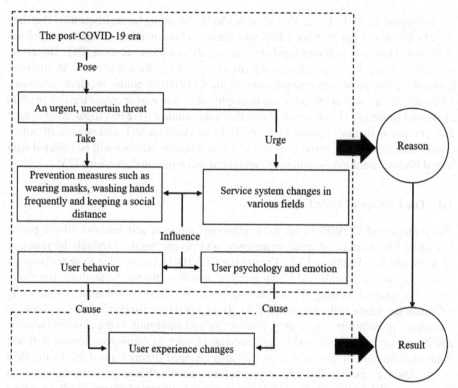

Fig. 2. The causal relationship between users' psychological, emotional, behavioral, and experience changes (devised by the authors based on the analysis)

promote physical activity; the use of music therapy, such as singing, to alleviate worries and fears; and a strong emphasis on the child's feelings [23]. Among adolescents, the COVID-19 has changed their leisure behaviors, which prompted researchers to innovate during the COVID-19 pandemic to promote health [28]. In the context of the COVID-19 pandemic, it is important to create acceptable experiences for users in order to alleviate the pressure caused by psychological, emotional and behavioral changes. Therefore, this paper will look for a usability design strategy to solve the user experience from the perspective of design and 'creation of cure'.

This research focuses on causality, starting from the source of the event, and looking for design strategies to solve user experience. As shown in Fig. 3 the analysis of the causal relationship in Fig. 2 shows that the uncertain threats and epidemic prevention measures in the post-COVID-19 era cannot be changed, but behaviors, psychology and emotions can be changed through certain design strategies. Therefore, this paper analyzes the potential usability design strategy of user experience under the COVID-19 situation from two aspects: psychological experience, emotional experience and behavioral experience.

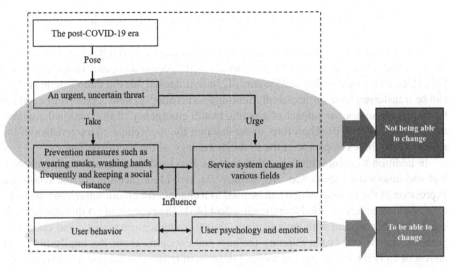

Fig. 3. Analysis of usability design strategy of user experience (devised by the authors based on the analysis)

2.1 Psychological and Emotional Experience Design Strategies

The literature suggests that a potential mechanism for understanding the relationship between psychological control and maladaptive emotional responses to current stressful public events may be empathy [29]. Among them, there is a complicated relationship between empathy and mental health development [30]. Therefore, the analysis of users' psychological and emotional experience can be combined.

Many articles combine user experience and usability research with mental models. For example, Lei et al. [31] discussed the influence of different mental models on user operation experience in 2016, Komang and Hendra [32] improved user experience of mobile learning applications by using mental models in 2020, and Zhang et al. [33] analyzed the usability of cookware interface by using user mental models. Therefore, the relevant theories of mental models are helpful to improve the usability of user experience and construct the usability strategies to deal with the psychological and emotional experience of users in the post-COVID-19 era.

In 1943, Kenneth Craik [34] proposed the concept of mental model. Mental model is a simplified knowledge structure or cognitive representation study of how a certain aspect of the world works, and it draws on the content of many disciplines such as psychology, organizational theory, economics, politics, and system dynamics [35]. Studies have shown that mental models can evolve from the form of a realistic logical framework to the logic we use to make decisions, learn and adapt [36]. Its knowledge structure can affect perception, information processing, problem solving, judgment, learning and decision-making [37]. Generally speaking, mental model is a script for the development process of certain things independently formed in people's mind after summarizing and learning experiences, which is often referred to as thinking set [38]. Donaldn [39] divides the mental model into three interrelated models, namely design model, user model and system model. Furthermore, when the user is in the context of a certain problem, the mental model will affect a person's focus and problem-solving actions and strategies [40].

Earlier studies suggested that in the fields of cognitive psychology and innovative design, creating and analyzing mental models will become a popular research method [41]. Recent research by Roy and Denzau [42] also proposed that the shared mental model can be transferred from an 'isolated' thinking to a broader 'system' organization, which has implications for the impact of a public health emergency of international concern, namely the COVID-19. Therefore, understanding the theoretical characteristics of the mental model helps to construct the usability strategy of the user experience.

In addition to mental models, art therapy is also used as a strategy for psychological and emotional experience. Art therapy can provide a medium for the emotional expression of the treated, which can be used as a channel for emotional release and self-expression to achieve a good therapeutic effect [43]. The process of art therapy can help users identify and deal with their feelings, thus forming a more realistic and optimistic point of view to resolve conflicting feelings and concerns about the family [44]. The arrival of COVID-19 has caused varying degrees of trauma to the public's psychology. Art therapy is an effective, non-verbal treatment method to solve trauma [45]. There are many theories used in art therapy, such as aesthetic theory [46], interpretative phenomenological analysis [47], and cognitive behavior theory [48]. In addition, art therapy uses a variety of art media, such as painting [49], music [50], clay [51], and images [52]. In general, the diversity of art therapy has potential application value for alleviating users' fear, anxiety, restlessness, stress and other psychological and emotional problems [53–55]. Moreover, the art intervention form of art therapy can start from the five senses of the person.

2.2 Behavioral Experience Design Strategy

User behavior research is an indispensable step in user experience research. It can collect user information, analyze user behavior patterns, and explore potential user psychology through various methods such as observation, interview, man-machine system analysis, and simulation of user behavior patterns, so as to provide guidance and evaluation criteria for design [56]. Shaker et al. [57] believe that the behavior and expression pattern of each game user can be mapped to user experience to create a more accurate user experience model. Baer [58] found that mindfulness intervention can alleviate behavioral problems in different areas, such as eating disorders and stress-related behaviors. The generalization of user behavior can be presented through behavior models, among which the existing behavior model types are Fogg behavior model and Lewin metal of behavior.

Fogg Behavior Model was proposed by Fogg [59], a teacher at Yale University, who thinks behavior(B) consists of three factors, namely motivation(M), ability(A) and trigger(T), which constitute the formula B=MAT. The formula indicates that a behavior can occur, the actor first needs to have the motivation to conduct the behavior and the ability to operate the behavior. When the motivation, ability and trigger reach the upper part of the behavior boundary, the behavior will occur successfully. Fogg's behavior model summarizes how to make products convince users, which is not only helpful to explore how to improve user's satisfaction with social functions, but also to find out the reasons for user behaviors [60]. In addition, Felebee [61] considers that the three theoretical foundations of Fogg's Behavior Model [62], Fogg's Behavior Grid [63] and Fogg's Persuasive Strategies [64] can be integrated when constructing an assessment of how persuasive technology can cause behavior reduction.

Lewin Metal of Behavior was proposed by American sociologist and psychologist Kurt Lewin [65] in his book 'Principles of Topological Psychology',who believes that human behavior is the product of the interaction between individuals and the environment, among which the factors affecting human behavior(B) can be summarized as personal(P) internal factors and external environmental(E) factors, that is, the formula $B = f (P, E)$. In this formula: 1) personal internal factors can consider physiological characteristics, ability, knowledge, and cognition, 2) external environmental factors can consider natural environment, social environment, and institutional environment. Therefore,Lewin metal of behavior can be used to analyze the travel behavior of traffic travelers [66], the consumption behavior of college students [67], and the behavior of garbage sorting [68]. It has gradually developed into a general paradigm for studying human behavior.

In addition to behavioral research, mindfulness intervention, Fogg behavior model and Lewin Metal of Behavior, art therapy can not only improve psychological and emotional problems, but also intervene in behavior problems. Art creation can provide a channel for emotional release and self-expression [69], and it has a certain therapeutic effect on many behavioral problems, such as aggressive behavior [70], behavioral difficulties [71], and drug abuse [72]. Therefore, art therapy can solve related behavioral problems, which has potential value for enhancing users' behavioral experience.

2.3 User Experience Model

Robert Rubino's Four Elements of User Experience. Robert Rubinoff's user experience model is mainly to quantify user experience, which is made up of four independent elements, namely branding, usability, functionality, and content [73].

Bernd Schmidt's Five Systems of User Experience. In the book 'Experiential Marketing', Bernd H. Schmitt [74] defines experiential marketing from the five systems of senses, emotions, thinking, behavior, and relevance through the means of seeing, listening, using, and participating, so as to study consumers' experience.

Whitney Quesenbery's 5E Principles of User Experience. Whitney Quesenbery [75] proposed the five E principles of user experience model, namely effective, efficient, engaging, error tolerant, and easy to learn, of which the five principles accounted for 20% respectively.

Peter Morville's Honeycomb Model of User Experience and Three Pies of Information Architecture. In his book Web Information Architecture, Peter and Louis [76] proposed the honeycomb model of user experience and the three pies of information architecture. The honeycomb model of user experience refers to the seven aspects of usefulness, availability, desirability, findability, accessibility, trust, and value, which go beyond availability and help people understand and prioritize requirements. In addition, the three pies of information architecture refer to ①scenarios: business goals, capital, politics, culture, technology, resources and restrictions; ②content: document/data type, content object, quantity, existing architecture; ③user: audience, tasks, needs, information search behavior, experience.

Jesse James' User Experience Elements. Jesse James [77] thinks that there are five main levels of user experience elements, namely, strategy level, scope level, structure level, framework level, and presentation level. The strategy layer corresponds to website goals and user needs, the scope layer corresponds to functional specifications and content requirements, the structure layer corresponds to interaction design and information architecture, the frame layer corresponds to information design, interface design, and navigation design, and the presentation layer corresponds to perceptual experience and visual design.

3 Potential Usability Design Strategy

In addition to analyzing psychological, emotional experiential strategies, behavioral experiential strategies and user experience models in the post-COVID-19 era, the core of user experience, empathy, technology, accurate information and whole-body interactive experience are also considered contents for the construction of potential usability design strategies. The core of user experience design is user-centered, which is a combination of ethnography, user observation, and information design [78]. User-centered design should start from grasping the needs of users and adopt a spiral design process to repeatedly evaluate and iterate to achieve the purpose of improving user experience [79].

In addition, understanding how to empathize with and create good interactions with users can not only improve the superficial experience, but also have the potential to profoundly influence users' attitudes and behaviors, in which technology is an important medium for understanding how digital experience affects user perception in the context of the COVID-19 [80]. Tucker and Ferson [81] believe that providing accurate information can better help people solve complex problems more easily and effectively. Therefore, in the post-COVID-19 era of uncertainty, fear and isolation, accurate information can become the glue that holds society together and pushes the community forward [80]. In the research of whole-body interactive experience, Carreras and Parés [82] believe that through user behavior, perception and reflection on the results of their behavior, a five-level framework based on concepts, symbols, semantics, user attitudes and user behavior can be established, so as to enable teenagers and children to have a unique whole-body interaction experience process.

Based on the analysis of the above contents, this paper starts from the problem of user experience changes under the background of COVID-19 to find the source of the event. By summarizing the corresponding countermeasures of psychological, emotional experience and behavioral experience, the potential usability strategy of user experience in the post-COVID-19 era is derived, as shown in Fig. 4.

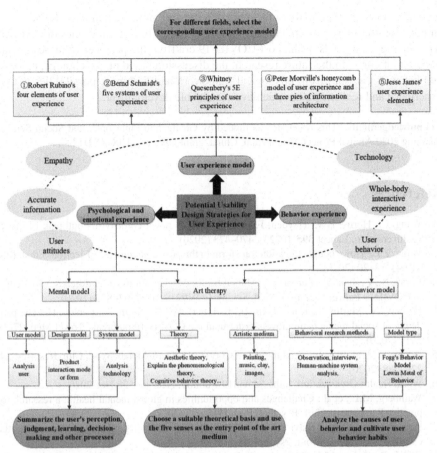

Fig. 4. Potential usability strategy framework for user experience in the post-COVID-19 era (devised by the authors based on the summary)

4   Conclusion

Based on the review of relevant literature, this paper summarized the changes of fear, trauma, stress, anxiety and depression in the psychological health and emotional performance of the public under the background of the COVID-19. Behavior habits will change based on prevention and control measures, such as frequent hand washing, wearing masks and maintaining social distance. The aspects of the user experience will change with psychological, emotional and behavioral changes in areas as diverse as telemedicine, airline services, and online education. Then, by analyzing the causal relationship between user experience changes, this paper proposes the design strategies of mental model and art therapy for psychological and emotional experience. The design strategies of behavioral model and art therapy are proposed for behavioral experience. In view of the changes of user experience, user experience models in different fields are proposed. Finally, by summarizing the corresponding countermeasures and relevant literature, this paper summarizes the logical framework of the potential usability design strategy for user experience in the post-COVID-19 era. This logical framework can deal with the practical needs of the post-COVID-19 era from the perspective of design and 'creation of cure'. In the future research, the discussion based on psychology, emotion and behavior can start from this logical framework and find more possibilities in user experience and realistic paths to achieve sustainable development.

Acknowledgements. This research was funded by Guangzhou Philosophy and Social Science Planning 2020 Annual Project, Guangzhou, China, grant number 2020GZYB12.

References

1. Wang, C., Horby, P.W., Hayden, F.G., Gao, G.F.: A novel coronavirus outbreak of global health concern. Lancet **395**(10223), 470–473 (2020)
2. Wang, Z.L.: How should education transform in the post-epidemic era? Electron. Educ. Res. **41**(04), 13–20 (2020)
3. Imran, N., Zeshan, M., Pervaiz, Z.: Mental health considerations for children & adolescents in COVID19 Pandemic. Pak. J. Med. Sci. **36**(COVID19–S4), S67–S72 (2020)
4. Depoux, A., Martin, S., Karafillakis, E., Bsd, R.P., Wilder-Smith, A., Larson, H.: The pandemic of social media panic travels faster than the COVID-19 outbreak. Travel Med. **27**(3), 1–11 (2020)
5. Dubey, S., et al.: Psychosocial impact of COVID-19. Diab. Metab. Synd. Clin. Res. Rev. **14**, 779–788 (2020)
6. World Health Organization. https://covid19.who.int/. Accessed 26 Dec 2020
7. Wainberg, M.L., et al.: Challenges and opportunities in global mental health: a research-to-practice Perspective. Curr. Psychiat. Rep. **19**(5), 28 (2017)
8. Pera, A.: Cognitive, behavioral, and emotional disorders in populations affected by the COVID-19 outbreak. Front. Psychol. **11**, 1–6 (2020)
9. Ghosh, R., Dubey, M.J., Chatterjee, S., Dubey, S.: Impact of COVID-19 on children: special focus on psychosocial aspect. Minerva Pediatr. **72**(3), 226–235 (2020)
10. Spinelli, M., Lionetti, F., Setti, A., Fasolo, M.: Parenting stress during the COVID-19 outbreak: socioeconomic and environmental risk factors and implications for children emotion regulation. In: Family Process, pp. 1–15 (2020). [published online ahead of print, 2020 Sep 28]
11. Ren, F.F., Guo, R.J.: Public mental health in post-Covid-19 era. Psychiatr. Danubina **32**(2), 251–255 (2020)
12. Healey, M.L., Grossman, M.: Cognitive and affective perspective-taking: evidence for shared and dissociable anatomical substrates. Front. Neurol. **9**, 1–8 (2018)
13. Preston, S.D., de Waal, F.B.M.: Empathy: its ultimate and proximate bases. Behav. Brain Sci. **25**(1), 1–20 (2002)
14. Depoux, A., Martin, S., Karafillakis, E., Preet, R., Wilder-Smith, A., Larson, H.: The pandemic of social media panic travels faster than the COVID-19 outbreak. J. Travel Med. **27**(3), 1–2 (2020)
15. Kramer, A.D.I., Guillory, J.E., Hancock, J.T.: Experimental evidence of massive-scale emotional contagion through social networks. Proc. Natl. Acad. Sci. USA **111**(24), 8788–8790 (2014)
16. World Health Organization. https://www.who.int/emergencies/diseases/novel-coronavirus-2019/advice-for-public. Accessed 28 Dec 2020

17. Wang, C., Horby, P.W., Hayden, F.G., Gao, G.F.: A novel coronavirus outbreak of global health concern. Lancet **395**(10223), 470–473 (2020)
18. Ferguson, N.M., Laydon, D., Nedjati-gilani, G., et al.: Impact of non- pharmaceutical interventions (NPIs) to reduce COVID- 19 mortality and healthcare demand. Imperial Coll. London, 1–20 (2020)
19. Manikandan, N.: Are social distancing, hand washing and wearing masks appropriate measures to mitigate transmission of COVID-19? Vacunas **21**(2), 136–137 (2020)
20. Centers for Disease Control and Prevention Homepage. https://www.cdc.gov/coronavirus/2019-ncov/your-health/need-to-know.html. Accessed 28 Dec 2020
21. Abtahi-Naeini, B.: Frequent handwashing amidst the COVID-19 outbreak: prevention of hand irritant contact dermatitis and other considerations. Health Sci. Rep. **3**(2), (2020)
22. Teo, S.S.S., Griffiths, G.: Child protection in the time of COVID-19. Paediatr. Child Health **56**(6), 838–840 (2020)
23. Jiao, W.Y., Wang, L.N., Liu, J., Fang, S.F., Jiao, F.Y., Pettoello-Mantovani, M., Somekh, E.: Behavioral and emotional disorders in children during the COVID-19 epidemic. J. Pediatr. **221**, 264–266.e1 (2020)
24. Ryu, W.H.A., Kerolus, M.G., Traynelis, V.C.: Clinicians' User Experience of Telemedicine in Neurosurgery During COVID-19. World Neurosurgery, E1–E9 (2020)
25. Vandekerckhove, P., Vandekerckhove, Y., Tavernier, R., de Jaegher, K., de Mul, M.: Leveraging user experience to improve video consultations in a cardiology practice during the COVID-19 pandemic: initial insights. J. Med. Internet Res. **22**(6), (2020)
26. Tuchen, S., Arora, M., Blessing, L.: Airport user experience unpacked: conceptualizing its potential in the face of COVID-19. J. Air Transp. Manage. **89**, (2020)
27. Chen, T.G., Peng, L.J., Jing, B.L., Wu, C.Y., Yang, J.J., Cong, G.D.: The impact of the COVID-19 pandemic on user experience with online education platforms in China. Sustainability **12**(18), 1–31 (2020)
28. Leon, M., Rodas, K., Greer, M.: Leisure behind bars: the realities of COVID-19 for youth connected to the justice system. Leisure Sci. **4**, 1–7 (2020)
29. Ma, X., Wang, X.: The role of empathy in the mechanism linking parental psychological control to emotional reactivities to COVID-19 pandemic: a pilot study among Chinese emerging adults. Pers. Indiv. Diff. **168**, (2021)
30. Schreiter, S., Pijnenborg, G.H.M., Rot, M.: Empathy in adults with clinical or subclinical depressive symptoms. J. Affect. Disord. **150**(1), 1–16 (2013)
31. Lei, T., Liu, X., Wu, L., Jin, Z., Wang, Y., Wei, S.: The influence of matching degree of the user's inherent mental model and the product's embedded mental model on the mobile user experience. In: Kurosu, M. (ed.) HCI 2016. LNCS, vol. 9732, pp. 320–329. Springer, Cham (2016). https://doi.org/10.1007/978-3-319-39516-6_31
32. Brata, K.C., Brata, A.H.: User experience improvement of Japanese language mobile learning application through mental model and A/B testing. Int. J. Electr. Comput. Eng. (IJECE) **10**(3), 2659–2667 (2020)
33. Zhang, L.F., Xu, K., Zhang, J.S.: Analyzing usability of cookers interface based on the user mental model. In: Liu, H., Yang, Y., Shen, S., Zhong, Z., Zheng, L., Feng, P. (eds.) 2nd International Conference on Applied Mechanics, Materials and Manufacturing (ICAMMM 2012), vol. 268–270, pp. 1958–1961. Trans Tech Publications Ltd., Laublsrutistr (2012)
34. Craik, K.: The Nature of Explanation, 1st edn. Cambridge University Press, Cambridge (1943)
35. Gary, M.S., Wood, R.E.: Unpacking mental models through laboratory experiments. Syst. Dyn. Rev. **32**(2), 99–127 (2016)
36. Cárdenas-Figueroa, A., Navarro, A.O.: Overview of mental models research using bibliometric indicators. Cogn. Process. **21**, 155–165 (2020)
37. Holyoak, K.J., Cheng, P.W.: Causal learning and inference as a rational process: the new synthesis. Ann. Rev. Psychol. **62**, 135–163 (2011)

38. Tenner, E.: The design of everyday things by Donald Norman (review). Technol. Cult. **56**(3), 785–787 (2015)
39. Norman, D.A.: Design principles for cognitive artifacts. Res. Eng. Des. **4**(1), 43–50 (1992)
40. Halford, G.S.: Children's Understanding: The Development of Mental Models, 1st edn. Psychology Press, London (1993)
41. Denzan, A.T., North, D.C.: Shared mental models: ideologies and institutions. Kyklos **47**(1), 3–31 (1994)
42. Roy, R.K., Denzau, A.T.: Shared mental models: insights and perspectives on ideologies and institutions. Kyklos **73**(3), 323–340 (2020)
43. Levy, B.: Art therapy in a women's correctional facility. Art Psychother. **5**, 157–166 (1978)
44. Stanley, P., Miller, M.M.: Short-term art therapy with an adolescent male. Arts Psychother. **20**, 397–402 (1993)
45. Kometiani, M.K., Farmer, K.W.: Exploring resilience through case studies of art therapy with sex trafficking survivors and their advocates. Arts Psychother. **67**, (2020)
46. Henley, D.R.: Aesthetics in art therapy: theory into practice. Arts Psychother. **19**, 153–161 (1992)
47. Papagiannaki, A., Shinebourne, P.: The contribution of creative art therapies to promoting mental health: using Iinterpretative phenomenological analysis to study therapists' understandings of working with self-stigmatisation. Arts Psychother. **50**, 66–74 (2016)
48. Sarid, O., Huss, E.: Trauma and acute stress disorder: A comparison between cognitive behavioral intervention and art therapy. Arts Psychother. **37**, 8–12 (2010)
49. Khadar, M.G., Babapour, J., Sabourimoghaddam, H.: The effect of art therapy based on painting therapy in reducing symptoms of separation anxiety disorder (SAD) in elementary School Boys. Procedia Soc. Behav. Sci. **84**, 1697–1703 (2013)
50. Register, D.M., Hilliard, R.E.: Using Orff-based techniques in children's bereavement groups: a cognitive-behavioral music therapy approach. Arts Psychother. **35**, 162–170 (2008)
51. Jang, H., Choi, S.: Increasing ego-resilience using clay with low SES (Social Economic Status) adolescents in group art therapy. Arts Psychother. **39**, 245–250 (2012)
52. Moon, C.: Art therapy: creating the space we will live in. Arts Psychother. **24**, 45–49 (1997)
53. Shella, T.A.: Art therapy improves mood, and reduces pain and anxiety when offered at bedside during acute hospital treatment. Arts Psychother. **57**, 59–64 (2018)
54. Kometiani, M.K.: Creating a vital healing community: A pilot study of an art therapy employee support group at a pediatric hospital. Arts Psychother. **54**, 122–127 (2017)
55. Gwinner, K.: Arts, therapy, and health: Three stakeholder viewpoints related to young people's mental health and wellbeing in Australia. Arts Psychother. **50**, 9–16 (2016)
56. Yang, R., Xiao, D.H.: Research on user behavior based on user experience. Art Des. (Theory) **04**, 90–92 (2007)
57. Shaker, N., Asteriadis, S., Yannakakis, G.N., Karpouzis, K.: Fusing visual and behavioral cues for modeling user experience in games. IEEE Trans. Cybern. **43**(6), 1519–1531 (2013)
58. Baer, R.: mindfulness training as a clinical intervention: a conceptual and empirical review. Clin. Psychol. Sci. Pract. **10**(2), 125–143 (2003)
59. Fogg Behavior Model Homepage. http://www.behaviormodel.org/. Accessed 30 Dec 2020
60. Wang, Y.H.: Research on mobile social product design based on Fogg behavior model. Technol. Innov. Appl. (08), 5–6+9 (2018)
61. Ferebee, S.S.: Successful persuasive technology for behavior reduction: mapping to Fogg's gray behavior grid. In: Ploug, T., Hasle, P., Oinas-Kukkonen, H. (eds.) PERSUASIVE 2010. LNCS, vol. 6137, pp. 70–81. Springer, Heidelberg (2010). https://doi.org/10.1007/978-3-642-13226-1_9
62. Fogg, B.J.: A behavior model for persuasive design. In: Proceedings of the 4th International Conference on Persuasive Technology (Persuasive 2009), pp. 1–7. Association for Computing Machinery, New York (2009)

63. Fogg, B.J.: The behavior grid: 35 ways behavior can change. In: Proceedings of the 4th International Conference on Persuasive Technology (Persuasive 2009), pp. 1–5. Association for Computing Machinery, New York (2009)

64. Fogg, B.J.: Persuasive Technology: Using Computers to Change What We Think and Do, 1st edn. Morgan Kaufmann, San Francisco (2003)

65. Lewin, K., Zhu P.L.: Principles of Topological Psychology. 1st edn. Peking University Press, Beijing (2011)

66. Luo, W., Sun, L.S., Wang, S.C., Rong, J.: Travel choice of car-sharing based on Lewin metal of behavior. J. Beij. Univ. Technol. **45**(5), 476–484 (2019)

67. Wu, Z.L., Liu, Z.S.: A study on college students' consumption behavior based on Lewin model. Chin. Collect. Econ. **10**, 101–102 (2012)

68. Wang, Y., Li, S.P., Xie, K.N.: Study on the influencing factors of household waste classification behavior based on Lewin behavior model. Ecol. Econ. **36**(01), 186–190+204 (2020)

69. Moore, R.W.: Art therapy with substance abusers: a review of the literature. Arts Psychother. **10**, 251–260 (1983)

70. Alavinezhad, R., Mousavi, M., Sohrabi, N.: Effects of art therapy on anger and self-esteem in aggressive children. Procedia Soc. Behav. Sci. **113**, 111–117 (2014)

71. Cortina, M.A., Fazel, M.: The art room: an evaluation of a targeted school-based group intervention for students with emotional and behavioural difficulties. Arts Psychother. **42**, 35–40 (2015)

72. Megranahan, K., Lynskey, M.T.: Do creative arts therapies reduce substance misuse? A systematic review. Arts Psychother. **57**, 50–58 (2018)

73. Sitepoint. https://www.sitepoint.com/quantify-user-experience/. Accessed 30 Dec 2020

74. Schmitt, B.H., Liu, Y., Gao, J., Liang, L.J.: Experiential Marketing. 1nd edn. Tsinghua University Press, Beijing (2004)

75. Quesenbery, W.: Balancing the 5Es of usability. Cutter IT J. **17**(2), 4–11 (2004)

76. Peter, M., Louis, R.: Information Architecture for the World Wide Web: Designing Large-Scale Web Sites, 3rd edn. O'Reilly Media, Sevastopol (2006)

77. Jesse, J.G.: The Elements of User Experience: User-Centered Design for the Web and Beyond, 2nd edn. New Riders Press, Berkeley (2010)

78. Gulliksen, J., Goransson, B., Boivie, I., Blomkvist, S., Persson, J., Cajander, A.: Key principles for user-centred systems design. Behav. Inf. Technol. **22**(6), 397–409 (2003)

79. Tarumoto, T., Chen, X.: User Experience and Usability Testing. 1st edn. People's Posts and Telecommunications Press, Beijing (2015)

80. Ponnada, S.: Reimagining the COVID-19 digital experience: the value of user empowerment and accessibility in risk communication. In: Walwema, J.; Hocutt, D.; Pigg, S. (eds.) SIGDOC 2020: 38th ACM International Conference on Design of Communication, pp. 54 (3 pp.). ACM, New York (2020)

81. Tucker, W.T., Ferson, S.: Strategies for risk communication: evolution, evidence, experience. Ann. New York Acad. Sci. **1128**, 1–137 (2008)

82. Carreras, A., Parés, N.: Designing an interactive installation for children to experience abstract concepts. In: Macías, J., Granollers, S.A., Latorre, P. (eds.) New Trends on Human–Computer Interaction, pp. 33–42. Springer, London (2009). https://doi.org/10.1007/978-1-84882-352-5_4

DUXU Case Studies

Improving the Withdrawal Functionality on ATM Using a UCD Framework. A Case Study

Joel Aguirre[1]($\boxtimes$) , Fiorella Falconi[1] , Rodrigo Serrano[2] ,
Arturo Moquillaza[1] , and Freddy Paz[1]

[1] Pontificia Universidad Católica del Perú, Lima32, Lima, Peru
{aguirre.joel,ffalconit}@pucp.edu.pe
{amoquillaza,fpaz}@pucp.pe
[2] SANMS Servicios de Ingeniería, Lima27, Lima, Peru

Abstract. Nowadays, the use of electronic payment methods has increased due to the COVID-19 pandemic. The use of cash has been limited to reduce interactions; however, in developing countries, there is still a strong necessity for this type of payment. The ATM is the only channel where people can get cash without interacting with someone else. In order to improve the experience of the clients in the ATM channel we designed a set of interfaces that allow clients to select the denomination of the bills they want to get for the intended withdrawal amount. In this case of study, we followed a design framework for ATM to propose a usable design for this new functionality. The framework allowed the team to execute the phases of a complete design process that is specific to ATM. After two iterations, the interfaces were approved. This solution showed promising results despite the fact of the completely virtual context.

Keywords: Heuristic evaluation · Design framework · Software design · Banking systems · Automated teller machine · User-centered design · Human-computer interaction

1 Introduction

Nowadays, the use of electronic payment methods has increased due to the COVID-19 pandemic [1]. The restrictions and social distancing have promoted even more the rising of e-commerce and digital transformation. This situation spreads rapidly to different sectors including the financial one [2].

In developing countries, bank branches are part of the daily life of most of the population. Even though people are transitioning to electronic payment methods, most transactions are still done at the bank branches and in cash [3]. This constitutes a tough challenge for developing countries in the attempt to control the current pandemic [2].

© Springer Nature Switzerland AG 2021
M. M. Soares et al. (Eds.): HCII 2021, LNCS 12780, pp. 565–580, 2021.
https://doi.org/10.1007/978-3-030-78224-5_39

In this sense, ATMs (Automated Teller Machine) represent relief for the bank branches [4] due to ubiquity [5]. As a self-service technology, an ATM reduces the interaction between people [6].

In recent months, the coronavirus has pushed customer transition to digital banking channels with an urgency that years of marketing couldn't accomplish [7]. ATM's are not just simple cash dispensers, they have become complex computers capable of doing more operations [8], they are now marketing tools; usability problems could affect the institutional image [9].

However, the processes involved in the development and testing of the ATM applications require an environment where physical interactions might be mandatory to get the best results possible. There are few tools specific to the ATM domain that help developers and designers to obtain usable interactive interfaces, one of these is the User-Centered Design Framework for the Design of Usable ATM Interfaces proposed by Aguirre et al. [10].

In previous studies, the authors have empirically demonstrated the utility of the framework previously mentioned. As the first example, a case study where the deposit functionality was improved following the simple process [10]. In this case, the process included methods such as Interviews, User Testing, and Field Observations. A second study on the use of a fast process to design a new functionality for the ATM [11]. This case still included methods that required physical interaction such as User Testing.

In this time, the context has changed dramatically, but the proposed framework includes a set of tools that are the optimal ones. The optimal process includes methods that are fast and simple to execute and also imply a low-cost for the project [10].

In this case study, we got the challenge to improve the withdrawal functionality. We followed the three phases specified in the framework: Analysis of context of use, User Requirements Specification, and Design and Evaluation of Interfaces. For each phase, we encourage the adoption of tools that help to complete the process with fewer face-to-face interactions in a virtual environment.

In the first phase, we used the verbatim analysis to know the experience of the final users, where we found pain-points directed to the withdrawal operation and the denominations of the bills available to the users. People desired to reduce the interaction in the transactions they made right after they leave the ATM. This means to get exact denominations at the withdrawals.

In the second phase, the method of Persona and Scenario of Use was supported with the application of the Analysis of the Competitor. Most banks have their functionalities and screens as public information, which allows us to apply the analysis without actually interacting with the competitor ATM.

In the third phase, some existing web tools helped the execution of the design of prototypes. After the design, the evaluation of the interfaces started with a virtual meeting with ATM domain experts, they identified some problems that allowed a second iteration to begin. In the second evaluation, we followed a Heuristic Evaluation process with aid of Usability experts that concludes with an approval result. The final proposal would improve the withdrawal functionality with a bill selection option.

As conclusions of this case study, in the first place, we found that this framework was able to successfully adapt to a virtual environment. In the second place, according to the client feedback, the proposal got an acceptable level of usability, and in the last place, we found the necessity of more virtual tools that help to cover the complete design process or, at least, some phases of the framework. For example, an automated software tool would help to assess the usability of the interfaces without face-to-face interaction, a condition that seems to persist in the upcoming years.

The article is divided as follows. The second section would detail the framework used and methods employed in each phase of the process. The third section would describe the case study and the details of the execution of each phase. And finally, the fourth section and fifth section show the results of the case study and the conclusions of the study.

2   User-Centered Design Framework

In the literature, the design frameworks or processes are focused on web and mobile interfaces. This is due to the increasing number of people using these technologies. However, in developing countries, the adoption of these technologies is not a generalized situation.

ATMs are one kind of self-service technology that allows people to get money in cash. These self-services are still in use, and because of their ubiquitous characteristic, still represent an important technology in peoples' daily life. In that sense, Aguirre et al. [10] proposed a framework for the design of usable ATM interfaces.

This framework consists of three phases or steps. According to the standard ISO 13047 [12] and ISO 9241 [13], this ATM design framework proposed these phases: Analyzing the context of use, Specification of user requirements, and Design and Evaluation (see Fig. 1).

This framework proposes a catalog of methods for each phase and, depending on the context of the project, these methods could be combined in a Simple Process, a Fast Process, and a Low Cost process. In previous studies, the fast methods and the simple methods were used [10,11], showing excellent results. In this study, due to the pandemic context, we had to use the optimal process, which proposed the methods that are simple, fast and low-cost. This process is ideal for virtual activities and to reduce interaction between the participants. Figure 2 shows the optimal methods as a process.

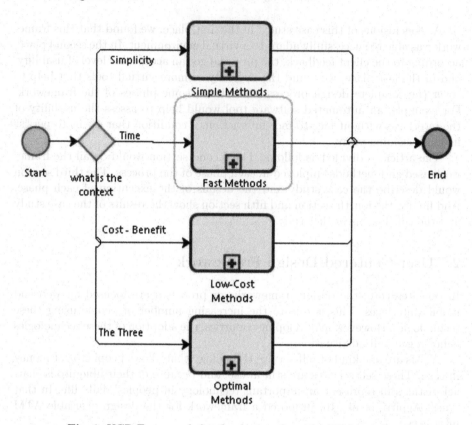

Fig. 1. UCD Framework for the design of usable ATM interfaces

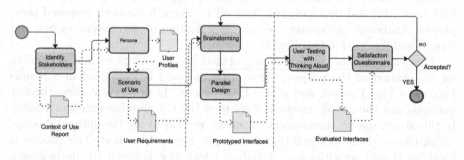

Fig. 2. Optimal UCD Framework for ATM Interfaces

2.1 Methods

According to the proposed framework, the optimal methods are detailed in the Table 1.

Table 1. Optimal methods for the design of usable ATM interfaces.

Phase	Method
Context	Identify Stakeholders
Requirements	Scenarios of use
	Persona
Design	Parallel design
	Brainstorming
Evaluation	User testing
	Satisfaction questionnaire

However, the real context of covid-19 forced us to exchange some methods such as 'User Testing' due to the gathering restrictions. The final set of methods employed is shown in the Table 2.

Table 2. Selected methods for the design of Bill Selection. interfaces.

Phase	Method
Context	Survey of existing users
Requirements	Scenarios of use
	Persona
Design	Software prototyping
	Brainstorming
Evaluation	Expert judgement
	Heuristic evaluation

3   Selection Bills Denominations in an ATM Withdrawal: A Case Study

This section describes how we employed the methods proposed in the ATM Framework used. The process focuses on the withdrawal functionality, the most used by final users. The context of the covid-19 pandemic forced the team to adapt the process to the new social restrictions.

3.1   Purpose of Study

The purpose of this study was to improve the interfaces of the withdrawal functionality, usability, and user experience. To achieve the goal, we employed a User-Centered Design Framework, specific to the ATM domain, for the design of the ATM withdrawal interfaces.

In collaboration with the ATM development team from one of the leading banks in Perú, we were required to propose a way for improving the withdrawal functionality, taking into consideration the whole pandemic context.

3.2   Methodology

The case was carried out following the process illustrated in Fig. 2. Furthermore, this process was executed in October, 2020, during the pandemic.

3.3   Analyzing the Context of Use

In this phase, it was necessary to understand the withdrawal context and how it has been changing through the pandemic. Due to the restrictions, we had to use different tools to gather enough and valuable information to understand how the context was going.

Survey of Existing Users. In order to obtain information from real customer, Moquillaza et al. [14] employed Verbatim Quotation. During the pandemic, the quality control division of the Bank continued addressing their customers' surveys to fulfill.

From these surveys, the verbatim is obtained as spontaneous opinions. The team detected that final users are complaining about the available bill denominations. It was stated that the bills combination the ATM made not always meets the requirements of the user.

In the pandemic context, people are hoarding money to feel safe and comfortable [7]. In many cases, the cash came from government benefits and support programs [7]. In the verbatim, the team also found that in the last year the queues in front of the ATM increased in size because users had to perform more than one withdrawal to obtain the combination of bills they desired. This directly affects the user experience.

3.4   Specifying the User Requirements

Competitor Analysis. For the competitor analysis, we went through the interfaces of the top three local competitors and found out that none of them had the option to select bills. In that sense, we had to research on competitors from other countries, such as Bank of America, Numerica Credit Union, and Chase. We found solutions where we could identify the number of screens involved in the functionality, if it is mandatory for the user, and if the functionality was placed before the withdrawal amount selection or after.

Due to the lack of local competitors, we took into consideration the one screen solution all the foreign competitors have. However, regarding the currencies, in Perú there are two that circulate and that the ATMs could dispense: the local currency 'Nuevos Soles' and US Dollars.

Table 3 shows the results of the analysis, giving an easy-to-read comparison between the competitors.

Table 3. Competitor analysis - comparison.

	National banks			Foreign banks		
	BCP	Scotiabank	Interbank	BoA	Numerica	Chase
Has bil selection?	NO	NO	NO	YES	YES	YES
Mandatory?	–	–	–	YES	YES	YES
Screens	–	–	–	1	1	1
Input before amount?	–	–	–	YES	YES	YES
Number of denominations?	–	–	–	3	3	3
Currency?	–	–	–	Dollars	Dollars	Dollars

Personas. For this method, we elaborated two typical user profiles to describe the final user that would interact with the functionality. First, Roberto Campos, who is presented in Fig. 3. And a female, Carla Sanchez, presented in Fig. 4.

In both profiles, we describe the values, goals, challenges, and frustration the person had. Also, it was necessary to describe their professional background, since a lot of people with different levels of education use ATMs. Their personal preferences were described, identifying their interests and needs, which motivated them into using the withdrawal functionality.

Scenarios of Use. After detailing the Persona, it was necessary to elaborate their scenarios of use. In both cases, the Personas wanted to withdraw specific amounts that caused a bad experience due to the combination of denominations. After that, the user requirements were specified and are shown in Table 4.

Table 4. Specified user requirements.

Requirement	Description
REQ01	The solution must be one-screen
REQ02	The solution must handle the two currencies
REQ03	The solution must not complicate the existing flow
REQ04	The solution must allow the user to select the desired amount of bill
REQ05	The solution must work on only buttons ATMs and touchscreen ATMs in a similar way
REQ06	The solution must inform the ATM limitations to the client
REQ07	The denominations must be the same available in the ATM

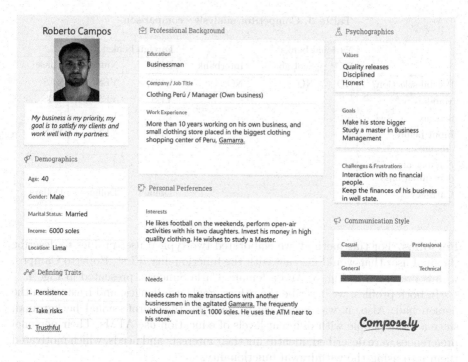

Fig. 3. Persona 1 - Roberto Campos

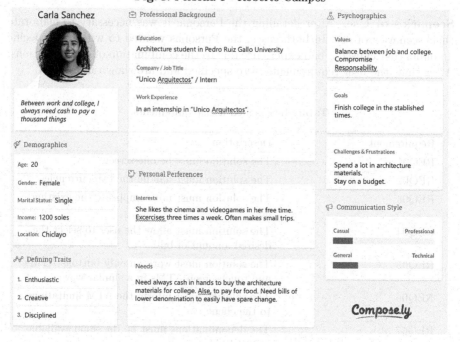

Fig. 4. Persona 2 - Carla Sanchez

3.5 Designing and Evaluating the Interfaces

Brainstorming. For the brainstorming session, we used a tool that helps us to carry it out virtually. This kind of web application already existed before the pandemic, but it was in this context when we really needed it the most. The brainstorming session was held through a video call. Everybody could give their opinion, and the application helps to have a more fluid session. In Fig. 5, we show how the virtual brainstorming session was held.

Software Prototyping. Based on the input given at the brainstorming and the wireframes proposed, we proceed to implement interactive prototypes. For that purpose, we used another web app, such as MarvelApp, that allowed us to easily prototype the high fidelity designs. These web apps have a share feature that facilitates the distribution of the prototypes to the evaluators. Also, the fact that the interactive prototypes were made in a web application meant that the evaluator won't have trouble opening them in their browser while evaluating remotely. Figure 6 shows one screen of the bill denomination functionality and Fig. 7 shows how to access the functionality, both screens are high fidelity prototypes.

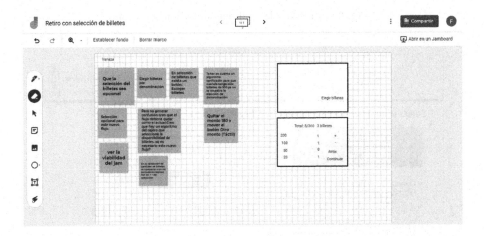

Fig. 5. Virtual brainstorming session

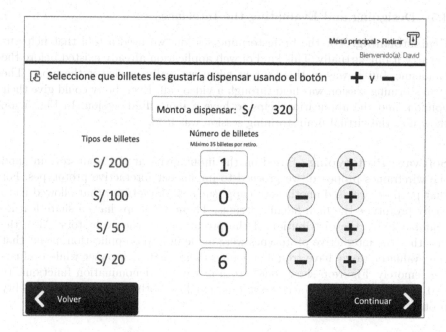

Fig. 6. Prototype for bill denomination selection

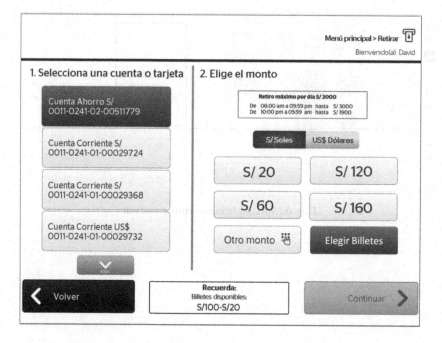

Fig. 7. Prototype for the selection of the new functionality

Expert Judgement. To carry out this evaluation method, we gathered again virtually through a video call with ATM domain experts. The experts that participated were part of the ATM Development team and the Reliability team. They could test the interactive prototypes through the web app employed and, after a few interactions, they gave their judgments by turns.

As a result, the experts identified problems with the designed proposal. For instance, the buttons to continue and to return should not be aligned with the plus and minus buttons. Also, to enter high numbers, the user must touch the plus button several times, and if he wanted to change it, it was impossible to correct it. The proposal was subject to a second evaluation through Heuristic Evaluation.

Heuristic Evaluation. This second evaluation followed the protocol proposed by Paz et al. [15] for Usability Heuristic Evaluations. This protocol consists of five phases: (1) planning, (2) training, (3) evaluation, (4) discussion, and (5) report. The protocol is illustrated in Fig. 8.

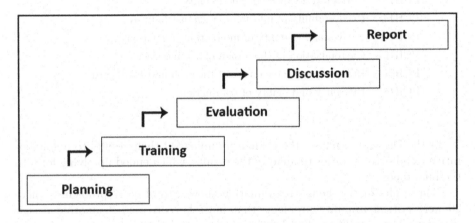

Fig. 8. Protocol to conduct heuristic evaluations proposed by Paz et al.

For the planning phase, first, we selected the evaluators who were part of the HCI-DUXAIT research group from PUCP, Perú. The heurístics to be employed in the evaluation were the Usability Heuristics for ATMs that Chanco et al. [16] proposed. The specific heuristics for ATM are listed in Table 5.

The Training phase was not necessary because the evaluation team had expertise performing heuristic evaluations. The Discussion and Report phases were held via video call.

For the Evaluation phase, we contacted each evaluator vía email and sent them the system prototype to be evaluated and gave them more than one week to perform the evaluation. Each evaluator had to test the prototypes, find usability problems, and associate them with the heuristics for ATM, classifying the problems by severity in a scale from 0 to 4.

Table 5. Usability Heuristics for ATM.

Heuristic	Description
PCH01	Visibility of system status
PCH02	Visibility of the progress and final status of the transaction
PCH03	Visibility and clarity of the relevant elements of the system
PCH04	Match between system and the real world
PCH05	User control and freedom
PCH06	Consistency between the elements of the system
PCH07	Error prevention
PCH08	Recognition rather than recall
PCH09	Adaptability of the functionalities to the user profile
PCH10	Aesthetic and minimalist design
PCH11	Help users recognize, diagnose, and recover from errors
PCH12	Appropriate session time distribution to display content
PCH13	Correct and expected functionality
PCH14	Recoverability of information against failures
PCH15	Early-stage visibility of interaction restrictions
PCH16	Customization in the design of the interface
PCH17	Prevention of the capture of the cash and bank card
PCH18	Efficiency and agility of transactions

In the Discussion phase, the evaluators uploaded their results to a collaborative cloud drive in order to analyze the results, which ended up giving form to the final report.

The results of this heuristic evaluation show a total of 47 problems, where 26 were critical usability problems that must be corrected in another design iteration. These problems had heuristics associated that helped the evaluators to identify the usability problem. The most associated heuristic was PCH06 (15.6%), followed by PCH07 (14.5%), and PCH18 (10.84%).

The problems were solved in a new iteration. The heuristic PCH06 refers to the consistency between elements of the screen. The proposal used different styles of buttons and labels were misused with textboxes. The proposal also did not prevent the user from falling into error, identified with PCH07. Also, the use of the Plus and Minus takes too much time, a problem identified with PCH18.

4   Final Results

Finally, to approve the interfaces, we had to solve the problems with severity 3 and 4. Figure 9 shows the one screen solution in a high fidelity interactive prototype for the bill selection.

To access the new functionality, the user must select first the corresponding button in the amount selection screen, and then press Continue. This way, we give the user control to change the decision to another amount. This screen is shown in Fig. 10.

To meet the user requirements, we show messages explaining the maximum quantity of bills that the ATM could dispense. Also, if the ATM has only one denomination available, the new functionality would be turned-off because of the lack of possible combinations.

After a final meeting, we discuss the final proposal with the evaluators to confirm that the problems with severity 3 and 4 were solved. With this done, the proposal met the required usability level to be approved.

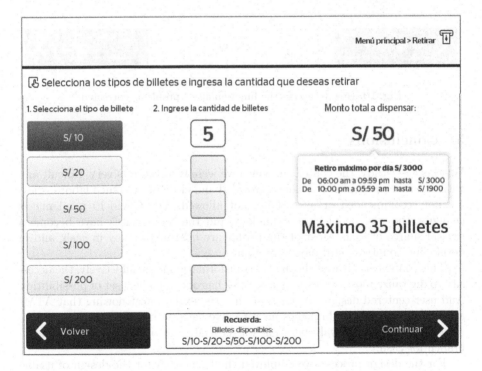

Fig. 9. The final proposal for a one-screen bill selection solution

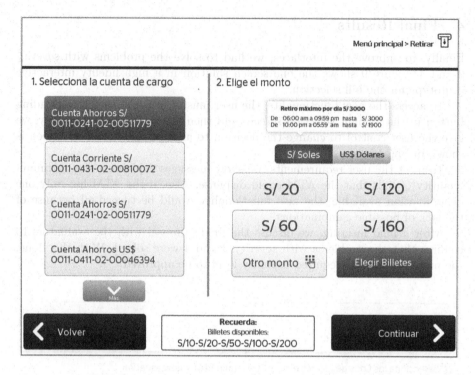

Fig. 10. How to access the functionality - problems corrected

5 Conclusions

For this case study, the context in which we were involved was very difficult and with several constraints. For safety, crowded and close places (such laboratories) are not recommended or even more, not allowed. The Covid-19 pandemic is changing the way people use technology and the self services have become a critical source of cash. Most of the people are hoarding money in cash, and in developing countries, still paying in cash.

This context motivated the digital transformation more effectively, the necessity to digitalize most of the daily activities has opened a new set of possibilities. And user-centered design processes are not the exception. Knowing that ATMs are the only way bank branches have to give cash without human interaction, improving the withdrawal operation was crucial to avoid people going into the branch for cash.

For the design process, we employed the framework for the design of usable ATM interfaces proposed by Aguirre following the optimal process. This process allowed us to employ methods that could be held in virtual sessions. The use of web applications was mandatory to achieve the completion of the process.

The evaluation of interfaces seemed a difficult task, since User Testing in the ATM domain regularly required the user interacting with a real ATM and was held typically at the ATM laboratory. We decided to evaluate the interfaces with Expert Judgment and a Heuristic Evaluation, since the latter should be complemented with another evaluation method. With the Heuristic Evaluation, we could evidence usability problems that affect the user experience in a high severity instead of only the appearance.

The use of virtual web applications helped to hold virtual sessions for Brainstorming, phases of the Heuristic Evaluation. The use of verbatim and data collected from other teams such as quality control divisions, helped us to obtain information of the context without running a real survey. This helped to overcome, in an easy and fast way, the pandemic constraints.

Finally, this process could be done virtually from start to end. Unfortunately, there is no web app or digital tool to perform the optimal process or any process of the ATM Framework. For future studies, we encourage the use of an application that helps to execute this or any other usability design process.

Acknowledgements. This case study was supported by the Human-Computer Interaction and Design of User Experience, Accessibility, and Innovation Technologies (HCI-DUXAIT PUCP) Research Group from PUCP in Lima, Perú. Also, we would like to acknowledge the support of the experts of the ATM domain, who contributed with their time and knowledge.

References

1. Hashem, T.N.: Examining the influence of COVID 19 pandemic in changing customers. Orientation towards e-shopping. Mod. Appl. Sci. **14**(8), 59 (2020). https://doi.org/10.5539/mas.v14n8p59
2. Agur, I., Peria, S.M., Rochon, C.: Digital financial services and the pandemic: opportunities and risks for emerging and developing economies. International Monetary Fund Special Issue on COVID-19, 1–13 (2020)
3. Hellmann, R.: In a mobile banking era, the ATM is more important than ever — ATM Marketplace. 11 June 2018. https://www.atmmarketplace.com/blogs/in-a-mobile-banking-era-the-atm-is-more-important-than-ever. Accessed Jan 2020
4. Mahmud, B., Islam, M.M., Naher, K.: Empirical study of the use of automated teller machine (ATM) among bank customers in Dhaka City, Bangladesh. Eur. J. Bus. Manage. **7**(1), 18–34 (2015)
5. Kaptelinin, V., Rizzo, A., Robertson, P., Rosenbaum, S.: Crafting user experience of self- service technologies. In: Proceedings of the 2014 Companion Publication on Designing Interactive Systems - DIS Companion 2014, pp. 199–202 (2014). https://doi.org/10.1145/2598784.2598798
6. Aguirre, J., Moquillaza, A., Paz, F.: Methodologies for the design of ATM interfaces: a systematic review. In: Ahram, T., Karwowski, W., Taiar, R. (eds.) IHSED 2018. AISC, vol. 876, pp. 256–262. Springer, Cham (2019). https://doi.org/10.1007/978-3-030-02053-8_39
7. Cluckey, S.: ATM & Self-service Softawer Trends, p. 49. Networld Media Group (2020)
8. Kamfiroozie, A., Ahmadzadeh, M.: Personalized ATMs: improve ATMs usability. In: Stephanidis, C. (ed.) HCI 2011. CCIS, vol. 173, pp. 161–166. Springer, Heidelberg (2011). https://doi.org/10.1007/978-3-642-22098-2_33

9. Camilli, M., Dibitonto, M., Vona, A., Medaglia, C.M., Di Nocera, F.: User-centered design approach for interactive kiosks: evaluation and redesign of an automatic teller machine. In: Proceedings of the 9th ACM SIGCHI Italian Chapter International Conference on Computer-Human Interaction: Facing Complexity, pp. 85–91. ACM, New York (2011). https://doi.org/10.1145/2037296.2037319

10. Aguirre, J., Moquillaza, A., Paz, F.: A user-centered framework for the design of usable ATM interfaces. In: Marcus, A., Wang, W. (eds.) HCII 2019. LNCS, vol. 11583, pp. 163–178. Springer, Cham (2019). https://doi.org/10.1007/978-3-030-23570-3_13

11. Aguirre, J., Benazar, S., Moquillaza, A.: Applying a UCD framework for ATM interfaces on the design of QR withdrawal: a case study. In: Marcus, A., Rosenzweig, E. (eds.) HCII 2020. LNCS, vol. 12202, pp. 3–19. Springer, Cham (2020). https://doi.org/10.1007/978-3-030-49757-6_1

12. International Standard: ISO 13407:1999. Human-centered design processes for interactive systems, Ergonomics of Human-System Interaction (1999)

13. International Standard: ISO 9241–210, Ergonomics of Human-System Interaction: Human-Centred Design for Interactive Systems. International Organization for Standardization, Suiza (2010)

14. Moquillaza, A., Falconi, F., Paz, F.: Redesigning a main menu ATM interface using a user-centered design approach aligned to design thinking: a case study (2019). https://doi.org/10.1007/978-3-030-23535-2_38

15. Paz, F., Paz, F., Pow-Sang, J., Collazos, C.: A formal protocol to conduct usability heuristic evaluations in the context of the software development process. Int. J. Eng. Technol. (UAE) **7**, 10–19 (2018). https://doi.org/10.14419/ijet.v7i2.28.12874

16. Chanco, C., Moquillaza, A., Paz, F.: Development and validation of usability heuristics for evaluation of interfaces in ATMs (2019). https://doi.org/10.1007/978-3-030-23535-2_1

Check-!n Toolkit for Capturing Guests' Momentary Experiences Without Disturbing Their Traveling

Jingrui An[✉], Yaliang Chuang, and Pengcheng An

Eindhoven University of Technology, Eindhoven 5612 AZ, The Netherlands
{j.an,y.chuang,p.an}@tue.nl

Abstract. In the experience economy, many companies invest tremendous resources and budgets in understanding customers' experiences and use the insights to design products or services that can make customers happy and satisfied. However, there is still a lack of further exploration of the details that influence consumers' experience of the journey, one important challenge is to capture and closely understand guests' momentary experience in each touch-point of their stay. These momentary experiences are details that cumulatively compose the whole experience of a guest's stay and imply rich design opportunities to improve the whole service. To tackle this challenge, we developed a low-threshold participatory toolkit 'Check-!n' for capturing customers' momentary experiences at the right moment in the right place based on the user sampling method. We used Airbnb as an example case to investigate this toolkit's usability and usefulness with six participants in 11 different Airbnb accommodations. The results show that the Check-!n toolkit is easy to use for capturing their momentary experience in the context. Moreover, the participants did not consider the toolkit to be interrupting their Airbnb experience. Conversely, the in-suit deliberations caused by the toolkit helped the participants to mindfully reflect on their underlying feelings at the sampling moments, which would otherwise go unspoken in the guest feedback. We demonstrate how the toolkit triggered the guest's momentary reflections in the Airbnb homes and their nuanced articulations in interviews. We therefore contribute a concrete case of sensitizing and capturing guests' experiences of Airbnb shared homes.

Keywords: Guest experience · Momentary · Airbnb shared home · Experience sampling toolkit

1 Introduction

In the Experience Economy [2], companies are striving to provide customers with great experiences that could delight the customers and maintain good impressions in customers' memories. Successful products and services are excellent in delivering unique experiences and engaging customers as loyal fans, such as Amazon Prime, Netflix, or Apple's iPod and iTunes store [13]. To create excellent experiences, designers and

© Springer Nature Switzerland AG 2021
M. M. Soares et al. (Eds.): HCII 2021, LNCS 12780, pp. 581–598, 2021.
https://doi.org/10.1007/978-3-030-78224-5_40

researchers used various research methods and techniques to understand users' behaviors, experiences, and perceptions, which all play a significant role in discovering and defining the right problems to be solved in experience design [14]. One such example is the journey map technique [25] which focuses on human experiences during a given period of time, where a sequence of interactions between the user and a service-product system takes place. Many entrepreneurs also used the journey map technique to envision the experiences they intend to deliver to the customers. For instance, Brian Chesky, the CEO and Co-Founder of Airbnb, used journey maps to analyze and define the experienceable process they want their customers to have with their services [43]. As a result, they illustrated the happy hosts and guests' journeys and used the comic-lick storyboards hang prominently in its headquarters to guide their product designs and developments.

However, in related research into Airbnb or similar shared accommodations, the journey map method was rarely applied to capture and evaluate users' authentic (or unfolding) experiences. In the majority of the studies, scholars often use analytic methods to examine guests' experience from their reviews posted on the platform, such as [7, 10, 39], or apply the post-hoc interview method, such as [8, 34]. The main critique of using those analytic is the in-congruence between the recalled and on-site experiences [34]. Because guests' experiences keep changing during their trips [32], some good experiences would be forgotten after the events that happened later [5]. Ultimately, when users tried to recall their experiences afterward, they might encounter the recall bias [33] or negative bias [22] rather than providing accurate information. Hence, the momentary experience needs to be captured on the spot to help us capture and study authentic, fine-grained guest experience.

In this research, we developed a research toolkit for capturing customers' experiences at the right time at the right place. Based on the experience sampling method [24], we created a paper-based folding card with various questions printed on different pages. The questions are phrased as prompts for users' momentary experiences. We named this toolkit "Check-!n" and in this paper, we use Airbnb as an exemplar case to investigate this toolkit's usability and usefulness with six participants during their Christmas holidays between December 2019 and January 2020. In total, there were 11 different Airbnb accommodations experienced by our participants. Every day, participants were asked to check the toolkit to reflect on their experiences in terms of the aspects that are mentioned by the prompt questions, and document their momentary experiences by taking photos using their smartphone (with the prompt question in the picture). The images were submitted to researchers right after they were taken. After the participant came back from the trip, we conducted a semi-structured interview with them individually to understand their experiences of using this Check-!n toolkit.

The results show that the Check-!n toolkit is easy to use for capturing their momentary experience in the context. It did not interrupt the participants' main activities while collecting valuable data for understanding their behaviors and feelings. Those photos not only can help researchers to investigate users' pain points but also can be used to create a vivid journey map that was highly aligned to the actual situations. Based on the findings, we envision that the Check-!n toolkit could help the host and designers of Airbnb to work together to fine-tune user experiences for future guests. Moreover,

This Check-!n toolkit could be adopted to various domains for investigating the user experiences easily at the right moment in the right place.

2 Related Works

2.1 Airbnb Experience

Despite some developments in the hospitality industry, discussions about memorable tourism accommodation experiences frequently revolve around Airbnb, the largest and most distinguished company in the quickly growing peer-to-peer short-term rental industry [37]. In fact, consumers want a more authentic experience, away from tourist traps and the masses of holidaymakers, hotels' trail into experience-making are often perceived as reactions to Airbnb's rise [3, 15]. Despite its fundamental importance, experience-related research remains underappreciated in the hospitality and tourism literature, such as the context of Airbnb [20, 30].

The lack of research into Airbnb's customer experience is mainly reflected in its excessive reliance on online reviews and data after the pos-hoc recall [16]. For example, several studies have analyzed the Airbnb website's reviews to highlight key aspects of the consumer experience, such as the sense of welcome [39], home location [11, 40], communication with the host [21], and amenities [17]. Additionally, A few studies also adopted the method of post-interview [8, 34]. However, we did not find any research that collected consumers' real-time experience through qualitative research, ample opportunities exist for more qualitative research to offer richer insights into the questions surrounding Airbnb [16].

2.2 Momentary Experience

The consumer experience including anticipated experience, momentary experience, episodic experience and cumulative experience [32], some momentary experiences would be forgotten by the events that happened later [5]. When consumers recall their experience, recall bias [33] or negative bias [22] would inevitably occur due to the stacking of experiences. Therefore, relying solely on recalled experiences can hardly surface the whole story of consumers' experience [34], which will confuse and even mislead researchers. As a result, capturing the momentary experience of consumers in the experience process will become the key to restore the user's journey.

The momentary experience will also change as the experience changes over time. Experience should be understood as a complex interaction between design attributes and contextual details where meanings and values will emerge in given contexts [35], it is very important to pay attention to consumer experience before, during, after and overtime of usage. For example, anticipated user experience for a product (before usage) will affect the momentary experience (during usage) [1]. Triggering users' deliberations on their momentary experience at the right moment in the right place would greatly help the researchers in charting the different parts of the customer journey. However, less research focuses on how to effectively capture momentary experience at different stages of experience at present.

2.3 Experience Sampling Method

As a commonly used method in user experience research, The Experience Sampling Method (ESM) becomes a potential way to capture consumers' momentary experiences. The ESM is a research procedure for studying what people do, feel, and think during their daily lives, it consists of asking individuals to provide systematic self-reports at random occasions during the waking hours of a normal week [24] and mainly including three distinct types [41]: Interval-contingent, Event-contingent and signal-contingent samplings. The methodological constructs for the later development of the ESM were provided by diary studies. The two types of diary studies can be distinguished: feedback studies and elicitation studies [9]. In the feedback study, participants answered a set of questions at a predetermined time-shot or event. In the elicitation study, participants captured media, such as photographs [44], as the event occurred and discussed the collected media with the researcher at a later point in time. Photos not only provide a way to elicit recall in a post-study interview, but can serve as the added value during data analysis [4].

However, both types of diary studies have their shortcomings, most prominently the participants' limitations to reliably reconstruct past events [19]. In some specific fields, such as tourism, the majority of participants' experiences are momentary, taking place in short episodes, rather than occurring over extended periods, a true understanding can be elusive [30]. Although Yue et al. [44] propose that photo-taking would greatly help to clarified non-specific nouns and disambiguation nouns, the majority of photos did not help researchers understand the participants' needs beyond what they had already included in text responses. In our opinion, taking photos can be a way to balance the advantages and disadvantages of on-the-spot reflection and post-hoc retrospection: on the one hand, photos can quickly record the results of participants' on-site reflection; on the other hand, the post-interview content explains the results of the reflection at that time, rather than the reflection of accumulation experience.

2.4 ESM on Mobile Devices

In the early stage, ESM was completed by taking notes in their diary or complete a questionnaire [31]. Following the introduction of the PDA (Personal Digital Assistant), such as smartphones and iPad, many studies have adopted such digital devices. With a constantly evolving software landscape, it is worthwhile to analyse the existing choices. The first mobile device application that could be used as a tool for the Experience Sampling Method was the ESP Package [26]. As smartphone use popularized, numerous smartphone software was involved in academic studies to improve participants' sampling experience, such as PIEL Survey [36], Qualiwall Tool [23], SurveySignal [18], Ilumivu, MetricWire, Instant Survey, and so on.

Most software tools support only a subsection of available questionnaire input types, a noticeable absent input type among the majority of analyzed software tools was the recording of multimedia data (image, video, audio). The capture of these types of multimedia data has been shown to be a useful addition during data collection [44]. In this paper, we want to focus on the role of photography in sample collection and try to make participants' photos contain more experience information. Ultimately, our goal is to collect sample information equal to or more than that based on questionnaires with a reduced on-site sampling workload.

3   Method

To break through the aforesaid limitation of ESM and capturing customers' momentary experience on the spot, we proposed our question-contingent sampling toolkit, a paper-based folding card with various questions printed on different faces. We further carried out an empirical study with six participants who stayed at different Airbnb accommodations during their separated trips in the winter holiday between December '19 and January '20. They first used our toolkit to collect their momentary experiences on the spots. After they came back from the trip, we conducted semi-structured interviews individually to investigate their experiences with our toolkit.

3.1   Toolkit Design

To maintain participants' enthusiasm in the short-term experience sampling and do not disturbing their authenticity experience, our sampling is in the form of photography, participants would quickly capture their reflections on the momentary experience by taking photos, instead of interrupting their experience by filling out the report. Our goal is to make the sampling process naturally interwoven with the Airbnb experience, encouraging participants to explore new environments with more reflectiveness. We believe that sensitizing guests is an effective way to capture authentic and fine-grained travel experiences. At the same time, the increased sensitivity of guests' experience would help the host evaluate room experience at the beginning of the rental business and timely adjust their services for potential problems.

The tourism experiences in Airbnb are the combination of environment, service and interactive experience, which would make self-reported evaluation more difficult. Therefore, we asked participants to evaluate each of their feelings and find the stimuli that affected them separately, instead of rating three different groups of emotions at the same times in self-report [24]. To sensitize the guests during the sampling process and find evidence of their feelings, we extracted 10 questions based on previous ESM self-report form [24] and Airbnb research [7, 27, 28, 45], asked participants to reflect on their momentary feeling on the spot, find the reason and take photos with the answer. Besides, we also interviewed with participants to further collect the explanation behind the reflection to fully activate the recorded moments of reflection, so as to understand the participants' mental models.

3.2   Procedure

Our toolkit including 'Check-!n' adventure cards, guest's feedback photos for elicitation [29], grid paper for activity track drawing and Airbnb web-page pictures of guest's room for experience contrast. The investigation including in-context momentary experience capturing and interpretation of reflective content.

In-context Momentary Experience Capturing. The 'Check-!n' adventure cards were used to sensitize the guest and capture their momentary experience in-context. When the guest arrived at the Airbnb, we asked them to reflect on the 10 questions in the cards (see Fig. 1) as they encountered each new experience. Each page of the cards has a keyword and a specific question, our questions including two parts: 1) Collecting participants' representative feelings from different degrees. According to the synthesis of the three groups of feelings in the previous scale [24], we used 'surprise', 'special', 'normal', 'disappointment' and 'uncomfortable' as an example to evaluate the experience in Airbnb context. 2) Some focus topics in previous Airbnb research. We choose home feeling [45], feeling of the host [7], local experience [27], personality behavior [28] and satisfaction-related experience [38] as examples. We presented these five factors to the participants in easy-to-understand keywords: 'Feels like home', 'host's lifestyle', 'different from home', 'settling in' and 'I can't wait to see'. For example, we ask our participants to find a corner that 'Feels like home', they will explore the 'Feels like home' in different contexts, find the specific physical objects or interaction that bring them home feeling, and take a picture of it with the 'Feels like home' page of the card.

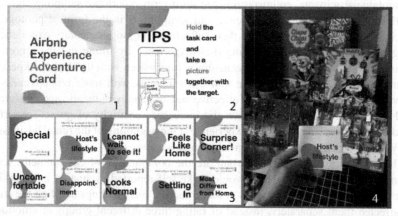

Fig. 1. The photo of folded 'Check-!n' cards. 2: The 'Check-!n' card instruction manual on the cover page. 3: 'Check-!n' cards 10 keywords with correspondent questions and the user instructions of the card: 1) Special: What's special about this apartment? 2) Host's lifestyle: What in the apartment told you something about the host? 3) I cannot wait to see it: What did you check first of the apartment? 4) Feels like home: What area makes you feel most like home? 5) Surprise Corner: What in the apartment surprise you? 6) Uncomfortable: Are there anything in the apartment that makes you feel uncomfortable? 7) Disappointment: Which part of the apartment is disappointed you? 8) Looks normal: Which part of the apartment looks basic? 9) Settling in: What did you do to makes you feel like home? 10) Most different from home: What is most different from your home? 4: An example of sampling by 'Check-!n' card

During the collection process, participants were encouraged to respond based on their understanding of the keyword rather than guessing the researcher's intentions. Besides, participants were usually asked to fill in the report after a certain time. However, the occurrence of momentary experience may be random, thus, our sampling process used

Event-contingent style [41], without limiting shooting order and numbers of the photo. In the end, the information in each photo contains the researcher's question, the participant's answers in their Airbnb, and the shooting time data from the smartphone.

Interpretation of Reflective Content. The memory of previous experiences would be modified by post-experience information [5] and most guests have a positive desire to share their fresh experiences after the trip. Therefore, when the guest came back with fresh memories and excitement, we conducted a timely semi-structured interview to ask them to explain the reflections on their experiences within 2 days. The goal of the interview is to help the researcher comprehend the context and reflection of the participants' momentary experience. The interview including the following three parts:

(i)   Participants explain their photos. The participants' photos carry the answers of their reflections on the momentary experience, we start to understand their experience from these photos. Each participant explained what in the photo, where did the photo take, the context of that moment and why it had been taken. These photos present the results of reflection, which means that our toolkit has helped participants complete their reflection and give answers on the spot, rather than sample what's going on without further thinking.

(ii) Participants draw their Airbnb layout on the grid paper, explain the location and relationship of the different kinds of momentary experience. Through the connection of these experiences, we get not only the experience journey at different times but also the track of participants in the Airbnb home. The time and tracks will help us build a dynamic user journey map.

(iii) The contrast of the participants' momentary experience between booking and encounters with Airbnb. After collecting the complete journey of participants, we presented the webpage photos of participants' Airbnb home to them again, so as to further understand the difference between participants' expectation at the moment of booking and the moment they encounter with the Airbnb.

3.3 Participants

We recruited participants by sending recruitment messages through online communities and local social networks via university, such as Facebook and What's App. We designed a pre-screening survey to get participants' demographic information, their previous major, and their Airbnb planning for the 2019 Christmas holidays. In this practice, we did not only want to verify the effectiveness of the toolkit in capturing momentary experiences in Airbnb but also compared the sampling experience of the past to our "Check -!n". Therefore, we selected six expert researchers (see Table 1) who have participated in SEM studies and familiar with a variety of sampling tools, including sampling by mobile phone. All of them had a strong interest in using the 'Check-!n' toolkit and had plans for one or more Airbnb experiences over the Christmas period. What's more, the members and timing of their trips are also selected as the representative of the candidates, we involved diverse kinds of participants to test the usability of the toolkit: The participants' travel form including solo travel, couples and multiple people. Some of them stay on the same Airbnb for several days, while others will change a new

Airbnb every day. At last, participants were required to explain our study to the Airbnb host and obtained the consent of the host before the study begins.

Table 1. Personal information about six participants, their partner, destinations, and the number of days they stay in each.

	Airbnb	Age	Gender	Partner(s)	Destination	Days
P1	1	25	M	None	Hamburg, Germany	5
P2	2	27	F	Three friends	Barcelona, Spain	2
	3				Madrid, Spain	1
P3	4	25	M	His girlfriend	Madrid, Spain	2
	5				Barcelona, Spain	2
	6				Paris, French	5
P4	7	24	M	A friend of him	Kassel, Germany	5
P5	8	30	F	Her husband	Eindhoven, Netherlands	1
P6	9	23	M	One friend and two pairs of couples	Madrid, Spain	1
	10				Seville, Spain	3
	11				Barcelona, Spain	2

3.4 Data Analysis

Transcriptions. All interviews were audio-recorded upon participants' permission. Then two co-coder conducted a thematic analysis [6] for transcribed recording. First, we read all transcriptions a few times to familiarize ourselves with the data, coded one transcription together at the sentence level to develop an initial codebook. For example, P3:5 said, *"I sleep on a sofa bed in the living room, at night the wind will pass over my head and I feel very cold."* We think that the toolkit captures experiences that can't be seen, so we code it as "invisible experiences". Second, we independently coded the same transcription of another session using the codebook. We added new codes to the codebook in that process. Once finished, we compared and discussed our coding, and converged on an updated codebook. Third, we coded the rest of the data using the updated code-book, which contains more than 50 unique codes, such as "encounter new objects", "Experience in different times", "The unattended corner", "Different from webpage photos" and so on. At the early stage of data analysis, we preliminarily grouped these codes into the theme according to similarity, examined, and ensured the codes were assigned to the correct theme. After the initial grouping, we further take image data into account to enrich and adjust the theme.

Image Data. We collected sampling photos and participant drawings of their Airbnb layout as image data. Following Yao et al.'s method [42], two co-coder coded all elements in every image, including objects in the picture (e.g., Space, objects, states), track flow on the layout (e.g., path, annotation), and other visual information (e.g., icons, colors). Over 30 codes emerged from the analysis, and all the codes were grouped into the aforementioned themes in the analysis of audio transcriptions. For example, we coded P5's stairs experience as "Experience over and over again" and grouped them in the preceding code "Experience in different times". After grouped all codes into the aforementioned themes, these themes are further merged into clusters and become our final result.

4 Usage of Check-!n Toolkit

We asked the participants to take the question on the cards into account and began sampling after they arrived at Airbnb. When participants encountered a new experience, they had to reflect on the questions in the card, send the answers to the first author via social media as soon as they photographed. At last, we received 122 photos from all participants (e.g. Right side of Fig. 2), two of the photos from P1:1 and P3:5 was excluded because the samples were not relevant to the Airbnb experience. Nine of the 11 Airbnb homes responded more than 90 percent of the questions, the other two homes had a response rate of 60 percent and 50 percent respectively. Besides, we collected 65 photos of participants' Airbnb on the website (e.g. Left side of Fig. 2), obtained 11 interview recordings for all the Airbnb home experience and collected 11 Airbnb layouts drawn by participants (see Fig. 3).

Fig. 2. A set of examples of Airbnb photos and on-site sample photos-Left: No.5 Airbnb home photos on the web-page, Right: On-site samples from P3.

5 Findings

Our evaluation objective is to validate the usefulness of toolkits, thus the presentation of our finding mainly emphasizes the theme-related usability of toolkits, while at the

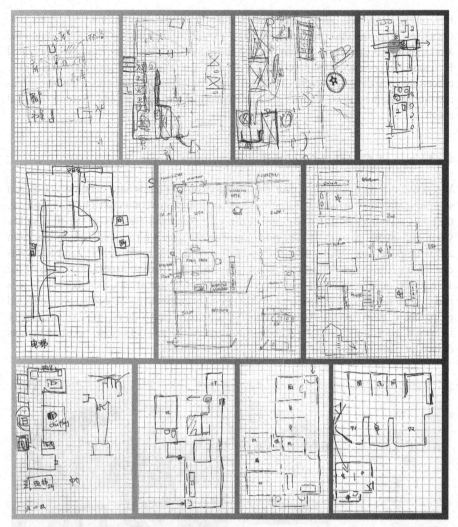

Fig. 3. Layout and supplementary information of 11 Airbnb homes drawn by six participants during the interview.

same time showing the thematic related with new insight that the toolkit has undisclosed compared to previous ESM research. The thematic analysis revealed three main themes of momentary experience addressing the evaluation objective:

5.1   Enriching Elements for Guest Experience

Interesting Sampling Process. Participants demonstrated a positive reaction to the using of 'Check-!n' card, despite having no prior knowledge about the basic concepts of the tools. They thought the behavior of taking photos in an unfamiliar environment was consistent with their motivation to explore the space. For instance, P5:8 reported 25 photos for our 10 questions: *"Compare with self-report scale, I felt very interesting when I used this card, just like taking Instagram style photos in a scenic spot."*. Meanwhile, they stated that sampling was accepted by other members of the room, some members even actively participate in the sampling process: *"When we were sitting together, my friend asked me where I put the cards and whether I had completed the tasks on the cards."* (P4:7). Furthermore, participants also actively use their own ways to make the samples convey more information: *"For comparison, I showed a photo of it on my phone next to the dishwasher, this is what it looks like when it started working[...]."* (P4:7). Although we didn't state the sampling numbers of each question, all of the participants actively reported two or more samples for some questions, these samples reflect their understanding of the questions from different perspectives, which will help researchers understand the multiple factors of different feelings.

Get in Touch with the New Experience. As participants reflected on the questions on the card, they further explored Airbnb and encountered new things: *"This traditional style elevator outside the door is not on the website, but I think is the most distinctive part of this Airbnb after explore."*(P2:3) The guest's exploration may help the host discover the unique features of the room. At the same time, in the process of sampling, the participant took the initiative to try a new experience in the room: *"When I try to answer the question 'different from home', I found a Christmas calendar on the display cabinet of the host that I had never bought and was very interesting after observation."*(P4:7) Participants also reflected on these momentary experience after encountered: *"The host put the introduction of nearby characteristic town on this shelf, I think it helps us know more about the local culture, which made me feel considerate from the host."* (P3:4)

Change Over Time. From sampling photos, participants showed the same interaction has different momentary experiences at different times. Although these photos were explained after the sampling, the participants could provide rich and vivid context and interpretation for their reflection. For example, the toolkit firstly captures the P5's experience on its first encounter with the stairs: *"The home in my hometown has only one floor, so the room with stairs made me feel very novel."*. (P5:8,10:25 pm) After the novelty wore off, we find the focus of her experience shifts from appearance to function: *"After using it a few times I feel tired and inconvenient to walk up the stairs."*(P5:8,10:44 pm) Although the long-term experience is not ideal, some unexpected discoveries are also captured: *"I was waiting for a night snack, and the sound on the wooden stairs reminds me of my husband coming up with food, the stairs made me feel surprised and expectant."* (P5:8,11:40 pm) By reflecting on the same thing from different perspectives at different times, the toolkit captures a rich variety of experiences.

Understanding the Host's Lifestyle. The interaction between host and guest has been mentioned as an authenticity experience in previous research, our toolkit reveals how could the room information details communicate the information of the host to the guest, which create a subtle connection between host and guest: *"The head of the bed is equipped with a socket, and tissues can be found in every corner of the room. I think the host is a very considerate person."* (P3:6), these positive experiences from the guest's point of view could guide other hosts improve their service. Furthermore, the toolkit reveals that participants construct host personalities by connecting clues in the room: "*Look at this little pot that it seems to be used a lot[...]The food was piled haphazardly on the bar[...]the host seemed to be a very casual person with a fast pace of life.*" (P1:1) Hosts are likely to ignore the impact of these details in the past, this feedback will benefit the reputation of the host if they adjust the display to avoid negative imagination from guests.

5.2 Uncovered Unremarkable Experience

Neglected Corners. In interviews, review photos on the website and drawing the layout helped participants uncover some overlooked experience of the corner: "*What's in this blank space?*" (Author pointed the blue dot area in the fourth picture of the first line on Fig. 3) "*I don't remember, let me see the pictures...It is a washing machine.*"(P3:5 Photo 1 in Fig. 2) At the same time, they also reflect on the reason why they ignore the experience, such as lack of function:"*The washing machine has no door and cannot be used, so we immediately ignore its existence.*" (P3:5) or the corner is in the experience blind spot: "*Is there an artwork above the sofa? I had no impression at all, my attention was drawn to the window across from the sofa.*" (P2:3) This feedback would help the host improve service details and focus the experience in places that guests can easily focus on.

Photos Differ From Reality. Participants exposed the hidden experience that they couldn't get from Airbnb web-page images. For example, they rated the degree of saturation (P6:10), sense of space (P3:4, P3:5), and lighting in some rooms (P6:10) as different from what they would expect from advertising picture: "*The objects in the room are the same as in the photo, but the colors are not as bright.*"(P6:10)" *The living room was very small and we were cramped in it, but you can't get that information in the photos.*" (P3:4) In Fig. 2 we could find an obvious gap of space and lighting from webpage photo (2 and 4 on the left) to on the spot feeling (Picture 'a' on the left). Through these momentary experiences, the host could reduce the gap between the photo and the reality: "*want the room to look same as the photo, not to fool me with special camera angles and filters.*" (P5)

Normal Experience. Participants reported several "normal" experiences that they felt did not exceed expectations: "*It was just an ordinary bed, just as I expected, without surprises or discomfort.*"(P3:4) It's worth noting, most of these normal experience feedback comes from beds and couch in the living room, and the following answers represent most of the reasons for shooting couch: "*We were tired after a long day of play, and we spend most of our Airbnb time lying on the couch together and playing with our phones. Compared to our own home, this ordinary sofa does not bring a different experience during travel.*" Therefore, the concentrated "normal" experience may indicate that the participants expect a better experience: "*The table next to the sofa is not high enough.*" (P3:5), "*The seating arrangement makes it difficult for us to get together.*" (P6:10) The sample suggests that the bed and common space might the key to further enhancing the experience.

Invisible Experience. Participants reported many experiences that they could not be represented in photographs, such as temperature (P5:8, P3:6), smells (P5:8), and noises (P1:1, P2:2, P3:4, P6:10). Nevertheless, they reflected and filmed the source of the experience and reported it in the interview:" *look at the old Windows in the picture, they have very poor sound insulation, I think it is the reason for the noise.*" (P2:2) The guest's reflection directly explains the root of the troubling experience, which rarely report to the host: "*I won't feedback the noise to the host, I'm leaving tomorrow anyway.*" (P2:2) Some guest even guesses "*The host won't fix the problem.*"(P3:4) Besides, a photo of P5:8 shows a blank wall, she explains: "*What I wanted to capture was the air in the room[...]When I reflected on the question of 'Host lifestyle', I mentioned the host's perfume made me feel good.*" We didn't find the attention to invisible experience in previous studies, while it might have a strong impact on the experience: "*This smell makes me live very comfortable, like the smell of my mother.*" (P5:8)

5.3 Pain Points of Using Check-!n

Insufficient Use Cards. The "Check-!n" card's whiteness affects camera lens metering in dark environments: "*When the room is dark and the camera focuses on the card, the photo becomes dark and blurry.*"(P4:7) We can also find this problem in the P5's samples (a and h in Fig. 2). "*Change the background color of the card.*" (P4:7) or "*Consider adopting electronic cards.*" (P2:2) may fix this problem. In addition, some questions on the card were missed collection by P3:5 and P4:7: "*I might forget to answer this question[...].*" (P3:5), one reason probably "*because I missed the page when I flipped through the card.*" (P3:5) Other reasons might be a few keywords are hard to understand: "*I am not sure about the meaning of 'normal'.*" or "*I didn't find appropriate objects to answer this question.*" (P6:10) In future research, it is necessary to ensure the comprehensibility of keywords while keeping the question open.

Barriers in the Interaction Flow. Participants reported small and fleeting frustration when they interact with the devices or space of the room. Such as lack of device availability (P5:8), living noise (P2:3), the sense of out of control: " *[...]I am not sure if the temperature adjustment was successful and feel the loss of control. I was instantly reflected that it is likely to create a negative experience for other guests as well.*" (P1:1) and missing of ancillary items: "*I was halfway through my breakfast cooking while I realized I even couldn't find any salt on the shelf, so I filmed the moment.*" (P2:3). However, "*Bad experiences will temporarily affect me, then I forgot about it.*" (P2:3), our toolkit would help the host capture these subtle obstacles in guest experience and try to fix them.

Inappropriate Spatial Arrangement. Momentary frustration caused by inappropriate layout and decoration also influenced our participants. The impact of these questions extends from the interactive level: " *The living room is quite small, while the host set up a big table, which made us feel very crowded.*" (P3:4) to the emotional level: "*Kitchen wall is covered with pictures of very greasy food, which makes me instantly lost my appetite.*" (P2:3). The negative experience of room arrangement was mostly reported after participants first encountering the room, while they didn't feedback to the host: *"We didn't communicate the uncomfortable details [...] we tolerated or ignored these negative experiences, then we adapted it."* (P2:3) Capturing and enhancing the guest's first encounter will become a topic of interest in the future.

6 Discussion

As a promising tool for user research on experience-centering services, the previous toolkit enables participants to gather authentic experiences from on-the-spot self-reports, providing rich data for their journey mapping. However, filling out these self-reports needs to take some time, which makes it difficult to capture momentary experiences. Although previous studies have involved the collection of images to make the user experience sampling easier, most of these images are used as auxiliary means to help record text information, and lack of purposeful information collection. As a result, in the post-hoc interview, participants term to feedback on cumulative UX rather than a specific reflection on each momentary experience.

Compared with the previous mobile self-report, our toolkit targeted questions for participants, transforms the collection of on-the-spot information into the collection of momentary experience reflection, and completes the sampling data recovery through simple interactive photography. In this study, all of the participants were able to use the "Check-!n" Toolkit, and their answers were successfully transmitted to the first author. When looking at the existing result, we found similar observations have been made: The mobile sampling tool can capture more "real" experiences [12], and it could help researchers map the user's journey [23]. Furthermore, as the research community has already drawn from past experiences with mobile experience sampling, we also suggest the need for a customizable experience sampling system [17]. In the data collection process, comparing the participants' recollections with the photographic cues they provided, we find that the recollection of the previous experience was indeed biased or missing [22, 33, 34] from the momentary experience record. In some of the photos in which participants tried to express their feelings, it was difficult to extract valuable coding from the photos [42] without their explanation. These development considerations and observations correlate with our experiences and current development goals.

Among the three themes obtained from the thematic analysis of the result, we find that the "Check-!n" toolkit has a positive effect on both experiences of sampling and participants' momentary experience collection. First, compared to traditional mobile self-reports, "Check -!n" sampling is considered to have less impact on the user experience process, the question-contingent sampling process sensitizes guests and enriches their experience, complementing Airbnb's brand promise of creating authentic experiences. Secondly, some overlooked unremarkable experiences of the guest were exposed. When hosts started launching rental services on Airbnb, these unremarkable experiences would help them further improve the guest experience with lower costs and subtle changes. Thirdly, participants' feedback on negative experiences became more specific, and their reflections reduced the bias of the researchers' analysis. At the same time, the participants' frustration has some resonance, in future studies, participants and researchers can analyze the data together for better interpretation.

When analyzing the answers obtained with the "Check-!n" toolkit, at least three issues can be noted. First, two Airbnb report rates were only 60% and 50%, the reason might the high similarity in the appearance of the cards, and the lack of page number and other marks, the participants missed these questions. Future development of the experience research toolkit should not only focus on collecting data, but also emphasize the participants' toolkit experience, avoid them inadvertently missing or even provide incorrect data due to usage issue. Second, Open-ended questions in the toolkit may confuse some participants, they may prudently give up answering these questions in the end. Future work needs to balance the openness and clarity of the sampling questions. Third, the information provides by the participants could lead to misinterpretations by the researchers. In the process of home layout drawing, after comparing sampling photos web page pictures, we found that some participants always exaggerated the room size of the part they emphasized. In future studies, it is possible to avoid misinterpretation by cross-testing participants' data from different aspects.

7 Limitation

We also acknowledge that there are still limitations regarding the presented tools. (1) This study invited expert user researchers to practice with the "check-!n" toolkit and compared the toolkit with the sampling methods they used in the past. The effectiveness of the toolkit was demonstrated by summarizing their feedback, without direct practice comparison to the previous sampling methods. Future research should invite more non-expert users to compare different sampling methods to get the advantages and disadvantages of the toolkit more specific. (2) Participants were mostly 23–30 years old and their perceptive and acceptance were not representative of those of other age groups. In the future, the research could be done on different age groups and special circumstances, such as the elderly or people with disabilities. (3) To ensure the diversity of data, we specially chose different forms of home-stay with limited participant numbers, including single and couple forms to stay. However, future research can refine the form to stay for a person or a family with larger sample size. (4) Our participants are all Asian researchers who are working in Europe, and our Airbnb homes are all European homes. Participants from other cultural groups and hosts from other regions can be explored in the future.

8 Conclusion

Users' momentary experience sampling Airbnb shared homes remains a relatively less explored sub-domain, suggesting unaddressed research opportunities. The practical case for Airbnb experience sampling shows that the "Check-!n" toolkit not only captures a user's momentary experience and enrich the details of their journey map but also helps researchers understand the user's on-site mental model. We believe that in the future, the "Check-!n" toolkit would further contribute to capturing momentary experiences in a different context, help researchers to further understand the design opportunities behind momentary experiences. Our toolkit also has the potential for further customize in niche areas, understand the impact of time and sequence of encounters in different momentary experiences.

References

1. Allam, A.H., Razak, A., Hussin, C.: User experience : challenges and opportunities. J. Res. Innov. Inf. Syst., 28–36 (2009). http://seminar.spaceutm.edu.my/jisri/download/F_FinalPu blished/Pub20_UserExperienceChallenges.pdf%5Cnhttp://seminar.utmspace.edu.my/jisri/download/F1_FinalPublished/Pub4_UserExperienceChallenges.pdf
2. Joseph Pine II, B., Gilmore, J.H.: Welcome to the experience economy. https://hbr.org/1998/07/welcome-to-the-experience-economy
3. Bearne, S.: Airbnb is forcing everyone to up their game: how hotels are changing tack. The Guardian (2018). https://www.theguardian.com/business-to-business/2018/apr/11/airbnb-is-forcing-everyone-to-up-their-game-how-hotels-are-changing-tack
4. Van Berkel, N., Ferreira, D., Kostakos, V.: The experience sampling method on mobile devices. ACM Comput. Surv. **50**, 6 (2017). https://doi.org/10.1145/3123988
5. Braun-LaTour, K.A., LaTour, M.S., Pickrell, J.E., Loftus, E.F.: How and when advertising can influence memory for consumer experience. J. Advert. **33**(4), 7–25 (2004). https://doi.org/10.1080/00913367.2004.10639171
6. Braun, V., Clarke, V.: Using thematic analysis in psychology. Qual. Res. Psychol. **3**(2), 77–101 (2006). https://doi.org/10.1191/1478088706qp063oa
7. Brochado, A., Troilo, M., Shah, A.: Airbnb customer experience: evidence of convergence across three Countries. Ann. Tour. Res. **63**, 210–212 (2017). https://doi.org/10.1016/j.annals.2017.01.001
8. Bucher, E., Fieseler, C., Fleck, M., Lutz, C.: Authenticity and the sharing economy. Acad. Manage. Discov. **4**(3), 294–313 (2018). https://doi.org/10.5465/amd.2016.0161
9. Carter, S., Mankoff, J.: When participants do the capturing: the role of media in diary studies. In: CHI 2005: Technology, Safety, Community: Conference Proceedings - Conference on Human Factors in Computing Systems (2005)
10. Cheng, M., Jin, X.: What do Airbnb users care about? An analysis of online review comments. Int. J. Hosp. Manage. **76**, 58–70 (2018). https://doi.org/10.1016/j.ijhm.2018.04.004
11. Cheng, M., Zhang, G.: When Western hosts meet Eastern guests: Airbnb hosts' experience with Chinese outbound tourists. Ann. Tour. Res. **75**, 288–303 (2019). https://doi.org/10.1016/j.annals.2019.02.006
12. Consoivo, S., et al.: Conducting in situ evaluations for and with ubiquitous computing technologies. Int. J. Hum. Comput. Interact. **22**(1–2), 103–118 (2007). https://doi.org/10.1207/s15327590ijhc2201-02_6
13. Senior, J., Bloch, N., Almquist, E.: The elements of value (2016). https://www.bain.com/insights/the-elements-of-value-hbr
14. Goodwin, K.: Designing for the Digital Age: How to Create Human-Centered Products and Services. Wiley, Indianapolis (2011)
15. Guttentag, D.: Progress on Airbnb: a literature review. J. Hosp. Tour. Technol. **10**(3), 233–263 (2019). https://doi.org/10.1108/JHTT-08-2018-0075
16. Guttentag, D.: Transformative experiences via Airbnb: is it the guests or the host communities that will be transformed? J. Tour. Futures **5**(2), 179–184 (2019). https://doi.org/10.1108/JTF-04-2019-0038
17. Hoffman, D.L., Novak, T.P.: Consumer and object experience in the internet of things: an assemblage theory approach. J. Cons. Res. **44**(6), 1178–1204 (2018). https://doi.org/10.1093/jcr/ucx105
18. Hofmann, W., Patel, P.V.: SurveySignal: a convenient solution for experience sampling research using participants' own smartphones. Soc. Sci. Comput. Rev. **33**(2), 235–253 (2015). https://doi.org/10.1177/0894439314525117

19. Iida, M., Shrout, P.E., Laurenceau, J.-P., Bolger, N.: Using diary methods in psychological research. In: APA Handbook of Research Methods in Psychology, vol 1: Foundations, Planning, Measures, and Psychometrics (2012). https://doi.org/10.1037/13619-016
20. Yang, Y., Jiang, H.R., Mavondo, F.: Destination marketing and visitor experiences: the development of a conceptual framework. J. Hosp. Mark. Manage. (2016). https://doi.org/10.1080/19368623.2016.1087358
21. Johnson, A.G., Neuhofer, B.: Airbnb – an exploration of value co-creation experiences in Jamaica. Int. J. Contemp. Hosp. Manage. (2017). https://doi.org/10.1108/IJCHM-08-2016-0482
22. Cherry, k.: What is the negativity bias? Verywellmind (2020). https://www.verywellmind.com/negative-bias-4589618
23. Kojo, I., Heiskala, M., Virtanen, J.-P.: Customer journey mapping of an experience-centric service by mobile self-reporting: testing the qualiwall tool. In: Marcus, A. (ed.) DUXU 2014. LNCS, vol. 8517, pp. 261–272. Springer, Cham (2014). https://doi.org/10.1007/978-3-319-07668-3_26
24. Larson, R., Csikszentmihalyi, M.: The experience sampling method. In: Flow and the Foundations of Positive Psychology, pp. 21–34. Springer, Dordrecht (2014). https://doi.org/10.1007/978-94-017-9088-8_2
25. Schneider, J., Stickdorn, M.: This is Service Design Thinking: Basics, Tools, Cases. Wiley (2011)
26. Mehl, M.R., Conner, T.S., Csikszentmihalyi, M.: Handbook of Research Methods for Studying Daily Life, The Guilford Press (2011)
27. Mody, M.A., Suess, C., Lehto, X.: The accommodation experiencescape: a comparative assessment of hotels and Airbnb. Int. J. Contemp. Hosp. Manage. 29(9), 2377–2404 (2017). https://doi.org/10.1108/IJCHM-09-2016-0501
28. Ka Yin Poon and Wei Jue Huang: Past experience, traveler personality and tripographics on intention to use Airbnb. Int. J. Contemp. Hosp. Manage. 29(9), 2425–2443 (2017). https://doi.org/10.1108/IJCHM-10-2016-0599
29. Pretto, A.: A type of interview with photos: the bipolar photo elicitation. Annee Sociologique (2015). https://doi.org/10.3917/anso.151.0169
30. Brent Ritchie, J.R., Hudson, S.: Understanding and meeting the challenges of consumer/tourist experience research. Int. J. Tour. Res. 11(2), 111–126 (2009). https://doi.org/10.1002/jtr.721
31. Schneider, B.: Review of experience sampling method: measuring the quality of everyday life. Eur. Psychol. (2008)
32. Seminar, D.: Demarcating user experience. User Experience White Paper. Seminar, pp. 1–12 (2011). http://www.allaboutux.org/files/UX-WhitePaper.pdf
33. Mahtani, K., Spencer, E.A., Brassey, J.: Recall bias (2017). https://catalogofbias.org/biases/recall-bias/
34. Sthapit, E., Jiménez-Barreto, J.: Exploring tourists' memorable hospitality experiences: an Airbnb perspective. Tour. Manage. Perspect. 28, 83–92 (2018). https://doi.org/10.1016/j.tmp.2018.08.006
35. Suri, J.F.: Designing experience: whether to measure pleasure or just tune in. Pleasure with products: beyond usability (2002)
36. PIEL Survey: Survey the moment. PIEL Survey. https://pielsurvey.org/
37. Ting, D.: Airbnb's response to Booking.com? We've got more listings. skift (2019). https://skift.com/2019/03/01/airbnbs-response-to-booking-com-weve-got-more-listings/
38. Tussyadiah, I.P.: Factors of satisfaction and intention to use peer-to-peer accommodation. Int. J. Hosp. Manage. 55, 70–80 (2016). https://doi.org/10.1016/j.ijhm.2016.03.005
39. Tussyadiah, I.P., Zach, F.: Identifying salient attributes of peer-to-peer accommodation experience. J. Travel Tour. Mark. 34(5), 636–652 (2017). https://doi.org/10.1080/10548408.2016.1209153

40. Tussyadiah, I.P., Zach, F.: Identifying salient attributes of peer-to-peer accommodation experience. J. Travel Tour. Mark. **34**(5), 636–652 (2017). https://doi.org/10.1080/10548408.2016.1209153

41. Wheeler, L., Reis, H.T.: Self-recording of everyday life events: origins, types, and uses. J. Pers. **5**, 339–354 (1991). https://doi.org/10.1111/j.1467-6494.1991.tb00252.x

42. Yao, Y., Basdeo, J.R., Kaushik, S., Wang, Y.: Defending my castle: a co-design study of privacy mechanisms for smart homes. In: Conference on Human Factors in Computing Systems – Proceedings, pp. 1–12 (2019). https://doi.org/10.1145/3290605.3300428

43. Kawi, Y.: How airbnb proved that storytelling is the most important skill in design. https://www.inc.com/yazin-akkawi/the-surprising-technique-airbnb-uses-to-better-sell-an-experience.html

44. Yue, Z., et al.: Photographing information needs: the role of photos in experience sampling method-style research. In: Conference on Human Factors in Computing Systems – Proceedings, pp. 1545–1554 (2014). https://doi.org/10.1145/2556288.2557192

45. Zhu, Y., Cheng, M., Wang, J., Ma, L., Jiang, R.: The construction of home feeling by Airbnb guests in the sharing economy: a semantics perspective. Ann. Tour. Res. **75**, 308–321 (2019). https://doi.org/10.1016/j.annals.2018.12.013

Content and Mechanism of Car Experience: A Case Study Based on Interpretive Phenomenological Analysis

Jingpeng Jia[✉] and Xueyan Dong

The College of Special Education, Beijing Union University, Beijing 100075, China
tjtjingpeng@buu.edu.cn

Abstract. Many studies have been carried out the car experience from functional view. Different from these studies, our study aims to find more detailed reason for customers to choose the car of interest from the perspective of the whole car experience. Such experience is that feeling of using a car product to form a comprehensive feeling of the automobile product. The effective study of car experience is necessary for thinking about car product innovation at a strategic level. However, reflection on this issue has not received sufficient involvement in previous studies. Therefore, we use a qualitative research based on phenomenological methods to interview a candidate. By analyzing the interview scripts, 19 kinds of experience elements are extracted in the car experience. We also discovered four main mechanisms of vehicle experience behavior, which provides useful strategic theoretical guidance for the innovative practice of automotive product experience for Generation Z customers. In addition, our study shows that descriptive phenomenon analysis and explanatory phenomenon analysis are effective method tools for carrying out scientific research on the vehicle experience.

Keywords: The whole car experience · Experience elements · Experience mechanism · Phenomenological method

1 Introduction

In this study we focus on the whole car experience which comes from the user's overall subjective feelings about a car product in the process of approaching and using the car [1]. Many practitioners of automobile enterprises believed that a full and in-depth understanding of the whole car experience is necessary for conduct product innovation. However, according to incomplete industry research, there are few researchers paying attention on the whole car experience. Existing experience design and research work on car products can be divided into five categories. First, color and material design research based on Kansei Engineering [2, 3]; second, modeling design research based on Kansei Engineering [4, 5]; third, car interaction system design based on human factor engineering which especially focuses on functions and usability [6]; fourth, operation experience research oriented to autonomous driving behavior [7, 8] fifth, research on interactive experience for speech recognition [9]. Based on the analysis of these studies,

© Springer Nature Switzerland AG 2021
M. M. Soares et al. (Eds.): HCII 2021, LNCS 12780, pp. 599–612, 2021.
https://doi.org/10.1007/978-3-030-78224-5_41

we found that they generally have a common feature: we are used to carrying out single point breakthrough research for a small problem, but rarely give consideration and exploration to the overall car experience problem. To address the problem, our study takes a typical z-generation car user as the research object, with the help of qualitative research based on phenomenological method, tries to form a profound insight into the following three aspects, so as to provide useful theoretical guidance for the innovative design practice of automobile products for z-generation users and also provide a new platform for the scientific research methods of car experience. Our study is conducted in three ways. (1) Explore the personality characteristics of the research object; (2) Extract the possible experience elements contained in the car experience from the viewpoint of the research object; (3) Summarize the behavior mechanism behind the whole car experience behavior. The following parts of the paper will explain the three ways in detail.

1.1 The Problem

According to the observation and analysis of experience design, automobile product innovation and academic research, the research on car experience lags behind, which is at least related to the following five reasons:

(1) It is influenced by the overall atmosphere of contemporary scientific research activities. Today, the mainstream scientific research paradigms accepted by the academic circles usually follow the two basic thinking principles: first, reductionist Philosophy [10]. For example, suppose a car can be disassembled into 100 parts. As long as each part is good, the function of the whole car can be ensured. Second, mathematical thinking. Based on mathematical thinking, only those can be described by mathematical language can be regarded as research objects. Moreover, accuracy is the requirement of both research process and research results. Due to the discipline of these two ways of thinking, the existing scientific research activities objectively tend to focus on local problems. For instance, generally speaking, scientific means correct. Therefore, this kind of single point breakthrough thinking has been widely accepted by many practitioners from various industries.

(2) It tends to be affected by the overall form of experience design industry. Specifically, throughout the existing experience design industry, it is composed of many experience design practices facing single point problems. For example: ease of use experience design, visual experience design, service experience design, interactive experience design and etc. Therefore, these practice frameworks are naturally applied to the experience design practice of automobile products.

(3) the whole car experience is too complicated. We talked many staff in car design consulting and market, and found that most of them confirmed that the car experience is something that everyone dares not touch. One potential reason is that the responsibility is too heavy, as the car experience means the whole car sales. If you claim to be studying the car experience, then Party A will ask you to be responsible for the car sales. Second, it is because the consciousness phenomenon of car experience is too complex. This is not only because it involves many elements: various forms of aesthetic experience, functional experience for all the elements of

the product, as well as the symbolic experience brought by the car and each part of the product for users. Another reason lies in that the whole car experience involves the whole process of the user's contact with the car product: watching ads, entering the store or watching the car online, actual driving, purchasing process, and the process of using the car. There is an elusive and complex relationship between these experience elements and each experience process.

(4) UX is regarded as a young subject, experience design is only more than ten years. Even the basic theoretical construction of UX is still in its infancy. The methodology construction is also in the initial stage of exploration. This is the case for the study of the whole car experience.

(5) it is influenced by the contemporary social and cultural atmosphere. Today, driven by commercial activities, instrumental rationality and efficiency almost dominate the rhythm of behavior in all areas of urban life: work, creation, learning, research, and even thinking. The pressure and tension brought by this rhythm rarely provide necessary opportunities for thinking about complex problems and breaking through the existing thinking paradigm.

1.2 Approaches

By observing the phenomenon of car experience and analyzing the existing scientific research methods, the author believes that the traditional scientific research paradigm based on quantitative thinking is not suitable for exploring the content and mechanism of car experience. Specifically, the whole car experience is a kind of human emotional experience, which is a kind of subjective conscious behavior. The emergence of the conscious behavior relies on the fuzzy and integrated emotional feelings brought by the experience object. Furthermore, this kind of emotion, especially the elements of aesthetic experience, is difficult to describe using quantitative measurement and simple concepts, and even difficult to express with language. Therefore, in order to present the content and mechanism of car experience, it is necessary to involve qualitative research methods.

Among all the qualitative research methods, phenomenological method is the most suitable for the study of consciousness and behavior. But for the whole car experience, there is still a problem worthy of exploration: should descriptive phenomenological research method or explanatory phenomenological research method be used. According to the consideration of the practical task of experience innovation of automobile products and the observation and thinking of the whole car experience phenomenon, the author finds that the research method based on phenomenology is suitable at the level of research strategy. But in the specific research practice, the car experience phenomenon contains not only the research objects suitable for descriptive phenomenology, but also the research objects appropriate for explanatory phenomenology.

It should also be pointed out that, like all other types of qualitative research, in terms of sampling quantity and research validity, qualitative research based on phenomenological methods also focuses on the depth and richness of information that can be extracted from each sample, which is the key to ensure the research validity [11]. Even if there is only one research sample, as long as the sample is sufficiently representative, it is likely to obtain good research validity due to the depth of the research. Moreover, even if the single case research results are not enough to provide sufficient support for solving a certain practice, they can at least provide valuable reference for other case research in terms of research perspective and formation hypothesis.

Based on the above considerations, the author tries to present the content and mechanism of car experience as much as possible through the combination of descriptive phenomenological analysis and explanatory phenomenological analysis, and through the interview study of single sample.

1.3 Author's Background

In qualitative research, it is generally believed a view, which is different from the quantitative research institute, that researchers themselves can be the main research tools. Researchers' knowledge background, critical thinking ability and sense of life for the research object play an important role in the quality of research results. Therefore, it is necessary to explain the knowledge background and experience of researchers. We believe this can provide important clues for other researchers to judge the quality of research results to avoid any omissions.

Jia Jingpeng, the first author of the paper, majored in interaction design (2011–2005). When being about to graduate, he found that good interactive products usually need the support of excellent dynamic elements, so he chose animation design major for in-depth study in the graduate stage. And he has published two books titled with animation movement law, and interface design. Afterwards, He found that it is difficult to see interaction design from a global perspective in 2012, therefore began to pursue a Ph.D. in philosophy and aesthetics, trying to answer curious questions. Through the study of aesthetics and phenomenological psychology, as well as the continuous attention to the field of interaction design. The author discovered three points. Firstly, the rise of experience design has brought a valuable paradigm shift to the traditional design industry, including interaction design. Secondly, phenomenological methods are very suitable for establishing an effective thinking perspective for the study of experience phenomenon. Thirdly, in the interaction of product innovation, the experience innovation of automobile product is quite representative. Because the consumption of car can reflect various human needs and underlying motives, and integrate almost all human civilization, technology and wisdom. Therefore, from 2017, the author began to pay attention to the experience design of all kinds of automobile products, and gradually found the importance of car experience design.

2   Related Work

On the one hand, the application of phenomenological methods is explored in the global. At present, the relevant exploration is mainly focused on psychological counseling, education and nursing. The research of this paper is an effort to promote the theoretical understanding of car experience phenomenon from the perspective of experience design, and also a new attempt to expand the application field of phenomenological method. The experience and lessons from the existing research cases based on phenomenological methods provide valuable reference for the research practice in the aspects of research design and data analysis.

On the other hand, the discovery of the limitations of the traditional scientific research paradigm using quantitative thinking only indicates that the quantitative thinking cannot be applied to all types of research objects. But this does not mean that we should completely abandon it. Because the research activities based on qualitative methods still need to adhere to the positivist principles of the traditional method, and confirm and falsify the research results. In addition, all kinds of quantitative research methods and related research techniques provided by the traditional paradigm play an important role in the verification of qualitative research and providing useful clues for qualitative research. In particular, the research of Kansei engineering based on EEG technology will provide important support for many confirmation tasks in car experience research. In the process of research, the author also found that this helping effect may appear in all stages of qualitative research. Therefore, the existing Kansei engineering research and the related research based on human factors method may provide an important reference for the qualitative research and design based on phenomenological method.

3   Research Process

According to the existing research on the phenomenon of user experience, any specific surface demand of users for products is the realization of the bottom motivation of human nature and personality characteristics in a certain situation. Therefore, in the research of car experience, we must strive to obtain the three findings. First, understand who the respondents are. That is to grasp the basic contents of the respondents in human motivation and personality characteristics, and what are the respondents' basic demands for real life under the promotion of these contents. Second, what are the experience elements that the respondents feel in the car experience. Third, what is the relationship between the underlying human motivation and personality characteristics and these experience elements. In order to accomplish the above tasks, the researchers carried out the following research activities.

3.1   Car Selection Report

To ensure the report to be fair, candidate was asked to choose the best cars for twice.

First Car Selection. From September 13 to 20, 2020, the first author was responsible for teaching the visual communication course to 72 grade 20 postgraduates majoring in user experience design from the Department of psychology of Beijing Normal University. September 13 is the first course, a total of eight hours. In the course, based on car products, the basic principles and practical methods of aesthetic research and aesthetic experience design are given. In order to help students to strengthen the sensitivity and self-examination ability of aesthetic experience, the author gave students an after-school homework of simulated car purchase. The job requirements are, first of all, at the auto home website (www.autohome.com.cn) search and understand the 44 models which given by lecturer. Second, through the comprehensive consideration of not limited to aesthetic factors, select five more cars from these 44 models that you feel most like, that is, the most likely to buy, and fill the model name in the form in the report template. And according to the degree of like in order, put your favorite car in the front place. In the corresponding position of the report, as much as possible to explain in detail the reasons for liking the car. Third, if you have a very tangled model that you want to buy and don't want to buy, you can list up to three models and write them in the corresponding position in the report template. Fourth, if none of the 44 models provided by the teacher has a favorite product, you can browse other models and choose your favorite model from them.

Second Car Selection. On September 19, 2020, we collected 72 car selection reports. In addition, through the communication with 72 students in these two weeks, we found some students with strong intention to buy a car. Combined with the details of these 72 assignments. In the way of two-way selection, 12 students were selected to enter the new automobile product experience design interest group. On October 3, the 12 students were asked to do the virtual car purchase homework again in the next week. And put forward two new requirements: first, through two weeks of new feelings for each model, the last selected model can be replaced and adjusted. Second, give a more detailed explanation of the reasons for choosing the car as far as possible. A week later, the researchers collected 12 points of second car selection report, and found that all the students adjusted the car selection content, and only one of them did not change the first favorite car. In addition, all the students gave a more detailed explanation of the reasons for choosing the car.

3.2   Analysis of Experience Elements of Automobile Products

Based on the subjective experience of car products formed in two virtual car purchase assignments, on October 11, the first author left a new assignment for the interest group: analysis of experience elements of automobile products. The specific requirements are: first, according to the two car selection experiences, please list the experience elements contained in the car experience. Please give each experience element a name and explain it. Second, for the experience elements of aesthetic type, please try to give the prototype of the experience, and try to depict the basic visual image of self-prototype or specific car type. On October 20, we received a total of 9 complete assignments, and further explained and answered the assignment requirements and analysis methods. In the next half month, students are encouraged to further improve the experience factor analysis report. As of November 7, we had received 10 improved assignments.

It should be pointed out that in the first three stages, the research objects are allowed to write the car purchase report and experience report based on their own subjective feelings and judgments, which effectively avoids any inducement or intervention that researchers may impose on the research objects. That is to say, the suspension of researchers' prior knowledge and experience is realized to the maximum extent.

3.3   Write-Up Car Experience Analysis Report

Through the communication with 12 interest group students during two months, it is found that some students have good performance in the ability of self-examination of experience. Combined with the detailed degree of 10 experience factor analysis assignments. The researcher chooses Mr. Su as a single case study object. Based on his two car selection reports and one final experience factor analysis report, this paper analyzes the personality characteristics, experience factors and behavior mechanism of car experience related to the underlying motivation. The first draft of the analysis report was completed on December 22. It should be pointed out that in order to give a clear interpretation of the experience elements and abstract refinement of the experience mechanism, we have integrated many assumptions based on empathy with Mr. Su's experience in the process of deep description and refinement of the experience elements and experience mechanism.

3.4 Confirmation and Amendment

In the week after December 23, 2020, researchers and Mr. Su conducted five rounds of confirmation and revision of the report. In this process, on the one hand, we confirmed with Mr. Su many hypotheses put forward in the previous stage, and corrected the mistakes of empathy contained in them. On the other hand, in order to provide specific direction guidance for car design practice, we inquiry about the remaining fuzzy content. The main method used is idiomatic language tracing. The researchers completed the improved version of the analysis report on January 2, 2021. Then the researcher asked Mr. Su to score each experience element in the improved manuscript based on the scale rules, so as to rethink and confirm the importance of different experience elements. Mr. Su sent the results to us on January 5. Accordingly, we revised the contents of the analysis report and completed the final version of the analysis report on January 10.

4 Results

In this part, we demonstrate our results in three aspects. First, Mr. Su's personality characteristics is demonstrated in Sect. 4.1; Sect. 4.2 shows Mr. Su's value of car experience elements. He identified 19 kinds of car experience: comfortable driving experience (95 points), unique feeling (95 points), elegant feeling (80 points), decent feeling (85 points), cultural experience (80 points), product strength (95 points), quality feeling (95 points), luxury feeling (75 points), spirit feeling (75 points), introverted quality (95 points), impractical appearance (20 points), novelty (75 points), high performance (65 points), cross-country and road performance balance (80 points), convergent aggressiveness (75 points), posture with potential energy (75 points), visual element restraint (90 points), word-of-mouth experience (80 points), pure sense (80 points), and balance between solemnity and dynamic (75 points). Due to the limited space, in this section, the five highest scoring experience elements will be introduced in Sect. 4.2. In Sect. 4.3, Mr. Su's car experience behavior mechanism.

4.1 Personality Traits

Mr. Su, from Qingdao, Shandong Province, is 24 years old. He has his bachelor of economics in 2018 and then went to work. When working, he felt that the rising period of the real estate industry has passed and wanted to switch to the Internet. So he resigned in 2020 and applied for a master's degree in user experience of Applied Psychology in Beijing Normal University to carry out full-time study.

In more than half a year of getting along with each other, we feel that Mr. Su usually seldomly talk much, but his mind is delicate. Although his intelligence level in the sense of intelligence is enough to help him get through the complex world, honesty and gratitude are still the clear background of his mind. Therefore, in the face of the pressure of reality, he may be good at calculation, but usually disdain to use the little cleverness that breaks through the ethical category. In a word, Mr. Su is a trustworthy person.

Perhaps it is because of the existence of this inner pure land that Mr. Su maintains a certain unconventional taste and pursuit of aesthetics and life. For example, Mr. Su has a special love for the unique oriental culture of Japan. For this reason, his Japanese listening and speaking has even reached the primary level. For another example, when talking about his preference for car consumption, Mr. Su said he appreciates the hidden state of life, likes elegant and unique things. He hopes that he is a person with heterogeneous taste and does not like tacky things. For example, BBA, which has been sought after, paid attention to and discussed by many people, is a representative of tacky stuff. In contrast, Mr. Su believes that Lexus demonstrates the taste of heterogeneity. For another example, in terms of living environment, Mr. Su prefers the quietness and cheerfulness of small towns. Although slightly away from the cutting-edge learning and work opportunities, it saves time-consuming, long-distance commuting, and avoids the rush and noise of metropolis.

But we are still born in a generation that needs competition and rushing, the inner pure land cannot afford food and clothing. Therefore, in the compromise with reality, Mr. Su's the inner pure land can only become a realistic self that is suitable for specific situations in a certain way.

Although Mr. Su holds unconventional values and beliefs, he still has to pay attention to society and others. For example, he pursues the uniqueness of taste, but also hopes that this uniqueness can gain the awareness and recognition of people around him. However, the ordinary heart is still around him. He said that just as he appreciates the hidden low-key feeling, he will never show this taste in an obvious way, but hopes to metaphorize it through his own words and the use of products. This illustrates that Mr. Su's attitude, which is that I hope you can know what I am. If you don't know, I won't take the initiative to say what I am. However, He also said frankly that the pursuit of non-vulgarity is just an ideal state of life, and now he does not have the strength to hide, that is to say, there is nothing to hide, but he is working towards the ideal state.

Every time when we saw him, we can feel that Mr. Su has something in his mind, and sometimes he is in a state of tension and anxiety. Later, we got along with him very well, and gradually seemed to know his thinking as usual. Although he was studying full-time, about two months after enrolled, he has thought about his employment prospects after graduation, including what position he could apply for and what income he could get, and constantly revised his resume and found related internships, which also delayed his knowledge learning. While Mr. Su's wisdom is clearly aware of the importance of bringing in new knowledge, we must also know the simple truth of devoting ourselves to cultivation and sharpening our swords without mistaking firewood. As a teacher of

Mr. Su, first author of the paper sometimes feels that his abandoning Buddhism and being possessed is too worldly. However, in the face of the pressure of living, we dare to ask who can maintain the most ideal decent state of Buddhism and care for all without considering rice. It can only be said that at present, he is in such a stage of life. In addition, he felt that his experience is still young to understand the industry so that he can only find a suitable position with the help of more internships.

It is certain that as long as the actual conditions permit, Mr. Su's personality traits will be realized almost all the time into all the specific life behaviors such as eating, wearing, living, using and walking.

4.2 Experience Elements

Comfortable Driving Experience. Mr. Su did not mention the experience element in the experience element analysis report, but in the second car selection report he clearly pointed out the need for comfortable driving experience.

Through further exchanges, Mr. Su believes that the comfortable driving experience includes four points. First, the smoothness of shifting and stepping on the accelerator. That is, in the process of acceleration and shifting, there will be no sense of frustration. Second, the sense of lightness. That is to say, the accelerator is sensitive, the acceleration line is linear, and the car cannot move without power. Third, the noise inside is acceptable. Fourth, the temperature inside the car is comfortable. Overall, he noted that Lexus's ES300 can provide him with a very comfortable driving experience as an example.

Mr. Su also pointed out that the experience of noise comfort should be divided into scenes. When taking the family on a trip, he probably wants to feel as quiet and comfortable as possible. While driving by himself out of the desire just for driving pleasure, he hopes to have pleasant engine sound into the cockpit when accelerating relatively hard. Therefore, we make a suggestion for car makers. The power output of 3000 rpm for the car can usually meet the needs of the family trip. Therefore, the engine noise below 3000 rpm should be suppressed as much as possible through engineering design. And a certain sound wave can be put into the cockpit when it is above 3000 rpm. Mr. Su agreed with the plan.

Sense of Uniqueness. Mr. Su did not mention the experience element in the report. However, in the second car selection report, he clearly expressed his need for a sense of uniqueness. The so-called sense of uniqueness is a sense of unconventionality. So what are stereotypes? For example, the cars from the well-known Germany brands Audi, BWM and Mercedes have been talked about too much, so they become cheesy. But Infiniti, Acura and Lexus are small and unique, not so tacky. But the need for such a niche is not too niche, but with high recognition. That is, when looking at the car from a distance, people will know that it is the car. He hopes this unique shape can also show a certain impact. The specific way to promote this effect is usually to have a unique brand design language in the appearance of the car, and to show a unique sense of design in the overall and local visual experience.

In addition, Mr. Su specially mentioned that showing impact power but not aggressive. This can let others feel my unique taste and I am an approachable person. For this reason, he said, for example, the front face design of the Lexus ES300, the edge of the air intake grille protrudes upward and extends to the hood, which has impact force but not aggressive, and this reminds him thinking of flowing water or air flow. It can be found that the flowing or streamlined body shape is of great help to create a non-offensive visual experience.

According to the confirmation with Mr. Su, he will appreciate a car because of the above-mentioned modeling features so as to obtain perceptual aesthetic experience. Besides, he hopes to own such a car to symbolize and metaphorize his own personality. At the same time, through the purchase of such a car, he will feel that he has practiced his own values and taste demands.

Product Power. According to our analysis on two reports and interviews, we found that Mr. Su gives great importance to the specific performance of a car's product strength. In his view, product strength refers to the specific feelings that the driving performance of a car can bring to a driver. The strength mainly includes: power experience, braking experience, driving experience, turning experience, transmission experience and body rigidity experience. These experiences include not only the actual driving experience, but also the cognitive experience of the specific situation of these performances. On the other hand, the strength of the enterprise and brand, and the historical heritage of the product are also the important components of the product strength.

In terms of cases, Mr. Su believes that the product strength of Audi RS6 is very good, and the main reason is the quality of RS6 in terms of performance. In addition, the product strength of Lexus ES300 is also very good. Because the driving is comfortable, NVH is excellent, and the hybrid system provides a very smooth and quiet driving experience at low speed; the appearance and interior design are unique and elegant, giving the driver the enjoyment of beauty, but also showing others the unique taste.

Sense of Quality. According to the comprehensive analysis of two reports and interviews, we found that the sense of quality is a kind of product experience that Mr. Su hopes to obtain. He failed to make more theoretical explanation for the connotation of the sense of quality, but pointed out that the feeling opposite to the high-quality texture is the sense of cheapness and lack of design. From the perspective of cases, He believes that the large vertical screen and many levels of menu give people a sense of lack of design and a sense of being cheap. For example, the central control design of the 2020 Ford Explorer. The deep brown leather material of ES300 and the wooden decorative board and mechanical buttons will not follow the trend, but also generate the feel of high quality.

Sense of Introvertedness. In the experience elements analysis report, Mr. Su pointed out, the introverted sense refers to the self-consistent and harmonious beauty of the visual feeling of the whole car by matching with appropriate design elements. Taking the Lexus ES300 as an example, he further described the sense. The ES300 body let him remind of the posture of a swan, giving him a feeling of self-confidence and introverted. But here the design of the front face in the car plays an important role. He also stated that the body shape with a sense of introverted should be the side without too complicated shoulder line and waist line. The opposite feeling of introverted is conflict, radical, strong and sharp. The third-generation Mercedes Benz S-class is also considered by him to be reserved.

In addition, Mr. Su agrees with our analysis: on the one hand, when seeing the introverted car, he can get aesthetic appreciation experience. On the other hand, Mr. Su also hopes to practice his attitude towards life, that is, his sense of identity, by buying a car with a sense of introvertedness. With the help of the symbolic function of the car, He also hope to show and express the low-key, introverted and confident personal character.

4.3 Mechanism of the Whole Car Experience

In the end, we found that the following four experience mechanisms can be extracted from Mr. Su's car experience phenomenon, while other more detailed experience mechanisms are implied in the narration of various experience elements.

First of all, the experience elements identified by Mr. Su can be classified into the following three types of experience: first, functional experience. It includes both usability experience and easy-to-use experience. Second, aesthetic experience. It is worth noting that in this process, in addition to the pure form of aesthetic pleasure, many specific aesthetic experience activities are inextricably linked with the functional performance of the car. For example, while Mr. Su enjoys the wonderful sound of the engine, his subconscious is still feeling the cognition of the power train of the engine and the satisfaction it brings. Third, symbolic experience. Among them, it includes not only helping him symbolize and express his own taste and identity with the help of some product attributes of cars, but also helping him feel his self-identity and taste behind the symbolic meaning of the car products.

Secondly, the realization of symbolic experience usually requires the realization of a certain function or aesthetic experience. In other words, if you want users to gain some kind of symbolic experience, corresponding aesthetic design elements or functional elements are required to be offered. For example, the high performance of the car is necessary for Mr. Su to express his taste and identity.

Thirdly, if we compare Mr. Su's personality traits with his demands for car experience, we will find that his personalized demands for car experience are all explicitly or implicitly related to his personality traits. The realization of personality traits is the intermediary of specific experience demands, which is the life situation of Mr. Su. Therefore, if you want to know what kind of car customers will like, you must first know the following three things: first, what kind of person customers are, which mainly refers to a deep understanding of their personality traits. This understanding includes not only a general grasp of their personality, but also an understanding of their short-term and long-term life goals, as well as their relationship Secondly, what is the social environment of customers. In particular, we need to understand the culture, technology and system that the operation of the society depends on. Third, what kind of role does customers need the car to play in his living environment.

Finally, the experience of automobile products is composed of five elements. First, automobile experience including the operation experience of mechanical parts, such as car interaction system and steering wheel. Second, cockpit experience. Third, appearance experience. Fourth, brand experience. Fifth, the whole car experience.

5 Discussion

Through this study, we have two important findings as following.

First of all, among the experience elements that Mr. Su can identify, aesthetic experience elements obviously occupy the main part. One worthy problem to discussing is that it is difficult to define these specific aesthetic experience elements in phenomenology. Because in all kinds of aesthetic activities, there is a clear structure and characteristics of common consciousness and behavior, which provides a full reference for the phenomenological definition of aesthetic concept. In contrast, the real features of various specific aesthetic experience activities only exist in the intuitive subjective feelings rather than in the description range of language. Therefore, in order to define and explain these experiential elements in the way of language, it is necessary to permit and accept the existence of certain fuzziness. That is to say, it is necessary to allow one or several of the following six ways to define and explain these experience elements phenomenologically.

1. Explain some experience elements with specific car design cases. For example, the side of the ES300 has the feeling of linear flow.
2. Use the subconscious prototype to illustrate experience elements. For example, swan is the prototype that can best interpret the sense of elegance in heart.
3. Give as detailed language description as possible for why a certain car design case carries certain experience elements;
4. Give as detailed language explanation as possible for why a certain prototype carries certain experience elements;
5. Give as detailed language explanation as possible for why a certain car design case can carry certain experience elements.
6. Describe the basic visual structure that a prototype can carry some experience elements. If the visual image of an aesthetic experience element can be accurately described, the sixth way of interpretation is obviously the most valuable for the innovative design practice of aesthetic experience, but it is also the most difficult to achieve. Because it puts forward quite high requirements for the aesthetic sensitivity of both the researcher and the studied, the abstraction of visual impression and the ability of hand-painted expression.

Secondly, as Dufrenne pointed out that the concrete schema that can be used to interpret a certain aesthetic subject is almost infinite [12]. In the same way, the possibility of design solutions that can carry the same aesthetic experience is almost infinite. Moreover, through this study, we found that the same is true for functional experience and symbolic experience. Therefore, in theory, for the interpretation of any experience element, we should look for as many design cases as possible to interpret the extension and connotation of the experience concept. However, such a wealth of information is likely to be difficult to not exceed the maximum length of a paper. So how should this kind of research be presented in the paper? We believe that academic publication of such research is of obvious importance. Only those the cases that can best interpret a certain experience concept should be put into the paper. The paper can not only show the new discovery of experience elements, but also show the new value of experience elements.

6   Conclusion

It should be noted that considering the limitation of space and the core purpose of providing theoretical guidance for car product innovation, we did not present the specific data analysis process in the paper. It's a pity to have an effective communication and discussion with readers on research methods. However, all the research results presented in this paper have been confirmed by the research object, so readers do not need to worry about the reliability of the research results.

In addition, with the help of several rounds of phenomenological interviews and data analysis, our study completed the research on the car experience phenomenon of Mr. Su, a typical car user in Z era. We found 19 kinds of experience elements of car products, as well as the experience mechanisms reflected. Through the analysis and reflection of the research activities and results, we believe that the combination of descriptive phenomenological analysis and explanatory phenomenological analysis constitutes an effective tool for car experience research. Besides, due to the in-depth research, the results of this research have certain guiding significance for the practice of car experience innovation for Z generation users. We admit that the validity of the research results remains to be further verified. According to the general experience of phenomenological qualitative research, we should look for more than five Z generation consumers to evaluate the effectiveness of the 19 experience elements identified by Mr. Su. The experience elements that are generally recognized by everyone can be regarded as the content with universal guiding significance. In addition, other respondents should be asked to rate the care of these 19 experience elements based on the same scale rules. It can help to further lock in the experience elements with the most universal guiding significance. In addition, it is helpful to find out the preference of car experience of consumers with different personality characteristics.

Acknowledgement. The publication of this research is supported by the funding project, Premium Funding Project for Academic Human Resources Development in Beijing Union University (No. 12210611609-039).

References

1. Norman, D.: Emotional Design: Why We Love (or Hate) Everyday Things. Basic Books (2005)
2. Gothelf, J., Seiden, J.: Lean UX. O'Reilly Media (2016)
3. Nielsen, J.: Usefulness, Utility, Usability: Why They Matter. Video, 20 Feb 2012. https://www.nngroup.com/videos/usefulness-utility-usability. Accessed 10 Sept 2017
4. Lokman, A.M.: The integration of quality function deployment and Kansei engineering: an overview of application. In: API 2016 (2016)
5. Mahut, T.: Interdependency between user experience and interaction: a Kansei design approach. Int. J. Interact. Des. Manuf. (2018)
6. Li, Y.: A posterior preference articulation approach to Kansei engineering system for product form design. Res. Eng. Des. (2019)
7. Howell, D.: Tesla Motors Earnings Scheduled: Black Ice Or Autopilot? Investor's Business Daily (2016)

8. Li, S., Yang, J.: Robust autopilot design for bank-to-turn missiles using disturbance observers. Aerospace & Electronic Systems (2013)
9. Casper, J., Catanzaro, B., Diamos, G.: Deep speech: scaling up end-to-end speech recognition. In: Computer Science (2014)
10. Bickle, J.: Precis of philosophy and neuroscience: a ruthlessly reductive account. Phenomenol. Cogn. Sci. **4**, 231–238 (2005)
11. Draper, P.: Reflexive methodology – new vistas for qualitative research. J. Adv. Nurs. (2001)
12. Rump, G.C.: The phenomenology of aesthetic experience. Leonardo (1973)

Design of Traditional Brand H5 Game Advertisement Based on EEG and Eye Movement Analysis: Example of MAXAM

JunXuan Li and RongRong Fu[✉]

College of Art Design and Media, East China University of Science and Technology, Xuhui District, 130 Meilong Road, 200237 Shanghai, People's Republic of China

Abstract. The acceptance of traditional brands is gradually decreasing among young people. Aiming at the problem, this research explores the promotion of recognition and acceptance of these brands through the design of H5 game advertisements. This paper takes MAXAM brand as an example to study its present situation. H5 game is designed by taking the Elemental Tetrad model as guidance and also integrating story, mechanism, aesthetics and technology. The design principle comprises of shaping a sense of mission and immersion, optimizing information feedback, and strengthening brand information output. An optimal design scheme is proposed by utilizing AARRR theory. After completing design, the transmission effect is evaluated via EEG combined with eye movement experiment and IPA analysis method. The results indicate that H5 game advertisements can enhance users' brain arousal to the brand, and also can improve somewhat the attention of target users to MAXAM hand cream and a stronger willingness to buy. H5 game advertisements can be used as a method of mobile propagation in the process of MAXAM brand renaissance according to the analysis of IPA effective sample data, and also provides a basic and effective reference for China's time-honored brands, similar to MAXAM, to update positioning and establish brand recognition, familiarity and audience satisfaction.

Keywords: H5 game · EEG and eye movement · MAXAM

1 Introduction

Shanghai's traditional brand MAXAM was once known as the "No. 1 cosmetics brand in China", unfortunately, it gradually declined after being bought up. After Shanghai Jahwa's heavy redemption, it is still tepid and hard to go back to its past return to prosperity. Hence force, the revival of MAXAM has been regarded as a key issue in the construction of Shanghai style brand. The MAXAM proposed that if MAXAM is to be revived, they need to establish brand reputation among women aged 22–28 [1].

H5 advertising, which is favored by young people, is rising because of its ability to achieve viral brand communication with minimal resources. Among them, H5 game advertising focusing on immersive experience interaction has become a new hot channel for brand communication. In recent four years, the study on H5 advertising in China

© Springer Nature Switzerland AG 2021
M. M. Soares et al. (Eds.): HCII 2021, LNCS 12780, pp. 613–626, 2021.
https://doi.org/10.1007/978-3-030-78224-5_42

has been on the rise. In 2018, Hu Liu and Liu Jie took experience communication as the entrance, pointing out that the topic volume and design hotspots of H5 games can bring huge communication effects to brands [2].

Therefore, the question that this article wants to explore is: Can H5 games bring a turn for the traditional brands? and how should we construct the H5 communication of MAXAM brand?

2   Analysis of the Status Quo of Research Objects

In the period when MAXAM was taken over by Unilever, MAXAM experienced the price reduction of Unilever, and then encountered the attack of a wide range of foreign brands, resulting in the reduction of brand positioning. MAXAM has also tried to launch a series of high-end products, but its market acceptance is rather low, which has not changed the low-end image of MAXAM in the hearts of consumers [3].

2.1   Analysis of MAXAM's Online Communication Channels

MAXAM has been actively trying to development network communication since 2011. So far, they have established a complete brand network communication system, including four main communication channels: brand official website, official Weibo, WeChat official account and e-commerce platform [4]. However, the integrity of the system does not mean that the system is perfect. The key points of MAXAM's network communication system are as follows:

1. The communication of the brand has many contacts, which easily makes people confused when receiving information.The official website dynamics always use "Shanghai Jahwa" as the subject, and the update is lagging and not obvious, which makes the brand image perceived by users fuzzy.

2. The interaction between the brand side and users is less. Neither the official website nor the WeChat official account has set up relevant exchange and feedback sections, and Weibo messages and Tmall evaluation are rarely responded.

3. The promotion conversion rate and reach rate of brand information dissemination through various channels are low, WeChat tweets have fewer contacts, the frequency of encountering their WeChat tweets is low, and the spreading effect is not obvious. In addition, there are many phantom fans on Weibo.

4. The purchase conversion rate of new products is low showing that MAXAM has been unsuccessful in product marketing, so that users' perception of MAXAM is almost the same as that of more than 30 years ago.

2.2   Analysis of Mobile H5 Advertising Form of MAXAM

Among the numerous mobile advertising types, H5 advertising is the closest to the trend of brand rejuvenation of MAXAM.

Compared with H5 graphic advertisement, H5 game will pay more attention to user interaction and immersive experience, and subtly imprint the brand image in the user's memory. When users tend to play it again, then brand-related information has the possibility of secondary dissemination, because the game is more competitive [5, 6]. In particular, the light-weight H5 game can meet the fragmented life rhythm of modern groups on the basis of ensuring the immersion experience. In summary, launching light-weight H5 game advertisement with distinct brand image from the mobile terminal makes it possible for MAXAM to spread its brand among young groups.

3 Optimization Strategy of MAXAM's H5 Advertising

Brand communication on the mobile terminal is a digital process, and the AARRR (Drainage-Activation-Retention-Monetization-Recommendation) model can be used as the main model to optimize the operations of MAXAM. For mobile terminal, the following three Rs are not strictly sequential. For example, users may not convert products, but they will still be stored in your H5 products and recommend them to others. The essence of this model is to cultivate users' loyalty through the process of "drainage, interaction, conversion, retention, and sharing", with emphasis on "activation" through interaction and viral communication through "recommendations".

The purpose of designing interactive and lightweight H5 games is to activate new user groups, so that users have a certain psychological familiarity and tendency to the brand, which provides the possibility for future product repurchase [7]. H5 games are shareable, and the brand side can also promote the sharing of users' interests by increasing rewards.

4 Optimized Design of MAXAM's H5 Advertisement

4.1 Design Principles of Brand H5 Game Advertising

Aiming at the three pain points (lack of brand story, less interaction with users, and low brand conversion rate) of MAXAM's advertising. We use the Elemental Tetrad model as a guide to design the H5 game with a combination of story, mechanism, aesthetics and technology, and propose the following three advertising design principles accordingly.

1. Create a sense of mission and immersion.
MAXAM's brand communication lacks an emotional reason for users to choose the brand. Based on the octagonal behavior analysis, the game should create a sense of mission for the users, so that the users can harvest feelings far higher than the game itself. It is also necessary to set a game scene with strong sense of substitution in combination with the actual situation, so that users can quickly perceive their own roles in the scene, and clarify their goals and tasks, so that users are more willing to immerse themselves in it.

2. Optimize information feedback.
MAXAM online communication channels interact less with users, which makes users lack the experience of being responded. The information feedback mechanism of H5 game advertisements is better than that of graphic advertisements, which can achieve "one operation, one feedback", so that usesr and the game have a stronger sense of interaction. H5 games with interesting immersive experience can make the brand directly

target the young group, thus greatly improving young users' favor for the brand and enhancing the possibility of advertising transformation [8].

3. Strengthen brand information output.

Brand information output density, brand awareness and brand credibility can affect the brand conversion rate. According to the feasibility, H5 advertising chooses to strengthen the brand information output to improve the conversion rate of MAXAM. The symbolic information of the brand and its products, such as logos, colors, styles, etc., are embedded in the H5 content to improve brand awareness. H5 game advertising logic architecture as follow (Fig. 1).

4.2 Design Framework

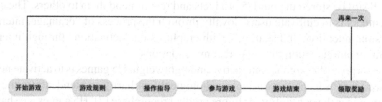

Fig. 1. H5 game advertising logic architecture

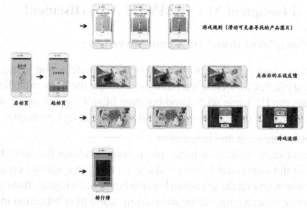

Fig. 2. H5 game advertising logic architecture process

4.3 Design Framework

1. Formal design

The target audience of H5 game is female users aged at 22–28, so the game style focuses on fashion and realism. The goal of the game is to find objects. Considering the difficulty of the game, the setting of hand speed score is increased, and the final score is taken as the measure of the game quality. H5 game advertising logic architecture process as shown in Fig. 2.

2. Content design

The game is designed around the series of MAXAM hand cream. The game elements are desserts, jewelry, gift boxes, cosmetics and other elements related to young female users. They are scattered on the table together with hand cream skin care products, fitting the scene of girls looking for things.

The goal of this H5 advertisement is to increase the exposure of MAXAM's various series of hand creams, and each interface of the game has been placed in the game. By increasing the frequency of user contact with the brand, it will increase the user's familiarity with the brand. For example, both the boot page and the start page have the brand logo of MAXAM. and the main color is MAXAM powder. During the game, the MAXAM classical image, light fragrance, fruit gel, and time series is applied.

3. Interaction Design

The H5 game will change the state of the hands in the boot page according to the login time, and the hands without login for a long time will produce fine lines. In addition, the page settings of the boot page and the end page are the same, and the interactive comparison diagram before and after playing the game is made. If there are fine lines on the picture of the hand before playing the game, the fine lines on the picture of the hand at the end of the game will fade or disappear, so as to give users a real sense of protection. At the same time, it gives users a psychological hint to care for their hands leading to users have a psychological orientation to buy hand cream.

4.4 Design Process and Effect Presentation

The name of the game "Looking for the Guardian" is consistent with the external touch-points of the brand "always guarding". "Shou" and "hand" are homophonic, which can make users associate with hand cream products (Fig. 3).

Fig. 3. H5 game advertising boot page, start page and leader board display

This design selects the H5 game mode of "treasure hunting", which accords with the age and acceptance of the target user in terms of game mode and difficulty. The scene selects multiple scenes where the user may use hand cream, and sets the user's desire to find the game background of hand cream in the chaotic life scene (Fig. 4).

Before the game starts, users can choose to view the rules of the game and the illustrations of various series of products. In order to complete the game more smoothly, most users will check the product icon for the first time, which can give users the impression of MAXAM related products. The setting of the game makes the user want to quickly identify the hand cream of MAXAM, which requires users to summarize

Fig. 4. Part of the H5 game level icon

spontaneously, and subconsciously find these symbol characteristics when there is a purchase demand (Fig. 5).

Fig. 5. H5 game advertising rules and product illustrations

During the game, according to the principle of "one operation corresponds to one feedback", we set the timing and scoring mechanism. When the user finds and clicks on the correct goal, the score will be calculated according to the speed. Moreover, when the user clicks on the wrong goal, the score will be deducted according to the number of errors (Fig. 6).

Fig. 6. H5 game advertisement right and wrong feedback diagram

After the end of the game, scores will be comprehensively given based on the user's correct operation rate and speed. H5 will automatically issue the corresponding rewards. Users click the score to query the reward content. The reward is MAXAM coupons, new product samples and random formal wear. When users click the "click to collect" button, the page will directly enter the flagship store of MAXAM, which ensures the user's service experience (Fig. 7).

Fig. 7. The display of H5 game advertisement score and reward

4.5 Enhancement of the brand's Achievable Effect

1. User satisfaction
The light-weight mini games are easy to use and have a certain degree of interest, which satisfies the entertainment of users in their leisure time and makes users establish emotional connection with the brand, also improves the user satisfaction of the brand.

2. Brand familiarity
Advertising expressions are consistent with brand contact points. When users play games, they will be mentally associated with the characteristics of the brand. And game advertising can easily stimulate users' desire to win or lose, so as to play games for many times, which increases the frequency of contact with brand information, and increases users' familiarity with the brand. Users' unintentional mention of the game in life can also improve the topic of the brand.

3. Brand loyalty
H5 game advertising in the gradual fit to complete the AARRR model is in the process of gradually cultivating brand loyalty. On the basis of brand awareness, users have accumulated a certain degree of satisfaction and brand familiarity. When they encounter similar products and brands, they are more inclined to choose the brand they are familiar with and feel satisfied with, which achieves the purpose of brand loyalty.

5 Design Evaluation

5.1 Objective Evaluation: EEG Combined with Eye Movement Analysis

Subject: The subjects were all female postgraduates aged at 22–28. All the subjects saw the sample pictures for the first time. And they are all right handedness, not suffering from color blindness or color weakness. Their naked eyes or corrected visual acuity greater than 1.0. They have no eye discomfort before the test, and they participated in the experiment voluntarily and were in good mental state. In EEG experiment and eye movement experiment, we selected 13 and 30 subjects meeting the experimental requirements as the experimental samples respectively.

Experiment: The experiment was carried out in a laboratory with good sound insulation and normal light. The indoor temperature was maintained at about 25 °C. In the whole process of the experiment, we keep the experimental environment quiet and try not to have other electromagnetic interference, so as to minimize the external interference to the subjects. The subjects were asked to face the wall and sit on a comfortable chair 1 m in front of the PC, and their muscles were relaxed.

Material: The experimental materials include 16 brand hand creams, such as MAXAM, Pechoin, L'Occitane, Mentholatum, Jo Malone London, KANS, WINONA, Herbacin, etc. In order to eliminate the interference of brand logo, the pictures do not display the brand logo. But they can only identify the brand through the appearance of brand products.

Material specifications: The EEG experiment material was black-and-white cross composition, with the size of 25.4 * 19.05 cm and the resolution of 300dpi. EEG experimental materials were played regularly in Latin square with blank pages in the middle to eliminate visual residue. The experimental materials of eye movement are all vertical composition, the size is 21 * 29.7 cm, and the resolution is 300dpi. The pictures are arranged in a 4 * 4 format. In order to eliminate the interference of experimental position, subjects took turns to use four experimental pictures to carry out untimely eye movement experiment.

1. EEG analysis

The experiment uses Muse2-Headband-Gray[1], the projects measured frequency band power of the EEG data, which is the other predominant paradigm in EEG research besides ERPs [9]. The experiment uses "prime probe" to simulate the real situation of brand evaluation.

Participants sat in a chair, read the experimental instructions under the guidance of the examiner, and the experiment will be started after collecting the EEG data for one minute in a meditation state. Participants need to complete a total of 8 groups of experiments (4 control groups and 4 experimental groups). Four control groups of experiments were conducted first, with four pictures of hand cream in each group. There will be a one-minute rest time between groups. The process of each group was the same, and the specific process is shown in Fig. 8. After the completion of the four groups of control group, the subjects were asked to play the game advertisement of H5, and then the experiment of the four groups of experimental groups was carried out, and the steps were the same as those of the control group.

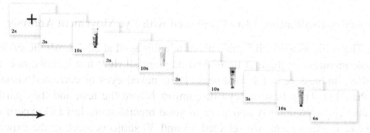

Fig. 8. EEG flow chart

---

[1] Muse is a light-weight rechargeable headband, which is equipped with 4 brain waves Electrodes: Two electrodes are located on the forehead (referred to as AF7 and AF8 in the standard 10–20 positioning system), the eyes are slightly upward, and the other two electrodes are in contact with the ears. In addition, it is also equipped with a spiral gauge and accelerometer, so that the head position can be calculated.

On Muse's official app, we can count the wake-up data of brain waves (Fig. 9).

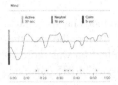

Fig. 9. App EEG wake-up data

In EEG experiment, the wake-up data statistics of the samples are as follows (Fig. 10):

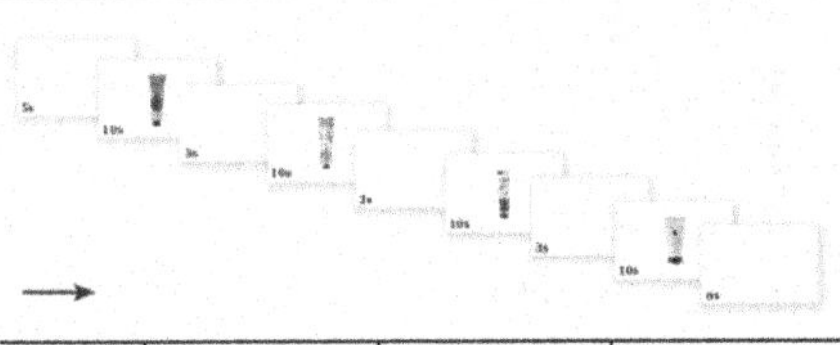

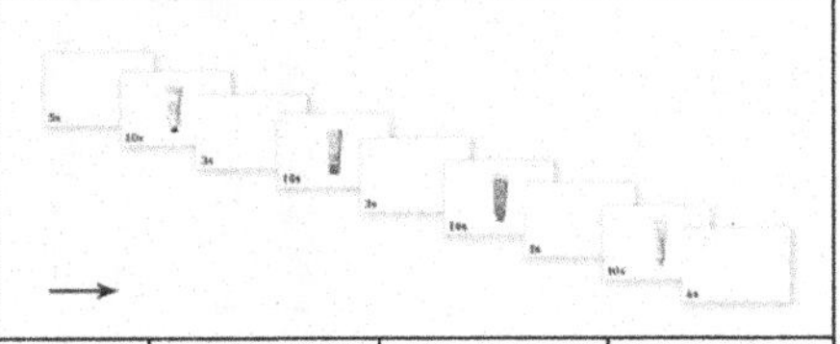

组别	Active	Neutral	Calm	组别	Active	Neutral	Calm
对照组1	18. 15384615	30. 23076923	11. 61538462	对照组2	23. 84615385	30. 30769231	5. 846153846
实验组1	9. 230769231	38. 76923077	12	实验组2	16. 46153846	34. 46153846	9. 076923077

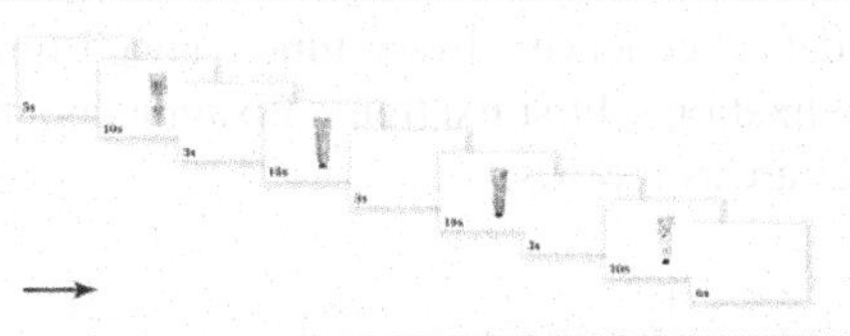

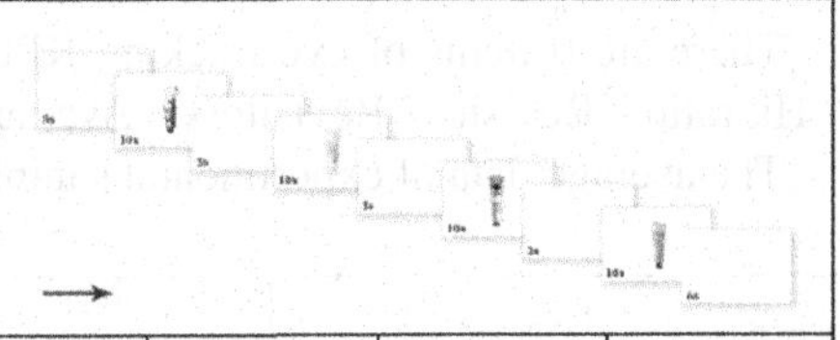

组别	Active	Neutral	Calm	组别	Active	Neutral	Calm
对照组3	17. 84615385	37. 23076923	4. 923076923	对照组M	17. 76923077	32. 92307692	9. 307692308
实验组3	19. 92307692	30. 53846154	9. 538461538	实验组M	19. 76923077	32. 92307692	7. 307692308

Fig. 10. Comparative statistics of EEG wake-up data

Combining H5 advertisements to analyze the results of the arousal level is as follows: after H5 game, the wake-up degree of group M (MAXAM) is enhanced, and the contrast effect is the best among the four groups. Two hand creams in group 1 have been used in H5 games, and the arousal degree of the experimental group is slightly lower than that of the control group, which may be related to the decline of the visual impact of the pictures when users watch the pictures for the second time; the hand creams in group 2 have not been used in H5 games, and the arousal degree of the experimental group is the most obvious decline compared with that of the control group in the four groups; there are three hand creams in group 3. In addition, Han Shu hand cream is very disturbing to the fruit gel series. During the trial play of the MAXAM H5 game, 1/3 of people did not distinguish between these two hand creams. Their colors are all pink, and their packaging styles are similar, which may be related to their increased arousal.

2. Eye movement analysis[2]

Eye movement data validation includes hotspot map and KPI data. The eye movement hot spot chart is shown in Table 1. Before the trial, the subjects' attention was scattered, but after the trial, the subjects' attention was more concentrated on the hand cream of MAXAM brand. The result showed that H5 game advertising can help increase users' attention to MAXAM brand products.

Table 1. Comparison of heat maps before and after being tried.

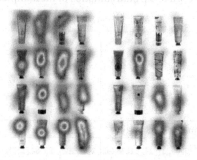

There are 9 items of eye tracking KPI data: Sequence、Entry time、Dwell time、Hit ratio、Revisits、Revisitors、Average fixation、First fixation、Fixation count。The average data of experimental samples are as follows:

产品系列	Sequence	Entry time	Dwell time	Hit ratio	Revisits	Revisitors	Average fixation	First fixation	Fixation count
果凝(对照组)	3.75	9578.925	2059.5	1	3.075	0.866071429	396.6	399	5.9
果凝(实验组)	4	9448.85	6246.425	0.9225	6.2	0.964285714	427.725	355.825	14.45
时刻(对照组)	2.75	6160.1	3515.775	1	4.5	0.857142857	367.275	384.3	9.675
时刻(实验组)	2.75	6493.225	7040.275	1	5.675	0.96875	458.65	302.05	15.45
轻香氛(对照组)	3.75	10050.875	1793.7	0.96425	3.15	0.714285714	333.4	319.775	5.25
轻香氛(实验组)	4	10816.1	6377.05	0.9285	4.2	1	501.15	563.7	12.375
经典(对照组)	3.75	9000.9	2279.325	1	3.45	0.571428571	325.65	350.1	6.85
经典(实验组)	3	7302.825	4806.95	0.96425	4.9	0.857142857	411.95	302.125	11.5

After eliminating part of the data, principal component analysis is used to concentrate the information,

KMO 和 Bartlett 的检验		
KMO值		0.69
Bartlett 球形度检验	近似卡方	52.043
	df	15
	p值	0

[2] In this study, SMI ETG eyeglasses eye tracker was used for eye tracking experiments. The sampling frequency was 60Hz and the resolution of HD lens was 1280 * 960p. Begaze3.7, which is matched with SMI ETG, was selected as the data processing software.

It can be seen from the above table that kmo is 0.690, greater than 0.6, which meets the premise requirements of principal component analysis, which means that the data can be used for principal component analysis. And the data passed Bartlett sphericity test ($P < 0.05$), indicating that the research data is suitable for principal component an analysis.

方差解释率表格						
编号	特征根			主成分提取		
	特征根	方差解释率%	累积%	特征根	方差解释率%	累积%
1	4.278	71.3	71.3	4.278	71.3	71.3
2	1.356	22.596	93.896	1.356	22.596	93.896
3	0.234	3.905	97.801	-	-	-
4	0.121	2.014	99.815	-	-	-
5	0.008	0.139	99.954	-	-	-
6	0.003	0.046	100	-	-	-

From the above table, we can see that there are two principal components extracted by principal component analysis, and the eigenvalue values are greater than 1. The variance interpretation rates of the two principal components are 71.300%, 22.596% and 93.896% respectively.

成份得分系数矩阵		
名称	成分	
	成分1	成分2
Dwell time（ms）	0.229	-0.064
Revisits	0.196	-0.371
Revisitors	0.21	0.154
Average fixation（ms）	0.213	0.257
First fixation（ms）	0.061	0.686
Fixation count	0.223	-0.187

When using principal component analysis to calculate the weight, we need to use "component score coefficient matrix" to establish the relationship between principal components and research items, and the equation is as follows:

线性组合系数及权重结果				
名称	主成分1	主成分2	综合得分系数	权重
特征根	4.278	1.356		
方差解释率	71.30%	22.60%		
Dwell time（ms）	0.4733	-0.075	0.3414	17.86%
Revisits	0.4045	-0.4321	0.2032	10.63%
Revisitors	0.435	0.1796	0.3736	19.55%
Average fixation（ms）	0.4399	0.2987	0.4059	21.24%
First fixation（ms）	0.127	0.7991	0.2887	15.11%
Fixation count	0.4621	-0.218	0.2984	15.61%

According to the weight calculation, the scores of each group are as follows:

产品系列	计算分数
果凝(对照组)	513.7706195
果凝(实验组)	1263.328675
时刻(对照组)	766.1505439
时刻(实验组)	1403.654518
轻香氛(对照组)	440.7809954
轻香氛(实验组)	1333.134155
经典(对照组)	530.7033493
经典(实验组)	994.1541289

In summary, many KPI data of eye tracking experiment once again show that H5 game advertising can help MAXAM improve its product attention.

To some extent, eye movement data cannot fully reflect the degree of preference. In order to make the experimental results objective and effective, the subjects were asked to choose three hand cream with the strongest desire to buy after each eye movement experiment. The subjective evaluation and eye movement data are combined to screen out the interest regions of the subjects. The purchasing desire of 30 subjects before and after playing H5 is shown in Table 2. The data in the table shows that after playing H5, the subjects' purchasing desire for MAXAM is significantly increased. At the same time, we found that the MAXAM at the same time, we found that MAXAM moments series is more popular among the subjects.

Table 2. Statistical table of purchase desire before and after being tried.

实验图片	序号	前购买意愿			后购买意愿		
	1	41	44	21	22	21	44
	5	12	41	22	12	11	22
	9	13	21	34	11	21	44
	13	14	43	21	14	12	43
	17	22	34	41	11	22	34
	21	22	14	42	22	12	11
	25	12	31	43	21	34	32
	29	14	22	43	11	22	43
	2	43	11	32	11	34	14
	6	12	11	14	11	12	14
	10	43	32	34	21	14	33
	14	42	11	34	14	11	42
	18	11	23	44	11	44	23
	22	23	31	33	23	31	33
	26	21	11	32	11	43	14
	30	32	23	24	34	44	14
	3	42	44	24	44	42	22
	7	21	14	34	43	21	13
	11	23	44	24	33	44	42
	15	23	33	44	22	33	44
	19	13	23	44	44	23	13
	23	44	33	41	44	43	33
	27	23	32	21	44	43	33
	4	21	14	42	21	11	33
	8	21	14	13	21	33	14
	12	23	21	13	12	22	33
	16	12	21	23	34	11	12
	20	33	42	11	33	11	42
	24	34	13	33	34	13	33
	28	23	34	33	33	11	23

Through the experimental analysis of EEG combined with eye movement, the results showed that H5 game advertising can enhance the target users' attention to the MAXAM hand cream to a certain extent. When they pay attention to the four series of hand cream involved in the MAXAM H5 game, the EEG is more active, and the target users' purchase intention is stronger.

5.2 Subjective Evaluation——IPA Analysis

In order to confirm the rationality of H5 advertising design more widely, the satisfaction evaluation was carried out in the form of questionnaire. Each link in the game was made into pictures, and the tested samples included 200 new target user groups of MAXAM (22–28 years old women). The satisfaction evaluation is carried out in the aspects of interface style, color matching, information transmission and so on.

The questionnaire was conducted from two dimensions of cognitive importance and player satisfaction. The importance of the questionnaire was multiple topics, and the percentage was calculated according to the answers. Most of the satisfaction was assessed by likert 7 scale, with 7–1 points in order of satisfaction. The evaluation index system of the questionnaire adopts the analytic hierarchy process, which divides the evaluation index satisfaction of players to H5 game into two levels: the first level is the target level (A) The second layer is the element layer (b). The player's evaluation of meijiajing H5 game includes eight target layers: boot page evaluation, start page evaluation, product graphic evaluation, level page evaluation, feedback mechanism evaluation, ranking evaluation, end page evaluation and reward page evaluation, and 29 element layers (hereinafter referred to as evaluation index) subordinate to the above eight target layers.

The questionnaire survey was performed in April 2020. A total of 428 samples were collected, including 218 target samples (answers by women aged at 22–28). SPSS was used to analyze the reliability of the questionnaire: the reliability coefficient was 0.982, which was greater than 0.9, indicating that the reliability of the research data was very high and could be used for further analysis.

In the follow-up structural research of satisfaction, IPA analysis method is used to construct a two-dimensional four quadrant grid [10] with the mean value of "importance" and "satisfaction" of the observed items as the intersection, the "importance" as the vertical axis, and the "satisfaction" as the horizontal axis. As shown in Fig. 11, the four quadrants formed are: advantage area, improvement area, opportunity area, and maintenance area [11] .

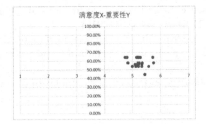
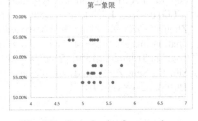

Fig. 11. IPA index factor quadrant chart   **Fig. 12.** Coon in the first quadrant

In order to subdivide the difference degree of importance and satisfaction of players to 28 indicators (C12 is suggested to be deleted due to reliability analysis), we performed IPA quadrant chart to evaluate players' satisfaction. The priority area is the area with high importance and satisfaction, indicating that these indicators are developing well. Among them, there are 27 evaluation indexes (including start page, start page, product diagram, level page, ranking list, end page and reward page). They are the advantages of MAXAM H5 game development and the core factors to attract players in the game. The maintenance area is the area with low importance and high satisfaction, which indicates that MAXAX H5 game develops well in feedback and continues to maintain.

6 Conclusion

By designing H5 games and evaluating the effectiveness of the design,we can find that H5 game advertising has a positive role in promoting the spread of traditional brands. At the same time, this study also plays a reference role for traditional brands similar to

MAXAM to become younger and arouse the audience's favor and reputation again. Of course, there are still some limitations in the sample collection of this study, and more in-depth work needs to be carried out to further verify the effectiveness.

References

1. Huang, K.: Reinventing MAXAM. Chinese SMEs **2014**(03), 36–37 (2014)
2. Hu, L., Liu, J.: Explore the design strategy of brand communication in DIY game HTML5 from "Experience Communication." Art Design **2**(03), 89–90 (2019)
3. Huang, C.: Dabao launched its first essence, is it feasible for old brands to enter high-end? Daily Chem. Sci. **41**(12), 4–12 (2018)
4. Cao, L.: A Study on Network Communication Strategies of Time-Honored Cosmetics Brand. Bohai University (2019)
5. Hu, L.: Research on the Performance Strategies of HTML5 Adevertising in China. JiNan University (2016)
6. Zhou, Y., Wang, F.: The manifestation and advantages of Html5 ads on mobile. New Media Res. **2**(01), 52–53 (2016)
7. Chen, J.: Advertising Design Research in Terminal based on HTML5 Technology. Jiangnan University (2017)
8. Sheng, C.: The Application of Mobile terminal Interactive Advertising under the Perspective of Immersive Experience. Zhejiang Gongshang University (2018)
9. Segawa, J.A.: Hands-on undergraduate experiences using low-cost electroencephalography (EEG) devices. J. Undergrad Neurosci. Educ. **17**(2), A119–A124 (2019)
10. Zhou, Y., Wei, X., Liang, F.: IPA-based integrated marketing communication of tourist destination image: a case study of two ancient water towns in the south of the Yangtze river. Tourism Tribune **2013**(9), 53–60 (2013)
11. Shi, L., Sun, Z.: A study on players' perception and evaluation of rural tourism catering **19**(05), 62–68 (2019)

Modular Approach to Designing 3D Printed Products: Custom HCI Design and Fabrication of Functional Products

Robert Phillips[1]([✉]), James Tooze[2], Paul Smith[3], and Sharon Baurley[1]

[1] Design Products, Royal College of Art, Kensington, UK
robert.phillips@rca.ac.uk
[2] University of Brighton, Product Design, UK
[3] Glasgow School of Art, Innovation School, Glasgow, UK

Abstract. Alongside bringing about new ways to make products, additive manufacturing (commonly referred to as 3d printing) opens up new ways to design them. This article explores a *speculative model and vision between HCI and Industrial design*, where the use of modular and modifiable 'CAD' parts coupled with intelligent systems could be used within lay user/retail settings to enable non-designers to create custom functional objects, with limit prior knowledge. Leading to design outputs that can be fabricated by on-site and on-demand additive manufacturing technologies. This article reports on a design workshop where cycling enthusiasts, supported by industrial designers, utilised, configured and modified a range of 'CAD parts' to create custom-made functional objects for additive manufacture. The study findings indicate the practicalities and challenges of implementing an 'HCI system' for the production of novel functional objects by novice designers, and signposts further investigation.

The article yields value to HCI researchers through design-led opportunities, based on technological review and workshop insights; developing sustainable, resilient and independent manufacture. The combination of digital manufacture, design opportunity and intelligent HCI systems offer; new HCI models, distribution, design file access, standards compliance, unique Intellectual Property and building functioning customised parts. The (current) Covid-19 context, reaffirms the researches study offering new and agile opportunities that HCI principles can support and build from. The article makes recommendations, forming a design-led HCI software 'blueprint'. Including guidelines on: part design, their interoperability, the design to production process, and embedding expertise and failure limitation within this process.

Keywords: HCI roadmap · User-designers · Digital manufacturing · On-demand · Modularity

Hypothesis: It was the researchers' hypothesis that due to the advances in four key areas (AM, CAD, AI and open design) it may be possible (in the near future) to develop an HCI system and retail service that allows the general public to custom design and have made functional products with relative ease. Guided by a 'design assistant' the user would follow a series of steps to help define their requirements, take important real-world

© Springer Nature Switzerland AG 2021
M. M. Soares et al. (Eds.): HCII 2021, LNCS 12780, pp. 627–646, 2021.
https://doi.org/10.1007/978-3-030-78224-5_43

measurements and criteria, and help them select the nearest fit in terms of existing objects or parts from which to create their novel design. This design would then be tested for performance, durability, and optimized accordingly prior to being fabricated on-site. The hypothesis rationale is founded on; *(1) the increase accuracy, affordability and usability of additive manufacture technologies - (machines, processes and materials); (2) the advances in usability and performance of CAD tools with features such as part libraries, FEA analysis, and other measures to improve speed and effectiveness of designers work; (3) the advances in AI and ML that offer the opportunity to embed or supplement a designers technical knowledge and (4) the open sharing and collaborative development of functional designs online.* Authors speculate this manufacturing approach benefits; resilience, circular economy and user-driven innovation.

1 Introduction

The order of this article; demonstrates a contextual design workshop, followed by a 'design vision' with state-of-the-art exemplars, combining contexts for a 'HCI retail experience', authors are aware it is unconventional.

3d printing materials and processes have seen significant development and investment [1], and technologies are now able to produce precision and high-performance parts, as evidenced in their use as critical functional components, for example in automated multi-material robot grippers, functional automotive parts, and medical devices. Computer Aided Design (CAD) tools are already excellent examples of systems with embedded expertise (snaps, guides, LCA, FEA, etc.), however they often have a steep learning curve, requiring considerable time to master. Design technology is progressing toward more intelligent systems with development of algorithmic controlled generative design systems. Yet, these are nascent and still often require expert intervention. Insights demonstrate the system would need to result in 'perfect first time' use, where the results generated are desirable and safe to use, a critical criterion for functional products. Linking together design knowledge and specific product domain knowledge, as well as manufacturing capability and other input data to achieve this basic level of functionality. Platforms, close to 'perfect first time' can be seen in website building platforms, such as WIX et al. [2], where users choose from predetermined features, guided by limited parameters and containing custom content all within a system that aims to guarantee a fully functional website. Mobile-based and lower cost scanning equipment, as well as AR/MR services offer the opportunity to take accurate real-world geometric data and measurements into CAD environments. The cycle industry was a primary industry to utilize; precision and adaptability of 3d printing, leading to a natural 'research through design' intervention. The cycle industry works to tight constraints including; stringent tolerances, human ergonomics, fit for purpose (lightweight road applications to rigorous off-road use), material and part optimization, durability, comfort, servicing requirements, environmental ingress, standardization, compliance and more. Rather than being a single product, bikes are essentially kits of parts, where off-the-shelf componentry works in chorus to rigorous tolerances. The industry is highly stratified and segmented; bikes are used across ranging environments, with large differences in the parts specification(s) aimed at professional vs amateur users. Keen cyclists often upgrade their bikes, changing parts to improve performance, comfort or aesthetics, suiting specific terrain or environmental conditions, and replace worn out or broken parts.

At the time of writing global supply chains, retail business and society in general has been challenged by Covid-19 and proved that localised production is viable. Covid-19 resulted in localised and global stock and material shortages. Amazon (the online retailer) has thrived [3], but the effect is to remove value from local economies and aggregate it off-shore. The disruption to global supply chains has resulted in shortages of mass-produced products – evident in the scarcity of bike parts. The response to the pandemic and the shortage of PPE across the world has seen rapid development of 3d printed alternatives (Prusa face shield) [4], which were designed openly and collaboratively, shared online and modified to create a multitude of versions to suit various material types and printers. This environmental 'event' has sparked powerful cultural, industrial and economic shifts that make on-demand digital fabrication in local retail not only possible, but viable, and necessary, in order to make supply chains more diverse and resilient.

This paper documents a workshop (repeated 4 times) exploring the challenges of what authors call *mass-configuration* within retail. As the technology, in the form of digital manufacturing and more specifically 3D printing, is becoming more accessible it brings with its opportunities for the general public, and by this we mean non-professional designers and makers, to create their own products. Scenarios are imagined where retail spaces offer the facilities that enable people to design and produce functional 3D printed artefacts. By functional artefacts we mean; products designed to serve a functional or technical purpose rather than being solely decretive or souvenir(s). We identify 3 overarching types of product creation scenarios:

1. *3D Print service;* where the retailer acts as service provider allowing customers to either print their own designs, ones that they have downloaded from the Internet or select from a range of products offered by the retailer. This type of product creation allows customers to make wholly custom objects for personal needs but does not offer a design framework for them to work within.
2. *Mass-customisation;* where the retailer offers customers a range of products that have been designed in such a way that the design is editable by the customer, prior to printing it out, in a limited way within known parameters, most probably with software tools. This type of product creation offers customers a design framework for them to work within but not the opportunity to make wholly custom objects for their own specific needs.
3. *Mass-configuration;* where the retailer offers customers the opportunity to modify and building upon a kit of virtual component parts and assemblies. Using software to modify them within known parameters as well as use them as building blocks for new parts and opportunities for customers to create wholly new parts. This type of product creation offers customers a design framework for them to work within as well as the opportunity to make wholly custom objects for their own specific needs.

We have undertaken this research, as converging factors increase the prevalence of 1 and 2 and potential rise to scenarios resembling 3.

1.1 Affordable and Capable Production Tools

The primary factor in these scenarios are the tools themselves; much has been written about the rise of Additive Manufacture (AM), commonly referred to as three-dimensional printing (3DP), and the opportunities that this range of technologies and associated materials offer [5–7]. What once were sequestered in research labs and in high value manufacturing centres are now within reach of a mass market. The cost barrier that restricts who owns them is being eroded and the range of printers within the reach of small businesses has grown exponentially over the last few years with developments in printing technologies emerging on the market that offer increased accuracy, various material properties, an increase in the speed of production and an increase in the structural properties of the parts produced. As well as produce parts with a higher degree of accuracy and most significantly parts that are homogenously strong in all directions and comparable in strength with those made using injection moulding. A number of 2019 [8, 9] articles highlight examples of 3DP technology utilised to produce 'functional products' opposed to pure prototyping or 'demonstrator' projects. Notable are the UK manufacturer of bicycle components Reynolds, who are producing 3DP metal parts. Also, the Razor Maker project, a pilot collaboration producing custom 3DP razors.

1.2 Making as a Movement

Another factor is 'information availability' in the public domain about 3D Printing and platforms for sharing 3D designs and encouraging making on the Internet. 3D Printing grew up alongside the Internet, and in tandem have been enabling disparate and interest specific networked communities to share what they are doing with one another with relative ease. A recent development for DIY and making enthusiasts, and an enabler of the nascent Maker Movement, are platforms such as Thingiverse (www.thingiverse. com) and Instructables (www.instructables.com), which act as repositories, guides and discussion boards for all manner of making projects. The Maker Movement can also be seen as manifest in the presence of open access maker spaces (*Techshop and Fab Labs*), magazines (www.makezine.com), making clubs (www.makerclub.org and www.diy.org) events (www.makerfaire.com), and successful start-up businesses (www.diydrones.com) and Local Motors (www.localmotors.com) that have their own active communities and collaborative development and content sharing platforms. Makerspaces and communities of makers, both physical and digital, foster openness and innovation as core to their philosophy and can avoid influence of mainstream innovation practice [10, 11]. This arrangement of the social and technical leading to 'information availability' is key to possibilities of new forms of production.

1.3 Design Tools and 3D Printing

In most cases to make 3D printed objects a 3D CAD (computer aided design) file will need to be generated. Mastery of CAD tools was once solely the preserve of professional designers, architects and engineers. More recently new CAD tools aimed squarely at the non-professional/novice markets (3dtin, Tinker CAD, Blokify) as well as more sophisticated free tools (Fusion 360, SketchUp, Blender, Sculptris) is abundant. Major CAD software developers such as; Autodesk Inc, and Dassault Systems have released free to use CAD tools aimed specifically at a young and novice sector that is enamoured by the potential of making things with digital fabrication tools. Autodesk released the 123D suite of tools, for desktop and tablet use, specifically created for 'people who want to make things themselves' [12]. Design tools targeted at children and the wider general public speak of a potential near future where there is a greater proficiency of the general public with 3D design software. One tool of note is Design Spark 3D (www.designspark. com) which is made available for free by Allied Electronics and RS Components and which allows users to import 3D CAD versions of parts both companies supply online. This allows users to create designs based on real parts without the need to measure or model them themselves, as well as automatically creating a bill of parts needed to realise their design. Some other CAD packages are also equipped libraries containing 3D models of standard parts such as nuts, bolts and bearings that users can customise to create non-standard parts.

Where the elements in these repositories are accurate and relate to parts in the real world, they can be considered *smart content*; as they are well-designed functional objects that were specifically created for others to utilise and be confident in their accuracy. Such objects that are simple parts but hard to model can act as a springboard for novice designers. Where parts imported from RS Components (www.rs-components.com) into Design Spark are the work of professional designers, the Open Structures project (www.openst ructures.net) is an online repository of parts, where all parts conform to a geometrical grid that builds 'a kind of collaborative Meccano to which everyone can contribute parts, components and assemblies' [13]. 3D Hubs (www.3dhubs.com) online platform connects people in needed of a 3D printing service with a community of over 20,000 globally distributed 3D printer owners. Major software providers [14] are beginning to offer algorithmically controlled generative design systems as part of their professional suite of products [15]. Generative design creates multiple alternative design solutions in response to set boundary conditions, for example material type or performance criteria. Coupled with the geometric freedoms of 3DP, generative design offers relatively unconstrained outcomes. These systems still require expert input to understand and define goals and boundaries. Yet a future can be imagined where intelligent systems can intervene where now an expert is required.

1.4 Mass-Customisation

Defined by Tseng & Jiao [15], Mass-customisation is "producing goods and services to meet individual customer's needs with near mass production efficiency". It is on one hand an offering of products to a mass market that have been designed specifically to allow for customer involvement to modify product designs, either formally or aesthetically within set variables that still allow single variants to be made together at high volume, and on the other a mechanism for manufacturers to offer wider choice. Mass customisation can therefore be thought of as having the capability to match both mass manufacture in terms of scale and efficiency, and custom manufacture in terms of suitability to the individual needs and wants [16]. In thinking about tailor's shops, it is evident that allowing people to make individual decisions from a framework or set of options is not a new phenomenon in product creation. What is a new phenomenon is the use of flexible fabrication tools and systems coupled with simple to use interfaces that allow the general public to customise prior to purchase mass produced goods that previously would have been standardised. Products as varied as footwear (www.nike.com/nikeid), 'all over print t-shirts', dolls (www.makie.me) and blended whiskey (www.whiskyble nder.com) are now being offered as customisable products. Manufacturing and design unite custom fabrication of goods to high streets.

1.5 Why Bikes?

Bikes are used for many purposes, varying greatly in their design accommodating multitudes of sports, contexts, and users. There are many bespoke niches and have needs that are yet to be met. Lead users involved in these niches are people that are at the leading edge of their discipline or personal hobby, 'positioned to benefit significantly by obtaining a solution to their needs' [17]. Bikes are a familiar territory for self-improvement and as they are an assembly of parts often from a wide range of manufacturers, open to modification and customisation. There is currently a wealth of evidence online of people designing and making personal bike related items on Instructables (www.instructa bles.com), Thingiverse (www.thingiverse.com), as well as bike specific websites such as bikehacks (www.bikehacks.com). Bikes are durable with Red bull changing advertising strategies to support 'extreme sports' operating at the edge of what is possible. During the current time, cycles are turned to as sustainable transport that is individual. Leading brands, i.e., 'Shimano' [18] produce group sets and assemblies that work across countless engineering and design visions for tolerances and inter-operability, set by industry and monopolising it. Finally, the equitable nature of the product is; rented [19], owned [20], a healthy transportation option [21], open to repair [22] and continually used throughout world wars and in times of hardship [23] (Fig. 1).

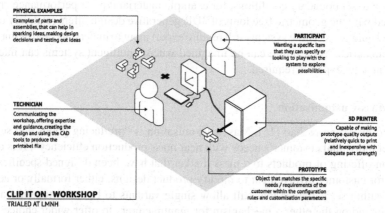

Fig. 1. Workshop's 'design vision' and then the operational functions of an optimal HCI system.

2   Method (Contextual Design Frame)

In order to trial the scenario of mass-configuration as a viable method to enable people to create their own products, either by building from the work of others or by creating a wholly new product; a workshop called *Clip-It-On* was run four times over two days. It was imagined that for this type of product creation the people who would participate would have specific interests and specific needs, people Von Hippel calls "lead users" [24]. The *Clip-It-On* workshops were run at *Look Mum No Hands* (LMNH), a bike themed café, repair workshop and accessories retailer, during the London Design Festival. As '*Clip-It-On*' suggests the co-design workshops focussed on clips that enable items; lights, cameras, phones, tools and anything else, to be mounted on to the frame of any bike. Although bike mounting attachments are currently available for sale, the purpose of the workshops was to explore the potential of creating custom solutions for individuals to explore, create and "imagine their ideal products" [25]. The 'uniqueness' of the product was derived from the item to be 'clipped on' to the bike, and then the design by which this was achieved. The workshop focused on the creation of something new that linked a standard component (bike mount) to a yet unimagined item, for example a banana. LMNH was chosen as a test venue as it has a large community following among cycle enthusiasts, drawing in specific interest and user groups (that might be) motivated to create their own products, as well as being located on a main cycle route within London, thereby enabling testing in "the richness of the real world in which the applications are placed" [26]. The LMNH café was large enough for researchers to establish a design and 3D print area.

3   Workshop Setup/Parameters

Over 2 days, open recruitment led to an 'inhouse set-up' in existing business with 20 self-selecting participants. The scenario envisioned is one where users build their ideas using a repository of pre-designed parts; six components were developed to form a 'kit of parts' that had changeable dimensions to connect/fit various items by using parametrized dimensions to a range of bike frame sizes. Parts were designed by looking at existing plastic bike accessories and then generating and physically testing designs optimised to the capabilities of the UP Printer (build orientation, printing resolution and material properties) as well as testing how they connect to each other to give various assembly options. 3D CAD software (Dassault Systems SolidWorks) was used to design parts, which allowed for them to be modified or adapted during the workshop. Each part had a preferred build orientation that corresponded to its optimum structural strength although the parts were not designed to meet any recognised safety standard. Not all elements of the kit of parts needed to be 3D printed. In order to connect parts and secure the assemblies to bike frames or items to assemblies, 30 mm M6 stainless steel bolts, sprung washers and M6 stainless steel wingnuts were used. Due to the exploratory nature of the workshops, all parts made, needed to be seen as 'prototypes' rather than 'finished products', which would be the case with the imagined scenario. Two PP3DP UP Printers (www.pp3dp.com) were chosen to fabricate parts as they are ready to use out of the box, while being very small and easy to transport, and capable of producing objects with a reasonable level of resolution. The UP is a low-cost desktop FDM (Fused Deposition Modelling) printer that uses reels of ABS (Acrylonitrile Butadiene Styrene) plastic filament to produce parts. ABS is a common thermoplastic that is used in many consumer products, as it has properties of "toughness and impact resistance, while being lightweight" [27].

3.1 The Consultation Process

The four workshop sessions were identically conducted. Four researchers acting as design technicians staffed the consultation. The technician's role was to help draw out, embody and realise the participant's ideas. In effect, mediating between the participant's ideas and the capabilities and constraints of the kit of parts, printer and design software, and taking on the role of the imagined 'embedded expertise'. The consultation space in LMNH consisted of a large table for participants and technicians to sit at, 4 laptops with Dassualt Systems SolidWorks, 2 UP 3D printers and a collective resource of digital cameras, sketchbooks, pens, pencils and measuring tools. The workshop followed a participatory design approach [28] where participants "engaged in a proposed design scenario, and developed design solutions with the technicians". Empathetic or co-design "get[s] people personally, emotionally engaged so they can reflect on a process" [29]. Co-design gathers "information about the contexts of people's interactions" comprehending applications, its practice provides "tools that create a fluency" [30]. This is in itself a form of engagement and Participatory Design (PD) involving users in "evaluative research: testing existing products or prototypes" [31]. The difference "between human-centred and user-centred design is huge as they don't address the same audience". "Human-centred design relates to people, user-centred design relates to consumers" [32]. The use of 'CAD operators' (i.e., design technicians) builds on Sinclair's practice [33] of exploring design territories in collaboration with technical mediators to provide software for users to explore ideas. Previous work on participatory design highlighted the need for "lay users to access to a technical third party to help translate their concepts into tangible, viable outcomes" [34].

Participants were briefed to ensure they understood the aims of the workshop, technological capabilities (3D printing), and the limitations of the workshop, namely that objects fabricated as a result of the workshop were 'prototypes', not finished products. Participants were also given a printed resource itemising the parts dimensions, their build direction, and a brief overview of the process. This also served as a reference and template for the technician and participant to draw on during the consultation. A number of copies of each part were printed, and available to hand on the table so participants could see and touch finished examples. The consultation process started by discussing the participant's object, how and where it might be attached to their bike. Participants were shown the range of clips, and discussed with the technicians, their or modifications. Once a brief/idea had been agreed, sketches and measurements taken, the technicians used CAD to alter and create new parts. The participants were consulted throughout this process, and the CAD models served as 'virtual prototypes' with which to discuss any required design changes. By building on the kit of parts, participants could be taken through 'small steps' of the design process, and so not be overwhelmed by the task of designing on their own and from scratch [35].

4 Results

Results are curated into; appropriate, tangible and diverse exemplars. Artefacts, motivations and participant needs created the LMNH workshop. *Pump mount* (Fig. 2) - This participant wanted to replace a lost component of an existing product. The bike pump they owned came with a mounting bracket that was subsequently damaged, and the producer doesn't sell replacement parts. 3D printing was of significant interest. *Banana Holder* (Fig. 3)–The participant wanted to mount something to hold a banana so that they could have an energy boost during long rides. The participant acknowledged the playfulness of the idea but was keen to engage in a workshop that combined design, 3D printing and cycling. *Light clip* - Similar to the Pump Mount - the free nature of the workshop was a key aspect for this participant, both in attendance and getting a free product. They wanted a clip to mount a light to their handlebars replacing a lost item.

Fig. 2. Pump mount, components from kit of parts.

Fig. 3. Banana Holder

Fig. 4. Seat mounted opener.

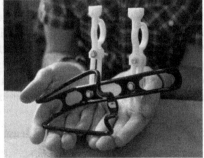

Fig. 5. Water bottle rack, custom built for hand-built bike.

Knitting wool spool holder - This participant wanted to use the workshop for technical experimentation; the justification behind the creation met no other needs other than for the individual to learn about 3D printing. The 'wool holder' was a bespoke object, fulfilling a very niche function and not (knowingly) in manufacture. *Ketchup Horn* - Two participants wanted to modify a bike horn, so it fired ketchup at inconsiderate/dangerous drivers, as London's roads are noisy, a standard horn has limited effect. *Seat mounted bottle opener* (Fig. 4) - This participant cycles to meet friends for picnics in the summer, forgetting their bottle opener and wanted to mount it onto her bike, drawn to the workshop to find out more about 3D printing. *Water bottle rack for a Penny Farthing* (Fig. 5) - This participant races Penny Farthings. She brought her bike to the workshop and described how she wanted to attach a water bottle, as her bike didn't have bottle cage mounts built into the frame (as modern bikes do). As she did not want to drill into the frame her solution was a clamp that held a bottle cage onto the frame. Penny Farthing racing is a niche sport and she couldn't find suppliers of this kind of product. She was also interested in 3D printing and the workshop in general. *Flag Clip* - This participant had recently been involved in an informal bike race and wanted to attach a small flag to their bike, showing their allegiance to charitable causes. They also thought it might 'look cool' to have it on their bike as a permanent feature. The participant brought a range of ideas as to how it might work as they worked as a professional designer; for example, they originally imagined the flag would be attached to the handlebars, but through consultation changed the location to under the seat.

5 Workshop Transferable Insights

In creating a facsimile of the scenario imagined there were a number of limiting factors. They were free to attend and the artefacts produced were offered at no cost and this perhaps meant that participants saw little or no risk in their involvement. It used entry point 3D printers, which are not best suited to commercial product quality, technical artefacts. It used designers to drive industry standard design software and contribute their expertise, instead of the participants driving the process and software themselves; and so, participants did not test any software or face the challenge of designing on their own. However, these factors should not be taken as negative, merely conditional; the workshops and wider research yielded a number of insights that would inform the requisite tools and resources needed to enable lay users to create technical products on-site and on-demand using 3D printing technology. Workshop findings have been grouped, addressing questions set out in the introduction.

5.1 Translating Participant's Ideas

Participants had no prior knowledge of the kit of parts, and so their ideas were quickly categorised into those that the kit could service and those that the kit could not. This task was undertaken, in the most part, by the technicians. To enable users to take on more of the design work it would be beneficial for them to be well informed as to the kit and its capabilities. In running the workshop, it was clear the technicians performed a number of roles in consultation with participants. To mediate the consultation using software these roles will need to be taken in to account:

1. Explaining the workshop process.
2. Identify elements of the kit that could be used and then explore modifications or additions that would deliver a solution in collaboration with the participant.
3. Explore solutions outside of the kit of parts, using their expertise to suggest and convey ideas to participants as well as stimulating participant led solutions.
4. Modify parts from the kit by altering dimensions or adding features.
5. Creating new parts that interact with parts from the kit.
6. Creating new parts or assemblies not linked to existing parts from the kit.
7. Communication of limitations of 3D printing within CAD, explaining decision making about form, part thickness, or surface finish, etc.

As the Participants were only asked to bring a 'thing and their bike', none came with preconceived designs, and as such all-design work was conducted with the technicians. There was a varying degree of engagement in the design process between participants and technicians: Some used drawing and dialogue to co-design solutions that were then realised in CAD by the technicians; others played more of a passive role where they explained their need and let the technician deliver them a solution, in which case CAD software was used to explain the final design. Analogue measuring and sketch tools aided exploration and communication for both the technicians and participants.

5.2 Effectiveness of Approach

It took time for participants to examine the parts and information supplied in the workshop in order to understand what was possible. Having the kit of parts 3D printed and physically for the participants to build tactile assemblies positively affected the design process and dialogue. It allowed solutions to be reached, and in some cases tested very quickly. Having more examples of assemblies, choices of materials, possible finishes, and off-the shelf components, would be beneficial. The kit, as it was used in the workshop, served as a useful base to build on; however, as a number of participants wanted solutions that did not utilise it, a more comprehensive toolkit would have been useful in order to limit the need to create entirely new parts. Technicians needed to rely heavily on their expertise as industrial designers to create solutions beyond the kit, and it was notable that solutions that used the kit required less time and effort than and those that deviated from it. The capability of the kit of parts was taken for granted by participants, and there was a general assumption that each part or assembly of parts would function effectively. This was of positive benefit as designs could progress quickly, but this also meant that participants did not scrutinise the parts in order to see if there was a better alternative, or if an improvement could be made. All elements of the kit must be rigorously designed to perform to a high standard, as users will expect this and use them accordingly. Constraints such as build orientation, material strength, maximum part size, and optimisation of build were solely within the technicians' remit; on occasion some of this information needed to be imparted to the participant to validate the technician's design outcome. Technicians made suggestions regarding the best mounting point for each item on the bike, whether additional features or a simpler design, would be preferable. For the most part, participants were not focussed on the constraints of the material or the 3D printing process, rather their interest was what could be achieved with it. When technicians explained the need for designs to be a certain way for strength or durability, the participants were happy to rely on their judgement.

6 Discussion (Updated Technologies)

There is a difficult line between; parametric, AI, fully Open Design and limiting participants capabilities. Open Design (OD) is a "catchall term for various on-and offline design and making activities, describ[ing] a design process that allows for (is open to) the participation of anybody (novice or professional) in collaborative development[s] of something" [36]. OD democratizes access to construction information in a post-industrial world, presenting opportunities for communities to sustainably respond to bespoke needs. EU 'right to repair' laws are transforming industry approaches, as "manufacturers [will] have to provide spare parts for 10 years" [37]. OD, unsettles hierarchies, manufacture, stimulating agency and responsibility "providing people the means to rip, mix and burn physical objects" [38]. Open Design cannot always be deployed as it relies on embedded knowledge. Authors re-reviewed the state of the art and the unification of three areas that have advanced since the LMNH workshop.

6.1 Digital Manufacture and Production in Retail Spaces

Over the past 2 years retail 'bricks-and-mortar' revenue has dropped by 14% with an online increase of 20%. With world leading brands producing augmented reality stores [39], live streaming instore experiences and even 'digital clothes' representing avatars (with billions in revenue) interactivity is transforming our current HCI and retail models. Netlooks (www.netlooks.fr/) is a collaboration of instore and digital ensuring that their glasses are personally fitted and adapted instore, based on sizing requirements and machine learning. Pixsweet.com a leading brand combining traditional toolmaking and 3d printing to manufacture 'Ice Pops' to any physical form and flavor. Whilst these projects are 'gimmicks' the foundations are based on function. Ellis Brigham, the world leading UK ski brand has a unique custom boot fit system 'Surefit' that builds onsite manufacture, deep staff expertise and personal taste to customize and adapt your sports equipment [40]. Adidas's 'Knit for you' is restraining the parameters of what it can make, but is getting a retail proven system stating "we need opportunities to be collaborators in experimenting with new ways to craft how our future works, and what it looks like" [41]. All of the retail exemplars; using off-the-shelf parts i.e. (assembly not making), not fully 'durable' or standards defined outputs and they do not interoperate within other constraints, highlighting the uniqueness of *Mass-configuration* research.

6.2 AI 'Decision Making'

AI is becoming a viable technology being considered for critical industry such as healthcare, where decision support systems are being considered for many specialisms and for many conditions. The application to manufacturing is less mature yet there is perceived benefit especially for additive manufacturing. Intelligent systems can automate some of the pre-process 'heavy lifting' making design decisions and 'repairing' parts prior to manufacture [42]. This type of decision support comes after a design is produced and retains knowledge sets concerning specific manufacturing processes. On the design side, generative design [43] adopts intelligent algorithms to 'create' digital artifacts within set parameters. CAD software such as Autodesk Dreamcatcher embed AI into the design system to automate geometric decision making [44]. It is plausible FEA analysis will follow, generating more efficient; parts, mechanisms informing artefacts design(s), i.e., 'torsional stiffness' is embedded into F1 race car design, but can (over time) review dynamic stresses & strains on dynamic components [43].

6.3 AR/VR: Experiences

AR and VR experiences are crossing a large divide, lowering high level experiences. Wieg water rides, specialise in providing VR experiences within 'water parks', both on water slides and snorkelling [45]. These truly compelling experiences partner the 'physical with the digital' leading to new opportunities, i.e., 'try digital products' before you make them and or buy them. The real estate industry (pre-covid) devised VR home viewings for properties and spaces (saving carbon impact, visiting locations without travelling). Could professionals get a view of 'racing courses' before the race and change/tailor parts. Mobile experiences (come on leaps and bounds) of how your smart phone can customise your personal experience, based on what it knows about you [46]. For example, when you are physically measured for clothing, can this data be used to determine your 'bike frame size' and or position to ensure optimum performance without injury over time? Invent Medical maps your size and scale (working of body and live anthropometrics), i.e., guaranteeing fit from different brands. Breezm, have revolutionized the 'eye ware' retail so there is perfect 'fit', without requiring overstocking in their outlets. Evidence of 'scanning' for fit is even entering the equine sector ensuring better hoof care for animals, with the limiting factor being the quality of scanning technologies, that will only improve in time. The final exemplar 'Maker Mask', is a custom Cloud service that fits a person's exact physical (face) size and complies to countless medical and functional standards. These rigorous standards are one of the last barriers uniting the retail/functional opportunities for 3D printing and the authors context. The Maker Mask, is not only a standard approach, but it is re-skilling participants;

> "Enabling communities to create necessary goods locally and quickly will lessen the spread of disease, protect more people, reduce burdens on medical facilities/DoD/governments, and give Americans something to be part of the solution to this pandemic, while building and training capability for the future" [47].

6.4 Unifying Enablers

The advancement of digital retail spaces, no doubt will advance into more and more digital spaces, due to covid-19 and producing more financially resilient models. For example, Fujitsu's "personal checkout" [48], is already transforming payment, personalization and the opportunity for more feedback between users and retailers. As input systems advance, 3dprinting resolution and more complex materials become mainstream, it is plausible that this type of work will lead manufacture (within certain domains) where consumer-led customizations in turn lead industry. For example, the Lego Builder platform has had "over 13,000 projects have been submitted to the LEGO Ideas platform" [49], where avid fans can create digital Lego, get crowd supporters and see their concepts translated into products and revenue.

6.5   Perceived Functions and Requirements

The proposed system (researched) needs to include the following;

- *Intelligent Leverage Points;* choosing when and how to inform decision making and or make suggestions, based on users' parameters.
- *Measure & Tolerances;* digital measuring equipment connected to the 'system', either scanning or measure, translating back into CAD.
- *Translation;* of ideas and mechanical detailing from the user to the screen.
- *Efficiencies;* material, production time & substitutions on appropriate existing parts, for example bolts or more durable hardware.
- *Contextually Durable;* through predictive FEA, outputs can leverage generative design processes based on activity; road bike, commuting or downhill.
- *Pre-flight Checks;* leveraging AR/VR people should be able to 'digitally' check the fit of the part, ensuring failure reductions and material sustainability.
- *Digital Standards;* checking parts and assemblies to high industrial standards through digital inputs to safeguard compliance of retailers, i.e., 'fit for purpose'.

6.6   Design Mediated by a Kit of Parts

The kit of parts served as a useful base to build on, however, as some participants wanted solutions that did not utilise it (e.g., mounting under seat), it should be refined and expanded through the use of workshops, such as *Clip-It-On*, to draw out insights and needs. The kit is seen to be the work of professional designers, where each part and the interconnectivity between parts have undergone much consideration. A vital aspect of the workshop and indeed overall scenario, was the focus on an interest/user group as a customer base. Understanding the untapped or underserved needs of a particular group is vital if the kit is to provide an effective platform to build on. However, if users are allowed to create new parts for the kit, as might be the case if the kit is open for all to expand upon, a rulebook or guidelines should be created to set the conditions for successful parts. By combining mass manufactured parts with those of the CAD repository, it is possible to limit the need for the 3D printer to be capable of printing multiple materials that possess various mechanical properties. As is the case with Design Spark, repositories used in retail could use proprietary non-printed parts that need to be purchased from the retailer. Parts could be functional (electrical or mechanical) components or convey brand identity. Various 3D printers and materials or processes, alongside other digital fabrication tools (such as laser cutters and CNC routers) could be used to fabricate parts as can be seen in the Open Structures project (www.openstructures.net). However, this will undoubtedly make engaging with the kit much more complex users and so might need sophisticated design software in order to overcome the complexity. Suites of these digital tools are currently seen in maker spaces (Tech Shop and Fab Labs) and would-be ideal test beds for further research. The kit of parts needs to be physical as well as digital. The real benefit of the on-site aspect of the scenario is the ability for users to play with physical parts, this helps them imagine and test out ideas. Much can be achieved with digital tools, but physical interaction is a fundamental element in comprehending functionalities and imagining new possibilities.

6.7 Design Mediated by Software Tools

The ideal scenario for the provision of point-of-sale design and fabrication is that consumers should be able to design for themselves. The consultation process revealed that in order to replace the role of the technician, their expertise and capability should be embedded into software tools. The design software would also be the primary means for users to understand the kit of parts and would need to not overly complicated for novice users, while also being sufficiently functional. The software would need to:

1. *Quick guides*; Enabling users in understanding the design and 3D print process/capabilities.
2. *Part selection;* making and informing interconnect decisions.
3. *Exemplars;* demonstrate possible assemblies (providing users to comment).
4. *Off-the-shelf parts;* Illustrate how to incorporate mass produced or non-printed parts into assemblies.
5. *Help users;* to choose attachment locations on to their chosen bike.
6. *Enable*; users to alter parts within functional parameters.
7. *Provide guidance;* informing the functional needs of products (such as load, stress, flexibility fit tolerance, ergonomics, etc.) and deliver analytical tools (such as FEA) to virtually test parts and certify them to required standards.
8. Preparing CAD parts for 3D print; taking into account build orientation for optimum strength and part nesting.

Although not explored in the workshop, it may be useful to import 3D models of standard bike dimensions/manufactured parts, i.e., handlebars etc. Elements or whole bike assemblies could be imported into CAD software, to virtually mount parts. Other elements such as lights and smart phones could be imported aiding designers. This should be applied broadly to items that would aid designing for any instance of scenario(s). Implementing the software, could be a CAD software plug-in to existing applications, or a stand-alone design tool. Alternatively, operating similarly to Wordpress (www.wor dpress.com), where the capability to create tailored tools and customisable kits of parts, allowing for multiple retail applications. Enabling brands to engage with custom on-site and on-demand manufacture at a relatively low entry point, with the added benefit of building upon a system that could be familiar to customers. The CAD tools can be, cloud-based CAD allowing users to generate ideas anywhere and allowing stores to operate as; interaction, demonstration centres, fabrication and pick-up points.

6.8 Potential Issues

In a scenario where authorship of a design is the result of collaboration, issues arise surrounding ownership and liability. Creative Commons (www.creativecommons.org) licensing allows for authorship to be attributed to the contributors of design project(s), while allowing for digital design content to be openly appropriated. This means users of on-site design and fabrication, as it is imagined, would forgo exclusive rights to their contribution/design while still being acknowledged for it. If the work of each customer was not be added to an archive for use by others they could retain some exclusivity, as is the case with some mass customisation (*Nike ID* and Makielab). In a scenario where the customer's designs can be shared, credit or financial reward can be paid to the author when it is used by others; a system of this kind is outlined in Jaron Lanier's book *Who Owns the Future*. In this case a design evolves over time and be the work of many individuals, with a system keeping track of the chain of contributions and ascribe authorship and reward proportionally. The cost of 3D printed artefacts are usually calculated based on 'material volume' in their construction (www.shapeways.com), and so costs could be calculated during the design process as parts are imported and modified. If the design is built upon the work of another user, payments can be factored into costs. Parts could be optimised for budget solutions based on material cost; however, this may result in products, vulnerable to failure. It is important to note that it was impossible to guarantee the effective functionality of anything designed and made during the workshop.

A significant hurdle to overcome if this type of practice is to become common-place. Technical products need to function in situations where they are subject to load, stress and environmental factors. If products are created through a part software and part user/customer collaboration, complications arise if that part fails. Responsibility must be taken by the service provider to mitigate any failure where possible, limiting risk where it is possible to predict and eliminate. Likewise, the service user must take responsi-bility when they deviate from any advised parameters. The challenge lies in attributing responsibility to aspects of the design artefact when legally required. 3D printing of functional artefacts in a retail environment would need to conform to industry standards by possibly using the model applied to 'mass-customisation' in order to limit technical or structural failure, as can be seen in MakieLab dolls. To ensure product safety standards, the software would embed restrictions on what lay users should and should not be able to edit. For the purposes of traceability digital 3D parts could be encoded with information, detailing location of manufacture, designer, material and printer used. Coded stamps or integrated markings into the 3D printed parts could offer quality control, provenance, or identify where liabilities lie in the case of accident or failure. Encoding a 3D printed product with this type of information might alter its value, if ever resold etc. The pitfalls outside of HCI territories and designers are;

- *Part accuracy;* if files are used in unspecified 3D printer.
- *Material failure,* temporal environments and miss use i.e., in different temperatures, hydrology's, etc. ware and failure will behave differently.
- *FEA limitations;* potential legal challenges, i.e., Terms and conditions of how 'output miss-use' as the products will remain between 'prototype and product'.

- *Intellectual Property;* how would it work if parts undergo development with 5 + users building on each other's work.
- *Interoperability,* how would the ownership model of the part work? Would you be able to edit it, own it or only use it in that system?

6.9 Potential Opportunities

- *Collaborative branding*; working through 'part sharing', partnering corporates and local makers, comprehending conditions and requirements.
- *Enabling cottage industries;* of bespoke needs and knowledge, supported by a digital economy, creating new commerce and legacy.
- *Complete stock control;* traceability 'code' embedded in part without being financially tied to a physical stock room.
- *Sustainable practice;* as parts is not 'over produced' and can be updated according to new EU law (right to repair).
- *Revisiting;* 'crowd' Intellectual Property that does not hinder progress but protects stakeholders' interests.
- *Digital experience(s);* (within bike context) going for 'VR ride' with custom components to perform for that location, trying before you fabricate.

6.10 Conclusion

It is more than credible that 3D printing and other digital manufacturing will be used in retail environments to make functional products. It is also credible that these products will be custom made, or customisable and delivered using digital manufacturing. Challenges also lie in how the process is managed to ensure quality outcomes, that allow for the creative authorship of the customer, that meet the needs of the customer, require the least effort or training from the customer, carry guarantees of use and can be attained at affordable costs. Customers will need some education prior to creating their custom product but this needs to be delivered with minimum of effort on their part. The workshops showed that while some customers were willing to spend time observing or participating with something they deemed interesting, others were more time limited and wanted information delivered quickly and concisely. Efficiencies can be delivered through the use of parametised CAD models, guided CAD tools and a comprehensive kit of parts, both printable and off the shelf. By combining a repository of parts with an intuitive CAD system it is possible for the novice to quickly understand the potential of building their ideas upon the expertise and work of others. Embedding design expertise into parts is an effective means to cater to novices, but what has been embedded needs to be understandable. The CAD system needs to be capable without being complex by automating all functions that are relevant to all products and guiding users through a step-by-step process. Analytical software should be used that virtually tests the product for use in certain conditions and under certain loads, and so certify it for a period of time and stipulate limits of use. Showing users exemplar designs that are formed from assemblies of parts would be effective as users can directly appropriate as well as understand the system of parts in use. It is important to note that the main focus of the scenario is to enable individual solutions rather than to invent new products, so many known factors can be in-built. Future retail environments may well have displays that showcase assembly options, libraries of parts, material choices and idea provoking images or text to inspire customers in choosing options or formulating ideas.

Bike culture was a good fit for this activity, and retail spaces that are tailored to cultural or hobby communities such as LMNH offer a knowledgeable target audience that have an understanding of their equipment as well as latent needs. This can be transferred to other groups i.e., extreme sports, robotics or prosthetics as well as more generally in homeware, footwear, toys and electronic devices. Furniture manufacturers *Unto This Last* and makers could use 'kits of parts' coupled with CAD to offer flexible products beyond the constraints of mass customisation or parametrised CAD, while still being tied to manufacturing capabilities. It is not proposed that this type of product offering will become the prevailing one, ousting mass produced goods sellers on the high street; however due to advances in software tools and fabrication technology the cost to implement it and the functional attributes of the printed artefacts are no longer prohibitive. Opportunities are seen for a provider of tailored systems for brands wanting to offer the imagined scenario; delivering a custom created kit of parts, CAD tools and design interface and manufacturing tools and material as well as support service. Beyond commercial space(s), Fab Labs could develop 'smart content' libraries, shared as common resources, with parts clustered by themes, with brands collaborations.

Acknowledgments. This work was supported by the Horizon Digital Economy Research Institute (EP/G065802/1) & conducted while the team were at Brunel University. The authors thank all workshop participants and *'Look Mum No Hands'* hospitality.

References

1. Tan, L.J., Zhu, W., Zhou, K.: Recent progress on polymer materials for additive manufacturing. Adv. Func. Mater. **30**(43), 2003062 (2020)
2. Wix: The Leader in Website Creation, 1 February 2021. https://www.wix.com/
3. Helmore, E.: Amazon third-quarter earnings soar as pandemic sales triple profits. Guardian, 29 October 2020. https://www.theguardian.com/technology/2020/oct/29/amazon-profits-lat est-earnings-report-third-quarter-pandemic
4. Prusa, J.: 3D printed face shields for medics and professionals. Prusa3D - 3D Printers from Josef Průša, 25 March 2020. https://www.prusa3d.com/covid19/
5. Jiménez, M., Romero, L., Domínguez, I. A., Espinosa, M.D.M., Domínguez, M.: Additive manufacturing technologies: an overview about 3D printing methods and future prospects. Complexity (2019)
6. Bourell, D., et al.: Materials for additive manufacturing. CIRP Ann. **66**(2), 659–681 (2017)
7. Pradel, P., Zhu, Z., Bibb, R., Moultrie, J.: Investigation of design for additive manufacturing in professional design practice. J. Eng. Des. **29**(4–5), 165–200 (2018)
8. Smith, A., Stirling, A.: Innovation, sustainability and democracy: an analysis of grassroots contributions. J. Self-Govern. Manage. Econ. **6**(1), 64–97 (2018)
9. O'Donovan, C., Smith, A.: Technology and human capabilities in UK Makerspaces. J. Hum. Develop. Capabil. **21**(1), 63–83 (2020)
10. Vialva, T.: The best 3D printed consumer products. 3D Printing Industry, 5 February 2019. https://3dprintingindustry.com/news/the-best-3d-printed-consumer-products-148352/

11. Lievendag, N.: Autodesk 123D Catch (Discontinued). 3D Scan Expert ,14 June 2019. https://3dscanexpert.com/autodesk-photogrammetry-review-123d-catch/
12. Warren, R.: Generative Design Meets Additive Manufacturing. Computer Aided Technology, 18 February 2020. https://www.cati.com/blog/2019/12/generative-design-meets-additive-manufacturing/
13. Open Structures, 3 April 2018. Open Structures. https://www.openstructures.net/home-page
14. Du, X., Jiao, J., Tseng, M.M.: Architecture of product family: fundamentals and methodology. Concurr. Eng. **9**(4), 309–325 (2001)
15. Tseng, M.M., Wang, Y., Jiao, R.J.: Mass customization. In: Laperrière, L., Reinhart, G., eds. CIRP Encyclopedia of Production Engineering, pp. 1–8. Springer, Heidelberg (2017). https://doi.org/10.1007/978-3-642-35950-7_16701-3
16. Fogliatto, F.S., Da Silveira, G.J., Borenstein, D.: The mass customization decade: an updated review of the literature. Int. J. Prod. Econ. **138**(1), 14–25 (2012)
17. Ro, C.: Will Covid-19 make urban cycling more inclusive? BBC Worklife, 30 July 2020. https://www.bbc.com/worklife/article/20200724-will-covid-19-make-urban-cycling-more-inclusive
18. Shimano: 2020–2021 SHIMANO Product Information Web. Shimano Specifications & Technical Documents, 5 November 2020. https://productinfo.shimano.com/
19. Matters, JELFT|Santander Cycles: Transport for London, 4 January 2021. https://tfl.gov.uk/modes/cycling/santander-cycles
20. Bike2Work Scheme: Government Cycle to Work Scheme - Bike2Work Scheme, 1 January 2021. https://www.bike2workscheme.co.uk
21. Harvard Health Publishing: The top 5 benefits of cycling. Harvard Health, 1 August 2020. https://www.health.harvard.edu/staying-healthy/the-top-5-benefits-of-cycling
22. Seppälä, M.: Top 5 (DIY) bicycle maintenance tips for beginners. Bikecitizens, 11 December 2017. https://www.bikecitizens.net/top-5-bicycle-maintenance-tips/
23. Catawiki: The forgotten role of bicycles in World War II, 3 July 2020. https://www.catawiki.com/stories/5385-the-forgotten-role-of-bicycles-in-world-war-ii
24. Hippel, E.V.: Democratizing innovation: the evolving phenomenon of user innovation. J. für Betriebswirtschaft **55**(1), 63–78 (2005)
25. Lofthouse, V.A., Lilley, D.: What they really, really want: user centered research methods for design. In: DS 36: Proceedings DESIGN 2006, the 9th International Design Conference, Dubrovnik, Croatia (2006)
26. Rogers, Y., et al.: Why it's worth the hassle: the value of in-situ studies when designing Ubicomp: (nominated for the best paper award). In: Krumm, J., Abowd, G.D., Seneviratne, A., Strang, T. (eds.) UbiComp 2007: Ubiquitous Computing: 9th International Conference, UbiComp 2007, Innsbruck, Austria, September 16-19, 2007. Proceedings, pp. 336–353. Springer, Heidelberg (2007). https://doi.org/10.1007/978-3-540-74853-3_20
27. Lynaugh, H., Li, H., Gong, B.: Rapid Fc glycosylation analysis of Fc fusions with IdeS and liquid chromatography mass spectrometry. MAbs **5**(5), 641–645 (2013)
28. Simonsen, J., Robertson, T. (eds.): Handbook of Participatory Design. Routledge, UK (2012)
29. Vaajakallio, K., Mattelmäki, T.: Collaborative design exploration: envisioning future practices with make tools. In: Proceedings of the 2007 Conference on Designing Pleasurable Products and Interfaces, pp. 223–238 (2007)
30. Sanders, E.B.N., Stappers, P.J.: Co-creation and the new landscapes of design. Co-design **4**(1), 5–18 (2008)
31. Heller, S., Vienne, V. (eds.): Citizen Designer: Perspectives on Design Responsibility. Skyhorse Publishing Inc., New York City (2003)
32. Sinclair, M., Campbell, I.: Classifying consumer involved product development (2014)

33. Phillips, R., Ford, Y., Sadler, K., Silve, S., Baurley, S.: Open design: non-professional user-designers creating products for citizen science: a case study of beekeepers. In: Marcus, A. (ed.) Design, User Experience, and Usability. Web, Mobile, and Product Design: Second International Conference, DUXU 2013, Held as Part of HCI International 2013, Las Vegas, NV, USA, July 21-26, 2013, Proceedings, Part IV, pp. 424–431. Springer, Heidelberg (2013). https://doi.org/10.1007/978-3-642-39253-5_47

34. Phillips, R.D., Blum, J.M., Brown, M.A., Baurley, S.L.: Testing a grassroots citizen science venture using open design, "the bee lab project". In: CHI 2014 Extended Abstracts on Human Factors in Computing Systems, pp. 1951–1956 (2014)

35. Tooze, J., Baurley, S., Phillips, R., Smith, P., Foote, E., Silve, S.: Open design: contributions, solutions, processes and projects. Des. J. **17**(4), 538–559 (2014)

36. Harrabin, B.R.: Climate change: 'Right to repair' gathers force. BBC News, January 2019. https://www.bbc.co.uk/news/science-environment-46797396

37. Lipson, H., Kurman, M.: Fabricated: The World of 3D Printing. John Wiley & Sons, Hoboken (2013)

38. Segran, E.: The 6 wildest ways we shopped in 2020. Fast Company, 1 January 2021. https://www.fastcompany.com/90585138/the-six-wildest-ways-we-shopped-in-2020

39. Segran, E.: Why this beauty startup is live-streaming everything inside its new store. Fast Company, 2 December 2020. https://www.fastcompany.com/90580782/why-this-beauty-startup-is-live-streaming-everything-inside-its-new-store

40. Ellis-Brigham: Ellis Brigham Surefit Guarantee - Ellis Brigham Mountain Sports. Surefit-Guarantee, 1 January 2021. https://www.ellis-brigham.com/surefit-guarantee

41. Adidas: adidas Knit for you - Knit for You, 1 January 2021. http://adidasknitforyou.com/

42. Venkat, V.: Artificial Intelligence and 3D printing: future of manufacturing. Medium, 25 October 2019.https://medium.com/@venkat34.k/artificial-intelligence-and-3d-printing-future-of-manufacturing-d84fb94b1c7d

43. Kanada, Y.: 3D printing of generative art using the assembly and deformation of direction-specified parts. Rapid Prototyping J. **22**, 636–644 (2016)

44. AutoDesk: Project Dreamcatcher draftr, 4 June 2020. https://www.autodesk.com/research/projects/project-dreamcatcher#:%7E:text=Dreamcatcher%20is%20a%20generative%20design,solutions%20that%20meet%20the%20objectives.

45. Wiegandwaterrides: Virtual Reality Waterslide, 12 December 2020. https://www.wiegandwaterrides.de/en/products/raft-slides/virtual-reality-waterslide

46. ricoh360: 12 November 2020. RICOH360|RICOH360. https://www.ricoh360.com

47. thisisyr: Home. YR, 28 September 2020. https://thisisyr.com/

48. Maker Mask, 8 September 2020. https://www.makermask.com/shop.html

49. Fujitsu: Self-Checkout Retail Solutions: Fujitsu EMEIA, 3 June 2020. https://www.fujitsu.com/emeia/solutions/industry/retail/self-checkout/

50. Alumni, D.: How the Crowd Saved LEGO. Digital Innovation and Transformation, 3 November 2015. https://digital.hbs.edu/platform-digit/submission/how-the-crowd-saved-lego/

The Effect of User Interface on Experiential Value for E-Book Platforms Users

Yen-Shan Tsai[1], Elena Carolina Li[2($\boxtimes$)], and Chih-Liang Yeh[1]

[1] Department of Information Communication, Yuan Ze University, Taoyuan City, Taiwan
[2] Department of Visual Arts, University of Taipei, Taipei City, Taiwan
elenali@utaipei.edu.tw

Abstract. The revenue of e-Book market was 14,747 million US$ in 2020 and is projected to reach 17,723 million US$ by 2025. The Experiential Value theory can measure the consumer experience, which includes four factors: consumer return on investment, service excellence, aesthetics, and playfulness. This study tried to explore the impact of the experiential value of the e-Book platforms on users and understand how the interface design affects users' experiential value through questionnaire surveys and interviews. A total of 325 valid questionnaires were collected. The results showed that users were lowest satisfied with the service excellence in the experiential value, and this factor was positively relevant to the other three factors. The results also showed that the users with purchasing experiences were more satisfied than the users without purchasing experiences. Base on the interview results, the following suggestions for the e-Book platforms: (1) Concise and beautifying e-Book platform interfaces. (2) Adjust the categorization of the e-Books. (3) Add a new service "Accumulate Reading Points," which can be converted into book-borrowing hours or contribute towards discounts when purchasing e-Books. (4) Make adjustments to the trial reading feature.

Keywords: Electronic book · Experiential value · User interface

1 Introduction

The revenue of e-Book market was 14,747 million US$ in 2020 and is projected to reach 17,723 million US$ by 2025 [1]. According to Statista [1], the penetration of e-Book users in China in 2020 was 26.1%, which ranked 1st in the world. The 2nd highest penetration was for users of the United States with 23.4%. Looking at global e-book revenue, the US market was at the top with a revenue of USD$ 6,071 million, Japan coming in second with USD$ 1,582 million, and China coming in 3rd at USD$ 1,406 million. Based on the aforementioned information, it is evident that Asia's outstanding user penetration and revenue implies that the Asian e-Book market has great potential.

Google Play Books was introduced into Taiwan in 2013, and Kobo e-Books were introduced in 2016. In 2017, Books.com.tw opened their e-Book Store, and TAAZE also followed suit by beginning to sell e-Books in Taiwan [2]. In addition, the Readmoo e-Book platform launched the e-book reader mooInk in 2017 and specifically designed

© Springer Nature Switzerland AG 2021
M. M. Soares et al. (Eds.): HCII 2021, LNCS 12780, pp. 647–660, 2021.
https://doi.org/10.1007/978-3-030-78224-5_44

the vertical/horizontal conversion for traditional Chinese readers [3]. Kindle added traditional Chinese, and the Zhuyin keyboard in 2018, and Amazon also launched its Taiwanese website in 2019 [2]. How will Taiwan's e-Book industry seize this opportunity to help customers have a comfortable and relaxing reading experience during the consumption process? This will be one of the key factors for the foundational competitiveness of Taiwan's e-Book market.

Pine II and Gilmore [4] proposed that experience is defined by companies becoming aware of focusing on their services and products, providing consumers with environments that they can experience on a personal level. The value created by the experiences has been used by companies in various markets. For example, Starbucks' brand experience provides a context that stimulates the senses and touches peoples' hearts. Consumers not only get to have coffee but also get to experience the atmosphere and brand created by Starbucks [5]. Huang and Zhang [6] mentioned that more and more consumers shop for products that make them happy, and fewer consumers will only make purchases based on brands. Kao, Huang, and Yang [7] also mentioned that consumer needs have become diversified, making traditional services and marketing models no longer capable of consumers.

Experiences are one of the best ways to satisfy consumers. Spiegelman [8] mentioned that in order to turn a one-time customer into an old customer, the experience consumption must bring value. The process of experience consumption is like appreciating art, placing emphasis on the essence of products or services, and not only thinking about its features or effectiveness [7]. Mathwick, Malhotra, and Rigdon [9] proposed that there are four aspects of experiential value: consumer return on investment, service excellence, aesthetics, and playfulness, emphasizing the contents of the experience throughout the consumption process rather than the product's brand and function.

There are countless researches on e-Books, most of which discuss the features of e-Books [10], future development trends [11], e-Book applications, and education using e-Books [12–14], e-Book business and profit model [15], and making libraries of e-Books [16, 17]. However, the impact of e-Book platforms on experiential value is rarely discussed. If the experience of using an e-Book platform can be improved, it should be able to further enhance the user's experiential value and thereby increase the willingness to purchase e-Books.

This study focuses on the e-Book purchasing process provided by e-Book platforms (including free reading and paid reading), and the consumer experiential value generated by the purchasing process as the core of this study. This study will look to understand the degrees of experiential value for e-Book platform users from the consumer's perspective, explore the needs and dissatisfaction of the consumers experiencing of the e-Book platforms so that e-Book suppliers can better understand the needs of e-Book users for the contents of the platforms, and adjust the interface designs of the e-Book platforms according to user needs. The purposes of this study is as follows: (1) To understand the factors that influence the experiential value of consumer experience in purchasing e-Books. (2) Derive the interface design suggestions of e-Book platforms using user experiential value of e-Book platforms.

Based on the research purposes, the scope and limitations of this study are as follows: (1) The scope of this study is limited to the use of e-Book platforms, and the readers of hardware devices are not included in this study scope. (2) This study mainly focuses on the process of consumers browsing and purchasing on e-Book platforms; however, the substantial financial issues involved in purchasing e-Books are beyond the research scope. (3) This study restricts the research participants to users who have experience in using e-Book platforms. Those who do not have relevant experience are not included as research participants.

2   Related Works

2.1   Electronic Books

McGuire and O'Leary [18] stated that readers are increasingly demanding convenience and relevance in hopes to find their favorite works easily, the medium of reading is easy to access and connect. As a result, many publishers have shifted their focus towards the e-Book market based on these needs.

Hao, Tsai, and Lin [19] defined e-Books as different types of media based on the device it is presented after texts, images, sounds, and animations are digitalized. Browne and Coe [20] defined that *eBooks as book-length publications in digital form*. Different scholars have different definitions of e-Books as some define them for their form of communication and others for their hardware and devices. This study defines e-Books as "Any text and picture content that are digitalized so that readers can use reading applications on readers, tablets, computers or mobile phones and other hardware devices to read".

There are significant differences between e-Books and paper books issued by traditional publishing houses. Pan [21] proposed that e-Books have advantageous features of being lightweight, take up less space, are environmentally friendly, contains lively content (not limited to text, the content can be more diverse and interactive), full-text search feature, shortened publishing process, no storage pressure, improved accuracy, personalized settings, and is easily accessible. E-Books have advantages that paper books do not have, but e-Books still have their limitations that also hinder the development and promotion of e-Books. Siriginidi [22] divides the limitations of e-Books into five major categories, among which three factors are related to the e-Book interface and platform: display, format factors, and haptic feedback. The details are as follows:

(1) Display: The color performance of the e-Book does not meet the quality requirements of the printed text.
(2) Format factors: The physical dimensions of the e-Book are fixed, it takes energy to use it, it is fragile, and it may be damaged if it is dropped.
(3) Haptic feedback: E-Books cannot recreate the thickness and touch of printed books, nor can people quickly flip through the pages to obtain information.

E-Book platforms are operated in diverse manners, while the common operating models are either B2C or C2C, which enables cross-platform (Windows, Mac, Android, iOS, etc.) and across devices. Some platforms will provide users with a trial reading feature before making purchases. The reading interface has bookmarks, a search feature, view book information, thumbnail previews, and a voice function. Users can directly read the text on the screen. The reading interface can also adjust the layout by switching between reading horizontally and vertically, adjusting font size and font type, and page-viewing color. Some platforms provide book-borrowing services and if users have already borrowed the e-Book before, they can get a discount by getting the borrowing fee deducted from the purchase price.

2.2 Experiential Value

Kotler and Armstrong [23] stated that in order to maintain a leading edge in the market, there must be innovative customer value. Felix, Laetitia, and Marle [24] defined experiential value as the benefits that customers obtain through joint participation. Babin, Darden, and Griffin [25] believe that there are two types of experiential value: utilitarian value and hedonic value. The former is the rational and task-based behavior of consumers, while the latter is the potential aesthetic, sensory entertainment that is experienced during the consumption process that amounts to joy. The combination of the two is the complete consumption experience.

Mathwick, Malhotra, and Rigdon [9] believe that experience consumption has an abundant amount of value. The perception of experiential value comes from people's perception of products or services, which is obtained through direct use or remote appreciation, and value enhancement is achieved through the process of interaction. Mathwick et al. [9] divides experiential value into four different aspects: Consumer return on investment, service excellence, aesthetics, and playfulness (Fig. 1); each aspect is explained as follows:

1. Consumer return on investment: Investment that includes financial, time, behavioral, and psychological resources that may produce returns. Using e-Book platforms as an example, consumer return on investment could be the price difference with actual books, the time costs of making purchases on e-Book platforms, etc.
2. Service excellence: refers to the services provided by service providers and the value obtained from the evaluation by the consumers. Using e-Book platforms as an example, service excellence could be the services provided by e-Book platforms such as payment methods, interface design, product recommendations, and book review features, etc.
3. Aesthetics: refers to the aesthetics perceived subjectively in the consumer experience, which is the five significant senses in the environment. Using e-Book platforms as an

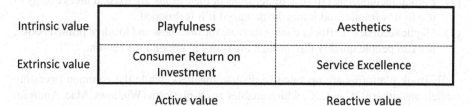

Fig. 1. Model of experiential value [9]

example, aesthetics may refer to the presentation of the e-Book platform interface, the cover and layout design of the e-Book, etc.

4. Playfulness: refers to the shopping opportunities, visual appeal, or consumers' pleasure of being served during the consumption process. Using e-Book platforms, playfulness may refer to the interactive content of the e-Books, the fun of making purchases on e-Book platforms, and other entertainment content.

Mathwick et al. [9] developed the Experiential Value Scale (EVS) after proposing the aforementioned four aspects of experiential value and believed that this scale could be used to evaluate the retail shopping experience, far exceeding the traditional scale combination that only values price and quality.

Hu and Zhang [26] conducted a study on university students' continuous use of mobile reading apps and found that experiential value has a significant impact on satisfaction. Maghnati, Ling, and Nasermoadeli [27] studied the relationship between smartphone user experiential marketing and experiential value. The results of the research confirmed that the higher the user experience, the higher the experiential value. Sreeram, Kesharwani, and Desai [28] studied the factors that affect online shopping satisfaction and loyalty. Among them, the playfulness value in experiential value is used as the contents of the research. The research results indicated that playfulness positively affects satisfaction and emphasizes that playfulness and economic values are important factors to improve consumer satisfaction and loyalty. These studies all use experiential value as the argument theory, and some use the EVS as the measurement standard for their research.

3 Research Method

This study process is divided into two phases: (1) Use the four aspects of experiential value as the contents of the questionnaire. After obtaining the data analysis results, understand the experiential value levels of e-Book platform users. (2) Select seven e-Book platform users to conduct interviews to understand the users' evaluation criteria and thoughts when filling out the questionnaire, further understand the users' experiences and suggestions on using e-Book platforms, and obtain possible interface improvement suggestions through the interview.

3.1 Questionnaire Survey

The questionnaire's participants were randomly sampled as the questionnaire selected the research participants that had experiences in using e-Book platforms, and divided them into two categories, "those who have purchasing experiences," and "those who don't have purchasing experiences". The reason for the two categories of "those who have purchasing experiences" and "those who don't have purchasing experiences" is to understand whether if the experiential value of the two groups will be different.

This study used Experiential Value Scale (EVS) as the basis to measure the experiential value of e-Book platform users. This study used Mathwick et al. [9] and Keng, Huang, Cheng, and Hsu [29] studies that proposed the four types of experiential value to design the questionnaire, dividing the questionnaire into five parts: six questions for consumer return on investment, six questions for service excellence, seven questions for aesthetics, six questions for playfulness, and basic information of the user. Table 1 was the Experience Value Scale in this study that referenced from Mathwick et al. [9] and Keng et al. [29].

Table 1. Experiential value scale for this study

Factors	Items
Consumer return on investment	1. Overall, I am happy with the prices of e-Book platforms 2. Reading e-Books make my life easier 3. Reading e-Books fit with my schedule 4. E-Books are a good economic value 5. The functions and classification of the e-Book platform fit my needs 6. The prices of e-Books I purchased from e-Book platforms are too high, given the quality of the merchandise
Service excellence	1. When I think of e-Book, I think of excellence 2. I think of e-Book as an expert in the reading it offers 3. E-Book is the best way to read 4. When it comes to reading, e-Book is my first preference 5. I intend to use e-Books in the future 6. In the future, e-Book is one of the first places I will look when I need to find certain kinds of reading
Aesthetics	1. The way e-Book displays its products is attractive 2. E-Book is aesthetically appealing 3. I like the way e-Books looks 4. I like the interface design of e-Books 5. I think e-Book is very entertaining 6. The expansion of the e-Book market increases my interest in e-Books 7. E-Book doesn't just a product, it entertains me
Playfulness	1. Reading e-Books get me away from it all 2. Reading e-Book makes me feel like I am in another world 3. When I am shopping from the e-Book platform, I feel very happy 4. I get so involved when I shop from e-Book platform that I forget everything else 5. I enjoy reading e-Books for its own sake, not just for the items I may have purchased 6. I read e-Books for the pure enjoyment of it

The five-point Likert scale was used to measure the participant's feelings and thoughts on the questions. The higher the score, the more the participant agreed with the contents of the questions. The questionnaire is an online questionnaire and before participants filled out the questionnaire, they are informed in advance that only people with "experiences in using e-Books" can fill out the questionnaire. An effective questionnaire is determined according to multiple choice questions having answers that aren't contradicting. In addition, questionnaires with answers that are conforming will also be considered invalid.

After the questionnaires were collected and invalid questionnaires were removed, the study uses descriptive statistics to analyze the basic data of the participants; reliability analysis was used to analyze whether if the questions were internally consistent or not. The Cronbach's Alpha was beyond the standard value of 0.7, which indicated that the questionnaire had good reliability.

Factor Analysis was used to test the validity of the questionnaire, and the Kaiser–Meyer–Olkin (KMO) measure of sampling adequacy and Bartlett test of sphericity were used to verify the feasibility of factor analysis. In this study, the reliability of each factor of the questionnaire (Cronbach's α value) must be higher than 0.7; the factor loading of each item must be higher than 0.4, and the cumulative variance of factor analysis must be greater than 50%. Having these values implied that the questionnaire was capable of effectively measuring its core concepts. This study removed the inappropriate questions based on these standards, and the factors were named based on the results of the factor analysis (including the connotation of each item and factor loadings).

Repeated measured ANOVA analysis was done to find the factors that significantly affected the experiential value of the participants. The Pearson correlation coefficient was used to acquire the correlation between the four experiential value factors. In addition, the Independent One-way ANOVA analysis was used to evaluate the degree of agreement for the experiential value of each factor between the two types of e-Book users (with purchasing experience and without purchasing experience). The standard α value for significance of the ANOVA analysis and Pearson correlation analysis was set at 0.05. If the p-value is less than 0.05, it implied that the results of the analysis had explanatory significance.

Before the questionnaire was officially released, this study conducted a pretest. A total of 69 valid questionnaires were collected in the pretest, and the effective questionnaire recovery rate was 75%. The questionnaire's reliability had a Cronbach's Alpha of .940, indicating that the questionnaire has high reliability and no one indicated that the questions were unclear or difficult to fill out.

3.2 Interview

After the questionnaire was distributed, this study conducted in-depth interviews as well to better understand e-Book users' experiences and suggestions for e-Book platforms. According to Nielsen [30] suggestion: If the interview is to test two groups of interviewees, at least 3–4 interviewees in each category are required. This study selected seven participants that filled out the questionnaire as interview participants, three individuals without e-Book purchasing experiences and four individuals with e-Book purchasing experiences.

The interview process was recorded with the consent of the interviewees to understand the reasons why they chose to fill in the scores of each item of the "Experiential Value Scale," and asked them about their experiences in using e-Book platforms.

The questions of the "Experience Value Scale" are used as interview questions, and there are extended interview questions based on the responses of the interviewees.

This study typed up the recordings of the interviews into transcripts and used the grounded theory as a basis to sort the transcripts. The criteria for selecting keywords lies in the labeling and sorting of key synonyms. If a synonymous keyword appears across more than four interviewees for the same item, it is determined that the item has a certain degree of positive or negative implication. This study looked at the transcripts based on the questionnaire items, the keywords were marked in bold font and then each item was compiled into "key answer sentences," and the results of each item were eventually summarized according to the results for each question. The results for each aspect of the experiential value were then consolidated into key sentences.

4 Results

4.1 Questionnaire Survey Results

This study collected a total of 325 valid questionnaires, and the response rate for valid questionnaires was 90%. There were 155 male participants that accounted for 47.7%, and there were 170 female participants that accounted for 52.3%. There are 151 people aged 14 to 24 years old; 144 people aged 25 to 39 years old; and 30 people aged over 40 (inclusive) years old. Among them, 39.0% of them were students (N = 127), 58.5% were employed (N = 190), and 2.5% were unemployed (N = 8). The average monthly income of the participants were as follows: 45.2% had monthly incomes below NTD $20,000 (N = 147); 40.9% had monthly incomes from NTD$ 20,001 to 40,000 (N = 133); 11.1% had monthly incomes from NTD$ 40,001 to 60,000 (N = 36), and 9 people had had monthly incomes of more than NTD$ 60,000.

The reliability of the entire Experiential Value Scale (25 items) had a Cronbach's Alpha of .954; this indicated that the questionnaire possessed high reliability. According to Bartlett's test of sphericity and the KMO test, the KMO value of this questionnaire was .953, which met the marvelous standard, and Bartlett's test of sphericity also reached the standard for significance ($p = .000 < .05$), which meant this scale was suitable for factor analysis. After factor analysis, four factors were obtained. The factor loading of each item is higher than 0.4, and the reliability of the four factors is higher than 0.7. The total variance of the scale is 68.21%, which meets the validity standard of the scale. The analysis results are shown in Table 2.

Repeated measured ANOVA for each factor was done next and the results indicated that some experiential values are significantly influential when purchasing/reading e-Books ($F = 7.370$, $p = .000 < .05$). The Post-hoc Bonferroni indicated that aesthetics ($M = 3.60$, $SD = 0.767$) and consumer return on investment ($M = 3.59$, $SD = 0.665$) had higher values, and service excellence ($M = 3.45$, $SD = 0.922$) had the lowest value while playfulness ($M = 3.52$, $SD = 0.828$) is in the middle. It can be seen that that aesthetics and consumer return on investment are the experiential value users feel the best about, followed by playfulness and finished off with service excellence being the lowest experiential value. The analysis results are shown in Table 3.

Table 2. Factor analysis of experiential value scale

Factors	Items	Factor loadings	Cronbach's α	% of Variance	Cumulative%
Consumer return on investment (CROI)	CROI3	.737	.714	24.275	24.275
	CROI1	.674			
	CROI4	.632			
	SE1	.453			
Service Excellence (SE)	SE6	.721	.893	16.602	40.877
	SE5	.712			
	CROI2	.632			
	SE3	.552			
	SE4	.546			
Aesthetics (A)	A1	.803	.929	16.452	57.329
	A2	.776			
	A4	.773			
	A3	.766			
	A5	.701			
	A7	.617			
	A6	.548			
	CROI5	.417			
Playfulness (P)	P1	.839	.885	10.878	68.207
	P4	.823			
	P2	.753			
	P6	.607			
	P3	.578			

Table 3. Summary table of repeated measured ANOVA

Resources	SS	df	MS	F	Post-hoc: Bonferroni
Between groups (A)	4.912	3	1.637	7.370***	Aesthetics (M = 3.60, SD = 0.767), consumer return on investment (M = 3.59, SD = 0.665) > playfulness (M = 3.52, SD = 0.828) > service excellence (M = 3.45, SD = 0.922)
Within groups					
Between-subjects (S)	615.522	324	1.900		
Error (A*S)	215.941	972	0.222		
Total	836.375	1299			

Notes: *** means $p < .001$.

Based on Pearson's correlation coefficient (Table 4), it can be seen that service excellence and aesthetics are highly correlated (>0.7), indicating that service excellence and aesthetics have a strong connection; the correlation of consumer return on investment with service excellence and aesthetics is moderate, and playfulness and service excellence also have a moderate correlation. These results infer that improving service excellence may improve consumer return on investment, aesthetics and playfulness.

Table 4. Results of Pearson correlation coefficient

	Consumer return on investment	Service excellence	Aesthetics
Service excellence	.643***		
Aesthetics	.639***	.807***	
Playfulness	.539***	.670***	.658***

Notes: *** means $p < .001$.

This study also compares the differences in experiential value between the two groups of "have or don't have e-Book purchasing experiences" through One Way ANOVA. It can be seen from Table 5 that users who have purchased e-Books have a higher degree of experience in the four aspects of experiential value than users who have not purchased e-Books. The reason is inferred that users who have purchased e-Books will not only have more advanced experiences due to their "consumption," they also get more features and services based on their consumption behavior.

Table 5. One way ANOVA of with (Y) or without (N) purchasing experience for e-Books

Factors	Groups	N	Means	SD	F
Consumer return on investment	Y	177	3.79	0.630	38.594***
	N	148	3.35	0.628	
Service excellence	Y	177	3.76	0.799	49.418***
	N	148	3.08	0.928	
Aesthetics	Y	177	3.80	0.697	28.444***
	N	148	3.37	0.780	
Playfulness	Y	177	3.75	0.758	34.683***
	N	148	3.24	0.823	

Notes: *** means $p < .001$.

4.2   Interview Results

All interviewees selected by this study have experience in using e-Book platforms and filled out the experiential value questionnaire in the first phase of this study. There are seven interviewees, three with no purchasing experiences (two females and one male) and four with purchasing experiences (three females and one male), between 20 and 39 years old. 'A' was used as the designation for those without purchasing experiences, and 'B' as the designation for those with purchasing experiences. The average duration of each interview was 40 min. The results of the interviews are as follows.

(1) Consumer return on investment

Six of the seven interviewees believed that the price of e-Books is reasonable. Only B6 thought that the price of e-Books was a bit expensive and that since e-Books have already saved the costs for fine printing, the prices should be lower. However, the general consensus was that the price-performance ratio of e-Books was good. Most of them felt that e-Books are convenient, easy to carry, do not occupy space, and can be instantly viewed. According to the results in Table 3, consumer return on investment (M = 3.59) is one of the four aspects experienced that was significantly better.

(2) Service excellence

Respondents A1, A2, and B6 all mentioned that reading e-Books caused fatigue, and B4 also mentioned that reading e-Books on mobile phones made reading speed too fast and was unable to experience flipping through the pages. In terms of reading choices, even though most of them preferred actual books (A2, A3, B4, B7), the interviewees also valued the convenience of e-Books (A1, A3, B5, B6, B7) and mentioned that e-Books resolve space issues (A3), and all of the interviewees gave positive answers when asked if they would continue using e-Books in the future.

Looking at Table 3, service excellence (M = 3.45) was one of the worst aspects of the four aspects experienced. In the service requirements of e-Books, the features that interviewees liked were different. This included the features of changing fonts and planning reading time (A3), trial reading (B4), free books (B5), discount activities (B5), book recommendations (B6) and the search feature (B7).

Interviewees with purchasing experiences usually paid more attention to selecting the e-Books they wanted to purchase more quickly (such as trial reading, recommendations, and search functions). The service requirements put forward by the interviewees included: calculating reading time (A1, B7), recording flipping records to jump pages next time when reading (A2), reader reviews (A2, B5), recommended books of interest (A2, B5), concise and beautified interfaces (B4, B6, B7), reading history can be turned into points to purchase or borrow books (B5), the contents of the samples can be selected by users (B5, B7), the interfaces looks like virtual bookcases (B6), real voiceovers (B6), improved book categorization (B4, B5, B7).

(3) Aesthetics

Visually, interviewees desired to have the same visual experiences printed books (A1, A3, B5, B6) and also preferred a cleaner and personalized interface (B4, B5). For features, interviewees hoped that they could be convenient (A2), interactive, and personalized (B5). Other interviewees expressed satisfaction with the features currently in use (A1, A3) or found them to be appropriate (B6, B7). Interviewees expressed their hope to make e-Book platforms look like virtual bookstores (A1), as well as making the interfaces more concise and beautified (B4, B6), hoped that e-Books were placed in categories that matched the contents (B4), wished that there would be more detailed categories, and provide the original region of the book for convenient searches (B5).

(4) Playfulness

Some interviewees were distracted while reading, possibly due to platforms having pop-up notifications (B4) or not being able to look at the screen for extended periods of time (A1). Interviewees purchasing or selecting e-Books enjoyed the convenience of purchasing and reading e-Books immediately (B4, B6), or enjoyed shopping around (B5, B7). Based on the results of the questionnaire analysis in Table 5, playfulness for those that have purchased e-Books is M = 3.75 and those who have not purchased e-Books is M = 3.24. The difference lies in the convenience of reading immediately after purchases and the joy experienced when purchasing e-Books, and individuals who haven't purchased e-Books prefer experiencing the joys of actual books.

The results of the interviews contained many design suggestions on aesthetics and excellent service. Past studies done by scholars also referred to the positive relationship between design and experiential value. Chang [31] pointed out that website experience design affects consumers' experiential value of the website, and therefore experience design can be used to enhance the experiential value and trust of consumers for shopping on websites, thereby increasing purchase motivation. Research done by Chang [32] had results indicating that the visual design of online platforms has the greatest amount of impact on consumers' experiential value. Based on the results of questionnaires and interviews, this study has four suggestions for the improvement of interface design and the features of e-Books.

1. Concise and beautifying e-Book platform interfaces (B4, B5, B6, B7): the ads on the homepages can be reduced and the interface can be beautified, making the selection of e-Books more intuitive.
2. Adjust the categorization of the e-Books (B4, B5, B7): make the categorization more detailed and have more depth, categorize books based on their original regions. For example, novel → light novel → Japanese light novel.
3. Add a new service "Accumulate Reading Points (B5):" the hours of reading e-Books can be accumulated into points, which can be converted into book-borrowing hours or contribute towards discounts when purchasing e-Books when the specified amount has been collected, and the platforms can allow borrowing books to make reading have additional value.
4. Make adjustments to the trial reading feature (B4, B5, B7): prevent reading blank pages, information pages and other pages that are not related to the content; allowing readers to easily determine whether if they want to purchase the e-Book through trial readings.

5 Conclusions

This study indicated that "service excellence" is the lowest experienced factor amongst the four aspects of experiential value. The results of correlation coefficient analysis pointed out that service excellence and consumer return on investment, aesthetics and playfulness have a medium to a high degree of correlation, especially aesthetics and service excellence have the highest positive correlation. In addition, users with experiences in purchasing e-Books have significantly higher levels of perceived experiential value than those without purchasing experiences across all four aspects. Among them, users with experiences in purchasing e-Books and users without experiences in purchasing e-Books have the lowest level of experience for "service excellence," especially users with no experiences in purchasing e-Books with an average value of merely 3.08 (Table 5). If e-Book platforms can make adjustments to service excellence, users will be more satisfied with the services of e-Book platforms.

This study also used interviews to understand users' experiences and suggestions on the use of e-Book platforms. Based on the results of the interviews, the following four improvement suggestions were made for e-Book platforms: making the e-Book platform interfaces more concise and beautified, adjust the categorization of books, provide a new service of "accumulating reading points" to redeem book-borrowing hours or discounts when purchasing books, and make adjustments to the trial reading feature. Hopefully, future research can confirm if experiential user values are improved after making adjustments to these four types of services.

References

1. Statista: Ebook-worldwide. https://www.statista.com/outlook/213/100/ebooks/worldwide Accessed 14 Jan 2021
2. Chiu, L.-L.: Amazon e-books will be launched in Taiwan. https://www.chinatimes.com/new spapers/20181112000196-260202 Accessed 10 Jan 2021
3. Readmoo: Readmoo Homepage. https://readmoo.com/ Accessed 10 Jan 2021
4. Pine II, B.J., Gilmore, J.H.: The Experience Economy. Harvard Business School Press, Boston (1999)
5. Liu, Y.-A., Hsieh, I.-M., Chen, Y.-H.: Exploring experiential marketing in the foodservice enterprise-a case study of starbucks coffee. J. Hum. Dev. Fam. Stud. **9**, 60–87 (2007)
6. Huang, S.-J., Zhang, Z.-X.: The research of the relationships among experience marketing, experiential value, customer satisfaction and customer loyalty: a case study based on L-brand-clothing. Serv. Ind. Manage. Rev. **8**, 31–53 (2010)
7. Kao, Y.-F., Huang, L.-S., Yang, M.-H.: Effects of experiential elements on experiential satisfaction and loyalty intentions: a case study of the super basketball league in Taiwan. Int. J. Revenue Manage. **1**(1), 79–96 (2007)
8. Spiegelman, P.: Live customer interaction and the internet join in 'internaction'. Direct Mark. **38**–41 (2000)
9. Mathwick, C., Malhotra, N., Rigdon, E.: Experiential value: conceptualization, measurement and application in the catalog and internet shopping. J. Retail. **77**, 39–56 (2001)
10. Lin, Y.-J., Lin, C.-C.: E-Book features that adolescent English learners in Taiwan favored. Taiwan J. TESOL **9**(1), 53–88 (2014)
11. Hu, T.-C., Lin, W.: The trend analysis of e-Book research in library and information studies. Res. Educ. Commun. Technol. **116**, 49–71 (2017)
12. Kung, H.-H., Luo, C.-L.: On the use of the e-book sing kids by kindergarteners for reading comprehension. Chaoyang J. Humanit. Soc. Sci. **10**, 34–49 (2017)
13. Liu, Y.-T.: Enhancing L2 digital reading for EFL learners. Engl. Teach. Learn. **39**(2), 33–64 (2015)

14. Wu, T.-T., Wang, I.-T., Chang, T.-L.: Impacts of integrating the team achievement division (STAD) strategy into the SQ4R-guided e-Book learning on students' English reading comprehension. Int. J. Digital Learn. Technol. 9(2), 53–84 (2017)
15. Yuh, Y., Hao, T.-Y.: A study of the influence of content marketing on the willingness of readers' eBook purchases. J. CAGST, 280–290 (2016)
16. Chang, W.-J., Wu, M.-M.: The eReading @ your library program: promotion strategies for rural libraries. Natl. Central Libr. Bull. 2, 71–98 (2016)
17. Zimerman, M.: E-books and piracy: implications/issues for academic libraries. New Libr. World 112(1/2), 67–75 (2011)
18. McGuire, H., O'Leary, B.: A Futurist's Manifesto: A Collection of Essays from the Bleeding Edge of Publishing. O'Reilly Media, Boston (2012)
19. Hao, T.-Y., Tsai, M.-H., Lin, S.-P.: A consumer behavior study of e-Book of college students. J. CAGST, 279–298 (2010)
20. Browne, G., Coe, M.: Ebook navigation: browse, search and index. Aust. Libr. J. 61(4), 288–297 (2012)
21. Pan, Y.-P.: Illustrated Science and Technology. Shu-Chuan Inc, Taipei (2011)
22. Siriginidi, S.R.: Electronic book technologies: an overview of the present situation. Libr. Rev. 53(7), 363–371 (2004)
23. Kotler, P., Armstrong, G.: Principles of Marketing. Prentice Hall, New Jersey (1999)
24. Felix, A., Laetitia, R., van Marle, E.: Perceived experience value, satisfaction and behavioural intentions: a guesthouse experience. Afr. J. Econ. Manage. Stud. 7(3), 419–433 (2016)
25. Babin, B.J., Darden, W.R., Griffin, M.: Work and/or fun: measuring hedonic and utilitarian shopping value. J. Consum. Res. 20(4), 644–656 (1994)
26. Hu, J., Zhang, Y.: Understanding Chinese undergraduates' continuance intention to use mobile book-reading apps: an integrated model and empirical study. Libri 66(2), 1–15 (2016)
27. Maghnati, F., Ling, K.C., Nasermoadeli, A.: Exploring the relationship between experiential marketing and experiential value in the smartphone industry. Int. Bus. Res. 5(11), 169–177 (2012)
28. Sreeram, A., Kesharwani, A., Desai, S.: Factors affecting satisfaction and loyalty in online grocery shopping: an integrated model. J. Indian Bus. Res. 9(2), 107–132 (2017)
29. Keng, C.-J., Huang, T.-L., Cheng, L.-C., Hsu, M.-K.: Modeling service encounters and customer experiential value in retailing: an empirical investigation of shopping mall customers in Taiwan. Int. J. Serv. Ind. Manage. 18(4), 349–367 (2007)
30. Nielsen, J.: Why you only need to test with 5 users. https://www.nngroup.com/articles/why-you-only-need-to-test-with-5-users/. Accessed 10 Jan 2021
31. Chang, H.-L.: Exploring the impact of website experience design on brand trust, experience value and customer loyalty from the perspective of experience marketing (Unpublished master thesis). National Ilan University, Ilan City, Taiwan (2018)
32. Chang, Y.-Y.: The effects of online store between relational bonds and experiential design on experiential value, relationship quality, and customer loyalty (Unpublished master thesis). Fu Jen University, New Taipei City, Taiwan (2016)

A Designer Embedded Book Space Experiment

Tao-Tao Yu [iD] and Teng Wen Chang[(⊠)] [iD]

National Yunlin University of Science and Technology, Yunlin, Taiwan
tengwen@yuntech.edu.tw

Abstract. The relationship between books and their readers are intimacy and personal. The texts are firsthand resources for readers experience personal journey while reading, and their own unparalleled inspiration. The reflection after reading could be represented in diverse fashions, most of them were written using words as reviews. Visualization of the book experience is another presentation are used as the interpretation by designers that are often belonged to designers' own collection. With these reflections, a single story allowed widening imaginaries and extended values. Sharing such unique presentation requires a unique setting. How to create and what are such interactive reading spaces, called Muse Space in a co-existing fashion in both physical bookshop and the collective drawing space associated with it is the problem this project wants to explore. Muse Space is comprised of three layers: physical environment, collective drawing space for visualization of book-inspired drawing and association and interactive tools for creating the book-inspired drawing are examined and analyzed in three research steps, namely (1) persona and journey map for contextual inquiry and requirement for physical and virtual spaces; (2) scenario planning for interactive behaviors of user centered installation design; and (3) information visualization for visual cue and feedback of collective drawing. Part of Muse Space's system had displayed and been test by several kinds of target users, with their feedback we could identify that Muse Space creates opportunities for readers to learn more knowledges from not only books but also other readers feedbacks and how to emphasize independent bookstores' superiorities with interactive tools.

Keywords: Experiment design · Bookstore · Interaction design · Drawing

1 Introduction

1.1 Background

Reading always play different roles in human activities in different life stages. For gaining knowledge we read for searching essential information, for hobbies we also read different literatures. Every book had recorded something the author owned, even fictional stories could express metaphors or theories. In order to encourage readers exploring those stories behind a book and provide a physical space with interactive digital design for these works are one of this experiment's purposes. Besides, how to guide the inspirations occurring during reading paper books being translated into well-recorded form through a customized physic field and been collected carefully by digital media are

© Springer Nature Switzerland AG 2021
M. M. Soares et al. (Eds.): HCII 2021, LNCS 12780, pp. 661–670, 2021.
https://doi.org/10.1007/978-3-030-78224-5_45

another objective for this experiment. After recorded in digital media, those transformed-inspirations would be visualized and releasing in online social communities. These exhibits will create different touch points from texts and finally increase possibilities spreading the paper books' content to audiences.

1.2 Target Groups and Persona

According to our contextual inquire process, the persona for Muse Space could be divided into: bookstore related workers, students or people related to assimilate large amounts of knowledges from books and others who have reading hobby.

As for bookstore-related workers such as clerks and owners, Muse Space with digital media system could offer several forms for displaying their products and also building display area. The upstream publishers can use Muse Space's online community to publicize events or released date. Muse Space also provide physic space with customized displaying forms which allow authors to hold activities with fans. Digital community afford digital platform to converge worldwide book lovers' community online.

The second parts of target groups generally determined on whether if they interested in exploring cognition, no matter if they are profession in related backgrounds or not. These people are willing to share and learn from others, getting used to have reflection or searching relative information after reading. Muse Space display books in different aspects and providing physical space for these people creating together. Those two target groups have maintained bookstores business as being both producer and consumer. Muse Space could afford their different demands and take parts in the business cycle. With these two personae, we then explore the interaction.

2 Reviews

Three groups of researches: reading habits, independent bookstore and co-existing spaces are reviewed. Reading habit provides the knowledge of the major behaviors: reading and its interpretation-like interaction for our experiment. Independent bookstore movement settle the theme and the context of Muse Space. Co-existing space and interaction among them provide the technology and concept for the implementation for this project.

2.1 Reading Habits

While e-book and digital media changes the world of bookstore and how people perceive the book, physical book reading still remains an unreplaceable experience. Several studies have indicated difference between paper-reading and e-reading regarded as most people understand and remember text better during paper [1]. This article also shown how human brain interpret texts with landscaping in mind, which known as mind-mapping. Visual symbol or texts position are confirmed in helping readers recalling plots. Besides visual senses, thickness of the pages and a simple movement such as turning page can also help human focus on reading. In order to interpret mind mapping construction during reader reading specific book, Muse Space provides a visualize form: Book Map to record them. These book maps will be collected and exhibited in Muse Space by digital online media. Book Map also identified as reader's review which could be provided to another reading habits' need: searching for reviews or recommendation before start reading. Most of readers will use mobile media combining with physical book reading to fulfill such needs. However, a distraction from physical book reading activity occurred. A space provides both a seamless transition between physical book reading activity and the information search digitally is needed to reader.

2.2 Independent Bookstores

Physic bookstores seem to be in decline in many countries, still there are researches showing different points of view. Li, J's study[2] shows that independent bookshops in Australia separated from others by providing unique services chaining with design. Independent bookstores also develop steady markets in Taiwan in several ways such as linking with local society and cultural meanings in experiences [3]. Not only spreading knowledge but also strengthen social cohesion, independent bookstore often symbolizes subculture community.

2.3 Co-existing Space

Following several forms of co-existing space studies, we could find dynamic interaction between users and information [4], visual forms using with co-existing space [5] and responsive skins [6]. Interactive tools could help users record not only their imaginations but also create chances for innovations.

Independent bookstores stand out with their corresponded needs from specialized target groups, that is to create a space for collecting readers' reviews in inspired-drawings and sharing them.

3 Scenario Planning

Following facilitation process by Yu and Lin [7], Fig. 1 shown difference between basic bookstore and additional new scenarios in Muse Space's. At least four scenarios generated from adding Book maps from Muse Space as touch points.

Basic Scenario. In basic bookstore, users browse books from showcase or book shelves in their first glances, the touch points between them are book cover's information included visual design, topics, author and left contents. Once if the information was attracted, user would pick up the book and start reading.

Scenario with Muse Space. There are four scenarios with touchpoints associated to book maps in Muse Space.

Scenario 1. in blue arrows. Displayed interactive Book maps which made from texts merged visual-drawing contain exquisite catalogs, user could explore selected books' contents in visual. Literal reviews also could be read in the display interface.

Scenario 2. in green arrows. Through browsing book maps, user could recognize more details with following book maps' objects and corresponded stories. The physical books exhibited on bookshelves next to the desk that user could easily find them and start reading.

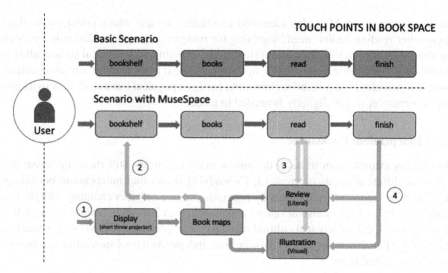

Fig. 1. Difference in scenarios between basic bookstores and Muse Space.

Scenario 3. in yellow arrows. During reading, user could search review or inspired drawing works through book maps to learn unexpected interpret.

Scenario 4. in red arrows. After enjoying reading, user share reflection with collective drawing or writing, with tools and environment in inspiring space during reading. Either written reviews or visual book maps will be collected and displayed in book maps together for extended communication.

These functions increase opportunities of contacting between user and book. Collecting reader's reflections provide different aspects that user could learn points of view they've never realized.

Based on these four scenarios, detailed user journey map could be analyzed and determined clearly.

4   Implementation

For creating specific space for book lovers, Muse Space integrated independent bookstore's features with interactive tools and space design. This research has conducted persona and followed by user journey (shown in Fig. 2) with 10 participants in background including bookstore owners, booklovers, publishers, book critic and interaction designers. Relationship between user and Muse Space are shown as Fig. 2 in journey map.

Following scenario-based user journey are divided into physic journey and virtual journey. Reading corner and Inspiring corner provide reader a place to stay, with online media which shown collective book maps and member ship as virtual setting. To make connection between these two types of user journey, the charming book selection are both initial and essential touch points to start up.

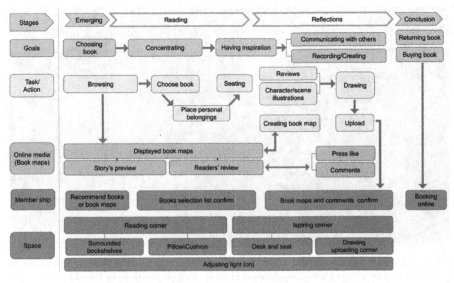

Fig. 2. User journey map framework in Muse Space.

4.1 Book Selection

Books display with book maps should be carefully matched the main idea of encouraging creation and displayed next to corresponded books. Selected literature series are generalized in mainly two inductions, "Indirect" and "Stories allowed multiple interpretation".

Indirect. Texts which conveying indirect meanings or scenes, the review from them depends on readers' immediate emotional regards. These texts are mostly article and emotional, also free in formats. etc. poem and essays.

Stories Allowed Multiple Interpretation. These stories contain impressive plots and characters, readers feel immersive with their encounter and stirring up their feelings. These series attracted readers start analyzing each character's outlooks or positions in the whole story. With basic story plots and world views, readers could make their own wishes to change some character's destiny with derivative works as reviews and drawing. etc. Fiction, biography and novels.

These books could be translated in multiple forms either visual forms or narrative texts. Diversity of the explanations also give inspirations to reader's own work.

4.2 Interaction Design

Book Maps. Media design allowed in Muse Space are visualization of book-inspired drawing and users' communities name as Book maps which transforms information visualization for visual cue and feedback of collective drawings. Following book map example as Fig. 3 shown was inspired from Love in a Fallen City [8] created by author.

This book map shows an antique style Chinese room responded to history background of story collection. Each object represented independent stories in short novels collection.

Fig. 3. Book map example about Love in a Fallen City, original presented in 1943 Chinese language novel by Eileen Chang, republished in short stories collections in Taiwan, 2010.

Tapping the object will linked to different stories in the book, it will show captured part's texts from specified stories. Reader could find corresponding sentences which symbolized each object in the full story. Via browsing book maps, user could recognize introduction and writing style quickly from captured part's texts about the whole book. This could be a familiar touch points for readers to get known about a book than just have a glance on book's cover. In classic way to display a book, bookstores make some exhibition board and put them in special stands or showcase. The critical touch points to get in a book still depends on whether readers take the book in hand and start look over it or not. Book maps provide different touch points to help readers get into stories plots without taking physic books. The physical selected books exhibited on bookshelves next to the desk that user could easily find original stories and continue experiencing completed stories. The displaying book map could also be an example for readers to transformed after-reading feedbacks in to visualize works, that is to create their own book map in their interpretation. Via membership system in apps, reader could record their inspired-drawings and uploaded online. Inspired-drawings will be displayed online in parts of book maps as Fig. 4 shown.

In reader reviews part in book maps, readers could display their inspired-drawings. Membership system allows readers creating personal account to join online community. With online accounts readers can share their book-inspired drawings and communicating with basics functions as pressing like and leaving comments.

Member Ship. Online member ship system offers services in commercial and social media, such as booking chosen book online. Members of Muse Space also have their own online communities to follow Muse Space's information and sharing their opinions together. Readers' reflections and official book maps also be offered only with membership beside physic display in Muse Space.

Fig. 4. Frame works of reader reviews which collect inspired-drawings' posts.

4.3 Space Design Framework

Fig. 5. Muse Space framework design shown in scenario-based sketch.

The main activities in Muse Space are reading and creating from collective books. Only selected themes books will be displayed in bookshelves and displayed in online media as book maps. Not only finding books from physical books display, book maps could collect more amount of books contents and information included story previews and multiple forms reader's reviews. Reader could comprehend books contents and easily find physic book near the display platform. After reader take selected book, the route will guide them into reading corner to start reading. If reader needs desk to make notes, inspiring corner offers writing table for reader to work. Reader could browse others reviews from book maps display in the space but also with their personal online member ship in mobile devices. The inspired book's drawings could be upload in either uploading corner or personal mobile devices (Fig. 5).

Reading Corner. Reading corner provide a self-seat spaces allowing readers to stay for reading chosen book. With bookshelves surrounded, every user has their own separated corner for seat and spacing. Every seat has storage space for reader putting their personal belongings. Several pillows and carpets will help user relaxing favorably. Personal adjusting light could customize reader's illumination while staying in corner.

Inspiring Corner. In inspiring corner, desks and chairs are important in human activities for creative works. Reader could move on the desk and start making notes from any imagination with pen and paper. After finishing creativity works, online media system will collect the works in digital files and upload them online in both membership community and digital display wall which surrounded Muse Space.

5   Reflections

5.1   User Feedback

High fidelity prototype of Book Maps and online community had been displayed by interactive short throw projector. Short throw projector could project book maps and user interface on table or wall which allowed users enjoy surfing them during reading by the table. In order to avoid the interruption while users switching to digital devices for checking online stuffs, interface projected on wall or table could rapidly allow users searching or recording some thoughts. Prototype of Muse Space had participated and tested in two case. One of them is Young Designer's Exhibition which open to public, another is private achievement exhibition in a design consultant company. Both of them are exhibited with illustrations arrange in introduction for each chapters of Love in a Fallen City as the Book map.

Users' feedback mostly emphasized that visual book maps increase their interests in exhibited books. Through a glance of visual book maps displaying, they recognize contents or atmosphere about the book easily. Since Love in a Fallen City is well-known in Taiwan academia, many users had already heard the title and author of it but still never want to try. Book map express the novel's history background with drawing and attract more people quickly have a look. Some of them might be interested in the drawings displaying in book maps but later realized that this book they've already heard but never think of start reading it. 70% of users who had operated book maps said they were willing to know more about Love in a Fallen City by reading it. Users already have reading habit also found that besides writing words, drawing could also help them express reflection from books. For users in design-oriented, Muse Space provide communities for them to share their feedbacks about stories and getting unexpected reflections from others in same stories.

In contrast, some literature-related users had given specific positive feed backs. A staff from National Museum of Taiwan Literature mentioned that showing texts in digital interactive display had been applied in their field. Book maps as a visual interactive display could make literature become more approachable. Another book review blogger responded that he typically shared his reviews on social media posts with words but never considered described in visual works such as book maps' drawing. As a blogger, he also looking forward to participate in Muse Space's membership's online community groups.

5.2 Lesson Learned

After collected user feed backs during prototype book maps display, building a co-existing space which allowing all scenarios related in book maps is essential. During analyzed user-centered reading experience scenario which occurred after book maps' existence, all terms of user journey maps are clearly generalized. In order to allow both physic and virtual events being co-existed, Muse Space's implementation are difficult to strike a balance.

Though prototype of book maps had received mostly positive feed backs, it still couldn't be able to afford interaction due to medical problem. Not only book maps displaying, figuring out how to merged both physic and virtual interaction in the same space at same time should be carefully arranged. After user drew or wrote down inspiration, those works should be collected and uploaded immediately, which need IoT technic supporting. Measuring light setting in order to assorted projector and screen which show digital media on surrounding wall and simultaneously not interrupting user's reading is also a critical problem.

6 Conclusion

Frame working with space design could be carefully plan in future and contains more digital tools to solve users demands. There still have many commercial managements with member ship system to keep this space survive. More details about reading space and inspiring space's devices should be evaluated. Though most space design in Muse Space are still in frame working, the book map of Love in a Fallen City still get optimistic responses in book-lovers. The knowledges which we learned from texts could be transformed in different ways of reviews and allowing more reflections and values. Infinite interpretations and resonating in plots make every relationship between readers and books unique and precious.

Acknowledgments. This research is a derivative experiment on original graduation project: Finger Muse initiated by Tao-Tao Yu and Chloe Lim. Authors would like to thank Ivy Lee from Or Book bookstore and Professor Chao-Ming Wang, Li-Shu Lu from National University of Science and Technology for supporting this research. Special thanks to Grace Lin from Scenario Lab and Rachel Lu, Cheng-Jun Hong, Doris Tien, Shih-Ting Tsai from SOFTLab for offering devices and experiment spaces and suggestions.

References

1. Jabr, F.: Why the brain prefers paper. Sci. Am. **309**, 48–53 (2013)
2. Li, J.: Choosing the right battles: how independent bookshops in Sydney, Australia compete with chains and online retailers. Aust. Geogr. **41**, 247–262 (2010)
3. Yu, H.-Y.: The production and consumption of "Experiencescapes" in Eslite Bookstores, Taiwan. Geography and Planning (GEOPL), vol. Ph.D., Cardiff University (2014)
4. Lai, I.-C., Chang, T.-W.: Dynamic interactions between users and information in a co-existence space. In: Orbak, H. (ed.) The eCAADe 2004 22nd conference, pp. 58–65, Copenhagen, Denmark (2004)
5. Lu, K.-T., Chang, T.-W.: Experience montage in virtual space. In: Proceedings of the 10th International Conference on Computer Aided Architectural Design Research in Asia, vol. 2, pp. 426–435. CAADRIA, New Delhi, India (2005)
6. Hsu, T.-M., Lin, C.-J., Wang, H.-A., Chang, T.-W.: Space breathes - an interactive bio-skin. In: 42nd Annual Conference of the Australian and New Zealand Architectural Science Association (ANZAScA) 2008 Conference, CDROM. New Castle University, New Castle, Australia (2008)
7. Yu, D.-J., Lin, W.-C.: Facilitating idea generation using personas. In: Kurosu, M. (ed.) HCD 2009. LNCS, vol. 5619, pp. 381–388. Springer, Heidelberg (2009). https://doi.org/10.1007/978-3-642-02806-9_44
8. Chang, E.: Love in a Fallen City. Short story collections from 1943. Crown Culture Corporation 皇冠文化, Taiwan (2010)

Author Index

Abujarad, Fuad II-343, II-389
Abulfaraj, Anas I-173
Adachi, Koji II-403
Aguirre, Joel I-225, I-327, II-565
Ahmed, Salman I-3
Ahumada, Danay II-34
Alam, Tanvir II-224
Aldrees, Asma II-3
Alenljung, Zackarias III-139
Almakramih, Hashem II-506
Almeyda, Silvana I-187
Alrehaili, Ahmed I-292
Alvarez, Jaime II-403
Amin, Mohammad Ruhul II-224
An, Jingrui II-581
An, Pengcheng II-581
An, Wa I-339, I-401
Argumanis, Daniela I-15
Ayabe, Rodrigo Crissiuma Figueiredo
       III-158

Ba, Shengqi I-523
Barbashova, Nadu I-457
Barbu, Roxana M. I-204
Basu, Rittika I-372
Baurley, Sharon II-627
Bertoline, Gary III-187
Bettoni, Marco Cesare I-351
Bombeke, Klaas III-171

Cai, Ming I-511, III-3
Cai, Sihao I-156
Cai, Yue II-252
Cantoni, Lorenzo II-88, III-326, III-340
Cao, Shunrong I-372
Cao, Tian II-178, II-195
Cao, Ting III-79
Cao, Wei II-60
Carr, Donald William I-533
Cavalcanti, Janaina Ferreira III-158
Chamberlain, Alan III-79
Chang, Teng Wen II-661
Chen, Chien-Hsiung III-15
Chen, Fengming II-43

Chen, Weiwen I-593
Chen, Xin II-420
Chen, Yali II-18
Chen, Ye I-339
Chen, Zhi I-511, III-3
Cheng, Xiandong I-523
Chiusaroli, Francesca I-426
Chuang, Yaliang II-581
Cisneros, Daniela II-210
Cohn, Dennis I-187
Cong, Yawen III-109
Costa de Souza, Maria de Fátima II-434
Coursaris, Constantinos K. II-450
Cueva, Rony I-100, III-439

da Silva, Anderson Gonçalves Barbosa
       III-158
Danış, Semih I-579
De Bruyne, Jonas III-171
De Marez, Lieven III-171
Demirel, H. Onan I-3
Deng, Qingxin II-420
Diamond, Sara I-372
Díaz, Jaime I-327, II-34
Dong, Xueyan II-599
Drapp, Jerica I-218
Duarte, Fernanda Carolina Armando III-158
Durnez, Wouter III-171

Edwards, Chelsea II-343
Elias, Herlander III-289
Esparza, Patricia III-439
Evans, Suzanne B. II-389

Fabri, Marc II-300
Falconi, Fiorella I-225, I-327, II-565
Faria Gomes, Renata II-434
Feng, Siqi I-156
Filgueiras, Ernesto III-371
Fornara, Nicoletta III-384
Fraenkel, Liana II-389
Freddolino, Paul P. II-450
Fritz, Michele C. II-450
Fu, RongRong II-132, II-613

Gaduel Thaloka, Tetteng　III-356
Gao, Ge　II-531
Gao, Xian　I-128
Gharawi, Mohammed　II-506
Giannakopoulos, Theodoros　I-477
Giménez, Araceli　I-457
Gong, Fengchen　III-187
Gong, Zhenxi　II-18
Gračanin, Denis　II-3
Gros, Jochen　I-385
Gross, Cary P.　II-389
Guo, Yu　I-637

Hai, Moushume　II-467
Hamid, Md Montaser　II-224
Han, Guizhong　I-533
Han, Xi　III-457
Hara, Eriko　II-403
Hasan, Khalad　II-224
He, Hao　I-523
Hibberd, Matthew　II-519
Hinojosa, Hilmar　I-327
Hochstetter, Jorge　II-34
Hu, Xiaomei　II-148
Huamán Monzón, Fernando　II-210
Huang, Dan　III-467
Huo, Ran　II-178
Hussain, Ajaz　I-372

Ichikawa, Daisuke　III-407
Ikawa, Yuma　III-303
Ismirle, Jennifer　II-343
Ito, Yuichi　III-407

Jia, Jingpeng　II-599
Jia, Tianjie　III-187
Jiang, Lijun　II-270
Jiang, Ming　I-544, III-268
Jiménez Sánchez, Juan Luis　I-48
Jin, Yucheng　II-531
Jing, Yuchen　III-268
Jordan, Philipp　I-34
Joundi, Jamil　III-171

Kagawa, Yoshihito　II-403
Kilani, Marwan　I-457
Killelea, Brigid K.　II-389
Kincaid, Jack A.　III-187

Kögel, Johannes　II-239
Kohr, Casey　III-187
Kolbeinsson, Ari　I-48
Kong, Yingao　II-160
Koyama, Toshihiko　II-403
Kuzminykh, Anastasia　II-224

Lacue, Ariana　II-467
LaLone, Nicolas　III-79
Lambert, Peter　III-171
Lantzouni, Marina　I-477
Lecaros, Adrian　I-242
Lee, Wan-Chen　I-67
Li, Elena Carolina　II-647
Li, Hui　III-25
Li, JunXuan　II-613
Li, Manhai　I-339, I-401
Li, Miao　III-467
Li, Peixuan　III-205
Li, Shuyue　III-66
Li, Wenhua　II-78
Li, Wenjing　I-87, III-315
Li, Xiangnuo　III-37
Li, Xiao　III-15
Li, Zhelin　II-270
Li, Ziyang　I-511, I-523, III-37
Liang, Rung-Huei　I-67
Lin, Fengze　II-43
Lin, Lan　III-256
Lindblom, Jessica　I-48, III-139
Liu, Hong　II-60
Liu, Jia　I-87, III-315
Liu, Jing　I-262
Liu, Miao　III-47
Liu, Naixin　III-66
Liu, Wei　I-156, I-544, II-531, III-268
Liu, Yi　I-442, II-107, II-121
Liu, Zaixing　II-270
Liu, Zhen　I-262, I-533, I-624, II-121, II-252,
　　　II-284, II-477, II-548, III-205, III-218,
　　　III-467, III-563
Liu, Zhensheng　I-593
Long, Jiaqian　III-109
Luo, Bao Quan　II-490
Luo, Ming Jun　II-78
Lv, Jinsong　II-160
Lyu, Yaru　I-544

Magnée, Maurice　II-373
Maguire, Martin　I-556

Majrashi, Khalid   II-506
Marcus, Aaron   I-413
Margaris, Dionisis   I-477
Matsuura, Akihiro   III-303
Maun, Rachael   II-300
Minagawa, Tatsuya   II-315
Miyata, Kazunori   I-278
Monti, Johanna   I-426
Moquillaza, Arturo   I-15, I-225, I-242, I-312,
     I-327, II-565, III-553
Morreale, Patricia   II-467
Motta, Isabela   III-483
Mougalian, Sarah S.   II-389

Nakajima, Tatsuo   III-396
Nakamura, Takashi   I-278
Namoun, Abdallah   I-292
Newbutt, Nigel   II-333
Nobile, Tekila Harley   III-326, III-356
Noris, Alice   III-340
Nucci, Antonio   II-519

Ochiai, Yoichi   II-315
Oechslin, Roman   I-457
Ouyang, Yiyu   I-442

Palmquist, Adam   I-48
Palomino, Fryda   I-312
Papangelis, Konstantinos   III-79
Patel, Yogesh   II-467
Paul, Gunther   III-503
Paz, Freddy   I-15, I-100, I-225, I-242, I-312,
     I-327, II-34, II-210, II-565, III-439,
     III-553
Paz, Freddy Asrael   I-327
Permatasari, Puspita Ayu   II-88
Phillips, Robert   II-627
Picco-Schwendener, Anna   III-356
Porter, Shane   III-503
Poulopoulos, Vassilis   I-477
Prabhala, Sasanka   I-218

Quaresma, Manuela   III-483, III-535
Quezada, Percy   I-100

Rabbi, Md Forhad   II-224
Reale, Cesco   I-457
Reeves, Matthew J.   II-450

Ren, Lingfeng   II-477
Ren, Pu   I-567
Rodrigues, Eulerson   III-371
Romaina, Juan-Carlos   III-524
Roncal, Asturias   II-467
Roshankish, Soheil   III-384
Ruiz, Cinthia   III-535
Şahin, Hilal   I-579

Sahua, Joe   III-553
Saldien, Jelle   III-171
Sangati, Federico   I-426
Sato, Hisashi   I-278
Schmidt, Matthew   II-333
Serrano, Rodrigo   II-565
Shen, Zuyu   II-531
Shi, Minghong   II-148
Shi, Zhengyu   I-603
Silva, Paula Alexandra   I-34
Silvennoinen, Johanna   I-115
Siyang, Zhong   II-60
Smith, Paul   II-627
Soares, Marcelo M.   II-361, III-66, III-109
Song, Fangli   III-90
Spiliotopoulos, Dimitris   I-477
Staal, Wouter   II-373
Steele, Adam   I-173
Su, Qixuan   II-107
Su, Zhanhong   III-218
Sun, Xin   I-128
Süner-Pla-Cerdà, Sedef   I-579
Suzuki, Hiroshi   III-233
Swierenga, Sarah J.   II-343, II-450

Tan, Hong Z.   III-187
Tanaka, Hiroki   III-396
Tang, Xuelin   I-593
Teunisse, Jan-Pieter   II-373
Thomas, Bruce   III-503
Tooze, James   II-627
Töre Yargın, Gülşen   I-579
Torres, Caroline   II-361
Trevorrow, Pip   II-300
Tsai, Yen-Shan   II-647
Tseng, Hsiu-Chen   I-67
Tubuku, Naoki   III-233
Tufail, Ali   I-292

Ulrich, Davis   II-389

Valente, João   III-371
van Dijk, Jelle   II-373
van Huizen, Niels   II-373
Van Kets, Niels   III-171
Van Wallendael, Glenn   III-171
van der Voort, Mascha   II-373
Vassilakis, Costas   I-477

Waardenburg, Thijs   II-373
Wallace, Manolis   I-477
Wan, Xi   II-531
Wang, Chen   III-245
Wang, Dawei   III-268
Wang, Di   I-637
Wang, LiMin   I-511, I-637
Wang, Qianying   II-531
Wang, Ruilin   I-156
Wang, Shi-Yi   II-389
Wang, Shuo   II-18
Wang, Tianxiong   I-128
Wang, Wei   III-90
Wang, Xi   I-401
Wang, Xiaohan   I-544
Wang, Xiaozi   I-533, I-624
Wang, Xinyang   III-109
Wang, Xiu   II-270
Wang, You   I-544
Wang, Zhe   I-567
Wang, Zhengyu   I-603
Werkmeister, Torsten   I-144
Woodward, Amanda T.   II-450
Woolley, Jacqueline D.   III-25
Wu, Cihui   III-563
Wu, Yanlin   II-160

Xi, Tao   III-457
Xiang, Wang   III-66
Xiao, Chang   I-652, II-548
Xiao, Jia Xin   II-78
Xiong, Wei   II-121
Xu, Yue   III-66

Yamamoto, Haruki   I-278
Yang, Chenhong   I-156
Yang, Mingjun   I-567
Yang, Shinan   III-47
Yang, Zulan   II-548
Yao, JingChuan   I-637
Yasumoto, Masasuke   III-407
Yeh, Chih-Liang   II-647
Yin, Wenjing   III-422
Yin, Yue   I-523
Yixin, Wan   II-60
Yu, DanDan   I-87, I-637
Yu, Haoxue   III-25
Yu, Junya   II-60
Yu, Tao-Tao   II-661
Yu, Yalan   II-132

Zallio, Matteo   I-495
Zapata Del Río, Claudia   I-187
Zeng, Jiayu   III-66, III-109
Zhang, Bowen   I-544
Zhang, Chengzhi   III-109
Zhang, Chi   II-148
Zhang, Chuqiong   I-652
Zhang, Fumei   II-178, II-195
Zhang, Ke   II-477, II-548, III-256
Zhang, Nan   II-160
Zhang, Ning   I-637
Zhang, Qi   I-544
Zhang, Yi   III-118
Zhang, Yinan   I-87
Zhang, Yiwen   I-544
Zhang, Zhengli   II-121
Zhang, Ziwei   III-268
Zhao, Liuyi   I-156
Zhou, Meiyu   I-128, I-603
Zhou, Yuwei   II-467
Zhou, Zhiwei   III-457
Zhu, Di   I-156
Zhu, Mingjian   II-43
Zhu, Yancong   III-268
Zhuang, Zihao   II-284
Zou, Jiapei   I-593

Printed in the United States
by Baker & Taylor Publisher Services